Lecture Notes in Computer Science 4422

Commenced Publication in 1973
Founding and Former Series Editors:
Gerhard Goos, Juris Hartmanis, and Jan van Leeuwen

Matthew B. Dwyer   Antónia Lopes (Eds.)

Fundamental Approaches to Software Engineering

10th International Conference, FASE 2007
Held as Part of the Joint European Conferences
on Theory and Practice of Software, ETAPS 2007
Braga, Portugal, March 24 - April 1, 2007
Proceedings

 Springer

Volume Editors

Matthew B. Dwyer
University of Nebraska
Lincoln, NE 68588, USA
E-mail: dwyer@cse.unl.edu

Antónia Lopes
University of Lisbon
1749–016 Lisboa, Portugal
E-mail: mal@di.fc.ul.pt

Library of Congress Control Number: 2007922338

CR Subject Classification (1998): D.2, F.3, D.3

LNCS Sublibrary: SL 1 – Theoretical Computer Science and General Issues

ISSN   0302-9743
ISBN-10   3-540-71288-7 Springer Berlin Heidelberg New York
ISBN-13   978-3-540-71288-6 Springer Berlin Heidelberg New York

Springer is a part of Springer Science+Business Media

springer.com

© Springer-Verlag Berlin Heidelberg 2007
Printed in Germany

Typesetting: Camera-ready by author, data conversion by Scientific Publishing Services, Chennai, India
Printed on acid-free paper   SPIN: 12032075   06/3142   5 4 3 2 1 0

Foreword

ETAPS 2007 is the tenth instance of the European Joint Conferences on Theory and Practice of Software, and thus a cause for celebration.

The events that comprise ETAPS address various aspects of the system development process, including specification, design, implementation, analysis and improvement. The languages, methodologies and tools which support these activities are all well within its scope. Different blends of theory and practice are represented, with an inclination towards theory with a practical motivation on the one hand and soundly based practice on the other. Many of the issues involved in software design apply to systems in general, including hardware systems, and the emphasis on software is not intended to be exclusive.

History and Prehistory of ETAPS

ETAPS as we know it is an annual federated conference that was established in 1998 by combining five conferences [Compiler Construction (CC), European Symposium on Programming (ESOP), Fundamental Approaches to Software Engineering (FASE), Foundations of Software Science and Computation Structures (FOSSACS), Tools and Algorithms for Construction and Analysis of Systems (TACAS)] with satellite events.

All five conferences had previously existed in some form and in various colocated combinations: accordingly, the prehistory of ETAPS is complex. FOSSACS was earlier known as the Colloquium on Trees in Algebra and Programming (CAAP), being renamed for inclusion in ETAPS as its historical name no longer reflected its contents. Indeed CAAP's history goes back a long way; prior to 1981, it was known as the Colleque de Lille sur les Arbres en Algebre et en Programmation. FASE was the indirect successor of a 1985 event known as Colloquium on Software Engineering (CSE), which together with CAAP formed a joint event called TAPSOFT in odd-numbered years. Instances of TAPSOFT, all including CAAP plus at least one software engineering event, took place every two years from 1985 to 1997 inclusive. In the alternate years, CAAP took place separately from TAPSOFT.

Meanwhile, ESOP and CC were each taking place every two years from 1986. From 1988, CAAP was colocated with ESOP in even years. In 1994, CC became a "conference" rather than a "workshop" and CAAP, CC and ESOP were thereafter all colocated in even years.

TACAS, the youngest of the ETAPS conferences, was founded as an international workshop in 1995; in its first year, it was colocated with TAPSOFT. It took place each year, and became a "conference" when it formed part of ETAPS 1998. It is a telling indication of the importance of tools in the modern field of informatics that TACAS today is the largest of the ETAPS conferences.

The coming together of these five conferences was due to the vision of a small group of people who saw the potential of a combined event to be more than the sum of its parts. Under the leadership of Don Sannella, who became the first ETAPS steering committee chair, they included: Andre Arnold, Egidio Astesiano, Hartmut Ehrig, Peter Fritzson, Marie-Claude Gaudel, Tibor Gyimothy, Paul Klint, Kim Guldstrand Larsen, Peter Mosses, Alan Mycroft, Hanne Riis Nielson, Maurice Nivat, Fernando Orejas, Bernhard Steffen, Wolfgang Thomas and (alphabetically last but in fact one of the ringleaders) Reinhard Wilhelm.

ETAPS today is a loose confederation in which each event retains its own identity, with a separate programme committee and proceedings. Its format is open-ended, allowing it to grow and evolve as time goes by. Contributed talks and system demonstrations are in synchronized parallel sessions, with invited lectures in plenary sessions. Two of the invited lectures are reserved for "unifying" talks on topics of interest to the whole range of ETAPS attendees. The aim of cramming all this activity into a single one-week meeting is to create a strong magnet for academic and industrial researchers working on topics within its scope, giving them the opportunity to learn about research in related areas, and thereby to foster new and existing links between work in areas that were formerly addressed in separate meetings.

ETAPS 1998–2006

The first ETAPS took place in Lisbon in 1998. Subsequently it visited Amsterdam, Berlin, Genova, Grenoble, Warsaw, Barcelona, Edinburgh and Vienna before arriving in Braga this year. During that time it has become established as the major conference in its field, attracting participants and authors from all over the world. The number of submissions has more than doubled, and the numbers of satellite events and attendees have also increased dramatically.

ETAPS 2007

ETAPS 2007 comprises five conferences (CC, ESOP, FASE, FOSSACS, TACAS), 18 satellite workshops (ACCAT, AVIS, Bytecode, COCV, FESCA, FinCo, GT-VMT, HAV, HFL, LDTA, MBT, MOMPES, OpenCert, QAPL, SC, SLA++P, TERMGRAPH and WITS), three tutorials, and seven invited lectures (not including those that were specific to the satellite events). We received around 630 submissions to the five conferences this year, giving an overall acceptance rate of 25%. To accommodate the unprecedented quantity and quality of submissions, we have four-way parallelism between the main conferences on Wednesday for the first time. Congratulations to all the authors who made it to the final programme! I hope that most of the other authors still found a way of participating in this exciting event and I hope you will continue submitting.

ETAPS 2007 was organized by the Departamento de Informática of the Universidade do Minho, in cooperation with

- European Association for Theoretical Computer Science (EATCS)
- European Association for Programming Languages and Systems (EAPLS)
- European Association of Software Science and Technology (EASST)
- The Computer Science and Technology Center (CCTC, Universidade do Minho)
- Camara Municipal de Braga
- CeSIUM/GEMCC (Student Groups)

The organizing team comprised:

- João Saraiva (Chair)
- José Bacelar Almeida (Web site)
- José João Almeida (Publicity)
- Luís Soares Barbosa (Satellite Events, Finances)
- Victor Francisco Fonte (Web site)
- Pedro Henriques (Local Arrangements)
- José Nuno Oliveira (Industrial Liaison)
- Jorge Sousa Pinto (Publicity)
- António Nestor Ribeiro (Fundraising)
- Joost Visser (Satellite Events)

ETAPS 2007 received generous sponsorship from Fundação para a Ciência e a Tecnologia (FCT), Enabler (a Wipro Company), Cisco and TAP Air Portugal.

Overall planning for ETAPS conferences is the responsibility of its Steering Committee, whose current membership is:

Perdita Stevens (Edinburgh, Chair), Roberto Amadio (Paris), Luciano Baresi (Milan), Sophia Drossopoulou (London), Matt Dwyer (Nebraska), Hartmut Ehrig (Berlin), José Fiadeiro (Leicester), Chris Hankin (London), Laurie Hendren (McGill), Mike Hinchey (NASA Goddard), Michael Huth (London), Anna Ingólfsdóttir (Aalborg), Paola Inverardi (L'Aquila), Joost-Pieter Katoen (Aachen), Paul Klint (Amsterdam), Jens Knoop (Vienna), Shriram Krishnamurthi (Brown), Kim Larsen (Aalborg), Tiziana Margaria (Göttingen), Ugo Montanari (Pisa), Rocco de Nicola (Florence), Jakob Rehof (Dortmund), Don Sannella (Edinburgh), João Saraiva (Minho), Vladimiro Sassone (Southampton), Helmut Seidl (Munich), Daniel Varro (Budapest), Andreas Zeller (Saarbrücken).

I would like to express my sincere gratitude to all of these people and organizations, the programme committee chairs and PC members of the ETAPS conferences, the organizers of the satellite events, the speakers themselves, the many reviewers, and Springer for agreeing to publish the ETAPS proceedings. Finally, I would like to thank the organizing chair of ETAPS 2007, João Saraiva, for arranging for us to have ETAPS in the ancient city of Braga.

Edinburgh, January 2007   Perdita Stevens
                                          ETAPS Steering Committee Chair

Preface

Software engineering is a complex enterprise spanning many sub-disciplines. At its core are a set of technical and scientific challenges that must be addressed in order to set the stage for the development, deployment, and application of tools and methodologies in support of the construction of complex software systems. The International Conference on Fundamental Approaches to Software Engineering (FASE) — as one of the European Joint Conferences on Theory and Practice of Software (ETAPS) — focuses on those core challenges. FASE provides the software engineering research community with a forum for presenting well-founded theories, languages, methods, and tools arising from both fundamental research in the academic community and applied work in practical development contexts.

In 2007, FASE continued in the strong tradition of FASE 2006 by drawing a large and varied number of submissions from the community — 141 in total. Each submission was reviewed by at least three technical experts from the Program Committee with many papers receiving additional reviews from the broader research community. Each paper was discussed during a 10-day "electronic" meeting. In total, the 26 members of the Program Committee, along with 101 additional reviewers, produced more than 500 reviews. We sincerely thank each them for the effort and care taken in reviewing and discussing the submissions.

The Program Committee selected a total of 30 papers — an acceptance rate of 21%. Accepted papers addressed topics including model-driven development, distributed systems, specification, service-oriented systems, testing, software analysis, and design. The technical program was complemented by the invited lectures of Jan Bosch on "Software Product Families: Towards Compositionality" and of Bertrand Meyer on "Contract-Driven Development."

FASE 2007 was held in Braga (Portugal) as part of the tenth meeting of ETAPS — for some history read the Foreword in this volume. While FASE is an integral part of ETAPS, it is important to note the debt FASE owes to ETAPS and its organizers. FASE draws significant energy from its synergistic relationships with the other ETAPS meetings, which gives it a special place in the software engineering community. Perdita Stevens and the rest of the ETAPS Steering Committee have provided extremely helpful guidance to us in organizing FASE 2007 and we thank them. João Saraiva and his staff did a wonderful job as local organizers and as PC chairs we appreciate how smoothly the meeting ran due to their efforts.

In closing, we would like to thank the authors of all of the FASE submissions and the attendees of FASE sessions for their participation and we look forward to seeing you in Budapest for FASE 2008.

January 2007

Matthew B. Dwyer
Antónia Lopes

Organization

Program Committee

Luciano Baresi (Politecnico di Milano, Italy)
Yolanda Berbers (Katholieke Universiteit Leuven, Belgium)
Carlos Canal (University of Málaga, Spain)
Myra Cohen (University of Nebraska, USA)
Ivica Crnkovic (Mälardalen University, Sweden)
Arie van Deursen (Delft University of Technology, The Netherlands)
Juergen Dingel (Queen's University, Canada)
Matt Dwyer (University of Nebraska, USA) Co-chair
Harald Gall (University of Zurich, Switzerland)
Holger Giese (University of Paderborn, Germany)
Martin Grosse-Rhode (Fraunhofer-ISST, Germany)
Anthony Hall (Independent Consultant, UK)
Reiko Heckel (University of Leicester, UK)
Patrick Heymans (University of Namur, Belgium)
Paola Inverardi (Universidad of L'Aquila, Italy)
Valérie Issarny (INRIA-Rocquencourt, France)
Natalia Juristo (Universidad Politecnica de Madrid, Spain)
Kai Koskimies (Tampere University of Technology, Finland)
Patricia Lago (Vrije Universiteit, The Netherlands)
Antónia Lopes (University of Lisbon, Portugal) Co-chair
Mieke Massink (CNR-ISTI, Italy)
Carlo Montangero (University of Pisa, Italy)
Barbara Paech (University of Heidelberg, Germany)
Leila Ribeiro (Federal University of Rio Grande do Sul, Brazil)
Robby (Kansas State University, USA)
Catalin Roman (Washington University, USA)
Sebastian Uchitel (Imperial College, UK and University of Buenos Aires, Argentina)
Jianjun Zhao (Shanghai Jiao Tong University, China)

Referees

M. Aiguier	A. Bazzan	A. Bucchiarone
M. Akerholm	D. Bisztray	S. Bygde
V. Ambriola	T. Bolognesi	D. Carrizo
J. Andersson	Y. Bontemps	G. Cignoni
P. Asirelli	J. Bradbury	V. Clerc
M. Autili	A. Brogi	A. Corradini

M. Caporuscio

R. Coreeia

S. Costa

M. Crane

C. Cuesta

O. Dieste

D. Di Ruscio

G. De Angelis

A. de Antonio

R.C. de Boer

F. Dotti

F. Durán

K. Ehrig

M.V. Espada

A. Fantechi

R. Farenhorts

M.L. Fernandez

X. Ferre

L. Foss

M. Fischer

B. Fluri

M. Fredj

J. Fredriksson

S. Gnesi

Q. Gu

R. Hedayati

S. Henkler

M. Hirsch

M. Katara

J.P. Katoen

F. Klein

P. Knab

P. Kosiuczenko

S. Larsson

D. Latella

B. Lisper

M. Loreti

Y. Lu

F. Lüders

R. Machado

G. Mainetto

S. Mann

E. Marchetti

C. Matos

S. Meier

Á. Moreira

A.M. Moreno

H. Muccini

J.M. Murillo

J. Niere

J. Oberleitner

A.G. Padua

H. Pei-Breivold

P. Pelliccione

A. Pierantonio

E. Pimentel

M. Pinto

M. Pinzger

P. Poizat

S. Punnekkat

G. Reif

G. Salaün

A.M. Schettini

P.Y. Schobbens

M.I.S. Segura

P. Selonen

L. Semini

S. Sentilles

M. Solari

T. Systa

M. ter Beek

G. Thompson

M. Tichy

M. Tivoli

E. Tuosto

F. Turini

A. Vallecillo

S. Vegas

A. Vilgarakis

R. Wagner

H.Q. Yu

A. Zarras

A. Zuendorf

Table of Contents

Distributed Systems

Specification

Services

Testing

Analysis

Design

Software Product Families: Towards Compositionality

Jan Bosch

Nokia, Technology Platforms/Software Platforms,
P.O. Box 407, FI-00045 NOKIA GROUP, Finland
Jan.Bosch@nokia.com
http://www.janbosch.com

Abstract. Software product families have become the most successful approach to intra-organizational reuse. Especially in the embedded systems industry, but also elsewhere, companies are building rich and diverse product portfolios based on software platforms that capture the commonality between products while allowing for their differences. Software product families, however, easily become victims of their own success in that, once successful, there is a tendency to increase the scope of the product family by incorporating a broader and more diverse product portfolio. This requires organizations to change their approach to product families from relying on a pre-integrated platform for product derivation to a compositional approach where platform components are composed in a product-specific configuration.

Keywords: Software product families, compositionality.

1 Introduction

Over the last decades, embedded systems have emerged as one of the key areas of innovation in software engineering. The increasing complexity, connectedness, feature density and enriched user interaction, when combined, have driven an enormous demand for software. In fact, the size of software in embedded systems seems to follow Moore's law, i.e. with the increased capabilities of the hardware, the software has followed suit in terms of size and complexity. This has lead to a constant struggle to build the software of embedded systems in a cost-effective, rapid and high-quality fashion in the face of a constantly expanding set of requirements. Two of the key approaches evolved to handle this complexity have been software architecture and software product families. Together, these technologies have allowed companies to master, at least in part, the complexity of large scale software systems.

One can identify three main trends that are driving the embedded systems industry, i.e. convergence, end-to-end functionality and software engineering capability. The convergence of the consumer electronics, telecom and IT industries has been discussed for over a decade. Although many may wonder whether and when it will happen, the fact is that the convergence is taking place constantly. Different from what the name may suggest, though, convergence in fact leads to a portfolio of increasingly diverging devices. For instance, in the mobile telecom industry, mobile phones have diverged into still picture camera models, video camera models, music

M.B. Dwyer and A. Lopes (Eds.): FASE 2007, LNCS 4422, pp. 1–10, 2007.

player models, mobile TV models, mobile email models, etc. This trend results in a significant pressure on software product families as the amount of variation to be supported by the platform in terms of price points, form factors and feature sets is significantly beyond the requirements just a few years ago. The second trend is that many innovations that have proven their success in the market place require the creation of an end-to-end solution and possibly even the creation or adaptation of a business eco-system. Examples from the mobile domain include, for instance, ring tones, but the ecosystem initiated by Apple around digital music is exemplary in this context. The consequence for most companies is that where earlier, they were able to drive innovations independently to the market, the current mode requires significant partnering and orchestration for innovations to be successful. The third main trend is that a company's ability to engineer software is rapidly becoming a key competitive differentiator. The two main developments underlying this trend are efficiency and responsiveness. With the constant increase in software demands, the cost of software R&D is becoming unacceptable from a business perspective. Thus, some factor difference in productivity is easily turning into being able or not being able to deliver certain feature sets. Responsiveness is growing in importance because innovation cycles are moving increasingly fast and customers are expecting constant improvements in the available functionality. Web 2.0 [7] presents a strong example of this trend. A further consequence for embedded systems is that, in the foreseeable future, the hardware and software innovation cycles will, at least in part, be decoupled, significantly increasing demands for post-deployment distribution of software.

Due to the convergence trend, the number of different embedded products that a manufacturer aims to bring to market is increasing. Consequently, reuse of software (as well as of mechanical and hardware solutions) is a standing ambition for the industry. The typical approach employed in the embedded systems industry is to build a platform that implements the functionality common to all devices. The platform is subsequently used as a basis when creating new product and functionality specific to the product is built on top of the platform. Several embedded system companies have successfully employed product families or platforms and are now reaching the stage where the scope of the product family is expanding considerably. This requires a transition from a traditional, integration-oriented approach to a compositional approach.

The contribution of this paper is that it analyses the problems of traditional approaches to software product families that several companies are now confronted with. In addition, it presents compositional platforms as the key solution approach to addressing these problems and discusses the technical and organizational consequences.

The remainder of this article is organized as follows. The next section defines the challenges faced by traditional product families when expanding their scope. Subsequently, section 3 presents the notion of compositional product families. The component model underlying composability is discussed in more detail in section 4. Finally, the paper is concluded in section 5.

2 Problem Statement

This paper discusses and presents the challenges of the traditional, integration-oriented approach to software product families [1] when the scope of the family is extended. However, before we can discuss this, we need to first define integration-oriented platform approach more precisely. In most cases, the platform approach is organized using a strict separation between the platform organization and the product organizations. The platform organization has typically a periodic release cycle where the complete platform is released in a fully integrated and tested fashion. The product organizations use the platform as a basis for creating and evolving theirs product by extending the platform with product-specific features.

The platform organization is divided in a number of teams, in the best case mirroring the architecture of the platform. Each team develops and evolves the component (or set of related components) that it is responsible for and delivers the result for integration in the platform. Although many organizations have moved to applying a continuous integration process where components are constantly integrated during development, in practice significant verification and validation work is performed in the period before the release of the platform and many critical errors are only found in that stage.

The platform organization delivers the platform as a large, integrated and tested software system with an API that can be used by the product teams to derive their products from. As platforms bring together a large collection of features and qualities, the release frequency of the platform is often relatively low compared to the frequency of product programs. Consequently, the platform organization often is under significant pressure to deliver as many new features and qualities during the release. Hence, there is a tendency to short-cut processes, especially quality assurance processes. Especially during the period leading up to a major platform release, all validation and verification is often transferred to the integration team. As the components lose quality and integration team is confronted with both integration problems and component-level problems, in the worst case an interesting cycle appears where errors are identified by testing staff that has no understanding of the system architecture and can consequently only identify symptoms, component teams receive error reports that turn out to originate from other parts in the system and the integration team has to manage highly conflicting messages from the testing and development staff, leading to new error reports, new versions of components that do not solve problems, etc.

In figure 1, the approach is presented graphically. The platform consists of a set of components that are integrated, tested and released for product derivation. A product derivation project receives the pre-integrated platform, may change something to the platform architecture but mostly develops product-specific functionality on top of the platform.

Although several software engineering challenges associated with software platforms have been outlined, the approach often proves highly successful in terms of maximizing R&D efficiency and cost-effectively offering a rich product portfolio. Thus, in its initial scope, the integration-oriented platform approach has often proven itself as a success. However, the success can easily turn into a failure when the organization decides to build on the success of the initial software platform and significantly broadens the scope of the product family. The broadening of the scope can be the result of the company deciding to bring more existing product categories under the platform umbrella or because it decides to diversify its product portfolio as the cost of creating new products has decreased considerably. At this stage, we have identified in a number of companies that broadening the scope of the software product family without adjusting the mode of operation quite fundamentally leads to a number of key concerns and problems that are logical and unavoidable. However, because of the earlier success that the organization has experienced, the problems are insufficiently identified as fundamental, but rather as execution challenges, and fundamental changes to the mode of operation are not made until the company experiences significant financial consequences.

platform   product

Fig. 1. Integration-oriented approach

The problems and their underlying causes that one may observe when the scope of a product family is broadened considerably over time include, among others, those described below:

1. **Decreasing complete commonality:** Before broadening the scope of the product family, the platform formed the common core of product functionality. However, with the increasing scope, the products are increasingly diverse in their requirements and amount of functionality that is required for all products is decreasing, in either absolute or relative terms. Consequently, the (relative) number of components that is shared by all products is decreasing, reducing the relevance of the common platform.

2. **Increasing partial commonality:** Functionality that is shared by some or many products, though not by all, is increasingly significantly with the increasing scope. Consequently, the (relative) number of components that is shared by some or most products is increasing. The typical approach to this model is the adoption of hierarchical product families. In this case, business groups or teams responsible for certain product categories build a platform on top of the company wide platform. Although this alleviates part of the problem, it does not provide an effective mechanism to share components between business groups or teams developing products in different product categories.

3. **Over-engineered architecture:** With the increasing scope of the product family, the set of business and technical qualities that needs to be supported by the common platform is broadening as well. Although no product needs support for all qualities, the architecture of the platform is required to do so and, consequently, needs to be over-engineered to satisfy the needs of all products and product categories.

4. **Cross–cutting features:** Especially in embedded systems, new features frequently fail to respect the boundaries of the platform. Whereas the typical approach is that differentiating features are implemented in the product (category) specific code, often these features require changes in the common components as well. Depending on the domain in which the organization develops products, the notion of a platform capturing the common functionality between all products may easily turn into an illusion as the scope of the product family increases.

5. **Maturity of product categories:** Different product categories developed by one organization frequently are in different phases of the lifecycle. The challenge is that, depending on the maturity of a product category, the requirements on the common platform are quite different. For instance, for mature product categories cost and reliability are typically the most important whereas for product categories early in the maturity phase feature richness and time-to-market are the most important drivers. A common platform has to satisfy the requirements of all product categories, which easily leads to tensions between the platform organization and the product categories.

6. **Unresponsiveness of platform:** Especially for product categories early in the maturation cycle, the slow release cycle of software platforms is particularly frustrating. Often, a new feature is required rapidly in a new product. However, the feature requires changes in some platform components. As the platform has a slow release cycle, the platform is typically unable to respond to the request of the product team. The product team is willing to implement this functionality itself, but the platform team is often not allowing this because of the potential consequences for the quality of the product team.

3 Towards Compositionality

Although software product families have proven their worth, as discussed above, there are several challenges to be faced when the product family approach is applied to an increasingly broad and diverse product portfolio. The most promising direction, as outlined in this paper, is towards a more compositional approach to product creation. One of the reasons for this is that in the integration-oriented approach all additions and changes to the platform components typically are released as part of an integrated platform release. This requires, first, all additions and changes for all components to be synchronized for a specific, typically large and complex, release and, second, easily causes cross-component errors as small glitches in alignment between evolving components cause integration errors.

The compositional approach aims to address these issues through the basic principle of independent deployment [6]. This principle is almost as old as the field of software engineering itself, but is violated in many software engineering efforts. Independent deployment states that a component, during evolution, always has to maintain "replaceability" with older versions. This principle is relatively easy to implement for the *provided interfaces* of a component, as it basically requires the component to just continue to offer backward compatibility. The principle however also applies to the *required interfaces* of a component. This is more complicated as this requires components to intelligently degrade their functionality when the required interfaces are bound to components that do not provide functionality required for new features. Thus, although the principle is easy to understand in abstract terms, the implementation often is more complicated, leading to situations where an R&D organization may easily abandon the principle.

If the principle of independent deployment is, however, adhered to, then a very powerful compositional model in the context of software product families is created: rather than requiring the evolution of each component or subsystem to be perfectly aligned, in this approach each component or subsystem can evolve separately. Because each component guarantees backward compatibility and supports intelligent degrading of provided functionality based on the composition in which the component is used, it facilitates a "continuous releasing" model, allowing new functionality to be available immediately to product derivation projects. In addition, quality issues can, to a much larger extent, be dealt with locally in individual components, rather than as part of the integration.

Although the approach described in this section has significant advantages for traditional product families, the broadening product scope of many families creates an increasing need for creating *creative configurations* [3]. Some typical reasons for creative configurations include:

- **Structural divergence:** As discussed earlier, the convergence trend is actually causing a divergence in product requirements. Components and subsystems need to be composed in alternative configurations because of product requirements that are deviating significantly from the standard product.
- **Functional divergence:** A second cause for requiring a creative configuration is where platform components need to be replaced with product specific components to allow for diverging product functionality.
- **Temporal divergence:** In some cases, the divergence between product requirements may be temporal, i.e. certain products require functionality significantly earlier than the main, high volume product segment for which the platform is targeted. Although every product family has leading, typically high-end, products feeding the rest of the product portfolio with new functionality, in this case the temporal divergence is much more significant than in those cases. This may, among others, be due to the need to create niche products or because of the need to respond more rapidly to changing market forces to an extent unable to be accounted for by typically slow platform development.
- **Quality divergence:** Finally, a fourth source of divergence is where specific quality attributes, e.g. security or reliability, require the insertion of behaviour *between* platform components in order to achieve certain quality requirements. Although the structure of the original platform architecture may be largely maintained, the connections between the components are replaced with behavioural modules that insert and coordinate functionality.

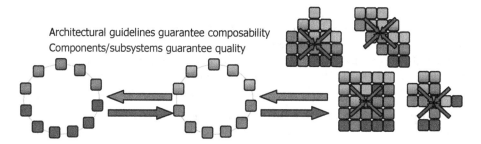

Architectural guidelines guarantee composability
Components/subsystems guarantee quality

Fig. 2. Compositional approach to software product families

In figure 2, the compositional approach is presented graphically. The main items to highlight include the creative product configurations shown on the right side and the fact that there are two evolutionary flows, i.e. from the platform components towards the products and visa versa.

In the paper so far, we have provided a general overview of the compositional approach to software platforms. However, this approach has bearing on many topics related to software product families. Below, we discuss a few of these.

Software variability management: In the research area of software product families, software variability management (SVM) is an important field of study. One may easily argue that the topics addressed in this paper can be addressed by employing appropriate variability mechanisms. In our experience, SVM is complementary to employing a compositional approach as the components still need to offer variation points and associated variants. In [5] we argue that SVM focuses primarily on varying behaviour in the context of stable architecture, whereas compositionality is primarily concerned with viewing the elements stable and the configurations in which the elements are combined to be the part that varies. In practice, however, both mechanisms are necessary when the scope of a product family extends beyond certain limits.

Software architecture: In most definitions of software architecture, the predominant focus is on the structure of the architecture, i.e. the boxes and lines. In some definitions, there is mention of the architectural principles guiding development and evolution [5], but few expand on this notion. In the context of compositional product families, the structural aspect of software architecture is become increasingly uninteresting from a design perspective, as the structure of the architecture will be different for each derived product and may even change during operation. Consequently, with the overall increase of dynamism in software systems, software architecture is more and more about the architectural principles. In [2], we argue that architectural principles can be categorized into architecture rules, architecture constraints and the associated rationale.

Software configuration management (SCM): At each stage of evolving an existing component, there is a decision to version or to branch. Versioning requires that the resulting component either contains a superset of the original and additional functionality or introduce a variation point that allows the functionality provided by the component to be configured at some point during the product derivation lifecycle. Branching creates an additional parallel version of the component that requires a selection during the product derivation. Although branching has its place in engineering complex software product families, it has disadvantages with respect to managing continued updates and bug fixes. It easily happens that, once branched, a component branch starts to diverge to the point that the product originally requiring the branching lacks too many features in the component and abandons it.

4   Component Model for Compositional Platforms

The Holy Grail in the software reuse research community has, for the last four decades, been that components not developed for integration with each other can be composed and result in the best possible composed functionality. In practice, this has proven to be surprisingly difficult, among others because components often have expectations on their context of use. In the context of the integration-oriented approach, we see that components typically have more expectations on components both providing and requiring functionality and that these expectations, paradoxically, that are less precisely and explicitly defined. In contrast, composition-oriented components use only explicitly defined dependencies and contain intelligence to handle partially met binding of interfaces.

For the software assets making up a product family, at least the components and subsystems need to satisfy a number of requirements in order facilitate composability. Different aspects of these requirements as well as additional requirements have been identified by other researchers as well.

- **Interface completeness:** The composition of components and subsystems should only require the information specified in the provided, required and configuration interfaces. Depending on the type of product family, compile-time, link-time, installation-time and/or run-time composition of provided interfaces and required interfaces should be facilitated and the composition should lead to systems providing the best possible functionality given the composition.
- **Intelligent degradation:** Components should be constructed such that partial binding of the required interfaces results in automatic, intelligent degradation of the functionality offered through the provided interfaces of the component. In reality, this can not be achieved for all required interfaces, so for most components the required interfaces can be classified as core (must be bound) and non-core (can be bound). This is mirrored in the provided interfaces that degrade their functionality accordingly. In practice, most non-core interfaces represent steps in the evolution of the component or subsystem.
- **Variability management:** Non-core interfaces and configurable internal behaviour are part of the overall variability offered by a component or subsystem and needs to be accessible to the users of the component through a specific configuration or variability interface.

One of the general trends in software engineering is later binding or, in general, delaying decisions to the latest point in the software lifecycle that is still acceptable from an economic perspective. Also for embedded systems, an increasing amount of configuration and functionality extension can take place after the initial deployment. However, for post-deployment composability to be feasible, again the software assets that are part of the product family need to satisfy some additional requirements.

- **Two descriptions:** A component requires an operational description of its behaviour (code) as well as an inspectable model of its intended behaviour.
- **Monitoring required interfaces:** For each required interface, a component has an inspectable model of the behaviour required from a component bound to the interface. This allows a component to monitor its providing components.
- **Self-monitoring:** In addition to monitoring its providing components, a component observes its own behaviour and identifies mismatches between specified and actual behaviour.
- **Reactive adjustment:** A component can initiate corrective actions for a subset of mismatches between required and actual behaviour of itself or of its providing components and is able to report other mismatches to the encompassing component/subsystem.

Concluding, although some of the techniques described in this section require more advanced solutions provided by the development environment, by and large the compositional approach can be implemented using normal software development tools and environments. The main transformation for most organizations is mostly concerned with organizational and cultural changes.

5 Conclusions

This paper discusses and presents the challenges of the traditional, integration-oriented approach to software product families when the scope of the family is extended. These problems include the decreasing complete commonality, increasing partial commonality, the need to over-engineer the platform architecture, cross–cutting features, different maturity of product categories and, consequently, increasing unresponsiveness of the platform.

   As a solution to addressing these concerns we present the compositional platform approach. This approach becomes necessary when the traditional integration-oriented approach needs to be stretched beyond its original boundaries. We have identified at least four types of divergence, i.e. structural divergence, functional divergence, temporal divergence and quality divergence. The compositional platform approach is based on the principle of *independent deployment* [6]. This principle defines rules that components need to satisfy in order to provide backward compatibility and flexibly in addressing partial binding of required interfaces. In particular, three aspects are necessary but not sufficient requirements: interface completeness, intelligent degradation and variability management.

   Although many product families implement or support a small slice of the principles and mechanisms, few examples exist that support a fully compositional platform approach. In that sense this paper should be considered as visionary rather than actual. However, the problems and challenges of the integration-oriented approach are real and as a community, we need to develop solutions that can be adopted by the software engineering industry.

References

1. J. Bosch, Design and Use of Software Architectures: Adopting and Evolving a Product Line Approach, Pearson Education (Addison-Wesley & ACM Press), ISBN 0-201-67494-7, May 2000.
2. Jan Bosch, Software Architecture: The Next Step, Proceedings of the First European Workshop on Software Architecture (EWSA 2004), Springer LNCS, May 2004.
3. Sybren Deelstra, Marco Sinnema and Jan Bosch, Product Derivation in Software Product Families: A Case Study, Journal of Systems and Software, Volume 74, Issue 2, pp. 173-194, 15 January 2005.
4. www.softwarearchitectureportal.org
5. R. van Ommering, J. Bosch, Widening the Scope of Software Product Lines - From Variation to Composition, Proceedings of the Second Software Product Line Conference (SPLC2), pp. 328-347, August 2002.
6. R. van Ommering, Building product populations with software components, Proceedings of the 24th International Conference on Software Engineering, pp. 255 – 265, 2002.
7. http://www.oreillynet.com/pub/a/oreilly/tim/news/2005/09/30/what-is-web-20.html

Contract-Driven Development

Bertrand Meyer
(Joint work with Andreas Leitner)

E.T.H. Zurich, Switzerland
Bertrand.Meyer@inf.ethz.ch

Abstract. In spite of cultural difference between the corresponding scientific communities, recognition is growing that test-based and specification-based approaches to software development actually complement each other. The revival of interest in testing tools and techniques follows in particular from the popularity of "Test-Driven Development"; rigorous specification and proofs have, for their part, also made considerable progress. There remains, however, a fundamental superiority of specifications over test: you can derive tests from a specification, but not the other way around.

Contract-Driven Development is a new approach to systematic software construction combining ideas from Design by Contract, from Test-Driven Development, from work on formal methods, and from advances in automatic testing as illustrated for example in our AutoTest tool. Like TDD it gives tests a central role in the development process, but these tests are deduced from possibly partial specifications (contracts) and directly supported by the development environment. This talk will explain the concepts and demonstrate their application.

M.B. Dwyer and A. Lopes (Eds.): FASE 2007, LNCS 4422, p. 11, 2007.
© Springer-Verlag Berlin Heidelberg 2007

EQ-Mine: Predicting Short-Term Defects for Software Evolution

Jacek Ratzinger[1], Martin Pinzger[2], and Harald Gall[2]

[1] Distributed Systems Group
Vienna University of Technology, Austria
ratzinger@infosys.tuwien.ac.at
[2] s.e.a.l. – software evolution and architecture lab
University of Zurich, Switzerland
{pinzger,gall}@ifi.unizh.ch

Abstract. We use 63 features extracted from sources such as versioning and issue tracking systems to predict defects in short time frames of two months. Our multivariate approach covers aspects of software projects such as size, team structure, process orientation, complexity of existing solution, difficulty of problem, coupling aspects, time constrains, and testing data. We investigate the predictability of several severities of defects in software projects. Are defects with high severity difficult to predict? Are prediction models for defects that are discovered by internal staff similar to models for defects reported from the field?

We present both an exact numerical prediction of future defect numbers based on regression models as well as a classification of software components as defect-prone based on the C4.5 decision tree. We create models to accurately predict short-term defects in a study of 5 applications composed of more than 8.000 classes and 700.000 lines of code. The model quality is assessed based on 10-fold cross validation.

Keywords: Software Evolution, Defect Density, Quality Prediction, Machine Learning, Regression, Classification.

1 Introduction

We want to improve the evolvability of software by providing prediction models to assess quality as soon as possible in the product life cycle. When software systems evolve we need to measure the outcome of the systems before shipping them to customers. Software management systems such as the concurrent versioning system (CVS) and issue tracking systems (Jira) capture data about the evolution of the software during development. Our approach, EQ-Mine uses this data to compute a number of features, which are computed for source file revisions in the pre- and post-release phases. Based on these evolution measures we then set up a prediction model.

To evaluate the defect density prediction capabilities of our evolution measures we apply three data mining algorithms and test 5 specified hypotheses. Results

M.B. Dwyer and A. Lopes (Eds.): FASE 2007, LNCS 4422, pp. 12–26, 2007.
© Springer-Verlag Berlin Heidelberg 2007

clearly underline that defect prediction models have to take into account different aspects and measures of the software development and maintenance [1]. In extension to our previous work on predicting defect density of source files [2] we use detailed evolution data from an industrial software project and include team structure and process measures.

The remaining paper is structured as follows. It starts with the formulation of our research hypotheses (section 2). Related work is discussed in section 3. In section 4 we describe the evolution measures used to build our defect prediction model. Our approach is evaluated on a case study in section 5. We finalize this paper with our conclusions and intent for future work in section 6.

2   Hypotheses

To guide the metrics selection for defect prediction and our evaluation with a case study, we set up several hypotheses. In contrast to previous research approaches (e.g. [3]) EQ-Mine aims at a fine-grained level. Our hypothesis are used to focus on different aspects of our fine grained analysis such as the severity of defects, the timing of predictions around releases, and the type of defect discovered (internal vs. external):

- *H1: Defect density can be predicted based on a short time-frame.* Previous research focused on the prediction of longer time-frames such as releases [4, 5]. In our research we focus on months as time scale and use two months of development time to predict defect densities for the following two months.
- *H2: Critical defects with high severity have a low regularity.* Prediction models build on the regularity of the underlying data and can predict events better that correspond to this regularity. We expect that defects that are critical are more difficult to detect as they "hide better" during the testing and product delivery.
- *H3: Quality predictions before a release are more accurate than after a release.* Project quality can be estimated in different stages of the development process. Some stages are more difficult to assess than others. Previous studies already indicated that the accuracy of data mining in software engineering varies over time (e.g. [5]). We expect that defects that are detected before a release date are easier to predict than defects that are reported afterwards.
- *H4: Defects discovered by internal staff have more regularity than defects reported by the customer.* For prediction model creation it is an important input to know where the defect comes from. Was it recognized by the internal staff (e.g. during testing) or does the defect report come from customer sites? We expect that internally and externally detected defects have different characteristics. As a result one group can be easier predicted than the other one.
- *H5: Different aspects of software evolution have to be regarded for an accurate defect prediction.* We use a large amount of evolution indicators for defect prediction. These indicators can be grouped into several categories such as

size and complexity measures, indicators for the complexity of the existing solution and team related issues. For defect prediction we expect that data mining features from many different categories are important.

3   Related Work

Many organizations want to predict software quality before their systems are used. Fenton and Neil provide a critical review of literature that describes several software metrics and a wide range of prediction models [1]. They found out that most of the statistical models are based on size and complexity metrics with the aim to predict the number of defects in a system. Others are based on testing results, the testing process, the "quality" of the development process, or take a multivariate approach.

There are various techniques to identify critical code pieces. The most common one is to define typical bug patterns that are derived from experience and published common pitfalls in a certain programming language. Wagner et al. [6] analyzed several industrial and development projects with the help of bug detection tools as well as with other types of defect-detection techniques.

Khoshgoftaar et al. [7] use software metrics as input to classification trees to predict fault-prone modules. One release provides the training dataset and the subsequent release is used for evaluation purpose. They claim that the resulting model achieved useful accuracy in spite of the very small proportion of fault-prone modules in the system. Classification trees generate partition trees based on a training data set describing known experiences of interest (e.g. characteristics of the software). The tree structure is intuitive and can be easily interpreted. Briand et al. [8] try to improve the predictive capabilities by combining the expressiveness of classification trees with the rigor of a statistical basis. Their approach called OSR generates a set of patterns relevant to the predicted object estimated based on the entropy H.

There are different reasons for each fault: Some faults exist because of errors in the specification of requirements. Others are directly attributable to errors committed in the design process. Finally, there are errors that are introduced directly into the source. Nikora and Munson developed a standard for the enumeration of faults based on the structural characteristics of the MDS software system [9]. Changes to the system are visible at the module level (i.e. procedures and functions) and therefore this level of granularity is measured. This fault measurement process was then applied to a software system's structural evolution during its development. Every change to the software system was measured and every fault was identified and tracked to a specific line of code. The rate of change in program modules should serve as a good index of the rate of fault introduction. In a study the application of machine learning (inductive) technique was tested for the software maintenance process. Shirabad et al. [10] present an example of an artificial intelligence method that can be used in future maintenance activities. An induction algorithm is applied to a set of pre-classified training examples of the concept we want to learn. The large size and complexity of systems, high staff turnover, poor documentation and the long periods of time these systems must be maintained leads to a lack of knowledge in how to proceed the maintenance of software systems.

Only a small number of empirical studies using industrial software systems are performed and published. Ostrand and Weyuker, for example, evaluated a large inventory tracking system at AT&T [4]. They analyzed how faults are distributed over different releases. They discovered that faults are always heavily concentrated in a relatively small number of releases during the entire life cycle. Additionally the number of faults is getting higher as the product matures and high-fault modules tend to remain high fault in later releases. So it would be worthwhile to concentrate fault detection on a relatively small number of high fault-prone releases, if they can be identified early.

4   Data Measures

To mine software development projects we use the data obtained from versioning system (CVS) and issue tracking system (Jira). CVS enable the handling of different versions of files in cooperating teams. This tool logs every change event, which provides the necessary information about the history of a software system. The log-information for our mining approach—pure textual, human readable information—is retrieved via standard command line tools, parsed and stored in the release history database [11].

Jira manages data about project issues such as bug reports or feature requests. This system give a historical overview of the requirements and their implementations. We extract the data based on its backup facility, where the entire issue data can be exported into XML files. These files are processed to import the information into our database. In a post-processing step we link issues from Jira to log information from CVS using the comments of developers in commit messages by searching for issue numbers. In addition we distinguish between issues created by developers and issues created by customers by linking issue reporters to CVS authors. Issues are counted as reported by internal staff when the issue reporter can be linked to a CVS author otherwise the issue is defined to be external (e.g. hotline).

4.1   Features

From the linked data in the release history database we compute 63 evolution measures that are considered as features for data mining. These features are gathered on file basis, where data from all revisions of a file within a predefined time period is summarized. To build a balanced prediction model we create features to represent several important aspects of software development such as the complexity of the designed solution, process used for development, interrelation of classes, etc. As previous studies [2, 3] discovered that relative features provide better performance in prediction than absolute ones, we decided that all our 63 features have to be relative. For EQ-Mina we set up the following categories of features for each file containing changes within the inspection period:

Size. This category groups "classical" measures such as lines of code from an evolution perspective: *linesAdded, linesModified,* or *linesDeleted* relative to the total *LOC* of a file. For example a file had three revisions within the learning period adding 3, 5, and 4 lines and this file had 184 lines before the learning period, we feed into the data mining: $(linesAdded = (3+5+4)/184) => (\sum$ defects$)$.

Other features of this category are *linesType,* which defines if there are more *linesAdded* or *linesModified.* Additionally, we regard *largeChanges* as double of the *LOC* of the average change size and *smallChanges* as half of the average *LOC.* We expect that this number is an important feature in the data mining, as other studies have found out that small modules are more defect-prone than large ones. [12, 13]

Team. The number of authors of files influences the way software is developed. We expect that the more authors are working on the changes the higher is the possibility of rework and mistakes. We define a feature for the *authorCount* relative to the *changeCount.* Further, the interrelation in people work is interesting. We investigate work rotation between the authors involved in the changes of each file as the feature *authorSwitches.* The number of people assigned to an issue and the authors contributing to the implementation of this issue is another feature we use for our prediction models.

Process orientation. In this category we assemble features that define how disciplined people follow software development processes. For source code changes developers have to include the issue number in their commit message to the versioning system. We define a feature regarding *issueCount* relative to *changeCount.* The developer is requested to also provide some rationale in the commit message. Thus, we use *withNoMessage* measuring changes without any commit comment as a feature for prediction.

In each project the distribution between different priorities of issues should be balanced. Usually, the number of issues with highest priority is very low. A high value may indicate problems in the project that have effects on quality and re-work amount. Accordingly, we investigate *highPriorityIssues* and *middlePriorityIssues* relative to the total number of issues. Also the time to close certain classes of issues provides interesting input for prediction and we use *avgDaysHighPriorityIssues* and *avgDaysMiddlePriorityIssues* in relation to the average number of days that are necessary to close an issue.

To get an estimation for the work habits of the developers we inspect the number of *addingChanges, modifyingChanges,* and *deletingChanges* per file. This information provides input to the defect prediction of files.

Complexity of existing solution. According to the laws of software evolution [14], software continuously becomes more complex. Changes are more difficult to add as the software is more difficult to understand and the contracts between existing parts have to retain. As a result we investigate the *changeCount* in relation to the number of changes during the entire history of each file. The *changeActivityRate* is defined as the number of changes during the entire lifetime of the file relative to the months of the lifetime. The *linesActivityRate* describes the number of lines of code relative to the age of the file in months.

We approximate the quality of the existing solution by the *bugfixCountBefore* before our prediction period relative to the general number of changes before the prediction period. We expect that the higher the fix rate is before the inspection period the more difficult it is to get a better quality later on. The *bugfixCount* is used as well as *bugfixLinesAdded*, *bugfixLinesModified*, and *bugfixLinesDeleted* in relation to the base measures such as the number of lines of code added, modified, and deleted for this file. For bug fixes not much new code should be necessary, as most code is added for new requirements. Therefore, *linesAddPerBugfix*, *linesModifiedPerBugfix*, and *linesDeletedPerBugfix* are interesting indicators, which measure the average lines of code for bug fixes.

Difficulty of problem. New classes are added to object-oriented systems when new features and new requirements have to be satisfied. We use the information whether a file was newly introduced during the prediction period as feature for data mining. To measure how often a file was involved during development with the introduction of other new files we use *cochangeNewFiles* as a second indicator. Co-changed files are identified as described in [15].

The amount of information necessary to describe a requirement is also an important source of information. The feature *issueAttachments* identifies the number of attachments per issue.

Relational Aspects. In object-oriented systems the relationship between classes is an important metrics. We use the co-change coupling between files to estimate their relationship. We use the number of co-changed files relative to the change count as feature *cochangedFiles*.

Additionally, we quantify co-changed couplings with features based on commit transactions similar to the size measures for single files: *TLinesAdded*, *TLinesModified*, and *TLinesDeleted* relative to lines of code added, modified, and deleted. The *TLinesType* describes if the transactions contained more lines added or lines modified. *TChangeType* is a coarser grained feature that describes if this file was part of transactions with more adding revisions or more modifying revisions.

For file relations we also use bug fix related features: *TLinesAddedPerBugfix* and *TLinesChangedPerBugfix* are two representatives. Additionally, we use *TBugfixLinesAdded*, *TBugfixLinesModified*, and *TBugfixLinesDeleted* relative to the *linesAdded*, *linesModified*, and *linesDeleted*.

Time constraints. As software processes stress the necessity of certain activities and artifacts, we believe that the time constrains are important for software predictions. The *avgDaysBetweenChanges* feature is defined as the average number of days between revisions. The number of days per line of code added or changed captured as *avgDaysPerLine*.

Peaks and outliers have been shown to give interesting events in software projects [15]. For the *relativePeakMonth* feature we measure the location of the peak month, which contains most revisions, within the prediction period. The *peakChangeCount* feature describes the number of changes happening during the peak month normalized by the overall number of changes. The number of changes is measured based on the months in the prediction period with feature *change-ActivityRate*. For more fine grained data the lines of code added and changed relative to the number of months is regarded for feature *linesActivityRate*.

Testing. We use testing metrics as an input to prediction models, because they allow estimating the remaining bug number. The number of bug fixes initiated by the developers itself provides insight into the quality attentiveness of the team and are covered by feature *bugfixesDiscoveredByDeveloper*.

4.2   Data Mining

For model generation and evaluation we use the data mining tool called Weka [16]. It provides algorithms for different data mining tasks such as classification, clustering, and association analysis. For our prediction and classification models we selected linear regression, regression trees (M5), and classifier C4.5. The regression algorithms are used to predict the number of defects for a class from its evolution attributes.

The following metrics are used to assess the quality of our numeric prediction models:

- *Correlation Coefficient* (C. Coef.) ranges from -1 to 1 and measures the statistical correlation between the predicted values and the actual ones in the test set. A value of 0 indicates no correlation, whereas 1 describes a perfect correlation. Negative correlation indicates inverse correlation, but should not occur for prediction models.
- *Mean Absolute Error* (Abs. Error) is the average of the magnitude of individual absolute errors. This assessment metrics does not have a fixed range like the correlation coefficient, but is geared to the values to be predicted. In our case the number of defects per file is predicted, which ranges from 1 to 6 and 16 respectively (see Table 1 and Table 2). As a result, the closer the mean absolute error is to 0 the better. A value of 1 denotes that on average the predicted value differs from the actual number of defects by 1 (e.g. 3,5 instead of 4).
- *Mean Squared Error* (Sqr. Error) is the average of the squared magnitude of individual errors and it tends to exaggerate the effect of outliers – instances with larger prediction error – more than mean absolute error. The range of the mean squared error is geared to the ranges of predicted values, similar to the mean absolute error. But this time the error metrics is squared, which overemphasize predictions that are far away of the actual number of defects. The quality of the prediction model is good, when the mean squared error is close to the mean absolute error.

The quality of our prediction models is assessed through 10-fold cross validation. For this method the set of instances is splitt randomly into 10 sub-sets (folds) and the model is build 10 times and validated 10 times. For each turn the classification model is trained on nine folds and the remaining one is used for testing. The resulting 10 quality measures are averaged to yield an overall quality estimation. Therefore, 10-fold cross validation is a strong validation technique.

5   Case Study

For our case study with EQ-Mine we analyzed a commercial software system from the health care environment. The software system is composed of 5 applications such as a clinical workstation or a patient administration system. This object-oriented system is built in Java consisting of 8.600 classes with 735.000 lines of code. For the clinical workstation a plug-in framework similar to the one of Eclipse is used and currently 51 plug-ins are implemented. The development is supported by CVS as the versioning system for source files and Jira as the issue tracking system. We analyzed the last two releases of this software system: One in the first half of 2006 and the other one in the middle of 2005.

Table 1. Pre-release: Number of files distinguishing between the ones with defects of all severities and files where defects with high severity were found

Number of defects per file (all severities)	Number of files	Number of defects per file (high severity)	Number of files
1	46	1	10
2	11	2	2
3	5	3	1
4	7	4	0
5	2	5	0
6	1	6	0

5.1   Experimental Setup

For our experiments we investigated 8 months of software evolution in our case study. We use two months of development time to predict the defects of the following two months, which builds up a 4 months time frame. We compare the predictions before the release date with the predictions after it, which results in a period of 8 months. Before the release we create prediction models for defects in general and for defects with high severity. These models can be compared to the ones after. After the release date we additionally distinguish defects discovered by internal staff vs. defects reported from the field (customer). With this experimental set up we test our hypotheses from Section 2.

Table 2. Post-release: Number of files distinguishing different types of defects

Number of defects with severity reported by	No. of files severity=all int. & ext.	No. of files severity=all internal staff	No. of files severity=all external customer	No. of files severity=high int. & ext.
1	46	30	32	21
2	21	12	7	1
3	8	6	1	0
4	6	4	1	0
5	5	4	0	0
7	1	1	0	0
12	1	1	0	0
16	1	1	0	0

5.2   Results

Short Time Frames. Our analysis focuses on short time frames. To evaluate H1 of Section 2 we use two months of development time to predict the following two months. Table 3 shows several models predicting defects before the release where the two months period for defect counting are laid directly before the release date and the other two months before this two target months are taken to collect feature variables for the prediction models. In the first Table 3(a) we can see that we obtain a correlation coefficient larger than 0.5, which is a quite good correlation. The mean absolute error is low with 0.46 for linear regression and 0.36 for M5 and the mean squared error is also low with 0.79 for linear regression and 0.67 for M5. In order to assess these prediction errors, Table 1 describes the defect distribution of the two target months. As mean squared error emphasizes outliers, we can state that the overall error performance of the prediction of all pre-release defects is very good.

Table 3. Prediction pre-release defects

	C. Coef.	Abs. Error	Sqr. Error		C. Coef.	Abs. Error	Sqr. Error
Lin. Reg.	0.5031	0.4604	0.7881	Lin. Reg.	-0.0424	0.1352	0.3173
M5	0.6137	0.3602	0.6674	M5	0.0927	0.0792	0.2589
(a) All defects				(b) High severity defects			

To confirm our first hypothesis Table 4(a) lists the quality measures for the prediction of post-release defects. There the values are not as good as for pre-release defects, but the correlation coefficients are still close to 0.5. Therefore, we confirm H1:

> We can predict short time frames of two months based on feature data of two months.

High Severity. Table 3(b) shows the results for the prediction models on pre-release defects with high severity. We get the severity level of each defect from the issue tracking system, where the defect reporter assigns severity levels. The quality measures for high severity defects differ from the prediction of all defects, because the number and distribution of high severity defects have other characteristics (see Table 1). It is interesting that linear regression has only a negative correlation coefficient. But also M5 can only reach a very low correlation coefficient of 0.10. The overall error level is low because of the small defect bandwidth of 0 up to 3.

Table 4. Prediction post-release defects

	C. Coef.	Abs. Error	Sqr. Error
Lin. Reg.	0.5041	0.9443	1.5285
M5	0.4898	0.7743	1.4152

(a) All defects

	C. Coef.	Abs. Error	Sqr. Error
Lin. Reg.	0.4464	0.9012	1.5151
M5	0.5285	0.688	1.3194

(b) Defects discovered internally
(through test + development)

	C. Coef.	Abs. Error	Sqr. Error
Lin. Reg.	0.253	0.3663	0.5699
M5	0.4716	0.2606	0.4574

(c) Defects discovered externally
(through customer + partner companies)

	C. Coef.	Abs. Error	Sqr. Error
Lin. Reg.	0.1579	0.1973	0.3175
M5	0.087	0.1492	0.3048

(d) High severity defects

For the post-release prediction of high severity defects in Table 4(d) the correlation coefficient of 0.16 is slightly better. The prediction errors are slightly worse, but this is due to the fact that there are more post-release defects with high severity than pre-release. However, we can conclude:

> Defects with high severity cannot be predicted with such a precision as overall defects.

Before vs. After Release. Our hypothesis H3 states that pre-release defects can be better predicted than the post-release ones. When we compare Table 3(a) with Table 4(a) we see that our hypothesis seems to be confirmed. The correlation coefficients of linear regression are very similar, but the prediction errors are higher for pre-release defects. This situation is even more remarkable for M5, as the pre-release correlation coefficient reaches 0.61 whereas the post-release remains at 0.49. For these prediction models also the two error measures are much higher for post-release. While comparing the defect distribution between pre-release in Table 1 with post-release in Table 2, we could believe that the high error rate is due to the fact that we discovered more files with many defects that occur post-release than pre-release. But when we repeat the model creation of post-release defects with a similar distribution to pre-release, we get still a mean absolute error of 0.68 and a mean squared error of 1.06, which is still clearly larger than for pre-release.

What about high severity defects? Are they still better predictable before a release than after? When we look at Table 3(b) and Table 4(d) we see a similar picture for this subgroup of defects. Only the correlation coefficient for linear regression is higher for post-release defects than for pre-release, because there are many more high severity defects after the release. This could be because the defects reported from customers are ranked higher than when they are discovered internally, in order to stress the fact that the defects from customers have to be fixed fast. When we repeat the model creation with similar distributions of pre-release and post-release we get similar correlation coefficients but higher prediction errors for post-release. Therefore, we can conclude that:

> Predictions of post-release defects have higher errors than for models generated for pre-release.

Discovered Internally vs. Externally. We show the difference between prediction of defects discovered by internal staff (testers, developers) vs. defects discovered externally (e.g. customer, partner companies) in Table 4(b) and Table 4(c). For internal defects the correlation coefficient is larger than 0.5, which is produced by the M5 predictor. Although it seems that the prediction error is lower for external defects than for internal ones, this result may be caused by the fact that there are no files with many externally discovered defects (see post-release defect distribution in Table 2). However, when we redo the prediction for internal defects with a similar distribution as for external defects, we get a mean absolute error of 0.48 and a mean squared error of 0.86 with a correlation coefficient of 0.47. As a result, we can partly reject H4 and conclude that:

> Defects discovered externally by customers and partner companies can be predicted with lower absolute and squared error than defects discovered internally by testers and developers.

Aspects of Prediction Models. To analyze the aspects of prediction models in more detail we created two cases using the C4.5 tree classifier: The first model distinguishes between files that are defect-prone vs. files without defects. The second tree model separates the files with just one defect from the ones with several defects. At each node in the tree, a value for the given feature is used to divide the entities into two groups: files with a feature value large/smaller than the threshold. The leafs of the decision trees provide a label for the entities (e.g. predicted number of defects). For each file such a tree has to be traversed according to its features to obtain the predicted class. If a node has no or only one successor than it is defined to be a leaf node for a part of the tree.

Tree 1 describes that the feature bearing the most information concerning defect-proneness is the location of the peak month, where the peak month is defined as the one containing the most change events for the analyzed file. Features on the second level are change activity rate and author count. Relative peak month and change activity rate represent the category of time constraints. Nevertheless, the tree is composed of features from many different categories. Author count and author switches belong to the team category. The number of resolved issues in relation to all issues referenced by source code revisions is an indicator for the process category, similar to the number of source adding changes in relation to the overall change count. Also the ratio of revisions without a commit message describes the process orientation of the development. The number of lines added per bug fix provides insight into the development process itself. *We conclude that not size and complexity measures dominate defect-proneness, but many people-related issues are important.*

tree root
relativePeakMonth
— changeActivityRate
— — resolvedIssues
— — — bugfixLinesAdded
— — — — withNoMessage
relativePeakMonth
— authorCount
— — addingChanges
— — — authorSwitches

Tree 1. Pre-release with/without defects

Tree 2 describes the prediction model evaluating the defect-prone files (one vs. several defects). This classification tree is much smaller than the previous one for prediction of defect-prone files. Nevertheless, it contains data mining features from many categories. The top level and the bottom level both regard lines edited during bug fixing, but on the first level the lines added to the file are of interest whereas at the bottom the relational aspect is central with lines deleted in all files of common commit transactions. Additionally, the team aspect plays an important role, as the number of author switches is the feature on the second level. The model is completed by features indicating the ratio of adding and changing modifications.

tree root
linesAddPerBugfix
— authorSwitches
— — addingChanges
— — — modifyingChanges
— — — — TBugfixLinesDel

Tree 2. Pre-release one vs. several defects

From these classifications we conclude that:

> Multiple aspects such as time constraints, process orientation, team related and bug-fix related features play an important role in defect prediction models.

5.3 Limitations

Our mining approach is strongly related with the quality of our data for the case study. As a result, validity of our findings is related with the data of the versioning and issue tracking system. Versioning systems register single events such as commits of developers, where the event recording depends on the work habits of the developers. However, we could show that an averaging effect supports statistical analysis [17] in general.

Our data rely strongly on automated processing. On one hand this ensures constancy, but on the other hand it is a source of blurring effects. In our case we extracted issue numbers from commit messages to map the two information systems. To improve the situation we could try to map from bug reports to code changes based on commit dates and issue dates as described in [5]. In our case this approach does not provide any valuable mappings, which we discovered on a random sample of 100 discovered matches.

We can only identify locations of defects corrections based on change data from versioning systems and derive from this information prediction models for components. Bug fixes can take place at locations different to the source of defects. Similar approaches are used by other researchers [5, 4, 3]. With predicting defect corrections, we provide insight into improvement efforts, as defect fixes could be places being in urgent need of code stabilization.

For our empirical study we selected software applications of different types such as graphical workstations, administrative consoles, archiving and communication systems, etc. We still cannot claim generalization of our approach on other kinds of software systems. Therefore, we need to evaluate the applicability of EQ-Mine on each specific software project. Nevertheless, this research work contributes to the existing empirical body of knowledge.

6 Conclusions and Future Work

In this work we have investigated several aspects of defect prediction based on a large industrial case study. Our research contributes to the body of knowledge in the field of software quality estimation in several ways. We conducted one of the first studies dealing with fine grained predictions of defects. We estimate the defect proneness based on a short time-frame. With this approach project managers can decide on the best time-frame for release and take preventive actions to improve user satisfaction. Additionally, we compare defect prediction before and after releases of our case study and discovered that in both cases an accurate prediction model can be established. In contrast to other studies, we investigated the predictability of defects of different severity. We could show that prediction of defects with high severity has lower precision. We also analyzed customer perceived quality, where defects reported by customers need other prediction models than defects discovered by internal staff such as testing.

In order to create accurate prediction models we inspected different aspects of software projects. Although size was already used in many other studies it is still an important input for prediction. We extend size measures with relational aspects, where we use the data about evolutionary co-change coupling of software entities. We can show that, for example, the number of lines added to all classes on common changes is as important for defect prediction of a class as the number of lines added to this particular class. Other aspects of our approach are the complexity of the existing solution and the difficulty of the problem in general, as they are causes of software defects. We include people issues of different types in our analysis to cover another important cause of defects. When a developer has to work on software that somebody else has initially written mistakes can occur, because she has to understand the design of her colleague. Factors such as author switches are covered by our team group of data mining features. The discipline of a developer does also influence defect probability. As a result we use indicators for process related issues. Finally, we include time constrains and testing related features into our defect prediction models. The models were created based on 63 data mining features from the 8 categories described.

In our future work we focus on the following topics:

- *Software Structure.* As we currently use evolution measures for quality estimations, we intend to enrich our models with information about software structures. Object-oriented inheritance hierarchies as well as data and control flow information provide many insights into software systems, which we will include in our quality considerations.
- *Automation.* Our analysis relies on automated data processing such as information retrieval, mapping of defect and version information, and feature computation. The model creation relies on scripts using the Weka data mining tool [16]. Integrated tools providing predictions and model details such as the most important features can help different stakeholders. On the one hand, developers could profit from this information best, when it is available in the development environment. On the other hand, project managers need a lightweight tool separated from development environments to base their decisions on.

Acknowledgments

This work is partly funded by the Austrian Fonds zur Frderung der Wissenschaftlichen Forschung (FWF) as part of project P19867-N13. We thank Peter Vorburger for his valuable input and thoughts to this research work. Special thanks go to André Neubauer and others for their comments on earlier versions of this paper.

References

1. Fenton, N.E., Neil, M.: A critique of software defect prediction models. IEEE Transactions on Software Engineering **25**(5) (1999) 675–689
2. Knab, P., Pinzger, M., Bernstein, A.: Predicting defect densities in source code files with decision tree learners. In: Proceedings of the International Workshop on Mining Software Repositories, Shanghai, China, ACM Press (2006) 119–125
3. Nagappan, N., Ball, T.: Use of relative code churn measures to predict system defect density. In: Proceedings of the International Conference on Software Engineering, St. Louis, MO, USA (2005) 284–292
4. Ostrand, T.J., Weyuker, E.J.: The distribution of faults in a large industrial software system. In: Proceedings of the International Symposium on Software Testing and Analysis, Rome, Italy (2002) 55–64
5. Schröter, A., Zimmermann, T., Zeller, A.: Predicting component failures at design time. In: Proceedings of the International Symposium on Empirical Software Engineering, Rio de Janeiro, Brazil (2006) 18–27
6. Wagner, S., Jürjens, J., Koller, C., Trischberger, P.: Comparing bug finding tools with reviews and tests. In: Proceedings of the International Conference on Testing of Communicating Systems, Montreal, Canada (2005) 40–55
7. Khoshgoftaar, T.M., Yuan, X., Allen, E.B., Jones, W.D., Hudepohl, J.P.: Uncertain classification of fault-prone software modules. Empirical Software Engineering **7**(4) (2002) 297–318
8. Briand, L.C., Basili, V.R., Thomas, W.M.: A pattern recognition approach for software engineering data analysis. IEEE Transactions on Software Engineering **18**(11) (1992) 931–942
9. Nikora, A.P., Munson, J.C.: Developing fault predictors for evolving software systems. In: Proceedings of the Software Metrics Symposium, Sydney, Australia (2003) 338–350
10. Shirabad, J.S., Lethbridge, T.C., Matwin, S.: Mining the maintenance history of a legacy software system. In: Proceedings of the International Conference on Software Maintenance, Amsterdam, The Netherlands (2003) 95–104
11. Fischer, M., Pinzger, M., Gall, H.: Populating a release history database from version control and bug tracking systems. In: Proceedings of the International Conference on Software Maintenance, Amsterdam, Netherlands, IEEE Computer Society Press (2003) 23–32
12. Moeller, K., Paulish, D.: An empirical investigation of software fault distribution. In: Proceedings of the International Software Metrics Symposium. (1993) 82–90
13. Hatton, L.: Re-examining the fault density-component size connection. IEEE Software **14**(2) (1997) 89–98
14. Lehman, M.M., Belady, L.A.: Program Evolution - Process of Software Change. Academic Press, London and New York (1985)
15. Gall, H., Jazayeri, M., Ratzinger (former Krajewski), J.: CVS release history data for detecting logical couplings. In: Proceedings of the International Workshop on Principles of Software Evolution, Lisbon, Portugal, IEEE Computer Society Press (2003) 13–23
16. Witten, I.H., Frank, E.: Data Mining: Practical machine learning tools and techniques. 2 edn. Morgan Kaufmann, San Francisco, USA (2005)
17. Ratzinger, J., Fischer, M., Gall, H.: Evolens: Lens-view visualizations of evolution data. In: Proceedings of the International Workshop on Principles of Software Evolution, Lisbon, Portugal (2005) 103–112

An Approach to Software Evolution
Based on Semantic Change

Romain Robbes, Michele Lanza, and Mircea Lungu

Faculty of Informatics
University of Lugano, Switzerland

Abstract. The analysis of the evolution of software systems is a useful source of information for a variety of activities, such as reverse engineering, maintenance, and predicting the future evolution of these systems.

Current software evolution research is mainly based on the information contained in versioning systems such as CVS and SubVersion. But the evolutionary information contained therein is incomplete and of low quality, hence limiting the scope of evolution research. It is incomplete because the historical information is only recorded at the explicit request of the developers (a *commit* in the classical checkin/checkout model). It is of low quality because the file-based nature of versioning systems leads to a view of software as being a set of files.

In this paper we present a novel approach to software evolution analysis which is based on the recording of *all* semantic changes performed on a system, such as refactorings. We describe our approach in detail, and demonstrate how it can be used to perform fine-grained software evolution analysis.

1   Introduction

The goal of software evolution research is to use the history of a software system to analyse its present state and to predict its future development [1] [2]. It can also be used to complement existing reverse engineering approaches to understand the current state of a system [3] [4] [5] [6]. The key to perform software evolution research is the quality and quantity of available historical information. Traditionally researchers extract historical data from versioning systems (such as CVS and SubVersion), which at explicit requests by the developers record a snapshot of the files that have changed (this is widely known as the checkin/checkout model).

We argue that the information stored in current versioning systems is not accurate enough to perform higher quality evolution research, because they are not explicitly designed for this task: Most versioning systems have been developed in the context of software configuration management (SCM), whose goal is to manage the evolution of large and complex software systems [7]. But SCM serves different needs than software evolution, it acts as a *management support discipline* concerned with controlling changes to software products and as a *development support discipline* assisting developers in performing changes to software products [8] [9]. Software evolution on the other hand is concerned with the phenomenon of the evolution of software itself. The dichotomy between SCM and software evolution has led SCM researchers to consider software evolution research as a mere "side effect" of their discipline [10].

M.B. Dwyer and A. Lopes (Eds.): FASE 2007, LNCS 4422, pp. 27–41, 2007.

Because most versioning systems originated from SCM research, the focus has never been on the quantity and quality of the recorded evolutionary information, which we consider as being (1) insufficient and (2) of low quality. It is insufficient because information only gets recorded when developers commit their changes. In previous work [11] we have analyzed how often developers of large open-source projects commit their changes and found that the number of commits per day barely surpasses 1 (one commit on average every 8 "working day" hours). The information is of low quality because there is a loss of semantic information about the changes: only textual changes get recorded. For example, to detect structural changes such as refactorings one is forced to tediously reconstruct them from incomplete information with only moderate success [12] [13]. Overall this has a negative impact on software evolution research whose limits are set by the quality and quantity of the available information.

This paper presents our approach to facilitate software evolution research by the accurate recording of *all semantic changes* that are being performed on a software system. To gather this change information, we use the most reliable source available, namely the Integrated Development Environment (IDE, such as Eclipse [1] or Squeak [2]) used to develop object-oriented software systems.

Modern development environments allow programmers to perform semantic actions on the source code with ease, thanks to semi-automatic refactoring [14] support. They also have an open architecture that tools can take advantage of: The event notification system the IDE uses can be monitored to keep track of how the developers modify the source code. From this information, we build a model of the evolution of a system in which the notion of *change* takes on a primary role, since people develop a software system by incrementally changing it [15]. The notion of incremental change is further supported by IDEs featuring incremental compilation where only the newly modified parts get compiled, *i.e.*, an explicit system building phase where the whole system is being built from scratch is losing importance.

In our model, the evolution of a system is the sequence of changes which were applied to develop it. These changes are operations on the program's abstract syntax tree at the simplest level. Through a composition mechanism, changes are grouped to represent larger changes associated with a semantic meaning, such as method additions, refactorings, feature additions or bug fixes. Thus we can reason about a system's evolution on several levels, from a high-level view suitable to a manager down to a concrete view suitable to a developer wishing to perform a specific task.

We store the change information in a repository, to be exploited by tools integrated in the IDE the programmer is using. After presenting our approach, we show preliminary results, based on the *change matrix*, an interactive visualization of the changes applied to the system under study.

Structure of the paper. Section 2 presents the principles and a detailed overview of our approach. Section 3 presents a case study we performed to validate our approach, in which we used the change matrix visualization to assess the evolution of projects done by students. Section 4 and 5 compare our approach to more traditional approaches to

---

[1] http://www.eclipse.org
[2] http://www.squeak.org

software evolution analysis. Section 6 briefly covers the implementation. In Section 7 we conclude and outline future work.

2   Change-Based Object-Oriented Software Evolution

Our approach to software evolution analysis is based on the following principles:

– *Programming is more than just text editing*, it is an incremental activity with semantics. If cutting out a piece of a method body and wrapping it into its own method body can be seen as cut&paste, it is in fact an *extract method* refactoring. Hence, instead of representing a system's evolution as a sequence of versions of text files, we want to represent it as a sequence of explicit changes with object-oriented semantics.
– *Software is in permanent evolution*. Modern Integrated Development Environments (IDE), such as Eclipse, are a very rich and accurate source of information about a system's life-cycle. IDEs thus can be used to build a change-based model of evolving object-oriented software and to gather the change data, which we afterwards process and analyze. Based on the analyzed data, we can also create tools which feed back the analyzed data into the IDE to support the development process.

Taming Change. Traditional approaches to evolution analysis consider the history of a system as being a sequence of program versions, and compute metrics or visualize these versions to exploit the data contained in them [16][17]. Representing evolution as a sequence of version fits the format of the data obtained from a source code repository. There is a legitimate doubt that the nature of existing evolution approaches is a direct consequence of the representation adopted by versioning systems, and is therefore limited by this.

The phenomenom of software evolution is one of *continuous change*. It is not a succession of program versions. Our approach fits this view because it models the evolution of a software system as a sequence of changes which have inherent object-oriented semantics, focusing on the phenomenon of change itself, rather than focusing on the way to store the information. We define semantic changes as changes at the design level, not at the behavioral level as in [18].

Modeling software evolution as meaningful change operations fits the inherently incremental nature of software development, because this is the very way with which developers are building systems. Programmers modify software by adding tiny bits of functionality at a time, and by testing often to get feedback. At a higher level features and bug fixes are added incrementally to the code base and at an even higher level the program incrementally evolves from one milestone version to another.

A consequence of this approach is that by recording only the changes we do not explicitly store versions, but we can reconstruct any version by applying the changes. In SCM this concept is called change-based versioning [9], however the fundamental difference between our approach and the existing ones is that the changes in our case feature fine-grained object-oriented semantics and are also first-level executable entities.

Our goal is to build a model of evolution based on a scalable representation of change. First we discuss how we represent programs, then we examine how we model changes and how we extract them from IDEs.

Representing Programs. Our model defines the history of a program as the sequence of changes the program went through. From these changes we can reconstruct each successive state of the program source code. We represent one state of the entire program as one abstract syntax tree (AST). Below the root are the packages or modules of the program. Each package in turn has children which are the package's classes. Class nodes have children for their attributes and their methods. Methods also have children. The children of a method form a subtree which is obtained by parsing the source code contained in the method. Thus each entity of a program, from the package level down to the program statement level, is represented as a node in the program's AST, as show in Figure 1.

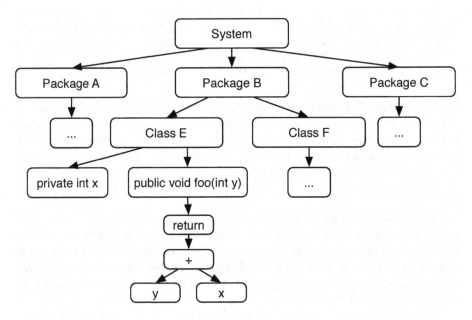

Fig. 1. We represent a state of a program as an abstract syntax tree (AST)

Each node contains additional information that is stored in properties associated with the node. The set of properties (and their values) defined on a node can be seen as its label or meta-information. Properties depend on the type of nodes they are associated to.

For instance, class nodes have properties like *name*, *superclass*, and *comment*. An instance variable has a *name* property. In a statically typed programming language it would also have a *type* property, as well as a *visibility modifier* in the case of Java. Methods have a *name* and could have properties encoding its type signature in a typed language. The property system is open so that other properties can be added at will.

Extracting the Changes. The type of semantic change information that we model is not retrievable from existing versioning systems [19]. Such detailed information about a software system can be retrieved from the IDEs developers are using to build software systems. IDEs are a good source of information because:

- They feature a complete model of a program to provide advanced functionalities such as code completion, code highlighting, navigation facilities and refactoring tools. Such a model goes beyond the representation at the file level to reference program-level entities such as methods and classes in an object-oriented system.
- They feature an event notification system allowing third-party tools to be notified when the user issues a change to the program. Mechanisms such as incremental compilation and smart completion of entity names take advantage of this.
- IDEs allow a user to automatically perform high-level transformations of programs associated with a semantic meaning, namely refactorings. These operations are easy to monitor in an IDE, but much harder to detect outside of it, since they are lost when the changed files are committed to a software repository [12] [13].

Since some IDEs are extensible by third parties with plugin mechanisms, our tools can use the full program model offered by the IDEs to locate and reason about every statement in the program, and can be notified of changes *without relying on explicit action by the developers*. This mechanisms alleviate the problems exhibited by the use of versioning systems: It is easier to track changes applied to an entity in isolation rather than attempting to follow it through several versions of the code base, each comprising a myriad of changes. Furthermore, after each notification, the IDE can also be queried for time and author information.

Representing the Changes. We model changes as first-class executable entities. It is possible to take a sequence of changes and execute it to build the version of the program represented by them. Changes can also be reversed (or undone) to achieve the effect of going back in time. Changes feature precise time and authorship information, allowing the order of the changes to be maintained. In contrast, most other approaches reduce the time information to the time where the change was checked in, following the checkin/checkout model supported by the versioning systems, such as CVS and SubVersion.

There are two distinct kinds of changes, (1) low-level changes operating at the syntactic level, and (2) higher-level changes with a semantic meaning, which are composed of lower-level changes.

1. **Syntactic Changes.** They are simple operations on the program AST, defined as follows:
   - A *creation* creates a node n of type t, without inserting it into the AST.
   - An *addition* adds a node n to the tree, as a child of another specified node m. If order is important, an index can be provided to insert the node n in a particular position in the children of m. Otherwise, n is appended as the last child of m.
   - A *deletion* removes the specified node n from its parent m.
   - A *property change* sets the property p of node n to a specific value v.

Using these low-level changes, we view a program as an evolving abstract syntax tree. A program starts as an empty tree and an empty change history. As time elapses, the program is built and the AST is populated. At the same time, all the change operations which were performed to build the program up to this point are stored in the change history.

2. **Semantic Changes.** To reason about a system, we need to raise the level of abstraction beyond mere syntactic changes. This is achieved by the composition mechanism. A sequence of lower-level changes can be composed to form a single, higher level change encapsulating a semantic meaning. Here are a few examples:

   – A sequence of consecutive changes involving a single method m can be interpreted as a single method *implementation*, or *modification* if m already existed.
   – Changes to the structure of a class c (attributes, superclass, name) are either a class *definition* or a class *redefinition*, if c existed before the changes. These kinds of changes form the *intermediate* changes.
   – At a higher level, some sequences of intermediate changes are *refactorings*[14]. They can be composed further to represent these higher-level changes to the program. For example, the "extract method" refactoring involves the *modification* of a first method $m1$ (a sequence of statements in $m1$ is replaced by a single call to method $m2$), and the *implementation* of $m2$ (its body comprises the statements that were removed from $m1$). In the same way, a "rename class" refactoring comprises the *redefinition* of the class (with a name change), and the *modification* of all methods because of the changed referenced class name.
   – We define a *bug fix* as the sequence of intermediate changes which were involved in the correction of the faulty behavior.
   – In the same way, a *feature* implementation is comprised of all the changes that programmers performed to develop the feature. These changes can be intermediate changes as well as any refactorings and bug fixes which were necessary to achieve the goal.
   – At an even higher level, we can picture *main program features* as being an aggregation of smaller features, and *program milestones* (major versions) as a set of high-level features and important bug fixes.

The composition of changes works at all levels, to allow changes to represent higher-level concepts. This property is a key point to the scalability of our approach. Without it, we would have to consider only low-level, syntactic changes, and hence be limited to trivial programs, because of the sheer quantity of changes to consider. In addition to composition, it is also possible to analyse the evolution of a system by considering subsets of changes. Thus a high-level analysis of a system would only take into account the changes applied to classes and packages, in order to have a bird's eye view of the system's evolution. The lower-level changes are still useful to analyse the evolution: Once an anomaly has been identified in a high-level strata of the system, lower-level changes can be looked at to infer the particular causes of a problem. For example, if a package or a module of the system needs reengineering, then its history in terms of classes and methods can be summoned. Once the main culprits of the problem have been identified, these few classes can be viewed in even more detail by looking at the changes in the implementation of their methods.

To sum up, we consider the program under analysis as an evolving abstract syntax tree. We store in our model all the change operations necessary to recreate the program at any point in time. At the lowest level, these operations consist of creation, addition and removal of nodes in the tree, and of modifications of node properties. These changes can be composed to represent higher-level changes corresponding to actions at the semantic level, such as refactorings, bug fixes *etc.*

3   Case Studies

Since our approach relies on information which was previously discarded, we can not use existing systems as case studies. We monitored new projects to collect all the information. Our case studies are projects done by students over the course of a week. These projects are small (15 to 40 classes), but are interesting case studies since the code base is foreign to us. There were 3 possible subjects to choose from: A virtual store in the vein of Amazon (Store), a simple geometry program (Geom), and a text-based role-playing game (RPG). Table 1 shows a numerical overview of the projects we have tracked (each project is named with a letter, from A to I). The frequency of the recorded changes was very high compared to a that of a classical versioning system: While the projects lasted one week, their actual coding time was in the range of hours. Considering this fact and that the students were novice programmers, our approach allows for an unprecedented precision with respect to the recording of the evolution.

Table 1. A numerical overview of the semantic changes we recovered from the projects

Project	A	B	C	D	E	F	G	H	I
Type	Geom	Store	Store	Store	Store	RPG	Geom	Store	RPG
Class Added	22	14	14	9	12	15	21	12	41
Class Modified	65	17	34	13	6	24	57	15	27
Class Commented	0	12	0	0	1	0	0	0	0
Class Recategorized	0	0	5	0	0	0	0	0	11
Class Renamed	0	0	0	0	1	1	0	0	1
Class Removed	10	1	5	5	0	3	6	2	18
Attributes Added	82	19	29	19	20	61	30	29	137
Attributes Removed	50	7	13	5	2	19	15	5	54
Method Added	366	119	182	164	117	237	219	135	415
Method Modified	234	69	117	140	81	154	143	118	185
Method Removed	190	20	81	32	13	38	117	21	106

The changes considered here are *intermediate-level* changes, one per semantic action the user did (in that case, mainly class and method modifications: the students were familiar with refactoring). The table classifies the changes applied to each project. We can already see some interesting trends: Some projects have a lot more "backtracking" (removals of entities) than others; usage of actions related to refactoring (commenting, renaming, repackaging entities) varies widely between projects.

In the remainder of the section, we concentrate on the analysis of one of the projects, namely the role-playing game project I (the last column of the table). More details on the other projects are available in the extended version of [11].

3.1 Detailing the Evolution of a Student Project

We chose project I for a detailed study, because it had the most classes in it, and was the second largest in statements. Project I is a role-playing game in which a player has to choose a character, explore a dungeon and fight the creatures he finds in it. In this process, he can find items to improve his capabilities, as well as gaining experience.

We base our analysis on the change matrix Figure 2 inspired by [17]. It is a timeline view of the changes applied to the entire system, described in terms of classes and methods (a coarser-grained version, displaying packages and classes is also available, but not shown in this paper).

The goal of the change evolution matrix is to provide the user with an overview of the activity in the project at the method level granularity over time. Time is mapped on the x-axis. Every method is allocated a horizontal band which is gray for the time period in which the method existed and white otherwise. The method bands are grouped by classes, and ordered by their creation time. Classes are delimited by black lines and are also ordered by their creation time, with the oldest classes at the top of the figure.

Changes are designed by colors: green for the creation of a method, blue for its removal and orange for a modification. Selecting a change shows the method's source code after the change is applied to the system. A restriction of the figure at this time of writing is that it does not show when a class is deleted.

Figure 2 is rotated for increased readability. Events are mapped on intervals lasting 35 minutes. Note that to ease comprehension the system size is reported on the left of the page, and sessions are delimited by rectangles with rounded corners in both the matrix and the graph size view. Also, the class names are indicated below the figure. Figure 3 represent the same matrix, but focused on the class Combat. Since its lifespan is shorter, we can increase the resolution to five minutes per interval.

Considering the classes and their order of creation (Figure 2), we can see that the first parcels of functionality were, in order: The characters; the weapons; the enemies; the combat algorithm; the healing items and finally the dungeon itself, defined in terms of rooms. We can qualify this as a bottom-up development methodology.

After seeing these high-level facts about the quality-wise and methodology-wise evolution of the system, we can examine it session by session. Each session has been identified visually and numbered. Refer to Figure 2 to see the sessions.

Session 1, March 27, afternoon: The project starts by laying out the foundations of the main class of the game, Hero. As we see on the change matrix, it evolves continually throughout the life of the project, reflecting its central role. At the same time, a very simple test is created, and the class Spell is defined.

Session 2, March 28, evening: This session sees the definition of the core of the character functionality: Classes Hero and Spell are changed, and classes Items, Mage, Race and Warrior are introduced, in this order. Since Spells are defined, the students define the Mage class, and after that the Warrior class as another subclass of Hero. This gives the player a choice of profession. The definitions are still very shallow at this stage, and the design is unstable: Items and Race will never be changed again after this session.

Session 3, March 28, night: This session supports the idea that the design is unstable, as it can be resumed as a failed experiment: A hierarchy of races has been

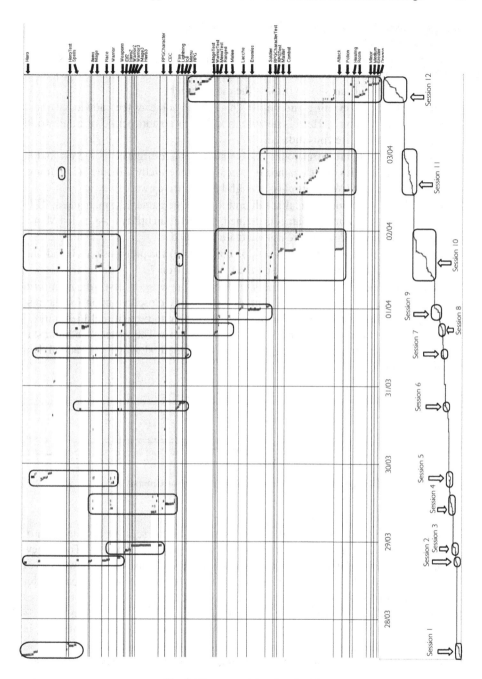

Fig. 2. Change matrix of project I

introduced, and several classes have been cloned and modified (Mage2, Hero3 *etc.*).
Most of these classes were quickly removed.

Session 4, March 29, afternoon: This session is also experimental in nature. Several classes are modified or introduced, but were never touched again: Hero3, CEC, RPGCharacter (except two modifications later on, outside real coding sessions). Mage and Warrior are changed too, indicating that some of the knowledge gained in that experiment starts to go back to the main branch.

Session 5, March 29, evening and night: This session achieves the knowledge transfer started in session 4. Hero is heavily modified in a short period of time, while Mage and Warrior are consolidated.

Session 6, March 30, late afternoon: This session sees a resurgence of interest for the offensive capabilities of the characters. A real Spell hierarchy is defined (Lightning, Fire, Ice), while the Weapons class is slightly modified as well.

Session 7, March 31, noon: The first full prototype of the game. The main class, RPG (standing for Role Playing Game) is defined, as well as an utility class called Menu. Mage, Warrior and their superclass Hero are modified.

Session 8, March 31, evening: This session consolidates the previous one, by adding some tests and reworking the classes changed in session 7.

Session 9, March 31, night: This session focuses on weapon diversification with classes Melee and Ranged; these classes have a very close evolution for the rest of their life, suggesting some data classes. At the same time, a real hierarchy of hostile creatures appears: Enemies, Lacche, and Soldier. The system is a bit unstable at that time, since Enemies experiences a lot of method which were added then removed immediately, suggesting renames.

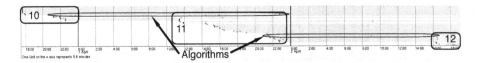

Fig. 3. Change matrix zoomed on the class Combat

Session 10, April 1st, noon to night: This intensive session sees the first iteration of the combat engine. The weapons, spells and characters are first refined. Then a new enemy, Master, is defined. The implementation of the Combat class shows a lot of modifications of the Weapon and Hero classes. An Attack class soon appears. Judging from its (non-)evolution, it seems to be a data class with no logic. After theses definitions, the implementation of the real algorithm begins. We see on Figure 3 –the detailed view of combat– that one method is heavily modified continuing in the next session.

Session 11, April 2, noon to night: Development is still heavily focused on the Combat algorithm. Classes of Potion and Healing are also defined, allowing the heroes to play the game for a longer time. This session also modifies the main combat algorithm, and at the same time, two methods in the Hero class, showing a slight degree of coupling. A second method featuring a lot of logic is implemented, as shown in Figure 3: several methods are often modified.

Session 12: April 3, afternoon to night: This last session finishes the implementation of Combat –changing the enemy hierarchy in the process–, and resumes the work on the entry point of the game, the RPG class. Only now is a Room class introduced, providing locality. These classes are tied to Combat to conclude the main game logic. To finish, several types of potions –simple data classes– are defined, and a final monster, a Dragon, is added at the very last minute.

4 Discussion

Compared to traditional approaches, extracting information from source control repositories, our change-based approach has a number of advantages (accurate information, scalable representation, and version generation), but also some limitations (portability, availability of case studies, and performance).

- **Accurate information.** The information we gather is more accurate in several ways. It consists of program-level entities, not mere text files which incurs extra treatment to raise the level of abstraction. Since we are notified of changes in an automatic, rather than explicit way, we can extract finer change information: Each change can be processed *in context*. The time information we gather is accurate up to the second, whereas a versioning system reduces it to the checkin time. Processing changes in context and in a timely manner allows us to track entities through their life time while being less affected by system-wide changes such as refactorings.
- **Scalable representation.** We represent every statement of a system as separate entities, and every operation on those statements as a first-class change operation. Such a precise representation enables us to reflect on very focused changes, during defined time period and on a distinct set of low-level entities. At the other end of the spectrum, changes can be composed into semantic level changes such as method modifications, class additions, or even entire sessions, while the entities we reflect on can be no longer statements, but methods, classes or packages. Thus our approach can both give a "big picture" view to a manager, as well as a detailed summary of the changes submitted by a developer during his or her last coding session.
- **Version generation.** Since changes are executable, we can also reproduce versions of the program. We can thus revert to version analysis and more traditional approaches when we need to.
- **Portability.** Our approach is currently both language-specific and environment-specific. This allows us to leverage to the maximum the properties of the target language and the possibilities offered by the IDE (in our case, Smalltalk and Squeak). However, it implies a substantial porting effort to use our approach in another context. Consequently, one of our goal is to extract the language and environment-independent concepts to ease this effort. Thus we will port our prototype to the Java/Eclipse platform. The differences in behavior between the two versions will help us isolate the common concepts.

- **Availability of case studies.** As mentioned above, we can not use pre-existing projects as case studies since we require information which was discarded previously. Solving this problem is one of our priorities. Beyond using student projects as case studies, we are monitoring our prototype itself for later study. This would be a medium-sized case study: At the time of writing, it comprised 203 classes and 2249 methods over 11681 intermediate changes. We also plan to release and promote our tools to the Smalltalk community (the language our tools are implemented in) soon. In the longer term, porting our tools to the Eclipse platform will enable us to reach a much wider audience of developers.
- **Performance.** Our approach stores operations rather than states of programs. The large number of changes and entities could raise performance concerns. It takes around one minute to generate all the possible versions of our prototype itself from the stored changes. The machine used was a 1.5 GHz portable computer, our prototype having around 11'000 intermediate changes.

5   Related Work

Several researchers have analysed the evolution of large software systems, basing their work on system versions typically extracted from software repositories such as CVS and SubVersion [20] [21] [22] [23] [24]. In most cases these approaches have specific analysis goals, such as detecting logical couplings [25] or extracting evolutionary patterns [4].

Several researchers raised the abstraction level beyond files to consider design evolution. In [22], Xing and Stroulia focus on detecting evolutionary phases of classes, such as rapidly developing, intense evolution, slowly developing, steady-state, and restructuring. They had to sample their data for their case study and used only the 31 minor versions of the project. Parsing and analysing the 31 versions took around 370 minutes on a standard computer, which rules out an immediate use by a developer. [26] presents a methodology to connect high-level models to source code, but has only been applied to a single version of a system so far. [23] describes how hierarchies of classes evolve, but still depends on sampling and the checkin/checkout model. [20] applies origin analysis to determine if files moved between versions. In [18], Jackson and Ladd present an approach to differencing C programs at the semantic level. They define semantic changes as dependency changes between inputs and outputs, while we are primarily interested in design-level changes.

All these and other known approaches cannot perform a fine-grained analysis because the underlying data is restricted by the data that can be extracted from versioning system, tying them to the *checkin/checkout* model. In [11], we outlined the limitations of this model to retrieve accurate evolutionary information. Versioning systems restrain their interactions with developers to explicit retrieval of the source (check out), and submission of the modified sources once the developer finishes his task (check in or commit). All the changes to the code base are merged together at commit time, and become hard to distinguish from each other. The time stamp of each modification is lost, and changes such as refactorings become very hard, if not impossible to detect. Even keeping track of the identity of a program element can be troublesome if it has been renamed.

Moreover, most versioning systems version text files. This guarantees language-independence but limits the quality of the information stored to the lowest common denominator: An analysis of the system's evolution going deeper than the file level requires the parsing of (selected) versions of the system and the linking of the successive versions. Such a procedure is costly [19]. Thus it is a common practice to first *sample* the data, by only retaining a fraction of the available versions. The differences between two versions retained for analysis becomes even larger, so the quality of the data degrades further.

Mens [27] presents a thorough survey of merging algorithms in versioning systems, of which [28] is the closest to our approach: operations performed on the data are used as the basis of the merging algorithm, not the data itself. However, the operations are not precised in the paper and are used only in the merge process. The change mechanism used by Smalltalk systems uses the same idea, but the changes are not abstracted. Smalltalkers usually don't rely on them and use more classic, state-based versioning systems. In addition, most of the versioning systems covered by Mens are not used widely in practice: most evolution analysis tools are based on the two most used versioning systems, CVS and SubVersion.

6   Tool Implementation

Our ideas are implemented for the Smalltalk language and the Squeak IDE in SpyWare, shown in Figure 4. From top to bottom, we see: the main window; a code browser on a version of project I; the change matrix of project I; and a graph showing the growth rate of the system.

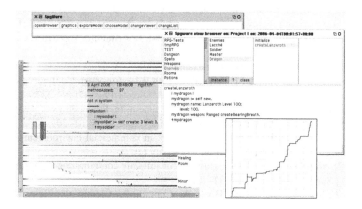

Fig. 4. Screen capture of SpyWare, our prototype

7   Conclusion and Future Work

We presented a fine grained, change-based approach to software evolution analysis and applied it to nine student projects, one of which was analyzed in detail. Our approach considers a system to be the sequence of changes that built it, and extract this information from the IDE used during development. We implemented this scheme and performed an evolution analysis case study based on a software visualization tool –the change matrix– we built on top of this platform.

Although our results are still in their infancy, they are encouraging as they allow us to focus on particular entities in a precise period of time once a general knowledge of the system has been gained. In our larger vision, we want a more thorough interaction of forward and reverse engineering to support rapidly changing systems. In this scenario, developers need this detailed analysis of part of the system as much as they need a global view of the systems' evolution.

We have only scratched the surface of the information available in these systems. We plan to use more advanced tools, visualizations, and methods (such as complexity metrics) to meaningfully display and interact with this new type of information, and envision other uses beyond evolution analysis.

References

1. Lehman, M., Belady, L.: Program Evolution: Processes of Software Change. London Academic Press, London (1985)
2. Gall, H., Jazayeri, M., Klösch, R., Trausmuth, G.: Software evolution observations based on product release history. In: Proceedings International Conference on Software Maintenance (ICSM'97), Los Alamitos CA, IEEE Computer Society Press (1997) 160–166
3. Mens, T., Demeyer, S.: Future trends in software evolution metrics. In: Proceedings IW-PSE2001 (4th International Workshop on Principles of Software Evolution). (2001) 83–86
4. Van Rysselberghe, F., Demeyer, S.: Studying software evolution information by visualizing the change history. In: Proceedings 20th IEEE International Conference on Software Maintenance (ICSM '04), Los Alamitos CA, IEEE Computer Society Press (2004) 328–337
5. Gîrba, T., Ducasse, S., Lanza, M.: Yesterday's Weather: Guiding early reverse engineering efforts by summarizing the evolution of changes. In: Proceedings 20th IEEE International Conference on Software Maintenance (ICSM 2004), Los Alamitos CA, IEEE Computer Society Press (2004) 40–49
6. D'Ambros, M., Lanza, M.: Software bugs and evolution: A visual approach to uncover their relationship. In: Proceedings of CSMR 2006 (10th IEEE European Conference on Software Maintenance and Reengineering), IEEE Computer Society Press (2006) 227 – 236
7. Tichy, W.: Tools for software configuration management. In: Proceedings of the International Workshop on Software Version and Configuration Control. (1988) 1–20
8. Feiler, P.H.: Configuration management models in commercial environments. Technical report cmu/sei-91-tr-7, Carnegie-Mellon University (1991)
9. Conradi, R., Westfechtel, B.: Version models for software configuration management. ACM Computing Surveys **30**(2) (1998) 232–282
10. Estublier, J., Leblang, D., van der Hoek, A., Conradi, R., Clemm, G., Tichy, W., Wiborg-Weber, D.: Impact of software engineering research on the practice of software configuration management. ACM Transactions on Software Engineering and Methodology **14**(4) (2005) 383–430
11. Robbes, R., Lanza, M.: A change-based approach to software evolution. In: ENTCS volume 166. (2007) to appear
12. Görg, C., Weissgerber, P.: Detecting and visualizing refactorings from software archives. In: Proceedings of IWPC (13th International Workshop on Program Comprehension, IEEE CS Press (2005) 205–214

13. Filip Van Rysselberghe, M.R., Demeyer, S.: Detecting move operations in versioning information. In: Proceedings of the 10th Conference on Software Maintenance and Reengineering (CSMR'06), IEEE Computer Society (2006) 271–278
14. Fowler, M., Beck, K., Brant, J., Opdyke, W., Roberts, D.: Refactoring: Improving the Design of Existing Code. Addison Wesley (1999)
15. Beck, K.: Extreme Programming Explained: Embrace Change. Addison Wesley (2000)
16. Gîrba, T., Lanza, M., Ducasse, S.: Characterizing the evolution of class hierarchies. In: Proceedings IEEE European Conference on Software Maintenance and Reengineering (CSMR 2005), Los Alamitos CA, IEEE Computer Society (2005) 2–11
17. Lanza, M.: The evolution matrix: Recovering software evolution using software visualization techniques. In: Proceedings of IWPSE 2001 (International Workshop on Principles of Software Evolution). (2001) 37–42
18. Jackson, D., Ladd, D.A.: Semantic diff: A tool for summarizing the effects of modifications. In Müller, H.A., Georges, M., eds.: ICSM, IEEE Computer Society (1994) 243–252
19. Robbes, R., Lanza, M.: Versioning systems for evolution research. In: Proceedings of IWPSE 2005 (8th International Workshop on Principles of Software Evolution), IEEE Computer Society (2005) 155–164
20. Tu, Q., Godfrey, M.W.: An integrated approach for studying architectural evolution. In: 10th International Workshop on Program Comprehension (IWPC'02), IEEE Computer Society Press (2002) 127–136
21. Jazayeri, M., Gall, H., Riva, C.: Visualizing Software Release Histories: The Use of Color and Third Dimension. In: Proceedings of ICSM '99 (International Conference on Software Maintenance), IEEE Computer Society Press (1999) 99–108
22. Xing, Z., Stroulia, E.: Analyzing the evolutionary history of the logical design of object-oriented software. IEEE Trans. Software Eng. **31**(10) (2005) 850–868
23. Gîrba, T., Lanza, M.: Visualizing and characterizing the evolution of class hierarchies (2004)
24. Eick, S., Graves, T., Karr, A., Marron, J., Mockus, A.: Does code decay? assessing the evidence from change management data. IEEE Transactions on Software Engineering **27**(1) (2001) 1–12
25. Gall, H., Hajek, K., Jazayeri, M.: Detection of logical coupling based on product release history. In: Proceedings International Conference on Software Maintenance (ICSM '98), Los Alamitos CA, IEEE Computer Society Press (1998) 190–198
26. Murphy, G.C., Notkin, D., Sullivan, K.J.: Software reflexion models: Bridging the gap between design and implementation. IEEE Trans. Software Eng. **27**(4) (2001) 364–380
27. Mens, T.: A state-of-the-art survey on software merging. IEEE Transactions on Software Engineering **28**(5) (2002) 449–462
28. Lippe, E., van Oosterom, N.: Operation-based merging. In: SDE 5: Proceedings of the fifth ACM SIGSOFT symposium on Software development environments, New York, NY, USA, ACM Press (1992) 78–87

A Simulation-Oriented Formalization for a Psychological Theory

Paulo Salem da Silva and Ana C. Vieira de Melo

University of São Paulo
Department of Computer Science
São Paulo – Brazil
salem@ime.usp.br, acvm@ime.usp.br

Abstract. In this paper we present a formal specification of a tradition-ally informal domain of knowledge: the Behavior Analysis psychological theory. Our main objective is to highlight some motivations, issues, con-structions and insights that, we believe, are particular to the task of formalizing a preexisting informal theory. In order to achieve this, we give a short introduction to Behavior Analysis and then explore in detail some fragments of the full specification, which is written using the Z for-mal method. With such a specification, we argue, one is in better position to implement a software system that relates to an actual psychological theory. Such relation could be useful, for instance, in the implementation of multi-agent simulators.

1 Introduction

Mathematical approaches have been successful in representing the universe of natural sciences and engineering. Modern Physics is, perhaps, the greatest ex-ample of this success. Yet, many important fields of study remain distant from formal structures and reasoning. Among these, we regard Psychology as partic-ularly interesting.

Roughly speaking, Psychology is divided into several schools of thought, and each one adopts its own definitions, methods and goals. As examples, we may cite Psychoanalysis, Cognitivism and Behaviorism. The later is further divided into several approaches, out of which *Behavior Analysis* [1], created by Burrhus Frederic Skinner, stands out. While not strictly built on formal terms, it does bear some resemblance to them through detailed and precise definitions. As a consequence, it suggests the possibility of a complete formalization.

With this in mind, we have designed a formal specification for agent behavior based on the Behavior Analysis theory. Its purpose is twofold. First, it should allow the construction of agent simulators following the principles of this psy-chological school. Second, it aims at demonstrating the possibility and the value, from a Software Engineering perspective, of formally specifying traditionally in-formal domains in order to build tools related to these domains.

The specification of the Behavior Analysis theory has been written with the Z formal method [2], and this paper presents its fundamental structure, but

M.B. Dwyer and A. Lopes (Eds.): FASE 2007, LNCS 4422, pp. 42–56, 2007.

does not go deep into all details. Our aim, here, is to highlight some issues, constructions and insights that, we believe, are particular to the task of formalizing a preexisting informal domain of knowledge. Moreover, we hope that our presentation argue in favor of this kind of formalization.

We are aware of some other works similar to ours either on their purposes or on their methods. A multi-agent specification framework written in Z, called SMART, can be found in [3]. One of the authors of this book is also involved in the formal modelling and simulation of stem cells [4]. Neuron models and simulations are common practice in the field of Computational Neuroscience [5,6]. We do not know, however, of attempts to formalize whole theories about *organism behavior*.

Sect. 2 details the process through which our specification was conceived. Naturally, we assume that the reader is not familiar with Psychology. Therefore, Sect. 3 presents a brief introduction to the fundamental elements of Behavior Analysis. Sect. 4 explores some fragments of the specification in detail, using them to illustrate relevant points. We expect the reader to know the basics of the Z formal method, which can be learned in works such as [2] and [7]. Sect. 5 summarizes our main results and further elaborates on them. Finally, Sect. 5 acknowledges the help we received.

2 Formalization Process

Although the formalization process we employed is not precise, it does follow a number of principles and practices which are worth registering. In this section we present this knowledge, as structured as possible.

Let us begin by tracing the two major steps that we went through, namely:

1. Definition of the main entities and relationships in the theory;
2. Addition of restrictions and further structure upon the entities and relationships.

The first step allow us to identify the elements upon which we should focus. This, we believe, is specially important if the domain being formalized is not entirely understood. In our case, we initially built an ontology [8,9] for the concepts of Behavior Analysis as described by Skinner in the book *Science and Human Behavior* [1]. Among the techniques we employed to accomplish this stage, the most relevant ones are the following:

- Map chapters or sections to subsystems. By doing this, we reused the general structure of the original theory;
- Build the ontology as the book is read. We adopted the discipline of editing the ontology at the end of sections or chapters;
- Register concepts in the ontology without structure and later organize them. This is important because sometimes it is not clear what a concept actually means or where it should be positioned in the ontology. As one gains more knowledge about the domain, it becomes simpler to organize the available concepts.

In the second step, then, we can focus our attention on the details of each entity and relationship identified in the previous step. More expressive formalisms might be needed at this point. In our work, we employed the Z formal method to this end. Z was chosen in part because of our prior experience with it, but also owing to the method's emphasis on axiomatic descriptions, refinement and modularization. Moreover, we used the Z/EVES tool [10] to help us write the specification.

To gain a deeper understanding of the identified entities, we also began to study other references, specially the book *Learning* [11], written by Charles Catania, a well known contemporary psychologist. The formal specification, thus, is mostly structured according to the views of Skinner himself, though we have used a modern reference to improve our understanding of specific topics. At this point, we found the following practices to be useful:

- Design subsystems to be as isolated as possible;
- Try to express new things in terms of what is available. We found that once some base concepts are set, much can be expressed using them;
- When defining an operation, try to account for all possible input cases. This helps spot conditions that have not being considered, either by the original theory, or by the formalization. We shall see an example of this in Sect. 4.2;
- When a concept is not clear, leave it as abstract as necessary. By not trying to formalize what is not well understood, one avoids having to change the formalization later on;
- When a concept may have multiple interpretations, provide an abstract definition followed by refinements that specialize it. We shall encounter an example of this in Sect. 4.2;
- Do not attempt to formalize all details of the theory at once. In our experience, such ambition is doomed to failure, for the more details are added, the harder it gets to connect each part of the specification to the others.

Such are the main practices we employed. In Sect. 4 we shall encounter some of them applied to an actual example.

3   A Brief Introduction to Behavior Analysis

We now present some fundamental ideas and elements of Behavior Analysis, upon which we have built our formal specification.

Behaviorism is a branch of Psychology created in the beginning of the 20th century. It was born mainly as an opposition to the dominating idea that the objective of Psychology was the study of the mind. Behaviorists rejected this position, claiming that it was too vague and unsuitable for scientific investigation. They asserted that the true purpose of Psychology should be the study of the *behavior* of organisms, which, they thought, was a precise concept and, therefore, within the realm of natural science.[1]

---

[1] See [12] for a classical exposition of these principles.

The Behaviorist tradition produced several important thinkers, from which Burrhus Frederic Skinner was, perhaps, the most notorious one. Between the decades of 1930 and 1950 he developed his own kind of Behaviorism, called Behavior Analysis.

In Behavior Analysis, the fundamental object of study is the *organism*. Organisms perceive their environments through *stimuli* and act upon such environments through *behavior*. Further, a relation is assumed to exist between stimuli and behavior, in such a way that behavior is, ultimately, determined by the stimulation received by the organism. Thus, the purpose of this science is the prediction and control of behavior.

This objective is pursued mainly through the classification of several phenomena concerning stimuli and behavior. The hope is that regularities can be discovered, leading to the formulation of behavioral laws. Let us first examine the ideas concerning stimulation, and then proceed to the points about behavior.

Each stimulus has an utility value. That is, it is either pleasant or painful, desired or feared. Some stimuli, called *primary*, possess utility values *a priori*, independently of prior experience. All others, called *conditioned*, have their utilities determined by primary stimuli during the organism's life.

The relations between primary and conditioned stimuli are modified through the process named *stimulus conditioning*. Essentially, it is a learning process that tries to relate the occurrence of certain stimuli to the occurrence of others. In other words, it allows organisms to formulate causal laws about their environments. As an example, consider a dog that is always fed after a whistle. Initially, only the presentation of food can make the dog salivate. With time, however, the dog learns that the whistle is related to the food, causing him to salivate with the whistle, prior to any food delivery. In this case, food is the primary stimulus, since it is naturally pleasant to the dog. The whistle, on the other hand, is a conditioned stimulus, which becomes related to food.

Stimulus conditioning also works the other way around. If the relation between two conditioned stimuli is not maintained, it tends to disappear. In the previous example, if the whistle is no longer followed by food, it is likely that, after some time, it won't elicit salivation.

Now let us proceed to the study of behavior. Behavior Analysis defines two main classes of behavior, namely, the class of *reflexes* and the class of *operants*. A reflex is characterized by an *antecedent stimulus*, which causes the organism to behave in some way. For instance, salivation is a reflex, since it is caused by the the presentation of food. Reflexes are innate to the organism. That is, they are not learning structures, they cannot be created nor modified in great extent. Operants, on the other hand, are far more flexible behavioral structures. An operant is defined by a *consequent stimulus*. The operant stands for the behavior that leads to this stimulus. That is, the behavior that operates in the environment in order to generate the stimulus. Notice that if a behavior no longer takes to a stimulus, or if the behavior required to reach that stimulus changes, the operant changes as well. They are, therefore, learning structures. As an example, suppose that a dog learns that the push of a button brings food to him. Then this button pushing behavior becomes an operant, for it is associated with a specific consequent stimulus.

It is through operant behavior that the most interesting issues arise in Behavior Analysis. Organisms can have their behavior changed by operations of *reinforcement* and *punishment*. Reinforcement is the presentation of pleasant stimuli as a reward for particular behaviors. Punishment, in turn, accounts for the presentation of unpleasant stimuli, in order to inhibit specific behaviors. There are many ways to perform these operations, called *schedules of reinforcement*. Each schedule modifies behavior in a distinct way.

There are other interesting concepts, but we shall limit ourselves to these, for they are sufficient to understand the examples that come in the next section. Moreover, most of the concepts discussed above are present explicitly in our specification. And how a simulator based on it could be useful? Once we define an organism, we can perform simulations to determine properties like:

- How frequent should reinforcement be in order to preserve behaviors of interest;
- How much time it takes to teach the organism a new behavior.

In general, simulations could replace some experiments usually done with real animals.

4   Results

As stated above, the specification is too large to be completely described in this paper. Therefore, in this section we do not present the whole specification, but some of its most significant parts, from which useful discussion can be drawn. Some schemata used might not be defined for this reason. Sect. 4.1 gives an overview of the specification's general structure, while Sect. 4.2 explores some of its most instructive parts in detail.

4.1   Specification Overview

The formalization's main goal is to allow the construction of a system that simulates the behavior of organisms according to the principles of Behavior Analysis. It is natural, therefore, to build a specification centered around the concept of "organism". The main object of our specification is an isolated organism, which receives stimuli from an environment and produces behavioral responses. It is modelled as a state machine according to the following principles:

- Time is discrete;
- At every instant, the state of the organism may change;
- At every instant, the organism may receive one stimulus;
- At every instant, the organism may produce a new behavioral response.

Changes in the state of the organism are given either spontaneously or as consequences of stimulation. These changes are controlled by several mechanisms, which we have divided into subsystems. Each subsystem is responsible for a particular aspect of behavior and is closely related to major concepts in the psychological theory. Thus, formally, an organism is a composition of several subsystems, as the following schema shows.

$$
\begin{array}{l}
\rule{0pt}{0pt}\text{\textit{Organism}} \\\hline
stimulationSubsystem : StimulationSubsystem \\
respondingSubsystem : RespondingSubsystem \\
driveSubsystem : DriveSubsystem \\
emotionSubsystem : EmotionSubsystem \\
\end{array}
$$

At every instant, the organism may receive a new stimulus, which is processed by all subsystems in no particular order. How these stimuli are generated or how the organism's behavior changes the environment is out of the specification's scope. Nevertheless, we do provide a simple definition of the simulation process with the following schema.

$$
\begin{array}{l}
\rule{0pt}{0pt}\text{\textit{Simulator}} \\\hline
organism : Organism \\
currentInstant : Instant \\
\end{array}
$$

4.2   Specification: Main Elements

Let us now proceed to the detailed examination of some parts of the specification. In what follows, we first explores some of the stimulation subsystem, and then give some details of operant behavior, defined in the responding subsystem.

Stimulation. The specification of stimulus processing is particularly suitable for the discussion of how traditional mathematical structures, such as graphs, can be used in formalization processes. The fact that these phenomena can be translated to well studied formal structures sheds new light on them. It allows us to consider possibilities that could have remained hidden prior to the formalization.

We begin by giving the main stimulation subsystem definition.

$$
\begin{array}{l}
\rule{0pt}{0pt}\text{\textit{StimulationSubsystem}} \\\hline
StimulationParameters \\
StimulusImplication \\
StimulusEquivalence \\
currentStimuli : \mathbb{P}\ Stimulus \\
stimulus\_status : Stimulus \rightarrow StimulusStatus \\
\end{array}
$$

Consider the several schema imports above. The first, *StimulationParameters*, merely defines the parameters that are given as input to the simulation. They define what is particular, *a priori*, to the organism being simulated. We shall not pursuit it in detail here. Our interest is in the other two, *StimulusImplication* and *StimulusEquivalence*. They carry the fundamental definitions that allow the formalization of stimulus conditioning operation. As we pointed out earlier, such operation allows organisms to learn about how their environment works. Let us first examine it informally and then, upon that, build a formal definition.

The behavior of organisms depends greatly on their power to learn how environmental stimuli are related. Sometimes, it is useful to consider two stimuli that are, in reality, different, to be equivalent. For example, if, through experimental procedures, we arrange that both the presence of a red light and of a green light are always followed by the same consequences (e.g., food), why should a hungry organism bother to distinguish between the colors? As far as the organism is concerned, the two lights are equivalent.

On the other hand, sometimes the appropriate relation is one that defines causality, not equivalence. In the previous example, we may arrange the procedure so that the red light is always followed by food. In this case, the learning takes the order of stimulation into account: though red light is followed by food, food is not necessarily followed by a red light. That is, the organism may establish an implication between red light and food.

We now proceed to the formalization of these ideas. Notice that causal laws are certainly reflexive, since a stimulus trivially causes itself. They are also transitive, in the sense that causality can be chained (e.g., stimulus s_1 causes s_2 which, in turn, causes s_3). Finally, in principle no symmetry is needed (e.g., if s_1 causes s_2, there is no need, at first, for s_2 to cause s_1). We are now in position to specify causality in the *StimulusImplication* schema. It also defines a function called *sCorrelation*, which accounts for the fact that some implications may be stronger than others.

   StimulusImplication
     $sCauses : \mathbb{P}(Stimulus \times Stimulus)$

     $sCorrelation : Stimulus \times Stimulus \nrightarrow Correlation$

     $\forall s_1, s_2, s_3 : Stimulus \bullet$

        $(s_1 \; \underline{sCauses} \; s_1) \wedge$

        $(((s_1 \; \underline{sCauses} \; s_2) \wedge (s_2 \; \underline{sCauses} \; s_3)) \Rightarrow (s_1 \; \underline{sCauses} \; s_3))$

     $\forall s_1, s_2 : Stimulus \mid s_1 \; \underline{sCauses} \; s_2 \bullet$

        $\exists c : Correlation \bullet ((s_1, s_2) \mapsto c) \in sCorrelation$

Stimulus equivalence relations, in turn, can be defined in terms of stimulus implication. We merely add the symmetry axiom and require the *sCorrelation* function to have the same value in both directions.

StimulusEquivalence _____
StimulusImplication

$equals : \mathbb{P}(Stimulus \times Stimulus)$

_____

$\forall s_1, s_2 : Stimulus \bullet$

   $(s_1 \ \underline{equals} \ s_2) \Leftrightarrow (s_1 \ \underline{sCauses} \ s_2) \wedge (s_2 \ \underline{sCauses} \ s_1)$

$\forall s_1, s_2 : Stimulus \mid s_1 \ \underline{equals} \ s_2 \bullet$

   $sCorrelation(s_1, s_2) = sCorrelation(s_2, s_1)$

With this, we have achieved a formal specification for the relations among stimuli. But we may continue our analysis, casting this specification in other terms. Notice that stimulus implication may be regarded as a directed graph (Fig. 1(a)), in which vertices represent stimuli and edges are the conditioning between stimuli. Similarly, stimulus equivalence can also be seen as a graph (Fig. 1(b)), but undirected. Furthermore, edges in both graphs might have weight, if the correlation of the conditioning is to be taken into account.

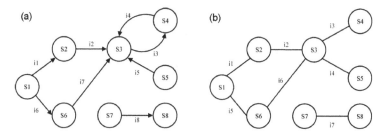

Fig. 1. (a) An example of stimulus implication represented as a directed graph; (b) An example of stimulus equivalence represented as an undirected graph

Regarding this stimuli graph, new psychological questions arise. In fact, we can use all our knowledge of Graph Theory and search algorithms to formulate questions, bringing new light to the psychological theory itself. For instance, consider the following:

- When looking for causal relations, which search strategy do organisms employ? Do they execute a depth- or breadth-first search?
- How deep can a search go? Is there some sort of memory limitation that prevents it from being exaustive?

Answers to these questions, of course, are left to psychologists. We must, however, model this lack of knowledge somehow. Fortunately, the Z formal method allows us to do this easily, as follows. For all operations that deal with stimulus implication and equivalence, we first define a more abstract version, containing only axioms that we are sure to hold. Then we provide one or more refinements that add assumptions to it. This allows experimentation with several possibilities and makes it easier to update the specification as we learn more about psychological phenomena.[2]

As an example, let us consider the schemata that specify how the utility of a stimulus is calculated. Recall from Sect. 3 that stimuli are divided into two classes, namely, primary and conditioned. Primary stimuli have utility values *a priori*, while conditioned stimuli have their utilities calculated in terms of the primary ones. Moreover, drives and emotions can influence this calculation. The more general version of stimulus utility, *StimulusUtility*, states that there exists a function that calculates the utility in terms of the stimulus, a set of emotions and a set of drives.

___ *StimulusUtility* _____

StimulationSubsystem

EmotionSubsystem

DriveSubsystem

$sUtility : Stimulus \rightarrow Utility$

$\exists f : Stimulus \times \mathbb{P}\, Emotion \times \mathbb{P}\, Drive \rightarrow Utility \bullet$
$\quad \forall s : Stimulus \bullet$
$\qquad sUtility(s) = f(s, activeEmotions, activeDrives)$

Clearly, this abstract definition does not relate conditioned to primary stimuli. The reason is that, as far as we can see, any such relation must contain assumptions that we are not sure to hold. Thus, the actual relation is given in refinements. A simple one is given by *StimulusUtility_Ref1* schema, which depends on another schema, *StimulusUtilityBase*. In this refinement, the calculation is performed by locating the best primary stimulus that can be reached through stimulus implication, and then applying emotional and driving filters.

___ *StimulusUtility_Ref1* _____

StimulusUtilityBase

StimulusEmotionalRegulator

StimulusDriveRegulator

$\forall s : Stimulus \bullet$
$\quad sUtility(s) = driveRegulator(s, emotionalRegulator(s, base(s)))$

<hr/>

[2] Notice that if the specification is implemented in an object-oriented language, this approach can be seen in terms of class inheritance.

```
┌─ StimulusUtilityBase ──────────────────────────────────
│ StimulusUtility
│
│ StimulusImplication
│
│ base : Stimulus → Utility
├────────────────────────────────────────────────────────
│ ∀ s : Stimulus •
│     (∃ p : primaryStimuli •
│         base(s) = primary_utility(p) ∧
│         (∀ q : primaryStimuli | s sCauses q •
│             primary_utility(p) ≥₁ primary_utility(q) ∧
│         (s sCauses p))) ∨
│     (∀ p : primaryStimuli •
│         ¬ (s sCauses p) ∧
│         sUtility(s) = neutral)
└────────────────────────────────────────────────────────
```

In the next section we shall make references to some of the entities presented here in order to show how different subsystems are related.

Operant Behavior. Operant behavior, as we have seen in Sect. 3, is the most important behavioral class within Behavior Analysis. We shall study it here from two perspectives. First, its formalization is not straightforward, and we shall examine some of the difficulties. Second, operant processing is not simple, but can be elegantly modeled to some extent.

Let us begin by defining an operant.

```
┌─ Operant ──────────────────────────────────────────────
│ StimulusUtility
│
│ antecedents : ℙ(ℙ Stimulus)
│
│ action : Action
│
│ consequence : Stimulus
│
│ consequenceContingency : (ℙ Stimulus) ⇸ Correlation
├────────────────────────────────────────────────────────
│ sUtility(consequence) ≠ neutral
│
│ ∅ ∈ antecedents
│
│ dom consequenceContingency = antecedents
└────────────────────────────────────────────────────────
```

The above schema states that an operant has an *action* which leads to a *consequence*. There are two important considerations to be made here. First, notice that we introduced the concept of action. From the study of Behavior Analysis, we realized that there are some terminological imprecisions; a behavior (i.e., what is actually performed by the organism) and a behavior *class* (i.e., a set containing behaviors that have some properties) are distinct concepts, but it is easy to confuse them. Thus, we adopted the notion of action to refer to what would traditionally be called a behavior or even a mechanical property of behavior.

The second consideration regards the fact that Behavior Analysis defines operants solely by a stimulus consequence. Thus, in principle, either no action should be defined within an operant, or all possible actions that lead to the consequence should be present. This approach, however, would neglect the fact that each action takes to the consequent stimulus in a different way. For instance, pushing either a red button or a green one might lead an animal to food. But, perhaps, the red button is more efficient and, hence, will be more strongly correlated with the consequence than the other.

The schema also defines a set of sets of stimuli, *antecedents*. This accounts for the fact that the stimuli currently present in the environment might change the chances of reaching the desired consequence. This is formalized by the function *consequenceContingency*, which takes antecedent stimuli to the probability of success.

Such details show that a formalization process is not just a matter of translation. Sometimes it is necessary to add notions and to infer, from unclear prose, what was actually meant.

We now move on to study some operations. In Z, we say that an operation is *total* if, and only if, its preconditions cover all possibilities. This concept will guide our analysis from here on.

Operants might be either created or modified. Here, we shall focus on operant modification, which can be achieved in four ways.

First, a new environmental condition might be learned. This is called a discrimination operation, for it allows the organism to discriminate among several environmental possibilities. Each possibility is defined by a set of *discriminative stimuli*.

DiscriminationOp

OperantOp

$discriminativeStimuli? \notin \mathrm{dom}\ consequenceContingency$

$consequence?\ \underline{sCauses}\ consequence$

$discriminativeStimuli? \in \mathrm{dom}\ consequenceContingency'$

$consequenceContingency'(discriminativeStimuli?) >_1 min\_correlation$

In the above schema we import *OperantOp*, which defines a general operation over an operant but is not necessary for the present discussion and, thus, is omitted.

Second, an already known environmental condition might lead to the operant consequent stimulus, which strengthens their relation.

$\quad$ *OperantConditioningOp* _____

$\quad$ *OperantOp*
_____

discriminativeStimuli? $\in$ dom *consequenceContingency*

consequence? $\underline{sCauses}$ *consequence*

consequenceContingency'(*discriminativeStimuli?*)
$\qquad \geq_1$ *consequenceContingency*(*discriminativeStimuli?*)

Third, a known environmental state might not lead to the desired consequence, which reduces their relation.

$\quad$ *ExtinctionOp* _____

$\quad$ *OperantOp*
_____

discriminativeStimuli? $\in$ dom *consequenceContingency*

$\neg$ (*consequence?* $\underline{sCauses}$ *consequence*)

consequenceContingency'(*discriminativeStimuli?*)
$\qquad \leq_1$ *consequenceContingency*(*discriminativeStimuli?*)

Finally, if neither the environmental condition is known, nor the consequence desired, the operant simply remains unchanged.

$\quad$ *NeutralOp* _____

$\quad$ *OperantOp*
_____

discriminativeStimuli? $\notin$ dom *consequenceContingency*

$\neg$ (*consequence?* $\underline{sCauses}$ *consequence*)

consequenceContingency'(*discriminativeStimuli?*)
$\qquad =$ *consequenceContingency*(*discriminativeStimuli?*)

Notice that these four definitions form a total operation: they cover all possibilities for the input variables *discriminativeStimuli?* and *consequence?*:

1. *DiscriminationOp* accounts for the case in which *discriminativeStimuli?* $\notin$ dom *consequenceContingency*.
2. *OperantConditioningOp* handles the case in which *discriminativeStimuli?* $\in$ dom *consequenceContingency* and *consequence?* $\underline{sCauses}$ *consequence*.
3. *ExtinctionOp* occurs when *discriminativeStimuli?* $\in$ dom *consequenceContingency* and $\neg$ (*consequence?* $\underline{sCauses}$ *consequence*).
4. *NeutralOp* accounts for the remaining case.

This model can be further refined by adding the notions of reinforcement and punishment. Each of these, in turn, can be either *positive* or *negative*. A positive reinforcement accounts for the provision of a pleasant stimulus (e.g., provision of food), while a negative reinforcement stands for the removal of an unpleasant stimulus (e.g., relief from pain through analgesics). Punishment is analogous. At last, there is the case in which the stimulus is neither pleasant nor painful. Hence, there are five possibilities.

$$
\begin{array}{|l}
\hline \textit{PositiveReinforcement} \\
\quad \textit{StimulusUtility} \\
\hline \quad \textit{consequence?} : \textit{Stimulus} \\
\hline \quad s\textit{Utility}(\textit{consequence?}) >_1 \textit{neutral} \\
\quad \textit{stimulus\_status}(\textit{consequence?}) = \textit{Beginning} \\
\hline
\end{array}
$$

$$
\begin{array}{|l}
\hline \textit{NegativeReinforcement} \\
\quad \textit{StimulusUtility} \\
\hline \quad \textit{consequence?} : \textit{Stimulus} \\
\hline \quad s\textit{Utility}(\textit{consequence?}) <_1 \textit{neutral} \\
\quad \textit{stimulus\_status}(\textit{consequence?}) = \textit{Ending} \\
\hline
\end{array}
$$

$$
\begin{array}{|l}
\hline \textit{PositivePunishment} \\
\quad \textit{StimulusUtility} \\
\hline \quad \textit{consequence?} : \textit{Stimulus} \\
\hline \quad s\textit{Utility}(\textit{consequence?}) <_1 \textit{neutral} \\
\quad \textit{stimulus\_status}(\textit{consequence?}) = \textit{Beginning} \\
\hline
\end{array}
$$

$$
\begin{array}{|l}
\hline \textit{NegativePunishment} \\
\quad \textit{StimulusUtility} \\
\hline \quad \textit{consequence?} : \textit{Stimulus} \\
\hline \quad s\textit{Utility}(\textit{consequence?}) >_1 \textit{neutral} \\
\quad \textit{stimulus\_status}(\textit{consequence?}) = \textit{Ending} \\
\hline
\end{array}
$$

$$
\begin{array}{|l}
\hline \textit{NeutralReinforcementOp\_1} \\
\quad \textit{OperantOp} \\
\hline \quad s\textit{Utility}(\textit{consequence?}) = \textit{neutral} \\
\hline
\end{array}
$$

Again, these possibilities account for all cases. We can integrate them with the previous schemata using the following formulae.

$$T\_FundamentalOperantOp \; \widehat{=} \; DiscriminationOp \vee OperantConditioningOp \vee$$
$$ExtinctionOp \vee NeutralOp$$

$$PositiveReinforcementOp\_1 \; \widehat{=} \; T\_FundamentalOperantOp \wedge$$
$$PositiveReinforcement$$

$$PositiveReinforcementOp\_2 \; \widehat{=} \; OperantFormationOp \wedge PositiveReinforcement$$

$$PositivePunishmentOp\_1 \; \widehat{=} \; T\_FundamentalOperantOp \wedge$$
$$PositivePunishment$$

$$PositivePunishmentOp\_2 \; \widehat{=} \; OperantFormationOp \wedge PositivePunishment$$

We may now combine all of the above and define a rather complex total operation.

$$T\_OperantOp \; \widehat{=} \; PositiveReinforcementOp\_1 \vee NegativeReinforcementOp\_1 \vee$$
$$PositivePunishmentOp\_1 \vee NegativePunishmentOp\_1 \vee$$
$$NeutralReinforcementOp\_1$$

5 Discussion

In this paper, we discussed the formalization of the Behavior Analysis psychological theory, a traditionally informal domain of knowledge. We argued that, though informal, such theory is sufficiently precise in order to allow a complete formal specification. Moreover, we tried to show that there is much to gain with such a formalization and that particular issues arise when dealing with it.

The formal specification brings new questions to the knowledge it formalizes. As such, it can be a theoretical tool for Psychology. For instance, we saw that graphs can be used to model certain stimuli properties. Furthermore, once implemented, experiments can be performed to validate the theory. Experiments that yield unexpected results might demonstrate that the underlying theory is not correct. And because a formal specification is responsible for the implementation, the faulty assumptions could be more easily located.

The construction of the ontology described in Sect. 2 was easy and fast. Moreover, its structure was simple enough in order to allow a person not familiar with formal specifications to read it. Therefore, it constituted an useful prototype, which could be used both to determine the value of further formalization and to allow an expert in the theory to validate the model.

The Z formal method allowed useful techniques, such as the definition of total operations and of refinement levels. Looking for total operations forces us to examine all possibilities of transformations. Hence, it helps spotting faults both in the specification and in the original theory. Different levels of refinements allow us to cope with incomplete information. Thus, when we are not sure about the details of a particular concept, we can nevertheless achieve a formalization, by breaking it into several levels of abstraction.

Z also encourages modularization through schemata and integration through schema calculus. We employed this facilities to divide as much as possible the concepts being formalized. We also found useful to group together into subsystems all concepts that relate to some major division of the theory. One of the advantages of this approach is that modifications in the specification tend to be localized.

The next step regarding this work will be the formal verification of properties of the specification (e.g., consistency). An implementation, then, will follow and conclude the project.

Acknowledgments

This work has been supported by CNPq (Conselho Nacional de Desenvolvimento Científico e Tecnológico) and FAPESP (Fundação de Amparo à Pesquisa do Estado de São Paulo). We also thank Walkiria Helena Grant, from the Institute of Psychology of the University of São Paulo, for proofreading our initial ontology.

References

1. Skinner, B.F.: Science and Human Behavior. The Free Press (1953)
2. Jacky, J.: The way of Z: practical programming with formal methods. Cambridge University Press, New York, NY, USA (1996)
3. d'Inverno, M., Luck, M.: Understanding Agent Systems. Springer (2003)
4. d'Inverno, M.: Modelling and simulating the behaviour of adult stem cells using agent-based systems (2006) http://www2.wmin.ac.uk/ dinverm/cell/index.htm.
5. Bush, P.C., Sejnowski, T.J.: Simulations of a reconstructed cerebellar purkinje cell based on simplified channel kinetics. Neural Computation **3**(3) (1991) 321–332
6. Lytton, W.W., Sejnowski, T.J.: Simulations of cortical pyramidal neurons synchronized by inhibitory interneurons. Journal of Neurophysiology **66**(3) (1991) 1059–1079
7. Woodcock, J., Davies, J.: Using Z: Specification, Refinement, and Proof. Prentice Hall (1996)
8. W3C: Web ontology language (2004) http://www.w3.org/2004/OWL/.
9. Informatics, S.M.: The protégé ontology editor and knowledge acquisition system (2006) http://protege.stanford.edu/.
10. Saaltink, M.: The Z/EVES 2.0 User's Guide. ORA Canada (1999)
11. Catania, C.A.: Learning. Prentice Hall (1998)
12. Watson, J.B.: Psychology as the behaviorist views it. Psychological Review (20) (1913) 158–177

Integrating Performance and Reliability Analysis in a Non-Functional MDA Framework*

Vittorio Cortellessa, Antinisca Di Marco, and Paola Inverardi

Università degli Studi di L'Aquila, Dipartimento di Informatica
{cortelle, adimarco, inverard}@di.univaq.it

Abstract. Integration of non-functional validation in Model-Driven Architecture is still far from being achieved, although it is ever more necessary in the development of modern software systems. In this paper we make a step ahead towards the adoption of such activity as a daily practice for software engineers all along the MDA process. We consider the Non-Functional MDA framework (NFMDA) that, beside the typical MDA model transformations for code generation, embeds new types of model transformations that allow the generation of quantitative models for non-functional analysis. We plug into the framework two methodologies, one for performance analysis and one for reliability assessment, and we illustrate the relationships between non-functional models and software models. For this aim, Computation Independent, Platform Independent and Platform Specific Models are also defined in the non-functional domains taken into consideration, that are performance and reliability.

1 Introduction

The recent evolution of software development activities based on models is rapidly moving the viewpoint of software engineers from a code-centric perspective to a model-centric one. Model-Driven Architecture [11] has substantially contributed to this change of perspective by providing techniques and tools for model creation and management along the software lifecycle. For example, numerous model transformation approaches finalized at the code generation through model refinements have been recently devised [9].

Software modeling is also a well-assessed practice in the non-functional domain. Since decades performance and reliability experts are use to build models for validating software/hardware systems vs non-functional requirements. However, these activities are not stably embedded in the software development process, thus non-functional models creation and management do not follow the same regular refinements applied to the software model.

In order to fill the gap between software development and non-functional validation, in the last few years the research has faced the challenge of automated

---

* This work has been partially supported by the IST EU project "PLASTIC" (www.ist-plastic.org), and partially supported by the MIUR project "FIRB-PERF" (Performance Evaluation of Complex Systems: Techniques, Methodologies and Tools).

M.B. Dwyer and A. Lopes (Eds.): FASE 2007, LNCS 4422, pp. 57–71, 2007.

generation of quantitative models for non-functional validation from software artifacts[1]. Several methodologies have been introduced that all share the idea of annotating software models with data related to non functional aspects and then translating the annotated model into a model ready to be validated.

None of these methodologies explicitly defines the roles of its models within an MDA context even if the approaches are often presented as *MDA-compliant*. In fact few approaches can be found in literature that aim at embedding non-functional validation activities and models within MDA.

In the reliability domain, UML profiles have been introduced in [13] and [12] to allow software reliability prediction at different levels of the MDA framework. In [13] the authors translate a set of annotated UML 2.0 Sequence Diagrams into an annotated LTS (Label Transition System) that is then interpreted as a Markov model. The solution of the Markov model provides estimations of the software system reliability. In [12], reliability aspects are introduced in a Platform Independent Model through an Abstract Reliability Profile. Then, at the Platform Specific level a new profile is defined that extends the UML Profile for EJB and allows the specification of the reliability support provided by the J2EE platform. Finally transformation rules have been defined to map the source model (PIM) onto the target model (PSM).

In [15] an approach have been defined in MDA that, starting from UML diagrams, derives an analysis model based on the Klaper language. The novelty of this approach is that the transformations are based on two techniques typically used in functional transformations, that are relational and graph grammar-based techniques.

In [17], MDA is viewed as a suitable framework to incorporate various analysis techniques into the development process of distributed systems. In particular, the work focuses on response time prediction of EJB applications by defining a domain model and a mapping of the domain onto a Queueing Network meta-model.

In [14], the authors aim at helping designers to reason on non-functional properties at different levels of abstraction, likewise MDA does for functional aspects. They introduce a development process where designers can define, use and refine the measurement necessary to take into account QoS attributes. Their ultimate goal is either to generate code for runtime monitoring of QoS parameters, or to provide a basis for QoS contract negotiation and resource reservation in the running system.

However, none of such approaches defines a global framework that embeds non-functional aspects within the whole MDA (i.e. at CIM, PIM and PSM levels) in an integrated manner. To fill this lack, in [5] we have introduced a framework that extends MDA to consider non-functional aspects. Such framework, called Non-Functional MDA (NFMDA), embeds, beside the typical MDA models and transformations, new models and transformations related to non-functional validation activities.

---

[1] The major references for this type of approaches in the field of software performance can be found in [1].

In this paper we provide two instances of the NFMDA framework, one related to performance (namely **PRIMA**) and another one to reliability (namely **COBRA**), both working at platform independent and platform specific level. Since automation is a key factor in MDA, we also discuss the tool support that should be provided to instantiate the NFMDA framework on new approaches.

Goal of this paper is to emphasize, through the instantiation of NFMDA on existing approaches in different non-functional domains, that platform independent/specific aspects actually occur also in non-functional domains, and to demonstrate that our framework nicely supports their manipulation through appropriate types of models and model transformations.

The paper is organized as follows: Section 2 briefly introduces the NFMDA framework, Section 3 discusses the issue of tool support in NFMDA; in Section 4 we instantiate the framework on two approaches for performance and reliability validation, and finally in Section 5 we give the conclusive remarks.

2   Non-Functional MDA Framework

In this section we summarize our extended view of MDA, already presented in [5] and illustrated in Figure 1. Beyond the canonical MDA models and transformations the NFMDA framework contains three additional types of models and three additional types of transformations/relationships (see the right side of Figure 1) that we have introduced to keep Non-Functional (NF) aspects under control. The new types of models are: CINFM, PINFM, PSNFM[2].

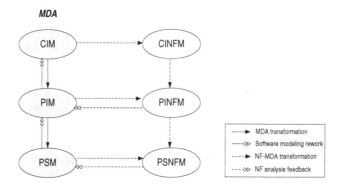

Fig. 1. The NFMDA framework

Figure 2 provides a graphical flavor of NFMDA. All NFMDA instances share the typical MDA models that are placed in the central cylinder of the figure. Each instance is represented as a wing departing from the cylinder, because each

---

[2] For sake of space we cannot provide details of the NFMDA framework, but they can be found in [5].

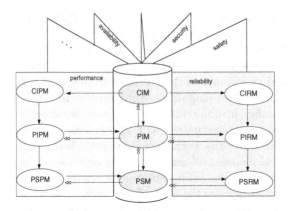

Fig. 2. Views of the NFMDA framework

NF property of a software/hardware system represents only a different view of the system, but it may need different models, languages and tools to be modeled and analyzed.

CINFM - A Computation Independent Non-Functional Model represents the requirements and constraints related to an NF aspect (such as performance, reliability, security, cost, etc) that can be formulated at different levels of detail (e.g. component level, functionality level, system level).

PINFM - A Platform Independent Non-Functional Model is a representation of the business logics of the system along with estimates of NF characteristics, such as the amount of resources that the logics needs to be executed.

PSNFM - A Platform Specific Non-Functional Model contains variables and parameters that represent the software structure and dynamics, as well as the platform where the software will be deployed. In an NF context a platform must include characteristics of the underlying hardware architecture such as the CPU speed and the failure probability of a hardware connection.

The new transformations and relationships we introduced among the models in Figure 1 are:

NFMDA horizontal transformation - It transforms a software model into the corresponding model suitable to evaluate an NF aspect of the system at any level in the MDA hierarchy. In Figure 1, CIM→CINFM, PIM→PINFM and PSM→PSNFM are horizontal transformations. The model transformations belonging to this class share a two-steps structure: the software model is first annotated with additional data, thereafter the annotated model is transformed into a model from which we estimate the NF aspect of interest.

NFMDA vertical transformation - Even though it seems to play in an NF domain a similar role to the one of MDA transformations, such transformation is instead intended to provide an input contribution to the horizontal transformation. In other words, often the horizontal transformations needs some input from the one-step-higher NF model in the hierarchy.

Two types of arrows with double empty peak also appear in Figure 1 to give completeness to the software NF analysis process, and they represent the reverse paths after the analysis takes place.

Dashed arrows with double empty peak represent the feedback that originates from the evaluation of an NF model. Continuous arrows with double empty peak are direct consequences of NF feedback. They represent the rework necessary on the software models to embed the changes suggested from the analysis.

3   Tool Support for the NFMDA Framework

Automation is undeniably a key factor in MDA approaches. To be embedded into the NFMDA framework, an NF validation approach should be supported by a tool that provides automation to all the validation steps, identified in Figure 1, that span from *model generation*, to *model analysis* and *results interpretation*.

However, any NF validation approach cannot be completely automated, as the annotation of software models with non-functional parameters is necessarily a manual step that has to be performed by experts of the non-functional domain of the approach[3].

In general, automated support for *model analysis* is available and download-able from the net. As opposite, due to the young age of the *model generation* field, few existing approaches generating quantitative models are supported by stable and reliable tools. Even the existing tools, quite often, do not deal with all the transformation rules defined in the approaches, due to the complexity of the transformations and/or the difficulty of the model representation.

However, several researchers are recently spending a lot of effort to implement their methodologies for NF validation of software artifacts in a more systematic way. Two alternative implementation techniques have been considered: (i) ad-hoc algorithms and (ii) model-transformation techniques.

Ad-hoc algorithms make use of programming languages like C and Java. All the logics of the model generation has to be carefully implemented, includ-ing the order in which the generation rules must be applied, the management of the internal representation of the source and target models and the traceability among source and target entities.

Model transformation techniques, instead, are based on languages and tools created to provide (general) means for transformations among models specified through meta-models [15]. In this case, the implementation must only cope with the model generation rules without taking care of the way such transformation is actually executed. Moreover, if a transformation language embeds traceability between models, then the approach can also provide a mechanism that traces back, on the source model, the analysis results.

Finally, *results interpretation* and consequent feedback generation are still open points in this domain. At the moment, few and primitive guidelines [18,19,4]

---

[3] The collection of values for the annotation parameters may be a non trivial activity, but it is out of scope of this paper.

or simple annotations of analysis results on the source models [2] have been proposed in the performance domain, but much work must still be done.

4   Two NFMDA Framework Instances

In this section we embed within the NFMDA framework two existing approaches to transform software models into NF models. The first approach is related to performance modeling and validation [7], the second one to reliability [8]. Both these approaches have been implemented with ad-hoc techniques for the generation and analysis of the quantitative model(s) they are based on.

It is worth noting that several NF validation approaches do not work at both the PIM and the PSM level, but they are suitable for just one of these levels [2,13]. Both approaches presented here work at all MDA levels, and they have been selected to show the complete instantiation of the NFMDA framework on two different NF domains.

4.1   Performance Analysis in MDA

The **PRIMA** methodology has been introduced in [7] and has evolved, on one side, towards validation of mobility-based software systems [10] and, on the other side, towards Component-Based Software Performance Engineering [3]. It was originally conceived as a model-based approach to estimate the performance of software systems ready to be deployed. Due to the type of performance models produced, **PRIMA** has the intrinsic capability of analyzing also software systems at a platform independent level. The prerequisites to apply the approach consist of: modeling the system requirements through an UML Use Case Diagram, modeling the software dynamics through UML Sequence Diagrams, and modeling the software-to-hardware mapping through an UML Deployment Diagram.

Figure 3 represents **PRIMA** as plugged into the NFMDA framework. CIM, PIM and PSM are shown in the left-hand side of the figure. In the right-hand side of the figure the additional models introduced in our framework are shown, which have been renamed in this specific instance as Computation Independent Performance Model (CIPM), Platform Independent Performance Model (PIPM), Platform Specific Performance Model (PSPM). Names of tools able to perform transformation steps have been reported on the edges corresponding to the transformations between models.

The system requirements are expressed by an Use Case Diagram that represents the Computation Independent Model of the system. The Use Case Diagram has been also reported as part of the Platform Independent Model because its annotated version is part of the transformation to the PIPM. The PIM is completed by the Sequence Diagrams that model the application dynamics through a set of system scenarios. Finally, the Platform Specific Model contains different types of information: the name of the platform (e.g. CORBA, J2EE, etc.) determining the type of code that must be generated, and a Deployment Diagram determining the software-to-hardware mapping of the application.

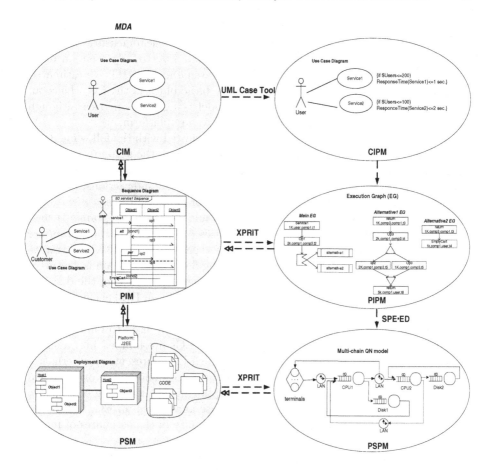

Fig. 3. The **PRIMA** approach

The topmost performance model, namely the CIPM, is obtained by the CIM (i.e. the Use Case Diagram) with annotations on use cases that express the performance requirements of the system. As an example, in Figure 3 a requirement on *Service1* entails that the average response time of such use case must not be larger than 1 second when the customers in the system are less than 200. A similar requirement is associated to *Service2*. The transformation CIM→CIPM can be easily achieved by annotating an Use Case Diagram within an UML CASE tool (e.g. Poseidon [21]).

The PIPM is represented by an Execution Graph (EG) [19]. An EG is basically a flow graph that models the software dynamics, and its building blocks are: basic nodes that model sequential operations, fork and join nodes that model concurrency, loop nodes that model iterative constructs, branching nodes that model alternative paths, and composite nodes that model separately specified macro-steps. In addition to the software dynamics, in an EG a *demand vector* is attached to each basic node to model the resources needed to execute the corresponding operation. It is worth to note that the amount of resource needed cannot be specified, at this level in the hierarchy, by classical measures like CPU time and disk accesses. Each element of the demand vector represents a high-level metric, such as *screen operation, message sending*, etc. [19]. An estimated amount of each metric can be attached to any basic block in the EG. Hence an EG is a Platform Independent Performance Model as high-level metrics, although representing performance data, are not bound to any platform.

In order to generate the PIPM, the PIM is annotated with the following data: (i) Use Case Diagram - probability that an actor enters the system and probability that the actor requires a certain use case (i.e. the operational profile); (ii) Sequence Diagram - size of messages exchanged over the interactions, probabilities over the branching points, average number of loop iterations.

The annotated PIM (i.e. Use Case Diagram and Sequence Diagrams) is then transformed into an EG as follows. Probabilities on the Use Case Diagram are combined to carry out the probability of each use case to occur. The latter represents also the probability that the corresponding Sequence Diagram is executed. Thereafter, an EG is built for each Sequence Diagram by visiting the diagram and piecewise translating each fragment encountered in an EG specific pattern. EG patterns are then combined following the structure of the Sequence Diagram. During the visit, the performance annotations are used to build demand vectors attached to EG basic blocks. Finally, all EGs are lumped into a single one that starts with a branching node, where each EG represents an alternative path. The probabilities over the outgoing paths correspond to the ones carried out from the Use Case Diagram[4]. The tool supporting the modeling of EGs (i.e. SPE·ED [22]) allows stand-alone and worst-case analysis of an EG. Obviously, the validity of the analysis undergoes the trustability of the estimates of model parameters.

In this step, the CIPM brings the target performance results that have to be compared with the one obtained from the PIPM solution. In Figure 3 the XPRIT label on the edges connecting (in both directions) PIM and PIPM represents the name of the tool that automates such transformation [6].

Going down in the hierarchy of Figure 3, the adopted PSPM is a multi-chain QN model. The semantics of the QN is as follows: each service center represents a hardware device, and the jobs traversing the network represent the software load of the devices.

In this approach the PSM→PSPM transformation makes a large use of the PIPM. First, the Deployment Diagram is annotated with information on the internal configuration of each host (i.e. number and speed of CPUs, number and access time of hard disks, etc.). This information is used in the transformation process to build the topology of the QN that represents the hardware platform. The EG structure determines the number of job classes (i.e. chains) that traverse the QN. The combination of values of demand vectors and performance information about the platform (e.g. CORBA) allow to determine the amount of

---

[4] For sake of space, we cannot provide more technical details of the transformation process; however, readers interested may refer to [7].

resources that each class of jobs requires to each hardware device [19]. In Figure 3 the XPRIT label on the edges connecting (in both directions) PSM and PSPM again indicates the tool that automates such transformation. The SPE·ED label on the edge connecting PIPM and PSPM indicated that the EG modeling tool also allows to elaborate the EG demand vectors in order to parameterize the QN.

It is obvious that at this level in the MDA hierarchy a different type of performance analysis is pursuable. The QN embeds all the software and hardware parameters that are needed for a canonical performance analysis. They have been collected and/or monitored on the actual deployed system. End-to-end response time, utilization and throughput of any platform device can be computed by solving the QN model, and the results can be compared to the measures of the actual system. Once validated, such model can be used for performance prediction. System configurations and workload domains that are unfeasible to experiment in the actual system can be represented in the model in order to study the behavior of the system under different (possibly stressing) performance scenarios.

The outputs of the PSPM evaluation represent the feedback on the PSM, which needs to be modified if performance do not satisfy the requirements. As illustrated in section 2, the model rework on the software side could propagate up to the higher level models in case no feasible change can be made on the PSM to overcome the emerging performance problems.

Behind PIPM/PSPM duality there is the intuitive concept that the performance analysis results can be expressed with actual time-based metrics only after a PIM is bounded to its platform and becomes a PSM. Obviously the results coming out a PIPM evaluation are not useful to validate the model against the system requirements, because they may take very different time values on different platforms. However, the following three types of actions can originate from this analysis.

(i) **Lower and upper bounds** on the system performance can be evaluated if some estimates of the performance of the possible target platforms are available. For example, if the lower bound on a system response time is larger than the corresponding performance requirement, then it is useless to progress in the development process as performance problems are intrinsic in the software architecture. It is necessary to rework on the software models. However, even when the results are not so pessimistic it is possible to take decisions that improve the software architecture.

(ii) In order to identify the most **overloaded components**, the utilization and/or queue length of each service center in our PIPM must be computed vs the system population. An overloaded component has a very long waiting queue and represents a bottleneck in the software architecture. Some rework is necessary in the PIM to remove the bottleneck.

(iii) Either as a consequence of the above decisions or as a planned performance test, different (functionally equivalent) **alternative software designs** can be modeled as PIMs, and then their performance can be compared through their PIPMs in order to select the optimal one.

4.2 Reliability Analysis in MDA

The methodology for reliability modeling and validation that we consider here has been first presented in [16] to estimate the reliability of a component-based software system as a function of the failure probabilities of components and the operational profile. Failures of hardware connections have then been embedded into the model [8]. In order to embed this approach into our NFMDA framework, we have further enhanced the reliability model by embedding failures of hardware sites. We have chosen this approach to the reliability validation for two main reasons: (i) it well suits to be interpreted in platform independent and platform specific views (as we show in this section), and (ii) well-founded transformations from UML models have been proposed to generate the reliability model [8]. For sake of readability, in the remainder of the paper, we will refer to this approach as **COBRA** (COmponent-Based Reliability Assessment).

In Figure 4 we show the **COBRA** approach as embedded into NFMDA. Software models are shown in the left-hand side of the figure and reliability models in the right-hand one. Following the naming that we have adopted in NFMDA, the reliability models are labeled as: Computation Independent Reliability Model (CIRM), Platform Independent Reliability Model (PIRM), and Platform Specific Reliability Model (PSRM). Again, names of tools able to perform transformation steps have been reported on the edges corresponding to the transformations between models.

The software models of **COBRA** (i.e. the ones on the left-hand side of the figure) are represented with the same UML diagrams as in **PRIMA**. Use Case Diagram represents system requirements and, together with Sequence Diagrams, represent the system dynamics at the platform independent level. The Deployment Diagram, together with Sequence Diagrams, represent the mapping of software to hardware in the PSM. In this case, the PSM does not include the software code and the name of the platform.

The topmost reliability model, namely the CIRM, can be obtained by the CIM with two different types of annotations: an annotation attached to an use case expresses a minimum reliability threshold that is required for the functionality corresponding to the use case; an annotation attached to the whole diagram represents a minimum reliability threshold required for the whole system. As an example, in Figure 4, we have annotated a 0.99 reliability threshold for the *Service1* use case, whereas a 0.982 threshold has been annotated for the whole system. We will consider here only reliability thresholds on the whole system. However, the same type of modeling and analysis can be applied at use case level by restricting the ranges of the reliability equations.

PIRM and PSRM are represented in **COBRA** by mathematical equations that link the reliability of the whole system to the failure probabilities of its components. The difference between the models is that in the PIRM the reliability of the system only depends on the failures of software components (independently of the platform they will be deployed), whereas in the PSRM the failures of the

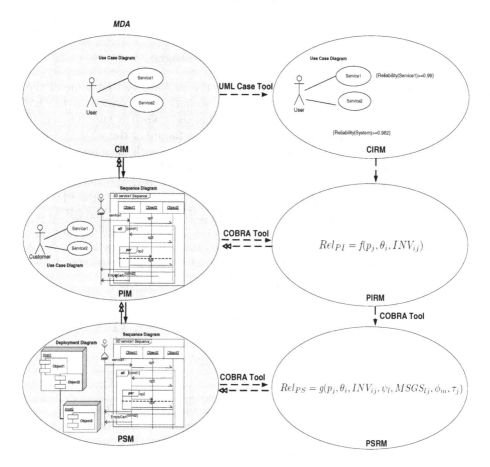

Fig. 4. The **COBRA** approach

platform sites and hardware connections are also taken into account. In both cases, the values assigned to the model variables are extracted from annotations on the UML diagrams of PIM and PSM.

In **COBRA** the PIRM is represented by the following equation [16]:

$$Rel_{PI} = \sum_{j=1}^{K} p_j \cdot \prod_{i=1}^{N} (1 - \theta_i)^{INV_{ij}} \tag{1}$$

where:

- N is the number of software components;
- K is the number of scenarios modeling the system dynamics;
- Rel_{PI} represents the system reliability at the platform independent level, that is the probability of no software failures during the system operation;
- θ_i represents the probability of failure on demand of the component i [20];

- INV_{ij} represents the number of invocations of component i within the dynamics of Sequence Diagram j;
- p_j is the probability of execution of Sequence Diagram j;

In practice, the system reliability in (1) is the probability that none of the components fails during the execution of the scenarios represented by the Sequence Diagrams. This type of reliability model is also known as *fail-and-stop*, in that any single failure of a component represents a failure of the whole system.

In order to generate the PIRM, the PIM is annotated with the following data: (i) Use Case Diagram - operational profile as in **PRIMA**; (ii) Sequence Diagram - number of invocations per component. The PIM→PIRM transformation in this case is trivial, in that values of annotations are extracted from the PIM and properly assigned to the variables of equation (1). In this domain, the CIRM has the same role as the CIPM, in that it brings the required reliability threshold that has to be compared with the one obtained from the PIRM solution.

Going down in the hierarchy of Figure 4, the PSRM is represented by an equation that takes into account also hardware failures, as follows:

$$Rel_{PS} = \sum_{j=1}^{K} p_j \cdot \left(\prod_{i=1}^{N} (1 - \theta_i)^{INV_{ij}} \cdot \prod_{l=1}^{C} (1 - \psi_l)^{MSGS_{lj}} \cdot \prod_{m=1}^{S} e^{-\phi_m \cdot \tau_j} \right) \quad (2)$$

where the following additional variables have been introduced:

- S is the number of platform sites;
- C is the number of hardware connections among platform sites;
- Rel_{PS} represents the system reliability at the platform specific level, that is the probability of no software/hardware failures during the system operation;
- ψ_l represents the probability of failure on demand of the hardware connection l;
- $MSGS_{lj}$ represents the number of messages exchanged over the connection l during the execution of Sequence Diagram j;
- ϕ_m represents the failure rate of the platform site m, that is the inverse of its Mean Time To Failure [20];
- τ_j is the execution time of scenario j over the targeted platform;

In practice, the system reliability in (2) is the probability that none of the components, the hardware connections and the platform sites fail during the execution of the scenarios represented by the Sequence Diagrams. Even in this case there is an underlying assumption of *fail-and-stop*, in that each type of failure induces a failure on the whole system.

Note that the failures of platform sites have been modeled by a continuous (exponential) failure rate, as opposite to all the other ones that have been modeled by probabilities of failures on demand (i.e. as originated from discrete time events). The rationale of this assumption is that hardware sites in practice are never idle (i.e. there are system processes always running), thus their failures may originate in any instant of time.

Obviously equations (1) and (2) represent only an example of reliability model that nicely fits into the NFMDA framework. Other assumptions can be made that bring to more sophisticated reliability models, such as considering error propagation among components or dependencies among hardware and software failures. However, it is out of scope of this paper to discuss limitations of non-functional models, as we have remarked in Section 1.

In order to generate the PSRM, the PSM is annotated with the following data: (i) Sequence Diagram - number of messages exchanged between pairs of components, execution time of the scenario; (ii) Deployment Diagram - probability of failure on demand of hardware connections, failure rates of platform sites. Similarly to the PIM→PIRM transformation, the values of annotations can be then extracted from the PSM and properly assigned to the variables of equation (2).

It is evident, by simply comparing equations (1) and (2), that the PIRM originates an optimistic evaluation of the system reliability, because the value of (1) will be always as large as the one in (2). However, an overestimation of system reliability can be accepted when failure data related to the hardware platform are not yet available, i.e. at platform independent level. In fact, a PIRM solution and sensitivity analysis may support early decisions in the software lifecycle, such as: (i) distributing the development and testing efforts over critical components, (ii) selecting COTS components to be plugged in an existing architecture, (iii) allocating computation complexity in software components and structuring the software architecture.

As soon as platform data are available, a PSRM can be generated and solved. The PSRM solution will support late decisions in the software lifecycle, such as the mapping of software components on platform sites, and the influence of a certain type of hardware connection on the whole system reliability.

The outputs of PIRM and PSRM represent, respectively, feedback on PIM and PSM. The latter ones can be modified if system reliability does not satisfy the requirements. The model rework on the software side could propagate up to the higher level models in case no feasible change can be made on the lower level models to overcome the emerging reliability problems.

5   Conclusions

NFMDA provides an unifying view on the NF validation in MDA, and it can be instantiated in several NF domains like performance, security, availability, etc. Platform Independent and Platform Specific concepts belong to many software validation processes, and bringing them to the evidence of an MDA structure is very advantageous to make these activities acceptable from the software engineering community.

In this paper we have shown how two existing approaches to the performance and reliability validation can be plugged into NFMDA framework. However, modern software systems claim for integrated validation of non-functional aspects, since the validation of a non-functional attribute in isolation (such as reliability) may not be meaningful due to intrinsic tradeoffs between attributes. For example, authentication mechanisms are usually introduced to improve the security of a system that, at the same time, may seriously degrade the system performance.

The NFMDA framework has been conceived to be compliant with the integrated validation of non-functional aspects, as there is no limitation on the types of non-functional models that can be generated. Obviously, the horizontal transformations may become very complex with a growing complexity of the non-functional models. However an integrated NF analysis, while increasing the complexity of the transformations, may save effort in model annotations (hence in parameter collection) because several parameters can be shared across non-functional attributes. A typical example of parameter sharing is represented by the operational profile. All non-functional aspects are heavily affected from the operational profile hence, once annotated on a software model, it can be used as input to several transformations towards different types of non-functional models.

Several directions may be taken in the future within this context.

First, basing on our experience, several other approaches match this framework in all its structure or in part of it, therefore they shall be easily plugged into NFMDA. We guess that this shall be one of the priorities for the future research in this field.

The suitability of the NFMDA framework for less established and more cross cutting NF aspects (such as security) shall be investigated. Likewise the practical applicability of the framework should be experimented on real case studies; however, experimentation should span over different application domains where different non-functional aspects can be critical.

Large investigation shall be devised to the feedback paths in the NFMDA framework, because the translation of validation results in actual design alternatives is still an open issue in all the NF domains. For example, the use of model transformation techniques that guarantee traceability would be helpful to straightforwardly report the analysis feedback on the software models.

Finally, the NFMDA framework represents the basis to enhance NF validation through: (i) the definition of languages and ontologies for representing CINFM, PINFM and PSNFM, and (ii) model transformation languages, techniques and tools targeting NF models.

References

1. S. Balsamo, A. Di Marco, P. Inverardi, M. Simeoni, Model-based Performance Prediction in Software Development: A Survey, *IEEE Trans. on Software Engineering*, 30(5):295-310, 2004.
2. S. Balsamo, M. Marzolla, A Simulation-Based Approach to Software Performance Modeling, *Proc. Joint 9th European Software Engineering Conference (ESEC) & 11th SIGSOFT Symposium on the Foundations of Software Engineering (FSE)*, pp. 363–366, Helsinki, FI, 2003.

3. A. Bertolino, R. Mirandola, CB-SPE Tool: Putting Component-Based Performance Engineering into Practice, *Proc. of CBSE 2004*, pp.233-248, 2004.
4. V. Cortellessa, A. Di Marco, P. Inverardi, Three Performance Models at Work: A Software Designer Perspective, *Electr. Notes Theor. Comput. Sci.*,vol. 97, pp. 219-239, 2004.
5. V. Cortellessa, A. Di Marco, P. Inverardi, Non-functional Modeling and Validation in Model-Driven Architecture, *Proc. of Sixth Working IEEE/IFIP Conference on Software Architecture (WICSA 2007)*, Mumbay, India, 2007 (To Appear).
6. V. Cortellessa V., M. Gentile, M. Pizzuti, XPRIT: an XML-based tool to translate UML diagrams into Execution Graphs and Queueing Networks, *Proc. of QEST 2004 (short papers)*, 2004.
7. V. Cortellessa, R. Mirandola, PRIMA-UML: a Performance Validation Incremental Methodology on Early UML Diagrams, *Science of Computer Programming*, Elsevier Science, 44(1):101-129, 2002.
8. V. Cortellessa, H. Singh, B. Cukic, E. Gunel, V. Bharadwaj, Early reliability assessment of UML based software models, *Proc. of 3rd ACM Workshop on Software and Performance*, 2002.
9. K. Czarnecki, S. Helsen, Classification of Model Transformation Approaches, *Proc. of OOPSLA03 Workshop on Generative Techniques in the Context of MDA*, 2003.
10. V. Grassi, R. Mirandola, PRIMAmob-UML: a methodology for performance analysis of mobile software architectures, *Proc. of WOSP 2002*, pp. 262-274, 2002.
11. J. Miller (editor), Model-Driven Architecture Guide, omg/2003-06-01 (2003).
12. G.N. Rodrigues, G. Robets, W. Emmerich, J. Skene, Reliability Support for Model Driven Architecture, *Proc. of WADS 2003, LNCS 3069*, pp.79-98, 2003.
13. G.N. Rodrigues, D. S. Rosenblum, S. Uchitel, Reliability Prediction in Model-Driven Development, *Proc. of Models Conference, LNCS 3713*, pp.339-354, 2005.
14. S. Rottger, S. Zschaler, Model-driven development for non-functional properties: refinement through model transformation, *Proc. of UML 2004*, LNCS 3273, pp.275-289, 2004.
15. A. Sabetta, D.C. Petriu, V. Grassi, R. Mirandola, Abstraction-raising Transformation for Generating Analysis Models, *Proc. of Models 2005 Satellite Events, LNCS 3844*, pp. 217-226, 2005.
16. H. Singh, V. Cortellessa, B. Cukic, E. Gunel, V. Bharadwaj, A Bayesian Approach to Reliability Prediction and Assessment of Component Based Systems, *Proc. of 12th IEEE International Symposium on Software Reliability Engineering*, 2001.
17. J. Skene, W. Emmerick, Model-driven performance analysis of Enterprise Information Systems, ENTCS 82(6), 2003.
18. C.U. Smith, L.G. Williams, Software performance antipatterns. *Proceedings of the 2nd international workshop on Software and performance (WOSP00)*, pp. 127–136, Ottawa, Ontario, Canada, 2000.
19. C.U. Smith, L.G. Williams, Performance Solutions: A Practical Guide to Creating Responsive, Scalable Software, Addison-Wesley, 2002.
20. K. Trivedi, Probability and Statistics with Reliability, Queuing, and Computer Science Applications, John Wiley and Sons, New York, 2001.
21. www.gentleware.com
22. www.perfeng.com

Information Preserving Bidirectional Model Transformations*

Hartmut Ehrig[1], Karsten Ehrig[2], Claudia Ermel[1], Frank Hermann[1], and Gabriele Taentzer[3]

[1] Department of Computer Science, Technical University Berlin, Germany
{ehrig,lieske,frank}@cs.tu-berlin.de
[2] Department of Computer Science, University of Leicester, United Kingdom
karsten@mcs.le.ac.uk
[3] Department of Mathematics and Computer Science, Phillips-University Marburg, Germany
taentzer@mathematik.uni-marburg.de

Abstract. Within model-driven software development, model transformation has become a key activity. It refers to a variety of operations modifying a model for various purposes such as analysis, optimization, and code generation. Most of these transformations need to be bidirectional to e.g. report analysis results, or keep coherence between models. In several application-oriented papers it has been shown that triple graph grammars are a promising approach to bidirectional model transformations. But up to now, there is no formal result showing under which condition corresponding forward and backward transformations are inverse to each other in the sense of information preservation. This problem is solved in this paper based on general results for the theory of algebraic graph transformations. The results are illustrated by a transformation of class models to relational data base models which has become a quasi-standard example for model transformation.

1 Introduction

Model transformation is a central activity in model-driven software development as it is used thoroughly for model optimization and other forms of model evolution. Moreover, model transformation is used to map models between different domains for analyzing them or for automatically generating code from them. Often a model transformation is required to be reversible to translate information back to source models. For example, a transformation of a domain-specific model to some formal model for the purpose of validation should be reversible to transform back analysis results stemming from the formal model. Reversible model transformations also play an important role in the presence of system evolution. Having usually a variety of different models around in the engineering process, the evolution of one model depends on the evolution of other models. To keep models coherent to each other, model transformations have to be reversible.

---

* This work has been partially sponsored by the project SENSORIA, IST-2005-016004.

M.B. Dwyer and A. Lopes (Eds.): FASE 2007, LNCS 4422, pp. 72–86, 2007.

Model transformations have been classified by Czarnecki, Mens et.al. [CH03, MG06]. Mens et.al. distinguish two main classes: endogenous and exogenous model transformations. While the former run within one modeling language, e.g. are used to model refactorings or other kinds of optimizations, the latter are used to translate models between different languages. In the context of this paper we concentrate on exogenous model transformations. A promising approach to reversible transformation is bi-directional model transformation, since only one transformation description is needed to deduce forward and backward transformations automatically.

A bi-directional model transformation can be well described by triple graph transformations as introduced by Schürr et.al. [KS06, Sch94]. The main idea is to relate a source and a target graph by some correspondence graph in between which is mapped to both graphs. In this way, source and target graphs are coupled and a basic structure for consistent co-evolution of the model graphs is established. Triple rules are used to formulate conditions for consistent co-evolution describing the simultaneous transformation of source and target graphs. It is often the case though that these graphs do not develop simultaneously: i.e. one graph evolves and the other one has to be updated accordingly. To capture this situation, Königs and Schürr showed that each triple rule can be split into a so-called source rule which changes the source graph only and a forward rule which updates the target accordingly. Furthermore, they lifted this result to transformation sequences in [KS06]. This means that we obtain for each triple transformation sequence a corresponding forward transformation and dually also a corresponding backward transformation sequence.

But up to now, there is no formal result showing under which conditions a given forward transformation sequence has an inverse backward sequence in the sense that both together are information preserving concerning the source graphs. The main result of this paper solves this problem under the condition that a given forward transformation sequence $G_1 \xRightarrow{tr_F^*} G_2$ is source consistent. Roughly speaking, that means G_1 can be generated by source rules only. This result is based on an extension of the result in [KS06] cited above, which allows to state a bijective correspondence between triple transformation sequences and combined match consistent source and forward transformation sequences. The proof of this extended result is based on the well-known Local Church–Rosser and Concurrency Theorem for graph transformations (see [EEPT06]) which are shown to be valid also for triple graph grammars.

All main concepts and results are illustrated at a running example, which is a model transformation from class models to relational data base models. This quasi-standard model transformation has been originally defined in the specification for QVT [OMG05] by the Object Management Group. Due to space limitations, we present a triple graph grammar for a restricted form of this model transformation.

In Section 2 we start with a review of triple graph grammar for graphs and introduce the running example in Section 3. Section 4 presents the main results concerning information preserving forward and backward transformations. In

Section 5 we discuss how to obtain a general theory for triple graph transformations which can be based also on typed and attributed graphs.

2   Review of Triple Rules and Triple Graph Grammars

Triple graph grammars [Sch94] have been shown to be a promising approach to consistently co-develop two related structures. They provide bidirectional transformation between a pair of graphs representing these structures which are connected using a third so-called correspondence graph together with its embeddings into the source and target graph. In [KS06], Königs and Schürr formalize the basic concepts of triple graph grammars in a set-theoretical way. In this section, we take up this formalization and present further steps of a theory of triple graph grammars in the following sections. We first base this formalization on simple graphs and will discuss the extension to typed, attributed graphs based on concepts from category theory in Section 5.

Definition 1 (Graph and Graph Morphism). *A graph $G = (V, E, s, t)$ consists of a set V of nodes (also called vertices), E of edges and two functions src, tar : $E \rightarrow V$, the source and target functions. Given graphs G_1, G_2 with $G_i = (V_i, E_i, src_i, tar_i)$ for $i = 1, 2$, a graph morphisms $f : G_1 \rightarrow G_2$, $f = (f_V, f_E)$, consists of two functions $f_V : V_1 \rightarrow V_2$ and $f_E : E_1 \rightarrow E_2$ that preserve the source and target functions, i.e. $f_V \circ src_1 = src_2 \circ f_E$ and $f_V \circ tar_1 = tar_2 \circ f_E$.*

Definition 2 (Triple Graph and Triple Graph Morphism). *Three graphs SG, CG, and TG, called source, connection, and target graphs, together with two graph morphisms $s_G : CG \rightarrow SG$ and $t_G : CG \rightarrow TG$ form a triple graph $G = (SG \xleftarrow{s_G} CG \xrightarrow{t_G} TG)$. G is called empty, if SG, CG, and TG are empty graphs.*

A triple graph morphism $m = (s, c, t) : G \rightarrow H$ between two triple graphs $G = (SG \xleftarrow{s_G} CG \xrightarrow{t_G} TG)$ and $H = (SH \xleftarrow{s_H} CH \xrightarrow{t_H} TH)$ consists of three graph morphisms $s : SG \rightarrow SH$, $c : CG \rightarrow CH$ and $t : TG \rightarrow TH$ such that $s \circ s_G = s_H \circ c$ and $t \circ t_G = t_H \circ c$. It is injective, if morphisms s, c and t are injective.

A triple rule is used to build up source and target graphs as well as their connection graph, i.e. to build up triple graphs. Structure filtering which deletes parts of triple graphs, are performed by projection operations only, i.e. structure deletion is not done by rule applications. Thus, we can concentrate our investigations on non-deleting triple rules without any restriction.

Definition 3 (Triple Rule tr and Triple Transformation Step).
A triple rule tr consists of triple graphs L and R, called left-hand and right-hand sides, and an injective triple graph morphism $tr = (s, c, t) : L \rightarrow R$.

$$L = (SL \xleftarrow{s_L} CL \xrightarrow{t_L} TL)$$
$$tr\downarrow \quad s\downarrow \quad c\downarrow \quad \downarrow t$$
$$R = (SR \xleftarrow{s_R} CR \xrightarrow{t_R} TR)$$

Given a triple rule $tr = (s, c, t)$:
$L \to R$, a triple graph G and
a triple graph morphism $m =$
(sm, cm, tm) : $L \to G$, called
triple match m, a triple graph
transformation step (TGT-step)
$G \xrightarrow{tr,m} H$ from G to a triple

$$
\begin{array}{c}
G = (SG \xleftarrow{sm} CG \xrightarrow{} TG) \\
H = (SH \xleftarrow{s_H} CH \xrightarrow{t_H} TH)
\end{array}
$$

graph H is given by three pushouts (SH, s', sn), (CH, c', cn) and (TH, t', tn) in
*category **Graph** with induced morphisms $s_H : CH \to SH$ and $t_H : CH \to TH$.*

Moreover, we obtain a triple graph morphism $d : G \to H$ with $d = (s', c', t')$
called transformation morphism. A sequence of triple graph transformation steps
is called triple (graph) transformation sequence, short: TGT-sequence. Furthermore, a triple graph grammar $TGG = (S, TR)$ consists of a triple start graph S
and a set TR of triple rules.

Remark 1 (gluing construction). Each of the pushout objects SH, CH, TH in
Def. 3 can be constructed as a gluing construction, e.g. $SH = SG +_{SL} SR$,
where the S-components SG of G and SR of R are glued together via SL
(see [EEPT06] Chapter 2 for more details).

3   Case Study: CD2RDBM Model Transformation

This case study presents a model transformation problem (see [BRST05,OMG05])
which occurs in several variants. It contains the transformation of class models
to relational database models. We will use it in this paper to illustrate the
triple graph grammar approach and especially, the conditions for information
preserving bidirectional transformations. In contrast to [BRST05], we present a
slightly restricted variant where the different treatment of persistent and non-
persistent classes is omitted, due to space limitations.

   The source language consists of class diagrams, while the target language
consists of schemes for database tables. A reference structure is established as
helper structure for the model transformation which relates classes with tables
and subclasses or attributes with columns. Associations are translated to foreign
keys. The relationship between the elements of the source and the target language
is documented in the TGG type graph in Fig. 1 where dashed edges represent
the morphisms s and t connecting the the source and the target graph via a
connection graph.

   Please note that this case study is given in the framework of triple graphs over
typed attributed graphs which is briefly discussed in Section 5. In that section,
we also show how to extend the basic theory presented in Sections 2 and 4, to
typed attributed graphs.

   Fig. 2 shows four of the triple rules for the $CD2RDBM$ model transformation.
Triple rule $Class2Table$ simultaneously creates a class and a table which are
related to each other. Since all triple rules are non-deleting, they are depicted in
a compact notation not separating the left from the right-hand side. All graph

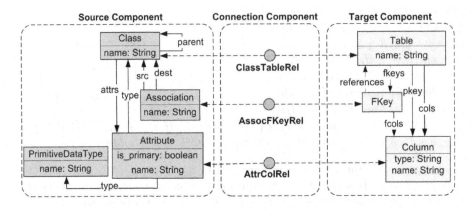

Fig. 1. TGG type graph for *CD2RDBM* model transformation

items which are newly created, are annotated by "{ new}". Those items occur in the right-hand side of a rule only. Triple rule *PrimaryAttribute2Column* creates columns and attributes. Given that a class is already related to some table, an attribute of this class is related to a column of the related table. By triple rule *SetKey*, the corresponding column for each primary attribute is set as primary key . A newly created subclass is related to the same table as its given superclass by triple rule *Subclass2Table*.

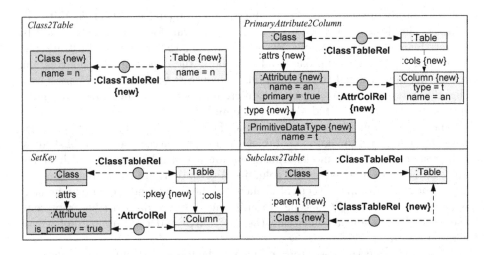

Fig. 2. TGG rules for *CD2RDBM* model transformation

Fig. 3 shows triple rule *Association2FKey* which creates associations related to foreign keys (FKey) pointing to columns of other tables. A similar triple rule *Attribute2FKey* (not depicted) creates class-typed attributes which are also related to foreign keys. Instead of the *:Association{new}* node in rule

Association2FKey, rule *Attribute2FKey* has an *:Attribute{new}* node, connected by an *:attrs{new}* edge to the upper class and a *:type{new}* edge to the lower class.

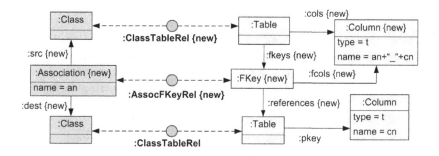

Fig. 3. TGG rule *Association2FKey*

4   Information Preserving Forward and Backward Transformations

The power of bi-directional model transformations is its potential to invert a forward transformation without specifying a new transformation. Deriving rules for forward and backward transformations automatically, we investigate the requirements for such a reversal to be fulfilled by triple graph transformations. A sufficient requirement for reversal is based on the notion of source transformation which is the projection of a triple graph transformation to its source component. It is sufficient to show that a source structure can be constructed by source transformations only. In this case, the forward transformation is called source consistent and we can show that it can be inverted, i.e. there is a backward transformation leading back to the same source structure as the original one.

For updating the changes of the source to the target graph and vice versa *forward* as well as *backward* rules are needed and they can be derived from a triple rule. In addition we can deduce a source rule tr_S and a target rule tr_T with empty connection and target or source component from a triple rule tr.

Definition 4 (Derived Triple Rules). *Given a triple rule tr as in Def. 3, a source rule tr_S, a target rule tr_T, a forward rule tr_F and a backward rule tr_B can be constructed as shown below:*

$$L_S = (SL \longleftarrow \emptyset \longrightarrow \emptyset)$$
$$tr_S\downarrow \quad s\downarrow \qquad \downarrow \qquad \downarrow$$
$$R_S = (SR \longleftarrow \emptyset \longrightarrow \emptyset)$$
$$\text{source rule } tr_S$$

$$L_F = (SR \xleftarrow{s \circ s_L} CL \xrightarrow{t_L} TL)$$
$$tr_F\downarrow \quad id\downarrow \qquad c\downarrow \qquad \downarrow t$$
$$R_F = (SR \xleftarrow{s_R} CR \xrightarrow{t_R} TR)$$
$$\text{forward rule } tr_F$$

$$L_T = (\emptyset \longleftarrow \emptyset \longrightarrow TL) \qquad\qquad L_B = (SL \xleftarrow{s_L} CL \xrightarrow{tot_L} TR)$$

$$tr_T \downarrow \qquad \downarrow \qquad \downarrow \qquad t\downarrow \qquad\qquad\qquad tr_F \downarrow \qquad s\downarrow \qquad c\downarrow \qquad\qquad \downarrow id$$

$$R_T = (\emptyset \longleftarrow \emptyset \longrightarrow TR) \qquad\qquad R_B = (SR \xleftarrow{s_R} CR \xrightarrow{t_R} TR)$$

$$\text{\textit{target rule} } tr_T \qquad\qquad\qquad\qquad \text{\textit{backward rule} } tr_B$$

Example 1 (derived forward and backward rules for triple rule Class2Table)
Fig. 4 shows the forward and backward rules derived from triple rule *Class2Table*
in Fig. 2 (a). In the forward rule a new table is created for an existing class. Vice
versa, in the backward rule a table exists already and the corresponding class is
created.

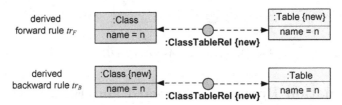

Fig. 4. derived forward and backward rules for triple rule *Class2Table*

Note that the source rule tr_S and the target rule tr_T can be obtained by projection of tr to source and target, respectively.

Definition 5 (Projection). *Given a triple graph* $G = (SG \xleftarrow{s_G} CG \xrightarrow{t_G} TG)$, *the
projection* $proj_T(G)$ *to the target is triple graph* $G_T = (\emptyset \xleftarrow{\emptyset} \emptyset \xrightarrow{\emptyset} TG)$ *and the
projection* $proj_S(G)$ *to the source is triple graph* $G_S = (SG \xleftarrow{\emptyset} \emptyset \xrightarrow{\emptyset} \emptyset)$.

A first important result shows that each TGT-sequence can be decomposed in
transformation sequences by corresponding source and forward rules and vice
versa, provided that their matches are consistent. Roughly spoken, match consistency means that the co-matches of source rule applications determine the
matches of corresponding forward rule applications.

The following Theorem 1 is partly given as Theorem 4.7 in [KS06] where
especially the bijective correspondence between *decomposition* and *composition*
is missing which however, is most important in this paper. Essential for this
bijective correspondence is the notion of match consistency for specific TGT-
sequences applying source and forward rules tri_S and tri_F of the same triple
rule tri for $i = 1, \ldots, n$.

Definition 6 (Match Consistency). *A TGT-sequence* $G_{00} \xRightarrow{tr1_S} G_{10} \Rightarrow \ldots \xRightarrow{trn_S}$
$G_{n0} \xRightarrow{tr1_F} G_{n1} \Rightarrow \cdots \xRightarrow{trn_F} G_{nn}$ *is called match consistent, if the S-component of
the match* $m1_F$ *of* $G_{n0} \xRightarrow{tr1_F} G_{n1}$ *is completely determined by the co-match* $n1_S$ *of*
$G_{00} \xRightarrow{tr1_S} G_{10}$ *and the transformation morphism* $d_1 : G_{10} \to G_{n0}$, *i.e.* $(m1_F)_S =$
$d1_S \circ (n1_S)_S$ *and similar for all matches of the forward transformations* tri_F
$(i > 1)$. *For* $n = 1$ *this means* $(m1_F)_S = (n1_S)_S$.

Theorem 1 (Decomposition and Composition of TGT-Sequences)

1. **Decomposition:** *For each TGT-sequence*

$$(1) \quad G_0 \xrightarrow{tr_1} G_1 \Longrightarrow \ldots \xrightarrow{tr_n} G_n$$

   there is a corresponding match consistent TGT-sequence

$$(2) \quad G_0 = G_{00} \xrightarrow{tr1_S} G_{10} \Rightarrow \cdots \xrightarrow{trn_S} G_{n0} \xrightarrow{tr1_F} G_{n1} \Rightarrow \cdots \xrightarrow{trn_F} G_{nn} = G_n.$$

2. **Composition:** *For each match consistent transformation sequence (2) there is a canonical transformation sequence (1).*
3. **Bijective Correspondence:** *Composition and Decomposition are inverse to each other.*

The proof is given in Section 5.2.

Remark 2. Moreover, we have $proj_T(G_{00}) = proj_T(G_{n0})$ and $proj_S(G_{n0}) = proj_S(G_{nn})$ in (2), due to the special form of triple rules $tr1_S, .., trn_S$ and $tr1_F, .., trn_F$, respectively. Dual results hold for target rules tr_T and backward rules tr_B (see the lower triangle in the figure on the right).

$$
\begin{array}{ccccc}
G_{00} & \xrightarrow{tr1_S} & G_{10} \cdots & \xrightarrow{trn_S} & G_{n0} \\
{\scriptstyle tr1_T}\Big\Downarrow & {\scriptstyle tr1} & & & \Big\Downarrow {\scriptstyle tr1_F} \\
\cdots & & \cdots & & \cdots \\
{\scriptstyle trn_T}\Big\Downarrow & & & {\scriptstyle trn} & \Big\Downarrow {\scriptstyle trn_F} \\
G_{0n} & \xrightarrow{tr1_B} & \cdots & \xrightarrow{trn_B} & G_{nn}
\end{array}
$$

Theorem 1 and its dual version lead to the following equivalence of forward and backward TGT-sequences which can be derived from the same general TGT-sequence.

Theorem 2 (Equivalence of Forward and Backward TGT-sequences).

Each of the following TGT-sequences implies the other ones assumed that the matches are uniquely determined by each other.

1. $G_0 \xrightarrow{tr_1} G_1 \xrightarrow{tr_2} G_2 \Longrightarrow \ldots \xrightarrow{tr_n} G_n$
2. $G_0 = G_{00} \xrightarrow{tr1_S} G_{10} \Longrightarrow \ldots \xrightarrow{trn_S} G_{n0} \xrightarrow{tr1_F} G_{n1} \Longrightarrow \ldots \xrightarrow{trn_F} G_{nn} = G_n$, which is match consistent. In this case we have: $proj_T(G_{00}) = proj_T(G_{n0})$, $proj_S(G_{n0}) = proj_S(G_{nn})$
3. $G_0 = G_{00} \xrightarrow{tr1_T} G_{01} \Longrightarrow \ldots \xrightarrow{trn_T} G_{0n} \xrightarrow{tr1_B} G_{1n} \Longrightarrow \ldots \xrightarrow{trn_B} G_{nn} = G_n$, which is match consistent. In this case we have: $proj_S(G_{00}) = proj_S(G_{0n})$, $proj_T(G_{0n}) = proj_T(G_{nn})$

Proof. Theorem 2 is a direct consequence of Theorem 1 concerning decomposition and composition of forward TGT-sequences and its dual version for target rules tri_T and backward rules tri_B where match consistency in Part 3 is defined by the T-components of the matches. The projection properties follow from Remark 2.2.

In the following we use the short notations for TGT-sequences introduced in Theorem 2:

1. $F \xrightarrow{tr^*} H$, with $F = G_0, H = G_n$ for sequence (1),

2. $F \xrightarrow{tr_S^*} G \xrightarrow{tr_F^*} H$, with $F = G_0, G = G_{n0}, H = G_n$ for sequence (2), and

3. $F \xrightarrow{tr_T^*} K \xrightarrow{tr_B^*} H$, with $F = G_0, K = G_{0n}, H = G_n$ for sequence (3).

Now we are able to address the main topic of this paper. We want to analyse under which conditions a forward TGT-sequence $G \xrightarrow{tr_F^*} H$ is information preserving in the sense that there is a backward TGT-sequence starting from $H_T = proj_T(H)$ and leading to H' such that the source graphs of G and H' are equal, i.e. $proj_S(G) = proj_S(H')$. That means sequence $G \xrightarrow{tr_F^*} H \xrightarrow{proj_T} H_T \xrightarrow{tr_B^*} H'$ is information preserving concerning the source component. In this case we say that $G \xrightarrow{tr_F^*} H$ is backward information preserving.

The condition under which we obtain backward information preservation is source consistency of $G \xrightarrow{tr_F^*} H$, i.e. G is generated by corresponding source rules tr_S^* such that $\emptyset \xrightarrow{tr_S^*} G \xrightarrow{tr_F^*} H$ is match consistent.

Definition 7 (Information Preserving Forward Transformation)

A forward TGT-sequence $G \xrightarrow{tr_F^*} H$ is

(1) **backward information preserving**, *if for $H_T = proj_T(H)$ there is a backward TGT-sequence $H_T \xrightarrow{tr_B^*} H'$ with $G_S = proj_S(G) = proj_S(H')$.*

$$G \xrightarrow{tr_F^*} H \xrightarrow{\quad proj_T \quad} H_T \xrightarrow{tr_B^*} H'$$
$$\underset{proj_S}{\searrow} \quad G_S \quad \underset{proj_S}{\swarrow}$$

(2) **source consistent**, *if there is a source TGT-sequence $\emptyset \xrightarrow{tr_S^*} G$ such that $\emptyset \xrightarrow{tr_S^*} G \xrightarrow{tr_F^*} H$ is match consistent.*

Remark 3. For backward transformations the terms forward information preserving and target consistency are defined dually.

Theorem 3 (Information Preserving Forward Transformation)

A forward TGT-sequence $G \xrightarrow{tr_F^*} H$ is backward information preserving, if it is source consistent.

Proof. $G \xrightarrow{tr_F^*} H$ is source consistent which implies the existence of (2) $\emptyset \xrightarrow{tr_S^*} G \xrightarrow{tr_F^*} H$ with $proj_S(G) = proj_S(H)$ being match consistent. By Theorem 2 with $G_0 = \emptyset$, $G_{n0} = G$, $G_{0n} = K$ and $G_n = H$ we obtain (3) $\emptyset \xrightarrow{tr_T^*} K \xrightarrow{tr_B^*} H' = H$ with $proj_T(K) = proj_T(H)$ being match consistent. Moreover, $proj_S(K) = proj_S(\emptyset) = \emptyset$ and the C-component of K is $\emptyset$ which implies $K = proj_T(H) = H_T$ leading to the diagram in Def. 7(1). Hence, $G \xrightarrow{tr_F^*} H$ is backward information preserving.

Remark 4. If $G \xrightarrow{tr_F^*} H$ is source consistent, then there is already a canonical backward transformation $H_T \xrightarrow{tr_B^*} H'$ with $H' = H$ and $H_T = proj_T(H)$

which is target consistent, i.e. $\emptyset \xrightarrow{tr_T^*} H_T \xrightarrow{tr_B^*} H'$ is match consistent. Vice versa, given a target consistent backward transformation there is a source consistent forward transformation according to Theorem 2. Similar results hold for backward TGT-sequences $K \xrightarrow{tr_B^*} H$.

Example 2 (backward information preserving CD2RDBM *model transformation sequence).* We consider a concrete forward transformation $G \Longrightarrow H$ from a given class model G to its extension H by the corresponding data base model (Fig. 5). The small class model in G (left part of Fig. 5) consists of two classes *Company* and *Person* with an association in between, and a third class *Customer* inheriting from class *Person*. Class *Customer* is equipped with an attribute. The transformation is performed by applying first the forward rules of rule *Class2Table* twice $(1, 2)$, and afterwards the forward rules of *SubClass2Table* (3), *PrimaryAttribute2Column* (4), *SetKey* (5), and *Association2FKey* (6) each once. In Fig. 5, the corresponding matches $(1..6)$ of this sequence are indicated by contours.

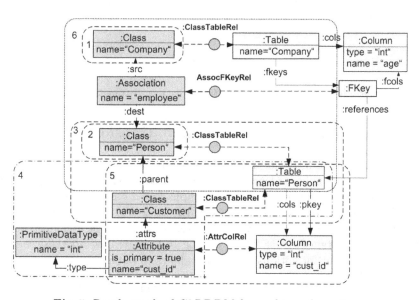

Fig. 5. Result graph of $C2RDBM$ forward transformation

This forward transformation is source consistent, since there is a transformation sequence $\emptyset \Longrightarrow G$. The co-matches of this source transformation sequence correspond to the matches of the forward transformation in Fig. 5, restricted to the source elements. It is easy to check that both transformation sequences are match consistent, i.e. the co-match of each source transformation step is not altered by forthcoming steps and is used again in its corresponding forward transformation step. Thus we can conclude from Theorem 3 that transformation $G \Longrightarrow H$ is backward information preserving, i.e. there is a backward transformation from $proj_T(H) \Longrightarrow H'$ and the source graph of H' is equal to G. The backward transformation with the matches of the corresponding backward rules is shown in Fig. 6 where $proj_T(H)$ is given in the right part of Fig. 6, and H' is the complete result graph in Fig. 6.

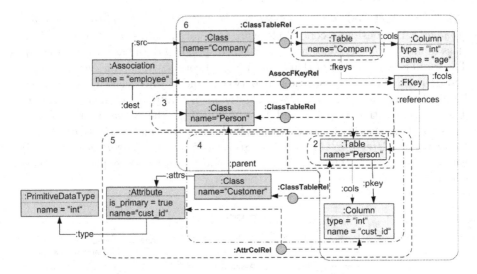

Fig. 6. Result graph of $C2RDBM$ backward transformation

5   General Theory of Triple Graph Transformations

In Section 2 we have introduced triple graphs and triple graph transformations based on simple graphs and graph morphisms (see Definition 1 - 3). In this section, we extend the concept to triple graphs based on typed, attributed and typed attributed graphs in the sense of [EEPT06]. WE can show that he corresponding categories are adhesive HLR categories. Thus, the general theory of adhesive HLR-systems in [EEPT06] can be instantiated by all these variants of triple graph transformations. That fact allows to obtain the well-known Local Church–Rosser and Concurrency Theorem for triple graph transformations which are used in a special case in the proof of Theorem 1. Further concepts and results which are presented in [EEPT06] and can be instantiated by triple graph transformation, include negative application conditions and critical pair analysis.

5.1   Triple Graph Transformations as Instantiation of Adhesive HLR Categories

Adhesive HLR categories and systems which are based on adhesive categories presented in [LS05], are a general categorical framework for several variants of graphs and graph transformation systems. One important instantiation of this framework are graph transformations based on simple graphs and graph morphisms (as in Section 2) leading to the category **Graphs**. Another important instantiation are attributed graphs and attributed graph morphisms (as in [EPT04]) leading to the category **AGraphs**. Roughly speaking, attributed graphs $AG = (G, D)$ are pairs of graphs G and data type algebras D where some of the domains of D are carrying the attributes of graphs G. Rule graphs are attributed by a common term algebra such that left and right hand side graph items may have arbitrary terms as attributes. Category **TripleGraphs** consisting of triple graphs and triple graph morphisms (as in Section 2), can be constructed as a diagram category over **Graphs** and also becomes an adhesive HLR category (see Fact 4.18 in [EEPT06]).

Analogously, category **TripleAGraphs** of attributed triple graphs is a diagram category over **AGraphs**. Moreover, given type graphs TG in **TripleGraphs** (resp. ATG in **TripleAGraphs**) we obtain category **TripleGraphs$_{TG}$** consisting of typed triple graphs (resp. **TripleAGraphs$_{ATG}$** consisting of typed attributed triple graphs) as slice categories over **TripleGraphs** (resp. **TripleAGraphs**) leading again to adhesive HLR-categories.

Theorem 4 (Adhesive HLR Categories for Triple Graph Transformations). *Categories* **TripleGraphs**, **TripleGraphs$_{TG}$**, **TripleAGraphs**, *and* **TripleAGraphs$_{ATG}$** *together with suitable classes* $\mathcal{M}$ *of monomorphisms are adhesive HLR categories.*

Proof. According to Theorem 4.15 in [EEPT06], diagram and slice categories over adhesive HLR categories **Graphs** and **AGraphs** are again adhesive HLR categories.

This result implies that the general theory of adhesive HLR systems can be applied to triple graph transformations based on categories **TripleGraphs**, **TripleGraphs$_{TG}$**, **TripleAGraphs**, and **TripleAGraphs$_{ATG}$**. In the following, we use the abbreviation **Triple**, if we mean one of these categories.

5.2   Proof of Theorem 1

Before proving Parts 1-3 of Theorem 1, we draw some conclusions from Theorem 4 above. From Theorem 5.12 in [EEPT06] for adhesive HRL-categories and Theorem 4 above we can conclude that the Local Church-Rosser Theorem is valid for each category **Triple**. We will use this result to show that "sequentially independent" steps $G_1 \xrightarrow{tr_1,m_1} G_2 \xrightarrow{tr_2,m_2} G_3$ can be commuted leading to $G_1 \xrightarrow{tr_2,m_2'} G_2' \xrightarrow{tr_1,m_1'} G_3$. Sequential independence means that there is a triple morphism $d : L_2 \to G_1$ with $g_1 \circ d = m_2$.

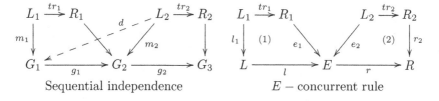

Sequential independence E − concurrent rule

From Theorem 5.23 in [EEPT06] and Theorem 4 above we can conclude that the Concurrency Theorem is valid. This result is used for the construction of E-concurrent rule $tr = tr_1 *_E tr_2$ for triple rules tr_1 and tr_2 given. Triple graph E with triple graph morphisms e_1 and e_2 is constructed by pushouts (1) and (2) above and $tr = r \circ l$.

We will use the following construction: Given triple rule $tr : L \to R$ with source rule $tr_S : L_1 \to R_1$, forward rule $tr_F : L_2 \to R_2$, $E = L_2$, $e_1 = (id, \emptyset, \emptyset)$ and $e_2 = id$, we obtain $tr_S *_E tr_F = tr$, because diagrams (3) and (4) below are pushouts in **Triple** and $tr_F \circ tr_S = tr$. Hence, tr is equal to the E-concurrent rule $tr_S *_E tr_F$.

$$
\begin{array}{ccc}
(SL \leftarrow \emptyset \to \emptyset) & \xrightarrow{tr_S} & (SR \leftarrow \emptyset \to \emptyset) \\
{\scriptstyle (id,\emptyset,\emptyset)} \downarrow & (3) & \downarrow {\scriptstyle (id,\emptyset,\emptyset)} \\
(SL \leftarrow CL \to TL) & \xrightarrow[tr_S = (s,id,id)]{} & (SR \leftarrow CL \to TL)
\end{array}
\qquad
\begin{array}{ccc}
(SR \leftarrow CL \to TL) & \xrightarrow{tr_F} & (SR \leftarrow CR \to TR) \\
{\scriptstyle id} \searrow & (4) & \downarrow {\scriptstyle id} \\
(SR \leftarrow CL \to TL) & \xrightarrow[tr_F = (id,c,t)]{} & (SR \leftarrow CR \to TR)
\end{array}
$$

Proof of Theorem 1

1. *Decomposition:* Given TGT-sequence (1) $G_0 \xRightarrow{tr_1} G_1 \Rightarrow \ldots \xRightarrow{tr_n} G_n$ we first consider case $n = 1$. TGT-step $G_0 \xRightarrow{tr_1} G_1$ can be decomposed uniquely into a match consistent TGT-sequence $G_0 = G_{00} \xRightarrow{tr_{1S}} G_{10} \xRightarrow{tr_{1F}} G_{11} = G_1$. In fact we have shown above that $tr1$ can be represented as E-concurrent rule $tr1 = tr1_S *_E tr1_F$. Using the Concurrency Theorem the TGT-step $G_0 \xRightarrow{tr_1} G_1$ can be decomposed uniquely into an E-related sequence as given above. In this special case an E-relation is equivalent to the fact that the S-components of the co-match of $G_{00} \xRightarrow{tr_{1S}} G_{10}$ and the match of $G_{10} \xRightarrow{tr_{1F}} G_{11}$ coincide which corresponds exactly to match consistency.

Using this construction for $i = 1, \ldots, n$ the transformation sequence (1) can be decomposed canonically to an intermediate version between (1) and (2) called

(1.5): $G_0 = G_{00} \xRightarrow{tr_{1S}} G_{10} \xRightarrow{tr_{1F}} G_{11} \xRightarrow{tr_{2S}} G_{21} \xRightarrow{tr_{2F}} G_{22} \Rightarrow \ldots \xRightarrow{tr_{nS}} G_{n(n-1)} \xRightarrow{tr_{nF}} G_{nn}$ where each subsequence $G_{(i-1)(i-1)} \xRightarrow{tr_{iS}} G_{i(i-1)} \xRightarrow{tr_{iF}} G_{ii}$ is match consistent. Moreover, $G_{10} \xRightarrow{tr_{1F}} G_{11} \xRightarrow{tr_{2S}} G_{21}$ is sequentially independent, because we have a morphism $d : L_2 \to G_{10}$, with $L_2 = (SL_2 \leftarrow \emptyset \to \emptyset)$ and $d = (m_{2S}, \emptyset, \emptyset)$. Morphism $m2 : L_2 \to G_{11}$ is the match of $G_{11} \xRightarrow{tr_{2S}} G_{21}$, because the S-components of G_{10} and G_{11} are equal according to forward rule $tr1_F$.

$$
\begin{array}{ccccccc}
G_{00} & \xRightarrow{tr_{1S}} & G_{10} & \xRightarrow{tr_{2S}} & G_{20} & \cdots \xRightarrow{tr_{nS}} & G_{n0} \\
{\scriptstyle tr_1} \searrow & & \downarrow {\scriptstyle tr_{1F}} & & \downarrow {\scriptstyle tr_{1F}} & & \downarrow {\scriptstyle tr_{1F}} \\
& & G_{11} & \xRightarrow{tr_{2S}} & G_{21} & \cdots \xRightarrow{tr_{nS}} & G_{n1} \\
& {\scriptstyle tr_2} \searrow & & & \downarrow {\scriptstyle tr_{2F}} & & \downarrow {\scriptstyle tr_{2F}} \\
& & \cdots & & & & \vdots \\
& & & {\scriptstyle trn} \searrow & & \downarrow {\scriptstyle trn_F} & \\
& & & & & & G_{nn}
\end{array}
$$

Now, the Local Church–Rosser Theorem mentioned above leads to an equivalent sequentially independent sequence $G_{10} \xRightarrow{tr_{2S}} G_{20} \xRightarrow{tr_{1F}} G_{21}$ such that $G_{00} \xRightarrow{tr_{1S}} G_{10} \xRightarrow{tr_{2S}} G_{20} \xRightarrow{tr_{1F}} G_{21} \xRightarrow{tr_{2F}} G_{22}$ is match consistent. The iteration of this shift between tr_{iF} and tr_{jS} leads to a shift-equivalent transformation sequence (2) $G_0 = G_{00} \xRightarrow{tr_{1S}} G_{10} \Rightarrow \cdots \xRightarrow{tr_{nS}} G_{n0} \xRightarrow{tr_{1F}} G_{n1} \Rightarrow \cdots \xRightarrow{tr_{nF}} G_{nn} = G_n$, which is still match consistent.

2. Composition: Vice versa, each match consistent transformation sequence (2) leads to a canonical sequence (1.5) by inverse shift equivalence where each subsequence as above is match consistent. In fact, match consistency of (2) implies that the corresponding subsequences are sequentially independent in order to allow inverse shifts in an order opposite to that in Part 1 using again the Local Church-Rosser Theorem. Match consistent subsequences of (1.5) are E-related as discussed in Part 1 which allows to apply the Concurrency Theorem to obtain the TGT-sequence (1).

3. Bijective Correspondence: The bijective correspondence of composition and decomposition is a direct consequence of the bijective correspondence in the Local Church–Rosser and the Concurrency Theorem where the bijective correspondence for the Local Church–Rosser Theorem is not explicitly formulated in Theorem 5.12 of [EEPT06], but is a direct consequence of the proof in analogy to Theorem 5.18.   □

6 Related Work and Conclusion

In this paper we dealt with bi-directional model transformations, a promising technique in model-driven software development to keep related models consistent or to evolve them into other models or executable code. Bi-directional transformations can be defined using triple graph grammars which were introduced by Schürr [Sch94]. In [KS06], Königs and Schürr considered a set-theoretical formalization of triple graph transformations. We took up this formalization and extended it on the basis of category theory. To cope with the situation that tools do not necessarily keep object identifiers while changing models, we consider projections to source and target graphs in between. This makes the reversal of transformations more complex, but also more flexible due to less requirements on tools. We have shown that forward transformations are backward information preserving, if their source graph can be created by corresponding source rules.

In [KS06], a comprehensive comparison with related model transformation approaches, especially with bi-directional ones, is given. For example, BOTL [MB03] and QVT [OMG05] are discussed and compared to triple graph grammars. Although offering the concept of bi-directional transformation, sufficient conditions for the existence of information preserving transformations have not been given for these approaches.

In Section 5, we considered the extension of triple graph grammars to types and attributes. While these extensions are straightforward, the addition of application conditions to triple rules requires future investigations. From the practical point of view, there is also a request for multiple source and target models, considering activities like multi-model requirement engineering and the creation of a platform independent design model. The idea of triple graphs can be extended in a straightforward way by replacing the span by some arbitrary network of graphs. This approach has already been followed for defining viewpoint-oriented specifications on the basis of distributed graph transformation in [GEMT00].

References

[BRST05] Jean Bézivin, Bernhard Rumpe, Andy Schürr, and Laurence Tratt. Model transformations in practice workshop. In Jean-Michel Bruel, editor, *MoD-ELS Satellite Events*, volume 3844 of *Lecture Notes in Computer Science*, pages 120–127. Springer, 2005.

[CH03] K. Czarnecki and S. Helsen. Classification of model transformation approaches. In *On-line Proc. of the 2nd Workshop on Generative Techniques in the context of Model-Driven Architecture, Anaheim*, 2003.

[EEPT06] H. Ehrig, K. Ehrig, U. Prange, and G. Taentzer. *Fundamentals of Algebraic Graph Transformation*. EATCS Monographs in Theoretical Computer Science. Springer, 2006.

[EPT04] H. Ehrig, U. Prange, and G. Taentzer. Fundamental theory for typed attributed graph transformation. In F. Parisi-Presicce, P. Bottoni, and G. Engels, editors, *Proc. 2nd Int. Conference on Graph Transformation (ICGT'04), Rome, Italy*, volume 3256 of *Lecture Notes in Computer Science*. Springer, 2004.

[GEMT00] M. Goedicke, B. Enders, T. Meyer, and G. Taentzer. Tool Support for ViewPoint-Oriented Software Development: Towards Integration of Multiple Perspectives by Distributed Graph Transformation. In *Int. Workshop on Applications of Graph Transformations with Industrial Relevance (AGTIVE'99), LNCS 1779*, pages 369 – 378. Springer, 2000.

[KS06] A. König and A. Schürr. Tool Integration with Triple Graph Grammars - A Survey. In *Heckel, R. (eds.): Elsevier Science Publ. (pub.), Proceedings of the SegraVis School on Foundations of Visual Modelling Techniques, Vol. 148, Electronic Notes in Theoretical Computer Science pp. 113-150, Amsterdam*, 2006.

[LS05] Stephen Lack and Pawel Sobociński. Adhesive and quasiadhesive categories. *Theoretical Informatics and Applications*, 39(2):511–546, 2005.

[MB03] Frank Marschall and Peter Braun. Model transformations for the mda with botl. In *Proc. of the Workshop on Model Driven Architecture: Foundations and Applications (MDAFA 2003), Enschede, The Netherlands*, pages 25–36, 2003.

[MG06] T. Mens and P. Van Gorp. A taxonomy of model transformation. In *Proc. International Workshop on Graph and Model Transformation (GraMoT05), number 152 in Electronic Notes in Theoretical Computer Science, Tallinn, Estonia, Elsevier Science*, 2006.

[OMG05] OMG. *MOF QVT Final Adopted Specification (05-11-01)*. http://www.omg.org/docs/ptc/05-11-01.pdf, 2005.

[Sch94] A. Schürr. Specification of Graph Translators with Triple Graph Grammars. In *G. Tinhofer, editor, WG94 20th Int. Workshop on Graph-Theoretic Concepts in Computer Science, volume 903 of Lecture Notes in Computer Science, pages 151-163, Springer Verlag, Heidelberg*, 1994.

Activity-Driven Synthesis of State Machines*

Rolf Hennicker and Alexander Knapp

Ludwig-Maximilians-Universität München
{hennicker,knapp}@ifi.lmu.de

Abstract. The synthesis of object behaviour from scenarios is a well-known and important issue in the transition from system analysis to system design. We describe a model transformation procedure from UML 2.0 interactions into UML 2.0 state machines that focuses, in contrast to existing approaches, on standard synchronous operation calls where the sender of a message waits until the receiver object has executed the requested operation possibly returning a result. The key aspect of our approach is to distinguish between active and inactive phases of an object participating in an interaction. This allows us to generate well-structured state machines separating "stable" states, where an object is ready to react to an incoming message, and "activity" states which model the computational behaviour of an object upon receipt of an operation call. The translation procedure is formalised, in accordance with the UML 2.0 meta-model, by means of an abstract syntax for scenarios which are first translated into I/O-automata as an appropriate intermediate format. Apparent non-determinism in the automata gives rise to feedback on scenario deficiencies and to suggestions on scenario refinements. Finally, for each object of interest the corresponding I/O-automaton is translated into a UML 2.0 state machine representing stable states by simple states and activity states by submachine states which provide algorithmic descriptions of operations. Thus the resulting state machines can be easily transformed into code by applying well-known implementation techniques.

1 Introduction

Scenario-based approaches describe system behaviour in terms of typical interactions between several objects participating, for instance, in a single use case. Scenarios are particularly useful in the analysis phase since they focus on the overall collaboration of objects to perform a particular task. However, scenarios do not show the complete behaviour of a single object which is left to the design phase where the objects' life-cycles can be described by state machines.

We propose a rigorous method to transform a set of scenarios, represented by UML 2.0 sequence diagrams, into state machines. Our general assumption is that each scenario is simple in the sense that it focuses only on one interaction sequence at a time. Hence, we will deliberately not consider more expressive notations for sequence diagrams (like, e.g., alternatives) which add computational complexity at the cost of clarity; cf. the discussion on the specification of conditional behaviour by Fowler [1].

---

* This research has been partially supported by the GLOWA-Danube project (01LW0303A) sponsored by the German Federal Ministry of Education and Research.

M.B. Dwyer and A. Lopes (Eds.): FASE 2007, LNCS 4422, pp. 87–101, 2007.
© Springer-Verlag Berlin Heidelberg 2007

Additional behaviour can be shown in separate sequence diagrams for (secondary) scenarios. The task then is to transform the set of sequence diagrams into a set of state machines, each showing the complete behaviour of a single object across the scenarios.

There are many approaches in the literature suggesting various strategies and solutions for state machine synthesis and analysis, like, e.g., [2,3,4,5]; see [6] for an overview. These approaches deal with asynchronous communication in the sense that the sender of a message is immediately ready for further activation and, in contrast to synchronous communication, does not wait until the receiver has executed its reaction to the incoming operation call. We claim that, as a consequence, the resulting state machines do not provide an adequate design model if we consider standard applications with synchronous operation calls and returns. The goal of this paper is to provide a synthesis algorithm that takes into account synchronous calls and their corresponding execution traces such that the resulting state machines can be easily transformed into a standard implementation with a single thread of control.

Our method is centred around the treatment of object activations that occur (in a sequence diagram) when an object has received an incoming message. During an activation an object may send messages to other objects, wait for corresponding results and finally provide a return value. We hence focus on reactive system objects where inactive phases, in which an object is waiting for an incoming message, and active phases, in which an object reacts to an incoming message, alternate. Inactive phases are considered as "stable" states. They may be given a name which will be used for matching different scenarios when generating state machines. During the translation different activations represented in different scenarios but caused by the same incoming message (after the same stable state) will be integrated into a single activity of an object. Activities can be considered as procedures in the sense of "Executable UML" [7]. They are modelled by UML 2.0 submachines with one entry point and, in general, several exit points representing different possible results (inferred from the different scenarios).[1] The overall state machine representing the life-cycle of an object is then obtained by integrating stable states and "activity" states (represented by submachine states). The generated state machines exhibit a general pattern with alternating stable and activity states. Any outgoing transition from a stable state leads to the entry point of an activity state and is labelled by an incoming message; upon completion of an activity a transition is fired which connects an exit point of the activity state with the next stable state.

Technically, our transformation sets out from a set of UML 2.0 interactions which are formalised, in accordance with the UML 2.0 meta-model, in terms of an appropriate abstract syntax for scenarios (see Sect. 2). Taking these scenarios as input, our synthesis procedure consists of the following four steps which are iteratively performed for each (system) object o.

1. *Projection of scenarios:* For each scenario the communications in which the object o under consideration participates are extracted. Such projections are usually computed in state machine synthesis approaches.
2. *Generation of behaviours from projected scenarios:* Each projected scenario is transformed into an equivalent but differently structured representation, called

---

[1] We do not use UML 2.0 activity diagrams to model activities because, in contrast to UML 1.x, the activity diagrams of UML 2.0 are not specialisations of state machine diagrams.

behaviour. A behaviour groups, for each incoming message, all subsequent outgoing messages sent by *o* into one activation capturing "the reaction" of object *o* for each synchronous operation call according to a particular scenario (see Sect. 3).

3. *Integration of behaviours into I/O-automata:* After the first two steps there is still one behaviour of system object *o* for each scenario. The different behaviours across all scenarios are now integrated on the basis of common (stable) states. The result is represented by an I/O-automaton with the incoming messages as input and the corresponding object activations (together with a return) as output (see Sect. 4.1). The non-deterministic transitions of the I/O-automaton serve as a basis for generating suggestions for scenario changes which are, in particular, directed towards behavioural completion (see Sect. 4.2).

4. *Translation of I/O-automata into UML 2.0 state machines:* Finally, the generated I/O-automaton is transformed into a UML 2.0 state machine with stable states and activity states. The activity states integrate possible different reactions to the same incoming message in a particular stable state (which may still have been present in an I/O-automaton) into one single activity (see Sect. 5). It is worth to note that, according to the abstract nature of the I/O-automata, translations into different concrete target representations are possible (e.g., generating instead of activity states procedural expressions of some action language [7]).

For ease of comparison of our synthesis procedure with the approaches from the literature (see Sect. 6) we base our description on a widely used automatic teller machine (ATM) example [2,5,8].

2 Scenarios

We introduce the sequence diagram language for describing scenarios by the well-known ATM example [2,5,8]. In the following we consider the case where an atm object reacts to a user who has inserted a card by validating the card with the help of the objects consortium and bank. The UML 2.0 sequence diagrams in Fig. 1(a) and Fig. 1(b) detail two possible scenarios which have been formulated in [2,5] with the difference, as pointed out in Sect. 1, that we consider here messages as synchronous operation calls which may provide return values.[2]

A scenario describes a sequence of communications between scenario participants. For scenario participants we distinguish between *user actors* (headed by stick figures) and *system objects* (depicted by boxes). A communication consists of a synchronous *operation call* (shown above a solid line with filled arrow head) and a *return* message with a *value* (shown above a dashed arrow with open arrow head). An operation call on a system object causes an *activation* (grey vertical rectangle) of the system object. Before and after an activation a system object is in a certain *state* which can be left implicit or be named explicitly (shown in a rounded rectangle).

---

[2] Note that both scenarios can be considered as "secondary" scenarios since they describe variations of the normal behaviour described by a primary scenario which is not considered here but could easily be included.

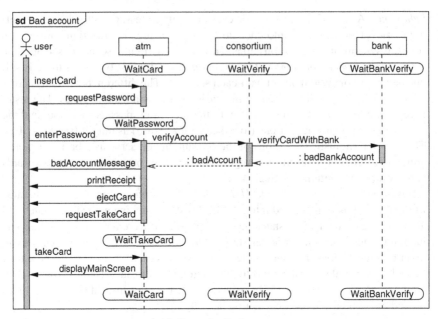

(a) Scenario: Bad account

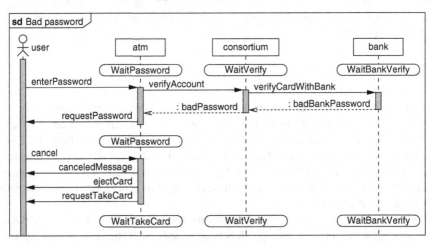

(b) Scenario: Bad password

Fig. 1. ATM example

The abstract syntax of our scenario language, which conforms to a subset of UML 2.0 interactions [9], is rendered in the following BNF grammar where we assume the domains *SystemObject* of system objects, *User* of user actors, *State* of states, *Operation* of operations, and *Value* of typed values.

$$Scenario ::= Communication^*$$
$$Communication ::= UserCommunication \mid SystemCommunication$$

$$UserCommunication ::= UserMessage\ Return$$
$$UserMessage ::= Object\ Operation\ User$$
$$SystemCommunication ::= State\ SystemMessage\ Return\ State$$
$$SystemMessage ::= Object\ Operation\ SystemObject$$
$$Return ::= Value\ |\ \text{void}$$
$$Object ::= SystemObject\ |\ User$$

In a sequence of communications, a user communication represents a message from a sending object to a receiving user actor together with its return; and a system communication a message from a sending object to a receiving system object again with its return. The first (pre-)state in a system communication represents the state of the receiving system object before actually receiving the message, the second (post-)state the state after having sent the return to the incoming message. We require that the post-state of a system communication equals the pre-state of the next system communication with the same receiving system object, which disallows spontaneous state changes on reactive system objects. The reaction of a system object o to an incoming message, i.e., its subsequent activation, is given implicitly by the sequence of all communications with o as sender before the next incoming message to o arrives. Hence, we do not consider nested activations caused by call-backs. Finally, we require that all returns are type correct in the sense that for a given operation either all return messages have no return value (represented by void) or all return messages have a return value of the same type.

Table 1. Tabular representation of the scenarios

(a) Scenario: Bad account

Pre state (rcv.)	Sender	Operation	Receiver	Return	Post state (rcv.)
WaitCard	user	insertCard	atm	void	WaitPassword
—	atm	requestPassword	user	void	—
WaitPassword	user	enterPassword	atm	void	WaitTakeCard
WaitVerify	atm	verifyAccount	consortium	badAccount	WaitVerify
WaitBankVerify	consortium	verifyCardWithBank	bank	badBankAccount	WaitBankVerify
—	atm	badAccountMessage	user	void	—
—	atm	printReceipt	user	void	—
—	atm	ejectCard	user	void	—
—	atm	requestTakeCard	user	void	—
WaitTakeCard	user	takeCard	atm	void	WaitCard
—	atm	displayMainScreen	user	void	—

(b) Scenario: Bad password

Pre state (rcv.)	Sender	Operation	Receiver	Return	Post state (rcv.)
WaitPassword	user	enterPassword	atm	void	WaitPassword
WaitVerify	atm	verifyAccount	consortium	badPassword	WaitVerify
WaitBankVerify	consortium	verifyCardWithBank	bank	badBankPassword	WaitBankVerify
—	atm	requestPassword	user	void	—
WaitPassword	user	cancel	atm	void	WaitTakeCard
—	atm	canceledMessage	user	void	—
—	atm	ejectCard	user	void	—
—	atm	requestTakeCard	user	void	—

Using a tabular notation, similar to the one suggested in the UML 2.0 superstructure specification [9, App. E], the sequence diagrams for the scenarios of the ATM example are represented by the two sequences of communications shown in Tab. 1. For missing returns void has been filled in. In our example, all states have user-defined names, but in general this is not necessary and states which were left implicit in the graphical representation of the sequence diagrams would be considered to be pairwise different and would be equipped with different artificial names. The symbol "−" is used in user communications where no states are needed for the user actor.

For deriving the behaviour of a given system object across many scenarios, we assume an ordering on the given set of scenarios such that the pre-state of the first communication of the system object in a successive scenario is already present as a state in one of its predecessor scenarios. For instance, the pre-state WaitPassword of atm in the second scenario Bad password occurs in the first scenario Bad account.

The scenario language differs from the MSC-based languages used in [5], [3], or [2] by three main concepts: the distinction between user actors and system objects, the use of activations and the use of return values. On the other hand, as discussed in Sect. 1, we deliberately do not include more complex constructs for interaction composition.

3   Generating Behaviours from Scenarios

For the synthesis of state machines from scenarios we focus (iteratively) on a single system object for which the different scenarios have to be integrated. In a first step, similarly to all other synthesis algorithms, a projection operation discards communications in a scenario that are not relevant for the system object o under consideration. More formally, given a system object o and a scenario S, the *projection* of S to o is defined as the scenario $proj(S, o)$ which consists of all those communications of S where o is either the sending or the receiving object. In our running example, the projection $proj$(Bad account, atm) to the system object atm yields the sequence of communications in Tab. 1(a) with the fifth line removed, and the projection $proj$(Bad password, atm) to atm yields the sequence of communications in Tab. 1(b) with the third line removed. If we focus on the system object consortium the projections $proj$(Bad account, consortium) and $proj$(Bad password, consortium) yield the communications shown in Tab. 2.

In the second step we transform for each system object each single projected scenario into an equivalent but differently structured representation, called *behaviour*, where for

Table 2. Projection of the scenarios to consortium

(a) Scenario: Bad account

Pre state (rcv.)	Sender	Operation	Receiver	Return	Post state (rcv.)
WaitVerify	atm	verifyAccount	consortium	badAccount	WaitVerify
WaitBankVerify	consortium	verifyCardWithBank	bank	badBankAccount	WaitBankVerify

(b) Scenario: Bad password

Pre state (rcv.)	Sender	Operation	Receiver	Return	Post state (rcv.)
WaitVerify	atm	verifyAccount	consortium	badPassword	WaitVerify
WaitBankVerify	consortium	verifyCardWithBank	bank	badBankPassword	WaitBankVerify

each incoming message (received in some state) the subsequent outgoing messages and the final return are grouped into one activation. After an activation has finished the object (possibly) changes its state. Thus, each (projected) scenario can be transformed into a block structure where each block consists of a pre-state, an incoming message, the corresponding activation and a post-state. The following grammar captures this intuition:

$$Behaviour ::= Block^*$$
$$Block ::= State\ InMessage\ Activation\ State$$
$$Activation ::= OutMessage^*\ Return$$
$$InMessage ::= Operation$$
$$OutMessage ::= Operation\ Object\ Return$$

From a scenario $S \in Scenario$ and a system object $o \in SystemObject$, the operation $beh(S, o)$ computes the *behaviour* of o in S, by first projecting S to o and then collecting all messages sent by o between two subsequent messages received by o:

$$beh : Scenario \times SystemObject \to Behaviour$$
$$beh(S, o) = act(proj(S, o), o)$$

$$act : Scenario \times SystemObject \to Behaviour$$
$$act(\varepsilon, o) = \varepsilon$$
$$act(\langle pre, \langle snd, op, o \rangle, ret, post \rangle\ cs, o) = \langle pre, op, \langle outs, ret \rangle, post \rangle\ act(rest, o)$$
$$\quad\quad where\ (outs, rest) = collect(cs, o)$$

$$collect : Communication^* \times SystemObject \to OutMessage^* \times Communication^*$$
$$collect(\varepsilon, o) = (\varepsilon, \varepsilon)$$
$$collect(\langle pre, \langle snd, op, rcv \rangle, ret, post \rangle\ cs, o) =$$

$$\begin{cases} (\varepsilon, \langle pre, \langle snd, op, rcv \rangle, ret, post \rangle\ cs) & if\ rcv = o \\ (\langle op, rcv, ret \rangle\ outs, rest) & if\ snd = o \\ \quad\quad where\ (outs, rest) = collect(cs, o) \end{cases}$$

where $\langle pre, \langle snd, op, rcv \rangle, ret, post \rangle \in Communication$ and $cs \in Communication^*$; ε denotes the empty sequence; sequence composition is denoted by juxtaposition; and angle brackets compound syntax fragments. The behaviours of atm and consortium for our running example scenarios Bad account and Bad password are given in Tab. 3.

Note that the construction of activations, based upon the function *collect*, marks a significant methodological and technical difference to the approaches in [5], [2], and [3], which has a crucial impact on the construction of UML 2.0 state machines described below.

4 Integrating Behaviours into I/O-Automata

The behaviours constructed in the last section are still split according to the original set of scenarios. The goal of the next step is to integrate for each system object its computed set of behaviours on the basis of shared states; these shared states must have been determined already by the modeller of the scenarios by giving them the same names. For the integration of behaviours we use as an intermediate format

Table 3. Behaviours for atm and consortium in each scenario

(a) Behaviour of atm in scenario Bad account

Pre state	Message in	Messages out	Return	Post state
WaitCard	insertCard	⟨requestPassword, user, void⟩	void	WaitPassword
WaitPassword	enterPassword	⟨verifyAccount, consortium, badAccount⟩ ⟨badAccountMessage, user, void⟩ ⟨printReceipt, user, void⟩ ⟨ejectCard, user, void⟩ ⟨requestTakeCard, user, void⟩	void	WaitTakeCard
WaitTakeCard	takeCard	⟨displayMainScreen, user, void⟩	void	WaitCard

(b) Behaviour of atm in scenario Bad password

Pre state	Message in	Messages out	Return	Post state
WaitPassword	enterPassword	⟨verifyAccount, consortium, badPassword⟩ ⟨requestPassword, user, void⟩	void	WaitPassword
WaitPassword	cancel	⟨canceledMessage, user, void⟩ ⟨ejectCard, user, void⟩ ⟨requestTakeCard, user, void⟩	void	WaitTakeCard

(c) Behaviour of consortium in scenario Bad account

Pre state	Message in	Messages out	Return	Post state
WaitVerify	verifyAccount	⟨verifyCardWithBank, bank, badBankAccount⟩	badAccount	WaitVerify

(d) Behaviour of consortium in scenario Bad password

Pre state	Message in	Messages out	Return	Post state
WaitVerify	verifyAccount	⟨verifyCardWithBank, bank, badBankPassword⟩	badPassword	WaitVerify

I/O-(input-/output-)automata before we finally construct concrete state machines. To use I/O-automata has several advantages: First, the integration process can be defined in terms of standard techniques for joining I/O-automata. Moreover, I/O-automata provide an abstract representation which is appropriate for feedback on problems in the integration process which can either be resolved by human manipulation of the scenarios or by choosing a default integration strategy. Finally, the intermediate representation paves the way for transforming scenario models into different concrete notations, like, in our case, UML 2.0 state machines or the "Executable UML" [7] or LTSA [5].

4.1 I/O-Automata

Formally, an *I/O-automaton* is a quadruple (Z, In, Out, δ) with Z its *states*, *In* the *input alphabet*, *Out* the *output alphabet*, and $\delta \subseteq Z \times In \times Out \times Z$ the *transition relation*. An *I/O-automaton with initial state* is a quintuple $(Z, In, Out, \delta, z_0)$ where (Z, In, Out, δ) is an I/O-automaton and $z_0 \in Z$ is the *initial state*.

Each single behaviour of a system object constructed in Sect. 3 can be seen as an I/O-automaton where the states in a behaviour are directly taken as the states of the automaton, the input messages as the input to the automaton, the activations, i.e., the sequences of output messages with final returns, as the output of the automaton, and each block as a transition. Given a scenario S and a system object o, the function $io(S, o)$ constructs

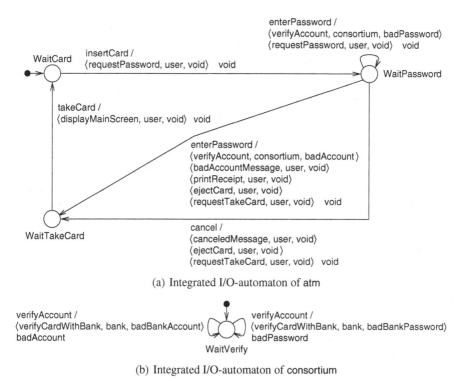

(a) Integrated I/O-automaton of atm

(b) Integrated I/O-automaton of consortium

Fig. 2. Integrated I/O-automata for atm and consortium

an I/O-automaton (Z, In, Out, δ) for the behaviour of o in S as follows: Z is given by the set of states in $beh(S, o)$; In is given by the set of in-messages in $beh(S, o)$; Out is given by the activations in $beh(S, o)$, i.e., the pairs of sequences of out-messages and returns; and δ is defined by requiring $(pre, in, (outs, ret), post) \in \delta$ iff $\langle pre, in, \langle outs, ret \rangle, post \rangle$ is a block in $beh(S, o)$.

The integration $intio(S_0, \{S_1, \ldots, S_n\}, o)$ of a given scenario S_0 with further scenarios $S_1, \ldots, S_n$ with respect to a system object o is now simply the (joined) I/O-automaton with initial state $(Z_0 \cup \cdots \cup Z_n, In_0 \cup \cdots \cup In_n, Out_0 \cup \cdots \cup Out_n, \delta_0 \cup \cdots \cup \delta_n, z_0)$ with $io(S_i, o) = (Z_i, In_i, Out_i, \delta_i)$ and z_0 the pre-state of the first block in $beh(S_0, o)$.

Figure 2(a) shows the integrated I/O-automaton of the atm object (with initial state) for the scenarios of our running example. Similarly, Figure 2(b) shows the integrated I/O-automaton of the consortium object.

4.2 Feedback

The integration of scenarios into a single I/O-automaton with initial state will, in general, result in a non-deterministic automaton. On the one hand, non-determinism reflects under-specification and thus is intentional. On the other hand, non-determinism can also be a symptom for incompleteness or errors in the original scenarios. Indeed, we would

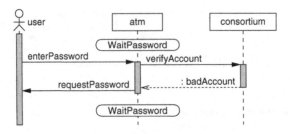

Fig. 3. Non-deterministic scenario Bad password (fragment)

expect different reaction sequences to an incoming message to be justified by different source states or by different returns in the sequence of outgoing messages of the reaction, and the user of the synthesis procedure will be warned about the possible error.

Suppose that for some source state and an input in the integrated I/O-automaton two sequences of outgoing messages of the following form appear:

$$m_1 \ldots m_{k-1} \langle op_k, rcv_k, ret_k \rangle \langle op_{k+1}, rcv_{k+1}, ret_{k+1} \rangle m_{k+2} \ldots c_l$$
$$m_1 \ldots m_{k-1} \langle op_k, rcv_k, ret'_k \rangle \langle op'_{k+1}, rcv'_{k+1}, ret'_{k+1} \rangle m'_{k+2} \ldots c'_n$$

If $ret_k = ret'_k$, but $op_{k+1} \neq op'_{k+1}$ or $rcv'_{k+1} \neq rcv'_{k+1}$ the user will be informed that ret_k and ret'_k should be different, in order to ensure deterministic behaviour. As a simple example, consider the scenario fragment in Fig. 3, which modifies the scenario Bad password of Fig. 1(b) by using as a return for verifyAccount the same value badAccount that has been used in the scenario Bad account. Then, the different continuations between the first and the (changed) second scenario indicate non-determinism which should be resolved by the user.

Similarly, suppose that some source state *pre* and an input *in* is followed by two sequences of outgoing messages, subsequent returns, and successor states of the following form:

$$\langle pre, in, \langle m_1 \ldots m_n, ret \rangle, post \rangle$$
$$\langle pre, in, \langle m_1 \ldots m_n, ret' \rangle, post' \rangle$$

If $ret \neq ret'$, the user will be warned that either ret should be the same as ret' or the activation sequences before should be different, because after exactly the same activation (for the same in-message and the same pre-state) there is no obvious reason to provide different return values. Analogously, if $ret = ret'$ but $post \neq post'$ a warning is issued.

5 Translating I/O-Automata into UML 2.0 State Machines

The generated I/O-automaton for the integrated behaviour of a system object in scenarios can be seen as a UML 2.0 state machine keeping the state-transition structure and only turning in-messages into triggers and sequences of out-messages with a return into effects. The drawback of this mere adaptation of the notation to UML is that it shows different activations following the same incoming message on different transitions retaining unnecessary non-determinism.

Fig. 4. Actions as state machine fragment

Thus, in order to obtain a comprehensive representation of the activity that follows an incoming message we transfer activations to state machines by discerning two kinds of states: *stable* states, in which a system object waits for a message; and *activity* states, in which the reaction to an incoming message is processed. The different sequences of outgoing messages and the subsequent returns mark different exits to such an activity state, in general leading to different (stable) successor states. In UML 2.0, submachine states provide the necessary structure for the activity states, with entry and exit points (shown as circles and crossed circles) encapsulating the internal behaviour of the contained state machine; simple states represent stable states. In fact, activity states capture procedures in the sense of "Executable UML" [7], but make case distinctions in procedure executions graphically explicit.

For integrating the reaction to an incoming message $in \in In$ in a state $z \in Z$ of an I/O-automaton with initial state $(Z, In, Out, \delta, z_0) = intio(S_0, \{S_1, \ldots, S_n\}, o)$ into a submachine, we first turn the outgoing operation calls in the activation set $R(z, in) = \{out \in Out \mid \exists z' \in Z . (z, in, out, z') \in \delta\}$ into state machine fragments: If (op, rcv) is a pair of an operation and a receiving object such that $\langle op, rcv, ret \rangle$ occurs in an $out \in R(z, in)$ with some return ret and if $(m_1 \ldots m_k \langle op, rcv, ret_1 \rangle) \ldots (m_1 \ldots m_k \langle op, rcv, ret_n \rangle)$ are all occurrences of (op, rcv) in $R(z, in)$ after a common prefix $m_1 \ldots m_k$ with $n > 0$ different returns $ret_1, \ldots, ret_n$, we construct a state machine fragment $M(z, in, m_1 \ldots m_k, op, rcv)$ of the form in Fig. 4 with r an auxiliary variable. In a next step, the different state machine fragments for out-messages in the activation set $R(z, in)$ are assembled into a single submachine: The transition for [r = ret_i] of $M(z, in, m_1 \ldots m_k, op, rcv)$ is merged to the incoming transition of $M(z, in, m_1 \ldots m_k \langle op, rcv, ret_i \rangle, op', rcv')$. Finally, we define an entry point for each $M(z, in, \varepsilon, op, rcv)$ and exit points for each $M(z, in, m_1 \ldots m_k, op, rcv)$ with $m_1 \ldots m_k$ a maximal sequence of out-messages in $R(z, in)$. The result of applying this procedure to enterPassword in the state WaitPassword in Fig. 2(a) is depicted in Fig. 5(a).

Having defined submachines for the activation sets $R(z, in)$ an integrated state machine can now be synthesised by introducing stable states from the I/O-automaton as simple states and connecting these by transitions to activity states as submachine states referencing the submachines from $R(z, in)$. For the two ATM scenarios the result of the translation of the I/O-automaton of atm in Fig. 2(a) is shown in Fig. 5(b). The states WaitCard, WaitPassword, and WaitTakeCard are the stable states, the states : insertCard, : enterPassword, : cancel, and : takeCard are the activity states of the state machine.

It is worth noting that for each system object the separation of stable and activity states leads to a sequential behavioural design model which can be directly implemented using the state pattern [10] or a straightforward implementation by means of state variables. The latter approach represents the incoming messages of a system object by methods which show a case distinction according to the stable states and

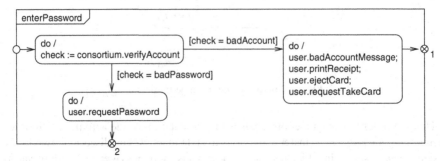

(a) UML 2.0 submachine for reaction of atm to enterPassword.

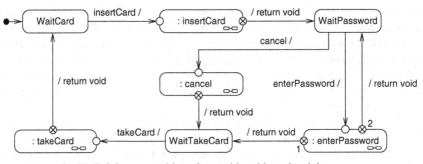

(b) UML 2.0 state machine of atm with stable and activity states.

Fig. 5. Synthesised state machines for atm

implement the behaviour of the activity states. Using Java as implementation language and recording the current state in an enumeration-typed variable `currentState`, the implementation of `enterPassword` takes the following form:

```
void enterPassword() {
  switch (currentState) {
    case WAIT_PASSWORD:
      VerificationResult check = consortium.verifyAccount();
      if (check == VerificationResult.BAD_ACCOUNT) {
        user.badAccountMessage(); ...
        currentState = State.WAIT_TAKECARD;
        return;
      }
      if (check == VerificationResult.BAD_PASSWORD) {
        user.requestPassword();
        currentState = State.WAIT_PASSWORD;
        return;
      }
      break;
    default:
  }
}
```

6   Related Work

To our knowledge, in contrast to all other approaches to state machine synthesis our method sets out from scenarios with a clear distinction between inactive (stable) states and activation phases that follow as a reaction to a synchronous operation call. Our approach is activity-driven in the sense that during the transformation process different activations occurring in different scenarios but following the same incoming message (in the same stable state) are integrated into one single activity which models the behaviour of an operation across many scenarios. Such a model can be easily translated into a sequential program.

In order to compare our results with the literature we can use the same ATM case study which, in an asynchronous environment, is modelled by the same scenarios as shown in Fig. 1, but deleting all states and replacing all synchronous and return messages by asynchronous messages [2,5] (we have omitted the initial outgoing displayMainScreen message). This example is also the basis for the detailed comparison in [5]. The crucial difference to the synchronous case is that instead of the return values badAccount and badBankAccount of the operations verifyAccount and verifyCardWithBank, respectively, now (call-back) messages are used to indicate the result of a verification.[3]

For the integration of the asynchronous scenarios different strategies have been proposed in the literature. According to [6], these approaches can mainly be categorised into synthesis algorithms which are based on matching conditions and algorithms which are based on matching events or actions.

As an instance of the first group, the integration procedure of Whittle and Schumann [2] is based on matching of pre-/post-conditions that the user has to provide (for incoming and outgoing messages) as an input to the transformation process. As a result, Whittle and Schumann obtain for the atm the state machine in Fig. 6(a) which has a completely different structure than the activity-based state machine for synchronous communication shown in Fig. 5. Also the hierarchical state machine developed in a last step in Whittle and Schumann's algorithm does not follow an activity-based integration strategy but groups states according to values of state variables in pre-/post-conditions. The approaches by Krüger et al. [3] and Uchitel et al. [5] are based on a similar strategy; here, explicit states, like in our scenarios, have to be provided, and Uchitel et al. also take into account combinations of basic scenario blocks.

The Fujaba approach to integrate scenarios into a state machine, proposed by Maier and Zündorf [4], is based on matching of send actions. In this way one would obtain for the above scenarios the state machine in Fig. 6(b) which in turn is not aimed at exhibiting the computational behaviour of operations. The SCED/MAS algorithm by Mäkinen and Systä [11] falls in the same category of event matching procedures, but also uses a learning procedure for synthesis.

---

[3] In the asynchronous approach, [2,5] distinguish also a further scenario where the user cancels the transaction before the consortium has called back the atm, which is not possible in the synchronous approach.

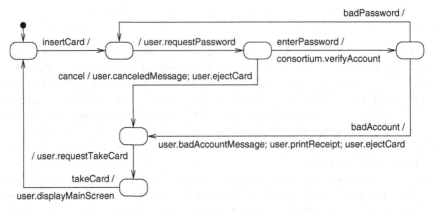

(a) According to Whittle and Schumann [2]

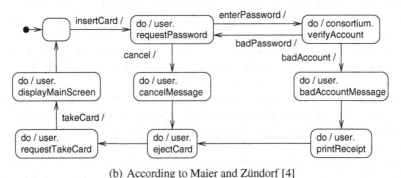

(b) According to Maier and Zündorf [4]

Fig. 6. Integrated atm state machine in asynchronous approaches

7   Conclusions and Future Work

We have described a model transformation procedure for synthesising an integrated UML 2.0 state machine from scenarios given as UML 2.0 interactions. The approach focuses on reactive objects, where activities are triggered by incoming synchronous messages. The transformation procedure constructs an intermediate I/O-automaton for the behaviour of a single object integrating the scenarios. The non-deterministic transitions of the I/O-automaton provide the basis for systematic feedback to the user of the transformation about integration problems, which will iteratively lead to more complete and refined scenarios. Finally, the integrated I/O-automaton is translated into a UML 2.0 state machine which describes the overall behaviour of an object distinguishing between stable and activity states. The activity states are represented by UML 2.0 submachines (with entry- and exit-points) modelling the reaction of an object to an operation call (occurring in a stable state).

A related distinction has been suggested by Tenzer and Stevens [12] who use protocol state machines to specify the permissible sequences of operation calls occurring in stable states and method state machines to model the execution of the actions of an operation. However, Tenzer and Stevens do not model state dependent reactions on operation calls and do not focus on a synthesis procedure but rather on the modelling of recursive calls and call-backs which we have not considered yet. Further steps to make our synthesis algorithm more complete concern message parameters, which can be easily added, and an extension to scenarios with both synchronous and asynchronous messages, which should work along the same lines as the current approach.

Finally, let us remark that our approach can be adjusted to a component-based framework where scenarios are used to identify provided and required interfaces of components and the synthesis procedure generates UML 2.0 protocol state machines for the ports of a component. In particular, the encapsulation of activities allows for independent refinement, of operation behaviour, on the one hand, and of the protocol on the other.

References

1. Fowler, M.: UML Distilled: Applying the Standard Object Modeling Language. Addison-Wesley, Boston–&c. (1997)
2. Whittle, J., Schumann, J.: Generating Statechart Designs from Scenarios. In: Proc. 22nd Int. Conf. Software Engineering (ICSE'00), IEEE Press (2000) 314–323
3. Krüger, I., Grosu, R., Scholz, P., Broy, M.: From MSCs to Statecharts. In Rammig, F.J., ed.: Distributed and Parallel Embedded Systems, Kluwer Academic, Boston–Dordrecht (1999) 61–71
4. Maier, T., Zündorf, A.: The Fujaba Statechart Synthesis Approach. In: Proc. 2nd Int. Wsh. Scenarios and State Machines: Models, Algorithms, and Tools (SCESM'03), Portland, Oregon (2003)
5. Uchitel, S., Kramer, J., Magee, J.: Synthesis of Behavioral Models from Scenarios. IEEE Trans. Softw. Eng. **29** (2003) 99–115
6. Liang, H., Dingel, J., Diskin, Z.: A Comparative Survey of Scenario-based To State-based Model Synthesis Approaches. In: Proc. 5th Int. Wsh. Scenarios and State Machines: Models, Algorithms and Tools (SCESM'06), Shanghai (2006) 5–12
7. Mellor, S.J., Balcer, M.J.: Executable UML — A Foundation for Model-Driven Architecture. Addison-Wesley, Boston–&c. (2002)
8. Blaha, M., Rumbaugh, J.: Object-Oriented Modeling and Design with UML. 2nd edn. Pearson Education, Upper Saddle River, N. J. (2005)
9. Object Management Group: Unified Modeling Language: Superstructure, version 2.0. (2005) http://www.omg.org/cgi-bin/doc?formal/05-07-04$^{(06/12/28)}$.
10. Gamma, E., Helm, R., Johnson, R.E., Vlissides, J.: Design Patterns. Addison-Wesley, Boston–&c. (1995)
11. Mäkinen, E., Systä, T.: MAS: An Interactive Synthesizer to Support Behavioral Modelling in UML. In: Proc. 23rd IEEE Int. Conf. Software Engineering (ICSE'01), IEEE Computer Society (2001) 15–24
12. Tenzer, J., Stevens, P.: Modelling Recursive Calls with UML State Diagrams. In Pezzè, M., ed.: Proc. 6th Int. Conf. Fundamental Approaches to Software Engineering (FASE'03). Volume 2621 of Lect. Notes Comp. Sci., Springer, Berlin (2003) 135–149

Flexible and Extensible Notations for Modeling Languages*

Jimin Gao, Mats Heimdahl, and Eric Van Wyk

Department of Computer Science and Engineering
University of Minnesota

Abstract. In model-based development, a formal description of the software (the model) is the central artifact that drives other development activities. The availability of a modeling language well-suited for the system under development and appropriate tool support are of utmost importance to practitioners. Considering the diverse needs of different application domains, flexibility in the choice of modeling languages and tools may advance the industrial acceptance of formal methods.

We describe a flexible modeling language framework by which language and tool developers may better meet the special needs of various users groups without incurring prohibitive costs. The framework is based on a modular and extensible implementation of languages features using attribute grammars and *forwarding*. We show a prototype implementation of such a framework by extending the *host language* Mini-Lustre, an example synchronous data-flow language, with a collection of features such as state transitions, condition tables, and events. We also show how new languages can be created in this framework by *feature composition*.

1 Introduction

Model-based development is gaining interest from the software industry, especially in the domain of safety critical systems. The aims are cost reduction and quality improvement through early defect removal through model testing and formal analysis, and automated code generation. There are currently many commercial and research tools that attempt to provide these capabilities [1,2,3,4,5].

In previous work [6] we discussed several factors that hinder the widespread adoption of formal methods and model-based development in practice. We also formulated several conjectures related to this topic, one of which is related to the work presented in this report: *"no modeling language will be universally accepted, nor universally applicable."* If a notation is not liked by the intended users it will simply not be used; a multitude of (domain-specific) languages is needed. Current languages and tools infrastructures are inflexible and make language customization and tool integration difficult and costly. As illustration, consider the following two scenarios.

---

* Different aspects of this work are partially funded by NSF CAREER Award #0347860, NSF CCF Award #0429640, and the McKnight Foundation.

M.B. Dwyer and A. Lopes (Eds.): FASE 2007, LNCS 4422, pp. 102–116, 2007.

First, a development team for an air-transport flight guidance system needs a modeling language. These systems are typically periodical and take actions when certain (generally rather complex) conditions hold. Due to the complexity of the conditions, condition tables, such as those found in RSML^{-e} [5] and SCR [4] would be useful when reviewing the models with domain experts and regulators. The developer's engineers prefer to use a data-flow language specifically designed for control systems, for example, Lustre. Thus, a language that is basically Lustre extended with RSML^{-e}-style tables would be desirable.

Second, a development team for pre-launch checkout software for a launch vehicle seeks a modeling language appropriate for capturing the complex sequences of events that must occur before it is safe to launch the vehicle. The team finds a pure data-flow language like Lustre unsuitable for the task (they would prefer an explicit notion of states and events), but they like the analysis support available for Lustre (numerous model checkers and theorem provers). The team finds the RSML^{-e} syntax more suitable for the task at hand, but does not find a commercial tool supporting the creation nor analysis of RSML^{-e} models. They wonder if the Lustre toolset could be extended with RSML^{-e} features to easily leverage existing analysis and code generation capabilities.

Because customizing commercial toolsets and building tools from the ground up to provide expanded language and analysis support is generally infeasible or too costly we believe a different view of modeling languages and tools is needed. Instead of treating each modeling language as a fixed, monolithic entity, and implementing its tool support based on that view, we adopt the notion of extensible languages—language implementations that are intended and optimized for future (front-end and back-end) additions (and possibly modifications). In this view, the artifacts include a *host language* and a set of *language extensions* that define desired language features not found in the host language.

The *flexible modeling language framework* described in this paper is based on the general idea that language extensions may introduce new constructs to the host language, new semantic analyses that, for example, ensure that the constructs defined in an extension are used correctly, and new translations to different target languages. In this framework, a domain-specific language can be easily created through inclusion of language extensions in the host language. In our domain, synchronous languages, (*e.g.*, Safe State Machines [2], SCADE [2], and SCR [4], to name just a few) are prevalent and all share the same semantic foundations. We believe that most (if not all) features of these languages can be implemented as extensions to a host language in our flexible language framework. Based on our experiences in model-based development, we believe that Lustre [7] is a suitable host language. First, Lustre is expressive enough to capture a large class of interesting behaviors and it has a simple and well-defined semantics suitable for analysis [8]. Second, there are commercial tools for Lustre that interest industrial users [2]. Here we use a reduced version (Mini-Lustre) that espouses the key features of full Lustre, but omits some rather involved and, for the purpose of this paper, less important ones.

In this framework, language features such as RSML^{-e}-style tables, Statecharts like events, and designated state variables do not need to be implemented in the host language but can instead be implemented as a language extension allowing us to address the needs of the developers in our first scenario.

The host-language is designed to have specific tool support; here, Mini-Lustre comes with support for semantic analysis such as type checking as well as a translation to a general purpose programming language and a number of translations from Mini-Lustre to the input languages of a number of analysis tools. Thus, to address the second scenario we create language extensions that (1) add the syntax and semantic analysis of the desired new language, (2) specify the translation of the new language constructs to the host language Mini-Lustre, and (3) hide the undesirable (concrete) syntax of Mini-Lustre so that the new language primarily uses the host language as an intermediate representation to take advantage of the translations to various analysis tools. Note that new translations from the host language to new analysis engines will automatically work to languages created by extending the host language.

To be useful, extensible language frameworks need two crucial characteristics. First, language constructs implemented as language extensions must have the same "look and feel" as constructs in the host language. That is, at a minimum, they should perform some semantic analysis to report error messages at the extension level and not rely on their translation to the host language for error checking. Thus, traditional macros are not an acceptable means for implementing language constructs as error checking is done on the constructs to which the macros expand. Second, language extensions must be composable so that various language extensions, implemented independently, can be imported into a host language in a cost-effective way. For some language extensions, the composition can be entirely automatic. The language user may just select language extensions from a list and the framework automatically builds the specification for the new extended language. This composition is possible for the first scenario above in which the host language Lustre is extended with RSML^{-e}-style tables. In other cases, composition may require more involvement from someone skilled in language development; this is the case in our second scenario where Lustre is extended with state variables and the underlying Lustre constructs such as nodes and data-flow equations need to be hidden (at last syntactically). Both forms of composition are demonstrated in Section 3.5.

Our extensible view of modeling languages may be realized using attribute grammars with *forwarding* [9]. The host language is implemented by writing an attribute grammar specification of the language. We have developed an attribute grammar specification language, called Silver for this purpose. The Silver tools automatically generate an attribute grammar evaluator for languages specified in Silver. Language extensions, such as the addition of tables suggested above, are implemented as attribute grammar fragments. The combination of the host language attribute grammar and the selected attribute grammar fragments that implement language extensions provide a specification for the new languages as required in our sample scenarios. Again, the Silver tools provide an automatic implementation for these new languages. We illustrate the feasibility of this approach by implementing solutions to the problems posed in each scenario.

Section 2 presents an implementation of Mini-Lustre as a Silver attribute grammar specification. Section 3 shows how extensions to Lustre can be implemented as attribute grammar fragments and composed to create new (extended) languages. These exercises provide a view of the power of this approach. Section 4 discusses related and future work and concludes.

2   Mini-Lustre: The Host Language

Lustre is a synchronous data flow language designed for programming reactive systems as well as for describing hardware. Lustre is synchronous in that it provides temporal determinism by partitioning physical time into discrete time points, at which computations react instantaneously to external events. This high-level paradigm is specially designed for abstracting the actual computation away from the complex timing constraints involved with control systems. In addition, Lustre specifies its computations using a data flow model, which enables natural parallelism and tractable analysis.

Consider the example in Fig. 1. It specifies partial functionality of an Altitude Switch (ASW), an avionics system that turns the power on for another system when the aircraft descends below a threshold altitude and turns it off when the aircraft ascends above the threshold plus a hysteresis factor. Here we focus on the AltStatus variable used to keep track whether the aircraft should be considered above or below the threshold. The initial value of AltStatus is undefined (Unknown ->) and thereafter assigned by the nested if-expression. We assign AltStatus the value Above if the altitude readings are reliable (AltQuality = Good) and we are either (1) classifying AltStatus for the first time (pre (AltStatus) = Unknown) and we are above the threshold or (2) AltStatus has been established and we are above the threshold plus the hysteresis. AltStatus is Below if altitude readings are reliable and the altitude is less than or equal to the threshold. If the altitude readings are not reliable AltStatus is Unknown.

```
type Status = enum { Unknown, Above, Below } ;

node ASW (AltQuality:Quality, AltThres:int, Hyst:int, Altitude:int)
     returns (AltStatus:Status) ;
 let AltStatus = Unknown ->
     if AltQuality = Good and Altitude > AltThres and
        (pre(AltStatus) = Unknown or Altitude > AltThres + Hyst) then Above
     else if AltQuality = Good and (not Altitude > AltThres) then Below
     else if not AltQuality = Good then Unknown
     else pre(AltStatus) ;     tel;
```

Fig. 1. ASW in Mini-Lustre

```
grammar lustre ;
nt Root, NodeList, Node, VarDeclList, VarDecl, Locals, EqList, Eq, Expr ;
syn attr pp      :: String occurs on Root, Node, Expr, VarDecl, ... ;
syn attr errors :: String occurs on Root, Node, Expr, ... ;
syn attr ctrans :: String occurs on Root, Node, Expr, ... ;

prod root r::Root ::= nl::NodeList
  { r.errors = nl.errors; r.pp = nl.pp; r.ctrans = ... nl.ctrans ...; }
prod nodeListCons nl::NodeList ::= n::Node nltail::NodeList { ... }
prod nodeListOne  nl::NodeList ::= n::Node   { ... }
prod node n::Node ::= name::Id inputs::VarDeclList outputs::VarDeclList
                      locals::VarDeclList eql::EqList
  { n.pp = "node " ++ name.lexeme ++ " (" ++ inputs.pp ++ ") " ++ ... ;
    n.errors = inputs.errors ++ outputs.errors ++ locals.errors ++ eql.errors ;
    n.ctrans = ... ;  }
prod varDecl vd::VarDecl ::= var::Id type::Type
  { vd.pp = var.lexeme ++ " : " ++ type.lexeme ;   }
prod equation eq::Eq ::= id::Id expr::Expr
  { eq.pp = id.lexeme ++ " = " ++ expr.pp ++ ";\n" ;
    eq.errors = ... ;  /* ensure id and expr have same type */ }
```

Fig. 2. A portion of the Silver specification of Mini-Lustre

We provide the attribute grammar (AG) specification for Mini-Lustre, which contains the characteristic features of full Lustre, such as node declarations and synchronous computation. The specification is written in Silver and shown in Fig. 2 and Fig. 3. In general, a Silver specification for a language consists of a series of declarations that define its concrete and abstract syntax as well as rules which assign values to attributes associated with nonterminals. To define the syntax, there are declarations for terminals, nonterminals (keyword **nt**), and productions (**prod**). Productions marked as *concrete* are used to construct the parser. They are as expected and thus not shown in Fig. 2 or Fig. 3. The AG portion of the specification consists of declarations for attributes (**attr**), and production-associated equations that define the values of attributes that label nonterminal nodes in a program's abstract syntax tree (AST). An attribute is synthesized (**syn**) if it propagates information up the abstract syntax tree; it is inherited (**inh**) if it propagates information down the AST. Note that the order of Silver declarations does not matter; values can be used before their definition.

The first line of the specification in Fig. 2 provides the name of this grammar. Grammar names are used in following sections in which the Silver **import** statement is used to combine attribute grammar specifications to create the specification for an extended language. Next, the nonterminals in the grammar are declared. Synthesized attributes **pp**, **errors**, and **ctrans** of type **String** are declared; these attributes, respectively, define a node's pretty-print or "unparsed" representation, the errors occurring on the node and its children, and its translation to C. The **occurs on** attribution clause specifies which nonterminals an attribute decorates. We will elide other nonterminal and attribution (**occurs on**) declarations as they can be inferred from the specification.

```
prod idref expr::Expr ::= id::Id  { ... }
prod and expr::Expr ::= lft::Expr rht::Expr
  { expr.pp = ... ; expr.errors = ... ; expr.ctrans = ... ; }
prod not expr::Expr ::= n::Expr { ... }
prod or expr::Expr ::= lft::Expr rht::Expr
  { expr.pp = "(" ++ lft.pp ++ " || " ++ rht.pp ++ ")" ;
    expr.errors = ... ;  /* check both lft and rht are bool */
    forwards to not( and( not(lft), not(rht) ) ); }
```

Fig. 3. Silver specifications of Mini-Lustre expressions (`Expr`)

A Mini-Lustre program (represented by a nonterminal `Root`) is a series of node definitions (represented by `NodeList`). The nonterminal `Root` on the left hand side of the production `root` is named `r`; the right hand side has a single `NodeList` nonterminal named `nl`. Equations defining the synthesized attributes of `r` are listed in curly brackets. For example, the last equation uses ellipses (...) to indicate that the value of the `ctrans` attribute on `r` is computed from the value of `ctrans` on `nl`. A node, defined by production `node`, is composed of a name (`name`), a list of input parameter declarations (`inputs` of type `VarDeclList`), a list of output parameters (`outputs`), a list of local variable declarations (`locals`), and a list of equations (`eql` of type `EqList`). Its attributes are defined as expected. There are several list constructs in Mini-Lustre and we will not show the productions for many of these as they are what one would expect and can be inferred. They will follow the pattern of using a "cons" and "one" production like those defined for `NodeList` in Fig. 2. The production `varDecl` binds identifier names to types. These bindings are stored in a symbol table that is passed to the equations in `eql` as expected. These are not shown since this is a straight-forward and common task in attribute grammars. The production `equation` will check that the identifier `id` and expression `expr` have the same type and generate an error message if they do not. It also defines its `pp` attribute as expected. Further definitions of `pp` are also what one would expect and are thus elided, though each production does have an explicit definition for it.

Of special interest is the production `or` which defines the disjunction of two expressions. It uses an extension to attribute grammars called *forwarding* [9] that is used extensively in defining the extensions to Mini-Lustre in Section 3. To use forwarding a production defines a construct that it is semantically equivalent to. It will *forward* queries for attributes that it does not *explicitly* define with an attribute definition to this "forwards-to" construct. The forwards-to construct will return its value for the queried attribute. In this case of `or`, the production states the semantic equivalent of `or(lft,rht)` is `not( and( not(lft)`, `not(rht)))`. When a construct created by the `or` production is queried for its `errors` or `pp` attributes, it returns the values specified by the explicit definitions. When queried for its `ctrans` attribute, it returns the value of `ctrans` on its semantically equivalent forwards-to construct. This is somewhat similar to macro expansion, where the forwards-to construct corresponds to the body of the macro. Unlike a macro definition of `or` the production with forwarding reports error messages on programmer-written specifications.

3   Mini-Lustre Extensions

In this section we define four language features that can be added to Mini-Lustre as modular language extensions. These features, RSML^{-e}-style tables, equals clauses, and state variables, and Statechart-like events, are all features that some but not all users of synchronous languages find useful. We also show how a simple "module" extension can hide host language syntax to in essence create a new language that is not an extension of the host. The goal of this section is to show in some detail how feature-rich modeling languages, tailored to specific domains or to user preferences, can be easily created by simply composing the host-language with the desired set of language features. Thus, the extensions, just like Mini-Lustre, capture the important characteristics of the features and not a full realization of them. This high-degree of modularity is achieved through the *forwarding* extension to attribute grammars.

3.1   Tables

Tables are used for specifying complicated boolean expressions, available in both RSML^{-e} and SCR. They have been shown to be useful when presenting specifications to domain experts, such as pilots and air traffic controllers [10, 11, 12]. An example of such a table is shown in Fig. 4 in which b, c1, c2, and c3 are boolean variables. In each row of the table there are "truth value" entries T (true), F (false),

```
b = table
  (c1 && c2) : T F ;
  ! (c2)     : T * ;
  (c3 || c2) : F T ;
  end;
```

Fig. 4. RSML^{-e} table

or * (don't-care) indicating the desired truthfulness of the preceding Boolean expression, *e.g.* c1 && c2 in the first row. A table is an alternative form of the Boolean expression that can be obtained by taking the conjunction of the expressions generated for each entry in a column and then taking the disjunction of these expressions generated for the columns. Therefore, the equation in Fig. 4 is semantically equivalent to the pure-Mini-Lustre code shown below:

```
b = ((c1&&c2) && !c2 && !(c3||c2)) || (!(c1&&c2) && true && (c3||c2));
```

The table extension is implemented as a Silver attribute grammar fragment, portions of which are shown in Fig. 5. This specification shows the abstract syntax productions and attribute definitions for error-checking and computing the pure-Mini-Lustre code to which the table construct translates (forwards to). A table is an alternative form of expression (nonterminal Expr) as defined by the production table. It consists of a number of rows (ExprRowList); each row (ExprRow) in turn consists of a (Boolean) expression and a list of truth-values (TruthValueList). Truth values (TruthValue) consist of the terminal TrueTV (marker T), FalseTV (marker F), or Star (marker *).

Several attributes are used to compute the pure-Mini-Lustre expression shown above that the table construct will forward to. The inherited attribute rowexpr is used to pass the Boolean expression in each row down to the truth values where a boolean expression in the host language is constructed (according to the truth value) and is passed up the AST in the attribute texpr. For example,

```
grammar lustre_tables ;
import  lustre ;

prod table t::Expr ::= erows::ExprRowList
{ t.errors = erows.errors ;
  forwards to disjunction(mapConjunction(transpose(erows.texprss ))) ; }

nt ExprRowList, ExprRow, TruthValueList, TruthValue ;

syn attr texprss :: [[Expr]] occurs on ExprRowList ;
syn attr texprs :: [Expr] occurs on ExprRow, TruthValueList ;
syn attr rlen :: Integer occurs on ExprRowList, ExprRow, TruthValueList ;
inh attr rowexpr :: Expr occurs on TruthValueList, TruthValue;
syn attr texpr   :: Expr occurs on TruthValue ;

prod exprRowCons erows::ExprRowList ::=
          erow::ExprRow erowstail::ExprRowList
{ erows.rlen = erow.rlen ;
  erows.errors = erow.errors ++ erowstail.errors ++
                    if erow.rlen == erowstail.rlen then "" else
                    "Error: rows need same num of cols";
  erows.texprss = cons(erow.texprs, erowstail.texprss ) ; }

prod exprRowOne erows::ExprRowList ::= erow::ExprRow
{ erows.errors = erow.errors ; erows.rlen = erow.rlen ;
  erows.texprss = [erow.texprs] ;    }

prod exprRow erow::ExprRow ::= e::Expr tvl::TruthValueList
{ erow.rlen = tvl.rlen ; erow.texprs = tvl.texprs ; tvl.rowexpr = e ;  }

func disjunction Expr ::= es::[Expr]
{ return if leng(es) == 1 then head(es)
    else or(head(es), disjunction(tail(es))) ; }

prod tvlistCons tvl::TruthValueList ::=
    tv::TruthValue tvltail::TruthValueList
{ tvl.rlen = 1 + tvltail.rlen ;
  tvl.texprs = cons (tv.texpr, tvltail.texprs );
  tv.rowexpr = tvl.rowexpr ; tvltail.rowexpr = tvl.rowexpr ;   }

prod tvlistOne tvl::TruthValueList ::= tv::TruthValue
{ tvl.rlen = 1; tvl.texprs = [tv.texpr]; tvl.rowexpr = tvl.rowexpr ; }

prod tvTrue tv::TruthValue ::= t::TrueTV { tv.texpr = tv.rowexpr ; }
prod tvFalse tv::TruthValue ::= f::FalseTV { tv.texpr = not(tv.rowexpr) ; }
prod tvStar  tv::TruthValue ::= s::Star { tv.texpr = true() ; }
```

Fig. 5. Silver table extension specification

for the first row of table in Fig. 4, the texpr attributes for the T and F markers have values of (c1 && c2) and ! (c1 && c2), respectively. A true constant is always created for a * entry. The synthesized attributes texpr, texprs, and texprss collect these Boolean expressions into a list of lists of Exprs that is passed up to the top ExprRowList node of the complete table. Both list types and list expressions are denoted using square brackets ([ ]). After a transposition of the list, the pure-Mini-Lustre translated table is formed. This construct is the forwards-to construct of the production table. Several utility functions, transpose, disjunction, conjunction, and mapConjunction, are defined for building the translated table. Only disjunction is shown, but the others are similar.

The other critical function computed by the attributes is to perform error checking. We need to check that all rows in the table have the same number of columns. This is a semantic analysis that *must* be performed on the extension constructs, as an incorrect number of columns in a row will *not* be detected on the translation to pure-Mini-Lustre. To accomplish this, that table production explicitly defines its errors attribute to be the errors reported on its child erows. To detect such errors, a row length attribute, rlen, is computed on truth value lists and expression row lists and compared on the exprRowCons production to detect any rows whose length differs from other rows. This analysis highlights the critical role played by forwarding. It allows us to define some attributes, such as ctrans *implicitly* via the translation to the host language and to define other attributes, such as errors, *explicitly* on the extension constructs. This ensures that semantic analyses can be carried out at the right level of abstraction.

The lustre_tables grammar specification provides a definition of Lustre extended with the table construct since it imports the grammar lustre. The Silver tools can take this specification and build an attribute evaluator that performs error checking and translations to C of the extended Mini-Lustre + tables language. In Section 3.5, we will see how several independently developed extensions such as those described in the following sections can be combined in creating an extended language.

```
grammar lustre_equals ;   import lustre ;
nt Cases ;   syn attr ifexpr :: Expr occurs on Cases;
prod equals e::Expr ::= cs::Cases
   { e.errors = cs.errors ++ ...; /* ensure e and vals in cs have same type */
     forwards to cs.ifexpr ; }
prod casesCons cs::Cases ::= val::Expr cond::Expr cs1::Cases
   { cs.errors = ... ; /* ensure cond is boolean type */
     cs.ifexpr = ifthenelse(cond, val, cs1.ifexpr) ; }
prod casesOtherwise cs::Cases ::= val::Expr
   { cs.errors = ... ; cs.ifexpr = val ; }
```

Fig. 6. The Silver specification of the equals clause extension

3.2   Equals Clauses

Specification in the state machine transition style is a popular approach in many domains and is the basic paradigm of languages such as Statechart, SCR, and RSML^{-e}. The *equals* clause construct implemented here as a language extension is one way to describe the transition choices of a state machine. An example of the equals

```
b = equals e1 if (c1 && c2)
    equals e2 if ! c1
    equals e3 if ! c2
    otherwise pre(b);
```

Fig. 7. Equals clauses

clause is shown in Fig. 7, where c1, c2, and c3 are Boolean variables, and e1, e2, and e3 are expressions of the same type as variable b. This equals clause is evaluated as follows: if the condition (c1 && c2) evaluates to true, the value of variable b is taken to be that of e1; otherwise if c1 is false, the value of b is e2; otherwise if c2 is false, the value of b is e3; and if none of the condition holds, b retains its original value (pre(b)). This equals clause can be translated to the pure-Mini-Lustre nested if-then-else expression shown below.

```
b = if (c1 && c2) then e1 else if (!c1) then e2
    else if (!c2) then e3 else pre(b);
```

Part of the AG specification of the equals clause extension is shown in Fig. 6. The complete equals clause (Cases) is defined as an expression (Expr) in production equals. The ifexpr attribute on nonterminal Cases holds the equivalent if-then-else expression, which is constructed in production caseCons. It is used as the forwards-to construct in the equals production. The errors attribute is defined explicitly, as in the table extension.

3.3   State Variables

Like the equals clause extension, state variables, representing communicating state machines, are an important element in the state transition style of software specifications. Here we show how the RSML^{-e} state variable construct that captures this notion can be implemented as a language extension built not only on the host language Mini-Lustre but also on the two previous extensions lustre_tables and lustre_equals.

Fig. 8 shows the same ASW specification from Fig. 1 rewritten with extended Mini-Lustre, complete with tables, equals clauses, and state variables extensions. The meaning of the state variable declaration is easy to infer from this example. What is different from the original equals clauses is that the *otherwise* clause is implied here. Although the mixture of Lustre node and state variable declarations may seem strange—for example, the variable AltStatus with its type is declared twice—an additional extension that defines *modules*, which forwards to the node declaration, can fix the syntax and then provide a complete package of features for the descriptions of state machine models.

Part of the attribute grammar specification of the state variable extension is shown in Fig. 9. The state variable production stateVar forwards to the semantically equivalent Mini-Lustre equation that uses the same ifexpr attribute defined on Cases used in the previous example. The inherited attribute

```
node ASW (AltQuality:Quality, AltThres:int, Hyst:int, Altitude:int)
        returns (AltStatus:Status) ;
let  state variable AltStatus : Status
        initial value : Unknown
        equals Above if table pre(AltStatus) = Unknown    : T * ;
                               AltQuality = Good           : T T ;
                               Altitude > AltThres         : T T ;
                               Altitude > AltThres + Hyst : * T ;
                      end table
        equals Below if table AltQuality = Good            : T ;
                               Altitude > AltThres         : F ;
                      end table
        equals Unknown if AltQuality = Good
      end state variable     tel;
```

Fig. 8. ASW in Mini-Lustre extended with state variables, equals clauses and tables

defaultExpr passes the expression to be used in the equation if none of the
conditions in the equals clauses are true. An aspect production is used to add
new attribute rules for attributes inStateVar and defaultExpr to productions
casesCons and equals imported from the grammar lustre_equals. The inherited attribute inStateVar is true on the Cases enclosed in a stateVar and
false otherwise. This is used on the casesOne production to raise an error if it,
instead of the casesOtherwise production, is used in the original equals clause
which requires an otherwise.

3.4   Events

Events are an extension to Mini-Lustre quite different from the previous ones.
Below is a fragment of an enhanced definition of AltStatus from Fig 1 written using Mini-Lustre extended with events. The complex conditions from the
original definition are abbreviated as C1, C2, and C3 here.

```
event AltClassEvt, AltLostEvt;
AltStatus = Unknown ->
            if catch(AltRcvEvt,C1) then throw(AltClassEvt,Above)
        else if catch(AltRcvEvt,C2) then throw(AltClassEvt,Below)
        else if catch(AltRcvEvt,C3) then throw(AltLostEvt,Unknown)    ...
```

A new declaration construct event is added to the language and used in
the declaration of two events. Here, an *altitude classified* event is thrown if
AltStatus is defined to be either Above or Below. If not, the AltLostEvt event
is thrown. In the assignment equation for AltStatus, two new constructs, throw
and catch, are used for the generation and consumption of events. The evaluation of throw(evt,e) produces the value e, and causes event evt to be generated in the next time step. An event remains active for only a single step and
catch(evt,e) returns true if the event evt is active at the current step and
e evaluates to true. Therefore throw is an expression with side-effects, clearly
a conceptual departure from the data flow model of Lustre. The event/action

```
grammar lustre_statevar ;
import lustre, lustre_tables, lustre_equals ;
inh attr inStateVar  :: Boolean occurs on Cases ;
inh attr defaultExpr :: Expr occurs on Cases ;

prod stateVar eq::Equation ::= id::Id type::Type init::Expr cs::Cases
{ cs.defaultExpr = pre(idref(id)) ; cs.inStateVar = true ;
  cs.errors = cs.errors ++ ... ; /* ensure init has correct type */
  forwards to equation(id, follow(init, cs.ifexpr)); }
prod casesOne cs::Cases ::= val::Expr cond::Expr
 { cs.errors = if cs.inStateVar then "" else "Error: Missing OTHERWISE clause";
   cs.ifexpr = ifthenelse(cond, val, cs.defaultExpr) ; }
aspect prod equals e::Expr ::= cs::Cases { cs.inStateVar = false; }
aspect prod casesCons cs::Cases ::= val::Expr cond::Expr cs1::Cases
 { cs1.defaultExpr = cs.defaultExpr ; cs1.inStateVar = cs.inStateVar ; }
```

Fig. 9. The Silver specification of the state variable extension

specification style can simplify some specifications and is an important feature
in languages like Statechart.

The specification using events above can be translated to pure-Mini-Lustre in
which events are translated into Boolean variables. A **throw** forwards to its second argument and a **catch** forwards to the conjunction of the Boolean variable
of the named event and its second argument. An equation for each new Boolean
variable is also generated by combining the conditions of the if-then-else constructs that enclose all **throw** constructs of the corresponding event. Below is
the equation generated for **AltClassEvt**.

```
AltClassEvt = false -> (pre(AltRcvEvt) && pre(C1)) ||
    (!(pre(AltRcvEvt) && pre(C1)) && (pre(AltRcvEvt) && pre(C2)) ;
```

The attribute grammar specification to create the above equation is not trivial
but is more verbose than it is complex. Essentially an inherited attribute of type
Expr is used to pass down the conditions of enclosing if-then-else constructs to
each **throw** construct. A synthesized attribute is used to compute the disjunction
of these expressions. Thus, the two **throw** constructs in the example correspond
to the disjunction of two expressions in its translation. The generation of these
equations requires a global transformation beyond the capabilities of macro-
based approaches. Due to space constraints the Silver implementation of events
is not shown.

3.5   Scenario Implementations

Silver has a flexible module system based on the **grammar** declarations seen in
the specifications above. Silver **import** statements can be used to easily compose
new and extended languages from these named grammars.

For Scenario 1, the desired language is created by composing the host language module **lustre** and language extension modules **lustre_tables** and
lustre_equals by the Silver specification in Fig. 10. The Silver tools read this

to build the attribute grammar for the specified language from the imported host and extensions. The import ... including syntax statement performs two functions. First it imports all the definitions of the attribute grammar constructs (productions, attributes, etc.) from the named module. These are used in the attribute grammar evaluation phase to perform error checking and translations as specified by the attributes. Second, the including syntax clause also add the concrete syntax specifications defined in the imported module. The specifications of the concrete syntax are given to a parser and scanner generator to build the parser and scanner for the extended language. In the specifications above we have not shown these as they are done in a traditional manner.

Many language extensions, including the tables, equals, state variable, and event extensions presented here are such that they can be automatically composed with other extensions to create, for example, the scenario1 language above. This means that no attribute grammar "glue" code needs to be written to compose the host language and the language extensions. In this case, the Silver specification above can be automatically generated from the list of extensions selected by the user.

```
grammar scenario1 ;
import lustre
  including syntax ;
import lustre_tables
  including syntax ;
import lustre_equals
  including syntax ;
```

Fig. 10. Scenario 1

For the second scenario, we create a new language that does not use the node construct of Mini-Lustre but replaces it with a simple module system for collecting state variables. This is similar to RSML^{-e} but is a smaller language meant to only demonstrate how new languages can be created in the framework. This is easily accomplished by a Silver specification that imports the lustre, lustre_statevar, lustre_tables, and lustre_equals modules, but uses a syntax hiding clause to block the importation of the concrete productions for nodes and equations from the host specification lustre. This specification also defines concrete syntax for a module construct that consists of a sequence of state variables. The abstract production for this module construct forwards to the expected translation in the host language Mini-Lustre. Space limitations prevent showing this specification, but the key point is that a new language is defined by hiding aspects of the host language and replacing them with the desired new ones.

4   Discussion

4.1   Related Work

Tools and techniques for language extensibility and modularity have been studied extensively in the area of programming languages and thus the description here is necessarily cursory. In the framework we have described, language extensions can define new language constructs, new semantic analyses on the extension-defined and host language-defined constructs, and translations to new target languages. There are existing tools and techniques that support each of these types of language extension, but no single approach supports them all. Closely related are various macro approaches, such as syntactic, hygienic, and programmable [13] macro systems. These allow new constructs to be defined but do not support semantic analysis of the new constructs.

There has also been a considerable amount of work on language modularity, *e.g.*, [14,15], from the perspective of attribute grammars. Higher-order functions as attributes provide the inspiration for some in seeking modular specifications, *e.g.*, [16], while object-oriented concepts of inheritance and objects motivate others, *e.g.*, [17]. Silver builds on much of this work and incorporates, for example, higher-order attributes [18]. Also of interest are Hedin's re-writable reference attribute grammars [19] in which a mechanism for rewriting the abstract syntax tree based on rewrite-rules is used. There, attributes are only retrieved from the rewritten tree; this differs from forwarding, which allows attributes to be retrieved from the original tree and the forwarded-to tree. This is critical for extensions like tables where we must do error checking on the original tree but want to get attributes for translations to target languages from the forwarded-to tree. Microsoft's Intentional Programming system (IP) [20] is the most closely related system to the extensible language framework used in this paper.

5   Conclusion

Silver was developed for building extensible languages based on attribute grammars with forwarding. It is a full-featured attribute grammar specification language with higher-order attributes [18], forwarding [9], a module system, polymorphic lists, and pattern-matching; it is freely available on the internet at `www.melt.cs.umn.edu`. We have used it to build an extensible versions of Java 1.4 called the Java Language Extender [21] and several modular extensions. One embeds the domain-specific language SQL into Java for static syntax and type checking of SQL queries; another adds general-purpose features such as algebraic data-types and pattern matching.

For users of synchronous languages, we can provide a flexible modeling language framework that allows a rich variety of modeling language features to be used. In the work presented here, we have showed how constructs such as condition tables, state variables, and events can be easily added to a host modeling language in a modular way. Note that these are not just lightweight syntactic extensions that do some error checking. Both the tables and the events extensions do a considerable amount of code transformation and manipulation to generate the host language constructs that they translate to via forwarding. The analysis and manipulation rely heavily on the expressive nature of attribute grammars.

We are currently building a much more complete implementation of Lustre and RSML^{-e} in this framework and exploring the feasibility of building higher-level abstractions as language extensions. It is our belief that a well-developed extensible language framework can be built that allows researchers and practitioners to more freely explore the wide range of possible language features that will help to more effectively specify software systems and ultimately make formal methods more appealing to a wider audience.

References

1. Berry, G., Gonthier, G.: The Esterel synchronous programming language: Design, semantics, implementation. Science of Comp. Prog. **19**(2) (1992) 87–152
2. Esterel-Technologies: Corporate web page. www.esterel-technologies.com (2004)
3. Harel, D., Lachover, H., Naamad, A., Pnueli, A., Politi, M., Sherman, R., Shtull-Trauring, A., Trakhtenbrot, M.: Statemate: A working environment for the development of complex reactive systems. IEEE Trans. on Soft. Engin. **16**(4) (1990)
4. Heitmeyer, C., Bull, A., Gasarch, C., Labaw, B.: SCR*: A toolset for specifying and analyzing requirements. In: Proceedings of the Tenth Annual Conference on Computer Assurance, COMPASS 95. (1995)
5. Thompson, J.M., Heimdahl, M.P., Miller, S.P.: Specification based prototyping for embedded systems. In: Seventh ACM SIGSOFT Symposium on the Foundations on Software Engineering. Volume 1687 of LNCS. (1999)
6. Van Wyk, E., Heimdahl, M.: Flexibility in modeling languages and tools: A call to arms. In: Proc. of IEEE ISoLA Workshop on Leveraging Applications of Formal Methods, Verification, and Validation. (2005)
7. Halbwachs, N., Caspi, P., Raymond, P., Pilaud, D.: The synchronous dataflow programming language Lustre. Proc. of the IEEE **79**(9) (1991) 1305–1320
8. Halbwachs, N., Lagnier, F., Ratel, C.: Programming and verifying real-time systems by means of the synchronous data-flow language lustre. IEEE Transactions on Software Engineering (1992) 785–793
9. Van Wyk, E., de Moor, O., Backhouse, K., Kwiatkowski, P.: Forwarding in attribute grammars for modular language design. In: Proc. 11th Intl. Conf. on Compiler Construction. Volume 2304 of LNCS. (2002) 128–142
10. Heninger, K.: Specifying software requirements for complex systems: New techniques and their application. IEEE Trans. on Software Engin. **6**(1) (1980) 2–13
11. Leveson, N., Heimdahl, M., Hildreth, H., Reese, J.: Requirements Specification for Process-Control Systems. IEEE Trans. on Software Engin. **20**(9) (1994) 684–706
12. Zimmerman, M.K., Lundqvist, K., Leveson, N.: Investigating the readability of state-based formal requirements specification languages. In: Proc. 24th Intl. Conf. on Software Engineering, ACM Press (2002) 33 – 43
13. Weise, D., Crew, R.: Programmable syntax macros. ACM SIGPLAN Notices **28**(6) (1993)
14. Ganzinger, H.: Increasing modularity and language-independency in automatically generated compilers. Science of Computer Programing **3**(3) (1983) 223–278
15. Kastens, U., Waite, W.M.: Modularity and reusability in attribute grammars. Acta Informatica **31** (1994) 601–627
16. Le Bellec, C., Jourdan, M., Parigot, D., Roussel, G.: Specification and implementation of grammar coupling using attribute grammars. In: Prog. Lang. Impl. and Logic Prog. (PLILP '93). Volume 714 of LNCS. (1993) 123–136
17. Hedin, G.: An object-oriented notation for attribute grammars. In: Proc. of European Conf. on Object-Oriented Prog., ECOOP'89, Cambridge Univ. Press (1989)
18. Vogt, H., Swierstra, S.D., Kuiper, M.F.: Higher-order attribute grammars. In: ACM PLDI Conf. (1990) 131–145
19. Ekman, T., Hedin, G.: Rewritable reference attributed grammars. In: Euro. Conf. on Object-Oriented Prog., ECOOP'04. Volume 3086 of LNCS. (2004) 144–169
20. Simonyi, C.: The future is intentional. IEEE Computer **32**(5) (1999) 56–57
21. Van Wyk, E., Krishnan, L., Bodin, D., Johnson, E.: Adding domain-specific and general purpose language features to Java with the Java language extender. In: Companion to the Proc. OOPSLA. (2006)

Declared Type Generalization Checker: An Eclipse Plug-In for Systematic Programming with More General Types

Markus Bach, Florian Forster, and Friedrich Steimann

Lehrgebiet Programmiersysteme
Fernuniversität in Hagen
D-58084 Hagen
bach.markus@gmx.net, florian.forster@fernuni-hagen.de,
steimann@acm.org

Abstract. The Declared Type Generalization Checker is a plug-in for Eclipse's Java Development Tools (JDT) that supports developers in systematically finding and using better fitting types in their programs. A type A is considered to fit better than a type B for a declaration element (variable) d if A is more general than B, that is, if A provides fewer members unneeded for the use of d. Our support comes in the form of warnings generated in the Problem View of Eclipse, and associated Quick Fixes allowing elements to be re-declared automatically. Due to the use of Eclipse extension points, the algorithm used to compute more general types is easily exchangeable. Currently our tool can use two publicly available algorithms, one considering only supertypes already present in a project, and one computing new, perfectly fitting types.

1 The Problem: Too Strong Coupling Due to Overly Specific Types

A class C is coupled to a type B if one or more declaration elements of C (i.e., fields, formal parameters, local variables, or methods with non-void return types) are declared with B as their type. Even though coupling between types cannot be eliminated completely (because without any coupling a type would be isolated from the rest of the system and therefore useless [1]), there is often a certain amount of unnecessary coupling which can be reduced in many cases by using a more general type than B. In fact, unnecessary coupling between C and B arises when a declaration element d in C is declared with B as its type and B offers more members than actually needed by d. In [2] we have shown that developers rarely use the best fitting type available in a program for typing declaration elements, and that by introducing new, better fitting types unnecessary coupling can be reduced to a minimum. However, we believe that developers cannot be blamed for not using more general types in a project as long as proactive tool support for indicating where which types can be used is lacking: programmers tend to think of their objects more in terms of the classes from which they

M.B. Dwyer and A. Lopes (Eds.): FASE 2007, LNCS 4422, pp. 117–120, 2007.

are instantiated, and less in terms of the generalizations they posses (which are often unknown, or at least not known to be useable in a given context).

2 The Solution: The Declared Type Generalization Checker

To support developers in becoming aware of — and in using — more general types, we implemented a tool, called the Declared Type Generalization Checker, as a plug-in for the Eclipse Java Development Tools (JDT) [6, 7][1]. This plug-in provides a new type of warning for the Problem View, which informs developers of unnecessary coupling arising from overly specific declaration elements (i.e., elements declared with types providing more members than actually needed). At the same time, the plug-in extends Eclipse's Quick Fixes by one that lets programmers re-declare elements with better fitting types. To compute these types and to perform the re-declaration, currently one out of two available algorithms for type generalization (and their associated refactorings) can be selected in the project properties tab of the plug-in.

2.1 Generation of Warnings

The Declared Type Generalization Checker is implemented as a builder that, if activated in a project's properties, is automatically started after each compilation of the project. Since compilation in Eclipse is itself implemented as a builder, the Declared Type Generalization Checker can take advantage of Eclipse's incremental build process — in particular, after a change only the compilation units affected by that change are rebuilt. This helps shorten checking times considerably (cf. Section 3).

The builder visits each declaration element of a compilation unit and invokes the algorithm selected for checking for possible generalizations (see Section 4). The results of each check are communicated to the IDE using its standard interface for builders.

2.2 Provision of Quick Fixes

With each warning a Quick Fix can be associated that triggers a refactoring introducing a more general type (thus resolving the warning). Whether such a Quick Fix exists depends on the algorithm chosen to generate the warning, which is selected in the project property settings. Currently, two such algorithms are available.

2.3 Algorithms Computing More General Types

For every project, the programmer can choose the algorithm the checker uses to generate the warnings. Currently, the available algorithms are the standard algorithms delivered with their corresponding refactorings, which also provide the Quick Fixes.

Generalize Declared Type. Generalize Declared Type is a standard refactoring of Eclipse distributed with JDT. After invocation of the refactoring on a declaration element d the developer is presented the type hierarchy for the declared type of d. In

---

[1] http://www.eclipse.org

this hierarchy, every supertype that can be used in the declaration of d (because it includes all members required from d) is highlighted and can be selected as the new type of d. Note that this refactoring does not necessarily reduce coupling to a theoretical minimum, as the new type may still contain excessive members, and the perfect generalization may not (yet) have been introduced (and therefore is not among the presented supertypes). Nevertheless, as [2] has shown, even if generalizations are available in a project, they are often not used.

Our Declared Type Generalization Checker uses the type inference algorithm employed by Generalize Declared Type to check whether a more general type is available (the basis for a warning); also, it launches the refactoring itself as the corresponding Quick Fix.

Infer Type. So-called type inference can compute type annotations for program elements independently of whether or how they are actually typed [3–5]. We designed our own type inference algorithm for Java [4] specifically to compute the most general type that can be used for a declaration element, and this independently of the types that already exist. Our algorithm is the basis of a new refactoring, called Infer Type[2], which can be characterized as an automatic version of the Extract Interface refactoring distributed with Eclipse's JDT and other Java IDEs. Since the types computed by Infer Type are always maximally general (meaning that no member can be removed without causing a static type error), types using only inferred types for their declaration elements are always maximally decoupled.

The type inference algorithm underlying Infer Type is used by our Declared Type Generalization Checker as an alternative to that of Generalize Declared Type in exactly the same way as described above.

3   Performance Evaluation

Checking every declaration element of a program for the availability of a more general type is a time-consuming task. To get an impression of how the systematic search for type generalizations influences the development cycle, we performed the measurements summarized in the following table.

PROJECT	NUMBER OF DECLARATION ELEMENTS	ALGORITHM			
		Generalize Declared Type		*Infer Type*	
		time	*warnings*	*time*	*warnings*
JUnit 3.8.1	1501	≈ 3.5 mins	205	≈ 8 mins	315
JHotDraw 6.0b1	7788	≈ 42 mins	1230	–	–

These times (obtained on a ThinkPad run at 2 GHz) may appear unacceptable, especially for Infer Type, but since they refer to full builds, they rarely occur in practice. What we found instead is that for average change/build cycles, the overhead incurred by the Declared Type Generalization Checker is reasonable. As for Infer Type, we hope to be able to present a more efficient implementation soon (see Section 5).

---

[2] http://www.fernuni-hagen.de/ps/prjs/InferType/

4 Extending the Declared Type Generalization Checker

As mentioned above, the algorithm used to compute more general types for declaration elements is variable. In fact, our tool accommodates further extensions, by allowing one to add other algorithms and refactorings. The corresponding extension point requires implementations of three methods, namely `boolean check-Type(...)`, `boolean hasResolution()`, and `IMarkerResolution2 getResolution()`. The first, `checkType`, answers for a given declaration element and its declared type whether a better matching type exists so that a corresponding warning can be generated. If it does, `hasResolution` tells the plug-in whether the extension can also offer a Quick Fix to resolve the issue (which is the case for both extensions currently in offered). If so, the method `getResolution` delivers an object that, through its `run` method, redeclares the declaration element in question (in the current extensions by starting a refactoring).

5 Availability

The Declared Type Generalization Checker can be installed from the update site http://www.fernuni-hagen.de/ps/prjs/DTGC/update/. It depends on the availability of the Generalize Declared Type refactoring (which is part of the standard distribution) and optionally also that of Infer Type (which is part of the Yoxos[3] distribution, but can also be installed separately from the link given in Footnote 2).

We are currently working on a new implementation of Infer Type that utilizes Eclipse's type constraint framework and that can handle Java generics. Once available, it will be offered as an alternative extension to our Declared Type Generalization Checker.

References

1. E Berard *Essays on Object-Oriented Software Engineering* (Prentice-Hall 1993).
2. F Forster "Cost and benefit of rigorous decoupling with context-specific interfaces" in: *Proceedings of the 4th International Conference on Principles and Practices of Programming in Java* (2006) 23–30.
3. J Palsberg, MI Schwartzbach "Object-oriented type inference" in: *Proceedings of OOPSLA* (1991) 146–161.
4. F Steimann, P Mayer, A Meißner "Decoupling classes with inferred interfaces" in: *Proceedings of the 2006 ACM Symposium on Applied Computing* (2006) 1404–1408.
5. T Wang, SF Smith "Precise constraint-based type inference for JAVA" in: *Proceedings of ECOOP* (2001) 99–117.
6. D Bäumer, E Gamma, A Kiezun "Integrating refactoring support into a Java development tool" in: *OOPSLA'01 Companion* (2001).
7. E Gamma, K Beck *Contributing to Eclipse* (Addison-Wesley Professional 2003).

---

[3] www.yoxos.com

S2A: A Compiler for Multi-modal UML Sequence Diagrams*

David Harel, Asaf Kleinbort, and Shahar Maoz

The Weizmann Institute of Science
{dharel,asaf.kleinbort,shahar.maoz}@weizmann.ac.il

Abstract. We report on S2A, a compiler that translates Modal UML Sequence Diagrams (MSDs), a UML-compliant version of Live Sequence Charts (LSCs), into AspectJ code. It thus provides full code generation of reactive behavior from visual inter-object scenario-based specifications. The S2A compiler is based on a compilation scheme presented by Maoz and Harel in [13].

1 Introduction

An important challenge of the inter-object, scenario-based approach to software specification is to find ways to construct executable systems based on it [3]. Many researchers have dealt with this challenge as a synthesis problem; see, e.g., [4,10,15], where inter-object specifications, given in variants of Message Sequence Charts (MSC) [9], are translated into intra-object state-based executable specifications for each of the participating objects. "Play-out" [8] is a recent example of a different approach. Instead of synthesizing intra-object state-based specifications for each of the objects, the play-out algorithm executes scenarios directly, keeping track of all user and system events for all objects simultaneously, and causing other events and actions to occur as dictated by the specified scenarios. No intra-object model for any of the participating components is built in the process. Play-out was defined for Live Sequence Charts (LSCs) [2,7], a rich extension of MSC that supports multi-modal scenario specifications.

In this paper we present S2A, a compiler that implements the play-out execution mechanism by translating inter-object scenario-based specifications, given in a variant of LSC that is UML-compliant — Modal Sequence Diagrams (MSD) — into AspectJ code. S2A is based on a compilation scheme presented by Maoz and Harel in [13]. It exploits the inherent similarity between the scenario-based approach and the aspect-oriented approach to software specification — in both, part of the system's behavior is specified in a way that explicitly crosses the boundaries between objects — and takes advantage of the similar unification semantics of play-out and AspectJ pointcuts. We consider S2A a significant step towards realizing the promise of visual scenario-based programming within real world software engineering.

---

* This research was supported by The John von Neumann Minerva Center for the Development of Reactive Systems at the Weizmann Institute of Science.

Section 2 very briefly reviews the MSD language, the play-out execution mechanism, and the compilation scheme; Section 3 concludes with a short discussion and future work directions.

2   Overview of S2A

MSD and LSC. The language of Modal Sequence Diagrams (MSD) is a visual formalism for scenario-based inter-object specifications, defined as proper UML profile that extends UML 2 Interactions [14] with a <<modal>> stereotype consisting of two attributes: *mode* and *execution mode*. Each element in an MSD interaction, e.g., a message, a constraint, has a *mode* attribute which can be either *hot* (universal) or *cold* (existential), and an *execution mode*, which can be either *monitor* or *execute*. MSD is a more standardized and slightly generalized version of Live Sequence Charts (LSC) [2] (i.e., in MSD, monitoring and execution are not divided into pre-charts and main-charts, *mode* and *execution mode* are orthogonal). The semantics of MSD is based on that of LSC, whose expressive power is comparable to that of various temporal logics [11] (a trace-based semantics for MSD was given in [6] using alternating Büchi automata). Thus, MSD allows not only to specify traces that "may happen", "must happen", or "should never happen", but also to divide the responsibility for execution between the environment, the participating objects, and the coordination mechanism. MSD notation is adopted from LSC: hot (resp. cold) elements are colored in red (resp. blue), execution (resp. monitoring) elements use solid (resp. dashed) line.

MSD Play-Out. MSD play-out is based on LSC play-out, presented by Harel and Marelly in [8][1]. Roughly, the execution mechanism reacts to events that are referenced in one or more of the MSDs; for each active MSD, instantiated following the occurrence of a minimal event in the partial-order induced by the diagram, the mechanism checks whether the event is enabled with regard to the current cut; if it is, it advances the cut accordingly; if it is violating and the current cut is cold (a cut is cold if all its elements are cold and is hot otherwise), it discards this active MSD copy; if it is violating and the current cut is hot, program execution aborts; if the event does not appear in the MSD, it is ignored. Conditions are evaluated as soon as they are enabled in a cut; if a condition evaluates to true, the cut advances accordingly; if it evaluates to false and the current cut is cold, the MSD copy is discarded; if it evaluates to false and the current cut it hot, program execution aborts. If the cut of an active MSD copy reaches maximal locations on all lifelines, the active MSD is discarded. Once all MSD's cuts have been updated, the execution mechanism chooses an event to execute from among the execution-enabled methods that are not violating any chart, if any.

Play-out requires careful event unification and dynamic binding mechanism. Roughly, two methods are unifiable if their senders (receivers) are concrete

---

[1] For a thorough definition of the LSC language and its operational semantics we refer the reader to [7].

instance-level (or already bound) and equal, or symbolic class-level of the same class and at least one is still unbound. When methods with arguments are considered, an additional condition requires that corresponding arguments have equal concrete values, or that at least one of them is free[2]. To implement this, S2A exploits the similarity between the unification semantics of play-out and that of AOP.

The Compilation Scheme. We briefly review the compilation scheme (see [13] for details). S2A translates each MSD into a *Scenario Aspect*, implemented in AspectJ. The Scenario Aspect simulates an alternating Büchi automaton whose states represent possible MSD cut states and whose transitions are triggered by aspect pointcuts. Each Scenario Aspect is locally responsible for listening to relevant events and advancing its cut accordingly. To construct the automaton, S2A statically analyzes the MSD by simulating a 'run' that captures all possible cuts; each cut is represented by a state; transitions correspond to enabled events.

In addition, and most importantly, S2A generates a single *coordinator* aspect, which collects cut state information (sets of enabled and violating events, including dynamic context, i.e., bound objects, arguments values) from all active scenario aspects, and, as necessary, uses a *strategy* (see below) to choose a method for execution. It then executes it using inter-type declarations inside generated wrapper methods.

The *strategy* is responsible for choosing the next method to execute, based on the information collected by the *coordinator*. S2A installation includes a default play-out strategy that implements basic (naïve) play-out (arbitrarily choosing a non-violating method from among the currently enabled methods). The user can implement a new strategy (by implementing the `IPlayOutStrategy` interface) and point the compiler to it in the compiler's configuration file.

3 Conclusions and Future Work

We presented S2A, a compiler for multi-modal UML Sequence Diagrams. S2A currently supports the following MSD language features: hot/cold (universal/existential) method calls and conditions, symbolic lifelines (class hierarchies and interfaces), symbolic, exact, and opaque method arguments, dynamic creation of objects, control structures (if-then-else, bounded and unbounded loops, switch-case), and (one step) anti-scenarios.

While we concentrate on scenario-based program *construction*, S2A can also be used for scenario-based *testing* of Java programs in general. This includes test execution and monitoring, similar to that implemented by tools such as the Rhapsody TestConductor [12]. No prior assumptions on the Java program under test are necessary.

We are continuing to develop S2A in a number of directions. First, the compilation scheme can be easily modified to generate code in aspect languages other than AspectJ (e.g., AspectC++) or extensions of AspectJ (e.g., TraceMatch [1]),

---

[2] The formal definitions of unification for LSCs can be found in [7].

possibly taking advantage of specific AOP features we have not yet exploited (e.g., aspect instantiation). This will create opportunities for code optimization as well as for widening the applicability of our approach to other application domains (e.g., embedded systems). Second, we are planning to implement better play-out strategies, such as *Smart Play-Out* [5], which uses model-checking to reduce nondeterminism in LSC execution. Third, we are enhancing the compiler with scenario-aware debugging capabilities (e.g., supporting breakpoints at the scenario's cut-state level).

UML models, source and generated code, executables of case studies, installation guide, as well as other resources, are available online at the S2A website: `http://www.wisdom.weizmann.ac.il/~maozs/s2a/`.

References

1. C. Allan, P. Avgustinov, A. S. Christensen, L. J. Hendren, S. Kuzins, O. Lhoták, O. de Moor, D. Sereni, G. Sittampalam, and J. Tibble. Adding trace matching with free variables to aspectj. In *Proc. 20th Conf. on Object Oriented Programming, Systems, Languages, and Applications (OOPSLA'05)*, pages 345–364, 2005.
2. W. Damm and D. Harel. LSCs: Breathing life into message sequence charts. *Formal Methods in System Design*, 19(1):45–80, 2001.
3. D. Harel. From Play-In Scenarios To Code: An Achievable Dream. *IEEE Computer*, 34(1):53–60, 2001.
4. D. Harel and H. Kugler. Synthesizing state-based object systems from LSC specifications. *Int. J. of Foundations of Comp. Science (IJFCS)*, 13(1):5–51, Feb. 2002.
5. D. Harel, H. Kugler, R. Marelly, and A. Pnueli. Smart Play-Out of Behavioral Requirements. In *Proc. 4th Int. Conf. on Formal Methods in Comp.-Aided Design (FMCAD'02), Portland, Or.*, volume 2517 of *LNCS*, pages 378–398, 2002.
6. D. Harel and S. Maoz. Assert and Negate Revisited: Modal Semantics for UML Sequence Diagrams. In *Proc. 5th Int. Workshop on Scenarios and State-Machines (SCESM'06) at the 28th Int. Conf. on Soft. Eng. (ICSE'06)*, Shanghai, 2006.
7. D. Harel and R. Marelly. *Come, Let's Play: Scenario-Based Programming Using LSCs and the Play-Engine*. Springer-Verlag, 2003.
8. D. Harel and R. Marelly. Specifying and executing behavioral requirements: the play-in/play-out approach. *Software and System Modeling*, 2(2):82–107, 2003.
9. ITU. International Telecommunication Union Recommendation Z.120: Message Sequence Charts. Technical report, 1996.
10. I. Krüger, R. Grosu, P. Scholz, and M. Broy. From MSCs to Statecharts. In F. J. Rammig, editor, *DIPES*, volume 155 of *IFIP Proc.*, pages 61–72. Kluwer, 1998.
11. H. Kugler, D. Harel, A. Pnueli, Y. Lu, and Y. Bontemps. Temporal Logic for Scenario-Based Specifications. In N. Halbwachs and L. D. Zuck, editors, *TACAS*, volume 3440 of *LNCS*, pages 445–460. Springer, 2005.
12. M. Lettrari and J. Klose. Scenario-based monitoring and testing of real-time UML models. In *Proc. 4th Int. Conf. on The UML*, Toronto, October 2001.
13. S. Maoz and D. Harel. From Multi-Modal Scenarios to Code: Compiling LSCs into AspectJ. In *Proc. 14th Int. Symp. Foundations of Software Engineering (FSE-14)*, Portland, Oregon, November 2006.
14. UML. Unified Modeling Language Superstructure Spec., v2.0. OMG, August 2005.
15. J. Whittle, R. Kwan, and J. Saboo. From scenarios to code: An air traffic control case study. *Software and System Modeling*, 4(1):71–93, 2005.

Scenario-Driven Dynamic Analysis
of Distributed Architectures

George Edwards, Sam Malek, and Nenad Medvidovic

Computer Science Department
University of Southern California
Los Angeles, CA 90089-0781
{gedwards, malek, neno}@usc.edu

Abstract. Software architecture constitutes a promising approach to the development of large-scale distributed systems, but architecture description languages (ADLs) and their associated architectural analysis techniques suffer from several important shortcomings. This paper presents a novel approach that reconceptualizes ADLs within the model-driven engineering (MDE) paradigm to address their shortcomings. Our approach combines extensible modeling languages based on architectural constructs with a model interpreter framework that enables rapid implementation of customized dynamic analyses at the architectural level. Our approach is demonstrated in XTEAM, a suite of ADL extensions and model transformation engines targeted specifically for highly distributed, resource-constrained, and mobile computing environments. XTEAM model transformations generate system simulations that provide a dynamic, scenario- and risk-driven view of the executing system. This information allows an architect to compare architectural alternatives and weigh trade-offs between multiple design goals, such as system performance, reliability, and resource consumption. XTEAM provides the extensibility to easily accommodate both new modeling language features and new architectural analyses.

1 Introduction

Many modern-day software systems are targeted for highly distributed, resource-constrained, and mobile computing environments. In addition to the difficulties inherent in traditional distributed system development, such as unpredictable network latencies and security concerns, this new environment forces software developers to cope with additional sources of complexity. For example, developers must assume an inherently unstable and unpredictable network topology; they must elevate resource utilization concerns to the forefront of design decisions; and they must take application power consumption profiles into account.

As the complexity associated with software development has increased in this new setting, software engineers have sought novel ways to represent, reason about, and synthesize large-scale distributed systems. The field of *software architecture* has advanced new principles and guidelines for composing the key properties of such systems [1]. In many cases, the concepts and paradigms developed through research in software architecture have drastically altered the way developers conceptualize

M.B. Dwyer and A. Lopes (Eds.): FASE 2007, LNCS 4422, pp. 125–139, 2007.

software systems. For example, in an effort to raise the level of abstraction used for describing large-scale distributed systems above the object-oriented constructs provided by previous software modeling technologies, such as UML 1.x, researchers have attempted to create architecture description languages (ADLs) and associated toolsets that provide the system modeler with higher-level architectural constructs. ADLs endeavor to capture the crucial design decisions that determine the ultimate capabilities, properties, and qualities of a software system [2]. ADL-based representations can be leveraged throughout the software development process for communication and documentation, examination and analysis, validation and testing, and refinement and evolution.

However, the software architecture community has struggled to invent modeling technologies that are semantically powerful as well as flexible and intuitive. ADLs have generally either focused on structural elements (to the detriment of other important system characteristics) or have relied on rigid formalisms that have a narrow vocabulary and cumbersome syntax [3]. The result is that, for many domains (including the mobile systems domain), crucial aspects of a system are not expressible in any of the existing ADLs. As just one example, power usage characteristics, while integral to mobile and embedded systems, are completely ignored by prominent ADLs.

In parallel with (and largely unaffected by) these developments, model-driven engineering (MDE) has emerged as a promising approach to distributed software system development that combines domain-specific modeling languages (DSMLs) with model transformers, analyzers, and generators [4]. DSMLs codify the concepts and relationships relevant in a particular domain as first-class modeling elements [6]. DSMLs also provide multiple model views and specify domain rules that define model validity (*i.e.*, well-formedness). Model transformers, analyzers, and generators examine and manipulate models to create useful artifacts such as component specifications and implementations, supplementary views of the system, or descriptions of emergent behavior.

The work described in this paper leverages the respective strengths of ADLs (*i.e.*, high-level, architectural description) and MDE (*i.e.*, domain-specific extensibility and model transformation) in support of a novel, scenario-driven approach to the modeling and analysis of distributed software architectures.

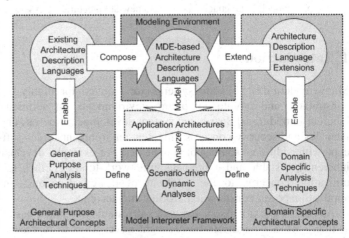

Fig. 1. Software architecture in the model-driven engineering context

Our approach combines extensible modeling languages based on architectural constructs with a model interpreter[1] framework that enables rapid implementation of customized dynamic analyses at the architectural level. The analyses provide statistical data quantifying emergent behaviors and cross-cutting system properties (*e.g.*, end-to-end latencies and system-wide power consumption).

In this manner, an architect can compare architectural alternatives and weigh trade-offs between multiple design goals. In particular, during the early design stages, a software architect can target high-risk events by modeling scenarios that represent unusual or dangerous conditions (*e.g.*, extremely heavy loading). The artifacts produced by our approach can be leveraged by an architect during other stages of the development cycle, as well. For example, during system maintenance and evolution, our approach can be used to assess the impact of modifications to the system (*e.g.*, replacing components with newer versions). A high-level view of the overall approach is shown in Figure 1.

Our initial study of the approach targets software development in distributed, resource-constrained, and mobile computing environments, which is a setting that presents significant challenges for software architects. To demonstrate the approach, we have developed the eXtensible Tool-chain for Evaluation of Architectural Models (XTEAM). XTEAM provides ADL extensions for mobile software systems and implements a corresponding set of dynamic analyses on top of a reusable model interpreter framework. Architectural models that conform to the XTEAM ADL are constructed in an off-the-shelf meta-programmable modeling environment. XTEAM model translators transform these architectural models into executable simulations that furnish measurements and views of the executing system over time.

In order for our approach to be successful, it must fulfill two key requirements:

R1: the language should be extensible to accommodate new domain-specific concepts and concerns as needed.

R2: the provided tool support should be flexible to allow rapid implementation of new architectural analysis techniques that take advantage of domain-specific language extensions.

This paper is organized as follows: Section 2 provides an overview of related work in software architecture and MDE. Section 3 describes how our approach reconceptualizes architectural description and analysis techniques in the MDE paradigm. Section 4 describes our complete tool-chain in detail in order to demonstrate the overall approach. In Section 5, we provide a discussion of the salient aspects of our work. We conclude the paper by summarizing and discussing future directions of this research effort.

2   Related Work

The approach described in this paper builds on previous projects and advancements in software architecture and model-driven engineering. However, our approach and associated tool-chain, XTEAM, exhibit several key differences from previous work.

---

[1] We use the term "interpreter" to denote a custom-built component that utilizes and manipulates models in order to perform functions such as transformation and analysis.

So that we may better illustrate these differences, this section provides an overview of related projects in software architecture and MDE. In Section 3, we examine more closely how our approach addresses the shortcomings of and represents an improvement over related techniques and technologies.

2.1 Model-Driven Engineering

The flexible nature of MDE has made it a suitable approach for representing different and arbitrarily complex concerns across a wide spectrum of application domains. Although a number of previous works have applied MDE to the analysis and synthesis of distributed and embedded software systems [5, 6, 9], they have either done so at a finer level of granularity than the system's software

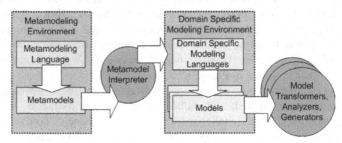

Fig. 2. High-level view of the model-driven engineering process as implemented in GME

architectural constructs, or have been tied to a particular implementation platform or analysis engine. While such approaches are very useful in specific contexts, they do not leverage the concepts and paradigms developed by the software architecture community in their modeling languages, and do not provide a framework that allows rapid implementation of customized analyses. Below we provide a brief overview of the most notable MDE projects related to our work.

Generic Modeling Environment. The MDE paradigm is realized via the appropriate tool support. One of the most widely used MDE tools is the Generic Modeling Environment (GME) [8]. GME is a meta-programmable, graphical modeling environment that enables the creation of domain-specific modeling languages (DSMLs) and models that conform to those DSMLs, as shown in Figure 2. GME also provides interfaces for custom-built components (*i.e.*, model interpreters) to access the information captured in models in order to conduct analysis or synthesize useful artifacts. To demonstrate the approach described in this paper, we have implemented a significant portion of XTEAM in GME.

MILAN. MILAN [6] comprises a DSML for embedded systems based on a dataflow representation, and a set of model translators that generate executable specifications for simulation engines. The dataflow formalism consists of nodes connected by directed edges. Functional, performance, and power simulations can all be generated from a single system model. MILAN also enables automated synthesis of software implementations from system models. While MILAN enables highly accurate simulations, the modeling language requires the developer to build system models using low-level constructs. As noted earlier, the MILAN language is based on a hierarchical dataflow representation. This is an appropriate formalism for signal processing systems, but is not sufficient for large-scale distributed architectures.

Attempting to build and maintain the model of such a system using dataflow can quickly become unmanageable and overwhelming. In contrast, the high-level structural and behavioral abstractions employed by ADLs allow the construction, review, and maintenance of large, complex models with reduced effort and potential for error.

WML and CUTS. The Workload Modeling Language (WML) is another DSML that enables dynamic analysis of component-based architectures [9]. WML allows the modeler to create descriptions of the resource utilization patterns of components for the purpose of evaluating system-wide quality-of-service (QoS) properties. WML models can be automatically transformed into the XML-based inputs required by the Component Workload Emulator Utilization Test Suite (CUTS). WML is tightly coupled to CUTS and requires that models be specified in terms of emulator constructs. The WML model interpreter performs a syntactic translation (from graphical models to XML) rather than a semantic translation (from architectural constructs to simulation constructs). Furthermore, the analysis provided by WML and CUTS is implemented in the emulator engine, rather than in the model interpreter, so the implementation of new analysis techniques would require *changes to* the infrastructure, rather than *utilization of* the infrastructure. Finally, WML does not capture component behavior in a generalized way that permits the representation of complex control flow paths.

2.2 Software Architecture

In this section, we examine two works that are relevant to XTEAM: Finite State Processes (FSP) [16], and xADL [7]. FSP is related to XTEAM because it is a modeling notation used to capture the behavior of software architectures; xADL is related because it is an *extensible* ADL. A number of other well-known ADLs provide some sort of static analysis capability; their relationship to XTEAM is considered in Section 3.

xADL. The eXtensible Architecture Description Language (xADL) was developed as a response to the proliferation of proposed ADLs, each of which had a different focus and addressed different architectural concerns. It was (correctly) observed that no single ADL could anticipate the needs of a wide variety of projects and domains. Consequently, the xADL language is inherently extensible and can be enhanced to support new domain-specific concepts. The language is defined by XML schemas; a "core" schema specifies standard architectural constructs common to all ADLs, while "extension" schemas — written by domain experts and tailored to the needs of specific projects — specify new modeling elements as needed. While xADL represents a promising step towards the flexibility and customizability required by contemporary large-scale distributed systems development, xADL's focus is primarily architectural representation rather than analysis, simulation, or the generation of implementation/configuration/deployment artifacts. xADL's supporting toolset consists of parsers and other syntactic tools that are semantically agnostic. Therefore, the xADL toolset cannot be extended to enforce semantic consistency within architectural models without modifying the toolset's implementation. This is in contrast to MDE, in which DSMLs ensure the construction of models that conform to domain-specific constraints, while model interpreters provide semantically-aware analysis. The result is that xADL, by itself, does not fully capitalize on the potential of architectural modeling.

FSP. FSP is a modeling notation for capturing the behavior of software architectural constructs in terms of guarded choices, local and conditional processes, action prefixes, and so on. FSP also allows for the construction of composite architectural constructs, in which the behavior of a composed element is defined in terms of the behavior of its constituents. While previous works have leveraged FSP models for analysis and simulation of a system's architecture [16], they have not focused on a number of concerns that are important for distributed systems executing in heterogeneous environments, including the structural aspects of an architecture, its deployment onto physical hosts, or extensibility of the notation.

3 Reconceptualization of ADLs

By recasting the concepts and techniques developed by the software architecture community in a model-driven engineering framework, the benefits of an architecture-based approach to large-scale distributed system development are preserved, while the shortcomings of the approach are diminished. The architecture-based approach to software modeling, and the ADLs that support that approach, suffer from two key drawbacks: inflexible notations with a narrow vocabulary, and supporting tools that enable only a limited set of analyses.

Note that these two drawbacks are the corollary of the requirements stated in Section 1. The hypothesis underlying this research is that these shortcomings can be addressed by representing ADLs (and compositions thereof) via domain-specific modeling languages (DSMLs), and performing architectural analysis via model interpreters. However, to achieve this result, two key challenges must be overcome:

- Development of ADLs, even with the benefit of MDE environments, is inherently challenging and requires both software architecture and metamodeling expertise.
- Implementation of custom-built model interpreters that access the information contained in models to perform architectural analyses requires significant effort.

In this section, we provide an overview of our approach for overcoming the above challenges in order to represent and analyze software architectures via MDE techniques and facilities. In Section 4, the conceptual strategies outlined here are made concrete through a detailed discussion of XTEAM and explanatory examples.

3.1 ADLs as Domain-Specific Modeling Languages

The first step in leveraging the MDE approach for software architecture is to codify ADLs as DSMLs within a MDE framework, such as that provided by GME. However, as mentioned above, the creation of semantically powerful, flexible, and intuitive ADLs is non-trivial; in fact, it requires a great deal of expertise in both software architecture and modeling languages. An ADL developer must command a thorough understanding of the central and elemental concepts in software architecture and must be adept in the mechanisms for codification of those concepts.

To overcome this challenge, we advocate an approach that avoids the creation of ADLs from scratch. Instead, we rely on *ADL composition* (*i.e.*, the combination of constructs from multiple ADLs) and *ADL enhancement* (*i.e.*, the definition of new, customized ADL constructs). MDE technologies capture the concrete syntax of DSMLs through *metamodels*. Once the metamodel for an ADL has been created, the ADL can be manipulated as needed for a given application domain. Thus, the composition and enhancement of ADLs is achieved through composition [10] and enhancement of their corresponding metamodels. Existing notations and languages can be reused to the greatest extent possible, and only incremental additions to the language are created as needed to enable a specific architectural analysis technique. In addition to reducing the burden of language development, this distinction is important for two reasons: (1) existing ADLs are based on well-understood concepts and generally provide formal semantics, which increases model understandability, and (2) utilization of common languages maximizes the potential for reuse of the tool infrastructure (modeling environments and model interpreters) across development projects and domains. Both ADL composition and enhancement are utilized in XTEAM.

ADL composition allows the various concepts and design information expressible in different ADLs to be captured in a single language, which then allows models that conform to the language to be utilized in a variety of ways and at multiple stages of the development cycle. Composition of ADL metamodels is simplified by the fact that most ADLs share a small set of common elements (*i.e.*, components, connectors, interfaces, and so on) [Medvidovic N., et al.: A Classification and Comparison Framework for Software Archite] that serve as the integration point. In Section 4, we describe in detail how features from multiple ADLs are seamlessly integrated in XTEAM.

Some system properties that are not addressed by a general-purpose ADL may be of significant concern for certain application domains. Furthermore, each type of architectural analysis requires certain types of information to be modeled and represented, which may not be supported by a general-purpose ADL. Therefore, ADL enhancement—the ability to incorporate domain-specific concepts via new extensions—is highly valuable in an architectural modeling tool. The metamodeling mechanism provided by GME makes this process straightforward and intuitive: the new information is added to the existing language by creating new elements or new attributes of existing elements. This ADL metamodel enhancement mechanism provides the means through which requirement R1 (stated in Section 1) is satisfied. We will further illustrate the motivation and utility of ADL enhancement through a detailed example in Section 4.

In this way, the mechanisms for language refinement, enhancement, and evolution are built into MDE tool-chains. As a consequence, the notations used can always be modified and the vocabulary expanded. As language extensions are developed, new types of analysis will become possible. In Section 4, we describe how a model transformation framework can be utilized to rapidly implement customized analyses.

3.2 Architectural Analyses as Model Interpreters

Typically, an ADL is accompanied by tool support that is geared specifically to the notations provided by the language, thus only allowing for limited types of analysis. On the other hand, the MDE paradigm advocates flexible tool support, where multiple model interpreters with different analysis capabilities can be utilized. This characteristic is absolutely necessary for reasoning about the varying and evolving concerns of large-scale software systems.

MDE tools, such as GME, provide interfaces for custom-built model interpreters to access and manipulate the information contained in models. However, building these tools from scratch requires significant effort. In many cases, a complex semantic mapping between languages is required that is difficult to define and implement. Such a mapping is required to transform architecture-based models, which are at a very high level of abstraction, into simulation models, which are at a much lower level. For this reason, our approach utilizes a *model interpreter framework* that allows the software architect to rapidly implement custom analysis techniques without knowing the details of complex semantic mappings (*e.g.*, the architecture-to-simulation mapping is achieved by the framework infrastructure "under-the-hood"). The interpreter framework provides "hook" methods for which the architect provides implementations that, taken as a whole, realize a specific analysis technique. The objects available to the architect in the implementation of the analysis technique are the architectural constructs defined in ADL extensions, not low-level simulation constructs. The model interpreter framework, through its "hook" methods, greatly simplifies the development of simulation generators, and thus provides the means through which requirement R2 is satisfied. Section 4 demonstrates the use of the XTEAM model interpreter framework in the implementation of a specific analysis technique.

Analysis techniques may be static or dynamic. Static analysis techniques rely on the formalisms underlying models to provide information about system properties or expose subtle errors without executing the system [11]. Many static analyses attempt to prove the "correctness" of a system, which may be useful in many scenarios, but suffers from the difficulty that system implementation must precisely match the model in order for the analysis to be relevant. Dynamic analysis, on the other hand, attempts to execute model-based architectural representations in order to illuminate their characteristics and behaviors at run-time. Dynamic analysis is more useful for comparing high-level design possibilities early in the development cycle because it does not require that a model be completely faithful to the eventual implementation to remain relevant. Static analysis has an important place in the development of certain types of software systems, but dynamic analysis is more relevant when an architect wishes to understand the system's behavior within the context of specific execution scenarios.

For these reasons, our approach has thus far focused on dynamic analysis through system simulation. Model interpreters synthesize executable specifications that run on a simulation engine. The simulation code is instrumented to record the occurrence of events (*e.g.*, message exchanges and component failures) and measurements of system properties (*e.g.*, observed latencies and memory usage). The results of a simulation run depend heavily on the environmental context (*e.g.*, the load put on the system) and may contain elements of randomness and unpredictability (*e.g.*, the timing of client requests). Consequently, we consider our approach to be *scenario-driven*, in that a given simulation run represents only one possible execution sequence. The software architect should choose the set of scenarios to be simulated to include high-risk situations and boundary conditions. While this simulation-based approach does not provide a formal proof of system behavior, it does allow the architect to rapidly investigate the consequences of fundamental design decisions (*e.g.*, choice of architectural style or deployment architecture) in terms of their impact on non-functional properties (*e.g.*, reliability, performance, or resource utilization).

4   The XTEAM Tool-Chain

In this section, we demonstrate the approach described in Section 3 in the eXtensible Tool-chain for Evaluation of Architectural Models (XTEAM), a model-driven architectural description and simulation environment for distributed, mobile, and resource constrained software systems. XTEAM composes existing, general-purpose ADLs, enhances those ADLs to capture important features of mobile software systems, and implements simulation generators that take advantage of the ADL extensions atop a reusable model interpreter framework.

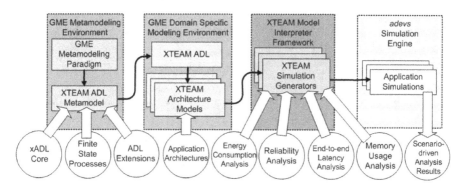

Fig. 3. The eXtensible Toolchain for Evaluation of Architecture Models

A high-level view of XTEAM is shown in Figure 3. Using GME's metamodeling environment, we created an XTEAM ADL metamodel by composing a structural ADL, the xADL Core [7], with a behavioral ADL, FSP [16]. GME uses the XTEAM metamodel to configure a domain-specific modeling environment in which XTEAM architectural models can be created. With this language basis, we were able to implement the XTEAM model interpreter framework, which provides the ability to generate simulations of application architectures that execute in the *adevs* [17] discrete event simulation engine. However, these simulations alone do not implement any architectural analysis techniques. To do so, we enhanced the XTEAM ADL metamodel with language extensions that capture system characteristics relating to energy consumption, reliability, latency, and memory usage, thereby demonstrating the fulfillment of requirement R1. We then utilized the extension mechanisms built into the model interpreter framework in such a way as to generate simulations that measure, analyze, and record the properties of interest, thereby demonstrating the fulfillment of requirement R2. We further elaborate on this process below.

4.1   Composing ADLs and Implementing a Model Interpreter Framework

Using the approach described in Section 3, XTEAM leverages previous work in software architecture through the composition of existing ADLs. We created metamodels for the xADL Core, which defines architectural structures and types common to virtually all ADLs, and FSP, which allows the specification of component behaviors. The integration of these metamodels was straightforward, as they capture largely orthogonal concerns.

For illustration, the metamodel for xADL Core is shown in Figure 4 (along with additional extensions that are discussed in the next subsection). Components and connectors represent the basic building blocks for architecture models. They contain interfaces that can be connected via links. Interface mappings denote the realization of an interface by the interface of a sub-component. The group element captures the membership of multiple components and connectors in a set. Components and connectors may contain substructures. Finally, several of the xADL Core elements include typed attributes, such as a generic description.

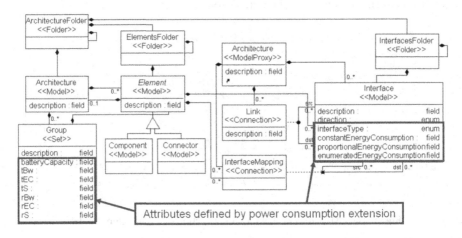

Fig. 4. The metamodel of xADL Core (with the energy consumption extension) as implemented in XTEAM

The combination of xADL and FSP allowed us to create executable architectural representations. Models conformant to the composed ADL contain sufficient information to implement a semantic mapping into low-level simulation constructs that can be executed by an off-the-shelf discrete event simulation engine [18], such as *adevs*. This semantic mapping is implemented by our model interpreter framework. The framework infrastructure synthesizes the low-level structures (*e.g.*, atomic and static digraph models) and logic (*e.g.*, state transition functions) needed by *adevs*. "Hook" methods provided by the framework allow an architect to generate the code needed to realize a wide variety of dynamic analyses. The following subsection explains this process in more detail through the use of concrete examples.

4.2 Domain-Specific Extensions and Architectural Analyses

In order to take advantage of the extensibility and flexibility afforded by the MDE approach, we implemented several domain-specific ADL extensions within the XTEAM metamodel, and then relied on the interpreter framework to efficiently implement analysis techniques that operate on the information captured in those extensions. As XTEAM targets the development of architectures for distributed, mobile, and resource constrained software systems, we chose to implement analyses that are highly relevant for that domain. Below we elaborate on our implementation of one such analysis in XTEAM and briefly describe three others.

4.2.1 Energy Consumption Extensions and Analysis

The energy consumption of executing software has traditionally been ignored by software engineers as they could rely on an uninterrupted, abundant energy source. In the mobile setting, this assumption no longer holds, and the energy consumption of software components can have an important impact on system longevity. The energy consumption estimation framework described in [13] provides a mechanism for estimating software energy consumption at the level of software architecture.

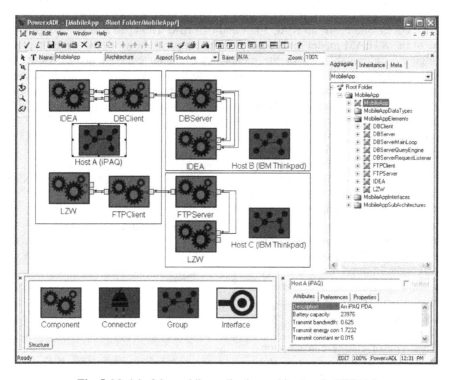

Fig. 5. Model of the mobile application architecture in XTEAM

At a high level, the energy consumption estimation framework defines the overall energy consumption of a software component as a combination of its computational and communication energy costs. The computational energy cost (due to CPU processing, memory access, I/O operations, *etc.*) is incurred whenever one of the component's interfaces is invoked, while the communication energy cost is incurred whenever data is transmitted or received over the wireless network. The estimation framework provides equations that enable the calculation of these energy costs based on a number of a parameters, including data sizes and values, the rate of energy consumption during data transmission, and network bandwidth. Enhancing the XTEAM metamodel with these values was straightforward: they were added as attributes to the appropriate elements (groups, which denote hosts in this context, and interfaces), as shown in Figure 4. Then, in our interpreter framework (recall Figure 3), we inserted the equations for energy consumption based on the parameters defined in the model. The communication energy cost equation was inserted into the "hook" methods that correspond to the sending and receiving of data between components. If the components are on different hosts, the communication energy cost is deducted from the hosts' total battery power. Similarly, the computational energy cost equation was inserted into the "hook" method corresponding to the invocation of an interface.Whenever one of these events occurs during the simulation run, the energy consumption values are calculated and recorded.

To illustrate the use of the energy consumption ADL extension and analysis, consider the example of a small mobile application in which we have three distributed, mobile hosts: an iPAQ PDA and two IBM Thinkpad laptops. A top-level view of the XTEAM model for the mobile application is shown in the screen capture in Figure 5 (although most of the model detail cannot be seen in this view). A database client and a FTP client are deployed to the PDA, while the corresponding servers each run on one of the laptops. Components that perform encryption and compression (respectively, IDEA and LZW open-source components) are also deployed on the PDA and laptops. When the DB client wishes to query the database, it encrypts the query using the local IDEA component and sends the query over the wireless network to the DB server, where it is decrypted. The DB server then retrieves the result of the query from the database, encrypts the results, and sends them back to the DB client. An analogous path is used for the FTP client, except that compression rather than encryption is performed.

By invoking our energy consu-mption simulation generator (built using the interpreter framework) on the mobile application model, the energy consumption on each host can be determined dynamically. Plotting these measurements as a function of time results in the exa-mple graph shown in Figure 6.

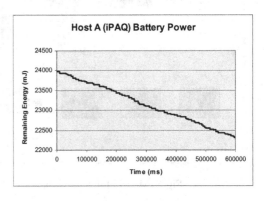

Fig. 6. Result of energy consumption analysis

This type of energy consumption estimation has a variety of uses in the scenario-driven analysis approach. First, the assignment of components to hosts, or deployment architecture, can have a significant effect on system energy consumption, and, in turn, its longevity. Our environment allows the architect to quickly model a set of potential deployment architectures, and then observe the energy consumption on each host over time. Moreover, the architect can determine whether a dynamic redeployment strategy is required in situations when the actual energy consumption rate differs significantly from expected rates. Conversely, given a requirement for the longevity of system services, the architect can begin to arrive at target energy usages for each component.

4.2.2 Other Extensions

We have also leveraged XTEAM to implement dynamic analysis capabilities for end-to-end latency, memory utilization, and component reliability. The implementation of ADL extensions and model interpreters for these analyses follows the same pattern as that used for energy consumption, and demonstrates the fulfillment of our original requirements. For example, we implemented the component reliability extension and analysis based on the technique described in [12]. This reliability estimation approach relies on the definition of component failure types, the probabilities of those failures at different times during component execution, and the probability of and time required for failure recovery. This type of analysis meets the primary criteria for implementation in XTEAM: it estimates the reliability of components at the level of software architecture. We extended the FSP-based behavior language in XTEAM to include failure and recovery events and probabilities. We also developed an analysis that determines if and when failures occur as the components in the system progress through different tasks and states. In general, we believe that given an architectural analysis technique that is applicable in a dynamic, simulated setting, our framework can be utilized to realize that technique through implementation of the appropriate hook methods.

5 Discussion

This section discusses our approach in the context of wider architectural development processes and activities. In particular, we see three cases where our approach is particularly relevant and unique: (1) providing rationale for fundamental architectural decisions, (2) weighing trade-offs among multiple conflicting design goals, and (3) understanding the results of composing independent components developed in isolation.

5.1 Providing Design Rationale

Early in the architectural development process, software architects are, in many situations, required to rely on their own intuition and past experience when weighing fundamental design questions. For example, the choice of a particular architectural style, the distribution of components across hosts, or the functionality allocated to components can dramatically effect the ultimate behaviors and properties of a system, but architects have very limited mechanisms for arriving at such decisions beyond their own knowledge and expertise and the collective wisdom of the architecture community. In other words, rationalizing such decisions using specific processes and tools is relatively rare. Our approach to software architecture provides a means of experimentation with fundamental design decisions and the rationalization of those decisions through quantifiable means. By generating and executing simulations of a distributed system, the consequences of crucial architectural choices can be better understood.

5.2 Weighing Architectural Trade-Offs

Nearly all non-trivial architectural decisions come down to trade-offs between multiple desirable properties. The relative importance of different system properties to the user (e.g., availability or performance) can be determined prior to architectural development, but the architect is still required to engineer the right balance between conflicting goals. Emphasizing one attribute over others will eventually yield diminishing returns, and usually this "tipping-point" between different qualities is anything but obvious. For example, given a system with both fixed and mobile hosts, deploying components to a mobile host will likely increase the availability and reduce the latency perceived by a client using that device, but will also drain the battery power faster. The "right" deployment (*i.e.*, that which maximizes the system's utility given users' quality-of-service preferences [14]) depends heavily on the wireless network characteristics, such as bandwidth and the frequency of disconnects, in addition to a number of other factors. Rather than relying on intuition or past development projects to achieve the right balance, our approach allows an architect to determine the relationships between various design goals and increase system utility experimentally.

5.3 Understanding Compositions of Off-the-Shelf Components

In the present day, independent teams or organizations are often responsible for producing components that are ultimately assembled to create a unified system. In such settings, detailed information about individual components (*e.g.*, resource consumption, failure rates) may be available, but the properties of their composition may not be well-understood. In such a case, our approach can produce accurate measurements of the emergent properties of the composed system. This knowledge ultimately enhances the architects' understanding of the system and increases their confidence in the ability of the composed system to meet end-user operational goals. Both of these outcomes serve to reduce the risk associated with a large-scale development and/or integration project.

6 Conclusions

This paper presented a software architecture-based approach to modeling and analysis of distributed architectures that leverages the domain-specific extensibility provided by model-driven engineering. Our approach addresses the significant shortcomings of previous ADLs by relying on a tool-chain that enables both modeling language and analysis extensibility. The dynamic analysis capabilities of the tool-chain allow an architect to better understand the consequences of architectural decisions, focus on aspects that have the greatest effect on a system's critical properties, weigh trade-offs between conflicting design goals, and better understand component compositions. We demonstrated and evaluated the approach on XTEAM, a suite of ADL extensions and model transformation engines targeted specifically for highly distributed, resource-constrained, and mobile computing environments. We believe our approach represents an improvement over traditional ADLs and exhibits significant differences from other MDE tools that have been developed for distributed systems development.

There are several ways in which we intend to extend this work. First, we will utilize the XTEAM tool-chain in the context of architectural development for a real-world security application that operates in an embedded, wireless environment. Second, we will integrate XTEAM with other complementary architecture-based development tools, including DeSi [14] and Prism-MW [15]. Third, we will determine more precisely the exact class of analysis techniques that can be implemented with our model interpreter framework, and evaluate the feasibility of supporting other classes of analysis techniques (*e.g.*, static analyses) via additional interpreter frameworks. Lastly, we will further define ways in which our approach can be integrated with widely-used architectural development processes, such as the Architecture Trade-off Analysis Method (ATAM).

Acknowledgments

The work described in this paper was sponsored by the National Science Foundation under Grant number ITR-0312780. Any opinions, findings, and conclusions expressed in this paper are those of the authors and do not necessarily reflect the views of the NSF. This material was also sponsored by Bosch. The authors wish to thank the anonymous reviewers for their detailed and helpful comments.

References

[1] Perry, D. E., Wolf, A.L.: Foundations for the Study of Software Architectures. ACM SIGSOFT Software Engineering Notes, pp. 40-52, Oct 1992.

[2] Medvidovic N., et al.: A Classification and Comparison Framework for Software Architecture Description Languages. IEEE Trans. on Software Engineering, 26(1), Jan 2000.

[3] Medvidovic, N., Dashofy, E. and Taylor, R.N.: Moving Architectural Description from Under the Technology Lamppost. Journal of Systems and Software, 2006.

[4] Schmidt, D.C.: Model-Driven Engineering. IEEE Computer, 39(2), pp. 41-47, Feb 2006.

[5] Karsai, G., Sztipanovits, J., Ledeczi, A., and Bapty, T.: Model-integrated development of embedded software. In Proceedings of the IEEE, 91(1), pp. 145-164, Jan 2003.

[6] Ledeczi, A., et al.: Modeling methodology for integrated simulation of embedded systems. ACM Transactions on Modeling and Computer Simulation, 13(1), pp. 82-103, Jan 2003.

[7] Dashofy, E., van der Hoek, A. and Taylor, R.N.: An Infrastructure for the Rapid Development of XML-based Architecture Description Languages. Proceedings of the 24th International Conference on Software Engineering, pp. 266 - 276, 2002.

[8] GME: The Generic Modeling Environment. http://www.isis.vanderbilt.edu/projects/gme/

[9] Paunov, S., et al.: Domain-Specific Modeling Languages for Configuring and Evaluating Enterprise DRE System Quality-of-Service. Proceedings of the 12th IEEE International Conference on Embedded and Real-Time Computing Systems and Applications, 2006.

[10] Ledeczi, A., et al.: On metamodel composition. Proceedings of the 2001 IEEE International Conference on Control Applications, pp. 756-760, 2001.

[11] Jackson, D., Rinard, M.: Software Analysis: A Roadmap. In The Future of Software Engineering, Anthony Finkelstein (Ed.), pp. 215-224, ACM Press 2000.

[12] Roshandel, R., et al.: Estimating Software Component Reliability by Leveraging Architectural Models. 28th International Conference on Software Engineering, May 2006.

[13] Seo C., Malek S., N. Medvidovic: An Energy Consumption Framework for Distributed Java-Based Software Systems. Tech. Report USC-CSE-2006-604, 2006.

[14] Malek, S.: A User-Centric Framework for Improving a Distributed Software System's Deployment Architecture. To appear in proceedings of the doctoral symposium at the 14th Symposium on Foundation of Software Engineering, Portland, Oregon, Nov. 2006.

[15] Malek, S., et al.: Prism-MW: A Style-Aware Architectural Middleware for Resource Constrained, Distributed Systems. IEEE Trans. on Software Engineering. 31(3), Mar. 2005.

[16] Magee, J., et al.: Behaviour Analysis of Software Architectures. Proceedings of the TC2 First Working IFIP Conference on Software Architecture (WICSA1), pp. 35 - 50, 1999.

[17] Adevs: A Discrete EVent System simulator. http://www.ece.arizona.edu/~nutaro/

[18] Schriber, T. J., Brunner, D.T.: Inside Discrete-Event Simulation Software: How it Works and Why it Matters. Proceedings of the Winter Simulation Conference, 2005.

Enforcing Architecture and Deployment Constraints of Distributed Component-Based Software

Chouki Tibermacine[1], Didier Hoareau[1], and Reda Kadri[1,2]

[1] VALORIA, University of South Brittany, Vannes, France
{Didier.Hoareau,Chouki.Tibermacine}@univ-ubs.fr
[2] Alkante, Cesson Sévigné, France
r.kadri@alkante.com

Abstract. In the component-based software development process, the formalisation of architectural choices makes possible to explicit quality attributes. When dealing with the deployment of such component-based software in dynamic networks, in which disconnections or machine failures can occur, preserving architectural choices becomes difficult to ensure, as current architecture-centric languages and their support mainly focus on steps prior to the deployment one. We present in this paper a family of languages that formalise not only architectural choices but deployment aspects as well, both as constraints. Then, we show how all of these constraints are reified in order to manage the deployment of a component-based software in this context of a dynamic hosting platform. The proposed solution defines an automatic deployment that ensures permanently, at run time, the preservation of architecture and deployment choices, and thus their corresponding quality attributes.

1 Introduction

Architectural choices should be preserved throughout the software lifecycle so that their associated quality attributes persist. For example, if we choose, at design-time, a particular architectural style like the pipe and filter [15], we should be able, at runtime, to enforce it so that maintainability and performance quality requirements can be ensured permanently.

In an MDE (Model-Driven Engineering) approach, we can define at architecture design-time an architecture description of a system with a given ADL, like Acme [4]. We can then transform this description into a component implementation in CORBA components (CCM) [10], for example. For a smooth transition, we can transit by a component diagram in UML 2 (or one of its profile, like CCM one), at component design-time. We showed in [16], how to formalize architectural choices at the different stages above using a family of constraint languages called ACL profiles: Acme ACL profile at architecture design stage, UML 2 ACL profile at component design stage and CCM ACL profile at component implementation stage. We also presented how these architectural choices (constraints) are preserved from one stage to another.

M.B. Dwyer and A. Lopes (Eds.): FASE 2007, LNCS 4422, pp. 140–154, 2007.

In this paper, we present how these choices can be preserved after the development has finished. We show how this can be achieved after the deployment of the component implementation in a distributed execution environment. Indeed, one of the characteristics of emerging distributed platforms is their dynamism. Such dynamic platforms are not only composed of powerful and fixed workstations but also of mobile and resource-constrained devices (laptops, PDAs, smart-phones, sensors, etc.). Due to the mobility and the volatility of the hosts, connectivity cannot be ensured between all hosts, e.g. a PDA with a wireless connection may become inaccessible because of its range limit. As a consequence, in a dynamic network, partitions may occur, resulting in the fragmentation of the network into islands. Machines within the same island can communicate whereas, no communication is possible between two machines that are in two different islands. Moreover, as some devices are characterized by their mobility, the topology of islands may evolve.

Dynamism in the kind of networks we target is not only due to the nature of the devices but also to their heterogeneity making difficult to base a deployment on resource's availability. When deploying component-based software in dynamic distributed infrastructures it is required that the deployed system complies permanently with its corresponding architecture choices. By taking advantages of changes in the environment (e.g. availability of a required resource), the initial deployment can evolve but any reconfiguration must respect initial architectural choices. This makes the running system benefit from the targeted quality attributes, and more particularly those which are dynamically observed, like performance or reliability.

In addition, we introduce in this paper the enrichment of architectural choices, during deployment-time, with constraints on resources and location. We show how we can use the same language to formalize this kind of constraints, and how we can check them at runtime. The proposed approach makes use of a transformation technique to evaluate ACL constraints. All architectural choices together with resource and location constraints are transformed into reified runtime constraints to be evaluated.

In the next section we present briefly how we can formalize architecture choices using a constraint language, and we illustrate this formalization by a short example of a client/server architectural style. In addition we show how to use this same language to describe resource and location requirements at component deployment stage. We present in section 3, the deployment process and the resolution mechanisms of these constrained component-based software in dynamic infrastructures. In section 4 implementation details and experiment results are given. Before concluding and highlighting the perspectives, we present some related work in section 5.

2   Formalizing Architectural Choices During Development

In order to make explicit architectural choices, like the use of a particular architecture style or the enforcement of general architecture invariants, we proposed

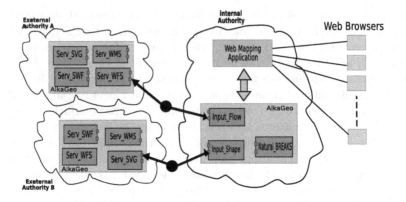

Fig. 1. Client/Server architecture of a Web mapping system

in [16] a constraint language named ACL (Architecture Constraint Language). Architectural choices are thus formalized as architecture predicates which have as a context an architectural element (component, connector, etc) that belongs to an architecture metamodel.

ACL is a language with two levels of expression. The first level encapsulates concepts used for basic predicate-level expression, like quantifiers, collection operations, etc. It is represented by a slightly modified version of UML's OCL [11], called CCL (Core Constraint Language). The second level embeds architectural abstractions that can be constrained by the first level. It is represented by a set of MOF architecture metamodels. Architectural constraints are first-order predicates that navigate in a given metamodel and which have as a scope a specific element in the architecture description. Each couple composed of CCL and a given metamodel is called an ACL profile. We defined many profiles, like the ACL profile for xAcme[1], for UML 2, for OMG's CORBA Components (CCM) or the profile for ObjectWeb's Fractal [1].

To illustrate our work, we briefly describe the development process of a component-based software we developed, from the architecture design stage to the deployment stage. We chose xAcme to illustrate the architecture design stage and the Fractal component model for the implementation stage.

2.1   Architectural Choices at Architecture Design Stage

As an answer to a request from a local community in Brittany (France), we developed a component-based software, called AlkaGeo. This software generates geographic information flow which is used by a Web Mapping Application (WMA). When using this application, our customer can access Web GIS data and maps, like land maps, through their browsers. This WMA is deployed in application servers of our provider (Internal Authority, in Figure 1).

---

[1] xAcme is an XML extension of Acme ADL.

The overall architecture of AlkaGeo is organized according to the client/server style. In this system we have two instances of this style. The first occurrence of this style can be seen in Figure 1 between the components (Input_Flow) asking for maps and data, in two different formats SVG and SWF, from server components (Serv_SVG and Serv_SWF). The second instance of the style is defined between clients (Input_Flow) requesting maps and data in the GML format from server components (Serv_WMS and Serv_WFS)[2]. AlkaGeo is deployed on different server providers (External Authorities), which have different resources and configuration, to which we do not have access. For the sake of brevity, we illustrate in this work just the GML flows service implemented by the Serv_WMS and Serv_WFS components.

The client/server style is characterized by the following constraints:

- There is no direct communication between Input_Flow components,
- Serv_WFS and Serv_WMS can accept requests from at most 40 different Input_Flow components,
- Input_Flow components can use at most one Serv_WFS component or one Serv_WMS component.

These three constraints can be described using ACL profile for xAcme as follows:

1. ```
context ClientServer:ComponentInstance inv:
ClientServer.subArchitecture.archInstance.linkInstance->select(1|
1.endPoint->forAll(p1,p2|p1.anchorOnInterface.componentInstance
.id = 'Input_Flow' and p2.anchorOnInterface.componentInstance
.id <> 'Input_Flow'))
```

   This constraint states that for all link instances between architecture instances, there should be no link which binds two components which are identified by Input_Flow.

2. ```
context ClientServer:ComponentInstance inv:
ClientServer.subArchitecture.archInstance.componentInstance
->forAll(c| ((c.id = 'Serv_WFS') or (c.id = 'Serv_WMS')) and
(c.linkInstance->select(1|1.componentInstance
.id = 'Input_Flow'))->size() <= 40)
```

   The constraint above stipulates that component instances with the identifier Serv_WFS and Serv_WMS should have at most 40 links with component instances with the identifier Input_Flow.

3. ```
context ClientServer:ComponentInstance inv:
ClientServer.subArchitecture.archInstance.linkInstance
->forAll(1|1.endPoint->select(1|1.endPoint->forAll(p1,p2|
(p1.anchorOnInterface.componentInstance.id = 'Input_Flow')
and ((p2..anchorOnInterface.componentInstance.id = 'Serv_WFS')
or (p2..anchorOnInterface.componentInstance.id = 'Serv_WMS')))
```

   The last constraint enforces the existence of at most one link between the component instance with the identifier Input_Flow and one of the two component instances identified by Serv_WFS and Serv_WMS.

---

[2] WMS and WFS are two standards of the Open Geospatial Consortium: http://www.opengeospatial.org/
```

ACL profile for xAcme is composed of CCL and a MOF metamodel of xArch. An xArch architecture instance is composed of a set of component instances, connector instances, link instances and logical groups of the previous architectural elements. Component or connector instances define a set of interface instances and optionally a sub-architecture for a hierarchical description. The sub-architecture defines a set of architecture instances and a list of mappings between inner and outer interface instances. Link instances bind two end points, each one references an interface instance. As we can see, the constraints above navigate in this xArch metamodel.

2.2   Architectural Choices at Component Design Stage

Before implementing our software, we decided to establish an intermediate UML model for a smooth transition. Indeed, recent experiments [13] showed also that some ADLs and the UML can be used in a complementary fashion, in order to make better analysis of software architectures. The constraints formalizing the client/server style can be described, at this stage, using the ACL profile for UML 2. The first constraint is expressed as follows:

```
context ClientServer:Component inv:
ClientServer.connector.end.role->forAll(r1,r2|(r1->oclAsType(Port)
.encapsulatedClassifier->oclAsType(Class)->oclAsType(Component)
.name = 'Input_Flow') and (r2->oclAsType(Port).encapsulatedClassifier
->oclAsType(Class)->oclAsType(Component).name <> 'Input_Flow'))
```

This constraint navigates in the UML 2 component metamodel. At the differences of the previous constraint, it manipulates connectors, roles, components and ports. The constraint above and the first constraint expressed in the previous subsection have the same semantics in the context where they are applied (on an xAcme architecture description and on a UML 2 component model).

In order to evaluate constraints, we use an intermediate ACL profile to which all architectural constraints specified in the different profiles are transformed. At a given stage of the development process, architecture choice preservation is achieved by the transformation of constraints specified in all upstream stages in this intermediate ACL profile to be evaluated.

2.3   Architectural Choices at Component Implementation Stage

Suppose that the system modeled above has been implemented in a component technology, like Fractal. The three constraints of the previous client/server style can be described at this development stage using ACL profile for Fractal. In the listing below, we illustrate the first constraint expressed in this profile:

```
context ClientServer:CompositeComponent inv:
ClientServer.binding->forAll(b|b.client.component.name= "Input_Flow"
and b.server.component.name <> "Input_Flow")
```

This constraint navigates in the MOF metamodel of Fractal component model which is presented in Figure 2. This metamodel abstracts components, which can be composite or primitive. Components can have interfaces of several types.

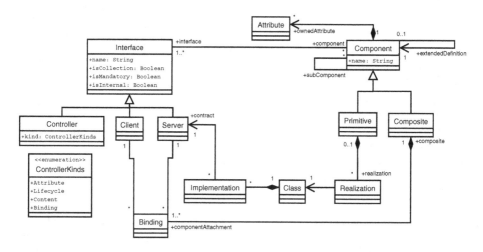

Fig. 2. The MOF metamodel of Fractal component model

Server interfaces are interfaces that specify provided functionalities. Client interfaces define required operations. Controller interfaces embed non-functional specifications, such as predefined operations which manage the lifecycle or the contents of a given component. A composite component specifies a set of bindings which are simple method invocation connectors. These bindings are attachments between client and server interfaces. Bindings can represent either hierarchical or assembly connectors (with analogy to UML's delegation and assembly connectors).

2.4 Resource and Location Requirements at Deployment Stage

In addition to these architecture constraints, the deployment of each component is governed by some resource and location requirements. Indeed, before deployment, we are unlikely to know what are the machines that are involved in the deployment and thus where to deploy each component. However, one can define for each component what are its requirements in terms of resources, that is, the characteristics of the machines that will host the component. For example, a Serv_SVG must be hosted by a machine that has at least 512 MB of free memory, a CPU scale greater than 1 GHz and is connected to the network by an interface with a bandwidth of at least 512 Kb/s. With regard to Input_Flows, each instance must be hosted by a machine that belongs to the Internal Authority provider.

Resource constraints can be defined using an ACL profile (i.e. a CCL and a metamodel), called R-ACL (Resources-ACL). R-ACL integrates in its metamodels concepts related to system resources and their properties. The resource constraints introduced above are described in R-ACL as follows:

1. Free memory $>=$ 512 MB:
   ```
   context Serv_SVG : Component inv :
   Serv_SVG . resource ->oclAsType (Memory ). free >= 512
   ```

2. CPU scale > 1 GHz (1000 MHz):

```
context Serv_SVG : Component inv :
Serv_SVG . resource ->oclAsType (CPU) . processors
->select (cpu : CPU_Model | cpu . speed >1000)->size ()>=1
```

3. Network interface bandwidth >= 512 Kb/s:

```
context Serv_SVG : Component inv :
Serv_SVG . resource ->oclAsType ( NetworkInterface ) . tx >= 512
```

4. Each instance of the component Input_Flow must be hosted by an internal authority machine:

```
context Input_Flow : Component inv :
Input_Flow . location ->forAll (h : Host | h
. group = 'Internal Authority ')
```

As discussed above these constraints navigate in the resources metamodel, but have as a scope only one specific architectural element, which is the component Server_SVG or Input_Flow. This element is of type Component which is a sub-meta-class of the meta-class ArchitecturalElement. This meta-class is the ancestor of all meta-classes in the Fractal metamodel[3].

Besides resource constraints, it is sometimes required to control the placement of the components, especially when several machine can host the same component. For example in the Client/Server system we designed, we would require that for reliability reasons (redundancy at the server side), all Serv_SVGs have to be located on distinct hosts. The following listing illustrates this constraint expressed in R-ACL.

```
context ClientServer : CompositeComponent inv :
ClientServer . subComponent->select (c1 , c2 : Component | c1 . name='Serv_SVG '
and c2 . name='Serv_SVG ' and c1 . location . id <> c2 . location . id )
```

The different categories of constraints are saved in XML documents. There is a style descriptor which contains the constraints formalizing an architecture style (the first category of constraints) and a deployment descriptor which embeds resource and location constraints (the second and the third category of constraints). These descriptors are used while deploying the system, as described in the next section.

3   Preserving Architectural Choices at Runtime

When the choice of the placement of every component has to be made, the initial configuration of the target platform may not fulfil all resources' requirements of the application and some needed machines may not be connected. We are thus interested in a deployment that allows the instantiation of the components as soon as resources become available or new machines become connected. We qualify this deployment as *propagative*. We propose a general framework to guarantee the designed architecture and its instances for each deployment evolution. We present first the requirements of a deployment driven by architecture choices

---

[3] This is omitted from Figure 2 for the purpose of clarity.

and resource specifications. Then, for the purpose of clarity, we detail first the deployment process in a non-partitioned network—this will allow us to focus on the dynamic resolution of constraints—then we take into account fragmentation within the environment.

3.1   From Architectural Constraints to Runtime Constraints

At design time, we are unlikely to know what are the machines that are involved in the deployment and thus what are their characteristics. Hence, a valid configuration of the client/server style presented in section 2, can only be computed at runtime. A valid configuration is a set of component instances, interconnected and for which, a target host has been chosen for every instance. Every architectural constraint (e.g. on bindings or number of instances) has to be verified and the selected hosts must not contradict the resource and location constraints.

Our approach consists in manipulating all the architectural and resource constraints at runtime in order to reflect the state of the deployed system with respect to these constraints. As it is detailed below, these runtime constraints are suited when considering reaction mechanisms to changes that can occur in the environment. The reified constraints are generated from the R-ACL constraints and correspond to a Constraint Satisfaction Problem (CSP). In a CSP, one only states the properties of the solution to be found by defining variables with finite domains and a set of constraints restricting the values that the variables can simultaneously take. The use of solvers such as Prolog IV [12] can then be used to find one or several solutions. On the one hand the use of dynamic constraints makes it possible to preserve architectural choices at runtime, on the other hand reified constraints allow detecting and reacting to changes that can occur with the environment. By identifying these different changes we will explicit the constraints that have to be reified and that will guarantee the preservation of the architecture's consistency all along its execution.

In the kind of network we qualify as dynamic, crashes (e.g. failure of machines, components) may happen and partitions may exist. In both cases, some components that were in use regarding other components can become unavailable. When dealing with a crash, if some repair mechanisms have been defined, these components can or must be redeployed. However because of the existence of islands, it is crucial to control the instantiation mechanism (and thus the number of instances). Indeed, the strategy consisting in redeploying a component each time this latter fails is not suited as the number of instances will not be consistent even if it is the case in each island. In order to overcome the instantiation of components in a dynamic network, we introduce a first type of constraints, named C_1:

C1. These constraints specify the number of instances allowed for each component. By fixing the minimum and the maximum of instances allowed of a component it is possible to control its instantiation which can be initiated due to the dynamism of the network. When a new resource, required by a component, becomes available, its instantiation is conceivable. In the same way, when a component becomes faulty or becomes out of reach, one may consider its substitution by a new instance. Due to partitions within the network, it is mandatory not only to have such a constraint but to maintain its consistency as well: the information about the current number of instances is a global one, and thus must be the same within each island.

In a dynamic network resources on machines may change in such a way that a required resource that was unavailable when the deployment was triggered, may become available later. Moreover, because of the mobility of the devices that compose the network we target, some machines that were out of reach until now may become accessible, inducing the availability of new (required) resources[4]. In order to take into account changes of resources and hosts, we introduced constraints C_2 and C_3:

C2. It is possible with R-ACL to define components' needs in terms of software and hardware resources. In order to react on resources'changes, resource constraints are reified and form constraints C_2;

C3. In the same way, location constraints have to be reified to take into account hosts mobility. When dealing with a constraint such specifying components Serv_SVG$_1$ and Serv_SVG$_2$ must reside on two distinct hosts, a deployment may initially not be possible due to the absence of one or several hosts. A solution can however be found as soon as the number of connected (and reachable) hosts is sufficient. Constraints C_3 correspond to the reification of location constraints.

The constraints presented above allow to react on changes of the environment, that is, the fluctuation of resources and the mobility and volatility of hosts, while controlling the number of instances of the components. When a component instance is created or withdrawn, the architecture of the application, i.e. the assembly of the components, has to be reconfigured : indeed, when a component is created, some bindings have to be added towards this component, and if the latter requires others, bindings to these components have also to be made. When dealing with the removal of a component, bindings towards and from this component have to be suppressed. The addition and suppression of bindings on any architecture must be done regarding the architectural constraints defined at design-time. For example, the client / server style of AlkaGeo specifies that at most 40 component Input_Flow can be bound to component Serv_WFS. Thus, we introduce three more constraints that are reified and that preserve the architectural constraints during bindings reconfiguration.

C4. When a component is instantiated in consequence of the availability of new resources or when a remote component becomes accessible, it is mandatory to add it into the architecture (i.e. to set up bindings) if the style descriptor specifies the interconnection of this component with others. Constraints of type C4 are the reification of information specifying a binding between two components or two types of components.

The previous constraints make it possible to detect that a binding between two components can be made once the style descriptor specifies such a binding and that the two components are reachable from each other. Even if a binding can be

---

[4] Besides, a resource used by a component may become unavailable (e.g. the amount of free memory).

made, some other aspects can prevent this creation. For example, the AlkaGeo application defines a client / server style which limits component Input_Flow to use at most one component Serv_WFS, and that every component Serv_WFS can only be used by at most 40 components Input_Flow. It is thus necessary, before creating a binding between a component Input_Flow and a component Serv_WFS to check that the number of connections respects the architectural choices. Constraints C5 and C6 reify these constraints:

C5. The number of "outgoing" bindings allowed on a client interface;

C6. The number of "incoming" bindings allowed on a server interface.

Each C_i corresponds to a set of constraints. These sets are sufficient to generate a valid configuration regarding to an architectural style. The deployment process that is presented in the next section relies on these constraints in order to build a mapping between the component instances and the hosts of the target platform.

3.2 Deployment Process: A Centralized Evolution

We will consider first a network in which no fragmentation into islands is possible (this assumption will not be considered in the next subsection). Further, we make the following assumptions: there is a dedicated machine, called DeployManager on which we can rely in order to maintain up-to-date the ids of the machines that are connected. When the deployment is triggered, some machines may not be connected. Besides, a machine that enters the network is detected by the DeployManager.

When the deployment is launched, style and deployment descriptors are sent to the DeployManager, which in turn broadcasts the descriptors to all the machines that are connected in the network. Each machine that receives these descriptors, creates the constraints described in the listing above depending on the deployment and style descriptors. Then a process is launched on each host. Locally, each machine maintains its own set of constraints (C1 to C6) and tries to make the deployment evolve until a (or multiple) solution(s) exist(s) for constraints C1, that is, some components can still be instantiated. The main steps of this process for a component C that can be deployed in a machine m_i are the followings:

- For each resource constraint associated with C, a dedicated probe is launched (e.g. a probe to get the amount of memory required by component C) in order to check if locally, all the required resources are available (C2). The observation of the resources is made periodically.
- If this is the case, that is, the component can be hosted locally, m_i sends its candidature to the DeployManager. This candidature indicates that m_i can host component C.
- The latter may receive several candidatures from other machines for the instantiation of C. The DeployManager has to resolve a placement solution regarding to constraints C3. Depending on location constraints, a placement solution may require a sufficient number of candidatures.

- Once a solution has been found, the DeployManager updates the deployment descriptor with the new information of placement and broadcasts it to all the nodes that are currently connected.
- When a new descriptor is received, m_i updates the set C1 and C3 in order to take into account the placement decision made by the DeployManager.
- m_i can then resolve some bindings towards newly instantiated (remote) components (C4) by sending a request to the machines hosting them. This is possible only if constraints C5 are still verified.
- When m_i receives a request of bindings, according to C6, it can accept or refuse this request and inform the sender of its answer.
- Depending on the answer, the definition domain that corresponds to the binding constraint (C4) is updated (removed from the constraint set if the binding is not possible or set to the remote host otherwise).

This process defines a propagative deployment driven by architectural and resources requirements. Since the observation of resources is made periodically, when a resource becomes available on a specific machine, this may yield the deployment to evolve. Similarly, when a machine enters the network, the DeployManager sends the current version of the style and deployment descriptors to this machine, making possible this newly connected machine to participate in the deployment evolution.

3.3   Deployment Evolution in a Partitioned Network

The deployment described above relies on a dedicated machine—the DeployManager—that orchestrates the evolution of the deployment regarding to the resolution of the location constraints. In front of islands, that is, the fragmentation of the network, the uniqueness of such a manager raises the problem of the propagative deployment in islands where no manager exists. We have addressed this aspect by considering the management of several managers. The main difficulties here are twofolds: first, how can we guarantee the architecture consistency if several managers make decisions independently to each other (e.g. we have to avoid the instantiation of the same component in two distinct islands)? Secondly, the management of multiple managers have to be faced with when two islands *merge*.

We have decided to use the results obtained in [6] in which we have defined a consensus algorithm to elect such a manager in networks where partitions can occur. This algorithm is based on a common view of the different machines to make a decision about the identity of an approved manager. Thus, the resolution of location constraints can be made in islands composed of a majority of machines. The consensus algorithm ensures that no contradictory decisions can be made in two different islands and that the latest version of the style and deployment descriptor exists in every island.

Unlike the centralized version of the propagative deployment, the deployment presented in partitioned network requires that the ids (thus the number) of the machines that will be involved in the deployment, be known. Indeed the used algorithm depends on a majority of connected machines, in order to terminate.

4 Implementation Status and Results

In order to validate our proposals, we enhanced and reused some existing prototype tools. The first tool is ACE (Architecture Constraint Evaluator). ACE is composed of an editor for ACL constraints. This editor assists developers to write their constraints by proposing the different navigation alternatives in the used metamodel (resources and location metamodel or architecture metamodel). After specifying these constraints, ACE makes some well-formedness checking and compiles them in order to generate the corresponding runtime constraints. This transformation process is performed starting from a Java implementation of the abstract syntax tree of the different constraints.

The constraints that are solved dynamically have been implemented with Cream[5]. Cream is a Java library for writing and solving constraint satisfaction problems or optimisation problems on integers. Every constraint generated from an R-ACL's one defines a relation on a variable taking its value in a finite domain. For the location constraints, the definition domain of each variable is not known before the deployment but is increased each time a candidature is received.

The deployment that has been presented in this paper relies on the discovery of the resources required by the components. For that, we used DRAJE (Distributed Resource-Aware Java Environment) [7], an extensible Java-based middleware developed in our team. Thus, hardware resources (e.g. processor, memory, network interface...) or software resources (e. g. process, socket, thread, directory...), can be modelled and observed in a homogeneous way. For every resource constraint of the deployment descriptor, a resource in DRAJE is created and a periodic observation is launched.

The performance of the deployment process depends on changes imposed by the execution environment such as resources availability and host connectivity. But, the propagative deployment requires the DeployManager to solve first a solution placement before the instantiation can go along. Hence, we have measured the impact of this computation. The preliminary results of this experiment showed that the time to obtain a placement solution (when all conditions are met) remains acceptable (less than 10 milli-seconds to deploy 50 Serv_SVG components) and corresponds to the complexity of the AllDiff constraint (i.e. each Serv_SVG must be hosted on a distinct machine) which is $O(n^2)$.

5 Related Work

Many ADLs provide capabilities to describe architecture choices. Medvidovic and Taylor in [8] make an overview of some existing ADLs offering capabilities to describe architectural styles and constraints in general. The description of architecture styles with these ADLs makes possible some reasoning about the modeled system, analyzing its structure and evaluating its quality. The difference between the work presented here and such ADLs is twofolds:

---

[5] http://kurt.scitec.kobe-u.ac.jp/~shuji/cream/

- First, design-level and deployment-level constraints are described in a homogeneous way in our approach. Indeed, the same language (ACL) is used throughout the software life-cycle to describe them. The majority of ADLs deals only with one kind of these constraints. Some ADLs focus on architectural style description, like Aesop [3]. Others, deal with deployment requirements specification, like in [6]. Even if an ADL deals with the two kinds of constraints at the same time, there is no means to describe them at different stages of the development process. In these ADLs, architecture design and deployment requirements should be addressed together and language constructs that are used to specify them are mixed. The approach we propose here targets the separation of concerns by providing a single constraint language, with many profiles; each profile can be used to deal with a particular concern (design choice formalization or deployment requirement description).
- Second, the approach proposed here is implementation technology-independent. An easy migration can be performed from one implementation technology to another, as demonstrated in [17]. However in existing works, constraint languages are tightly coupled with ADLs, and constraints are parts of architecture or component descriptions. This makes difficult migration between technologies, because whole architecture descriptions should be translated.

We share similarities with researches on self-healing and self-organizing systems. Indeed, in the approaches presented in [5,14], a system architecture to deploy is not described in terms of component instances and their interconnections but rather by a set of constraints that define how components can be assembled. In both cases the running system is modelled by a graph. The main difference with our work is that reconfigurations of the systems are explicitly defined in a programmatic way while this is achieved automatically by the resolution of the constraints (C1 to C6) in our approach.

In [9], the authors present an approach to deploy software components in resource constrained environments. The deployment process is initiated by the Continuous Analysis component which maintains up-to-date the current topology of the running application. This component is responsible of initiating the necessary operations to deploy a part of the architecture if there is a difference between the current and desired configuration. The deployment of a given component is performed starting from an architecture description specified with an ADL called PitM ADL, which is interpreted by the Prism architecture middleware. Besides this centralized version, the authors specified a distributed ownership of the deployment process in which several Continuous Analysis components are responsible of the deployment of a local subsystem. This distributed process differs from ours as it relies on the division of the system into subsystems which cannot be done *a priori* in a network with evolving topology; such dynamic networks are not considered by the authors.

The work presented in [2] shares the same motivation to define high level deployment description with regard to constraints on the application assembly and on the resources the hosts of the target platform should meet. The authors present the Deladas language that allows the definition of a deployment goal in terms of architectural and location constraints. A constraint solver is used to generate a valid configuration of the placements of components and reconfiguration of the placement is possible when a constraint becomes inconsistent. This centralized approach requires, contrary to ours, a full knowledge of the identity of the different hosts that may participate in the deployment. Moreover, the current version of Deladas does not consider resource requirements.

6   Conclusion and Future Work

Preserving architectural choices throughout the development process of a software is an important aspect. Indeed, in order to implement a software that complies with the initial requirements, architectural choices should be formalized at all stages. In addition, at a given stage, architectural choices defined in upstream stages should be preserved. This makes possible a traceability of quality attributes implemented by these choices. After the implementation of this system comes its deployment. Another aspect is important in the life-cycle of the developed software. It is related to the preservation of architectural choices after its deployment (during its execution). Indeed, this makes the system benefit from the quality attributes, associated to these choices, which can be dynamically observed, like performance or reliability. In the example introduced in section 2, the client/server style is formalized and enforced dynamically, in order to benefit from the dynamic quality attributes guaranteed by this style (like, scalability and interoperability).

In this paper, we presented an approach to formalize, as constraints, architecture choices made throughout a component-based software life-cycle. We illustrated how we can use the same formalization language (ACL) to describe resource and location requirements that appear at deployment stage. We showed how these constraints are checked while deploying the implemented system in a dynamic infrastructure. Indeed, in this kind of platforms the availability of resources and hosts cannot be predicted. Faced with the environment evolution (disconnection and reconnection of nodes), we presented a deployment process that checks permanently the constraints to enforce architecture choices with respect to deployment requirements. The constraints that are checked dynamically are obtained after transforming ACL static constraints into runtime (CSP) ones.

We are working now on defining architecture patterns as libraries which are automatically transformed into their equivalents at runtime. This will, as we think best, make easier architecture description, more specifically architectural style formalization, and will simplify considerably the deployment of its implementation according to the proposed approach. Even if not considered in this article, the management of network failures[6] is one of our current work. The main difficult aspect resides in the automation of the re-deployment regarding the constraints resolution mechanism.

---

[6] In the case of a partitioned network, one can notice that the distinction between the failure of a machine and its inaccessibility is a hard problem.

References

1. E. Bruneton, C. Thierry, M. Leclercq, V. Quéma, and S. Jean-Bernard. An open component model and its support in java. In *Proceedings of CBSE'04*, Edinburgh, Scotland, may 2004.
2. A. Dearle, G. N. C. Kirby, and A. J. McCarthy. A framework for constraint-based deployment and autonomic management of distributed applications. In *Proceedings of ICAC'04*, pages 300–301, 2004.
3. D. Garlan, R. Allen, and J. Ockerbloom. Exploiting style in architectural design environments. In *Proceedings of FSE'94*, pages 175–188, New Orleans, Louisiana, USA, 1994.
4. D. e. a. Garlan. Acme: Architectural description of component-based systems. In G. T. Leavens and M. Sitaraman, editors, *Foundations of Component-Based Systems*, pages 47–68. Cambridge University Press, 2000.
5. I. Georgiadis, J. Magee, and J. Kramer. Self-organising software architectures for distributed systems. In *Proceedings of WOSS'02*, pages 33–38, Charleston, South Carolina, USA, 2002.
6. D. Hoareau and Y. Mahéo. Constraint-Based Deployment of Distributed Components in a Dynamic Network. In *Proceedings of ARCS'06*, volume 3864 of *LNCS*, pages 450–464, Frankfurt/Main, Germany, March 2006. Springer Verlag.
7. Y. Mahéo, F. Guidec, and L. Courtrai. A Java Middleware Platform for Resource-Aware Distributed Applications. In *Proceedings of ISPDC'03*, pages 96–103, Ljubljana, Slovenia, October 2003. IEEE CS.
8. N. Medvidovic and N. R. Taylor. A classification and comparison framework for software architecture description languages. *IEEE TSE*, 26(1):70–93, 2000.
9. M. Mikic-Rakic and N. Medvidovic. Architecture-level support for software component deployment in resource constrained environment. In *Proceedings of the 1st International IFIP/ACM Conference on Component Deployment (CD'02)*, pages 31–46, Berlin, Germany, 2002.
10. OMG. Corba components, v3.0, adpoted specification, document formal/2002-06-65. Object Management Group Web Site: http://www.omg.org/docs/formal/02-06-65.pdf, June 2002.
11. OMG. Uml 2.0 ocl final adopted specification, document ptc/03-10-14. Object Management Group Web Site: http://www.omg.org/docs/ptc/03-10-14.pdf, 2003.
12. I. Prolog. constraints inside, 1996. *Prolog IV reference manual*, 1996.
13. R. Roshandel, B. Schmerl, N. Medvidovic, D. Garlan, and D. Zhang. Understanding tradeoffs among different architectural modeling approaches. In *Proceedings of WICSA'04*, pages 47–56, June 2004.
14. B. Schmerl and D. Garlan. Exploiting architectural design knowledge to support self-repairing systems. In *Proceedings of SEKE'02*, pages 241–248, Ischia, Italy, 2002.
15. M. Shaw and D. Garlan. *Software Architecture: Perspectives on an Emerging Discipline*. Prentice Hall, 1996.
16. C. Tibermacine, R. Fleurquin, and S. Sadou. Preserving architectural choices throughout the component-based software development process. In *Proceedings of WICSA'05*, Pittsburgh, Pennsylvania, USA, November 2005.
17. C. Tibermacine, R. Fleurquin, and S. Sadou. Simplifying transformations of architectural constraints. In *Proceedings of SAC'06*, Dijon, France, April 2006.

A Family of Distributed Deadlock Avoidance Protocols and Their Reachable State Spaces*

César Sánchez, Henny B. Sipma, and Zohar Manna

Computer Science Department
Stanford University, Stanford, CA 94305-9025
{cesar,sipma,manna}@CS.Stanford.EDU

Abstract. We study resource management in distributed systems. Incorrect handling of resources may lead to deadlocks, missed deadlines, priority inversions, and other forms of incorrect behavior or degraded performance. While in centralized systems deadlock avoidance is commonly used to ensure correct and efficient resource allocation, distributed deadlock avoidance is harder, and general solutions are considered impractical due to the high communication overhead. However, solutions that use only operations on local data exist if some static information about the possible sequences of remote invocations is known.

We present a family of efficient distributed deadlock avoidance algorithms that subsumes previously known solutions as special instances. Even though different protocols within the family allow different levels of concurrency and consequently fewer or more executions, we prove that they all have the same set of reachable states, expressed by a global invariant. This result enables: (1) *a design principle*: the use of different protocols at different sites does not compromise deadlock avoidance; (2) *a proof principle*: any resource allocation protocol that preserves the global invariant and whose allocation decisions are at least as liberal as those of the least liberal in the family, guarantees absence of deadlock.

1 Introduction

Middleware services play a key role in the development of modern distributed real-time and embedded (DRE) systems. DRE systems often consist of a variety of hardware and software components, each with their own protocols, interfaces, operating systems, and API's. Middleware services hide this heterogeneity, allowing the software engineer to focus on the application, by providing a high-level uniform interface, and handling management of resources and communication and coordination between components. However, this approach is effective only if these services are well-defined, flexible and efficient.

In this paper we focus on resource allocation services for DRE systems. Computations in distributed systems often involve a distribution of method calls over

---

* This research was supported in part by NSF grants CCR-01-21403, CCR-02-20134, CCR-02-09237, CNS-0411363, and CCF-0430102, and by NAVY/ONR contract N00014-03-1-0939.

M.B. Dwyer and A. Lopes (Eds.): FASE 2007, LNCS 4422, pp. 155–169, 2007.

multiple sites. At each site these computations need resources, for example in the form of threads, to proceed. With multiple processes starting and running at different sites, and a limited number of threads at each site, deadlock may arise. Traditionally three methods are used to deal with deadlock: prevention, avoidance and detection. In *deadlock prevention* a deadlock state is made unreachable by, for example, imposing a total order in which resources are acquired, such as in "monotone locking" [1,4]. This strategy can substantially reduce performance, by artificially limiting concurrency. With *deadlock detection*, common in databases, deadlock states may occur, but are upon detection resolved by, for example, roll-back of transactions. In embedded systems, however, this is usually not an option, especially in systems interacting with physical devices.

Deadlock avoidance methods take a middle route. At runtime a protocol is used to decide whether a resource request is granted based on current resource availability and possible future requests of processes in the system. A resource is granted only if it is *safe*, that is, if there is a strategy to ensure that all processes can complete. To make this test feasible, processes that enter the system must announce their possible resource usage. This idea was first proposed in centralized systems by Dijkstra in his Banker's algorithm [2,3,13,11], where processes report the maximum number of resources that they can request. When resources are distributed across multiple sites, however, deadlock avoidance is harder because the different sites may have to consult each other to determine whether a particular allocation is safe. Consequently, a general solution to distributed deadlock avoidance is considered impractical [12]; the communication costs involved simply outweigh the benefits gained from deadlock avoidance over deadlock prevention.

We study distributed deadlock avoidance algorithms that do not require any communication between sites. Our algorithms are applicable to distributed systems in which processes perform remote method invocations and lock local resources (threads) until all remote calls have returned. In particular, if the chain of remote calls arrives back to a site previously visited, then a new resource is needed. This arises, for example, in DRE architectures that use the *WaitOnConnection* policy for nested up-calls [9,10,14]. Our algorithms succeed in providing deadlock avoidance without any communication overhead by using static process information in the form of call graphs that represent all possible sequences of remote invocations. In DRE systems, this information can usually be extracted from the component specifications or from the source code directly by static analysis.

In this paper we analyze the common properties of a family of deadlock avoidance protocols that include the protocols we presented in earlier papers [8,7,6]. We show that the two protocols BASIC-P introduced in [8] and LIVE-P presented in [6] are the two extremes of a spectrum of protocols that allow, going from BASIC-P to LIVE-P, increasing levels of concurrency. Despite these different levels of concurrency, and thus executions permitted, we prove that all protocols in the family have the same set of reachable states. The significance of this result is that it allows running different protocols from the family at different sites without compromising deadlock. In addition, it considerably simplifies proving correct modifications and refinements of these protocols, as proofs reduce to showing that the new protocol preserves the same invariant.

The rest of this paper is structured as follows. Section 2 describes the computational model and Section 3 introduces the protocols. Section 4 characterizes the different levels of concurrency by comparing allocation sequences for the different protocols, and Section 5 presents the proof that all protocols have the same set of reachable states. Section 6 concludes with some remarks about the design principle enabled by our results and some open problems.

2   Computational Model

We model a distributed system as a set of sites that perform computations and a call graph, which provides a static representation of all possible resource usage patterns. Formally, a distributed system is a tuple $\mathcal{S} : \langle \mathcal{R}, \mathcal{G} \rangle$ consisting of

- $\mathcal{R} :$ $\{r_1, \ldots, r_{|\mathcal{R}|}\}$, a set of sites, and
- $\mathcal{G} :$ $\langle V, \rightarrow, I \rangle$ a call graph specification.

A call graph specification $\mathcal{G} : \langle V, \rightarrow, I \rangle$ consists of a directed acyclic graph $\langle V, \rightarrow \rangle$, which captures all the possible sequences of remote calls that processes can perform. The set of initial nodes $I \subseteq V$ contains those methods that can be invoked when a process is spawned. A call-graph node $n{:}r$ represents a method n that runs in site r. We also say that node n resides in site r. If two nodes reside in the same site we write $n \equiv_{\mathcal{R}} m$. An edge from $n{:}r$ to $m{:}s$ denotes that method n, in the course of its execution may invoke method m in site s.

We assume that each site has a fixed number of pre-allocated resources. Although in many modern operating systems threads can be spawned dynamically, many DRE systems pre-allocate fixed sets of threads to avoid the relatively large and variable cost of thread creation and initialization. Each site r maintains a set of local variables V_r that includes the constant $T_r \geq 1$ denoting the number of resources present in r, and a variable t_r that represents the number of available resources. Initially, $t_r = T_r$.

The execution of a system consists of processes, created dynamically, executing computations that only perform remote calls according to the edges in the call graph. When a new process is spawned it starts its execution with the graph node whose outgoing paths describe the remote calls that the process can perform. All invocations to a call graph node require a new resource in the corresponding site, while call returns release a resource. We impose no restriction on the topology of the call graph or on the number of process instances, and thus deadlocks can be reached if all requests for resources are immediately granted.

Example 1. Consider a system with two sites $\mathcal{R} = \{r, s\}$, a call graph with four nodes $V = \{n_1, n_2, m_1, m_2\}$, where n_1 and m_1 are initial, and edges:

$$\rightarrow \boxed{n_1 \quad r} \rightarrow \boxed{n_2 \quad s} \qquad \rightarrow \boxed{m_1 \quad s} \rightarrow \boxed{m_2 \quad r}$$

This system has reachable deadlocks if no controller is used. Let sites s and r handle exactly two threads each. If four processes are spawned, two instances of

n_1 and two of m_1, all resources in the system will be locked after each process starts executing its initial node. Consequently, the allocation attempts for n_2 and m_2 will be blocked indefinitely, so no process will terminate or return a resource. This allocation sequence is depicted below, where a • represents an existing process that tries to acquire a resource at a node (if • precedes the node) or has just been granted the resource (if • appears after the node).

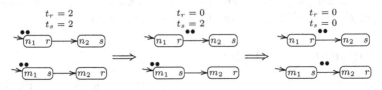

Our deadlock avoidance solution consists of two parts: (1) the offline calculation of *annotations*, maps from call-graph nodes to natural numbers; and (2) a run-time *protocol* that controls resource allocations based on these annotations. Informally, an annotation measures the number of resources required for a computation. The protocols grant a request based on the remaining local resources (and possibly other local variables) and the annotation of the requesting node.

Protocol. A *protocol* for controlling the resource allocation in node $n : r$ is implemented by a program executed in r before and after method n is dispatched. This code can be different for different call-graph nodes even if they reside in the same site. The schematic structure of a protocol for a node $n{:}r$ is:

$$
n :: \left[\begin{array}{l}
\boxed{\begin{array}{l} \textbf{when } En_n(V_r) \textbf{ do} \\ \quad In_n(V_r, V'_r) \end{array}} \quad \left.\right\} \text{ entry section} \\[1.2em]
\boxed{f()} \qquad\qquad\qquad \left.\right\} \text{ method invocation} \\[0.8em]
\boxed{Out_n(V_r, V'_r)} \quad\; \left.\right\} \text{ exit section}
\end{array} \right]
$$

Upon invocation, the entry section checks resource availability by inspecting local variables V_r of site r. If the predicate $En_n(V_r)$, called the enabling condition, is satisfied we say that the entry section is *enabled*. In this case, the request can be granted and the local variables are updated according to the relation $In_n(V_r, V'_r)$ (where V'_r stands for the local variables after the action is taken). We assume that the entry section is executed atomically, as a *test-and-set*. The method invocation section executes the code of the method, here represented as $f()$, which may perform remote calls according to the edges outgoing from node n in the call graph. The method invocation can only terminate after all its invoked calls (descendants in the call graph) have terminated and returned. The exit section releases the resource and may update some local variables in site r, according to the relation $Out_n(V_r, V'_r)$. In_n is called the entry action and Out_n is called the exit action.

Annotations. Given a system $\mathcal{S}$ and annotation α, the annotated call graph $(V, \rightarrow, \dashrightarrow)$ is obtained from the call graph $(V, \rightarrow)$ by adding one edge $n \dashrightarrow m$ between any two nodes that reside in the same site with annotation $\alpha(n) \geq \alpha(m)$. A node n "depends" on a node m, which we represent $n \succ m$, if there is a path in the annotated graph from n to m that follows at least one $\rightarrow$ edge. The annotated graph is acyclic if no node depends on itself, in which case we say that the annotation is acyclic.

3 A Family of Local Protocols

Our goal is to construct protocols that (1) avoid deadlock in all scenarios, (2) require no communication between sites, and (3) maximize resource utilization (grant requests as much as possible without compromising deadlock freedom).

The first protocol we proposed was BASIC-P [8], shown in Fig. 1 for a node $n{:}r$ with annotation $\alpha(n) = i$. Upon a resource request, BASIC-P checks whether the number of available resources is large enough, as indicated by the annotation i. This check ensures that processes (local or remote) that could potentially be blocked if the resource is granted, have enough resources to complete. The correctness of BASIC-P is based on the acyclicity of the annotations:

$$n :: \begin{bmatrix} \begin{bmatrix} \textbf{when } i \leq t_r \ \textbf{do} \\ t_r\text{--} \end{bmatrix} \\ f() \\ t_r\text{++} \end{bmatrix}$$

Fig. 1. The protocol BASIC-P

Theorem 1 (Annotation Theorem for Basic-P [8]). *Given a system $\mathcal{S}$ and an acyclic annotation, if* BASIC-P *is used to control resource allocations then all executions of $\mathcal{S}$ are deadlock free.*

Example 2. Reconsider the system from Example 1. The left diagram below shows an annotated call graph with $\alpha(n_1) = \alpha(n_2) = \alpha(m_2) = 1$ and $\alpha(m_1) = 2$. It is acyclic, and thus by Theorem 1, if BASIC-P is used with these annotations, the system is deadlock free.

Let us compare this with Example 1 where a resource is granted simply if it is available. This corresponds to using BASIC-P with the annotated call graph above on the right, with $\alpha(n) = 1$ for all nodes. In Example 1 we showed that a deadlock is reachable, and indeed this annotated graph is not acyclic; it contains dependency cycles, for example $n_1 \rightarrow n_2 \dashrightarrow m_1 \rightarrow m_2 \dashrightarrow n_1$. Therefore Theorem 1 does not apply. In the diagram on the left all dependency cycles are broken by the annotation $\alpha(m_1) = 2$. Requiring the presence of at least two resources for granting a resource at m_1 ensures that the last resource available in s can only be obtained at n_2, which breaks all possible circular waits. $\square$

$$n :: \left[\begin{array}{l} \left[\begin{array}{l} \textbf{when } 1 \leq t_r \textbf{ do} \\ \qquad t_r\text{--} \end{array} \right] \\ f() \\ t_r\text{++} \end{array} \right] \qquad\qquad n :: \left[\begin{array}{l} \left[\begin{array}{l} \textbf{when } i \leq p_r \, \wedge \, 1 \leq t_r \textbf{ do} \\ \qquad \langle p_r\text{--}, \ t_r\text{--} \rangle \end{array} \right] \\ f() \\ \langle t_r\text{++}, \ p_r\text{++} \rangle \end{array} \right]$$

If $i = 1$ If $i > 1$

Fig. 2. The protocol EFFICIENT-P

The protocol BASIC-P can be improved using the observation that processes requesting resources to execute nodes with annotation 1 can always terminate, in spite of any other process in the system. This observation leads to EFFICIENT-P (shown in Fig. 2), which uses two counters: t_r, as before; and p_r, to keep track of the "potentially recoverable" resources, which include not only the available resources but also the resources granted to processes in nodes with annotation 1. A similar version of the Annotation Theorem for EFFICIENT-P establishes that in the absence of dependency cycles, EFFICIENT-P can reach no deadlocks.

The proof of the Annotation Theorem for BASIC-P and EFFICIENT-P [8] relies on showing that the following global invariant φ is maintained:

$$\varphi \overset{\text{def}}{=} \bigwedge_{r \in \mathcal{R}} \bigwedge_{k \leq T_r} \varphi_r[k] \qquad \text{with} \qquad \varphi_r[k] \overset{\text{def}}{=} A_r[k] \leq T_r - (k-1).$$

where $a_r[k]$ stands for the number of active processes running in site r executing nodes with annotation k and $A_r[k]$ stands for $\sum_{j \geq k} a_r[j]$, that is, $A_r[k]$ represents the number of active processes running in site r executing nodes with annotation k or higher. In [6] we exploited this fact by constructing the protocol

$$n :: \left[\begin{array}{l} \left[\begin{array}{l} \textbf{when } \varphi_r^{(i)} \textbf{ do} \\ \qquad a_r[i]\text{++} \end{array} \right] \\ f() \\ a_r[i]\text{--} \end{array} \right]$$

Fig. 3. The protocol LIVE-P

LIVE-P, shown in Fig. 3, which grants access to a resource precisely whenever φ_r is preserved. This protocol not only guarantees absence of deadlock, it also provides, in contrast with BASIC-P, individual liveness for all processes. Its enabling condition, $\varphi_r^{(i)}$, is exactly the weakest precondition for φ_r of the transition that grants the resource:

$$\varphi_r^{(i)} \overset{\text{def}}{=} \left(\begin{array}{c} \bigwedge_{k > i} A_r[k] \qquad \leq T_r - (k-1) \\ \wedge \\ \bigwedge_{k \leq i} A_r[k] + 1 \leq T_r - (k-1) \end{array} \right)$$

We use $\varphi_r^{(i)}[j]$ for the clause of $\varphi_r^{(i)}$ that corresponds to annotation j. Observe that $\varphi_r^{(i)}[j]$ is syntactically identical to $\varphi_r[j]$ for $j > i$. Moreover, for $j \leq i$, $\varphi_r^{(i)}[j]$ implies $\varphi_r[j]$.

To compare the protocols we restate BASIC-P and EFFICIENT-P in terms of the notation introduced for LIVE-P. The enabling condition of BASIC-P becomes:

$$n :: \left[\begin{bmatrix} \textbf{when } \chi_r^{(i)}[1] \textbf{ do} \\ a_r[i]\texttt{++} \end{bmatrix} \right]$$
$$f()$$
$$a_r[i]\texttt{--}$$

$$n :: \left[\begin{bmatrix} \textbf{when } \varphi_r^{(i)}[1] \wedge \chi_r^{(i)}[2] \textbf{ do} \\ a_r[i]\texttt{++} \end{bmatrix} \right]$$
$$f()$$
$$a_r[i]\texttt{--}$$

(a) 1-EFFICIENT-P (b) 2-EFFICIENT-P

Fig. 4. BASIC-P and EFFICIENT-P restated using strengthenings

$$A_r[1] \leq T_r - (i-1)$$

which is, as we will see, stronger than $\varphi_r^{(i)}$, that is, the enabling condition of BASIC-P implies that of LIVE-P. Given $k \leq i$ we define the k-th strengthening formula for a request in node $n{:}r$ with annotation i as:

$$\chi_r^{(i)}[k] \stackrel{\text{def}}{=} A_r[k] \leq T_r - (i-1)$$

It is easy to see that the following holds for all $k \leq j \leq i$,

$$\chi_r^{(i)}[k] \rightarrow \varphi_r^{(i)}[j] \quad \text{and therefore} \quad \chi_r^{(i)}[k] \rightarrow \bigwedge_{k \leq j \leq i} \varphi_r^{(i)}[j].$$

Also, if φ_r holds before the resource is granted, then $\varphi_r^{(i)}[j]$ also holds for all $i \geq j$, since the formulas for $\varphi_r^{(i)}[j]$ and $\varphi_r[j]$ are identical in this case. Hence:

$$\chi_r^{(i)}[k] \rightarrow \bigwedge_{k \leq j} \varphi_r^{(i)}[j]. \tag{1}$$

Finally, if $\varphi_r^{(i)}[j]$ is satisfied for all values less than k, and $\chi_r^{(i)}[k]$ is ensured, $\varphi_r^{(i)}$ can be concluded:

$$(\bigwedge_{j<k} \varphi_r^{(i)}[j]) \wedge \chi_r^{(i)}[k] \rightarrow (\bigwedge_{j<k} \varphi_r^{(i)}[j]) \wedge (\bigwedge_{j \geq k} \varphi_r^{(i)}[j])$$

$$\leftrightarrow \bigwedge \varphi_r^{(i)}[j]$$

$$\leftrightarrow \varphi_r^{(i)}.$$

Therefore, if a protocol ensures that for some k, both $\bigwedge_{j<k} \varphi_r^{(i)}[j]$ and the k-strengthening $\chi_r^{(i)}[k]$ hold, then φ_r is an invariant.

In general, the lower the value of the strengthening point k, the less computation is needed to compute the predicate (the number of comparisons is reduced) but the less liberal the enabling condition becomes. In the case of $k = 1$ the strengthening is $\chi_r^{(i)}[1]$, and the protocol obtained (see Fig. 4(a)) is equivalent

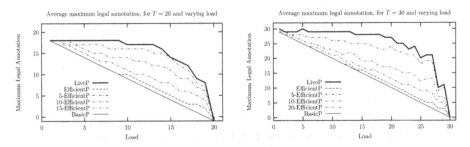

Fig. 5. A comparison of BASIC-P, k-EFFICIENT-P and LIVE-P

to BASIC-P. Note that this protocol is *logically* equivalent to BASIC-P: the result of the enabling condition, and the effect of the input and output actions on future tests are the same. The implementation of BASIC-P introduced earlier uses a single counter t_r, while in this restated version, several counters are used: $a_r[i]$ and $A_r[1]$. However, the effect on $A_r[1]$ of the increments and decrements of $a_r[i]$ are independent of i. Therefore, these actions can be implemented as $A_r[1]$++ and $A_r[1]$-- respectively. Similarly, with a strengthening point of $k = 2$ we obtain a protocol equivalent to EFFICIENT-P, shown in Fig. 4(b).

The general form of our family of protocols can now be given as k-EFFICIENT-P, shown in Fig. 6. It covers the full spectrum of protocols with BASIC-P, which is equivalent to 1-EFFICIENT-P, at one end and LIVE-P, which is equal to T_r-EFFICIENT-P at the other end of the spectrum. The protocols k-EFFICIENT-P can be implemented in several ways. The simplest implementation needs space $O(k \ log \ T_r)$ to store k counters and requires $O(k)$ operations per allocation decision. A more sophisticated implementation using an *active tree* data-structure still needs $O(k \ log \ T_r)$, but requires only $O(log \ k)$ operations per allocation decision [6]. Fig. 5 presents some experimental results that compare concurrency levels allowed by the different protocols. The figures depict the maximum annotation allowed by each protocol as a function of the load (total number of active processes). The load is created by annotations picked uniformly at random.

$$n :: \left[\begin{array}{l} \left[\textbf{when } (\bigwedge_{j<k} \varphi_r^{(i)}[j]) \wedge \chi_r^{(i)}[k] \textbf{ do} \\ \qquad\qquad a_r[i]\text{++} \end{array} \right] \\ f() \\ a_r[i]\text{--} \end{array} \right]$$

Fig. 6. The protocol k-EFFICIENT-P

4   Allocation Sequences

In this section we compare the set of runs allowed by each protocol. We capture these sets by languages over an alphabet of allocations and deallocations.

Given a call graph $(V, \rightarrow)$ let the set $\overline{V}$ contain a symbol $\overline{n}$ for every n in V. The allocation alphabet Σ is the disjoint union of V and $\overline{V}$. Symbols in V

are called allocation symbols, while symbols in $\overline{V}$ are referred to as deallocation symbols. Given a string s in Σ^* and a symbol v in Σ we use s_v for the number of occurrences of v in s, and $|s|_n$ to stand for $s_n - s_{\overline{n}}$. A *well-formed* allocation string s is one for which every deallocation occurs after a matching allocation, that is, for every prefix p of s, $|p|_n \geq 0$. An *admissible* allocation sequence is one that corresponds to a prefix run of the system, according to the call graph. This requires (1) that the string be well-formed, (2) that every allocation of a non-root node is preceded by a matching allocation of its parent node, and (3) that every deallocation of a node is preceded by a corresponding deallocation of its children nodes. Formally,

Definition 1 (Admissible Strings). *A well-formed allocation string s is called admissible if for every prefix p of s, and every remote call $n \to m$: $|p|_n \geq |p|_m$.*

Admissible strings ensure that the number of child processes (callees) is not higher than the number of parents (caller processes), so that there is a possible match. For brevity, we simply use *string* to refer to admissible string.

We say that a protocol is *completely local* if all the enabling conditions are determined by: (1) the annotation of the call-graph node requested, and (2) the set of active processes in the local site and their annotations. It is easy to see that the protocols k-EFFICIENT-P are completely local. We use the values of $a_r[\cdot]$ and $A_r[\cdot]$ as the (abstract) global states of the system since these values capture all effects of completely local protocols in the outcomes of future requests. The initial state of the system, denoted by Θ, is $a_r[i] = A_r[i] = 0$ for all sites r and annotations i.

Given a state σ and a protocol P, if the enabling condition of P for a node n is satisfied at σ we write $En_n^P(\sigma)$. For convenience, we introduce a new state $\bot$ to capture sequences that a protocol forbids, and require that $En_n^P(\bot)$ does not hold. We denote by $P(s)$ the[1] state reached by P after exercising the allocation string s, defined inductively as $P(\epsilon) = \Theta$ and:

$$P(s\,n) = \begin{cases} In_n^P(P(s)) & \text{if } En_n^P(P(s)) \\ \bot & \text{otherwise} \end{cases} \qquad P(s\,\overline{n}) = \begin{cases} Out_n^P(P(s)) & \text{if } P(s) \neq \bot \\ \bot & \text{otherwise} \end{cases}$$

We say that a string s is accepted by a protocol P if $P(s) \neq \bot$. The set of strings accepted by P is denoted by $\mathcal{L}(P)$, and we use $P \sqsubseteq Q$ for the partial order defined by language inclusion $\mathcal{L}(P) \subseteq \mathcal{L}(Q)$.

Example 3. Reconsider the system in Example 1. The allocation sequence that leads to a deadlock is $s : n_1 n_1 m_1 m_1$. Even though $n_1 n_1 m_1$ is in $\mathcal{L}(\text{BASIC-P})$, the enabling condition of m_1 becomes disabled, so $\text{BASIC-P}(s) = \bot$ and $s \notin \mathcal{L}(\text{BASIC-P})$.   □

---

[1] All our protocols are deterministic but the results can be adapted for non-deterministic protocols as well.

Lemma 1. *The following are equivalent:*

(i) $\mathcal{L}(P) \subseteq \mathcal{L}(Q)$.
(ii) *For all strings s and allocation symbols n, if $En_n^P(P(s))$ then $En_n^Q(Q(s))$.*

Proof. We prove both implications separately:

– Assume $\mathcal{L}(P) \subseteq \mathcal{L}(Q)$, and let s and n be such that $En_n^P(P(s))$. Since $s \in \mathcal{L}(P)$ then $s \in \mathcal{L}(Q)$. Moreover, $s \cdot n \in \mathcal{L}(P)$ and then $s \cdot n \in \mathcal{L}(Q)$. Hence, $En_n^Q(Q(s))$.
– Assume now (ii). We reason by induction on strings:
  • First, both $\epsilon \in \mathcal{L}(P)$ and $\epsilon \in \mathcal{L}(Q)$.
  • Let $s \cdot n \in \mathcal{L}(P)$. Then $En_n^P(P(s))$, so also $En_n^Q(Q(s))$. Hence, $s \cdot n \in \mathcal{L}(Q)$.
  • Let $s \cdot \overline{n} \in \mathcal{L}(P)$. This implies $s \in \mathcal{L}(P)$ and by inductive hypothesis $s \in \mathcal{L}(Q)$. Then $s \cdot \overline{n} \in \mathcal{L}(Q)$, as desired.

Therefore (i) and (ii) are equivalent.   □

Let P, Q be any two of BASIC-P, EFFICIENT-P, k-EFFICIENT-P and LIVE-P. We showed in Section 3 that the entry and exit actions are identical for all these protocols. Therefore, if s is in the language of both P and Q then the states reached are the same, i.e., $P(s) = Q(s)$. It follows that if for all states σ, $En_n^P(\sigma)$ implies $En_n^Q(\sigma)$, then $\mathcal{L}(P) \subseteq \mathcal{L}(Q)$.

Lemma 2. *If j-EFFICIENT-P allows an allocation then k-EFFICIENT-P also allows the allocation, provided $j \leq k$.*

Proof. Let $j \leq k$. It follows from the definition that $\chi_r^{(i)}[j]$ implies $\chi_r^{(i)}[k]$. Moreover, by (1), $\chi_r^{(i)}[j]$ implies $\bigwedge_{j \leq l \leq k} \varphi_r^{(i)}[l]$. Consequently,

$$\underbrace{\bigwedge_{l<j} \varphi_r^{(i)}[l] \wedge \chi_r^{(i)}[j]}_{En_n^{j\text{-EFFICIENT-P}}} \rightarrow \underbrace{\bigwedge_{l<k} \varphi_r^{(i)}[l] \wedge \chi_r^{(i)}[k]}_{En_n^{k\text{-EFFICIENT-P}}}$$

Therefore if j-EFFICIENT-P allows a request so does k-EFFICIENT-P.   □

Lemma 2 states that the enabling condition of k-EFFICIENT-P becomes weaker as k grows, that is, the enabling condition of BASIC-P is stronger than that of EFFICIENT-P, which in turn is stronger than k-EFFICIENT-P, which is stronger than LIVE-P. An immediate consequence of Lemma 2 is:

$$\text{BASIC-P} \sqsubseteq \text{EFFICIENT-P} \sqsubseteq \ldots \sqsubseteq k\text{-EFFICIENT-P} \sqsubseteq \ldots \sqsubseteq \text{LIVE-P}$$

The following examples show that these language containments are strict:

$$\text{BASIC-P} \not\sqsupseteq \text{EFFICIENT-P} \not\sqsupseteq \ldots \not\sqsupseteq k\text{-EFFICIENT-P} \not\sqsupseteq \ldots \not\sqsupseteq \text{LIVE-P}$$

which is depicted in Fig 7(a).

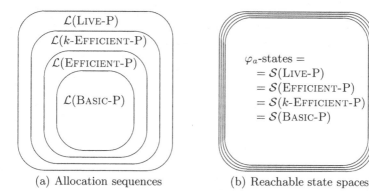

(a) Allocation sequences   (b) Reachable state spaces

Fig. 7. Comparison of the family of protocols

Example 4. Consider the following call-graph, with initial resources $T_r = 2$.

$$\boxed{n_2 \quad r} \xrightarrow{2} \boxed{n_1 \quad r}^1$$

$$\boxed{m_1 \quad r}^1$$

The string $m_1 n_2$ is accepted by EFFICIENT-P but not by BASIC-P. This system can be generalized to show that there is a string accepted by k-EFFICIENT-P but not by j-EFFICIENT-P (for $j < k$). Consider the following annotated call graph, with initial resources $T_r = j + 1$.

$$\boxed{n_{j+1} \quad r} \xrightarrow{j+1} \boxed{n_j \quad r} \xrightarrow{j} \boxed{n_{j-1} \quad r} \xrightarrow{j-1} \cdots \longrightarrow \boxed{n_1 \quad r}^1$$

$$\boxed{m_j \quad r} \xrightarrow{j} \boxed{m_{j-1} \quad r} \xrightarrow{j-1} \cdots \longrightarrow \boxed{m_1 \quad r}^1$$

The string $m_j n_{j+1}$ is accepted by k-EFFICIENT-P, but is not accepted by j-EFFICIENT-P.   □

5   Reachable State Spaces

The reachable state space of a protocol P, denoted by $\mathcal{S}(P)$, is the set of global states that P can reach following some admissible allocation sequence. Clearly, for two protocols P and Q, if their actions are equivalent and $P \sqsubseteq Q$ then every state reachable by P is also reachable by Q. Indeed any allocation string that reaches a state for P also reaches that same state for Q.

Lemma 3. *For every two protocols P and Q with the same entry and exit actions, if $P \sqsubseteq Q$ then $\mathcal{S}(P) \subseteq \mathcal{S}(Q)$.*

Consequently,

$$\mathcal{S}(\text{BASIC-P}) \subseteq \mathcal{S}(\text{EFFICIENT-P}) \subseteq \ldots \subseteq \mathcal{S}(k\text{-EFFICIENT-P}) \subseteq \ldots \subseteq \mathcal{S}(\text{LIVE-P})$$

Let $\mathcal{S}(\varphi_a)$ describe the set of states that satisfy φ and that are reachable by some admissible allocation string. In the rest of this section we show that the above containment relation collapses into equalities by proving

$$\mathcal{S}(\text{BASIC-P}) \;=\; \mathcal{S}(\text{LIVE-P}) \;=\; \mathcal{S}(\varphi_a)$$

The proof relies on the existence of a *preference order* on the nodes of the annotated call graph, such that, if allocations are made following this order, then every allocation request that succeeds in LIVE-P also succeeds in BASIC-P.

5.1   Preference Orders

A *preference order* of an annotated call graph is an order on the nodes such that, if all allocations in a given admissible string are performed following that order, then (1) the sequence obtained is also admissible, and (2) higher annotations for each site are visited first. This will allow us to show that BASIC-P can reach all φ_a-states.

Given a call graph, a total order $>$ on its nodes is called topological if it respects the descendant relation, that is, if for every pair of nodes n and m, if $n \to m$ then $n > m$. Analogously, we say that an order $>$ respects an annotation α if for every pair of nodes n and m residing in the same site, if $\alpha(n) > \alpha(m)$ then $n > m$. A total order that is topological and respects annotations is called a preference order.

Lemma 4. *Every acyclically annotated call graph has a preference order.*

Proof. The proof proceeds by induction on the number of call-graph nodes. The result trivially holds for the empty call graph. For the inductive step, assume the result holds for all call graphs with at most k nodes and consider an arbitrary call graph with $k + 1$ nodes.

First, there must be a root node whose annotation is the highest among all the nodes residing in the same site. Otherwise a dependency cycle can be formed: take the maximal nodes for all sites, which are internal by assumption, and their root ancestors. For every maximal (internal) node there is $\to^+$ path reaching it, starting from its corresponding root. Similarly, for every root there is an incoming $\dashrightarrow$ edge from the maximal internal node that resides in its site. A cycle exists since the (bipartite) subgraph of roots and maximal nodes is finite, and every node has a successor (a $\to^+$ for root nodes, and a $\dashrightarrow$ for maximal nodes). This contradicts that the annotation is acyclic.

Now, let n be a maximal root node, and let $>$ be a preference order for the graph that results by removing n, which exists by inductive hypothesis. We extend $>$ by adding $n > m$ for every other node m. The order is topological since n is a root. The order respects annotations since n is maximal in its site. $\square$

5.2   Reachable States

A global state of a distributed system is *admissible* if all existing processes (active or waiting) in a node n are also existing, and active, in every node ancestor of

n. That is, if the state corresponds to the outcome of some admissible allocation sequence.

Theorem 2. *The set of reachable states of a system using* LIVE-P *is precisely the set of φ_a-states.*

Proof. It follows directly from the specification of LIVE-P that all reachable states satisfy φ. Therefore, we only need to show that all φ_a-states are reachable.

We proceed by induction on the number of active processes in the system. The base case, with no active process, is the initial state of the system Θ, which is trivially reachable by LIVE-P. For the inductive step, consider now an arbitrary φ_a-state σ with some active process. Since the call graph is acyclic and finite, there must be some active process P in σ with no active descendants. The state σ' obtained by removing P from σ is an admissible φ_a-state (all the conditions of admissibility and the clauses of φ are either simplified or identical); by the inductive hypothesis, σ' is reachable by LIVE-P. Since σ is obtained from σ' by an allocation that preserves φ (otherwise σ would not be a φ_a-state), then σ is reachable by LIVE-P. □

Theorem 2 states that for every sequence s that leads to a φ_a-state there is a sequence s' arriving at the same state for which all prefixes also reach φ_a-states. The sequence s' is in the language of LIVE-P.

Perhaps somewhat surprisingly, the set of reachable states of BASIC-P is also the set of all φ_a-states. To prove this we first need an auxiliary lemma.

Lemma 5. *In every φ_a-state, an allocation request in site r with annotation k has the same outcome using* BASIC-P *and* LIVE-P, *if there is no active process in r with annotation strictly smaller than k.*

Proof. First, in every φ_a-state, if BASIC-P grants a resource so does LIVE-P, by Lemma 2. We need to show that in every φ_a-state, if LIVE-P grants a request of k and $a_r[j] = 0$ for all $j < k$, then BASIC-P also grants the request. In this case,

$$T_r - t_r = A_r[1] = \sum_{j=1}^{T_r} a_r[j] = \sum_{j=k}^{T_r} a_r[j] = A_r[k], \tag{2}$$

and since LIVE-P grants the request, then $A_r[k] + 1 \leq T_r - (k-1)$ and $A_r[k] \leq T_r - k$. Using (2), $T_r - t_r \leq T_r - k$, and $t_r \geq k$, so BASIC-P also grants the resource. □

Theorem 3. *The set of reachable states of a system using* BASIC-P *is precisely the set of φ_a-states.*

Proof. The proof is analogous to the characterization of the reachable states of LIVE-P, except that the process P removed in the inductive step is chosen to be a minimal active process in some preference order $>$. This guarantees that P has no children (by the topological property of $>$), and that there is no active process in the same site with lower annotation (by the annotation respecting property of $>$). Consequently, Lemma 5 applies, and the resulting state is also reachable by BASIC-P. □

Theorem 3 can also be restated in terms of allocation sequences. For every admissible allocation string that arrives at a φ_a-state there is an admissible allocation string that arrives at the same state and (1) contains no deallocations, and (2) all the nodes occur according to some preference order. It follows from Theorem 3 that $\mathcal{S}(\text{BASIC-P}) = \mathcal{S}(\varphi_a)$, and hence, as depicted in Fig 7(b):

$$\mathcal{S}(\text{BASIC-P}) = \mathcal{S}(\text{EFFICIENT-P}) = \ldots = \mathcal{S}(k\text{-EFFICIENT-P}) = \ldots = \mathcal{S}(\text{LIVE-P}).$$

6   Applications and Conclusions

We have generalized our earlier distributed deadlock avoidance algorithms by introducing a family of protocols defined by strengthenings of the global invariant φ. The most liberal protocol, LIVE-P, also ensures liveness, at the cost of maintaining more complicated data-structures (which require a non-constant number of operations per allocation request). The simplest protocol, BASIC-P, can be implemented with one operation per request, but allows less concurrency.

We have shown that all the reachable state spaces of the protocols are the same. This result allows a system designer more freedom in the implementation of a deadlock avoidance protocol, because it follows that every local protocol P that satisfies the following conditions for every request is guaranteed to avoid deadlock:

(1) if BASIC-P is enabled then P is enabled, and
(2) if P is enabled then LIVE-P is enabled

This holds because all P-reachable states satisfy φ, and from those states BASIC-P guarantees deadlock freedom. Informally, (2) guarantees that the system stays in a safe region, while (1) ensures that enough progress is made. This result implies, for example, that the combination of different protocols at different sites is safe. If a site has a constraint in memory or CPU time, then the simpler BASIC-P is preferable, while LIVE-P is a better choice if a site needs to maximize concurrency.

This result also facilitates the analysis of alternative protocols. Proving a protocol correct (deadlock freedom) can be a hard task if the protocol must deal with scheduling, external environment conditions, etc. With the results presented in this paper, to show that an allocation manager has no reachable deadlocks, it is enough to map its reachable state space to an abstract system for which all states guarantee φ, and all allocation decisions are at least as liberal as in BASIC-P. This technique is used in [5] to create an efficient distributed priority inheritance mechanism where priorities are encoded as annotations, and priority inheritance is performed by an annotation decrease. Although this "annotation decrease" transition is not allowed by the protocols presented here, since the resulting state is still a φ-state, it is also reachable by BASIC-P (maybe using a different sequence). Therefore, deadlocks are avoided.

Topics for further research include (1) the question whether LIVE-P is optimal, that is, does there exist a completely local protocol P that guarantees deadlock avoidance such that LIVE-P $\sqsubseteq P$, and (2) the question whether k-EFFICIENT-P is optimal with $O(k \, log \, T_r)$ storage space.

References

1. Andrew D. Birrell. An introduction to programming with threads. Research Report 35, Digital Equipment Corporation Systems Research Center, 1989.
2. Edsger W. Dijkstra. Cooperating sequential processes. Technical Report EWD-123, Technological University, Eindhoven, the Netherlands, 1965.
3. Arie N. Habermann. Prevention of system deadlocks. *Communications of the ACM*, 12:373–377, 1969.
4. James W. Havender. Avoiding deadlock in multi-tasking systems. *IBM Systems Journal*, 2:74–84, 1968.
5. César Sánchez, Henny B. Sipma, Christopher D. Gill, and Zohar Manna. Distributed priority inheritance for real-time and embedded systems. In Alex Shvartsman, editor, *Proceedings of the 10th International Conference On Principles Of Distributed Systems (OPODIS'06)*, volume 4305 of *LNCS*, Bordeaux, France, 2006. Springer-Verlag.
6. César Sánchez, Henny B. Sipma, Zohar Manna, and Christopher Gill. Efficient distributed deadlock avoidance with liveness guarantees. In Sang Lyul Min and Wang Yi, editors, *Proceedings of the 6th ACM & IEEE International Conference on Embedded Software (EMSOFT'06)*, pages 12–20, Seoul, South Korea, October 2006. ACM & IEEE.
7. César Sánchez, Henny B. Sipma, Zohar Manna, Venkita Subramonian, and Christopher Gill. On efficient distributed deadlock avoidance for distributed real-time and embedded systems. In *Proceedings of the 20th IEEE International Parallel and Distributed Processing Symposium (IPDPS'06)*, Rhodas, Greece, 2006. IEEE Computer Society Press.
8. César Sánchez, Henny B. Sipma, Venkita Subramonian, Christopher Gill, and Zohar Manna. Thread allocation protocols for distributed real-time and embedded systems. In Farn Wang, editor, *25th IFIP WG 2.6 International Conference on Formal Techniques for Networked and Distributed Systems (FORTE'05)*, volume 3731 of *LNCS*, pages 159–173, Taipei, Taiwan, October 2005. Springer-Verlag.
9. Douglas C. Schmidt. Evaluating Architectures for Multi-threaded CORBA Object Request Brokers. *Communications of the ACM Special Issue on CORBA*, 41(10):54–60, October 1998.
10. Douglas C. Schmidt, Michael Stal, Hans Rohnert, and Frank Buschmann. *Pattern-Oriented Software Architecture: Patterns for Concurrent and Networked Objects, Volume 2*. Wiley & Sons, New York, 2000.
11. Abraham Silberschatz, Peter B. Galvin, and Greg Gagne. *Operating System Concepts*. John Wiley & Sons, Inc., New York, NY, Sixth edition, 2003.
12. Mukesh Singhal and Niranjan G. Shivaratri. *Advanced Concepts in Operating Systems: Distributed, Database, and Multiprocessor Operating Systems*. McGraw-Hill, Inc., New York, NY, 1994.
13. William Stallings. *Operating Systems: Internals and Design Principles*. Prentice Hall, Inc., Upper Saddle River, NJ, Third edition, 1998.
14. Venkita Subramonian, Guoliang Xing, Christopher D. Gill, Chenyang Lu, and Ron Cytron. Middleware specialization for memory-constrained networked embedded systems. In *Proc. of 10th IEEE Real-Time and Embedded Technology and Applications Symposium (RTAS'04)*. IEEE Computer Society Press, May 2004.

Precise Specification of Use Case Scenarios

Jon Whittle

Dept of Information & Software Engineering
George Mason University
4400 University Drive
Fairfax, VA 22030
jwhittle@ise.gmu.edu

Abstract. Despite attempts to formalize the semantics of use cases, they remain an informal notation. The informality of use cases is both a blessing and a curse. Whilst it admits an easy learning curve and enables communication between software stakeholders, it is also a barrier to the application of automated methods for test case generation, validation or simulation. This paper presents a precise way of specifying use cases based on a three-level modeling paradigm strongly influenced by UML. The formal syntax and semantics of *use case charts* are given, along with an example that illustrates how they can be used in practice.

1 Introduction

Since their introduction, use cases have become a method of choice for elaborating software requirements. A use case—defined by Cockburn as a description of "the system's behavior under various conditions as the system responds to a request from one of the stakeholders" ([Coc00])—is typically represented as a combination of a UML use case diagram [BRJ05] and loosely structured text in one of many suggested template formats. The templates show the main sequence of steps that define a use case as well as some additional sequences that may capture exceptions, alternatives or extensions. The templates are usually related at a more abstract level using a UML use case diagram ([OMG05]) in which use cases are given graphically by ellipses and the actors that trigger those use cases are shown using standardized icons. Use cases are almost exclusively defined in an informal way—use case diagrams have no commonly agreed semantics and the semantics of the text templates is deliberately left unspecified in UML because there are no restrictions on what kind of text can be given.

The informality of use cases makes them very easy to use but is a barrier to the application of automated analysis methods such as test case generation, simulation, validation etc. Usually, little attention is paid to how different use cases interact—whether, for example, they can execute sequentially or concurrently, whether there are inconsistencies, or whether they are complete.

Many attempts have been made to introduce rigor into use case descriptions, ranging from structural restrictions on the text that can be used in templates (e.g., [Smi04, Wil04]) to the development of a formal semantics for aspects of use

M.B. Dwyer and A. Lopes (Eds.): FASE 2007, LNCS 4422, pp. 170–184, 2007.

case diagrams (e.g., [Ste01, OP99]). Approaches based on formalizing the text in templates usually define a restricted grammar for a subset of natural language and may also enforce that words in the text come from a dictionary. Approaches for defining a formal semantics for use cases focus on poorly specified constructs in UML use case diagrams, such as the UML ⟨⟨include⟩⟩ and ⟨⟨extend⟩⟩ relationships [Ste01] or the generalization of use cases [Iso04]. This paper takes a different approach. It gives an alternative, precisely defined, graphical language for use cases. It does not attempt to formalize UML's notion of a use case.

UML2.0 ([OMG05]) introduces interaction overview diagrams, a notation based on activity diagrams, for specifying relationships between interaction diagrams (e.g., sequence diagrams). Interaction overview diagrams (IODs) can be used to more precisely describe use cases as a set of interaction diagrams connected by activity diagram relationships, e.g., concurrency. IODs are based on high-level message sequence charts (hMSCs) [Uni04], a well-established notation for specifying interactions originally developed for the telecommunications domain. Whilst IODs provide much needed expressiveness for relating interaction scenarios, their semantics is still somewhat unclear since neither activity nor interaction diagrams have a formal semantics. In addition, IODs model only a single use case at a time and do not specify relationships *between* use cases. Nevertheless, IODs are an important step in precise use case modeling and form the basis for the *use case charts* presented in this paper.

In this paper, *use case charts*, a 3-level notation based on extended UML activity diagrams, is proposed as a way of specifying use cases in detail. The main application of use case charts to date has been to simulate use cases but use case charts are also precise enough for test generation and automated validation.

The idea behind use case charts is illustrated in Figure 1. For the purposes of this paper, a use case is considered to be a set of scenarios, where a scenario is an expected or actual execution trace of a system. The functionality of a system can be given as a set of use cases—that is, a set of sets of scenarios.

A use case chart specifies the scenarios for a system's use cases as a 3-level description: level-1 is the *use case chart*, an extended UML activity diagram in which the nodes are use cases; level-2 is a set of *scenario charts*, or extended activity diagrams where the nodes are scenarios; level-3 is a set of UML2.0 ([OMG05]) interaction diagrams. Each level-1 use case node is defined by a level-2 scenario chart (i.e., a set of connected scenario nodes). Each level-2 scenario node is defined by a UML2.0 interaction diagram. In Figure 1, 7 use cases are connected in a level-1 use case chart that starts with an initial use case and then forks into 4 "threads". Each of these 7 use cases is defined by a level-2 scenario chart. In Figure 1, the scenario chart for the use case at the source of the dashed arrow is shown. In this scenario chart, there are three scenario nodes. Each node is defined by a UML2.0 interaction diagram.

Semantically, control flow of the entire use case chart starts with the initial node of the use case chart (level-1). Flow then passes between use case nodes along the edges of the level-1 activity diagram. When flow reaches a use case chart node at level-1, level-2 scenario chart defining this node is executed, with

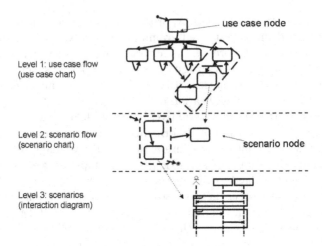

Level 1: use case flow
(use case chart)

Level 2: scenario flow
(scenario chart)

Level 3: scenarios
(interaction diagram)

Fig. 1. Use Case Charts

flow starting from the scenario chart's initial node. Flow exits a scenario node when a final node is reached. Scenario charts may have two types of final nodes— a final success node represents successful completion of the scenario chart and a final failure node represents completion but with failure. Flow only continues beyond the current use case node if a final success node is reached in the use case's defining scenario chart. The semantics of each scenario chart is similar to that for high-level message sequence charts (hMSCs) [Uni04]. Each scenario chart node is defined by a UML2.0 interaction diagram. Hence, when flow passes into a scenario chart node, the defining interaction diagram is executed. When the interaction diagram completes, flow returns to the level-2 scenario chart, exits the scenario node at that level and continues with the next scenario node.

The intention is to reuse as much of the notation of UML2.0 as possible. This makes it easy for practitioners to learn the language. The activity diagrams used are a restriction of UML2.0 with some additional features. Although use case charts rely on the notation of UML activity diagrams, the semantics is quite different. UML2.0 activity diagrams are a general purpose modeling language for workflow modeling and business process modeling. Their (informal) semantics is petri-net based [OMG05]. In contrast, the formal semantics for use case charts is a denotational, trace-based semantics.

2   Example of Use Case Charts

Figures 2, 3 and 4 give an example of how use case charts can be used to precisely describe use cases. The system under development is an automated train shuttle service in which autonomous shuttles transport passengers between stations [Sof05]. When a passenger requires transport, a central broker asks all active shuttles for bids on the transport order. The shuttle with the lowest bid wins. A complete set of requirements for this application is given in [Sof05]. Figure 2 shows a use case chart that includes use cases for initialization of the system, maintenance and repair of shuttles, and transportation (split into multiple use cases). Each use case node in Figure 2 is defined by a level-2 scenario chart—Figure 3 is the scenario chart for Carry Out Order. Figure 4 is a level-3 interaction diagram for the scenario chart defining Make A Bid.

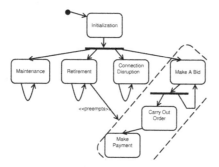

Fig. 2. Shuttle System Use Case Chart

Figure 2 shows that the shuttle system first goes through an Initialization use case. After that, four use cases execute in parallel. If the Make A Bid use case is successful, it can be followed by Carry Out Order or another bidding process (executed in parallel). The Retirement use case represents the case when the shuttles are shut down. It preempts any activity associated to Make A Bid. This is represented by a stereotyped preemption relationship that applies to a region. A region is a set of nodes enclosed in a dashed box.

Figure 3 is a description of what happens in the Carry Out Order use case. Transportation of passengers takes place and the broker is informed of success. The asterisk in the region represents the fact that the region may execute in parallel with itself any numbers of times, i.e., there may be multiple concurrent transports. The requirements of the problem state that during transport, shuttles may not move to intermediate stations except to pick up or drop off passengers. This is captured by introducing a negative scenario node with a stereotyped negation arrow. Note that scenario charts must have at least one final success or final failure node. A final success node represents the fact that execution of the use case has successfully completed and is depicted graphically as in Figure 3. A final failure node says that the use case completes but that execution should not continue beyond the use case. This is given graphically using the final flow node of activity diagram notation, i.e., a circle with a cross through it[1]. As an example, suppose that the passenger transport cannot be completed for some reason. This could be captured by introducing a scenario node capturing the

---

[1] Note that this is not the standard UML2.0 interpretation for the final flow node.

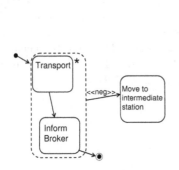

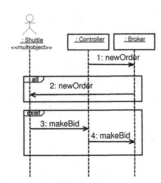

Fig. 3. Shuttle System Scenario Chart for Carry Out Order

Fig. 4. Shuttle System Interaction Diagram for a scenario in Make A Bid

failure and then an arrow to a final failure node. In this case, when the final failure node is reached, the Make Payment use case in Figure 2 will not execute, i.e., payment will not be paid for an unsuccessful transport.

Each scenario node in Figure 3 is described by a UML2.0 interaction diagram. Figure 4 shows an interaction diagram that is part of the Make A Bid use case. This particular example is shown to illustrate extensions that use case charts introduce to UML2.0 interaction diagrams, namely, multiobjects and universal/existential messages. We introduce two new interaction operators, **exist** and **all**. We also introduce a stereotype ⟨⟨multiobject⟩⟩ which denotes that an interaction applies to multiple instances of a classifier. In the figure, Shuttle is stereotyped as a multiobject which means that multiple shuttles may participate in the interaction. There are two interaction fragments. In the first, the Broker sends messages to *all* shuttles. In the second, there must be *at least one* makeBid message to Controller followed by at least one makeBid message to Broker.

The activity diagrams used in use case and scenario charts are a restricted version of UML2.0 activity diagrams but with some additional relationships between nodes. They are restricted in that they do not include object flow, swimlanes, signals etc. They do include additional notations, however. The abstract syntax is defined in Section 3. The concrete syntax reuses as much of the activity diagram notation as possible. Informally, the allowed relationship types between nodes (either in use case or scenario charts) are given as follows, where, for each relationship, X and Y are either both scenario nodes or both use case nodes:

1. X continues from Y (i.e., the usual activity diagram arrow)
2. X and Y are alternatives (the usual alternative defined by a condition)
3. X and Y run in parallel (the usual activity diagram fork and join)
4. X preempts Y—i.e., X interrupts Y and control does not return to Y once X is complete, shown by the stereotype ⟨⟨preempts⟩⟩ from X to Y.
5. X suspends Y—i.e., X interrupts Y and control returns to Y once X is complete, shown by the stereotype ⟨⟨suspends⟩⟩ from X to Y.

6. X is negative—i.e., the scenarios defined by X should never happen. This is shown by an arrow stereotyped with $\langle\langle neg \rangle\rangle$ to X and where the source of the arrow is the region over which the scope of the negation applies.
7. X may have multiple copies—i.e., X can run in parallel with itself any number of times. This is shown by an asterisk attached to node X.

In addition, use case charts and scenario charts may have regions (graphically shown by dashed boxes) that scope nodes together. Relationships of type (4), (5) may have a region as the target of the arrow. Relationships of type (6) may have a region as the source of the arrow. All other arrows do not link regions. (8) may also be applied to a region.

Arrow types (4), (5) and (6) are not part of UML2.0 activity diagrams (although there is a similar notation to (4) and (5) for interruption). Activity diagrams do have a notion of region for defining an interruptible set of nodes. Regions in use case charts are a general-purpose scoping mechanism not restricted to defining interrupts. In addition to the arrow and region extensions, there are minor extensions to interaction diagrams.

3   Use Case Chart Syntax

The abstract syntax for interaction diagrams is not given as it is assumed to be the same as in UML2.0 except for the multiobject, universal/existential message extensions.

3.1   Abstract Syntax for Scenario Charts (Level-2)

The abstract syntax of a scenario chart is given first. The abstract syntax for use case charts is almost the same since both are based on activity diagrams.

Definition 1. *A scenario chart* $(S, R_S, E_S, s_0, S_F, S_{F'}, L_S, f_S, m_S, L_E)$ *is a graph where* S *is a set of scenario nodes,* $R_S \subseteq \mathcal{P}(S)$ *is a set of regions,* $E_S \subseteq (\mathcal{P}(S \cup R_S) \times \mathcal{P}(S \cup R_S) \times L_E)$ *is a set of edges with labels from* L_E, $s_0 \in S$ *is the unique initial node,* $S_F \subset S$ *is a set of final success nodes,* $S_{F'} \subset S$ *is a set of final failure nodes,* L_S *is a set of scenario labels,* $f_S : S \to L_S$ *is a total, injective function mapping each scenario node to a label and* $m_s : S \cup R_S \to \{+, -\}$ *is a total function marking whether or not each scenario or region can have multiple concurrent executions. The labels in* L_S *are references to an interaction diagram.* L_E *is defined to be the set* $\{normal, neg, preempts, suspends\}$. L_S *is the set of words from some alphabet* Σ.

This definition describes a graph where edges may have multiple source nodes and multiple target nodes. This subsumes the notion of fork and join from activity diagrams which can be taken care of by allowing edges to have multiple source nodes and/or multiple target nodes. Multiple source nodes lead in the use case chart graphical notation to a join and multiple target nodes lead to a fork. An edge with both multiple sources and multiple targets is equivalent to a join followed by a fork. Regions are a scoping mechanism used to group nodes. As stated previously, the intuition behind final success and final failure nodes is that a final success node denotes successful completion of the scenario chart; a final failure node denotes that the scenario chart completes but unsuccessfully. Definition 1 omits the notion of conditions on edges, for the sake of clarity, but it is enough to say that guards could be placed on arrows leaving a node.

3.2   Abstract Syntax for Use Case Charts (Level-1)

The abstract syntax for a use case chart is almost identical except that a use case chart has only one type of final node (for success) and each use case node maps to a scenario chart not an interaction diagram. Only one type of final node is required for use case charts because there is no notion of success or failure—either a use case chart completes or it does not.

Definition 2. *A use case chart $(U, R_U, E_U, u_0, U_F, L_U, f_U, m_U, L_E)$ is a graph where U is a set of nodes, $R_U \subseteq \mathcal{P}(U)$ is a set of regions, $E_U \subseteq (\mathcal{P}(U \cup R_U) \times \mathcal{P}(U \cup R_U) \times L_E)$ is a set of edges, $u_0 \in U$ is the unique initial node, $U_F \subset U$ is a set of final nodes, L_U is a set of scenario chart labels, $f_U : U \rightarrow L_U$ is a total, injective function mapping each use case node to a scenario chart label and $m_U : U \cup R_U \rightarrow \{+, -\}$ is a total function marking whether each use case or region can have multiple concurrent executions. The labels in L_U are references to a scenario chart. L_E is as given in Definition 1.*

4   Use Case Chart Semantics

A trace is a sequence of events where an event may be the sending of a message, $!x$, or the receipt of a message, $?x$.

Definition 3. *The semantics of a 3-level use case chart, U, is a pair of trace sets, (P_U, N_U), where P_U is the set of positive traces for U and N_U is the set of negative traces for U.*

Positive traces are traces that are possible in any implementation of the use case chart. Negative traces may never occur in a valid implementation of the use case chart. An implementation satisfies a use case chart if every positive trace is a possible execution path and if no negative trace is a possible execution path.

4.1   Semantics of UML2.0 Interaction Diagrams (Level-3)

The semantics for UML2.0 interaction diagrams follows the one given by Haugen & Stølen [HHRS05], extended to include **all** and **exist** fragments.

A message, x, in a UML2.0 interaction has two events—a send event, $!x$, and a receive event, $?x$. In any valid event trace, the send event must come before the receive event. In UML2.0, as shown in Figure 5, messages can be composed using interaction fragments, where a fragment has an interaction operator and a

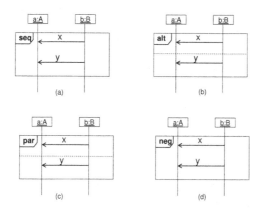

Fig. 5. UML2.0 Interaction Fragments

number of interaction operands. For example, Figure 5(b) shows an alternative fragment with two operands; 5(c) shows a parallel fragment with two operands; and 5(d) shows a negative fragment with a single operand. The default operator in UML2.0 is the sequential operator, **seq** (Figure 5(a)), which represents weak sequencing. Any messages not explicitly contained within a fragment are by default assumed to be contained within a **seq** fragment.

A message is a triple (s, tr, re) of a signal s, a transmitter instance, tr, and a receiver instance, re. Each transmitter instance has a type, $tr : Tr$. Similarly, $re : Re$. Let M denote the set of all messages and L the set of all lifelines. An event is a pair of kind and message: $(k, m) \in \{!, ?\} \times M$. Let E denote the set of all events. A trace is a sequence of events. Let $tr(e)$ denote the transmitter for event e and $re(e)$ denote its receiver. Let H be the set of valid event traces, that is, event traces such that for any message x, the send event, $!x$, comes before the receive event, $?x$. Define the following operators on traces. $h_1 \frown h_2$ is trace concatenation. $h_1|_B$ is the trace h_1 restricted to events in the event set B — i.e., all events not in B are removed.

The semantics for the four fragments in Figure 5, as well as for universal/existential messages, is summarized in Figure 6. e is an event and d_i is an interaction diagram, for all i. The semantics of a single event is a single positive trace. Interaction operators are represented textually using the keywords **neg**, **alt**, **par** and **seq**. For example, **neg** d represents an interaction diagram d that is negated by a negative interaction fragment.

For **alt**, the set of positive traces is the union of the set of positive traces from each operand. The set of negative traces is the union of the set of negative traces from each operand. The **neg** operator simply negates all traces—its set of negative traces is the union of the positive and negative traces of its operand. This captures the fact that the negation of a negative trace remains negative.

par is defined by interleaving traces from each of its operands. In Figure 6, ‖ denotes interleaving and is formally defined below. **par**'s positive traces are the

$$[\![e]\!] = (e, \emptyset)$$

$$[\![\mathbf{neg}\ d]\!] = (\emptyset, p \cup n)$$

$$[\![d_1\ \mathbf{alt}\ d_2]\!] = (p_1 \cup p_2, n_1 \cup n_2)$$

$$[\![d_1\ \mathbf{par}\ d_2]\!] = (p_1 \| p_2, (n_1 \| p_2) \cup (n_1 \| n_2) \cup (p_1 \| n_2))$$

$$[\![d_1\ \mathbf{seq}\ d_2]\!] = (p_1 \succeq p_2, (n_1 \succeq p_2) \cup (n_1 \succeq n_2) \cup (p_1 \succeq n_2))$$

$$[\![\mathbf{all}\ d]\!] = (\mathbf{all}\ p, \mathbf{all}\ n)$$

$$[\![\mathbf{exist}\ d]\!] = (\mathbf{exist}\ p, \mathbf{exist}\ n)$$

$$\text{where}\ (p, n) = [\![d]\!], (p_1, n_1) = [\![d_1]\!]\ \text{and}\ (p_2, n_2) = [\![d_2]\!]$$

Fig. 6. UML2.0 Interaction Diagram Semantics

interleavings of positive traces from both operands. Its negative traces are the interleavings of negative traces from both operands, or a positive trace from one operand with the negative trace from the other operand. Interleaving is defined as follows for trace sets s_1, s_2 (adapted from [HHRS05]):

$$s_1 \| s_2 = \{h \in H \mid \exists o \in \{1,2\}^\infty \cdot \pi_2((o,h)|_{\{1\} \times E}) \in s_1 \wedge \pi_2((o,h)|_{\{2\} \times E}) \in s_2\}$$

The infinite sequence o is an oracle to resolve non-determinism in the interleaving. π_2 is a projection operator returning the second element in a pair. Any trace in the set $s_1 \| s_2$ is an interleaving of events from a trace in s_1 with events from a trace in s_2.

seq fragments are defined in UML2.0 to have a weak sequencing semantics ([OMG05]): the ordering of events within each operand is maintained; events on different lifelines from different operands may come in any order; events on the same lifeline from different operands are ordered such that an event from the first operand comes before an event from the second operand. Any **seq** fragment joins traces from each of its operands in a way that satisfies these three constraints. Informally, the positive traces for **seq** are all possible ways of joining a positive trace from the first operand and a positive trace from the second operand. The negative traces for **seq** are those derived from joining a positive trace from the first operand with a negative trace from the second, or a negative trace from the first with either a positive or negative trace from the second.

The definition in Figure 6 relies on a definition of $\succeq$, weak sequencing for trace sets (adapted from [HHRS05]), which captures formally the three constraints stated above. $ev(l)$ is the set of events that take place on lifeline l.

$$s_1 \succeq s_2 = \{h \in s_1 \| s_2 \mid \exists h_1 \in s_1, h_2 \in s_2 \cdot \forall l \in L \cdot h|_{ev(l)} = h_1|_{ev(l)} \frown h_2|_{ev(l)}\}$$

The semantics for the multiobject extensions are now given. Consider first the interaction operator **all** applied to a single positive event trace, **all** $e_1, e_2, \ldots$. The resulting positive traces are all those that can be derived by replacing each e_i by its *image under* **all**. If t_i is a receive event where the receiving instance is a multiobject, then the image under **all** is the trace $e_{i_1}, e_{i_2}, \ldots$ where each e_{i_j} is the same event as e_i but with a different receiver, namely, instance j. The corresponding send event is also replaced by a set of send events, one for each instance j. The same logic applies if e_i is a send event where the sending instance is a multiobject. In this case, e_i is replaced by a set of send events, one for each instance of the multiobject, and the corresponding receive events for the new send events are added.

For an event e, define $e \frown_{(I, re)}$, where I is a set of type instances, as a concatenation of copies of e where each element of the concatenation has the receiver of e replaced by an element of I. Similarly, $e \frown_{(I, tr)}$ is a concatenation of copies of e where each element of the concatenation has the transmitter replaced by an element of I. Furthermore, $\frown_{e_i \in h}$ defines repeated concatenation indexed over the events e_i of an event trace h. If $tr(e) : Tr$ and $re(e) : Re$, then let $inst_{tr}(e)$ denote the set of all instances of Tr (including $tr(e)$ itself). Similarly, $inst_{re}(e)$ is the set of all instances of Re (including $re(e)$).

Now define **all** e as follows:

$$
\textbf{all } e = \begin{cases}
e \frown_{(inst_{tr}(e), tr)} & \text{if } tr(e) \text{ is a multiobject} \\
e \frown_{(inst_{re}(e), re)} & \text{if } re(e) \text{ is a multiobject} \\
\frown_{e_i \in e} \frown_{(inst_{tr}(e), tr)} e_i \frown_{(inst_{re}(e), re)} & \text{if both } tr(e) \text{ and} \\
& re(e) \text{ are multiobjects} \\
e & \text{otherwise}
\end{cases}
$$

The intent of this definition is to effect the replacement of events by multiple events, one for each instance, as described above. In the case that an event has a multiobject receiver and a multiobject transmitter, the definition describes a "nested" replacement, in which the replacement is first done for the transmitter and then the result is processed with receiver replacement.

For a trace h, $h[e'/e]$ is defined as the trace h with all occurrences of event e replaced by e'. Multiple replacements are separated by commas and applied sequentially. Now define **all** h for an event trace $h = e_1, e_2, \ldots$ as follows:

$$
\textbf{all } h = h\left[(\textbf{all } e_1)/e_1, (\textbf{all } e_2)/e_2, \ldots\right]
$$

The definition extends naturally to a set of traces, s:

$$
\textbf{all } s = \{h \in H \mid h = (\textbf{all } h_1) \wedge h_1 \in s\}
$$

The definition of the semantics of **all** applied to an interaction diagram, as given in Figure 6, is now clear. The case for **exists** is similar and is not presented here, for lack of space.

This concludes the definition of the trace-based semantics for UML2.0 interaction diagrams. UML2.0 contains other constructs not considered here.

4.2   Semantics of Scenario Charts (Level-2)

The semantics is extended to scenario charts in the natural way—the semantics is also given as a pair of a set of positive traces and a set of negative traces.

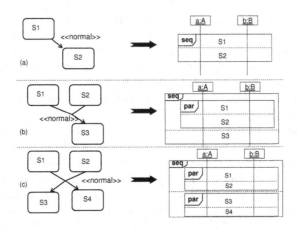

Fig. 7. Flattening Scenario Charts

Edges of type *normal* in scenario charts can be given a semantics by "flattening" the edge—i.e., create a new interaction diagram that takes the interaction diagrams represented by the source and target of the edge and connects them using an interaction fragment with a particular interaction operator. See Figure 7. Normal edges with only one source and target scenario node can be flattened using the **seq** interaction operator for sequential composition. This captures the weak sequential semantics of one-to-one *normal* edges. Many-to-many *normal* edges are flattened using the **par** interaction operator. This is because the semantics of a one-to-many edge is defined to be a forking and that of a many-to-one edge is defined to be a joining of "threads". Hence, a many-to-many edge can be replaced by a fork and join in the usual activity diagram notation. Since *normal* edges can be eliminated in this way, their semantics is not explicitly given here but the semantics is assumed to be that of the equivalent "flattened" interaction diagram. This leaves only edges of type *neg*, *preempts* and *suspends*.

In what follows, c_1 **preempts** c_2 informally means that scenario node c_1 preempts scenario node c_2. c_1 **suspends** c_2 means that c_1 suspends c_2 and c_1 **negative during** c_2 means that c_1 can never happen during the execution of c_2. $c_1 \to c_2$ denotes a normal edge between scenario nodes. Edges can also be between sets of scenario nodes. c_1* denotes that multiple occurrences of c_1 can occur in parallel. The semantics for preemption, suspension and negation are given only for one-to-one edges, but can be extended to many-to-many edges. Figure 8 summarizes the semantics. In this figure, c_1, c_2 are scenario nodes defined by interaction diagrams d_1 and d_2, respectively. C_1 and C_2 are sets of scenario nodes defined by sets of interaction diagrams D_1 and D_2 where there is a bijective mapping from C_i to D_i. **par** X, for a set of interaction diagrams $X = \{x_1, x_2, \ldots\}$, is shorthand for x_1 **par** x_2 **par** $\ldots$ $size(X)$ returns the number of elements in X. If $size(X) = 1$, X' refers to its only element. $prefix(h)$ denotes the set of prefixes of event trace h.

$$[\![C_1 \rightarrow C_2]\!] \begin{cases} D_1' \textbf{ seq } D_2' & \text{if } size(D_1) = 1 \wedge size(D_2) = 1 \\ (\textbf{par } D_1) \textbf{ seq } D_2' & \text{if } size(D_1) > 1 \wedge size(D_2) = 1 \\ D_1' \textbf{ seq } (\textbf{par } D_2) & \text{if } size(D_1) = 1 \wedge size(D_2) > 1 \\ (\textbf{par } D_1) \textbf{ seq } (\textbf{par } D_2) & \text{if } size(D_1) > 1 \wedge size(D_2) > 1 \end{cases}$$

$$[\![c_1 \textbf{ preempts } c_2]\!] = \\ (\{h \in H \mid \exists h_1 \in p_1, h_2 \in H, h' \in p_2 \cdot h = h_2 \frown h_1 \wedge h_2 \in prefix(h')\} \\ , n_2)$$

$$[\![c_1 \textbf{ suspends } c_2]\!] = \\ (\{h \in H \mid \exists h_1 \in p_1, h_2 \in p_2, h_{2a}, h_{2b} \in H \cdot h = h_{2a} \frown h_1 \frown h_{2b} \wedge h_2 = h_{2a} \frown h_{2b}\} \\ , n_2)$$

$$[\![c_1 \textbf{ negative during } c_2]\!] = (p_2, n_2 \cup p_1 \| p_2)$$

$$[\![c_1 *]\!] = d_1 \textbf{ par } d_1 \textbf{ par} \ldots$$

where c_1, c_2 are defined by interaction diagrams d_1, d_2 respectively
and $(p_1, n_1) = [\![d_1]\!]$, $(p_2, n_2) = [\![d_2]\!]$

Fig. 8. Semantics for Edges in Scenario Charts

For preemption, a positive trace for (c_1 **preempts** c_2) is any trace made up of a prefix of a positive trace of c_2 concatenated with a positive trace of c_1. Note that a preempting scenario cannot have negative traces. Furthermore, (c_1 **preempts** c_2) does not introduce any new negative traces because preempting traces have no effect on the original negative traces. The case for suspension is similar except that control returns to the suspended scenario once the suspending scenario is complete.

In the case of negation, the positive traces of (c_1 **negative during** c_2) are simply the positive traces of c_2. Negative traces, however, can be any trace that is an interleaving of a positive trace of c_2 with a positive trace of c_1. This, in effect, defines a monitor for traces of c_1—if a positive c_1 trace occurs at any point, even with events interleaved from c_2, then this defines a negative trace. Note that c_1 cannot have negative traces.

The semantics for multiple concurrent executions (the asterisk notation) is given by interleaving and hence can be described in terms of flattening using **par** operators. The number of **par** operators is unbounded since there can be any number of executions of the node.

Regions are sets of connected nodes and so, their semantics is a pair of trace sets. Hence, their semantics is not given explicitly here but follows the same rules as in Figure 8.

Figure 8 defines the semantics for single edges. This is extended to an entire scenario chart as follows. A path through a scenario chart is a (possibly infinite) sequence of scenario nodes $s_0, s_1, s_2 \ldots$ where s_0 is the unique initial node. If the path is finite, it must be ended by either a final success or final failure node. A path is maximal if it is not a proper prefix of any other path. The set of positive traces of a scenario chart is the set of traces that follow a maximal path through the chart. Similarly, for the set of negative traces.

4.3   Semantics of Use Case Charts (Level-1)

The semantics for use case charts is essentially the same as for scenario charts because both a scenario and a use case are given meaning as a pair of trace sets. For use case charts, however, the meaning of a *normal* edge is given by strong not weak sequential composition. Operationally, this means that before execution can continue along an edge to the next use case, *all* participants in the interaction must complete (where completion is defined below). In contrast, in scenario charts, some participants may complete and continue to the next node while others remain in the current node. Strong composition is chosen to define use case charts because nodes represent use cases. Use cases are considered modular functional units in which the entire unit must complete before control goes elsewhere. Strong composition enforces the modularity. Semantically, strong composition of traces is defined to be concatenation.

A use case chart node completes if and only if its defining scenario chart reaches a final success or final failure node. If the scenario chart reaches a final success node, control continues to the next use case node. If the scenario chart reaches a final failure node, the use case "thread" terminates. Semantically, each trace in a scenario chart is either infinite, ends with a final success node (a success trace) or a final failure node (a failure trace). Suppose a use case chart has two nodes, u_1 and u_2, connected by a single edge from u_1 to u_2. Then the positive trace set of the use case chart is the union of three trace sets: the positive infinite traces of u_1, the set of traces formed by concatenating positive success traces from u_1 with positive traces from u_2, and the set of positive failure traces from u_1. The first of these three trace sets captures the fact that infinite traces of u_1 never reach u_2. The second of the trace sets captures strong composition and the final trace set corresponds to the case when traces in u_1 end at a final failure node. This is captured formally in Figure 9.

For any use case node, u_i, let $s(u_i)$, $f(u_i)$ denote the set of positive traces of u_i that end in a final success and final failure node, respectively, and let $inf(u_i)$ denote the infinite set of positive traces. Then the set of positive traces of u_i is the disjoint union of $s(u_i)$, $f(u_i)$ and $inf(u_i)$. In Figure 9, the definition of concatenation is extended to sets of traces, in the natural way, as follows:

$$s_1 \frown s_2 = \{h \in H \mid \exists h_1 \in s_1, h_2 \in s_2 \cdot h = h_1 \frown h_2\}$$

where s_1, s_2 are trace sets. For negative traces, the final success and final failure nodes have no effect; negative traces are composed using strong composition. Finally, only normal edges are affected by final success and final failure nodes, i.e., preemption, suspension and negation edges retain the same semantics.

$$[\![c_1 \rightarrow c_2]\!] = (inf(c_1) \cup f(c_1) \cup (s(c_1) \frown p_1), (n_1 \frown p_2) \cup (n_1 \frown n_2) \cup (p_1 \frown n_2))$$

Fig. 9. Semantics for Normal Edges in Use Case Charts

5   Related Work

At first glance, use case charts look quite similar to hMSCs [Uni04] and UML2.0 [OMG05] IODs. However, in IODs, there are only two levels of hierarchy — activity diagrams connect references to interaction diagrams but use cases are not handled. In hMSCs, nodes can be references to other hMSCs so there is an unlimited number of levels. However, there is no semantic difference between nodes at different levels—references to hMSCs are just syntactic sugar and can be flattened to references to basic MSCs—so there are in effect only two levels, interactions and references to interactions. Use cases again are not handled.

Use case charts contain relationships that do not exist in UML or hMSCs, as noted in Section 2. Finally, there is a formal semantic model for use case charts. There is no official formal semantics for UML2.0 IODs. Although one can infer a semantics for UML2.0 activity diagrams (or at least part of them) because the UML specification [OMG05] bases the semantics on petri-nets, the semantic assumptions of generic UML activity diagrams do not carry over to IODs because a number of restrictions and modifications are made to the activity diagrams used in IODs. The semantics given here for use case charts is declarative. It is also possible to define an operational semantics based on petri-nets but this is outside the scope of this paper.

Activity diagrams and hMSCs can, of course, be used in a variety of ways to support use-case based development. Some authors (e.g., [MB02]), for example, suggest the use of activity diagrams to connect use cases. Others (e.g., [Man01]) suggest to define each use case by an hMSC. The former approach does not consider how to use activity diagrams to define each use case. The latter only connects use cases using a standard UML use case diagram. Use case charts essentially combine these two approaches in that activity diagrams are used both to relate use cases and to define those use cases. As such, the contribution of this paper is more in the formal semantics than the syntax.

6   Conclusion

This paper presented a precise notation for specifying use cases. The notation is based on UML and is defined on three levels: use cases, scenarios and interactions. A formal syntax and semantics of the notation is presented. Use case charts are precisely and unambiguously defined, and can therefore be executed. A project is currently underway to implement a simulator for use case charts that is compliant with the semantics defined in this paper. This will enable users to immediately execute their use cases and validate the use case specification. Clearly, use case charts require a degree of rigor and effort above and beyond what is normal for use case definition. The author feels, therefore, that the notation is most beneficial when applied to the specification of systems with stringent functional requirements. Use case charts have been applied on a number of industrial case studies, most notably a transaction-based weather data system that is part of a NASA air traffic control application.

References

[BRJ05]   G. Booch, J. Rumbaugh, and I. Jacobson. *The Unified Modeling Language User Guide, 2nd Edition*. Addison-Wesley Professional, 2005.

[Coc00]   Alistair Cockburn. *Writing Effective Use Cases*. Addison-Wesley Longman Publishing Co., Inc., Boston, MA, USA, 2000.

[HHRS05]   Øystein Haugen, Knut Eilif Husa, Ragnhild Kobro Runde, and Ketil Stølen. Stairs: Towards formal design with sequence diagrams. *Journal of Software and System Modeling*, 4(4):355–367, 2005.

[Iso04]   Sadahiro Isoda. On UML2.0s abandonment of the actors-call-use-cases conjecture. *Journal of Object Technology*, 4(6), 2004.

[Man01]   Nikolai Mansurov. Automatic synthesis of SDL from MSC and its applications in forward and reverse engineering. *Comput. Lang.*, 27(1/3):115–136, 2001.

[MB02]   Stephen J. Mellor and Marc Balcer. *Executable UML: A Foundation for Model-Driven Architectures*. Addison-Wesley, Boston, USA, 2002.

[OMG05]   OMG. Unified Modeling Language 2.0 specification, 2005. http://www.omg.org.

[OP99]   Gunnar Overgaard and Karin Palmkvist. A formal approach to use cases and their relationships. In *First International Workshop on The Unified Modeling Language UML'98*, pages 406–418. Springer-Verlag, 1999.

[Smi04]   Michal Smialek. Accommodating informality with necessary precision in use case scenarios. *Journal of Object Technology*, 4(6), 2004.

[Sof05]   Software Engineering Group, University of Paderborn. Shuttle system case study, 2005. http://www.cs.uni-paderborn.de/cs/ag-schaefer/CaseStudies/ShuttleSystem/.

[Ste01]   Perdita Stevens. On use cases and their relationships in the unified modelling language. In *FASE '01: Proceedings of the 4th International Conference on Fundamental Approaches to Software Engineering*, pages 140–155, London, UK, 2001. Springer-Verlag.

[Uni04]   International Telecommunication Union. Recommendation Z.120: Message sequence chart. Technical report, 2004.

[Wil04]   Clay Williams. Towards engineered, useful use cases. *Journal of Object Technology*, 4(6), 2004.

Joint Structural and Temporal Property Specification Using Timed Story Scenario Diagrams*

Florian Klein and Holger Giese

Software Engineering Group, University of Paderborn,
Warburger Str. 100, D-33098 Paderborn, Germany
fklein@upb.de, hg@upb.de

Abstract. Complex software systems, and self-adaptive systems in particular, are characterized by complex structures and behavior. For their design, appropriate notations for the specification of properties that integrate structural and temporal aspects are required. We present Timed Story Scenario Diagrams (TSSD), a visual notation for scenario specifications that takes structural system properties into account and provides an integrated way of discussing system state evolution. We present the key features of the notation and demonstrate how the patterns of the Specification Pattern System [1,2] can be encoded using TSSDs. We also discuss how TSSDs can be derived from textual specifications in a straight-forward manner, using a case study.

Keywords: Property Specification, Temporal Logic, Visual Specification Language.

1 Introduction

As part of the trend towards more intelligent, efficient, and flexible software-intensive systems (cf. self-adaptive systems [3,4]), dynamic software architectures which permit structural adaptation at run-time are beginning to displace static architectures and models. While this allows building more flexible systems, designing and validating adaptable systems poses new challenges to software engineers. In order to express requirements and commitments concerning the evolution of the structure over time, appropriate integrated notations for the specification of properties covering structural and temporal aspects are required as these are closely intertwined.

The need for formal specifications expressed using logics or automata is a major obstacle for the adoption of formal verification techniques by practitioners. We do not only need techniques for the description of structural and temporal properties which are sufficiently expressive and provide the essential theoretical concepts, but which are appropriate for use by normal designers, requirements engineers, or even informed stakeholders who can handle UML class diagrams (domain experts or engineers from outside the software domain) rather than experts on logic.

---

* This work was developed in the course of the Special Research Initiative 614 - Self-optimizing Concepts and Structures in Mechanical Engineering - University of Paderborn, and was published on its behalf and funded by the Deutsche Forschungsgemeinschaft.

M.B. Dwyer and A. Lopes (Eds.): FASE 2007, LNCS 4422, pp. 185–199, 2007.

For specifying **structural properties**, the UML only provides a textual specification language, the OCL [5]. The writing of OCL properties requires that the developer translates his/her concrete ideas about the required structural properties from the familiar structural view in form of UML Class and Object Diagrams into an often intricate textual syntax. When reading OCL, a complicated and error prone translation in the opposite direction is required. This mental mapping problem is the reason why OCL with its textual appearance is rarely used in practice, as the UML's popularity is in large part due to its visual nature and the accessibility of its structural modeling concepts (see also [6]).

Several approaches try to overcome this problem. Constraint diagrams [7] visualize constraints as restrictions on sets using Euler circles, spiders and arrows and constraint trees [8]. VisualOCL [9] focuses on mapping OCL syntax to a visual format as closely as possible, thus facilitating the parsing of structural constraints. However, the resulting visually complex diagrams have only little relation with the original UML specification so that a similar gap results. In contrast, Story Patterns (cf. [10]) extend UML Object Diagrams and thus avoid this gap. However, they have deficits when it comes to quantification and negation.

For **temporal properties**, temporal logics such as LTL or CTL [11] represent the standard. However, as reported in [2], even experts have serious problems handling the intricate nature of these logics. Even in projects with trained experts, employing them is often impossible, as the resulting property specifications will usually be unintelligible to domain experts from other disciplines that need to participate in the effort. Specification patterns for temporal properties represent an attempt to alleviate this problem. As outlined in [2], many useful temporal properties can be constructed using a small set of elementary building blocks. This idea has been extended and applied to real-time systems in [12]. However, while applying the patterns is intuitive, the resulting formulas themselves are no more transparent or readable than before.

Scenarios in form of UML sequence diagrams [13], Triggered Message Sequence Charts (TMSCs) [14], or Live Sequence Charts (LSC) [15] have been proposed as a more accessible means for the description of temporal properties. Visual Timed event Scenarios (VTS) [16] are an alternative which focuses on scenarios for pure events, rather than the interaction of predefined units. Therefore, they provide a more intuitive notion of temporal ordering than Sequence Diagrams, which require specifying a sequence of interactions that 'enforces' this ordering.

The existing approaches which combine **structural and temporal properties** are mostly extensions of the OCL towards the description of dynamics. Through the introduction of additional temporal logic operators in OCL (e.g., eventually, always, or never), the specification of required behavior by means of temporal restrictions among actions and events is enabled, e.g., [17]. Temporal extensions of the OCL that consider real-time issues have been proposed for events in OCL/RT [18] and for states in RT-OCL [19]. As temporal logic alone already causes an even more demanding mental mapping problem (cf. [2]), integrating the OCL and some temporal logic concepts at the textual level does not yield a sufficiently comprehensible solution.

In [20], an embedding of graph patterns into LTL formulas is proposed in order to be able to capture structural properties. This approach tackles the theoretical aspects of the proposed integration rather than the design of a practical specification language, which would suffer from the intricate nature of the underlying LTL.

The only notation that takes an approach similar to ours is a recent proposal [21] for writing temporal graph queries. The approach extends Story Diagrams [22] – an extension of UML Activity Diagrams with Story Patterns – by annotating unary forward or past operators from LTL with additional explicitly encoded time constraints. It requires the explicit specification of an accepting automaton rather than employing the idea of scenarios. In cases where only partial orders of events or time constraints between partially ordered situations have to be specified, the encoding of the time constraints in the automaton will therefore become rather complex.

We can conclude from our analysis of the state of the art that no existing approach fully supports the joint specification of structural and temporal properties in the desired scenario-based manner. The notations either lack support for one of the aspects or seem unsuitable for the intended audience, as they require handling the combination of two notations that already seem forbiddingly complex own their own.

In this paper, we demonstrate that the outlined requirements for jointly specifying structural and temporal properties in a comprehensible manner can be met by a visual language. First, we outline how *Story Decision Diagrams* (SDD) [23] can be used to capture structural requirements. SDD are an extension of Story Patterns [10], combining the intuitive concept of matching structural patterns with decision diagrams, which foster a consecutive if-then-else decomposition of complex properties into comprehensible smaller ones. We then introduce *Timed Story Scenario Diagrams* (TSSD), a new notation inspired by the Visual Timed Event Scenario approach [16], as a way of capturing temporal properties. They provide conditional timed scenarios describing the partial order of specific structural configurations.

The paper is structured as follows: After providing a short introduction to SDDs as a means of capturing structural properties in Section 3, we introduce TSSDs, which employ SDDs as basic building blocks for capturing joint structural and temporal properties, in Section 3. We then demonstrate the capabilities of TSSDs by showing that the Property Specification Pattern System proposed in [1,2] can be easily described in a compositional manner in Section 4 and outline how to systematically derive TSSDs from given textual description by a systematic stepwise transformation process in Section 5. Finally, the conclusions of the paper and outlook on future work is presented.

2   Specifying Structural Properties

The fundamental abstraction underlying our approach is the idea of interpreting instance situations of an object-oriented system as graphs. We map each object/value to a node and each attribute/association to an edge of a labeled graph. The theory of graph transformation systems (cf. [24]) provides the formal semantics that are typically missing from UML-based notations, which allows reasoning about states and behavior of object-oriented systems modeled using a visual notation.

The system structure is modeled using UML Class Diagrams characterizing all possible system states. Figure 1 provides the example that is used in the case study below, a networked system of elevators.

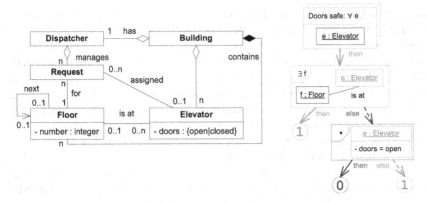

Fig. 1. Elevator class diagram — SDD illustrating basic syntax

Story Patterns are an extended type of UML Object Diagram (cf. [10]) that allow expressing properties as specific object configurations (in accordance with a given Class Diagram). They provide a notation for forbidding individual elements, but no negation of subgraphs, disjunction, implication, or modularity, which limits their use for the encoding of more complex properties.

Story Decision Diagrams (*SDD*) are an extension that remedies the shortcomings of Story Patterns while retaining an accessible visual notation. An SDD is a directed acyclic graph (DAG). Each node contains a *Story Decision Diagram Pattern* (*SDDP*) specifying an elementary structural property, basically a Story Pattern without forbidden elements. Pattern elements bound by one node remain bound in subsequent nodes.

During evaluation, the nodes are processed starting from the root node with an empty binding. Each node in the SDD can essentially be seen as a local if-then-else decision based on the current binding. If a match is found, we extend the binding and follow the solid **then** connector, if no match is found, we leave the binding unchanged and follow the dashed **else** connector. When a binding reaches a (1) or (0) *leaf node*, it evaluates to *true* or *false*, respectively. SDDs are thus similar to decision trees, but allow sharing isomorphic subtrees and leaf nodes to reduce diagram size. Like in decision diagrams, consecutive conditions correspond to logical conjunction or, equivalently, implication, i.e. if a then b else c corresponds to $(a \Rightarrow b) \wedge (\neg a \Rightarrow c)$. SDDs allow multiple **then** or **else** connectors per node as a way of expressing alternatives.

As all pattern elements are positive, negation is expressed by switching the **then** and **else** connectors, i.e. a match leads to failure and no match leads to success. By appropriately chaining the corresponding nodes, complex negative conditions can be expressed. In absence of negation, the leaf nodes are implied and can be omitted.[1]

SDDs allow **quantification** over the free variables of each node. Accordingly, we differentiate between **existential** nodes, which require that at least one of the bindings they propagate reaches a (1) leaf node, and **universal** nodes, which require this of every propagated binding. If an **existential** node binds *explicitly* named variables var_i to objects or links, it is marked with $[\exists \, var_i^+]$. If the node only binds *anonymous* variables

---

[1] Note that color is used to make diagrams more readable, but redundant at the semantic level.

to links, it is marked with $[\exists\_]$. If the node contains no free variables at all, it becomes a *guard* node – marked with $[\bullet]$ – that sends the original binding down the appropriate connector depending on the specified constraints on attributes. A **universal** node containing the free variables var_i is marked with $[\forall\ var_i^+]$. If no matching binding exists, the expected semantics of $\forall$ quantification require that the expression evaluate to true, i.e. an **else** connector to **(1)** is implied. Finally, it is possible to specify *cardinalities* for a node's **then** connector that constrain the number of extensions that may be generated for the same original binding. If too few or many bindings are found, the original binding is propagated down the **else** connector. The SDD in Figure 1 illustrates the basic concepts, requiring that every **elevator** is at a **floor** or else the **doors** are not **open**.

Most visual specification techniques lack the capability to compose complex properties by referencing other properties. SDDs support the composition of specifications by means of **Embedded Story Decision Diagrams** (ESDD). ESDDs are defined as patterns with free variables that are bound depending on the respective current context. The ESDD definition begins with a λ node that defines the pattern's name and rebinds variables of the host node to the local roles. If a node contains a reference to an ESDD, represented by the UML pattern symbol, a binding only matches the node if it also fulfills the embedded pattern. ESDDs are evaluated like normal SDDs, but introduce a local scope. In Figure 2, an ESDD is defined, expecting a **floor** and an **elevator** as its parameters.

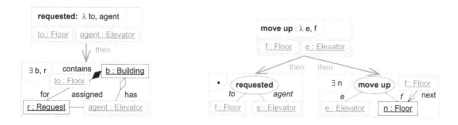

Fig. 2. Simple ESDD definition — Recursive ESDD definition

It is possible to define ESDDs recursively (see Figure 2), providing a way to encode reachability and other transitive properties. The formal semantics of SDDs is defined in [25], where we define the semantics of recursive ESDDs using least fixed points and demonstrate that ESDD evaluation terminates on arbitrary finite graph structures.

3   Specifying Temporal Properties

The temporal behavior of a system can be described as a sequence of states. As we model the system as a *graph transformation system*, each of these states corresponds to a graph. Between states, the identity of nodes and edges is preserved. The idea behind **Timed Story Scenario Diagrams** (TSSD) is to use the ordering of incidences of structural properties in order to specify temporal properties as sets of valid orderings. The diagrams are thus directed acyclic graphs consisting of nodes, each containing the specification of a structural property, and edges, constraining the ordering of incidences.

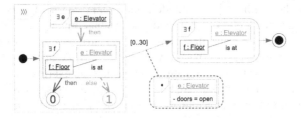

Fig. 3. Basic Example of the TSSD syntax

While TSSDs were designed with SDDs in mind, the structural properties could be encoded using any sufficiently expressive formalism.

Figure 3 is a basic example presenting the key elements of a TSSD. Whenever an elevator is not at a floor, it has to reach a floor within 30 time units. Meanwhile, the doors of the elevator must not be open, which is indicated by the (forbidden) guard on the transition. Using the overview in Figure 4, we now systematically introduce the elements of the TSSD syntax. The formal semantics of TSSDs is defined in [25].

Each node of a TSSD defines a **situation**. While a situation characterizes a set of states, calling it a state would be misleading, as multiple situations of the same TSSD can be incident, i.e. active, at the same time. A labeled situation can be referenced in other places in order to reduce diagram size and avoid redundancies. Bindings are shared between subsequent situations on the same path through the TSSD so that variables cannot be rebound in later situations. If bindings were not retained, it would be difficult to specify properties such as 'If an elevator is assigned a request, it needs to complete it.' because any elevator completing any request would complete the scenario.

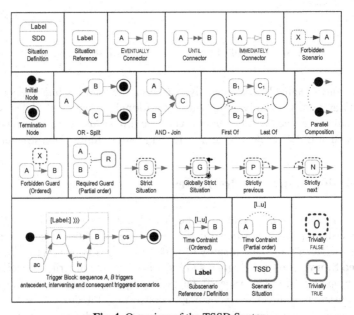

Fig. 4. Overview of the TSSD Syntax

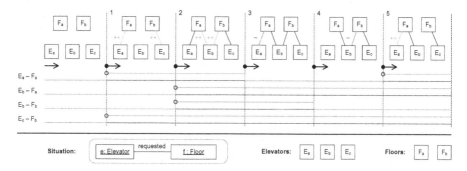

Fig. 5. The relationship between a situation and its observations

When matching a situation, its SDD generates a result set consisting of the alternative candidates, i.e. the bindings that satisfied the SDD. As SDDs may contain ∀ quantification and can then only be satisfied by *sets* of valid bindings, the result set actually contains candidate sets, even though these typically only contain a single binding. Each valid candidate set in the result set is called an **observation** of the situation. However, as the SDD encodes a structural property, whose incidence is typically not limited to a single point in time but spans an interval, the situation could generate infinitely many observations for the same candidate set. An observation is thus made only at the specific time when a structural property is first present after being absent. Figure 5 illustrates this for a situation encoding that a specific elevator is requested at a specific floor. As the truth value of this property changes over time for the different pairs, observations (marked by small circles) are only generated where the truth value changes from $false$ to $true$. For the pair (E_a, F_a), two observations are generated, one a time 1 and one at time 5.

The observations for a scenario are then placed in relation to each other using **temporal connectors** between situations specifying their temporal ordering. The *eventually connector* ($A \longrightarrow B$) denotes that an observation for situation B is eventually made after an observation for situation A (or simultaneously). The *until connector* ($A \longrightarrow\!\!\!\!\blacktriangleright B$) denotes that an observation for situation A is made and that the specific observation remains valid until a compatible observation for situation B is made. Otherwise, the connector ceases to be enabled. The *immediately connector* ($A \longrightarrow\!\!\!\!\vartriangleright B$) denotes that an observation for situation B is made at the same time as the corresponding observation for situation A. The connector is thus only enabled in a single state.

As situations generate sets of observations and as bindings are retained across situations, the indicated temporal ordering only makes sense when applied to compatible pairs of observations, i.e. if the candidate set of the more recent observation actually evolved from the candidate set of the earlier observation. For example, Figure 3 constrains the movement of a single elevator, independently of any other elevator. This same argument applies to multiple observations based on the same candidate set (such as the pair (E_a, F_a) in Figure 5) as well – a subsequent observation should not be invalidated just because the structure matched by the antecedent reappears. $A \longrightarrow B$ therefore does not imply that all compatible A need to occur before B, but rather that a compatible A exists before B. Such a sequence of correctly ordered compatible observations is called a **trace**. As there may be multiple antecedent observations with identical bindings, a single observation can extend multiple traces. As a binding may later be extended in multiple ways, each trace may furthermore be extended by several concurrent observations, resulting in a set of alternative traces.

Pseudostates control the scope of the scenario and encode logical operators. The initial node ● always matches exactly once, as soon as possible. The descriptive, sequential character of TSSDs implies the assumption that time is bounded in the past. The termination node ⊙ marks the end of a branch of a TSSD and always matches as late as possible, i.e. the current state during runtime monitoring or the last state of a finite system. In conjunction with an ──▶ connector, a ⊙ node can thus express that a property, e.g. safety, should hold globally. A trace starts at an initial node and is completed once it has reached a termination node. A system execution path π then fulfills a TSSD if a completed trace to a ⊙ node exists within a prefix of π.

While TSSDs need to be acyclic, each situation may have multiple successors and predecessors. If the TSSD forks, both branches progress independently and in parallel. Observations are only partially ordered. Disjunction can be expressed using multiple ⊙ nodes on independent branches, as one successfully completed trace is sufficient. If a situation has multiple ingoing temporal ordering edges, observations for all situations directly preceding it need to exist. Multiple incoming connectors thus correspond to conjunction. Predecessor branches that do not begin in an initial node can be used to make statements concerning the past. While the *eventually* connector then serves as the *past* operator, *until* can be used to emulate *since* as time is assumed to be bounded in the past. If there are multiple initial nodes in a single diagram, we require a satisfying trace from every initial node, which can be used to create the parallel composition of multiple TSSDs.

As a way of expressing logical ¬ and negate whole scenarios, it is possible to turn branches of a TSSD or the entire diagram into **forbidden scenarios**. In the style of SDD connectors, required situations and connectors are drawn with solid (dark) green lines, while forbidden situations and connectors use dashed (dark) red lines. Forbidden scenarios are defined by means of *inhibiting connectors*. Normally, a connector is disabled and becomes enabled when it is reached by an appropriate trace. Inhibiting connectors are enabled and become disabled if a trace reaches them. Inhibiting connectors mark the end of a forbidden scenario and thus are the connectors leading from forbidden to required elements. In the presence of an inhibiting connector, the subsequent required situation is thus only enabled if *no* trace completing the forbidden branch exists. The semantics of all other situations and connectors in a forbidden scenario is unchanged. Forbidden scenarios may branch and join in any situation of the diagram. If they join in a ⊙ node, they must never occur. As multiple ⊙ nodes represent alternatives, a required and a forbidden scenario leading to different ⊙ nodes still represent alternatives.

Additional **guards and time constraints** can appear directly on the temporal connectors defining the ordering of situations or on dedicated *constraint edges* connecting any two situations regardless of their relative position in the diagram. Constraint edges have no direction. Guards are situations that are forbidden *between* two situations. They are drawn with a bolder dashed border and connected to the connector or constraint edge in question. For convenience, the notation provides support for specifying required guards as well. We also directly support some commonly used idioms in connection with guards: While the observation semantics ensure that the same observation could not have been made earlier, we may want to require that the situation should not yet have matched at all. While this can be achieved using a dedicated guard, we allow 'bending' the forbidden guard onto the situation itself, which then becomes *strictly next*. Likewise, a *strictly previous* situation needs to be the *last* possible observation. Finally, a *strict* situation without any connectors is forbidden between any two situations unless explicitly required, or, if it is globally strict, also between situations and pseudostates.

Time constraints allow setting a lower bound l and an upper bound u for the permitted delay between two observations for two situations A and B within the same trace or related traces. A time constraint can either be placed directly on a temporal connector ($A \xrightarrow{[l...u]} B$) or on a dedicated constraint edge ($A \cdots [l \ldots u] \cdots B$). In case of multiple constraints, the more restrictive bounds dominate the less restrictive ones. The dedicated pseudostates *first of* and *last of* allow specifying (time) constraints between the earliest and the latest observation for two sets of situations.

TSSDs provide **quantification** on different levels. As observations are generated by SDDs, a situation can be observed as structurally equivalent but distinct instances of the same pattern. This is quite different from typical event- or message-based approaches that do not consider structure and cannot differentiate between multiple (concurrent) instances of the same event. E.g., if an elevator needs to complete any one accepted request, it is not sufficient to only match the first accepted request. The TSSD keeps matching freshly accepted requests, as it might otherwise miss the one that is actually completed. This is the reason why a TSSD, which represents a *set* of (potential) scenarios, can 'be' in many states at once. Candidate sets provide another level of quantification, e.g. 'If all requests are approved (at the same time), then eventually all (these) requests have to be completed (at the same time)', which could be written by universally quantifying over all approved requests in the first situation.

The characteristic response and precedence relationships in scenarios are encoded by means of **trigger** blocks. Whenever the sequence within the trigger block has been observed in its entirety, the corresponding trace becomes a *root trace*. The TSSD is then only fulfilled if every root trace successfully completes the triggered scenario. On the other hand, if the trigger is never completed, there is no root trace and the TSSD places no constraints on the system behavior. Borrowing from Live Sequence Charts [15], we distinguish between *universal* TSSDs, which possess a trigger and need to be fulfilled every time it matches, and *existential* TSSDs, which are implicitly triggered by their initial node and need to match once during the execution of the system. It is possible to have multiple triggers in the same TSSD. An important feature is the ability to trigger antecedent and intervening triggered scenarios. In order to support this, only those previous situations that are directly connected to an initial node are considered as preconditions when evaluating whether a trigger block is completed. A trigger containing the trivially *true* situation matches in every state and allows encoding properties such as fairness ('always occurs eventually *again*').

Subscenarios provide a way to define and reference whole scenarios and thus provide a concept for modularity. A subscenario definition begins with a special λ situation for rebinding roles and parameters. A subscenario invocation works in a similar fashion to ESDD invocations, however, as we may need to reference bindings that have been created by the subscenario, the invocation itself needs to take place inside a second λ-node that allows exporting the generated bindings. *Scenario situations* are situations that contain another TSSD and can be seen as in-place subscenario definitions. Most notably, they can be used as 'parentheses' for encoding $\vee$-joins. A subscenario is evaluated in the given context of the surrounding scenario, i.e. its initial and $\odot$ node cannot match earlier/later than the subscenario's predecessor/successor situations.

The expressiveness of TSSDs is discussed in [25], where we show that any LTL and TPTL (LTL with clocks) formula can be encoded using TSSDs.

4   Specification Pattern System

The Property Specification Pattern System (cf. [1],[2]) proposes to address the problem of making formal specification techniques and verification accessible to practitioners. The idea is to allow users to construct complex properties from basic, assuredly correct building blocks by providing generic specification patterns encoding certain elementary properties (existence, absence, universality, bounded existence, precedence (chains), and response (chains)), each specialized for a set of different scopes (globally, before R, after Q, between Q and R, after Q until R). We now demonstrate how the patterns of the Specification Pattern System can be encoded using Timed Story Scenario Diagrams. A convenient quality of TSSDs is that they allow us to define the scopes and the properties separately as orthogonal concepts and then simply plug the appropriate property into the desired scope.

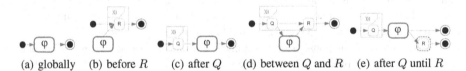

(a) globally   (b) before R (c) after Q (d) between Q and R (e) after Q until R

Fig. 6. The scopes encoded as TSSDs (for a property φ)

In Figure 6, we define the scopes as TSSDs. The scopes *before*, *after*, *between*, and *until* are encoded using trigger blocks where φ is the triggered scenario. As the table shows, all definitions except the definition of *until* are very compact. The last case requires an additional $\odot$ node because TSSDs provide no direct encoding of for the operator $\tilde{U}$ (weak until) so that the property that R may occur or not needs to be encoded explicitly. This omission is intentional as we believe that, in the context of a scenario notation, it is more intuitive to explicitly specify that the scenario might be successfully completed in an earlier situation using the standard syntax for completion ($\odot$) instead of introducing some additional, less obvious syntax for a $\tilde{U}$ connector.

In Figure 7, we define the ten different properties. Inbound connectors link to possible preconditions, outbound connectors encode success and lead to possible postconditions. *Existence*, *absence*, and *universality* are trivially encoded using the standard syntax for required and forbidden scenarios. *Bounded existence* is encoded by enumerating the acceptable sequences, i.e. 0, 1, or 2 occurences. As the number of occurences

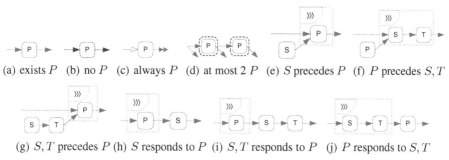

(a) exists P (b) no P (c) always P (d) at most 2 P (e) S precedes P (f) P precedes S, T

(g) S, T precedes P (h) S responds to P (i) S, T responds to P (j) P responds to S, T

Fig. 7. The properties φ encoded as TSSDs)

is relevant, all situations are strict so that no additional occurences are permitted between the observations of a trace. Again, the weak progress (no occurence of P is also acceptable) is encoded by additional outbound connectors. When it comes to encoding response and precedence chains, the notation excels – quite unsurprisingly, as this is the use case for which it was designed. Triggers are designed for expressing response (and its dual, precedence), while sequences such as S, T are *the* basic concept in TSSDs.

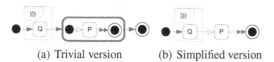

(a) Trivial version   (b) Simplified version

Fig. 8. Always P after Q

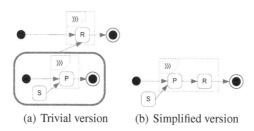

(a) Trivial version   (b) Simplified version

Fig. 9. Always S precedes P before R

These property definitions can now simply be substituted for φ by completing them with an intial node as their precondition and ⊙ nodes as their postcondition(s). While the trivial form of each combined pattern obtained using this mechanistic approach already yields useable results, simplified versions can be derived using two simple transformations that basically correspond to the elimination of redundant parentheses in mathematical expressions: A scenario situation with a single ⊙ node can be eliminated by connecting each situation inside the scope whose predecessor is the scope's intial node to each of the scope's predecessor nodes, and by connecting each situation inside the scope whose successor is the scope's ⊙ node to each of the scope's successor nodes (see Figure 8). Secondly, if both the surrounding scenario and the scenario situation contain trigger blocks, these blocks are merged (see Figure 9).

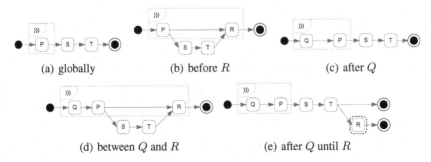

Fig. 10. Response (1,2), simplified versions

Figure 10 lists all simplified variants of the (1,2) response chain pattern. Note how the simplified forms are quite natural expressions of the original requirements. Disregarding the Specification Pattern System's distinction between scopes and properties, e.g. S, T responds to P after Q actually translates to 'after the sequence Q, P, the sequence S, T needs to follow', which is exactly what the TSSD expresses.

5   Deriving Specifications from Textual Requirements

We now discuss how structural and temporal property specifications can be derived from informal textual requirements in a systematic manner. As our case study, we use an elevator system. The application is in part inspired by an example property given in [2], but extends the system from a single elevator to a large building with an arbitrary number of floors and elevators. The following requirements are provided for the system: (1) **Safety**: Whenever an elevator is not at a floor, its doors may not be open. (2) **Responsive**: Every request for an elevator is assigned to one elevator by the central dispatcher. (3) **Progress**: An elevator may not stay between floors for more than 30 seconds. (4) **Progress**: If requests have been assigned to an elevator, it may not be idle for more than 22 seconds. (5) **Purposeful**: An elevator may only move towards some assigned request. (6) **Fairness**: Concurrent requests must be fulfilled within 300 seconds of each other. (7) **Fairness**: When a request for a specific floor has been assigned to an elevator, it may only arrive at this floor at most twice before opening its doors.

Using standard OOA techniques, we extract the class diagram in Figure 1 from the requirements. As the safety property (1) is a structural requirement, we encode it as an SDD. As suggested by the vertical lines, we decompose the textual requirement into the semantically relevant blocks | every elevator | not at a floor | doors must not be open |, which can be directly translated into SDD nodes | ∀ elevator | ∃ at a floor | • door = open |. After switching the connectors where negation is required, this results in the SDD in Figure 1.

Property (2) is not purely structural, unless requests are created with an assignment. We therefore interpret it as | Every time | a request is (created) | it then | afterwards | is assigned to one elevator |. We first encode the two structural terms ∃ request (Figure 11(a)), and ∃ elevator assigned to request with a cardinality of [1..1] (Figure 11(b)). | Every time | ... | then | becomes a trigger block around ∃ request, while

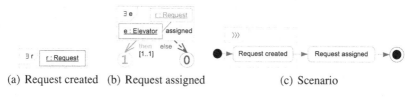

(a) Request created (b) Request assigned   (c) Scenario

Fig. 11. Deriving a TSSD

| afterwards | becomes an eventually connector (Figure 11(c)), resulting in the TSSD in Figure 12(a).

Property (3) is encoded using the same schema, but additionally introduces a time constraint [0..30] between the two situations. Combined with a guard enforcing requirement (1), this yields Figure 3.

For property (4), we interpret idleness as | Every time | an **elevator** with assigned requests | is **at a floor** | then | it needs to move within [0..22] |. The trigger block includes the first two situations, while there are two alternative triggered scenarios, resulting in the TSSD in Figure 12(b).

The difficulty in encoding property (5) is in detecting the direction of the movement from a sequence of states in the trigger, which is achieved by the sequence **elevator at floor**, eventually **elevator at next floor** for the up-direction. The triggered scenario is then simply encoded by the recursive ESDD in Figure 2 that traverses **floors**, upwards, until it finds a **request** or fails. The result is seen in Figure 12(c).

Property (6) becomes | Every time | two concurrent requests exist | then | each | is eventually | completed | within 300 seconds of the other |. After the trigger block, the | each | introduces two ∨-branches. The | within | time constraint results in a constraint edge across the two branches, yielding the TSSD in Figure 12(d).

Property (7) is the famous example that results in a rather unwieldy LTL formula (cf. [2]). It can be expressed using the bounded-existence-between pattern above. However, we believe that a slightly stronger interpretation of the requirement better reflects what is expected of an elevator, namely that it eventually opens its door when it is requested (i.e. as a strong instead of a weak until). We therefore encode the requirement as | Every time | an **elevator** is **requested for** a floor | then | it eventually | is **at the floor** | for the first time | and eventually opens its **doors** | or eventually | is **at the floor** | for the second time | and eventually opens its **doors** |. It is the explicit

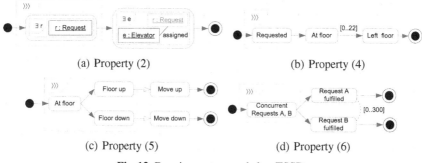

(a) Property (2)   (b) Property (4)

(c) Property (5)   (d) Property (6)

Fig. 12. Requirements encoded as TSSDs

requirement | for the first/second time | that turns being at the floor into a strict situation. The case that | is at the floor | never matches is omitted here as it is a necessary precondition for opening the doors at the floor. The first structural property is encoded by the ESDD in Figure 2. Property (7) is then encoded by the TSSD in Figure 13.

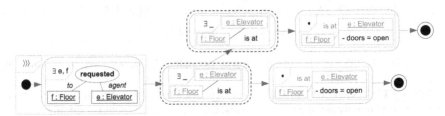

Fig. 13. The elevator may only arrive twice before opening the door

6   Conclusion and Future Work

The combination of TSSDs with SDDs allows the joint specification of structural and temporal properties that is required in the context of complex software-intensive systems, in particular self-adaptive systems. We have shown that all Property Specification Patterns proposed in [1,2] can be easily encoded and derived in a compositional manner using TSSDs (see [25] for the full catalogue). We have demonstrated that the mapping from textual property descriptions to SDD/TSSD specifications is fairly direct as the notations support many common intuitions (implication, precedence etc.).

We are currently developing tool support for the specification, monitoring, and verification of TSSDs, which will allow us to further evaluate them in larger case studies with requirements engineers and domain experts.

References

1. Dwyer, M.B., Avrunin, G.S., Corbett, J.C.: Property Specification Patterns for Finite-state Verification. In: 2nd Workshop on Formal Methods in Software Practice, ACM Press (1998)
2. Dwyer, M.B., Avrunin, G.S., Corbett, J.C.: Patterns in property specifications for finite-state verification. In: ICSE '99: Proceedings of the 21st international conference on Software engineering, Los Alamitos, CA, USA, IEEE Computer Society Press (1999) 411–420
3. Musliner, D., Goldman, R., Pelican, M., Krebsbach, K.: Self-adaptive software for hard real-time environments. IEEE Intelligent Systems **14** (1999)
4. Oreizy, P., Gorlick, M.M., Taylor, R.N., Heimbigner, D., Johnson, G., Medvidovic, N., Quilici, A., Rosenblum, D.S., Wolf, A.L.: An Architecture-Based Approach to Self-Adaptive Software. IEEE Intelligent Systems **14** (1999) 54–62
5. Object Management Group: UML 2.0 Object Constraint Language (OCL) Specification (2003) http://www.omg.org/docs/ptc/03-10-14.pdf.
6. Diskin, Z., Kadish, B., Piessens, F., Johnson, M.: Universal arrow foundations for visual modeling. In: Diagrams '00: Proceedings of the First International Conference on Theory and Application of Diagrams, London, UK, Springer-Verlag (2000) 345–360
7. Kent, S., Howse, J.: Mixing visual and textual constraint languages. In France, R., Rumpe, B., eds.: UML'99, Fort Collins, CO, USA, October 28-30. 1999, Proceedings. Volume 1723 of LNCS., Springer (1999) 384–398

8. Kent, S., Howse, J.: Constraint trees. In Clark, T., Warmer, J., eds.: Object Modeling with the OCL. Springer (2002) 228–249

9. Bottoni, P., Koch, M., Parisi-Presicce, F., Taentzer, G.: A visualization of OCL using collaborations. Lecture Notes in Computer Science **2185** (2001) 257–271

10. Köhler, H., Nickel, U., Niere, J., Zündorf, A.: Integrating UML Diagrams for Production Control Systems. In: Proc. of the 22nd International Conference on Software Engineering (ICSE), Limerick, Irland, ACM Press (2000) 241–251

11. Clarke, E.M., Grumberg, O., Peled, D.: Model Checking. MIT Press (2000)

12. Konrad, S., Cheng, B.H.C.: Real-time specification patterns. In: ICSE '05: Proceedings of the 27th international conference on Software engineering, New York, NY, USA, ACM Press (2005) 372–381

13. Object Management Group: UML 2.0 Superstructure Specification. (2003) Document ptc/03-08-02.

14. Sengupta, B., Cleaveland, R.: Triggered Message Sequence Charts. In Griswold, W.G., ed.: Proceedings of the Tenth ACM SIGSOFT Symposium on the Foundations of Softare Engineering (FSE-10), Charleston, South Carolina, USA, ACM Press (2002)

15. Harel, D., Marelly, R.: Playing with Time: On the Specification and Execution of Time-Enriched LSCs. In: Proc. 10th IEEE/ACM Int. Symp. on Modeling, Analysis and Simulation of Computer and Telecommunication Systems (MASCOTS 2002), Fort Worth, Texas, USA (2002) (invited paper).

16. Alfonso, A., Braberman, V., Kicillof, N., Olivero, A.: Visual Timed Event Scenarios. In: ICSE '04: Proceedings of the 26th International Conference on Software Engineering, Washington, DC, USA, IEEE Computer Society (2004) 168–177

17. Bradfield, J., Kuester Filipe, J., Stevens, P.: Enriching OCL Using Observational mu-Calculus. In Kutsche, R.D., Weber, H., eds.: Fundamental Approaches to Software Engineering (FASE 2002), Grenoble, France. Volume 2306 of LNCS., Springer (2002)

18. Cengarle, M., Knapp, A.: Towards OCL/RT. In Eriksson, L.H., Lindsay, P., eds.: Formal Methods – Getting IT Right, International Symposium of Formal Methods Europe, Copenhagen, Denmark. Volume 2391 of LNCS., Springer (2002) 389–408

19. Flake, S., Mueller, W.: An OCL Extension for Real-Time Constraints. In: Object Modeling with the OCL: The Rationale behind the Object Constraint Language. Volume 2263 of LNCS. Springer (2002) 150–171

20. Gadducci, F., Heckel, R., Koch, M.: A fully abstract model for graph-interpreted temporal logic. In: Proc. of the Theory and Application of Graph Transformations. Volume 1764 of Lecture Notes in Computer Science. (2000) 310–322

21. Rötschke, T., Schürr, A.: Temporal Graph Queries to Support Software Evolution. In: Graph Transformation: 5th International Conference, ICGT 2006, Rio Grande do Norte, Brazil, September 17-23, 2006. (2006) 1–15

22. Fischer, T., Niere, J., Torunski, L., Zündorf, A.: Story diagrams: A new graph rewrite language based on the unified modeling language. In Engels, G., Rozenberg, G., eds.: Proc. of the 6th International Workshop on Theory and Application of Graph Transformation (TAGT), Paderborn, Germany. LNCS 1764, Springer Verlag (1998) 296–309

23. Giese, H., Klein, F.: Beyond Story Patterns: Story Decision Diagrams. In Giese, H., Westfechtel, B., eds.: Proc. of the 4th International Fujaba Days 2006, Bayreuth, Germany. Volume tr-ri-06-275 of Technical Report., University of Paderborn (2006)

24. Rozenberg, G., ed.: Handbook of Graph Grammars and Computing by Graph Transformation : Foundations. World Scientific Pub Co (1997) Volume 1.

25. Klein, F., Giese, H.: Integrated Visual Specification of Structural and Temporal Properties. Technical Report tr-ri-06-277, Computer Science Department, University of Paderborn (2006)

SDL Profiles – Formal Semantics and Tool Support

R. Grammes and R. Gotzhein

Computer Science Department, University of Kaiserslautern

Abstract. Over a period of 30 years, ITU-T's Specification and Description Language (SDL) has matured to a sophisticated formal modelling language for distributed systems and communication protocols. The language definition of SDL-2000, the latest version of SDL, is complex and difficult to maintain. Full tool support for SDL is costly to implement. Therefore, only subsets of SDL are currently supported by tools. These SDL subsets - called *SDL profiles* - already cover a wide range of systems, and are often sufficient in practice. In this paper, we present a formalised approach for extracting the formal semantics for SDL profiles from the complete SDL semantics. Based on this formalisation, we then define a notion of profile consistency. Finally, we present our SDL-profile tool, and report on our experiences.

1 Introduction

Over a period of 30 years, ITU-T's Specification and Description Language (SDL) [1] has matured from a simple, informal graphical notation for describing a set of communicating finite state machines to a sophisticated formal modelling technique with graphical syntax, data types, structuring mechanisms, object-oriented features, formal semantics, support for reuse, companion notations, and commercial tool environments. This development has led to an expressive and sophisticated language for a wide range of domains. On the other hand, the language definition of SDL-2000, the latest version of SDL, is complex and difficult to maintain. Full tool support for SDL is costly to implement. Therefore, all commercial tool providers have decided to support subsets of SDL only. These SDL subsets are targeted towards specific domains and companies, where, due to their reduced complexity, they are preferred by engineers. Following the notion of UML profiles [2], which enable the specialisation of UML for specific domains, we call these subsets *SDL profiles.*

While the use of SDL profiles is today's state-of-the-practice, their definition is not reflected in the SDL standard. One could argue that this is of no particular importance, since the full language definition covers all possible subsets. However, a drawback is that engineers working with a well-defined SDL profile only are still confronted with the entire language definition. Also, the task of tool builders to show conformance to the language definition is highly complex, in particular if the optimisation potential of a particular SDL profile is to be exploited.

M.B. Dwyer and A. Lopes (Eds.): FASE 2007, LNCS 4422, pp. 200–214, 2007.

To solve these problems, one could think of defining a separate standard for each SDL profile of interest. This, however, creates other problems arising from the extra work to define and maintain these standards, and from keeping them consistent. In this paper, we address these problems and present a formalised, tool-based approach for extracting, for a given SDL profile, the formal semantics from the standardised SDL semantics.

This paper is organised as follows: Section 2 gives a brief overview over the language definition of SDL, in particular, the formal semantics. Section 3 outlines our approach to the extraction of the formal semantics for SDL profiles. In Section 4, it is shown how the approach has been formalised. Consistency of SDL profiles is defined in Section 5. We present our tool chain for the extraction approach in Section 6, survey related work in Section 7, and draw conclusions in Section 8.

2   Language Definition of SDL

In this section, we survey the definition of SDL, and briefly present ASMs, the formalism used to define the dynamic semantics of SDL.

2.1   Specification and Description Language (SDL)

The Specification and Description Language (SDL) [1] is a formal language standardised by the International Telecommunications Union (ITU). It is widely used both in industry and academia. SDL is based on the concept of asynchronously communicating finite state machines, running concurrently or in parallel. SDL provides language constructs for the specification of nested *system structure*, *communication* using channels, signals and signal queues, *behaviour* using extended finite state machines, and *data*.

In 1988, the semantics of SDL was formally defined, upgrading the language to a formal description technique. In 1999, a new version of the language, referred to as SDL-2000, was introduced. Since the formal definition of the semantics was assessed as being too difficult to extend and maintain, a new formal semantics, based on Abstract State Machines (see Section 2.2), was defined from scratch [3]. In November 2000, the formal semantics of SDL-2000, the current version of SDL, was officially approved to become part of the SDL language definition [1]. It covers all static and dynamic language aspects, and consists of two major parts (for a detailed survey, see [3]):

- The *static semantics* of SDL defines well-formedness conditions on the concrete syntax of SDL. Furthermore, transformations map extended features of SDL to core features of the language, reducing the complexity of the dynamic semantics. The static semantics contains over 5600 lines of specification.
- The *dynamic semantics* of SDL defines the dynamic behaviour of well-formed SDL specifications, based on ASMs. At the core of the dynamic semantics is the SDL Virtual Machine (SVM), providing a signal flow model and several types of agents. Agents go through an initialisation phase, creating the

nested structure of an SDL system, and an execution phase, forwarding signals and executing extended state machines. Behaviour primitives form the instruction set of the SVM, defining basic actions such as sending signals, setting timers or calling procedures. A *compilation function* maps actions from transitions in an SDL specification to instructions of the SVM. The dynamic semantics contains over 3700 lines of ASM specification.

2.2 Abstract State Machines

Abstract State Machines (ASMs) [4,5] are a general model of computation introduced by Yuri Gurevich. They combine declarative concepts of first-order logic with the abstract operational view of distributed transition systems. ASMs are based on many-sorted first-order structures, called *states*. A state consists of a *signature* (or vocabulary) containing domain names, function names and relation names, together with an interpretation of these names over a base set. Intuitively, it can be viewed as a memory snapshot of the ASM, where locations - identified by functions and parameter values - are mapped to result values.

The computation model of *distributed ASMs* is based on a set of autonomously operating *ASM agents*. Starting from an initial state, the agents perform concurrent computations and interact through shared locations of the state. The behaviour of ASM agents is determined by *ASM programs*, consisting of *ASM rules*. Complex ASM rules are defined as compositions of guarded update instructions using a small set of rule constructors. From these rules, update sets, i.e. sets of memory locations and new values, are computed. These update sets define state transitions that result from applying all updates simultaneously.

3   Outline of the Extraction Approach for SDL Profiles

SDL profiles are self-contained subsets of SDL, targeted towards specific domains and companies. In comparison to the full SDL language definition, SDL profiles have reduced complexity, a result that is useful for both engineers and tool builders. In [6], the SDL Task Force has identified an SDL profile called SDL+, which focuses on the state machine aspect of SDL and adds functionality for testing[1]. However, no formal semantics is provided for SDL+. In [7], we have identified a hierarchy of SDL profiles, some of which are supported by our configurable transpiler ConTraST [8].

An SDL profile, as a subset of the complete SDL specification, can be characterised by its reduced concrete and abstract syntax, by defining a reduced language grammar. For the reduced language grammar, well-formedness conditions and transformations have to be taken into account. Some well-formedness conditions and transformations become dispensable. A problem arises when, through the reduction of the grammar, a well-formedness condition cannot be met, and the resulting language is empty. This occurs when language constructs are removed, while language constructs that depend on them remain in the subset.

---

[1] For SDL profiles, we only regard the parts of SDL+ that are included in SDL.

Likewise, transformations are affected if a language construct in the subset is transformed to a language construct that has been removed. These problems are avoided by taking self-contained subsets of the language, like the SDL subsets implicitly defined by tool providers.

We define SDL profiles by *extracting* the profile definition from the complete SDL language definition. To obtain a particular SDL profile, we remove parts correspondig to language features not included in the profile from the formal syntax and semantics. While the syntax extraction for a given SDL profile is straightforward, the extraction of the formal semantics has turned out to be difficult. To solve this problem, we have considered two approaches:

– **ASM rule coverage.** With each SDL profile, an ASM rule coverage comprising all ASM rules of the SVM that may be evaluated in some execution of some SDL specification written in that SDL profile can be associated. While this approach is semantically sound, it is practically infeasible. For a given SDL specification, the concurrent, non-deterministic nature of the SVM may lead to a very large number of possible executions. Furthermore, the number of SDL specifications that can be written in a given SDL profile is extremely large. Therefore, the worst-case complexity of an algorithm for ASM rule coverage is far too high to be of any use for practical purposes.

– **Dead ASM rule recognition.** Instead of computing the ASM rule coverage of a set of SDL specifications, we can develop safe criteria to recognise ASM rules that are never evaluated for a given SDL profile. For instance, if the SDL language module *timer* is to be removed, we can safely remove all ASM rules that are used for setting and resetting SDL timers, including the corresponding ASM domains, functions, and relations. It is important here that dead ASM rule recognition works in a conservative way, i.e. ASM rules must only be removed if it can be formally proven that they are not evaluated for a given SDL profile. The degree of reduction that can be achieved this way thus depends on the completeness of the criteria that can be defined. Unlike the ASM rule coverage approach, dead ASM rule recognition is practically feasible. Therefore, we have followed this approach, and will present safe criteria as well as some heuristics below.

4   Formalisation

We now formalise our approach for extracting the formal semantics of SDL profiles from the complete SDL semantics. The formalisation gives a precise definition of the removal process, which leads to deterministic results, and provides the foundation for tool support for the removal process. Finally, a formal definition is necessary in order to make precise statements about the consistency of SDL profiles. Since the formal syntax definition can be easily defined in a modular fashion, making its reduction straightforward, we focus on the reduction of the formal semantics definition.

4.1 Reduction Profile

SDL profiles characterise subsets of the set of valid SDL specifications, by defining subsets of the concrete and abstract syntax of SDL. The abstract syntax of SDL influences the dynamic semantics, which is the focus of our work, in two ways:

- The abstract syntax yields part of the SDL Virtual Machine (SVM) data structure (ASM signature, see Figure 1). For each element of the abstract grammar, a domain of the same name is introduced in the ASM signature. For example, the following non-terminals of the abstract grammar, which are only relevant for SDL specifications with timers, are also domains in the signature of the ASM: *Timer-name*, *Timer-identifier*, *Timer-definition*, *Timer-active-expression*, *Set-node*, and *Reset-node*.
- In the case of SDL actions (assignments, setting timers, ...), a compilation function maps parts of the abstract syntax to domains of the formal semantics definition that form the SVM. For example, the compilation of a *Set-node* in the abstract syntax tree leads to the creation of an element of the domain SET in the ASM signature.

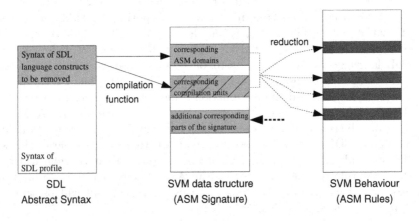

Fig. 1. Concept of the extraction process

Featuring the extraction approach, we remove SDL language modules from the formal language definition. Language modules consist of sets of SDL language constructs, and their corresponding grammar rules. These grammar rules are removed from the formal syntax definition. Furthermore, they form the starting point for the reduction of the formal semantics definition (see Figure 1). Starting from the removed parts of the formal syntax definition, we can identify corresponding domains in the ASM signature, as described above. These domains are empty in the initial state of the SVM, and, since they are not modified by the SVM, will be empty in all reachable states, too. This observation is fundamental for recognising dead ASM rules of the SVM.

Apart from domains corresponding to elements of the abstract grammar of a language module, other domains, functions and predicates in the SVM signature correspond to specific language modules. For example, *SignalSaved* is a predicate that corresponds to the *save* feature in SDL. If it holds, the signal being examined is not discarded, if no valid transition is found. These elements of the SVM signature are removed in addition to domains corresponding to elements of the abstract grammar. However, we need to prove that these elements are not needed for the given SDL profile.

In order to perform dead ASM rule recognition, we collect all parts of the ASM signature that correspond to language modules not included in the SDL profile in a *reduction profile*. The reduction profile is a list of domains, functions and predicates from the SVM signature to be removed in the extraction process. This list can be derived from the abstract syntax and the compilation function, however, domain knowledge is still required. We specify a default value (**true** or **false**) for predicates, and assume the special element **undefined** and the empty set as default values for functions and domains. These elements are removed from the formal semantics definition according to a set of extraction rules formally defined in the following sections. The complete formalisation can be found in [9].

$$
\begin{array}{|l|}
\hline
\textit{Save-signalset} \\
\textit{SignalSaved} = \text{false} \\
\hline
\end{array}
$$

Fig. 2. Reduction profile for 'save' feature

Figure 2 shows the smallest possible reduction profile corresponding to a language feature. It specifies all grammar elements and predicates used to defer the consumption of input signals.

4.2 Formalisation Signature

For the formal definition of the extraction process, we have decided to use a functional approach, defining functions that recursively map the original formal semantics to the reduced formal semantics. These functions are based on a concrete grammar for Abstract State Machines [10]. The input of the reduction is the SDL formal semantics definition from [11] and a reduction profile r, as described in Section 4.1.

To formalise the extraction, we define a function *remove*, which maps a term from the grammar G of ASMs and a set of variables V - an initially empty set of locally undefined variables from the ASM formal semantics - to a reduced term from the grammar G. Additionally, we introduce three mutually exclusive binary predicates, namely $undefined_r$, $true_r$ and $false_r$. These predicates hold for expressions of the ASM that are determined as true, false or undefined/empty, respectively, in any state, given the information in the reduction profile.

$$remove : G \times V \to G$$
$$undefined_r : G \times V \to \mathsf{Boolean}$$
$$true_r : G \times V \to \mathsf{Boolean}$$
$$false_r : G \times V \to \mathsf{Boolean}$$

The *remove* function is defined on all elements of the grammar G. Predicates $true_r$ and $false_r$ are defined on boolean and first-order logic expressions, and predicate $undefined_r$ on all expressions. In the following sections, we omit the index r from the predicates.

The function *remove* is defined recursively - a given term is mapped to a new term by applying the mapping defined by *remove* to the subterms. In case none of the predicates *undefined*, *true* and *false* holds, the current term is not reduced any further. This assures in particular that *remove* corresponds to the identical mapping if the reduction profile r is empty. In other cases, subterms can be replaced or omitted depending on which of the predicates hold.

4.3   Formal Definition of *true* and *false*

Identifying expressions as always true (false) is an important step in the reduction process. Predicates *true* and *false* hold for some first-order expressions that are true (false) in every state of the ASM. Generally, this is undecidable for first-order expressions.

Predicates of the ASM can be included in the reduction profile together with a default value **true** or **false**. Boolean-valued functions *true* and *false* introduced in Section 4.2 hold directly for these predicates. For general first-order expressions, we define the functions *true* and *false* recursively.

Predicate *undefined* holds for expressions that evaluate to the empty set or the special element **undefined** in every state, as defined by the reduction profile. Therefore, we can derive that equating an expression e with the empty set or the special ASM element **undefined** always yields **true** if *undefined* holds for expression e. Likewise, such an expression is never unequal to the empty set or **undefined**. With an expression e_2 being an empty set, we can determine the element-of operator to yield **false** in every state of the ASM. These considerations are reflected in the following definitions:

$$true(e = \mathsf{undefined}, \mathcal{V}) \text{ iff } undefined(e, \mathcal{V})$$
$$false(e \neq \mathsf{undefined}, \mathcal{V}) \text{ iff } undefined(e, \mathcal{V})$$
$$true(e = \emptyset, \mathcal{V}) \text{ iff } undefined(e, \mathcal{V})$$
$$false(e \neq \emptyset, \mathcal{V}) \text{ iff } undefined(e, \mathcal{V})$$
$$false(e_1 \in e_2, \mathcal{V}) \text{ iff } undefined(e_2, \mathcal{V})$$

In the SVM, a state s is a tuple with several elements. An element is selected from the tuple using the **s-** operator together with the element type, for example

s.s-*Save-signalset* for the set of saved signals in this state. Given the reduction profile in Figure 2, *false* holds for the expression $sig \in s.\mathtt{s}\text{-}Save\text{-}signalset$ for all signals *sig* and all SDL states *s*.

The result of *true* and *false* for a boolean expression is derived from its subexpressions, and can be defined in a truth table. Table 1 defines if *true* (T), *false* (F), *undefined* (U) or none of these predicates (-) hold for the disjunction.

Table 1. Truth table for disjunction

$e_1 \vee e_2$	T	F	U	-
T	T	T	T	T
F	T	F	F	-
U	T	F	U	-
-	T	-	-	-

Further boolean connectors and quantified expressions are defined in a similar fashion in [9].

4.4 Formal Reduction of ASM Rules

Rules specify transitions between states of the ASM. The basic rule is the *update rule*, which updates a location of the state to a new value. All together, there are seven kinds of rules for ASMs, for all of which we have formalised the reduction. Below, we show the formalisation of the reduction for two rules.

The mapping of the **if**-rule depends on which predicate holds for the guard *exp* of the rule. If the guard always evaluates to `true` (`false`), the **if**-rule can be omitted, and removal continues with subrule R_1 (R_2). If the guard is undefined, the rule is syntactically incorrect, and should not be reachable[2]. If none of the predicates hold, the removal is applied recursively to the guard and the subrules of the **if**-rule, leaving the rule itself intact.

$$\begin{array}{lll} \multicolumn{3}{l}{\mathit{remove}(\textbf{if}\ \text{exp}\ \textbf{then}\ R_1\ \textbf{else}\ R_2\ \textbf{endif}, \mathcal{V}) =} \\ \quad \mathit{remove}(R_1, \mathcal{V}) & \text{iff} & \mathit{true}(\text{exp}, \mathcal{V}) \\ \quad \mathit{remove}(R_2, \mathcal{V}) & \text{iff} & \mathit{false}(\text{exp}, \mathcal{V}) \\ \quad \text{skip} & \text{iff} & \mathit{undefined}(\text{exp}, \mathcal{V}) \\ \quad \textbf{if}\ \mathit{remove}(\text{exp}, \mathcal{V})\ \textbf{then}\ \mathit{remove}(R_1, \mathcal{V}) & & \text{otherwise} \\ \quad\quad \textbf{else}\ \mathit{remove}(R_2, \mathcal{V})\ \textbf{endif} & & \end{array}$$

Figure 3 shows an **if**-rule with a guard expression for which *false* holds, given the reduction profile in Figure 2. The **if**-rule is removed except for the else-branch, which is empty.

[2] This is a proof obligation that we have to verify manually. However, so far this has only occurred in very few cases, which were the result of errors in the reduction profile.

if *sig* ∈ *s*.s−*Save*−*signalset* **then**
...
endif

Fig. 3. if-Rule with unsatisfiable guard condition

The **choose**-rule nondeterministically takes an element from the finite set defined by the constraint exp and binds it to the variable x. If no element satisfies the constraint, as in the case where *false* holds, choose is equivalent to skip.If *true* or *undefined* hold for the constraint, the **choose**-rule is invalid since it ranges over a potentially infinite set.

$remove($**choose** $x :$ exp R **endchoose**, $\mathcal{V}) =$

skip	iff	$false(\text{exp}, \mathcal{V}) \vee true(\text{exp}, \mathcal{V}) \vee$ $undefined(\text{exp}, \mathcal{V})$
choose $x : remove(\text{exp})\ remove(R, \mathcal{V})$ **endchoose**		otherwise

5 Consistency of SDL Profiles

We call a set of SDL profiles *consistent*, if any specification that can be stated in all of these profiles behaves exactly the same way in each profile. Deriving the profiles from a common language definition enables us to make statements about consistency, because, unlike profiles defined independently, the derived profiles share many common parts.

A run of an ASM is a sequence of states, where each subsequent state is the result of firing all rules which conditions are true on the preceding state. For non-deterministic, multi-agent ASMs, the legal behaviour is given by a set of runs, each run in the set describing a possible execution of the system. Two SDL profiles are considered consistent, if they yield the same set of runs of their respective ASMs for all specifications contained in both profiles.

In order to prove consistency, it is sufficient to show that only dead ASM rules are removed. This property does not follow automatically from the formally defined operations for removal, since they rely on heuristics in some parts. However, based on these operations, it is possible to derive proof obligations that have to be verified in order to prove consistency.

For example, during removal, an if-rule can be replaced by the subrule in the **then**-block of the rule, if the predicate *true* holds for the guard. To prove consistency, it is sufficient to prove that for all specifications of the SDL profile, the guard evaluates to **true** in all reachable states[3]. Likewise, if the predicate *false* holds for the guard, we have to prove that for all specifications of the SDL profile, the guard evaluates to **false** in all reachable states. In case *undefined* holds for the guard, we have to prove that the **if**-statement can not be reached at all.

---

[3] This condition is stronger than necessary. It would suffice to show that the guard is always **true** for all reachable states that lead to the firing of the if-rule.

Figure 4 shows a part of the formal language definition that was removed as part of the save feature of SDL, which is used to defer the consumption of input signals. For SDL profiles that do not contain the save feature, no grammatical elements of *Save-signalset* exist. Therefore, selecting the *Save-signalset* for any state yields **undefined**, and selecting *Signal-identifier-set* for the element **undefined** yields the empty set. Since *Save-signalset* is not modified in the formal language definition, this holds for any reachable state of the ASM. An element can not be contained in an empty set, therefore the guard is always false, and omitting the **if**-statement leads to a consistent definition for specifications without save.

if *Self.signalChecked.signalType* $\in$
        *sn.stateAS1.s−Save−signalset.s−Signal−identifier−***set** **then**
       Self.SignalSaved := *True*
endif

Fig. 4. Removed part of formal semantics definition

Choose. Choose nondeterministically selects an element that satisfies the constraint given by expression *exp*. If a **choose**-rule is removed, we have to prove consistency by proving the expression *exp* to be `false` in any reachable state, and therefore - according to the semantics of ASMs - the **choose**-rule equates to an empty update set. Alternatively, we can prove that the **choose**-rule can not be reached.

Boolean Expressions. Parts of boolean expressions are removed if they have no influence on the final result, for example if *true* holds for a subexpression of a conjunction. In this case, the proof obligation is to show that the subexpression is always true for specifications of the SDL profile.

Proof obligations on boolean expressions can be split into proof obligations on subexpressions, as shown for $\wedge$ and $\vee$ below. For example, in order to prove consistency for predicate *true* on $e_1 \wedge e_2$, we can prove consistency for predicate *true* on e_1 and e_2.

$$true(e_1 \wedge e_2) \text{ iff } true(e_1) \text{ and } true(e_2) \tag{1}$$

$$false(e_1 \wedge e_2) \text{ iff } false(e_2) \text{ or } false(e_2) \tag{2}$$

$$true(e_1 \vee e_2) \text{ iff } true(e_1) \text{ or } true(e_2) \tag{3}$$

$$false(e_1 \vee e_2) \text{ iff } false(e_1) \text{ and } false(e_2) \tag{4}$$

Proof obligations for ASM rules and expressions can be inserted into the reduced formal semantics definition by the SDL-profile tool described in the following section. In order to prove consistency, we show that all generated proof obligations hold. Currently, this verification is done manually.

6   SDL-Profile Tool

Based on the formalisation provided in Section 4, we have implemented a tool called SDL-profile tool in order to automate the reduction process, providing visible results. The tool reads the formal semantics definition, performs the *remove* operation based on a *reduction profile*, and outputs a reduced version of the formal semantics. Figure 5 shows the sequence of steps performed during the removal, and the tools used for each step.

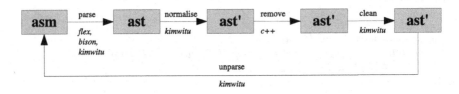

Fig. 5. Tool chain of the SDL-profile tool

6.1   Tool Chain

Parser. The *parser* takes an ASM specification as input and creates an abstract syntax tree representation of the specification as output. It is generated out of specifications of the lexis, grammar and abstract syntax of Abstract State Machines, as used in the formal semantics of SDL-2000 [10]. The specification of the abstract syntax is translated by kimwitu++ [12] to a data structure for the abstract syntax tree, using C++ classes. Scanner and parser are generated by flex and bison, respectively. Apart from minor differences, the parser is identical to the parser used in [13].

Normalisation. The *normalisation* step transforms the abstract syntax tree to a pre-removal normal form. The transformation is specified by rewrite rules on the abstract syntax tree. The rewrite rules are translated to C++ functions by the kimwitu tool. The main function of the normalisation step is to split up complicated abstract syntax rules, in order to make the definition of the remove function easier.

Remove. The *remove* step is the implementation of the removal formalised in Section 4. For each type of node (called *phylum*) in the abstract syntax definition, a remove function is introduced. The remove function performs removal for each term of the respective phylum, for example the terms IfThenElse, Choose, and Extend for the *rule* phylum. It returns a term of the respective phylum as result – for example the remove function for rules always returns a term of type rule.

For a term of a phylum, removal starts by checking conditions consisting of the predicates *true*, *false* and *undefined*, as defined in the formalisation of the reduction process. If a condition evaluates to true, a modified term is returned, calling remove recursively on the subterms of the term if necessary. For example, for the rule term IfThenElse, if the predicate *true* holds for expression *exp*, removal continues with the **then**-part, if the predicate *false* holds for expression *exp*, removal continues with the **else**-part. If *undefined* holds for the expression *exp*, the rule term Skip is returned.

```
IfThenElse(exp, r1, r2):  {
    if (eval_true(exp,V)) { return remove(r1,V); };
    if (eval_false(exp,V)) { return remove(r2,V); };
    if (eval_undef(exp,V)) { return Skip(); };
    return IfThenElse(remove(exp,V), remove(r1,V), remove(r2,V));
}
```

Cleanup. The *cleanup* step transforms superfluous rules resulting from the removal step to a post-removal normal form. The normal form is achieved by defining term rewrite rules in kimwitu. Unlike removal, the rewrite rules apply anywhere where their left hand side matches, and are applied as long as a match is found. The cleanup step only removes trivial parts of the ASM specification. The resulting specification is semantically equivalent to the specification before the cleanup step.

Iteration. Given a completely defined reduction profile, only one run of the SDL-profile tool is needed to generate a reduced ASM semantics definition. In case the reduction profile is incomplete, the profile tool can identify further names in the ASM signature that can be removed, and iterate the removal process.

Unparsing. Unparsing traverses the abstract syntax tree and outputs a string representation of every node. The result is a textual representation of the formal semantics tree in the original input format. Therefore, the output of the profile tool can be used as the input for a subsequent run of the profile tool. We also provide different output formats, for example a Latex document of the formal semantics, or a compilation to C++.

6.2   Application of the SDL-Profile Tool

Given an ASM formal semantics definition and a reduction profile, the SDL-profile tool generates a reduced formal semantics definition in the original format. In order to validate the removal process, we compare the original semantics definition with the reduced version. For this, we have used graphical diff-based tools (tkdiff) to highlight the differences between the versions. Using the SDL-profile tool, we have created reduction profiles for several language modules, such as timers, exceptions, save, composite states and inheritance. We have also created reduction profiles for language profiles like SDL+ and Core, resulting in formal semantics definitions that, with small modifications, match these SDL profiles.

SELECTTRANSITIONSTARTPHASE ≡
  if (*Self. currentExceptionInst* ≠ *undefined*) **then**
    Self. agentMode3 := *selectException*
    Self. agentMode4 := *startPhase*
  elseif (*Self. currentStartNodes* ≠ ∅) **then**
    ...
  else
    ...
  endif

SELECTTRANSITIONSTARTPHASE ≡
  if (*Self. currentStartNodes* ≠ ∅) **then**
    ...
  else
    ...
  endif

Fig. 6. Macro SELECTTRANSITIONSTARTPHASE before and after reduction

Figure 6 shows an excerpt of the formal semantics definition before and after applying the SDL-profile tool, using a reduction profile for SDL exceptions. The reduction profile contains, besides other function and macro names, the function name *currentExceptionInst*, which is interpreted as *undefined* in the context below. Therefore, the predicate *false* holds for the guard of the **if**-rule, and the first part of the **if**-rule is removed.

7   Related Work

A modular language definition can be found in the language specification of UML [2]. The abstract syntax of UML is defined using a meta-model approach, using classes to define language elements and packages to group language elements into medium-grained units. The core of the language is defined by the Kernel package, specifying basic elements of the language such as packages, classes, associations and types. However, each meta-model class has only an informal description of its semantics, limiting a precise definition of subsets to the language syntax.

UML has a profile mechanism that allows metaclasses from existing metamodels to be extended and adapted, using stereotypes. Semantics and constraints may be added as long as they are not in conflict with the existing semantics and constraints. The profile mechanism has been used to define a UML profile for SDL, enabling the use of UML 2.0 as a front-end for SDL-2000 [14].

ConTraST [8] is an SDL to C++ transpiler that generates a readable C++ representation of an SDL specification by preserving as much of the original structure as possible. The generated C++ code is compiled together with a runtime environment that is a C++ implementation of the formal semantics defined in Z100.F3. ConTraST is based on the textual syntax of SDL-96, and supports SDL profiles syntactically through deactivation of language features, and semantically by suppressing unreachable parts of the runtime environment for a given profile, as identified by the SDL-profile tool.

In [15], the concept of program slicing is extended to Abstract State Machines. For an expressive class of ASMs, an algorithm for the computation of a minimal slice of an ASM, given a slicing criterion, is presented. While the complexity of the algorithm is acceptable in the average case, the worst case complexity is exponential. ASM slicing does not cover indeterminism, which usually occurs in language definitions.

8   Conclusions and Outlook

In this paper, we have introduced the concept of SDL profiles as well-defined subsets of SDL, leading to smaller, more understandable language definitions. Tool support can be based on these profiles, leading to faster tool development and less expensive tools. Based on the smaller language definitions, code optimisations can be performed when generating code from a specification. Deriving the formal semantics of SDL profiles from a common formal semantics definition allows us to compare the formal semantics of different SDL profiles, and to make assertions about their consistency.

To achieve deterministic results, we have formalised the extraction of the formal semantics for SDL profiles from the complete formal semantics of SDL-2000. The extraction is based on recognising and removing dead ASM rules from the formal semantics definition, starting from a reduced ASM signature. The reduction of the ASM signature is derived from the abstract syntax of removed language modules. The extraction has been automated by the SDL-profile tool, providing visible results. This tool has been used to create several language profiles for SDL-2000, by removing SDL language modules from the formal semantics definition, such as exceptions, timers, save and composite states. The reduction achieved is significant. The formal semantics definition for SDL+ has been reduced to less than 2300 lines of specification, and less than 1100 lines for a small core of SDL, from about 3700 lines of the complete formal semantics.

Based on the formally defined process for the derivation of formal language definitions for SDL profiles, we can define precise criteria for the consistency of SDL profiles. Currently, some consistency criteria have to be verified manually. Our future work will focus on improving the extraction process, so that further criteria can be checked automatically.

References

1. ITU Recommendation Z.100: Specification and Description Language. Geneva (1999)
2. OMG Unified Modelling Language Specification: Version 2.0 (2003) www.omg.org.
3. Glässer, U., Gotzhein, R., Prinz, A.: The Formal Semantics of SDL-2000 - Status and Perspectives. Computer Networks, Elsevier Sciences **42** (2003) pp. 343–358
4. Gurevich, Y.: Evolving Algebras 1993: Lipari Guide. In Börger, E., ed.: Specification and Validation Methods. Oxford University Press (1995) 9–36

5. Gurevich, Y.: May 1997 draft of the ASM guide. Technical Report CSE-TR-336-97, EECS Department, University of Michigan (1997)
6. SDL Task Force: SDL+ - The Simplest, Useful 'Enhanced SDL-Subset' for the Implementation and Testing of State Machines (2005) www.sdltaskforce.org.
7. Grammes, R.: Formal Operations for SDL Language Profiles. In Gotzhein, R., Reed, R., eds.: SAM 2006: Language Profiles - 5th International Workshop on System Analysis and Modelling (SAM 2006), Kaiserslautern, Germany. Volume 4320 of LNCS., Springer (2006) pp.51–65
8. Fliege, I., Grammes, R., Weber, C.: ConTraST - A Configurable SDL Transpiler And Runtime Environment. In Gotzhein, R., Reed, R., eds.: SAM 2006: Language Profiles - 5th International Workshop on System Analysis and Modelling (SAM 2006), Kaiserslautern, Germany. Volume 4320 of LNCS., Springer (2006) pp.222–234
9. Grammes, R., Gotzhein, R.: SDL Profiles - Definition and Formal Extraction. Technical Report 350/06, Department of Computer Science, University of Kaiserslautern (2006)
10. Glässer, U., Gotzhein, R., Prinz, A.: An Introduction To Abstract State Machines. Technical Report 326/03, Department of Computer Science, University of Kaiserslautern (2003)
11. ITU Study Group 10: Draft Z.100 Annex F3 (11/00) (2000)
12. von Löwis, M., Piefel, M.: The Term Processor Kimwitu++. In Callaos, N., Harnandez-Encinas, L., Yetim, F., eds.: SCI 2002: The 6th World Multiconference on Systemics, Cybernetics and Informatics, Orlando, USA (2002)
13. Prinz, A., von Löwis, M.: Generating a Compiler for SDL from the Formal Language Definition. In Reed, R., Reed, J., eds.: SDL 2003: System Design. Volume 2708 of LNCS., Springer (2003) pp. 150–165
14. ITU Study Group 17: UML Profile for SDL. Draft Recommendation Z.109 (2005)
15. Nowack, A.: Slicing Abstract State Machines. In Zimmermann, W., Thalheim, B., eds.: Abstract State Machines 2004. Advances in Theory and Practice, Lutherstadt Wittenberg, Germany. Volume 3052 of LNCS., Springer (2004) 186–201

Preliminary Design of BML: A Behavioral Interface Specification Language for Java Bytecode*

Lilian Burdy, Marieke Huisman[1], and Mariela Pavlova[2],**

[1] INRIA Sophia Antipolis, France
[2] Ludwig-Maximilians-Universität München, German

Abstract. We present the Bytecode Modeling Language (BML), the Java bytecode cousin of JML. BML allows the application developer to specify the behaviour of an application in the form of annotations, *directly* at the level of the bytecode. An extension of the class file format is defined to store the specification directly with the bytecode. This is a first step towards the development of a platform for Proof Carrying Code, where applications come together with their specification and a proof of correctness. BML is designed to be closely related with JML. In particular, JML specifications can be compiled into BML specifications. We briefly discuss the tools that are currently being developed for BML, and that will result in a tool set where an application can be validated throughout its development, both at source code and at bytecode level.

1   Introduction

The use of formal methods to show conformance of an implementation *w.r.t.* a specification has become an accepted technique for the development of security-critical applications. Various tools exist that allow to specify and validate complex functional or security properties, using different techniques such as runtime assertion checking, testing and verification condition generation. However, often these techniques are restricted to source code level programs, while for many applications, and in particular for mobile code, one needs to be able to also specify and verify the executable (or interpreted) code.

Different possible reasons for this exist: the executable code may not be accompanied by its (specified) source, or one simply does not trust the compiler. And in an attempt to avoid *all* possible security threats, sometimes security-critical applications are directly developed at the executable level. Thus, it is essential to have the means to specify *and* to verify an application directly at this level, without the use of a compiler, and both specification and verification techniques should be tailored directly to the particularities of executable code.

* This work is partially funded by the IST programme of the European Commission, under the IST-2003-507894 Inspired project and the IST-2005-015905 MOBIUS project.
** Research done while at INRIA Sophia Antipolis.

M.B. Dwyer and A. Lopes (Eds.): FASE 2007, LNCS 4422, pp. 215–229, 2007.

Moreover, in order to capture all relevant security requirements, the specification language used should be expressive enough for this.

Proof Carrying Code (PCC) is a typical example where the need to specify and verify executable code directly is imperative, in particular when one wishes to capture complex security policies that cannot be checked with a type checker. PCC is a possible solution to support the secure downloading of applications on a mobile device. The executable code of an application comes together with a specification, and the necessary evidence from which the code client can easily establish that the application respects its specification. In such a scenario, the code producer, who *has* to produce a correctness proof, will often prefer to do the verification at source code level, and then compile the specification and the proof into the level of executable code. Realising a platform to support this scenario is one of the goals of the MOBIUS project (see http://mobius.inria.fr).

This paper describes the low-level specification language that we propose to specify the security requirements for mobile device applications. Since the most common execution framework for mobile devices is the J2ME platform, our language is tailored to Java bytecode, and thus to the verification of *unstructured* code. To be able to translate source code level specifications into bytecode level specifications, our specification language is also designed to be closely related to the Java Modeling Language (JML) (see http://www.jmlspecs.org).

Over the last few years, JML has become the *de facto* specification language for Java source code programs. Different tools exist that allow to validate, verify or generate JML specifications (see [9] for an overview). Several case studies have demonstrated that JML can be used to specify and improve realistic industrial examples (see *e.g.* [8]). One of the reasons for its success is that JML uses a Java-like syntax. Specifications are written using preconditions, postcondition, class invariants and other annotations, where the different predicates are side-effect-free Java expressions, extended with specification-specific keywords (*e.g.* logical quantifiers and a keyword to refer to the return value of a method). Other important factors for the success of JML are its expressiveness and flexibility, and its ability to characterise typical security requirements.

Therefore, we define a variation of JML especially tailored to bytecode, called BML, short for Bytecode Modeling Language. BML supports the most important features of JML. Thus, we can express functional properties of Java bytecode programs in the form of *e.g.* pre- and postconditions, class and object invariants, and assertions for particular program points like loop invariants. Because of the close connection with JML, JML source code level specifications can be compiled into BML bytecode level specifications without too much difficulty, basically by compiling the source code predicates into bytecode predicates. This allows to do development and verification at source code level, while still being able to ship bytecode level proofs. To the best of our knowledge, no other specification language with similar design goals exists for Java bytecode. Notice that, even though the design of BML was motivated by the need to specify security requirements for mobile device applications, just as JML, BML is a general specification language that can be used for different kinds of applications and analyses.

Section 2 quickly summarises the relevant features of JML. Section 3 gives a detailed account of BML, describing its syntax and semantics, while Section 4 proposes a format to store BML specifications in a class file. Section 5 discusses the compilation from JML to BML, while Section 6 wraps up and discusses tool support and related and future work.

2   A Short Overview of JML

This section gives a short introduction to JML, by means of an example. Throughout the rest of this paper, we assume that the reader is familiar with JML, its syntax and its semantics. For a detailed overview of JML we refer to its reference manual [15]. Where necessary, we refer to the appropriate sections of this manual. A detailed overview of the tools which support JML can be found in [9].

To illustrate the different features of JML, Figure 1 shows an example class specification, defining the class Bill. It contains an abstract method round_cost, that computes the cost of a particular round. The method produce_bill is supposed to sum up the costs of the different rounds.

In order not to interfere with the standard Java compiler, JML specifications are written as special comments (tagged with @). Method specifications contain

```
/* @author Hermann Lehner, Aleksy Schubert
 * The Bill class provides an abstract implementation of the bill
 * functionality. It calculates the aggregate cost for series of investments
 * based on the cost of a single round (to be implemented in subclasses). */
abstract class Bill {
  private int sum;  //@ invariant sum>=0;

  /* This method gives a cost of a single round.
   * @param x is the number of the particular round
   * @return the cost of the investment in this round, below <code>x</code> */
  //@ ensures 0 <= \result && \result <= x;
  abstract int round_cost(int x) throws Exception;

  /* This method calculates the cost of the whole series of investments.
   * @return <code>true</code> when the calculation is successful and
   *             <code>false</code> when the calculation cannot be performed */
  //@ requires n > 0;
  //@ ensures sum <= \old(sum)+n*(n+1)/2;
  public boolean produce_bill(int n){
    try{//@ loop_modifies sum, i;
        //@ loop_invariant 0 <= i && 0 <= sum && i <= n + 1 &&
        //@                   sum <= \old(sum)+(i-1)*i/2;
        for (int i=1;i<=n;i++) { this.sum = this.sum + round_cost(i); }
        return true;
    } catch (Exception e){ return false; } } }
```

Fig. 1. Class Bill with JML annotations

preconditions (keyword **requires**), postconditions (**ensures**) and frame conditions (**assignable**). The latter specify which variables *may* be modified by a method. In a method body, one can annotate all statements with an **assert** predicate and loops also with invariants (**loop_invariant**), variants (**decreases**) and loop frame conditions (**loop_modifies**). The latter is a non-standard extension of JML, introduced in [11], which we found useful to make program verification more practical. One can also specify class invariants, *i.e.* properties that should hold in all visible states of the execution, and constraints, describing a relation that holds between any two pairs of consecutive visible states (where visible states are the states in which a method is called or returned from).

The predicates in the different conditions are side-effect free Java boolean expressions, extended with specification-specific keywords, such as \result, denoting the return value of a non-void method, and \old, indicating that an expression should be evaluated in the pre-state of the method.

JML allows to declare special specification-only variables: logical variables (with keyword **model**) and so-called **ghost** variables, that can be assigned to in special **set** annotations.

In Figure 1, the specification for **round_cost** states that the result of the method should be positive, but less than the number of the round. The specification for **produce_bill** requires that we compute at least one round, and then ensures an upper-bound on the outcome of the method. We use a loop invariant and loop frame condition to prove the method body correct. Finally, the class invariant specifies that the **sum** field is always positive.

3   The Bytecode Modeling Language

Basically, BML has the same syntax as JML with two exceptions:

1. specifications are not written directly in the program code, they are added as special attributes to the bytecode; and
2. the grammar for expressions only allows bytecode expressions.

Syntax for BML predicates. Figure 2 displays the most interesting part of the grammar for BML predicates, defining the syntax for primary expressions and primary suffixes[1]. Primary expressions, followed by zero or more primary suffixes, are the most basic form of expressions, formed by identifiers, bracketed expressions *etc.*

Since only bytecode expressions can be used, all field names, class names *etc.* are replaced by references to the constant pool (a number, preceded by the symbol #), while registers are used to refer to local variables and parameters. The register **lv[0]** of a non-static method always contains the implicit argument **this**, the other registers contain the parameters and the local variables declared inside a method body. Compilers often reuse local variable registers throughout the execution of a single method. Thus, when *e.g.* type checking an annotation

---

[1] See **http://www-sop.inria.fr/everest/BML** for the full grammar of BML.

predicate ::= ...

unary-expr-not-plus-minus ::= ...
      | *primary-expr* [*primary-suffix*]...

primary-suffix ::= . *ident* | ([*expression-list*]) | [*expression*]

primary-expr ::= #*natural*   % reference in the constant pool
    | lv[*natural*]   % local variable
    | *bml-primary*
    | *constant* | super | true | false | this | null | (*expression*) | *jml-primary*

bml-primary ::= cntr   % counter of the operand stack
    | st(*additive-expr*)   % stack expressions
    | length(*expression*)   % array length

Fig. 2. Fragment of grammar for BML predicates and specification expressions

containing a local variable, it has to be taken into account at which point in the code the annotation is evaluated (but notice that this is not more complicated than reusing the same local variable name in different block statements).

We can use the stack counter (cntr) and stack expressions (st(e), where e is some arithmetic expression) to describe intermediate states of a computation. These are not used in method specifications. We also add a special expression length(a), denoting the length of array a. Since the source code expression a.length is compiled into a special bytecode instruction arraylength, we also need a special specification construct for this at bytecode level.

In Java source code, one can usually leave the receiver object this implicit. But compilation into bytecode makes this object explicit, *i.e.* instructions such as putfield *always* require that the receiver object is loaded on the operand stack. In analogy with this, BML specifications require that the receiver object is written explicitly in expressions (see Figure 3 below).

In JML, many special keywords are preceded by the symbol \, to ensure that they will not clash with variable names. For BML, we do not have to worry about this: all variable names are replaced by references to the constant pool or local variable registers. Therefore, the new keywords are written without a special preceding symbol. However, for convenience, we keep the symbol for keywords that are also JML keywords.

At the moment, the use of pure methods is not part of the BML grammar, as there is still ongoing research on the exact semantics of method calls used in specifications. However, we believe that if the theoretical issues have been settled, eventually any tool supporting BML should also support this[2].

Class and method specifications. BML contains equivalent constructs for all specification constructs of JML Level 0 (see [15, §2.9]), which defines the features that should be understood and checked by all JML tools. It also contains several constructs from JML level 1, that we find important to be able to write meaningful

---

[2] In fact, we think that both at source code and at bytecode level, specifications will benefit significantly from being allowed to use method calls in them.

specifications for the example applications studied in the MOBIUS project, namely static invariants; object and static constraints; and loop variants.

We choose to keep the notion of loop specification in BML, even though there is no high level loop construct in bytecode. But to be able to prove termination, one needs to prove decrease of a loop variant, which makes the treatment of loops different from the treatment of other statements. Also, experiences with verification of realistic case studies have shown that it is beneficial to know which variables may be modified by the code block that corresponds to the loop. For this, we use the special clause `loop_modifies`. This allows to write concise specifications, and to efficiently generate proof obligations using a weakest precondition calculus. Moreover by keeping the notion of loop specification explicit in BML, we keep the correspondence with JML specifications more direct.

As mentioned above, specifications are stored as special attributes in the class file. This means that every class contains a table with invariant and constraint annotations, while each method has extra attributes containing its specifications. Finally, the code for the method body is annotated with local annotation tables for the assert annotations and the loop specifications. Section 4 defines the precise format of these attributes.

Since the bytecode and BML specifications are two separate entities, they should be parsed independently. Concretely this means that the grammar of BML is similar to the grammar of type specifications, method specifications and data groups of JML [15, §A.5, A.6, A.7], restricted to the constructs in JML level 0, plus the constructs of JML level 1 mentioned, but with the changes to the grammar for predicates and specification expressions, as mentioned above.

An example BML specification. To show a typical BML specification, Figure 3 presents the BML version of the JML specification of method `produce_bill` in Figure 1. Notice that the field `sum` has been assigned the number 24 in the constant pool, and that it is always explicitly qualified with `lv[0]` (denoting this). Further, `lv[1]` denotes the parameter `n`, while `lv[2]` denotes the local variable `i`.

The class invariant gives rise to the following BML specification (stored in the class file as a special user-specific attribute, as explained below):

```
invariant:  #24 >= 0
```

This expression is not qualified with `lv[0]`, as it is implicitly quantified over all objects that are an instance of a subclass of class `Bill` (*cf.* the JML semantics [15, §8.2]).

Structural and typing constraints for BML specifications. BML specifications have to respect several structural and typing constraints, similar to the structural and typing constraints that the bytecode verifier imposes over the class file format. Examples of typing constraints that a BML specification must respect are the following:

```
{| requires lv[1] > 0
   ensures lv[0].#24 <= \old(lv[0].#24) + lv[1] * (lv[1] + 1) / 2 |}
 0 iconst_1
 1 istore_2
 2 goto 22
 5 aload_0
 6 aload_0
 7 getfield #24 <Bill.sum>
10 aload_0
11 iload_2
12 invokevirtual #26 <Bill.round_cost>
15 iadd
16 putfield #24 <Bill.sum>
19 iinc 2 by 1
loop_invariant 0 <= lv[2] && 0 <= lv[0].#24 && lv[2] <= lv[1] + 1 &&
               lv[0].#24 <= \old(lv[0].#24) + (lv[2] - 1) * lv[2]/2
entry loop:
22 iload_2
23 iload_1
24 if_icmple 5
27 iconst_1
28 ireturn
29 astore_3
30 iconst_0
31 ireturn
```

Fig. 3. Bytecode + BML specification for method `produce_bill` in class `Bill`

- field access expression $e.ident$ is well-typed only if e is of a subtype of the class where the field described by the constant pool element at index $ident$ is declared;
- array access expression $e_1[e_2]$ is well-typed only if e_1 is of array type and e_2 is of integer type; and
- predicate $e_1 <: e_2$ is well-typed only if the expressions e_1 and e_2 are of type `java.lang.Class` (which is the same as the JML type `\TYPE`).

Examples of structural constraints that a BML specification must respect are the following:

- all references to the constant pool must be to an entry of the appropriate type; for example, for field access expression $e.ident$, $ident$ must reference a field in the constant pool; while for expression `\type(`$ident$`)`, $ident$ must be a reference to a constant class in the constant pool;
- every $ident$ in a BML specification must be a correct index in the constant pool; and
- if the expression $lv[i]$ appears in a BML method specification, i must be a valid index in the method's local variables table.

These checks are best implemented as an extension of the bytecode verifier.

Semantics of BML expressions. The semantics of BML specifications follows the semantics of JML specifications [15]. But, just as a JML specification can be mapped into a more fundamental Hoare triple specification, we can also define a semantics for BML in terms of a basic logic for Java bytecode, namely the so-called MOBIUS base logic. This logic will be the core of the PCC platform developed within the project. This logic (see [7] for an earlier version, without exceptions) has been proven sound in Coq *w.r.t.* a formalisation of the virtual machine. On top of this, a direct verification condition generator has been proven sound, also in Coq. And, as a first step towards efficient tool development, a translation of bytecode into guarded commands has been defined and proven correct, *w.r.t.* verification condition generation [16].

Defining the mapping of BML specifications into this MOBIUS base logic is defined in two steps. First the evaluation of predicates is defined over the program state (*i.e.* over the heap, store and operand stack), and second the complete BML specifications are translated into judgements of the MOBIUS base logic. Notice that this embedding allows to use the verification condition generator for the MOBIUS base logic also for BML specifications.

Judgements in the MOBIUS base logic are of the form $G, Q \vdash \{A\} \, pc \, \{B\} \, (I)$, where G is a proof context, and Q the local annotation table, *i.e.* the table that associates assert annotations with particular instructions. Further, A is a (local) precondition, relating the state at label pc with the initial state, while B is a (local) postcondition, relating the initial, current and final state, and I is a (local) invariant, *i.e* a predicate that is supposed to hold throughout execution of the current method.

Mapping class specifications (invariants and constraints) and method specifications into the MOBIUS base logic is straightforward. Since the MOBIUS base logic only has one postcondition, the normal and exceptional postconditions are combined into a single postcondition, specifying with a case distinction which conditions should hold if the state is normal or exceptional, respectively. Frame conditions are also added to the postconditions, specifying explicitly which variables are allowed to be changed. Since predicates in the MOBIUS base logic specify properties over the whole heap, this can be expressed directly: all locations that are not mentioned in the frame condition of the method (evaluated in the pre-state of the method) should be unchanged. Methods with multiple specifications are translated only after desugaring them into a single method specification *cf.* [20].

Assert and set statements are inserted directly in the local annotation table[3]. However, for loop specifications some manipulations are necessary to produce the appropriate assert annotations, due to the unstructured nature of bytecode. The loop invariants can be added directly to the local annotation table, but loop variants and loop frame conditions first are transformed into a sequence of assert and set annotations (after introducing appropriate ghost variables).

---

[3] In fact, at the moment, the MOBIUS base logic does not support ghost variables; but these will be added in the near future.

This transformation is done at the level of BML, after which we can add the annotations to the local annotation table.

The transformation of the loop variant basically proceeds as follows. Let variant be the expression declared in the decreases clause. We declare ghost variables loop_init (initially set to true) and loop_variant (whose initialisation is not essential). If l is the program point where we enter the loop, then at that point we add an assertion

```
//@ assert !loop_init ==> (0 <= variant && variant < loop_variant);
```

followed by:

```
//@ set loop_init = false; set loop_variant = variant;
```

This ensures that every time the loop entry point l is reached again, the decrease of the loop variant is checked. Only a path that goes through the loop can set loop_init to false.

For transforming loop frame conditions, we use again that in the MOBIUS base logic we can express properties of the heap. We make a transformation into a sequence of assert and set statements, declaring ghost variables to remember the old heap and all locations mentioned in the loop frame condition, and a ghost variable loop_init as above. Then we assert at the entry point of the heap that if loop_init does not hold, any location that is not mentioned in the loop frame condition should remain unchanged. Notice that this assertion cannot be directly expressed in BML, but it can be expressed in the MOBIUS base logic. Finally, in the MOBIUS base logic we add appropriate ghost variable updates to remember the old heap and the locations of the loop frame condition when the loop was first entered.

4   Encoding BML Specifications in the Class File Format

To store BML specifications together with the bytecode it specifies, we encode them in the class file format. Recall that a class file contains all the information related to a single class or interface, *e.g.* its name, which interfaces it implements, its super class and the methods and fields it declares. The Java Virtual Machine Specification [17] prescribes the mandatory elements of the class file: the constant pool, the field information and the method information. The constant pool is used to construct the runtime constant pool upon class or interface creation. This will serve for loading, linking and resolution of references used in the class. The JVM specification allows to add user-specific information to the class file ([17, §4.7.1]) as special user-specific attributes. We store BML specifications in such user-specific attributes, in a compiler-independent format[4]. To ensure that the augmented class files are executable by any implementation of the JVM, the user-specific attributes cannot be inserted in the list with bytecode

---

[4] Another possibility would be to use metadata to encode the specifications, but this is only supported in Java 1.5, and it is (currently) not directly compatible with JML.

```
Ghost_Field_attribute {              BMLMethod_attribute {
    u2 attribute_name_index;            u2 attribute_name_index;
    u4 attribute_length;                u4 attribute_length;
    u2 fields_count;                    formula requires_formula;
    { u2 access_flags;                  u2 spec_count;
      u2 name_index;                    { formula spec_requires_formula;
      u2 descriptor_index;               u2 assignable_count;
    } fields[fields_count]; }            formula assignable[assignable_count];
                                         formula ensures_formula;
                                         u2 exsures_count;
                                         { u2 exception_index;
                                           formula exsures_formula;
                                         } exsures[exsures_count];
                                       } spec[spec_count]; }
```

Fig. 4. Attributes for ghost field declarations and method specifications

instructions. Instead BML annotations are stored separately from the method body, and where necessary the annotations contain the index of the instruction that they specify. The use of special attributes ensures that the presence of BML annotations does not have any impact on the application's performance, *i.e.*, the augmented class file should not slow down loading or normal execution of the application. requirement is important for mobile.

For each class, we add the following information to the class file:

- a second constant pool which contains constant references for the BML specification expressions;
- an attribute with the ghost fields used in the specification;
- an attribute with the model fields used in the specification;
- an attribute with the class invariants (both static and object); and
- an attribute with the constraints (both static and object).

Apart from the second constant pool, all extra class attributes basically contain the name of the attribute, the number of elements it contains, and a list with the actual elements.

If a model or a ghost field is dereferenced in the specification, then a **constantFieldRef** is added to the second constant pool as the Java compiler does for any dereferenced Java field in the original constant pool of the class. Note that in this way, the BML encoding will not affect the JVM performance. In particular, if we would use the original constant pool for storing constants originating from specifications, the search time in the original constant pool might degrade significantly (especially for a large specification).

The left-hand column of Figure 4 shows the format of the ghost fields attribute. This should be understood as follows: the name of the attribute is given as an index into the constant pool. This constant pool entry will be representing a string "Ghost_Field". Next we have the length of the attribute, which should be $2 + 6*$**fields_count** (the number of fields stored in the list). The **fields** table stores all ghost fields. For each field we store its access flags (*e.g.* `public` or `private`), and the name index and descriptor index, both referring to the constant pool. The first must be a string, representing the (unqualified) name of the variable, the latter is a field descriptor, containing *e.g.* type information. The tags **u2** and **u4** specifies the size of the attribute, 2 and 4 bytes, respectively. The model field attribute is similar.

In a similar way, we define attributes for class invariants and constraints, containing a list of invariants and constraints, respectively. These contain the predicate, a tag whether the invariant (constraint) is defined over instances or static, and appropriate visibility modifiers.

The JVM specification prescribes that the attribute with method information at least contains the code of each method. We add attributes for the method specification, set statements, assert statements, and loop specifications.

The attribute for lightweight behaviour specifications is shown in the right-hand column of Figure 4 (heavyweight behaviour specifications are handled similarly). The global requires formula is the disjunction of all preconditions in the different specification cases of the method. For each specification case, we then have a precondition (**spec_requires_formula**), a list of assignable expressions, a postcondition (**ensures_formula**) and a list of exceptional postconditions (stored in the **exsures** attribute). If a clause is not explicitly specified, its default value will be stored here.

The attributes for set and assert statements and loop specifications have the same format as *e.g.* the ghost variable attribute: a length entry and a list of elements. The elements storing set and assert statements do not only keep the appropriate predicate or expression, but also an index to the appropriate point in the bytecode. Similarly, the elements for loop specifications contain the loop specification (invariant, variant and frame conditions), plus an index to the bytecode instruction that corresponds to the entry of the loop. If the specification does not contain a loop variant, we indicate this, using a special tag for the **decreases** clause.

5   Compiling JML Specifications into BML Specifications

Since it is often easier and more intuitive to specify and verify at source code level, we have defined a compiler from JML to BML: JML2BML. BML is designed to be very close to JML, so the correspondence between the original and the compiled specification is straightforward. Notice that in principle, the same can be done for the proofs, *i.e.* a source code level proof can be compiled into a bytecode level proof. It is future work to define this in full detail, but some work in this direction has already been done [6].

The JML specification is compiled separately from the Java source code. In fact, JML2BML takes as input an annotated Java source file *and* the Java class file produced by a non-optimising compiler with the debug flag set.

From the debug information, we use in particular the **Line_Number_Table** and the **Local_Variable_Table** attributes. The presence of these attributes is optional [17], but almost all standard non-optimising compilers can generate them. The **Line_Number_Table** links line numbers in the Java source code with the Java bytecode instructions. The **Local_Variable_Table** describes the local variables that appear in a method.

To compile loop invariants appropriately, the control flow graph corresponding to the list of bytecode instructions resulting from the compilation of a method body must be a *reducible control flow graph*, *i.e.* every cycle in the graph must have exactly one entry point (see [1]). Note that this is not a serious restriction; all non-optimising Java compilers produce reducible control flow graphs and in practice even most hand-written bytecode is reducible.

The compilation from JML specifications into BML is defined in several steps. As mentioned above, we assume that the Java source code has been compiled with the debug flag set, and that we have access to the generated class file.

Compilation of ghost and model field declarations. Ghost and model variables declared in the specification are compiled into the special class attributes that contain all ghost variable and model variable declarations.

Linking and resolving of source data structures. The JML specification is transformed into an intermediate format, where the identifiers are resolved to their corresponding data structures in the class file. The Java and JML source identifiers are linked to their identifiers on bytecode level, *i.e.* the corresponding indexes either from the second constant pool or from the **Local_Variable_Table** attribute. This is similar to the linking and resolving stage of the Java source code compiler.

Locating instructions for annotation statements. Annotation statements, like loop specifications and asserts are associated with the appropriate point in the bytecode program, using the **Line_Number_Table** attribute.

A problem is that a source line may correspond to more than one instruction in the **Line_Number_Table**. This makes it complicated to identify the exact loop entry instruction in the bytecode, and thus to know to which instruction the compiled loop specification should be associated. To solve this, we use the following heuristics: if the control flow graph of the bytecode is reducible and we search from an index in the **Line_Number_Table** that corresponds to the first line of a source loop, then the first loop entry instruction found will be the loop entry corresponding to this source loop. We do not have a formal correctness proof for this algorithm, because it depends on the particular implementation of the compiler, but experiments show that the heuristic works successfully for Sun's non-optimising Java compiler.

Compilation of JML predicates. JML predicates are Java boolean expressions. However, the JVM does not provide direct support for several integral types, such as byte, short, char, or for booleans. Instead, they are encoded as integers. Therefore, the compiler wraps up the boolean expressions in the JML specification by a conditional function, returning 1 if the predicate is true, 0 otherwise.

Generation of user-specific class attributes. Finally, the complete specification is compiled into appropriate user-specific attributes, using the format defined in the previous section.

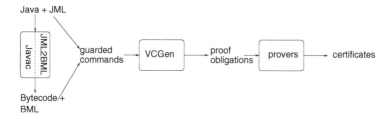

Fig. 5. Overview of MOBIUS tool set

6   Conclusions and Related Work

This paper presents the Bytecode Modeling Language (BML). BML allows one to specify and verify an application directly at the level of bytecode. Its syntax and semantics are directly inspired by the source code level specification language JML. The possibility to reason direct at the level of bytecode, without relying on a compiler, is of major importance for guaranteeing the security of applications (for example in a context of mobile code, where some applications are written in bytecode directly, to avoid security problems related with compilation). However, to make such verifications tractable, it is important that the specification language is intuitive and provides a sufficient degree of abstraction, without the need to talk too much about the internal structure of the state (heap, store *etc.*). BML does exactly this: it is designed to be close to the source code level specification language JML and provides a high level of abstraction. It is designed for program verification, and its semantics supports the development of a verification condition generator for unstructured code. Moreover, because of its close connection with JML, it is not too complicated to compile source code level specification into bytecode level specifications. The BML language as we have defined it now, corresponds roughly to JML level 0, *i.e.* that part of JML whose semantics is relatively well understood. However, more advanced constructs of JML can be easily added to BML, if required.

Tool support. As part of the MOBIUS project, we plan to develop a program verification tool set that supports both JML and BML. Figure 5 outlines the general architecture of this tool set. Thus, both Java/JML and bytecode/BML can be used as input application. Annotated programs are translated into a guarded command format, for which an appropriate verification condition generator is used to generate proof obligations that can be discharged with a theorem prover (either automatic or interactive). To support the PCC platform, the provers will be instrumented to produce certificates. In addition, source code applications annotated with JML can be compiled into bytecode annotated with BML.

The development of the JML subcomponent of the tool set will be based on experiences with ESC/Java [13] and JACK [11]. Several tools and algorithms (notably the compiler and the verification condition generator) for BML have already been implemented, see [10,19], but more work is needed to cover the whole language. Moreover, to make the tool set usable in practice, we will also need a tool to inspect and write BML specifications directly, and a run-time checker for BML specifications. The latter can be implemented by a code transformation, inserting explicit run-time checks in the bytecode, or by extending the virtual machine to take the user-specific attributes with specifications into account. It is also important to have tool support for checking the structural and typing constraints for BML specifications. Such a tool can be built as an extension the Java bytecode verifier.

Our initial experiments with compilation of specifications has shown that there exists indeed a correspondence between the proof obligations generated at source and at bytecode level, modulo differences in elimination of trivial goals, handling of boolean expressions, and the naming convention of generated variables [19]. Moreover, when the proofs are done with the Coq prover, different names are generated for hypotheses at source code and bytecode level. It is future work to clean up the compilation, so there is a one-to-one correspondence.

Related work. The interest in specification and verification of bytecode applications is quite recent, and not too much work has been done in that direction. Several logics have been developed to reason about bytecode, *e.g.* by Bannwart & Müller [4] and within the MRG project [3]. However, in this work the main focus was the development of a sound proof system, while the focus of BML is to write understandable specifications for bytecode. JVer is a tool to verify annotated bytecode [12]. However, as specification language they use a subset of JML, *i.e.* a source code level specification language.

The development of BML is clearly inspired by the development of the JML specification language [15]. Both JML and BML follow the Design by Contract principle introduced first in Eiffel [18]. The Boogie project [5] introduces in similarly the Design by Contract principles into the C# programming language, both at source code level and for CIL, the .NET intermediate language. The possibility to check a property at run-time, using the `assert` construct, has been long adopted in the C programming language and recently also in Java (Java 1.5, see [14, §14.10]).

Finally, we should mention the Extended Virtual Platform project[5]. This project aims at developing a framework that allows to compile JML annotations, to allow run-time checking [2]. However, in contrast to our work, they do not intend to do static verification of bytecode programs. Moreover, their platform takes JML-annotated source code files as starting point, so it is not possible to annotate bytecode applications directly.

Acknowledgements. We thank Lennart Beringer and Olha Shkaravska for discussions about the semantics of BML.

---

[5] See http://www.cs.usm.maine.edu/~mroyer/xvp/.

References

1. A.V. Aho, R. Sethi, and J.D. Ullman. *Compilers: Principles, Techniques, and Tools.* Addison-Wesley, 1986.
2. S. Alagić and M. Royer. Next generation of virtual platforms. Article in `odbms.org`, 2005. Available from `http://odbms.org/about_contributors_alagic.html`.
3. D. Aspinall, L. Beringer, M. Hofmann, H.-W. Loidl, and A. Momigliano. A program logic for resource verification. In K. Slind, A. Bunker, and G. Gopalakrishnan, editors, *Theorem Proving in Higher Order Logics (TPHOLs'04)*, volume 3223 of *LNCS*, pages 34–49. Springer, 2004.
4. F.Y. Bannwart and P. Müller. A logic for bytecode. In F. Spoto, editor, *Bytecode Semantics, Verification, Analysis and Transformation (BYTECODE)*, volume 141 of *ENTCS*, pages 255–273. Elsevier, 2005.
5. M. Barnett, B.-Y. E. Chang, R. DeLine, B. Jacobs, and K.R.M. Leino. Boogie: A modular reusable verifier for object-oriented programs. In *Formal Methods for Components and Objects (FMCO '05)*, LNCS. Springer, 2005.
6. G. Barthe, T. Rezk, and A. Saabas. Proof obligations preserving compilation. In R. Gorrieri, F. Martinelli, P. Ryan, and S. Schneider, editors, *Proceedings of FAST'05*, volume 3866 of *LNCS*, pages 112–126. Springer, 2005.
7. L. Beringer and M. Hofmann. A bytecode logic for JML and types. In *ASIAN Symposium on Programming Languages and Systems (APLAS 2006)*, 2006.
8. C. Breunesse, N. Cataño, M. Huisman, and B. Jacobs. Formal methods for smart cards: an experience report. *Science of Computer Programming*, 55:53–80, 2005.
9. L. Burdy, Y. Cheon, D. Cok, M. Ernst, J. Kiniry, G.T. Leavens, K.R.M. Leino, and E. Poll. An overview of JML tools and applications. *STTT*, 7(3), 2005.
10. L. Burdy and M. Pavlova. Java bytecode specification and verification. In L.M. Liebrock, editor, *proceedings of SAC'06*. ACM, 2006.
11. L. Burdy, A. Requet, and J.-L. Lanet. Java Applet Correctness: a Developer-Oriented Approach. In *Formal Methods (FME'03)*, number 2805 in LNCS, pages 422–439. Springer, 2003.
12. A. Chander, D. Espinosa, N. Islam, P. Lee, and G. Necula. JVer: A Java Verifier. In *Proceedings of the Conference on Computer Aided Verification (CAV'05)*, 2005.
13. D. Cok and J.R. Kiniry. ESC/Java2: Uniting ESC/Java and JML. In G. Barthe, L. Burdy, M. Huisman, J.-L. Lanet, and T. Muntean, editors, *CASSIS*, volume 3362 of *LNCS*, pages 108–128. Springer, 2004.
14. J. Gosling, B. Joy, G. Steele, and G. Bracha. *The Java Language Specification, Third Edition.* Sun Microsystems, Inc., 2005.
15. G.T. Leavens, E. Poll, C. Clifton, Y. Cheon, C. Ruby, D. Cok, P. Müller, and J. Kiniry. JML reference manual. `http://www.cs.iastate.edu/~leavens/JML/jmlrefman/jmlrefman_toc.html`, 2005.
16. H. Lehner and P. Müller. Formal translation of bytecode into BoogiePL, 2007.
17. T. Lindholm and F. Yellin. *The Java^{TM} Virtual Machine Specification. Second Edition.* Sun Microsystems, Inc., 1999.
18. B. Meyer. *Object-Oriented Software Construction.* Prentice Hall, 2nd rev. edition, 1997.
19. M. Pavlova. *Specification and verification of Java bytecode.* PhD thesis, Université de Nice Sophia-Antipolis, 200x.
20. A.D. Raghavan and G.T. Leavens. Desugaring JML method specifications. Technical Report TR #00-03e, Department of Computer Science, Iowa State University, 2000. Current revision from May 2005.

A Service Composition Construct
to Support Iterative Development

Roy Grønmo[1], Michael C. Jaeger[2], and Andreas Wombacher[3]

[1] SINTEF, P.O.Box 124 Blindern, N-0314 Oslo, Norway
`Roy.Gronmo@sintef.no`
[2] Technische Universität Berlin, FG FLP, Sek. FR6-10, Franklinstrasse 28/29,
D-10587 Berlin, Germany
`mcj@cs.tu-berlin.de`
[3] School of Computer and Communication Sciences, Ecole Polytechnique Federale de
Lausanne (EPFL), CH-1015 Lausanne, Switzerland
`andreas.wombacher@epfl.ch`

Abstract. Development of composed services requires a continues adaptation of the composed service to the changing environment of offered services. Services may no longer be available or may change performance characteristics, price, or quality of service criteria after they have been selected and used in a composition. The replacement of such a service requires a good understanding why this service got selected in the first place. This is hard to accomplish as it is known from software maintenance. Therefore we propose an approach where the conceptual task implemented by a selected service as well as the relationship between task and selected service is explicated and maintained during the complete life cycle of a composed service. This covers the design of the composition, derivation of service search criteria, and the execution of the composed service. The approach has been validated by an implementation in the Service Composition Studio (SERCS) supporting the iterative development of composed services.

1 Introduction

The vision of the service-oriented architecture (SOA) is that there are numerous available services that can be reused by other parties when developing new services. SOA involves searchable registries, such as UDDI for Web services, and technological infrastructure regarding textual descriptions in XML for bindings and protocols. Most attention has been given to Web services, but now also grid and other service types are proposed to be part of the infrastructure. The goal is that services may be easily found, that the services may be reused and composed into new service compositions, and that the binding and execution of these services work seamlessly. Numerous composition languages and tools have been proposed (eg. BPEL [13], OWL-S [5]) to aid the user when building service compositions. The important question which we will try to answer in this paper is: *What should be the main characteristics of a composition language in order to support the iterative service composition development?* When we investigate this question we assume to some extent that the SOA visions have been properly

M.B. Dwyer and A. Lopes (Eds.): FASE 2007, LNCS 4422, pp. 230–244, 2007.
© Springer-Verlag Berlin Heidelberg 2007

addressed and that there are lots of available, searchable services, possibly with associated Quality-of-Service (QoS) offerings and semantic information.

We define a composition model to be a representation of a larger task into smaller, more basic tasks. The decomposing is done to break a complex task into smaller, more manageable tasks for which we hope to find existing services. If existing services are found for each particular task, then we may solve the large task by calling other, already defined services in the right order. In general, there may be competing services from different providers and with different QoS offerings, but with the same functionality. Thus, these services are alternative candidates for the same task in our composition model.

It is absolutely crucial that the service composition development is iterative since there are a number of factors which might change over time. The pool of available services will change continuously. Some services will be withdrawn, others will be introduced, and the available services may also change their QoS even though their functionality remains intact. Some services may become temporarily or permanently unavailable. Even if there are established contracts with the service providers to ensure that a specific service is available and delivers the QoS as promised, there may be competing services from other vendors with lower price and better QoS offerings available since the time we previously searched for services.

An example for such fast changing service offerings can be observed in emergency situations. Here the situation changes fast and emergency teams request context-specific services. Thus, the teams iteratively have to adapt the composed service depending on the changing situation and context. In emergency situations a lot of resources of different locations and organizations are involved to handle the situation. An example of such a situation has been the Oder flood in Germany 1997. Certain parts of Germany along the river Oder were flooded by the river and emergency teams from all over Germany were sent to support the local authorities in fighting the flood [14]. A lot of resources were needed to secure cities, houses, and embankments along the river. In particular, several ten thousands of people have been involved in this situation. The emergency teams were sent to different locations to help, and they were coordinated by a hierarchic crisis management.

The emergency teams had to navigate to the different locations in an unknown area with the constrained infrastructure imposed by the flood. Each team offers a composed service as help to the crisis management, and in case the offer gets rejected they finish their operation. Otherwise, they are assigned a location for their operation and have to find their way to that location. To illustrate the benefits of our approach in such a scenario, a *determineBestRoute* service is investigated to find the best route to the assigned location. The used *determineBestRoute* service is applied iteratively, and dependent on the assigned location and the status of the flood, different service providers should be selected. In particular, the emergency team already working at the assigned location should provide the route service, because they are most familiar with the local situation. We focus on the *determineBestRoute* service, and use it as a running example within this paper.

This paper is organized as follows; Section 2 gives a motivation for the paper by explaining how existing approaches fail to provide sufficient support for iterative service composition development; Section 3 introduces our contribution, which is a composition construct and its application within a composition language; Section 4 shows how the composition construct enables search and discovery; Section 5 shows how the composition construct enables execution; Section 6 shortly describes the implementation in the SERCS tool; Section 7 discusses our approach; and Section 8 summarizes with conclusions.

2   Related Work

This section describes some of the proposed composition languages and tools, which we have placed in three main groups. We focus on how they support the iterative development, and why they are not sufficient for iterative development.

First we define two key concepts, **task** and **service**, where one or both are present (perhaps with different terms) in any service composition language. A task (also commonly called goal) represents a requirement specification for what we want to accomplish. When the tasks are sufficiently defined, they may be used to search for existing services. A **task** will typically contain a syntactic interface represented by an operation name, input and output parameters. We anticipate also the description of QoS requirements (throughput, availability or the time delay etc.) and of the semantics of the service elements. The semantic information may include an ontology reference for the inputs and outputs, classification specifications of the service operation, preconditions and postconditions. A **service**, on the other hand, will contain enough information so that an execution can bind to a unique service and invoke it. If we look at Web services as an example, then the four values of WSDL file, service name, port name and operation name will be enough information to call the Web service. Implicitly, then the information of input and output parameters are also given through the unique operation inside the WSDL file. The necessary binding information will vary between service types.

Existing languages and tools can be placed in three groups related to the task and service concepts: pure task-based, evolving from task-based to service-based, and pure service-based. In the following we investigate these groups by identifying languages or tools that belong to each group:

- **Pure task-based.** Pure task-based approaches provide only task constructs as editable constructs to the user. These approaches may have an equivalent to the service construct, but the services will be automatically selected and executed, and the user cannot operate at the service level. Peer's [11] PDDL tool and Ponnekantis' SWORD tool [12] represent two approaches for expressing overall composition tasks (termed goal and rule), and to automatically generate an executable service composition. Peer uses AI planning techniques on goals defined in PDDL, while SWORD relies on a knowledge-base of axioms for each Web service, and a rule-based expert system to generate the executable composition. We fear that the approaches will not scale to handle the large number of available services in the open SOA environment, especially since they deal with automatic decomposition. Tsalgatidou et al. suggest the USQL language [16] to define requirements for single tasks in isolation. Pure task-based approaches without automatic transition to execution, must always be combined with a service-based execution approach in order to sufficiently support service composition.

- **Evolving from task-based to service-based.** The approaches in this group start out with modeling task-based composition that evolves to a service-based composition when suitable services are identified for each task. The services typically replace the tasks, and the tasks are no longer in active use at the later development stage. Traverso and Pistore [15] present an approach to automatically transform OWL-S [5] process models into executable BPEL documents. An OWL-S process model represents a task-based composition model for which Traverso and Pistore automatically find perfect matches among a set of Web services (theoretically a global registry of services). Perfect matches are then used to build a BPEL document which represents a service-based composition model. Agarwal et al. [1] transform an abstract BPEL document with service types (corresponding to tasks) into a concrete BPEL document with bindings to service instances (corresponding to services). Agarwal et al. allow for the process to be non-automatic with human intervention to select appropriate services, negotiate service-level agreement etc., and to manually define necessary transformations in order to use services. Cardoso and Sheth [4] present a workflow language implemented in the METEOR tool where a service template is a task and a service object is a service according to our definition. The service template is first used to search for service objects, then the developer selects a single service object to replace the service template.

All the approaches in this group typically start with an original composition graph consisting of nodes representing tasks. The graph is then transformed into a graph with service nodes, where all the task nodes are replaced by service nodes. The problem with this approach is that we have lost all the original information about the tasks which were designed to search for services. The service nodes lack the QoS requirements, and may also have less generalized input and output parameters as well as possibly lacking the appropriate link to semantic definitions. Thus, we are not able to sufficiently repeat the search for services after some period of time. The iterative development in a continuously changing Web environment is not supported properly.

- **Pure service-based.** Pure service-based approaches provide only service constructs and have no equivalent to the task construct. The languages in this group are focused on making executable service compositions. The pure service-based group includes the graphical alternatives BPMN [3], JOpera [10], KEPLER [2] and the textual alternatives BPEL [13] and USCL [10]. Pure service-based approaches provide no help to define tasks and provide limited or no help to search for services, which means that the iterative development is not sufficiently supported.

The first and last approaches may also be combined so that we use one tool for maintaining a pure task-based composition and another tool for pure service-based composition. The problem with this approach is that we now have two compositions that are identical with respect to control flow and number of nodes. This implies a need to maintain the control flow in two places, one for each of the two compositions. Furthermore the relationship between a task and a service are only implicitly defined by their positions in the two different compositions, such as when we have two equivalent graph structures. When the task-based graph is used to perform a service search, the results will have to be manually registered into the corresponding service-based graph. The solution is likely to be error-prone and this is not satisfactory.

All the existing tools can be placed in one of the three groups above which all have their limitations. These limitations lead to requirements for a service composition language in order to sufficiently handle the iterative development:

- **Service discovery.** The composition can be used as a basis for search and discovery of services to fulfill specific tasks. This means that the tasks need to be associated with QoS requirements and semantic annotation.
- **Service execution.** The composition can be used as a basis for execution, that means calling the part services in the correct order. The services need to be associated with data and control flow including necessary data transformations.
- **Composition using a single structure.** The composition can be represented as a single structure to avoid the error-prone maintenance issue of maintaining several structures or graphs with duplication of control flow or other information.

3   The Approach

Our contribution is based around a new service composition construct, which we call the task-service construct. We illustrate the usefulness of the construct by introducing a graphical composition language with task-service nodes as the basic building block.

3.1   The Task-Service Construct

The task-service construct is used to bridge the task composition part with the service composition part. The task-service construct can be viewed as a composite node containing one task part with zero or more services. The task part can be viewed as a requirement specification, and the services represent actual matches to the task specification. Although there are many differences in the information content of a task and a service (Section 2), we also see that the syntactic information of inputs, outputs and operation name shall be represented for both a task and a service. Still we register this information as separate objects. The reason is that we allow for matching services that are not perfect matches. There may for instance be minor differences with respect to the syntactic way of representing the input and output. Conceptually we may treat such services as matches, which we expect will give more alternative services for the composition developer. The composition developer may still choose to only allow perfect matches today, or in the future especially if the semantically described services become widespread. We will discuss how to handle the mismatching part later by using data transformations. A metamodel of the task-service construct is depicted in the left hand side of Figure 1.

Notice that we allow to register multiple services as matches of the task specification. There may be many competing services providing the same service with different (or similar) QoS offerings. Having many alternatives is particularly useful due to varying service performance and availability over time. This will make the service composition less dependent on single services, as alternative services may be used in place of temporarily unavailable ones. The control flow behavior of the services associated to a task is related to the discriminator pattern identified by Aalst et al. [17].

Considering the emergency scenario in Section 1, the *determineBestRoute* task will be represented by a *determineBestRoute* task-service, where the task is to determine the best route which can be provided by different services like eg. mapquest, map24, or a local authority of the emergency scenario. All services provide a route service although QoS attributes as well as the actual input and output may differ slightly. In particular, in the emergency case the local authority may provide the best information within their territory, while routes to get initially to the specific area of the emergency can be better provided by other service providers.

3.2   The Graphical Composition Language

The task-service construct is the basic building block of our composition language, which has been implemented in the SERCS tool. In the following we present the main concepts of the composition language depicted in the right part of Figure 1. We use graphical symbols to represent the metamodel concepts and a dotted line shows the relationship for three main concepts of the task-service construct. We present the provided constructs in three groups.

Regular nodes. This group contains two node types: task-graph and task-service (section 3.1). The task-graph node consists of a task part and an entire subgraph. Thus we have a construct that can be repeated at arbitrary many levels to create a recursive decomposition structure. A subgraph consists of two or more nodes, which are either task-service or task-graph nodes. All leaf nodes are task-service nodes.

Control flow. This group contains initialNode, finalNode, sequence, and-split, and-join, xor-split, xor-join. These well-known basic control flow constructs have quite logical names and a normal interpretation. An initialNode has exactly one outgoing edge, and a finalNode has exactly one incoming edge. There is exactly one initialNode and one finalNode for each graph. A finalNode within a subgraph terminates only the flow of the subgraph and the flow continues in the enclosing graph. The outermost finalNode terminates the whole composition execution. Furthermore, a regular node must have exactly one incoming edge and one outgoing

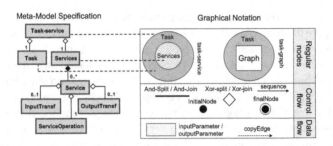

Fig. 1. The composition language

edge. This means that all the control flow is handled explicitly by the control flow constructs listed above. The proposed model represents a combination of structured flow models because each graph must have exactly one starting and one single ending node, and arbitrary models because no restrictions on the combination of control flow constructs are given [7].

Data flow. This group contains copyEdge, inputParameter, outputParameter and dataTransformation. Any number of inputParameters and outputParameters may be associated with the task parts of task-graph and task-service nodes, a service in a task-service node, and with dataTransformation services. A parameter has a name and a type which covers the syntactic definition and offers support for a semantic description. Parameters cannot appear as standalone objects and the set of inputParameters and the set of outputParameters (associated with an object) are unordered. A copyEdge connects a source parameter to a target parameter, and implies a deep copy. There may be an arbitrary number of outgoing copyEdges from a parameter, but there may only be one incoming copyEdge to a parameter. Furthermore these copyEdges may be connected between parameters at different nesting levels, which means that there may be a copyEdge from a parameter to another parameter within a subgraph. A data transformation has inputParameters and outputParameters. Each service in a task-service node is associated with two specialized data transformations: inputDataTransformation and outputDataTransformation. The dataTransformations act as mediators between the task and its services within a service-node. Data transformation techniques are a large matter on its own which we do not have enough space to explore in this paper. We assume that some kind of apparatus is available to do so. We also allow dataTransformations to be applied to inputParameters and outputParameters involving tasks only, but this is not important for the scope of this paper.

Now that we have introduced a composition language, based upon the task-service construct, we may take a closer look at the construct. We could require that realizing services for a task (in the task-service construct) were perfect matches so that the inputs and outputs corresponded one-to-one in both numbers, types and semantics. We feel that this would be too rigid, and that we would exclude a number of relevant services with only minor data format mismatches. This could be so

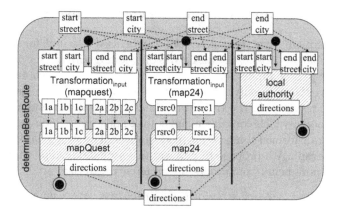

Fig. 2. A task-service example

simple that two different services have the same logical data input, but their syntactic XML tags are different. When we allow such mismatches to occur we need to use the transformation service on input and on output to build a bridge between a task and its service.

To illustrate the introduced concepts, we apply the definition on the scenario in Section 1. The task *determineBestRoute* (see Figure 2) should be operated on the input parameters of the starting street and city as well as the destination street and city. The output of the task is a route description. The *determineBestRoute* task can be implemented by services from mapquest, map24, or a local authority. Since these services are right now not directly provided as Web services we use the corresponding input and output parameters of the Web forms of the corresponding sites. All services have a single output parameter containing the route description. However, the input parameters required by the

- mapquest are 1a(2a) for the street, 1b(2b) for the zip code, and 1c(2c) for the city of the start and the destination respectively;
- map24 are rsrc0 and rsrc1 for the start and destination address respectively including all information;
- local authority are street and city of start and destination respectively.

As a consequence, a transformation service for mapquest and map24 is needed, while direct copyEdges can be used for the local authority. Figure 2 illustrates the scenario, where the different alternative services are depicted next to each other in the figure. Be aware that this is not a correct task-service construct since there are several initial and final nodes. However, we decided to depict it in such a way to represent the set of services implementing a particular task. In addition, the example covers several principles of our approach while others like e.g. graphs could not be considered due to the space limitations.

4   Using the Composition for Service Discovery

This section explains how the composition can be used to search for services. The main idea is that we look at the task parts only and ignore the service parts, because the task part contains all required information for the search. In our composition language there are only two kinds of regular nodes available, task-graph and task-service. Therefore, in the transformation to query documents we introduce a plain task node, which contains a single task node only. Plain task nodes are only used in transformed composition models and will never appear in an editable composition graph. We propose to perform two sequential steps which separate processing requirements from processing preference criteria:

1. *Search.* At first, a search is performed for each task-service node. The task part is transformed into a proper query denoting the requirements about the requested service covering syntactic interface definitions, semantic descriptions, and QoS constraints. How to actually represent such information in a query language will differ for each application case. Currently, there is no de-facto standard for such a query language. If the search does not identify suitable services, either the requirements must be reconsidered or the required functionality must be implemented.
2. *Select.* If more than one service is available that matches the requirements, a sorted list is desired where one can start with the closest matches first. In addition, QoS preference criteria can be considered selection criteria, e.g. to select the cheapest service. This step can include the negotiation and establishment of a QoS contract with the providers of the candidate services. This step will end with a chosen list of services.

After the appropriate services have been identified, the composition must be updated. All the necessary binding details of the chosen services must be registered within the service part of the corresponding task-service node for which we performed the search.

5   Using the Composition for Execution

This section shows how the outermost task-graph node (representing the entire composition) can be transformed into an executable document. In the transformation to an executable document we introduce the plain service node, which contains a single, executable service operation only. Plain service nodes are only used in the transformed composition models and will never appear in an editable composition graph. We assume that at least one service is identified for each of the task-service nodes. An algorithm comprised of two main steps are used to transform the graph into a one-level graph (no subgraphs) with service nodes only, and no tasks (except for the main composition itself which is a task-graph node).

Step 1: Replace task-service nodes by an explicit subgraph structure (transitions labeled 1 in Figure 3). The task-service node defines an implicit structure which we will transform into an explicit structure (using our composition language) in this transformation step. We must assume that the necessary Input-Transformation and the OutputTransformation specifications are defined already and are associated with the service. If not, then the specification is only partial and we cannot generate a fully executable document. (If the data transformations are omitted, we assume that the service is a perfect match of the task, and the control flow becomes trivial.) The task-service node is replaced by a task-graph node, where the task part remains the same and the subgraph is produced as described in the following text. If there is a single service inside the task, then the following sequentially ordered subgraph is produced: initialNode, InputTransformation, ServiceNode, OutputTransformation, finalNode. If there is more than one service (S1 in Figure 3), then we introduce an and-split after the initialNode and an xor-join before the finalNode. There will be parallel branches in between with the sequentially ordered triple InputTransformation, ServiceNode and OutputTransformation for each service. Notice that we allow an and-split to be followed by an xor-join, meaning that control-flow continues when the first parallel flow arrives and the other flows, produced in the and-split, are terminated or ignored. The decision on executing the alternative services in parallel has been made to achieve robustness of the implemented services. This approach is applicable as long there is no cost associated with the alternative services, otherwise this approach is far too expensive. A more detailed discussion of robustness and its implications can be found in [6].

Step 2: Flattening subgraphs (transitions labeled 2 in Figure 3). This transformation step can be applied to all task-graph nodes except the outermost node representing the whole composition. We flatten a task-graph node by replacing it with the entire subgraph (except the initialNode and its outgoing edge, and the finalNode and its incoming edge) inserted into the parent graph. This is possible since we only allow graphs with a single outgoing edge from the initial-Node, and a single incoming edge to the finalNode. Notice that we also remove the task part of the original task-graph node in the process. The removal of the task part will be semantics-preserving with respect to the control and data flow. We do not show a proof of the claim in this paper, but illustrate in Figure 4 that the task part is redundant for the execution logics of task-service node. The input and output parameters of the task part are redundant since they are simply copied to and from the transformation services on input and output. Thus we can detach the task part and attach all its incoming and outgoing data flow (labeled df-in and df-out) and control flow edges (labeled cf-in and cf-out) to the transformation services instead.

We need to repeat steps one and two until there are no more task-graph nodes, and no more task-service nodes left. It is trivial to see that this approach can be supported by an algorithm that is guaranteed to terminate. The following observations should be sufficient to convince the reader; None of the two steps introduce task-service nodes; The first step reduces the number of task-service nodes; The second step reduces the number of task-graph nodes.

We have now produced a composition graph which is flattened, and that only uses basic control and data flow constructs, data parameters and a service node representing an executable service. These language concepts are supported by

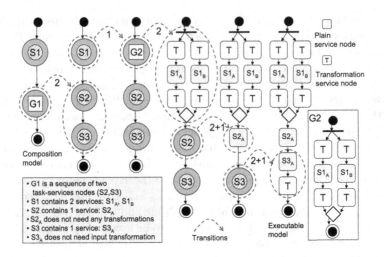

Fig. 3. Example: Transformation to an executable model

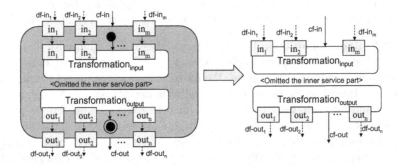

Fig. 4. Task parts are removed as part of the collapsing of subgraphs

most of the service composition languages and thus we believe that our composition language is transformable to most of these languages.

Figure 3 shows how a composition graph is transformed. The main task-graph node representing the whole composition surrounds the first subgraph structure and it is not shown in the figure. The first subgraph contains two regular nodes to be executed in sequence: a task-service node with the service part named S1, and a task-graph node with the subgraph named G1. Further details necessary to carry out the transformation are given in the text box at the bottom of the figure. Seven transitions (The last four transitions in the figure are combined into two) are needed to produce the final executable graph structure containing only plain services (including transformation services) and common control-flow constructs. For each transition we mark by an adjacent number which of the two algorithm steps are used. The rightmost box shows the subgraph structure named G2, which is produced as an intermediate step in step two of the example transformation.

6   Implementation in SERCS

Our approach has been validated by implementing a tool called the Service Composition Studio (SERCS, pronounced *circus*) with the service composition language as its core. The design principle of the language is built around the task-service construct presented in this paper. Furthermore it is based on UML 2 activity models [9] regarding both graphical layout and most of the core concepts. The language can be viewed as a UML profile in that there are several extensions for QoS and semantic information as well as the enforcement of the task-service node construct. SERCS is an Eclipse-based tool with a GNU Public License. The graphical user interface of SERCS offers functionality to develop compositions, search for composition-relevant services and run service compositions. Figure 5 shows a model of *determineBestRoute* in the SERCS tool.

SERCS provides the ability to transform the task part of a task-service node in SERCS into USQL documents [16], perform a call to the externally defined USQL engine [16] to search for services, and to bring the found services back into the service part of the corresponding task-service node. The transformation is defined by XSLT with SERCS composition files as input and USQL documents as output. The transformation definition follows the approach described in Section 4 of searches for a single task in isolation, since this is the only alternative currently provided by the USQL engine.

SERCS provides the ability to apply an XSLT-defined transformation from a SERCS composition into a USCL document [10], and to perform a call to the externally defined JOpera engine [10] which executes the composition. USCL has its own sub composition construct which can be used to directly support the task-graph node. Thus we skipped step two of the algorithm in Section 5.

We have introduced a new graphical tool since existing languages do not support the task-service construct. We could have extended existing tools, but then we would not be able to enforce the use of the task-service construct. SERCS compositions are independent of the actual query and execution language. Thus alternative transformations could have been defined, such as a transformation from SERCS compositions to BPEL as the target execution language.

A running service composition, to be used in emergency situations, has been developed by the SERCS tool. A person at the emergency location uses a mobile phone to call the emergency help desk. Based on the mobile phone position, a number of steps is performed which finally delivers a map displaying the optimal driving route to the closest available ambulance. This composition consists of five task-graph nodes, fourteen task-service nodes, fifteen Web services, one Grid service, one Peer-to-Peer service and a number of data transformation services.

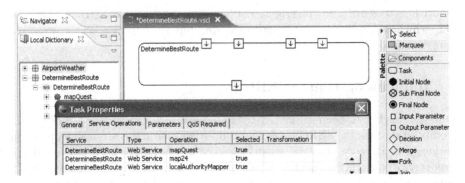

Fig. 5. Screenshot of the example within the SERCS tool

7   Discussion

Section 4 and Section 5 show that the requirements (final part of Section 2) of service discovery and service execution are satisfied by our composition language. The requirement of a single structure is satisfied since the **task-service** construct enables us to use a single graph for representing tasks and services.

A possible limitation with our approach is the manual decomposition. The composition developer manually proposes a decomposition which has a set of leaf tasks. It may be the case that a leaf task, T1, cannot be realized by a single service but that there are two services, S1 and S2, that can be executed in sequence to realize the leaf task. In our approach there is no way to determine this automatically. However, it may be that the search results for T1 returns S1 and/or S2 indicated to be partial matches, and that these give the composition developer a clue to revise T1 into a new subcomposition graph.

In our composition language we require that all services in a composition model belong to a task. This may seem too rigid and bothersome for cases where we know in advance exactly which service we want to use. The SERCS tool allows the user to insert such a service directly into the composition and the tool will automatically generate a **task-service** node with a task part based on the imported service. This will result in a task which initially lacks QoS requirements. It may also lack semantic descriptions if the imported service is not semantically described. We do allow for tasks that lack QoS and even semantic requirements, because currently the major part of service providers does not provice such description. It may even be argued that it is more relevant to associate QoS requirements only with the outermost task since the aggregated QoS is more interesting than how it distributes to the individual parts.

The automatic task production based on an imported service leads naturally to a question: *Are the explicit tasks redundant since they could be automatically generated by a transformation tool whenever we want to search for services?* Although this may work fine for some composition examples, we think that this in general is not satisfactory. This is because the automatic deducible task may be a poor task since it depends strongly on how well the service is described semantically. In many cases the semantic information may be missing or it may be that its interface is too specialized leading to missing matches of relevant services. In some cases it will also be relevant with local QoS requirements. Consider a service composition with several tasks of which one of them deals with a payment transaction. We may want to force a local QoS restriction of good security and high encryption level only to the payment service. Such local QoS requirements cannot be automatically deduced from a service since a service in the best case only advertises its own QoS offering.

The Web Service Modelling Ontology (WSMO) [8] contains description languages for tasks (Goals), services (Webservices) and a mapping (such as our Data-Transformation) between task and service with the wgMediator. Up to our knowledge there is however no tool that enforces the coupling between a WSMO task and a service. Thus WSMO services may exist without a defined task, and there may be tasks which are not aware of existing mappings to services. This is a limitation for iterative service composition development.

The discussion of task-service right now focuses on stateless services, that is, a service associated to a task represents a service with a single request-response communication. Statefull services are maintaining an internal state and require several request-response communications, which may require an extension of the proposed approach on service discovery. We leave this to future work.

8   Conclusions and Future Work

Our contribution is a task-service construct which introduces a strong coupling between the definition of *what* we want to accomplish with *how* it can be accomplished by existing services. The task part defines the requirements for what we want to accomplish, and the service part defines all the discovered services that are capable of performing the task. When this task-service construct is the basic building block in a composition language, as within our SERCS tool, we achieve the benefits of maintaining a single graph which can be used both for service discovery and for executing service compositions. This benefit is crucial in an ever-changing SOA environment. We advocate for an iterative composition development with regular searches for newly introduced services. The service composition should take advantage of these new services and strive to always find the most appropriate services based on their QoS offerings.

Further research is needed to explore the effects of run-time search and selection on performance. Important topics to investigate for such run-time handling include trust, semantic precision and failure handling.

Acknowledgement. The work of Roy Grønmo has been partially supported by the European Commission under the contracts IST-FP6-004559 (SODIUM) and FP6-26514 (SWING).

References

1. Agarwal et al. A service creation environment based on end to end composition of Web services. In *International conference on World Wide Web*, 2005.
2. B. Ludäscher et al. Scientific Workflow Management and the Kepler System. *Concurrency and Computation: Practice & Experience, Special Issue on Scientific Workflows*, 2005.
3. BPMI.org. Business Process Modeling Notation (BPMN) Version 1.0, May 2004.
4. J. Cardoso and A. P. Sheth. Semantic E-Workflow Composition. *Journal of Intelligent Information Systems*, 21(3):191–225, 2003.
5. David L. Martin et al. Bringing Semantics to Web Services: The OWL-S Approach. In *Revised Selected Papers of the Intl Workshop Semantic Web Services and Web Process Composition (SWSWPC'04)*, San Diego, California, USA, July 2004.
6. M. C. Jaeger and H. Ladner. A Model for the Aggregation of QoS in WS Compositions Involving Redundant Services. *Journal of Digital Information Management*, 4(1):44–49, March 2006.
7. B. Kiepuszewski, A. H. M. ter Hofstede, and C. Bussler. On Structured Workflow Modelling. In *Proceedings of the 12th International Conference on Advanced Information Systems Engineering (CAiSE'00)*, volume 1789 of *LNCS*, pages 431–445, Stockholm, Sweden, June 2000. Springer Press.
8. R. Lara, D. Roman, A. Polleres, and D. Fensel. A Conceptual Comparison of WSMO and OWL-S. In *Web Services, European Conference (ECOWS 2004)*, September 2004. Erfurt, Germany.
9. O. M. G. (OMG). UML 2.0 Superstructure Specification, OMG Adopted Specification ptc/03-08-02, August 2003.
10. C. Pautasso and G. Alonso. The JOpera visual composition language. *Journal of Visual Languages and Computing (JVLC)*, 16(1-2):119–152, 2005.
11. J. Peer. A PDDL Based Tool for Automatic Web Service Composition. In *Proceedings of the Second Intl Workshop on Principles and Practice of Semantic Web Reasoning (PPSWR)*, St. Malo, France, September 2004.
12. S. R. Ponnekanti and A. Fox. SWORD: A Developer Toolkit for Web Service Composition. In *Proc. of the Eleventh International World Wide Web Conference (WWW*, Honolulu, Hawaii, USA, 2002.
13. Satish Tatte (Editor). Business Process Execution Language for Web Services Version 1.1, February 2005.
14. F. Schiersner. Fallstudien: Die Oder-Flut im Sommer 1997. http://www.krisennavigator.de/kafa1-d.htm.
15. P. Traverso and M. Pistore. Automated Composition of Semantic Web Services into Executable Processes. In *The Semantic Web - ISWC 2004: Third International Semantic Web Conference,Hiroshima*, Hiroshima, Japan, November 2004.
16. A. Tsalgatidou, M. Pantazoglou, and G. Athanasopoulos. Specification of the Unified Service Query Language (USQL), Technical Report, June 2006.
17. W. M. P. van der Aalst, A. H. M. ter Hofstede, B. Kiepuszewski, and A. P. Barros. Workflow patterns. *Distributed and Parallel Databases*, 14(1):5–51, 2003.

Correlation Patterns in Service-Oriented Architectures

Alistair Barros[1], Gero Decker[2], Marlon Dumas[3], and Franz Weber[4]

[1] SAP Research Centre, Brisbane, Australia
alistair.barros@sap.com
[2] Hasso-Plattner Institute, University of Potsdam, Germany
gero.decker@hpi.uni-potsdam.de
[3] Queensland University of Technology, Brisbane, Australia
m.dumas@qut.edu.au
[4] SAP AG, Walldorf, Germany
franz.weber@sap.com

Abstract. When a service engages in multiple interactions concurrently, it is generally required to correlate incoming messages with messages previously sent or received. Features to deal with this correlation requirement have been incorporated into standards and tools for service implementation, but the supported sets of features are ad hoc as there is a lack of an overarching framework from which their expressiveness can be evaluated. This paper introduces a set of patterns that provide a basis for evaluating languages and protocols for service implementation in terms of their support for correlation. The proposed correlation patterns are grounded in a formal model that views correlation mechanisms as means of grouping atomic message events into conversations and processes. The paper also provides an evaluation of relevant standards in terms of the patterns, specifically WS-Addressing and BPEL, and discusses how these standards have and could continue to evolve to address a wider set of correlation scenarios.

1 Introduction

Contemporary distributed system architectures, in particular service-oriented architectures, rely on the notion of message exchange as a basic communication primitive. A message exchange is an interaction between two actors (e.g. services) composed of two events: a message send event occurring at one actor and a message receive event at another actor. These events are generally typed in order to capture their purpose and the structure of the data they convey. Examples of event types are "Purchase Order", "Purchase Order Response", "Cancel Order Request", etc. Event types are described within *structural interfaces* using an interface definition language such as WSDL [12]. Sometimes, message exchanges are related to one another in simple ways. For example, a message exchange corresponding to a request may be related to the message exchange corresponding to the response to this request. Such simple relations

M.B. Dwyer and A. Lopes (Eds.): FASE 2007, LNCS 4422, pp. 245–259, 2007.

between message exchanges are described in the structural interface as well (e.g. as a WSDL operation definition).

The above abstractions are sufficient to describe simple interactions such as a weather information service that provides an operation to request the forecasted temperature for a given location and date. However, they are insufficient to describe interactions between services that engage in long-running business transactions such as those that arise in supply chain management, procurement or logistics. In these contexts, message event types can be related in complex manners. For example, following the receipt of a purchase order containing several line items, an order management service may issue a number of stock availability requests to multiple warehouses, and by gathering the responses from the warehouses (up to a timeout event), produce one or several responses for the customer. Such services are referred to as *conversational services* as they engage in multiple interrelated message exchanges for the purpose of fulfilling a goal. Conversational services are often related to (business) process execution, although as we will see later, conversations and processes are orthogonal concepts.

The need to support the description, implementation and execution of conversational services is widely acknowledged. For example, enhancements to the standard SOAP messaging format and protocol [12] for correlating messages have been proposed in WS-Addressing [7]. However, WS-Addressing merely allows a service to declare (at runtime) that a given message is a reply to a previous message referred to by an identifier. This is only one specific type of relation between interactions that has a manifestation only at runtime (i.e. it does not operate at the level of event types) and fails to capture more complicated scenarios where two message send (or receive) events are related not because one is a reply to another (or is caused by another), but because there is a common event that causes both. This is the case in the above example where stock availability requests are caused by the same "purchase order" receive event.

Another upcoming standard, namely WS-BPEL [9], provides further support for developing conversational services. In particular WS-BPEL supports the notion of *process instance*: a set of related message send and receive events (among other kinds of events). Events in WS-BPEL are grouped into process instances through a mechanism known as *instance routing*, whereby a receive event that does not start a new process instance is routed to an existing process instance based on a common property between this event and a previously recorded send or receive event. This property may be the fact that both messages are exchanged in the context of the same HTTP connection, or based on a common identifier found in the WS-Addressing headers of both events, or a common element or combination of elements in the message body of both events. Thus, WS-BPEL allows developers to express event types, which are related to WSDL operations, and to relate events of these types to process instances. It also allows developers to capture ordering constraints between events related to a process instance, which ultimately correspond to causal dependencies (or causal independence).

Despite this limited support for message event correlation, there is currently no overarching framework capturing the kinds of event correlation that service-oriented architectures should support. As a result, different approaches to event correlation are being incorporated into standards and products in the field, and there is no clear picture of the event correlation requirements that these standards and products should fulfill.

In this setting, this paper makes three complementary contributions: (i) a unified conceptualization of the notions of conversation, process and correlation in terms of message events (Section 2); (ii) a set of formally defined *correlation patterns* that cover a spectrum of correlation scenarios in the context of conversational services (Sections 3, 4 and 5); (iii) an evaluation of the degree of support for these correlation patterns offered by relevant Web service standards (Section 6). Together, these contributions provide a foundation to guide the design of languages and protocols for conversational services.

2   Classification Framework

When talking about correlation we mainly deal with three different concepts: events, conversations and process instances. An event is an object that is record of an activity in a system [11]. Events have attributes which describe the corresponding activity such as the time period, the performer or the location of the activity. We assume that a type is assigned to each event. In the area of service-oriented computing, where emphasis is placed on communication in a distributed environment, the most important kinds of events include message send and receipt events. In addition to these *communication events* that capture the externally visible behavior of actors, we consider *action events*, which are records of internal activities or internal faults within an actor, as well as *timeout events*. A message send event is directly caused by an action event that *produces* the message in question, while a message receipt event normally leads to (i.e. causes) an action event that *consumes* the message in question. We postulate the existence of a causal relation between communication events and action events. In addition, we postulate the existence of a causal relation between send events and their corresponding receipt events. Figure 1 illustrates these causal relations.

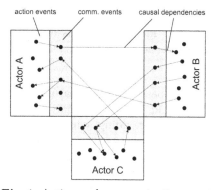

Fig. 1. Action and communication events

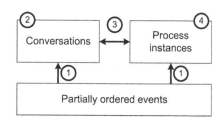

Fig. 2. Framework for classifying correlation patterns

Events can be grouped in different ways, e.g. all events occurring at one particular actor can be grouped together. Since this work deals with event correlation in conversational services, we consider two types of event grouping: conversations and process instances. Conversations are groups of communication events occurring at different actors that all correspond to achieving a certain goal. Boundaries of conversations might be defined through interaction models (choreographies) or might not be defined in advance but rather discovered a posteriori. Process instances are groups of action events occurring at one actor. Boundaries of process instances are determined by process models.

Figure 2 illustrates a framework for classifying correlation patterns. At the bottom there are partially ordered events. We assume that each event has a timestamp, but since events may be recorded by different actors with discrepant clocks, we may not be able to linearly order all events using their timestamps. However, we can use the timestamps to linearly order events recorded by a given actor (assuming a perfect clock within one actor). From there, we can derive a partial order between events recorded by different actors using the relation between message send events and their corresponding receipt events as formalized below. In the case of multiple clocks within one actor due to decomposition into distributed components, causal relations between action events occurring in different components can replace the pure timestamp-based ordering. But for the sake of simplicity, we assume that all events within one actor are totally ordered.

Conversations and process instances are sets of correlated events. The different patterns describing the relationships between events, conversations and process instances are grouped into four categories (for numbering see Figure 2).

1. Mechanisms to group events into conversations and process instances. These *correlation mechanisms* are presented in Section 3.
2. Having identified conversations, we can examine how conversations are structured. In previous work we investigated common interaction scenarios between participants within one conversation [2]. The *conversation patterns* in Section 4 present relationships between different conversations.
3. Relationships between conversations and process instances are covered in Section 5.
4. Common patterns of action events within one process instance have been studied in [1]. Additional work is required to identify patterns describing the relationships between different process instances, but this is outside the scope of this paper.

The proposed patterns are formally described based on the idea of viewing events from a post-mortem perspective. This could be seen as analyzing logs of past events. This view is taken for the sake of providing a unified formal description. In practice the patterns will not necessarily be used to analyze event logs, but rather to assess the capabilities of languages that deal with correlation in SOAs. A language will be said to support a pattern if there is a construct in the language (or a combination of constructs) that allows developers to describe or implement services which, if executed an arbitrary number of times, would generate event logs that satisfy the conditions captured in the formalization of the correlation pattern. In the sequel, we use the following formal notations:

- E is the set of events
- $CE, AE \subseteq E$ are the communication and action events ($CE \cap AE = \emptyset$)
- A is the set of actors
- $<_t \subseteq E \times E$ partially orders the events occurring at the same actor according to their timestamps
- $<_c \subseteq E \times E$ is the causal relation between events, including pairs of corresponding send and receipt events as well as corresponding communication and action events
- $<$ is a partial order relation on E being the transitive closure of $<_t$ and $<_c$: $< := (<_t \cup <_c)^+$.
- $Conv \subseteq \wp(CE)$ and $PI \subseteq \wp(AE)$ are sets of sets of communication and action events corresponding to groupings of events into conversations (Conv) and process instances (PI), respectively. These sets will in principle be generated using correlation mechanisms as discussed below.

3   Correlation Mechanisms

The correlation mechanism patterns focus on how events can be correlated to different process instances and more importantly to different conversations.

The purpose of correlation is to group messages into traces based on their contents (including message headers). Current web service standards do not impose that every message must include a "service instance identifier". Hence, assuming the existence of such identifier may be unrealistic in some situations. Other monitoring approaches in the field of Web services have recognized this problem and have addressed it in different ways, but they usually end up relying on very specific and sometimes proprietary approaches. For example the Web Services Navigator [4] uses IBM's Data Collector to log both the contents and context of SOAP messages. But to capture correlation, the Data Collector inserts a proprietary SOAP header element into every message.

To achieve a general approach to correlation in SOAs, we need to make as few assumptions as possible. In this paper, we assume that message events contain a timestamp and data (i.e. contents), but not necessarily a message identifier. a message identifier as part of their contents, but this is not part of our assumptions. Thus, message event correlation can be performed based on data or based on timestamp. Secondly, we assume that two events can be correlated in the following cases: (1) Both events have a common property, e.g. there exists a function that when applied to both events yields the same value. For example, two events can be correlated simply because they are performed by the same actor, or because they refer to the same purchase order. (2) One event is a cause of the other (directly or transitively), or there is a third event which is a cause (directly or transitively) of both events, or both events are a common cause (directly or transitively) of a third event.

Accordingly, we introduce two categories of correlation mechanisms: *function-based correlation* (case 1 above) and *chained correlation* (case 2). Different flavors of each category are presented, some based on data and others on time. The application of a particular function-based or chained correlation mechanism or a combination of different mechanisms leads to a *correlation scheme*. Such schemes are sets of sets of correlated events that might be interpreted e.g. as conversations or process instances later on. Different combinations are discussed in this section.

3.1   Function-Based Correlation

Functions assign labels to an event. Events with common labels are then grouped together. We distinguish three correlation mechanisms in this category: the first two deal with correlation based on data, while the third deals with correlation based on time. Strictly speaking, the first two patterns could be merged into a single one (i.e. the second pattern subsumes the first one). However, we treat them separately since, as discussed later, existing standards tend to support the first one but not the second.

C1. Key-based correlation. One or a set of unique identifiers are assigned to an event and all events with at least one common identifier are grouped together.
Example: a process instance identifier or a conversation identifier is attached to each event. Identifiers can be single values or compositions of several values.

C2. Property-based correlation. A function assigns a label to an event depending on the value of its attributes. In contrast to key-based correlation not only equality can be used in the function. Operators such as "greater", "less", "or" and "not" must be available in the function.
Example: all events involving customers living less than 50km away from the city centers of Brisbane, Sydney or Melbourne are grouped together (label = "metropolitan") as opposed to the others (label = "rural").

C3. Time-interval-based correlation. This is a special kind of property-based correlation. A timestamp is attached to an event and a corresponding label is assigned to the event if the event happened within a given interval.
Example: all events that happen in July 2006 could be grouped together (e.g. label = "07/2006") as opposed to those happening in August (label = "08/2006").

Function-based correlation can be formalized in the following way: Let *Label* be the set of all labels and $F \subseteq \{f \mid f : E \rightarrow Label\}$ a set of partial functions assigning labels to an event. Then the set of sets of correlated events is $\{C \subseteq E \mid \exists l \in Label \ (\forall e \in E \ [\exists f \in F \ (l = f(e)) \Leftrightarrow e \in C])\}$.

This formalization uses one set of labels. However, in practice we would distinguish between different types of labels, e.g. intervals, product groups.

As an extension to function-based correlation relationships between the labels can be considered ($R_L \subseteq Label \times Label$). E.g. we could assume a hierarchical order of keys where several keys have a common super-key. In this case events could be grouped according to their keys attached as well as according to some super-key higher up in the hierarchy. Let us assume e.g. a set of line items that all belong to the same order. In this example events could be grouped according to the line item ID or according to the order ID.

3.2 Chained Correlation

The basic idea of chained correlation is that we can identify relationships between two events that have to be correlated (grouped together). This relationship might be explicitly captured in an event's attributes or might be indirectly retrieved by comparing attribute values of two events. Starting from these binary relationships we can build chains of events that belong to the same group.

Since we assume that grouping events to process instances will mostly be done by using unique identifiers, chained correlation becomes important mostly for identifying conversations within our framework. In the case of conversations we especially look at the relationships between message exchanges. Depending on whether chained correlation is done based on message data or based on time, we can identify two chained correlation mechanisms.

C4. Reference-based correlation. Two events are correlated, if the second event (in chronological order) contains a reference to the first event. This means that if there is some way of extracting a datum from the second event (by applying a function) that is equal to another datum contained in the first event. This datum therefore acts as a message identifier, and the second message refers to this message identifier in some way.

C5. Moving time-window correlation. Two events involving the same actor are related if they both have the same value for a given function (like in function-based correlation) and they occur within a given duration of one another (e.g. 2 hours). There might be chains of events where the time passed between the first and last event might be very long and others where this time is rather short.

Chained correlation can be formalized as follows: Let $R \subseteq E \times E$ be the relations between two events that have to be grouped together. Then the set of sets of correlated events is $\{C \subseteq E \mid \forall e_1 \in C, e_2 \in E \ [e_1 \ R^* \ e_2 \Leftrightarrow e_2 \in C]\}$.

3.3 Aggregation Functions

Sometimes only a limited number of events are grouped together although according to function-based or chaining correlation mechanisms more events would fulfill the criteria to be part of the group. For example, only a maximum number of 10 items are to be shipped together in one container. More items are requested to be shipped and might have the same destination or arrive timely according to the defined moving time window.

In this paper, we do not deal with correlation mechanisms that include such maximality requirements. We envisage that the framework could be extended to capture such scenarios by means of an aggregation function agg that takes as input a set of correlated events and produces a boolean (i.e. $agg : \wp(E) \to \{true, false\}$). A correlation scheme could then be constrained to only produce sets of events that satisfy a given aggregation function.

4   Conversation Patterns

The Service Interaction Patterns proposed in [2] describe recurrent interaction scenarios *within* one conversation. The following patterns focus on relationships *between* different conversations.

C6. Conversation Overlap. Some interactions belong to multiple conversations. Each conversation also contains interactions that are not part of others.
Example: during a conversation centering around delivery of goods a payment notice is exchanged. This payment and other payments is the starting point for a conversation centering around the payment.
Two conversations C_1, C_2 overlap if $C_1 \cap C_2 \neq \emptyset \wedge C_1 \setminus C_2 \neq \emptyset \wedge C_2 \setminus C_1 \neq \emptyset$.

C7. Hierarchical Conversation. Several sub-conversations are spawned off and merged in a conversation. The number of sub-conversations might only be known at runtime.
Example: as part of a logistics contract negotiation between a dairy producer and a supermarket chain a set of shippers are to be selected for transporting goods from the producer to the various intermediate warehouses of the chain. Therefore, negotiation conversations are started between the chain and each potential available shipper.
A conversation $C_1 \in Conv$ has two sub-conversations $C_2, C_3 \in Conv$ if $\exists C_p \in Conv$ $(C_1, C_2, C_3 \subset C_p \wedge \forall e_2 \in C_2, e_3 \in C_3 \; [\exists e_{11}, e_{12} \in C_1 \; (e_{11} < e_2 \wedge e_{11} < e_3 \wedge e_2 < e_{12} \wedge e_3 < e_{12})])$.

C8. Fork. A conversation is split into several conversations and is not merged later on. The number of conversations that are spawned off might only be known at runtime.
Example: an order is placed and the different line items are processed in parallel.
A split from a conversation $C_1 \in Conv$ into the two conversations $C_2, C_3 \in Conv$ occurs if $\exists C_p \in Conv$ $(C_1, C_2, C_3 \subset C_p \wedge \forall e_1 \in C_1, e_2 \in C_2, e_3 \in C_3 \; [e_1 < e_3 \wedge e_1 < e_2])$.

C9. Join. Several conversations that do not originate from the same fork are merged into one conversation. The number of conversations that are merged might only be known at runtime.
Example: several orders arriving within one week are merged into a batch order.
A join between two conversations $C_1, C_2 \in Conv$ into one conversation $C_3 \in Conv$ occurs if $\exists C_p \in Conv$ $(C_1, C_2, C_3 \subset C_p \wedge \forall e_1 \in C_1, e_2 \in C_2, e_3 \in C_3 \; [e_1 < e_3 \wedge e_2 < e_3])$.

C10. Refactor. A set of conversations is refactored to another set of conversations. The numbers of conversations that are merged and spawned off might only be known at runtime. This pattern generalizes Fork and Join.
Example: goods shipped in containers on different ships have reached a harbor where they are reordered into trucks with different destinations.
A refactoring from two conversations $C_1, C_2 \in Conv$ into the two conversations $C_3, C_4 \in Conv$ occurs if $\exists C_p \in Conv$ $(C_1, C_2, C_3, C_4 \subset C_p \wedge \forall e_1 \in C_1, e_2 \in C_2, e_3 \in C_3, e_4 \in C_4 \; [e_1 < e_3 \wedge e_1 < e_4 \wedge e_2 < e_3 \wedge e_2 < e_4])$.

5 Process Instance to Conversation Relationships

So far, we have considered conversations and process instances separately. Below, we consider relationships between process instances and conversations, as well as relationships between action events and communication events. First, we classify the relationships between process instances and conversations according to multiplicity, and we derive three patterns from there (C11 – C13). Next, we consider relationships between the start and the end of process instances and conversations, and derive another three patterns (C14 – C16). Finally, we consider scenarios that deviate from the usual case whereby one action event is related to one communication event, and derive two more patterns (C17 & C18).

To formalize these patterns, we introduce the notion of *actor*. A process instance is executed by exactly one actor. We rely on a relation $\approx \in \wp(AE) \times \wp(AE)$ where $p_1 \approx p_2$ means that the process instances p_1 and p_2 are executed by the same actor. Also, we introduce a relation $\diamond \subseteq \wp(CE) \times \wp(AE)$ indicating that at least one event in a conversation C is causally related to at least one event in a process instance p. $\diamond = \{(C, p) \in \wp(CE) \times \wp(AE) \mid \exists e_1 \in C\ e_2 \in p\ (e_1 <_c e_2 \vee e_2 <_c e_1)\}$.

C11. One Process Instance – One Conversation. A process instance is involved in exactly one conversation and there is no other process instance involved in it and executed by the same actor.
Example: a purchase order is handled within one process instance.
A one-to-one mapping for a process instance $p \in PI$ to conversation $C \in Conv$ occurs if $p \diamond C \wedge \forall q \in PI\ [(p \neq q \wedge p \approx q) \Rightarrow \neg q \diamond C] \wedge \forall D \in Conv\ [C \neq D \Rightarrow \neg p \diamond D]$.

C12. Many Process Instances – One Conversation. Several process instances executed by the same actor are involved in the same conversation.
Example: an insurance claim is handed over from the claim management department to the financial department. The different departments have individual process instances to handle the case.
A many-to-one mapping for a set of process instances $PI' \subseteq PI$ to conversation $C \in Conv$ occurs if $\forall p_1, p_2 \in PI'\ [p_1 \approx p_2] \wedge \forall p \in PI'\ [p \diamond C]$.

C13. One Process Instance – Many Conversations. One process instance is involved in many conversations.
Example: a seller negotiates with different shippers about shipment conditions for certain goods. The shipper offering the best conditions is selected before shipment can begin.
A one-to-many mapping for a process instance $p \subseteq PI$ to a set of conversations $Conv' \in Conv$ occurs if $\forall C \in Conv'\ [p \diamond C]$.

C14. Initiate Conversation. A process instance has the role of the initiator of a conversation if the conversation is started within the process instance.
Example: a buyer places a purchase order and triggers a conversation concerning the negotiation about the price.
A process instance $p \in PI$ is an initiator of a conversation $C \in Conv$ if $\exists e_1 \in p\ e_2 \in C\ (e_1 <_c e_2 \wedge \neg \exists f \in C\ (f < e_2))$.

C15. Follow conversation. A process instance p has the role of a follower in a conversation it participates in, if the conversation was created within another process instance. Process instance p may be created because of a message received in the context of the conversation in question.

Example: a shipping order that is part of a multi-party conversation for procuring some products comes in to a shipment process and is processed in a new instance of this process.

A process instance $p \in PI$ is a follower in a conversation $C \in Conv$ if $\neg \exists e_1 \in p\, e_2 \in C\ (e_1 <_c e_2 \wedge \neg \exists f \in C\ (f < e_2))$. A process instance is created because of a message in a conversation if $\exists e_1 \in p\, e_2 \in C\ (e_2 <_c e_1 \wedge \neg \exists g \in p \setminus C\ (g < e_1))$.

C16. Leave Conversation. A process instance decides to no longer take part in a conversation.

Example: a carrier can no longer commit to delivery request and terminates involvement in a shipment contract.

To formalize this pattern we introduce the notion of action event types and conversation types. Functions $AET : AE \rightarrow Type$ and $CT : \wp(CE) \rightarrow Type$ assign a type to each action event and conversation. Leave Conversation occurs if $leave \in Type$ is the event type corresponding to leave actions and $lc \in Type$ is the type of conversation that is to be left and for all possible process instances p: $\neg \exists e_1, e_2 \in p\, e_3 \in CE\ (AET(e_1) = leave \wedge e_1 < e_2 \wedge CT(e_3) = lc \wedge e_3 < e_2)$.

C17. Multiple Consumption. A communication event is consumed (multiple times) by several actions, possibly belonging to different process instances.

Example: an account detail change is requested by a supplier and immediately processed. As part of a more complex fraud pattern this request leads to investigating potential fraud.

A communication event c is consumed several times if $\|\{e \in AE \mid c <_c e\}\| > 1$.

C18. Atomic Consumption. One action event is caused by several communication actions.

Example: a shipment is started when 500 shipment requests for the same destination are collected (see more detailed example in Section 6).

An atomic consumption of a set of communication actions $C \in \wp(CE)$ has occurred if $\exists e \in AE\ (\forall c \in C\ [c <_c e])$.

6   Assessment of BPEL 1.1 and BPEL 2.0

In this section, we provide an assessment of BPEL 1.1 and 2.0 specifications for support of the correlation patterns. Since BPEL directly concerns conversational processes, it provides a more comprehensive insight into the capabilities of Web services middleware vis-a-vis of event correlation than standards at lower levels of the WS stack. Table 1 summarizes the assessment, where "+" indicates direct support for a pattern, "+/–" partial support and "–" no support.

The mechanism in BPEL for relating action events to messages (i.e. communication events) is that of *correlation set*. A message can match one or more correlation sets. A BPEL inbound or outbound communication action (e.g. invoke, receive, reply, onMessage, pick) specify one or more correlation sets. These enable the execution engine to determine properties that a message produced or consumed by that action should have.

A process starts a conversation by sending a message and this sending action determines the values of properties in a correlation set, that then serve to identify the communication actions within a process instance that belong to the conversation in question. The conversation is continued by other processes receiving messages containing values of the correlation set. When a message is received which has the same value for a correlation set as the value of a message previously sent as part of a conversation, the message in question is associated with this conversation. Immediately we can see that *key-based correlation* is supported. However, only equality applies so *property-based correlation* is not supported, and no explicit support is available for *time-interval based correlation*.

From a post-mortem perspective, each message produced or consumed by the service can be related to a conversation as follows: the message log is scanned in chronological order, and a message is either related to a new conversation if it corresponds to a communication action that initializes a correlation set, or is related to a previously identified conversation if the values of its correlation set match those of a message sent by the previous service conversation.

Explicit support for *reference-based correlation* is possible when WS-Addressing is used for SOAP message exchange by BPEL processes. In the WS-Addressing standard, a message contains an identifier (*messageID* header) and may refer to a previous message through the *relatesTo* header. If we assume that these addressing headers are used to relate messages belonging to the same conversation in a chained manner, it is possible to group a service log containing all the messages sent or received by a service into traces corresponding to conversations. Similarly, correlations can be made through the *replyTo* header of a given message (say M), containing an URI uniquely identifying a message in question. When another message M' is observed that has the same URI this time in the *To* header, M and M' can be correlated.

Chaining through sliding windows, addressed in the *moving time-window correlation* pattern, cannot be supported through BPEL. Sliding windows require that events are buffered, however this aspect is left open in the BPEL specifications. A hand-coded solution is to implement buffering through one (continuously running) process instance, but this leads to convoluted code.

Conversation overlap occurs when different correlation sets are used in related message activities of two processes. By way of illustration, consider a process that initiates a conversation through an invoke, which has a corresponding receive in the targeted recipient, having the same correlation set (e.g. PurchaseOrder) as the invoke. Through subsequent message exchanges, reference to a different correlation set is made (e.g. Invoice), providing new data to correlate a different conversation between the two processes.

For conversational structuring, BPEL 1.1 and BPEL 2.0 have a major difference. Both of them allow correlation sets to be defined not only on a per scope basis. However, in BPEL 1.1, either the number of sub-conversations has to be known at design-time (one branch of a "parallel flow" is assign to each conversation), or the conversations in question must be entertained one after the other as opposed to concurrently. In BPEL 2.0, a "parallel foreach" construct, allows an unbounded number of conversations to be entertained concurrently. As such, we can see that *hierarchical conversation, conversation fork* and *conversation join* can be fully supported in BPEL 2.0, though only partially supported in 1.1.

The number of correlation sets in and across process instances allows for different conversation multiplicities. Patterns C11–C13 are thus supported. A process can *initiate* a conversation, if in one of its invoke activities, the correlation set's initiate attribute is set to "yes" (with the initiate attribute in the corresponding receive in the participant also set to "yes"). Subsequent message actions of the initiator should then have the initiate attribute be set to "no". Similarly, a process instance *follows* a conversation when one of its receive actions initiates a correlation set, thus signifying that the process instance becomes aware of a conversation. All subsequent actions referring to this correlation set should have the initiate attribute set to "no". For *Leave Conversation*, in BPEL 1.1 unsubscription from a conversation cannot be expressed. Once values are given to a correlation set, a subscription for corresponding messages exists until the process instance terminates. In BPEL 2.0, a subscription ends as soon as the execution of the scope where a correlation set is defined is closed.

One source of limitation of BPEL with respect to correlation, is the fact that every message arriving at a port is eagerly correlated to a process instance. In other words, when a message addressed to a Web service is received by the BPEL engine, its headers and contents are inspected and the message is consumed immediately for instance creation or instance routing, or it is rejected. This model is not suitable to capture scenarios where correlation can not be determined on a per-message basis, as in the case of the atomic consumption pattern. Consider the following scenario: A shipment aggregation service receives shipment requests from multiple customers and aggregates them into bundles. When the service receives a shipment request, it either: (i) creates a new bundle for the shipment's destination if there is no existing bundle for that destination; or (ii) assigns the request to an existing bundle for the same destination. When a bundle reaches a certain size, the corresponding bundle is closed and a delivery route is computed for it. Subsequent messages to the same destination are then assigned to a new bundle. If a bundle has been opened for more than a given time window, it is escalated to a human operator. Thus, shipment requests are aggregated in bundles based on their destination, until a bundle either reaches a given size (e.g. 10 requests) or a given age (e.g. 4 hours).

In this scenario, when a shipment request is received and no existing request for that destination is awaiting correlation, the message is buffered. It is only later that a process instance is created to deal with either that request alone, or a combination of requests with the same destination. Due to the "per event" nature of its correlation mechanism, BPEL does not support such scenarios involving *multiple consumption* or *atomic consumption*.

Table 1. Support for correlation patterns in BPEL 1.1 and 2.0

Correlation Patterns	BPEL 1.1	BPEL 2.0
C1. Key-based correlation	+	+
C2. Property-based correlation	−	¬
C3. Time-interval-based correlation	−	−
C4. Reference-based correlation	+	+
C5. Moving time-window correlation	−	−
C6. Conversation overlap	+	+
C7. Hierarchical conversation	+/−	+
C8. Conversation fork	+/−	+
C9. Conversation join	+/−	+
C10. Conversation refactor	+/−	+
C11. One process instance – one conversation	+	+
C12. Many process instances – one conversation	+	+
C13. One process instance – many conversations	+	+
C14. Initiate conversation	+	+
C15. Follow conversation	+	+
C16. Leave conversation	−	+
C17. Multiple consumption	−	−
C18. Atomic consumption	−	−

The proposed patterns can be used to analyze other languages for Web service implementation, such as the Web Service Choreography Description Language (WS-CDL [10]). WS-CDL uses equality of identity tokens to identify conversations. Therefore, WS-CDL directly supports *key-based correlation* but does not support *property-based correlation*. Like BPEL, WS-CDL can also be used in combination with WS-Addressing leading to direct support for *reference-based correlation*. The timeout attribute for interactions in WS-CDL provides a realization both of *time-interval-based correlation* and of *moving time-window correlation* (note that it is out of the scope of WS-CDL to specify how the individual participants handle the required message buffering). *Conversation overlap* can be realized in WS-CDL through the use of several sets of identity tokens. However, like in BPEL 1.1 there is only partial support for *hierarchical conversation*, *conversation fork* and *conversation join* since WS-CDL provides no construct to capture an unbounded number of branches that execute in parallel. WS-CDL is a language for describing interactions between multiple Web services from a global perspective. It does not deal with the individual behavior of each service, and hence does not have a notion of process instance. Therefore, the patterns from section 5 are irrelevant for WS-CDL.

7   Related Work

Two programming languages for Web service implementation propose alternative correlation mechanisms to BPEL's one: XL [6] and GPSL [5]. XL directly supports the concept of conversation. Conversations are identified by unique

URIs that are included in a SOAP header (similar to WS-Addressing "relatesTo" header). Conversation patterns define when should new conversation URIs be created versus when should existing conversation URIs be reused. With respect to BPEL, XL adds a concept of *conversation timer* which can deal with our time-interval-based correlation pattern. A conversation timer is armed when a service receives the first message related to a conversation: If a message is received by the service after the timeout, this message is treated as part of a new conversation. Arguably, one can achieve a similar effect in BPEL 2.0 using scoped correlation sets combined with alarms and faults, but this would require convoluted code. On the other hand, XL suffers from similar limitations as BPEL when it comes to dealing with multiple consumption and atomic consumption.

GPSL on the other hand relies on the concept of *join pattern* to capture correlation scenarios such as the shipment aggregation service above. A join pattern is a conjunction of message channels and a filtering condition: when messages are received over a channel they are stored in a buffer until there is a join pattern consuming them. For a join pattern to fire, there must be a combination of messages (one per channel in the join pattern) which satisfies the filter. This feature corresponds to the "atomic consumption" pattern. Timeouts are conceptually treated as messages coming from a "timer service", thus enabling time-interval-based correlation. Also, GPSL deals with "multiple consumption" by allowing a service to send (or re-send) a message to itself: so once a message is consumed, the service can put it back again in the corresponding channel.

Concepts similar to join patterns have been considered in the context of complex event processing [11], where they are called *event patterns*. IBM's Active Correlation Technology [3] for example, provides a rule language to capture event patterns such as "more than four events of a given type happen in a sliding window of 30 seconds". Event rule languages can capture arbitrarily complex correlation patterns. But the question that we attempt to answer is: how much of this event correlation technology is needed in SOA?

Patterns of correlation in enterprise applications are presented in [8]. But this work only considers reference-based correlation as supported by WS-Addressing.

8   Conclusion and Outlook

This paper introduced a framework for classifying and describing correlation scenarios in SOAs, with an emphasis on stateful services that engage in long-running business transactions. Using this framework, we described a set of patterns that can be used to evaluate the correlation mechanisms of standards and tools for service implementation. In particular, we evaluated two successive versions of BPEL and showed that, while the later version supports a larger set of correlation patterns than the earlier, it still does not support certain patterns due to its approach of correlating and consuming messages immediately upon receipt, as well as its inability to deal with time as a factor in determining correlation.

The framework points into the direction of patterns of relationships between process instances. In many scenarios, different process instances compete for the same messages, thus creating dependencies between them. A classification and in-depth study of these dependencies constitutes an avenue for future work. Furthermore, the framework can be extended to cover more sophisticated correlation patterns such as those found in the area of complex event processing. An extended version of the framework could provide a basis for evaluating the correlation mechanisms of languages and systems for event processing in general.

Acknowledgments. The second author conducted this work while visiting SAP Research Centre, Brisbane. The third author is funded by a fellowship co-sponsored by SAP and Queensland Government.

References

1. W. van der Aalst, A. ter Hofstede, B. Kiepuszewski, and A. Barros. *Workflow Patterns*. Distributed and Parallel Databases, 14(3):5–51, July 2003.
2. A. Barros, M. Dumas, and A. ter Hofstede. Service Interactions Patterns. In *Proceedings of the 3rd International Conference on Business Process Management (BPM)*, Nancy, France, September 2005, pages 65–80. Springer, 2005.
3. A. Biazetti and K. Gajda. *Achieving complex event processing with Active Correlation Technology*. IBM Technical Report, November 2005. http:// www-128.ibm.com/developerworks/autonomic/library/ac-acact/
4. W. De Pauw, M. Lei, E. Pring, L. Villard, M. Arnold, and J.F. Morar. "Web Services Navigator: Visualizing the Execution of Web Services" *IBM Systems Journal* 44(4):821-845, 2005.
5. D. Cooney, M. Dumas, and P. Roe. GPSL. A Programming Language for Service Implementation. In *Proceedings of the 8th International Conference on Fundamental Approaches to Software Engineering (FASE)*, Vienna, Austria, March 2006, pages 3–17. Springer, 2006.
6. D. Florescu, A. Grünhagen, and D. Kossmann. XL: an XML programming language for Web service specification and composition. *Computer Networks* 42(5):641–660, 2003.
7. M. Gudgin, M. Hadley, and T. Rogers (editors). *Web Services Addressing 1.0 – Core*. W3C Recommendation, May 2006. http://www.w3.org/Submission/ ws-addressing/
8. G. Hohpe, B. Woolf. *Enterprise Integration Patterns: Designing, Building, and Deploying Messaging Solutions*. Addison-Wesley, 2003
9. D. Jordan and J. Evdemon (editors). *Web Services Business Process Execution Language Version 2.0* Public Review Draft. OASIS WS-BPEL Technical Committee, August 2006. http://docs.oasis-open.org/wsbpel/2.0/ wsbpel-specification-draft.pdf/
10. N. Kavantzas, D. Burdett, T. Fletcher, Y. Lafon, and C. Barreto (editors). *Web Services Choreography Definition Language Version 1.0*. W3C Candidate Recommendation, November 2005. http://www.w3.org/TR/ws-cdl-10/
11. D. Luckham. *The Power of Events: An Introduction to Complex Event Processing in Distributed Enterprise Systems*. Addison-Wesley, 2001.
12. S. Weerawarana, F. Curbera, F. Leymann, T. Storey, and D. Ferguson. *Web Services Platform Architecture : SOAP, WSDL, WS-Policy, WS-Addressing, WS-BPEL, WS-Reliable Messaging, and More*. Prentice Hall PTR, 2005.

Dynamic Characterization of Web Application Interfaces

Marc Fisher II, Sebastian Elbaum, and Gregg Rothermel

University of Nebraska-Lincoln
{mfisher,elbaum,grother}@cse.unl.edu

Abstract. Web applications are increasingly prominent in society, serving a wide variety of user needs. Engineers seeking to enhance, test, and maintain these applications and third-party programmers wishing to utlize these applications need to understand their interfaces. In this paper, therefore, we present methodologies for characterizing the interfaces of web applications through a form of dynamic analysis, in which directed requests are sent to the application, and responses are analyzed to draw inferences about its interface. We also provide mechanisms to increase the scalability of the approach. Finally, we evaluate the approach's performance on six non-trivial web applications.

1 Introduction

Consider a flight reservation web application, such as Expedia. Such an application compiles data from multiple airlines, and provides a web site where customers can search for flights and purchase tickets. The site itself consists of HTML forms that are displayed to the customer in a web browser. Within these forms, the customer can enter information in fields (e.g. radio buttons, text fields) to specify the parameters for a flight (e.g. departure date, return date, number of passengers). The web browser then uses this entered information to assemble a request that is sent to a form handler. The form handler is a component that serves as an interface for the web application. This form handler could be responsible for queries submitted via multiple different forms, such as forms for round-trip flights or one-way flights.

Proper understanding of the interface exposed by the form handler can help engineers generate test cases and oracles relevant to the underlying web applications. Such an understanding may also be useful for directing maintenance tasks such as re-factoring the web pages. Finally, as we shall show, information that helps engineers comprehend web application interfaces may also help them detect anomalies in those interfaces and the underlying applications.

An understanding of web application interfaces can also be valuable for third party developers attempting to incorporate the rendered data as a part of a web service (e.g. a site that aggregates flight pricing information from multiple sources). Although web applications that are commonly used by clients may provide interface descriptions (e.g. commercial sites offering web services often offer

M.B. Dwyer and A. Lopes (Eds.): FASE 2007, LNCS 4422, pp. 260–275, 2007.

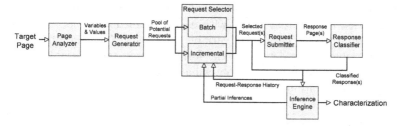

Fig. 1. WebAppSleuth architecture

a WSDL-type [1] description), many sites do not currently provide such support mechanisms. Moreover, as we shall show, the level of interface understanding that could be useful for comprehension and anomaly detection goes beyond that usually provided by such interface descriptions, and could serve as a complement to a WSDL description.

To support the various activities of both the engineers of sites, and third party developers incorporating information from other sites, we have been researching methods for automatically characterizing the properties of and relationships between variables and values in web application interfaces. In this paper, we present a methodology for characterizing the interface of a web application. Our methodology involves making requests to a target web application, and analyzing the application's responses to draw inferences about the variables and values that can be included in a request and the relationships among those variables and values. We identify three specific types of inferences, all of which have the ability to find anomalous behavior in and help increase understanding of web applications. To enhance the scalability of the approach, we provide a family of techniques for selecting requests to submit to the application.

We report the results of empirical studies of this approach, in which we apply it to six non-trivial, real-world web applications from various sources (academic, government, and commercial). Our studies show that our inferences are useful for finding anomalous behavior in these applications. In addition, we show that for these applications, our request selection techniques can reduce the number of requests needed to find correct inferences and filter out incorrect inferences, enhancing the scalability of the approach.

2   Methodology

Our methodology works by selectively submitting requests to a web application, and using the responses to those requests to discover relationships between variables and values in the application. Figure 1 shows the overall architecture for our web application interface characterization methodology, WebApp-Sleuth, with various processes (sub-systems) in the methodology shown as boxes. WebAppSleuth begins with a *Page Analyzer* process, which statically analyzes a target page containing a form generated by the web application. The *Page*

Analyzer identifies all variables associated with the fields in the form, and then associates a list of potential values with each identified variable. For each pull-down, radio-button, or check-box variable, the *Page Analyzer* obtains values from the possible values defined in the form. For text-type variables, the *Page Analyzer* prompts the user to supply values that may elicit a correct response from the web application.

Next, the *Request Generator* creates a pool of potential requests by exploring all combinations of values provided for each variable, as well as cases where variables are missing. Given this pool of requests, the *Request Selector* determines which request or requests will be submitted to the target application. There are two general request selection modes: *Batch* (requests are selected all at once) and *Incremental* (requests are selected one at a time guided by a feedback mechanism). The *Request Submitter* assembles the http request, sends it to the web server, and stores the response. This response is classified by the *Response Classifier*. The selected request and the classified response are then fed into the *Inference Engine*, which infers various properties about the variables and values used in submitted requests.

Currently, our methodology analyzes a single form handler within a web application. The form handler is assumed to be stateless and deterministic with respect to its inputs. Numerous important web applications satisfy (or mostly satisfy) these requirements, including applications that support travel reservation searches (e.g. Expedia), mapping applications (e.g. MapQuest), product searches (e.g. BuyAToyota's used car search) and other search sites (e.g. NSF's funding search). For sites that do not fully satisfy these requirements, it is often possible to approximate them by temporarily controlling the state (for developers characterizing their own site) or by limiting the time frame within which the site is accessed to limit potential changes to the underlying state.

In the following sections, we explain (1) how we classify responses, (2) how we use requests and responses to generate inferences, and (3) how we select the requests we are submitting, including methods that use previously submitted requests with responses and generated inferences to guide the request selection process.

2.1 Classifying Responses

After submitting each request, we classify the response. The user must choose between one of two methods for classification depending on the types of responses received and the types of inferences they wish to make. For some sites, the response is either some piece of information (i.e. a map for MapQuest) or an error message. Therefore our first method is to classify responses as either "Valid" (returns the request information) or "Invalid" (returns an error message). To classify these types of responses, our methodology searches for substrings in the result that match simple regular expressions.

Our second method is to extract a set of results from the response (for the inference algorithms that require valid/invalid classification, an empty set is invalid, and any non-empty set is valid). For example, for BuyAToyota the response page includes a set of identifiers representing cars, possibly with links to additional pages with more cars. We collect this set of identifiers (iterating through the additional pages if necessary), and store these as the classification for the request.

2.2   Discovering Inferences

We have devised a family of inference algorithms to characterize the variables that are part of a web application interface, and the relationships between them. The algorithms operate on the list of variable-value pairs that are part of each submitted request, and on the classified responses (valid/invalid or a set of returned results) to those requests.

To facilitate the explanation of the subsequent algorithms we use examples that are further explored in our study in Section 3. Also, we simplify the terminology by defining a *valid request* as one that generates a valid response from the application, and defining an *invalid request* as one that generates an invalid response. For space reasons, detailed algorithms and descriptions are omitted, but can be found in [2].

Variable Classes and Values. It is common for web applications to evolve, incorporating additional and more refined services in each new deployment. As an application evolves, it becomes less clear what variables are *mandatory* (required in every valid request), and what variables are *optional* (may be included or absent in a valid request). Distinguishing between these classes of variables is helpful, for example, to anyone planning to access the web application interface, and to developers of the web application who wish to confirm that changes in the application have the expected results in the interface.

In addition to assisting developers with evolving applications, we can identify anomalies in the application by finding *mandatorily absent* variables (variables absent in every valid request). There are two potential reasons mandatorily absent variables may be identified: 1) the web page or web application contains a error (e.g. a field was left in a form but is no longer used by the web application) or 2) additional requests are needed to provide an appropriate characterization of that variable.

Our algorithm identifies as mandatory any variable that appears in all valid requests and is absent in at least one invalid request. Our algorithm identifies as optional any variable that appears in at least one valid request and is absent in at least one valid request. Our algorithm identifies as mandatorily absent any variable that is absent in all valid requests and appears in at least one invalid request.

In addition to finding mandatory, optional, and mandatorily absent variables, we also find the range of values for variables that produced valid responses. This allows us to detect values that never return valid results. These values could indicate that there are problems with the web application (e.g. the form includes a value for a variable that is no longer used in the application), that more requests need to be made, or that there exists an opportunity for improving

Table 1. MapQuest Requests and Variable Implications

	$address$	$city$	$state$	zip	Implication	At least one-of
1	absent	absent	present	absent	$address \implies$	$state$
2	absent	absent	absent	present	$address \implies$	$state \lor zip$
3	present	absent	absent	present	$address \implies zip$	$state \lor zip$
4	present	present	present	absent	$address \implies zip \lor (city \land state)$	$state \lor zip$
5	present	present	present	present	$address \implies zip \lor (city \land state)$	$state \lor zip$

the web application (e.g. a possible value for a variable represents a value that does not exist in the current state of the database, and filtering the values in the form based on this state could be useful).

To find the range of values, our algorithm keeps track of the values that appear in requests (distinguishing between those that appear in valid and invalid requests) and reports a list of values that appeared in valid requests for each variable. To reduce the number of falsely reported value inferences, the algorithm reports an inference for a variable only after all values included for that variable have been used at least once.

Variable Implication. Sometimes a request that contains a particular variable can be valid only if other specific variables are present. Identifying such relationships between variables is helpful for understanding the impact of application changes, and for avoiding sending incomplete requests to the application.

To investigate this type of relationship, we began by defining the notion of implication as a conditional relationship between variables p and q, namely: if p is present, then q must be present. After examining existing implications on many sites we decided to expand our attention to implications in which the right hand side is a proposition in *disjunctive normal form* and does not contain negations or the constant TRUE. This guarantees that our implications are satisfiable but not tautological. Further, this type of implication (referred to henceforth as a "standard" implication) is relatively simple to understand because it can easily be mapped to the variables' expected behavior.

Our technique constructs an implication for each variable in the application by iterating through submitted requests, and adding clauses to the implication for requests in which the set of variables present is not a superset of the variables in any other clause in the implication. For a basic notion of how our technique operates consider Table 1, which shows the process for constructing the *address* implication for MapQuest across a sequence of requests. For the first two requests, *address* is not present in the request, so we do not update the implication. The third row includes *address* and *zip*, so we need to add the clause *zip* to the right side of the implication. The next request includes *address*, *city*, and *state*, but does not include *zip* (the only variable included in the clause in the implication so far), so we add the clause *city* ∧ *state* to the implication. Finally, the fifth request includes all four variables, a superset of the variables included in either of the existing two clauses, so a new clause is not needed.

In addition to standard implications, we use a similar algorithm to detect two other types of inferences. One of these is the "at least one-of" inference. This inference is a proposition in disjunctive normal form like those found on the right side of our implications. Only one of these is created per site. The last column of Table 1 shows how an "at least one-of" inference is found for the MapQuest site.

The other type of inference is value-based implication. This inference is an implication in which the left side has the form of $p = q$, where p is a variable and q is some value for that variable. We create one of these for each value of each variable in the site.

Value Hierarchies. It is often the case that when given two values for a variable, one of them should always return a subset of the results returned for the other value. Consider the case for real estate search engines, which typically provide a "minimum price" variable. As the minimum price increases, if all other variables are held constant, the returned results should be a subset of the results for lower minimum prices. Such relationships cause a hierarchy of values to exist. In the case of minimum price, this is a simple linear hierarchy with each lower price subsuming all of the results of the higher prices.

We represent hierarchy relationships as a graph, with a node for each value, and directed edges $p \rightarrow q$ indicating that $q \subseteq p$.

Most constrained inputs (i.e. radio button or pull-down inputs) should have a hierarchical relationship between their different values. When this is the case, the graph is a directed acyclic graph with a single root node, where that root node represents an "all" or "don't care" value for the variable (Figure 2(a)).

Anomalies in the structure of these graphs can be useful for finding problems in the web application. For example, a common anomaly seen in the applications used for our study in Section 3 is the presence of values without edges leading to them from the "all" value. This usually indicates that there were results that did not appear when the variable was set to its "all" value, but did appear under some other circumstance.

There are two special cases of the hierarchy pattern that appear often enough in web sites to warrant special consideration. The "flat" pattern (Figure 2(b)) often occurs when the underlying application looks only for exact matches of the values for the variable (excluding the "all" value).

The other special case is the "ordered" pattern (Figure 2(c)). This represents variables with values that indicate progressive restriction. The minimum price variable mentioned above is an example of this case.

Similar to our methodology for finding implications, our hierarchy inference methodology begins by creating a potential hierarchy for each variable in the application. Each potential hierarchy has two n by n boolean arrays, where n is the number of possible values for the associated variable. One of the arrays, *subset*, keeps track of whether we have found a case in which the subset relationship holds between the two values. The other array, *notSubset*, keeps track of whether we have found a case where the subset relationship does not hold

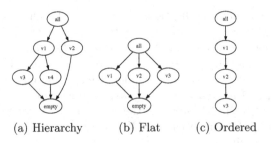

(a) Hierarchy   (b) Flat   (c) Ordered

Fig. 2. Example Hierarchies

between the two values. Each of these arrays is initialized with "false" in each of their cells. Then, as each request *R1* is submitted and classified, these arrays are updated.

To display hierarchical relationships, we iterate through all the possible combinations of values. If the cell in the *subset* array is "true" and the cell in the *notSubset* array is "false", we place an edge between the nodes. Beyond this there are two optimizations that can be made to make the graph more readable. The first is to combine values that return the same result into a single node (frequently we find several values that always return the empty set). The second optimization is to remove "transitive" edges from the graph. A transitive edge is any edge (u, v) where there also exist edges (u, u_1), ... (u_n, v). Currently our tool outputs the graph in dot format, which can then be read into GraphViz [3].

2.3   Selecting Requests

One of the fundamental challenges for characterizing a web application through directed requests is to control the number of requests. Larger numbers of requests imply larger amounts of time required to collect request-response data (for Expedia, one of the sites we study in Section 3, each request took about 30 seconds) and this slows down the inferencing process. In addition, our techniques are sensitive to the state of the underlying database, so when applying them to a live web application, we need to limit the time frame within which the requests are made to obtain consistent results.

To address these problems, the *Request Selector* can either select a sample of requests from the pool up-front, or it can operate incrementally by selecting a request based on previous results and continue selecting requests until the user no longer wishes to refine the inference set.

We consider two batch selection approaches. The first approach, Random, simply selects a set of random requests from the pool of requests without repetition. The second approach, Covering-Array, utilizes covering arrays [4] to determine the set of requests to submit. In general, covering arrays ensure that all n-way combinations of values are covered by the selected requests. For a given site with m variables, we consider all n, such that $1 \leq n < m$ (when $n = m$, all generated requests are included). We used a tool developed by Cohen et al. [5] that uses simulated annealing to find covering arrays.

We consider one incremental approach, Inference-Guided, which selects requests based on requests already submitted and inferences already derived. To select which request to submit, for each unsubmitted request, this approach determines an award value, and selects the request with the highest award value. To determine an award value for each unsubmitted request R_u, we consider those requests that differ from some submitted request R_s in one variable (all other unsubmitted requests are assigned an award value of 0). We focus on this set of requests because it seems that similar requests are likely to return similar results, and we can therefore use the classification of R_s as a predictor for the classification of R_u. The award value of R_u is equal to the number of potential inferences that would be changed if R_u has the same classification as R_s.

Inference-Guided selection requires that some requests be submitted before it can begin to compute award values for other requests. We use two approaches for this. One approach begins by randomly selecting the initial requests. Another approach uses the Covering-Array tactic (for $n = 2$) to select an initial set of requests to submit, and then incrementally selects additional requests.

3   Empirical Evaluation

The goal of our study is to assess whether our methodology can effectively and efficiently characterize real web sites. In particular, we wish to answer the following research questions:

RQ1: What is the effectiveness of the characterization? We would like our characterization to be useful for understanding and finding anomalies in web applications. Therefore, we examine the inferences generated for various sites, and consider how they reflect the observed behavior of those sites.

RQ2: What is the tradeoff between effectiveness and efficiency? As the number of requests submitted to a web application increases, the quality of the inferences we can obtain should improve. However, the number of requests that can be made is limited by practical considerations. Therefore, we examine how the quality of inferences varies as requests are selected.

3.1   Objects of Analysis

Our objects of analysis (see Table 2) are six applications from various domains and implemented by various organizations. Three of them, MapQuest, Expedia, and Travelocity, have been used in other studies [6,7] and are among the top-40 performers on the web [8]. BuyAToyota is an application to search for Toyota certified used cars at local dealerships. NSF is an application supporting searches for NSF funding opportunities. UNL is a job search application maintained by the University of Nebraska - Lincoln human resources department.

Table 2. Objects of Analysis

Object	Relevant variables identified by Page Analyzer			Variables considered for analysis	Size of request pool
	Text Box	List Box	Check & Radio		
MapQuest	4	0	0	4	16
Expedia	4	5	2	9	49,996
Travelocity	4	7	1	9	49,996
BuyAToyota	2	5	0	5	33,408
NSF	1	7	0	7	72,576
UNL	2	4	0	4	42,345

Table 2 lists the numbers of variables identified by our *Page Analyzer* on the main page produced by each of our target web applications, at the time of this analysis, subdivided into basic input types, the numbers of those that we used for our analysis, and the total of number requests in the initial request pool for each of these applications. To keep the total number of requests manageable, we limited the variables and values for those variables that we considered as well as choosing relatively static web sites. When choosing which variables and values to consider, we attempted to select them such that an interesting, but representative range of behaviors for the web applications was explored. As we show in Section 3.4, we did not always achieve this.

3.2 Variables and Measures

Our study requires us to apply our inferencing algorithms on a collected data set of requests and responses to characterize the objects of study. Throughout the study we utilize four request selection procedures corresponding to those described in Section 2.3: Random, Covering-Array, Inference-Guided (Random), and Inference-Guided (Covering-Array).

To quantify the impact of the request selection algorithms, we compute the recall and precision as we select requests. To compute recall and precision, we had to define a set of inferences as a baseline (the "expected" inferences). For each application, we defined this set as the set of inferences reported when all requests were selected. *TotalExpectedInf* is the cardinality of this set. Then, after submitting a subset of the requests, S, we can define two additional values. The first, *ReportedExpectedInf$_S$*, is the number of inferences from the set of expected inferences that were reported after submitting S. The second, *ReportedInf$_S$*, is the total number of inferences reported after submitting S. Finally we get:

$$Recall_S = ReportedExpectedInf_S \, / \, TotalExpectedInf$$
$$\text{and}$$
$$Precision_S = ReportedExpectedInf_S \, / \, ReportedInf_S$$

Note that *Recall$_S$* is 100% when the methodology reports all of the expected inferences after submitting S, and that *Precision$_S$* is 100% if we report no unexpected inferences after submitting S.

3.3   Design and Setup

We applied the WebAppSleuth methodology to each of the objects of study. This involved tailoring our request submission and response classification routines as described in Section 2.1. For three of the sites (MapQuest, Travelocity, and Expedia), we used the valid/invalid classification method. For the remaining three sites we were able to collect a set of results (cars for BuyAToyota, funding opportunities for NSF, and jobs for UNL).

To expedite the exploration of several alternative request selection mechanisms and inference algorithms without making the same set of requests multiple times, we performed all the requests in the pool, and then applied the different mechanisms and algorithms to these results. This controlled for potential changes in the state of the web applications by giving a common set of response pages to operate on, while still obtaining results identical to what would have occurred had we applied the analysis to the site directly.

We performed the analysis 25 times with each type of *Request Selector* to control for the randomness factor in the request selection algorithms. For the Random and Inference-Guided selection each of these 25 runs selected one request at a time and generated inferences after each request, continuing until all the requests in the pool were selected. For Covering-Array, we selected 25 sets of requests for each level of interaction from one to one less than the number of variables in the application, and generated inferences for each of these sets of requests.

3.4   Results

We present the results in two steps, corresponding to our two research questions. First, we show and discuss the characterization provided by the methodology for

Table 3. Inferences Found for each Web Application

Website	Type	Inferences
MapQuest	Optional	*address, city, state, zip*
	Implications	*city* $\implies$ *zip* $\vee$ *state, address* $\implies$ *zip* $\vee$ *(city* $\wedge$ *state)*
Expedia	Mandatory	*depCity, arrCity, depDate, retDate, depTime, retTime*
	Optional	*adults, seniors, children*
	Implications	*(adults* $\vee$ *seniors)*
	Values	*children*: 1 of 4 values
Travelocity		**All inferences from Expedia**
	Implications	*(adults* $= 0)$ $\implies$ *seniors, (seniors* $= 0)$ $\implies$ *adults*
BuyAToyota	Optional	*model, year, price, mileage, distance*
	Implications	*(year* $= 2006)$ $\implies$ *model*
	Values	*model*: 13 of 28 values, *price*: 5 of 7 values
	Hierarchies	*model*: Flat, missing 3 edges from "all" value, empty values, *mileage*: Ordered, *year*: Flat, *price*: Ordered
NSF	Mandatory	*pubSelect, fundType, queryText*
	Optional	*month, day, year, organization*
	Values	*organization*: 46 of 48 values
	Hierarchies	*fundType*: Flat, *organization*: Missing edges from "all" value, empty values, other anomalies, *year*: Ordered
UNL	Values	*fte*: 7 of 8 values, *category*: 7 of 9 values
	Hierarchies	*fte*: Flat, missing 5 edges from "all" value, empty value, *category*: Flat, missing 1 edge from "all" value, empty value, *reportsTo*: Flat, *title*: Flat

Table 4. Summary of Anomalies Found in Sites

Site and Symptom	Significance
Expedia and Travelocity: *children* had 3 invalid values	We did not consider the age variables associated with the *children* variable
Expedia: missing implications	Site returned flights in some cases when the total number of travelers was 0
BuyAToyota: missing values for *model* and *price*	We limited our search geographically, excluding results that would have filled in the missing values
BuyAToyota: *year* = 2006 ⟹ *model*	New cars were added to site as we collected requests
BuyAToyota: *model* hierarchy was flat	Models such as "Camry" did not include submodels such as "Camry Solara"
BuyAToyota: misplaced value in hierarchy	"> 100,000" miles functioned like "< 32, 767" miles
NSF: *queryText* variable was mandatory	Blank value for *queryText* treated different than not including *queryText*
NSF: missing values for *program*	We limited our search to active funding opportunities, excluding archived funding opportunities that would have filled in the missing values
NSF: *fundType* hierarchy was flat	Aggregate values such as "Standard or Continuing Grant" not treated proper aggregates
NSF: *program* hierarchy had numerous anomalies	Problems with application logic
NSF: inconsistent treatment of missing variables	Design inconsistency makes maintenance more difficult
NSF: missing implication (*pubSelect* = "After") ⟹ *day* ∧ *month* ∧ *year*	Site treated "After" the same as "Ignore" if dependent values were missing
UNL: *fte* and *category* had missing values	Certain values of these fields did not appear in database
UNL: *title* hierarchy was flat	Titles such as "Assistant Professor" and "Assistant Professor-Political Science" returned disjoint sets of results
UNL: missing edges in *fte* and *category* hierarchies	Either problems with application logic or the database state changed as we submitted requests

each target web application when the entire pool of requests is utilized. Second, we analyze how the characterization progresses as the requests are submitted and analyzed, utilizing four different request selection mechanisms.

RQ1: Effectiveness of the Characterization. Table 3 presents the inferences derived from the requests we made and the responses provided by each of the target applications. Overall, we were able to find anomalies on five of the six web applications, suggesting that our methodology can be used to help improve the dependability or usability of web applications. Table 4 summarizes all of the anomalies found. For space reasons we discuss just two of these in detail, the others are discussed in Reference [2].

The first example anomaly is for Expedia and Travelocity. On these applications we looked at sets of variables and values for which we expected to get identical results. However, there were two value-based implications found for Travelocity that did not appear in Expedia. These implications were the result of Travelocity never returning a list of flights if the total number of selected passengers was 0, while in some cases Expedia would return a list of flights. Since flight search in both of these sites is just the first step in a process for purchasing tickets and since Expedia's behavior has changed since the original set

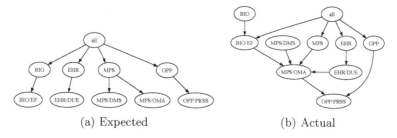

(a) Expected   (b) Actual

Fig. 3. NSF Organization Hierarchy

of requests was submitted, this difference in behavior indicates that the earlier version of Expedia probably contained a fault.

The second example anomaly was on NSF. The NSF grant search application includes a variable, organization, that allows the user to select which NSF program they are interested in. Figure 3(a) shows the expected hierarchy for an interesting subset of the values for the organization variable, while Figure 3(b) shows the hierarchy that was actually generated. The first thing to note is some missing edges (e.g. between all and BIO and between MPS and MPS/DMS). In addition, the value MPS/OMA is a child of multiple values: BIO/EF, MPS, MPS/DMS, and EHR/DUE. This occurred because particular grants could belong to multiple programs and, in this case, only one grant offered through MPS/OMA appeared in our results, and it belonged to the other programs as well. Finally, OPP/PRSS appears at the bottom as a descendant of every other node as no grants were ever returned for this value.

RQ2: Effects of Request Selection. Figure 4 presents our results with respect to the precision and recall of the Inference-Guided and Random request selection techniques, for three of the six web applications (with only 16 requests, MapQuest is too small an example for request selection to be useful, Travelocity had results nearly identical to Expedia and NSF had results similar to Buy-AToyota). In each of the graphs, the x-axis represents the number of requests selected from the pool, and the y-axis represents the average recall (left column) or precision (right column) over the 25 runs. Each of the lines represents one of the request selection techniques, and the legend below indicates which line corresponds to which technique.

On two applications, Expedia and UNL, Inference-Guided request selection (with Random or Covering-Array seeds) had average recall equal to or better than Random or Covering-Array request selection regardless of the number of requests selected. On these objects we see little difference between the two Inference-Guided techniques or between the Random and Covering-Array techniques (when considering the graphs for the Covering-Array technique, the points of interest are the corners of the "steps" as these represent the collected data points, while the other points along these plots are meant to aid in their interpretation). For BuyAToyota, all the techniques were only slightly different in terms of recall throughout the process.

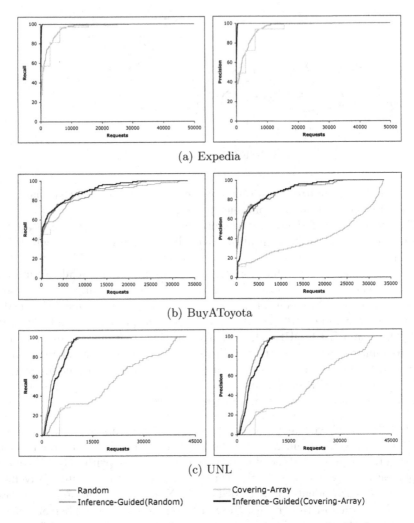

(a) Expedia

(b) BuyAToyota

(c) UNL

——— Random   ········· Covering-Array
——— Inference-Guided(Random)   ——— Inference-Guided(Covering-Array)

Fig. 4. Recall and precision vs percent of requests submitted

For all of the web applications, Inference-Guided request selection (with Random or Covering-Array seeds) had average precision equal to or better than Random or Covering-Array request selection throughout the request selection process. Again, there was little difference between Inference-Guided (Random) and Inference-Guided (Covering-Array) or between Random and Covering-Array.

These results are encouraging because they show that we can often dramatically reduce the number of requests required, while still reporting most correct inferences and few incorrect inferences. In particular, for the application with just valid and invalid classifications (Expedia) we needed fewer than 650 requests (1.3% of the pool) to achieve 100% recall and precision with the Inference-Guided techniques, and 21,500 requests (43% of the pool) with Random selection. The addition of set classification and hierarchy inferences makes request selection less effective, but we can still reduce reported incorrect inferences quickly using Inference-Guided selection. In addition, it appears that using Covering-Array techniques does little overall to improve the recall and precision of reported inferences (either by itself in comparison to Random or as a seeding technique for Inference-Guided instead of using random seeding).

4   Related Work

There has been a great deal of work to help identify deficiencies in web sites, to provide information on users's access patterns, and to support testing of web applications [9,10,11,12,13]. Among these tools, our request generation approach most resembles the approach used by load testing tools, except that our goal is to generate a broad range of requests to characterize the variables in the web application interface. There are also tools that automatically populate forms by identifying known keywords and their association with a list of potential values (e.g., zipcode has a defined set of possible values, all with five characters). This approach is simple but often produces incorrect or incomplete requests, so we refrained from using it in our studies to avoid biasing the inferencing process.

Our work also relates to research efforts in the area of program characterization through dynamic analysis [14,15,16,17,18,19]. These efforts provide approaches for inferring program properties based on the analysis of program runs. These approaches, however, target more traditional programs or their byproducts (e.g., traces) while our target is web application interfaces. Targeting web applications implies that the set of properties of interest to us are different and that we are making inferences on the program interface instead of on the program internals.

Recent approaches also attempt to combine dynamic inference with input generation [20,21]. These approaches use dynamic inference techniques to classify the behavior of the program under generated inputs to determine the usefulness of these inputs for finding faults. Our approach differs in that we want to avoid executing new inputs that will not help our characterization due to the high cost of their execution and the large number of potential requests.

In our own prior work, we have made several inroads into the problems of automatically characterizing the properties of and relationships between variables in web application interfaces. In earlier work [7] we presented static approaches for analyzing HTML and JavaScript code to identify variable types, and a dynamic approach for providing simple characterizations of the values allowed for variables (e.g., a variable cannot be empty). However, deeper characterizations of web application interfaces were not obtainable through the mechanisms that we considered. More recent work [6] presented our techniques for finding mandatory, optional and valid value and implication inferences as well as a less general version of our Inference-Guided request selection technique. This work did not consider classification of sets of results, hierarchy inferences, or the application of covering array techniques to request selection, and looked at only three of the six applications we examined here.

5   Conclusion

We have presented and evaluated what we believe to be the first methodology for semi-automatically characterizing web application interfaces. This methodology submits requests to exercise a web application, and analyzes the responses to make inferences about the variables and values within the application interface. As part of the methodology we have introduced a family of selection mechanisms for submitting requests more efficiently. Further, the results of an empirical study of six web applications from a variety of domains indicate that the methodology can effectively derive inferences that can help with anomaly detection or understanding of the web application interface and that our Inference-Guided request selection technique can reduce the number of requests required to get correct inferences and filter out incorrect ones.

These results suggest several directions for future work. First, we would like to extend our methodology to work with different types of web applications. Second, the current non-automated steps of the methodology, customization of the request submission and response classification routines, required between four and eight hours for each of the sites we studied. Hence, we plan on leveraging patterns in web applications along with clustering techniques to build heuristic methods for automating these parts of WebAppSleuth. Finally, we will explore additional types of inferences.

Acknowledgements. Thanks to M. Cohen who provided us with her tool for generating covering arrays. K.-R. Chilakamarri participated in the early portions of this work. This work was supported in part by NSF CAREER Award 0347518, the EUSES Consortium through NSF-ITR 0325273 and the ARO through DURIP award W911NF-04-1-0104.

References

1. Christensen, E., Curbera, F., Meredith, G., Weerawarana, S.: Web services description language. http://www.w3.org/TR/wsdl (2001)
2. Fisher II, M., Elbaum, S., Rothermel, G.: Dynamic characterization of web application interfaces. Technical Report UNL-TR-CSE-2006-0010, University of Nebraska - Lincoln (2006)
3. GraphViz. http://www.graphviz.org/ (2006)
4. Cohen, D., Dalal, S., Fredman, M., Patton, G.: The AETG system: An approach to testing based on combinatorial design. IEEE Trans. on Softw. Eng. **23**(7) (1997) 437–444
5. Cohen, M., Colbourn, C., Gibbons, P., Mugridge, W.: Constructing test suites for interaction testing. In: Int'l Conf. on Softw. Eng. (2003) 38–48

6. Elbaum, S., Chilakamarri, K.R., Fisher II, M., Rothermel, G.: Web application characterization through directed requests. In: Int'l Workshop on Dynamic Analysis. (2006)

7. Elbaum, S., Chilakamarri, K.R., Gopal, B., Rothermel, G.: Helping end-users "engineer" dependable web applications. In: Int'l Symp. on Softw. Reliability Eng. (2005) 31–40

8. Consumer top 40 sites. http://www.keynote.com/solutions/performance_indices/consumer_index/consumer_40.html(2006)

9. Benedikt, M., Freire, J., Godefroid, P.: VeriWeb: Automatically testing dynamic web sites. In: Int'l WWW Conf. (2002)

10. Elbaum, S., Rothermel, G., Karre, S., Fisher II, M.: Leveraging user-session data to support web application testing. IEEE Trans. on Softw. Eng. (2005) 187–201

11. Ricca, F., Tonella, P.: Analysis and testing of web applications. In: Int'l Conf. on Softw. Eng. (2001) 25–34

12. Software QA and Testing Resource Center: Web Test Tools. http://www.softwareqatest.com/qatweb1.html (2006)

13. Tilley, S., Shihong, H.: Evaluating the reverse engineering capabilities of web tools for understanding site content and structure: A case study. In: Int'l Conf. on Softw. Eng. (2001) 514–523

14. Ammons, G., Bodik, R., Larus, J.: Mining specifications. In: Symp. on Principles of Prog. Lang. (2002) 4–16

15. Ernst, M., Cockrell, J., Griswold, W., Notkin, D.: Dynamically discovering likely program invariants to support program evolution. In: Int'l Conf. on Softw. Eng. (1999) 213–224

16. Hangal, S., Lam, M.: Tracking down software bugs using automatic anomaly detection. In: Int'l Conf. on Softw. Eng. (2002) 291–301

17. Henkel, J., Diwan, A.: Discovering algebraic specifications from Java classes. In: Eur. Conf. on OO Prog. (2003) 431–456

18. Savage, S., Burrows, M., Nelson, G., Sobalvarro, P., Anderson, T.: Eraser: A dynamic data race detector for multithreaded programs. ACM Trans. on Comp. Systems 15(4) (1997) 391–411

19. Yang, J., Evans, D.: Dynamically inferring temporal properties. In: Workshop on Prog. Analysis for Softw. Tools and Eng. (2004) 23–28

20. Pacheco, C., Ernst, M.: Eclat: Automatic generation and classification of test inputs. In: Eur. Conf. on OO Prog. (2005) 504–527

21. Xie, T., Notkin, D.: Tool-assisted unit test selection based on operational violations. In: Int'l Conf. on Auto. Softw. Eng. (2003) 40–48

A Prioritization Approach for Software Test Cases Based on Bayesian Networks

Siavash Mirarab and Ladan Tahvildari

Department of Electrical and Computer Engineering,
University of Waterloo, Ontario, Canada N2L 3G1
{smirarab,ltahvild}@uwaterloo.ca

Abstract. An important aspect of regression testing is to prioritize the test cases which need to be ordered to execute based on specific criteria. This research work presents a novel approach to prioritizing test cases in order to enhance the rate of fault detection. Our approach is based on probability theory and utilizes Bayesian Networks (BN) to incorporate source code changes, software fault-proneness, and test coverage data into a unified model. As a proof of concept, the proposed approach is applied to eight consecutive versions of a large-size software system. The obtained results indicate a significant increase in the rate of fault detection when a reasonable number of faults are available.

Keywords: Test case Prioritization, Regression Testing, Bayesian Networks.

1 Introduction

Prioritizing existing test cases from earlier versions of software is one of the main techniques used to address the problem of regression testing. Regression testing is considered as one of the most expensive tasks in software maintenance activities [1]. Such a technique uses the test-suite developed for an earlier version of a software system to conform the new added requirement in the current version. Selecting all or a portion of the test-suite to execute which is referred to as Regression Selection Techniques (RST) can be very costly [2,3,4]. Furthermore using RST, testers do not have the option to adjust their test-effort to their budget. To provide the missing flexibility, researchers have introduced prioritization techniques [5,6] by means of which testers can order the test cases based on certain criteria, and then run them in the specified order and as much as they can afford. To further assist testers to adjust the cost and effort, models of cost-benefit analysis are introduced [7]. During the past ten years, there has been much research on techniques of prioritization [8,9,10,11,12,13].

Despite all the above-mentioned research activities, empirical studies indicate that there is a significant gap between optimal solutions to prioritization problem and proposed techniques [9]. Also, they show that the performance of different techniques depend largely on the target software system. Furthermore, one can imply that techniques using more than one factor typically perform better than

M.B. Dwyer and A. Lopes (Eds.): FASE 2007, LNCS 4422, pp. 276–290, 2007.

those with one criterion. Therefore, to fill the mentioned gap, we need to build techniques which can incorporate a diverse range of available data, from test coverage to history of fault detection.

In this paper, we present a novel test-suite prioritization framework which integrates various sources of information into one single model. Our technique is based on a probabilistic specification of the problem. Similar to the definition of Kim *at el.* [10], our prioritization approach is based on ordering test cases according to their success probability. The proposed process uses conditional probability and utilizes a Bayesian Network [14] model which takes advantage of source code modification information, univariate measures of fault-proneness, and test coverage data. We evaluate the performance of our technique using APFD (Average Percentage Faults Detected) [5] measure on eight consecutive versions of a large-size Java application augmented with hand-seeded faults; we then compare our results to some of the common techniques from literature. The results show that when there are reasonable number of faults in the source code, our proposed novel technique is capable of achieving better values of APFD in the comparison with other techniques.

The rest of the article is organized as follows: Section 2 deals with the problem statement. Then, our proposed approach to solve the problem is presented. Section 4 gives a brief introduction to Bayesian Networks (BN) while elaborating on how we have designed our BN model. Section 5 discusses the obtained results after applying our techniques on a large size case study. Finally we make conclusion and point out some future directions for this research work.

2 Problem Statement

The classic definition of test case prioritization is based on finding a permutation of test cases which can maximize an award function [5]. Kim *et al.* look at the same problem from a probabilistic point of view. They describe prioritization as: *i*) applying an RST technique, *ii*) assigning a selection probability to each of the remaining tests, *iii*) drawing a test case using the assigned probabilities, and *iv*) repeating until time is exhausted. Adopting the probabilistic nature of their description and with some modification, a prioritization can be considered as:

1. Gathering all "useful" evidences $\mathcal{E}_i$ from software system.
2. Using a "prioritization technique" to assign a probability of success to each test case t_i in test-suite $\mathbb{T}$, given all the evidences $P(\mathcal{T}_j|\mathcal{E}_1,\ldots,\mathcal{E}_n)$.
3. Selecting and running a test case from $\mathbb{T}$ based on the defined probability model.
4. Updating the $P(\mathcal{T}_j|\mathcal{E}_1,\ldots,\mathcal{E}_n)$ values when applicable.
5. Repeating step 4 until release criteria is met.

We do not think of the first step in Kim's description as a part of prioritization; thus, it is taken out. Moreover, in this approach some sort of selection is automatically done when low probabilities are assigned to test cases. However, in practice one may prefer to apply some less costly selection techniques before prioritization in order to reduce the size of test-suite. "Useful" evidence in step 1 means all information the "prioritization technique" of step 2 is interested in (e.g. test coverage information, code change). In step 2, the main part of this process, we have a set of random variables t_i, each of which reflect the outcome of a test case t_i from $\mathbb{T}$. These variables have two possible values of "Success" (meaning that a defect is detected) and "Failure". The event of "Success" in t_i is denoted as $\mathcal{T}_i$. A "prioritization techniques" is a systematic way to estimate all $P(\mathcal{T}_j|\mathcal{E}_1,\ldots,\mathcal{E}_n)$s. Step 3 is also slightly different than Kim's. Although the notion of drawing test cases using assigned probabilities is interesting in that it gives all test cases some selection chance and helps discover the residual faults, it is not the only option. One may simply order test cases according to their probability, particularly when experimentation is involved deterministic nature of the later approach is more appropriate. Step 4 is an important addition to previous definitions which provides a feedback mechanism to add the learned information from each test execution (e.g. its outcome) to the model defined in step 2. Note that this mechanism includes, but is not limited to the techniques of [5] where feedback is used while ordering test cases not after each run. Finally, in step 5 we generalize the stopping condition to "met release criteria" which can be anything from testing time exhaustion to reliability requirement satisfaction [15].

The proposed view of prioritization can be applied to existing techniques. In the following, two families of existing techniques are briefly described in accordance with the aforementioned view of prioritization problem.

- **Coverage-based Techniques.** The most important aspect of any technique is the set of evidences it takes advantage of. In this family of prioritization techniques, the evidence variable is the number of code elements that are covered by each test case. For example, at method level coverage-based technique, the number of covered methods is used to estimate the probability of success for each test case:

$$P(\mathcal{T}_j|\mathcal{E}) = \frac{the\ number\ of\ methods\ covered\ by\ t_i}{total\ number\ of\ methods}$$

- **Change-coverage Techniques.** In this family of techniques both information of test coverage and source code change are used as the evidence. At block level, for example, the estimation of success probability is:

$$P(\mathcal{T}_j|\mathcal{E}) = \frac{the\ number\ of\ changed\ blocks\ covered\ by\ t_i}{total\ number\ of\ changed\ blocks}$$

The main part of the described process is step 2 where one should estimate the probability of success for each test case. The problem that this paper addresses is to build such techniques. In the following section, our approach to solve this problem is described.

3   Proposed Approach

Our approach addresses the prioritization problem by: *i*) extracting different sets of evidence from the source code, *ii*) integrating all information to a single Bayesian network model, and *iii*) using probabilistic inference to compute $P(T_j|\mathcal{E})$ values. Fig. 1 illustrates a high-level schema of this approach. The first

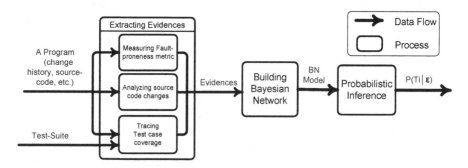

Fig. 1. Three Phases of Proposed Approach

step in performing prioritization is to gather all useful information that is to be included in the model. Our current solution exploits three sources of information: *software quality metrics*, *test coverage measures*, and *change analysis data*. *Extracting evidences* is undertaken in order to provide the necessary data for the next phase, *Building Bayesian Network*, in which an inclusive probabilistic model to relate these data is built. The details and rational behind using these evidences will be covered in the next section, where we give an in-depth description of the second phase. The last phase is to employ the probabilistic inference algorithms to associate to each test case its probability of success given the collected evidences. Note that the first and last phases are well-established research works and here we just make use of the existing contributions to implement them.

4   Building Bayesian Network

In this section, first we introduce Bayesian Networks briefly and then elaborate further on the second phase of our proposed process through which the other phases are more clarified.

4.1   Background: Bayesian Network

Bayesian Network (BN) is a special type of "probabilistic graphical models" [14]. A BN is a directed acyclic graph consisting of three elements: *nodes* representing random variables, *arcs* representing probabilistic dependency among those variables, and *Conditional Probability Distribution Table (CPT)* for each variable, given its parents. The nodes can be either evidence or latent variables.

An evidence variable is a variable of which we know its values (i.e. it is measured). Arcs specify the causal relation between variables. Each node has a table which includes the probabilities of outcomes of its variable given the values of its parents.

Bayesian networks reflect the belief of experts about the problem domain. They can be used to answer probabilistic queries. For example, based on the evidence (observed) variables, the posterior probability distributions of some other variables can be computed (probabilistic inference). However, designing a BN model is not a trivial task. There are two facets to modeling a BN, designing the structure and computing the parameters. Regarding the first issue, the notions of conditional independence and causal relation [16] can be of great help. Intuitively, two events (variables) are conditionally independent if knowing the value of some other variables makes the outcomes of those events independent. It is important to make sure that conditionally independent variables are not connected to each other. Designing based on causal relationships is one way to achieve that. For computing the parameters, expert knowledge, statistical learning, and probabilistic estimations can be used. One potential problem is that we may know how a variable is dependent on each of its parents, but do not have its distribution conditioned on all parents. In these situations, "noisy-OR" assumption can be helpful. The noisy-OR assumption gives the interaction between the parents and the child a causal interpretation and assumes that all causes (parents) are independent of each other in terms of their influence on the child [14]. More formally, this assumption asserts whatever prevents one parent to cause a child is independent from what prevents the other parents to cause the child.

4.2   Proposed BN Model

Empirical studies conducted in the literature indicate that an important factor in performance of a technique is the evidences it utilizes [9]. The rational behind using Bayesian networks for prioritization is to unify various types of evidences in one single model.

As mentioned in Section 4.1, modeling is the main focus in solving the problems using BN. A description of how three basic elements of a BN is designed in our approach follows:

Nodes. There are three categories of nodes in these models:

• **ce :** These variables represent change in the elements of the program. Each software element in the considered level of granularity (i.e. a class) has a node of this type. These variables can take a value of "Changed" or "Unchanged".

• **fe :** This category reflects our belief whether each element is faulty. Similar to the previous family, each element of the program has one node and each node can have the values of "Faulty", or "Non-Faulty".

• **t :** These variables represent the outcome of a test case which can be "Success" or "Failure". Each test case has one node of this type and the probability distributions of these nodes are what we are looking for $P(T_i|\mathcal{E})$.

Arcs. Each arc in a BN indicates a causal relation between variables of two connected nodes. There are two set of arcs in our network:

• **ce − fe :** Each **fe** node is the child of the corresponding (i.e. of the same code element) **ce** node. The existence of these arcs reflect the causal relation that changes to elements of software can introduce faults in the same element.

• **fe − t :** Each **t** node is the child of some **fe** nodes. These arcs imply the causal relation between presence of fault in a software element and success of test cases that examine that element.

In Fig. 2 the overall structure of the designed model is illustrated. Each **ce** node is connected to one **fe** node and the **fe** nodes are connected to an arbitrary number of **t** nodes.

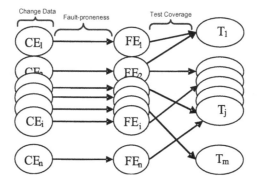

Fig. 2. The Structure of the Bayesian Network

CPT. Each category of nodes has its own Conditional Probability Table:

• $P(ce_i)$ **:** **ce** nodes are not the child of any other node, so their distribution is not conditional. These nodes are the only "observed" variables of the model. In a simple model, $P(ce_i = Changed)$ can be set to either 0 or 1, meaning that software is either "Changed" or "Unchanged". However, they also can be used to represent the amount of change an element has gone through. In this case ce_i variables mean the effective change of the element and $P(ce_i = Changed)$ reflects our belief that the element has been effectively changed.

$$P(ce_i = Changed) = ChangeIntensity(e_i)$$

In this formula, $ChangeIntensity(e_i)$ is a function which returns how much semantic change the element e_i has gone through. This function can be implemented with algorithms as simple as Unix diff. In our study, we have used an algorithm presented in [17] which uses byte code to estimate similarity between two versions of a program.

- $P(\mathbf{fe}_i|\mathbf{ce}_i)$: Each $\mathbf{fe}$ nodes is a child of one and only one parent, which is the corresponding $\mathbf{ce}$ variable. Considering that both $\mathbf{fe}$ and $\mathbf{ce}$ can take two values, the CPT will contain 4 values, two of which are trivial, since $P(\mathbf{fe} = Faulty|\mathbf{ce}) = 1 - P(\mathbf{fe} = Non\text{-}Faulty|\mathbf{ce})$. Therefore, we need to estimate two values: $P(\mathbf{fe} = Faulty|\mathbf{ce} = Changed)$ and $P(\mathbf{fe} = Faulty|\mathbf{ce} = Unchanged)$. In general, the probability of presence of fault in software is called fault-proneness and is profoundly studied in literature [18,19]. It is empirically shown that one can approximately predict the fault-proneness of code elements using software metrics. To build these models of fault-prediction, there are two major options: *multivariate* and *univariate* models. Univariate models estimate fault-proneness using one single metric. Multivariate models, on the other hand, are a linear combination of univariate models. To use multivariate models, one should "train" the model on a second program and apply the potentially biased model to the system in question. As empirically evaluated in [18], using this approach, multivariate models do not necessarily generate better results; thus, in this work we use univariate models. The aforementioned studies (and also an empirical study on the relation between APFD and software metrics [20]) indicate that measures of complexity and coupling are better indicators of fault-proneness. One specific study [19] has shown that coupling is a significantly better measure than other metrics. Although our model can fit in any software metric, here we use measures of coupling as an indicator fault-proneness:

$$P(\mathbf{fe}_i = Present|\mathbf{ce}_i = Changed) = \frac{\alpha\, CBO(e_i)}{\max(CBO(e_x))} + \delta_1,\ (\alpha + \delta_1 \leq 1)$$

In this formula, e_i is an element of the system, say a class, and CBO (Coupling between Objects) is an object-oriented metric from Chidamber and Kemerer suite [21] which counts the number of classes to which a given class is coupled (i.e. uses its methods and/or fields). The choice of this metric is based on the mentioned empirical studies. The dominator is a normalization factor and α and δ_1 bound the probability of fault introduction.

As for $P(\mathbf{fe}_i = Faulty|\mathbf{ce}_i = Unchanged)$, estimating this value is tricky because it represents the less probable situation that an element is faulty, even though it is not changed. This can happen because of residual faults (from previous versions) or because of the impact of changes in other elements. Estimating both causes is hard and calls for more thorough empirical studies. In current modelling we use the following formula:

$$P(\mathbf{fe}_i{=}Faulty|\mathbf{ce}_i{=}Unchanged) = \frac{\beta\, f\text{-}out(e_i)}{\max(f\text{-}out(e_x))} + \delta_2\,,\ (\beta + \delta_2 \ll \alpha + \delta_1 \leq 1)$$

Here, $f\text{-}out$ (fan out), is a measure of the number of classes an specific class is coupled to (i.e. uses them) [22]. Using this metric is mostly in order to capture change impacts. As known, the more fan out a class has, the more it is endangered by changes of other classes. The important invariant is that the probability of fault presence in unchanged elements should be much less than in changed elements. Let $\gamma = \frac{\alpha + \delta 1}{\beta + \delta 2}$. By adjusting γ (the change effect factor) we can control the degree to which the presence of change in an element raises our belief in its fault-proneness.

- $P(\mathbf{t}_i|\mathbf{fe}_1 \ldots \mathbf{fe}_n)$: Unlike the other node types, $\mathbf{t}$ nodes can have more than one parent. That is due to the fact that a test case may be able to find faults from different elements of the software. These values can be determined according to the coverage information of a test case. Normally, the information of test coverage is available only when test cases are executed and prioritization does not have any justification. The solution is to use the coverage information from previous versions for the current program. To further enhance the reliability of this solution, one may use heuristics of [12] (however, we believe even without these heuristics, the estimation is reasonable). Having test coverages, we estimate:

$$P(\mathbf{t}_i = Success|\mathbf{fe}_j = Faulty) = Cov(t_i, e_j)$$

Where $Cov(t_i, e_j)$ is a function returning the percentage of the code element j covered by test case i. This formula estimates the relation between a test case and one single element. However, to build the CPT we need the probability of success for a test given all combinations of values of $\mathbf{fe}$ variables. In this situation, the table would become enormous and its size would grow exponentially with the number of covered elements by a test. In order to cope with this problem, we make the noisy-OR assumption, explained in Section 4.1. The assumption is that the relation of a test case to an element is independent from its relation to any other element. It can be argued that the ability of a test case to reveal a fault in one element is not related to its fault revealing ability in other elements, hence the assumption. Having the noisy-OR assumption we can say:

$$P(\mathbf{t}_i|\mathbf{fe}_1 \ldots \mathbf{fe}_n) = 1 - (1 - P_0) \prod_j \frac{(1 - P(T_i|\mathbf{fe}_j = Faulty))}{1 - P_0} \qquad (1)$$

In this formula, P_0 is $P(T_i|\mathbf{fe}_1 = Non\text{-}Faulty, \ldots, \mathbf{fe}_n = Non\text{-}Faulty)$. This value (also called "leak") is the probability of a test case succeeding even though all of its related elements are non-faulty. This value should be zero unless the information of coverage is incomplete or there exists an integration fault. For consideration of these causes, a very small constant can be assigned to leak parameter. Formula 1 is a straight-forward usage of noisy-or formula (justification of this formula can be found in BN references such as [16]).

In this model $\mathbf{ce}$ nodes are observations and to estimate the distribution of $\mathbf{t}$ nodes (the desired variables), we need to perform probabilistic inference. There are many inference algorithms introduced for BNs which generally fall into two categories of exact and sampling algorithms. Due to well-structured nature (three layers of independent variables) of our network, we can use exact inference even for large systems. Details of how inference algorithms work are out of the scope of this paper but the general idea is first compiling the directed graph into a tree, and then updating the probabilities in the tree.

5 Experiment

To evaluate the proposed approach, we have built a semi-automated environment for test case prioritization. As a proof of concept, eight consecutive versions of Apache Ant [23] with a catalogue of 10 prioritization techniques are examined.

5.1 Prioritization Environment

To assist future experiments of test case prioritization, a semi-automated framework is implemented. Fig. 3 depicts a high-level schema of this system.

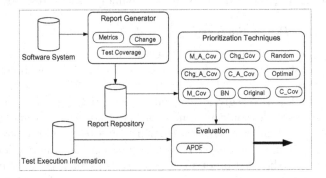

Fig. 3. The High-Level Schema of the Framework

The first subsystem, "Report Generator", is mostly implemented using external tools. To collect software metrics, a tool called ckjm [24] is used; for gathering coverage information Emma [25] is utilized and the change information is obtained from Sandmark [17] which is a watermarking program but provides interesting change track algorithms. In the second subsystem, "Prioritization Techniques", different techniques of prioritization are implemented. This subsystem uses generated reports from the first subsystem. For implementing the BN technique we have used Smile Library [26]. Finally, the last subsystem, "Evaluation", is responsible for measuring evaluation metrics (merely APFD).

5.2 Experiment Setup

Subject Program. Performing experiments in test case prioritization calls for many artifacts some of which are very expensive to gather. In particular, the subject program needs to have many faulty versions. Do *et al.* [27] have built a repository of C and Java open source programs with hand seeded faults called "Software-artifact Infrastructure Repository (SIR)". From their Java repository,

Table 1. Eight Consecutive Versions of Apache Ant

Metric Name	v0	v1	v2	v3	v4	v5	v6	v7
Faults Count	0	1	1	2	4	4	1	6
Test Case Count	0	28	34	52	52	101	104	105
Number of Classes	143	229	343	343	533	537	537	650
Lines Of Code (K)	23	37	57	57	95	97	97	124

Apache Ant has the most number of seeded faults and has a reasonable size (Table 1). We have used this program for all of our experimentation.

Evaluation Metric. To be able to compare our results to other empirical studies (esp. those of [8] as one of the rare studies focusing on Java programs), APFD is used as the evaluation metric. This metric aims to calculate fault detection rate by measuring the weighted average of the percentage of faults detected over the test suite execution period. APFD values range from 0 to 100 and higher numbers indicate faster fault detection rates. Its precise definition can be found in [5]. However, this metric has some drawbacks, for example, it neither takes into account the cost of each individual test nor the severity of faults.

Prioritization Techniques. In this study, ten prioritization techniques are examined. Table 2 lists these techniques. The first three are control techniques: Optimal is the best possible order computed in a greedy manner; Random orders randomly (the average of 50 runs); and Original is the original order of test cases. The next six techniques are based on [8] and use coverage information. Their difference is in evidences used, granularity level, and use of feedback mechanism. Here, feedback means adjusting the coverage information after adding any test case to the order such that elements that are already covered do not affect next selections ([8]). Finally, BN represents our approach where the parameters are set as: $\alpha = 0.8$, $\delta_1 = \delta_2 = 0.1$, and $\gamma = 8$.

Table 2. Prioritization Techniques Used in the Experimentation

Name	Evidences	Level	Feedback
Optimal	Fault Matrix	N/A	Yes
Random	Nothing	N/A	No
Original	Nothing	N/A	No
C_Cov (Class Coverage)	Coverage	Class	No
M_Cov (Method Coverage)	Coverage	Method	No
C_A_Cov (Class Additional Coverage)	Coverage	Class	Yes
M_A_Cov (Method Additional Coverage)	Coverage	Method	Yes
Chg_Cov (Change Coverage)	Coverage+Change	Class	No
Chg_A_Cov (Change Additional Coverage)	Coverage+Change	Class	Yes
BN	All	Class	No

5.3   Discussion on Obtained Results

The results of the case study are depicted in Fig. 4. Almost all techniques perform better than "random" and "original" (the two control techniques). As far as the level of granularity for coverage information is concerned, there is no meaningful difference between class level and method level techniques. This result is in accordance with past empirical studies (although to our knowledge, class-level coverage were not previously inspected), and suggests using class level coverage information which is much easier to obtain. Also, it is evident that techniques employing the feedback mechanism (or "additional techniques") bring about better results. Although using change data leads to a 2% increase in the average APFD value (Table 3), there is no strong evidence that they outperform techniques with merely coverage information.

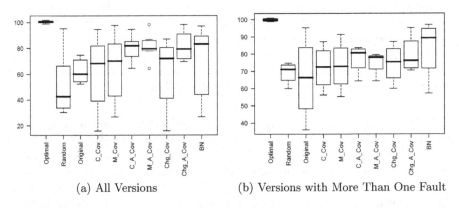

(a) All Versions   (b) Versions with More Than One Fault

Fig. 4. Boxplot Diagram of the Experiment Results

As for BN technique, the median of its AFPD values among all versions is better than all other techniques (however not significantly). When considering average instead of median, although it is performing better than most of the techniques, it is not the best when we consider all the versions of the subject program (Table 3). More specifically, in average BN is performing better than all techniques without feedback mechanism, but worse than additional techniques. Note that BN as implemented in this experimentation does not take the advantage of any feedback. Taking a closer look at the data, we noticed that in many versions, BN technique is achieving the best performance. To inspect why the average performance of BN is not the best, the fault information of the subject program should be considered. There are three versions of the ant case study which are seeded only with one fault. The results indicate that on these three versions, BN achieves less fault detection rate than the other techniques. However, one can argue that one single fault does not provide a reliable basis for comparison of techniques. Thus, we took out the versions with one fault (three versions were such) and compared the results again.

Fig. 4 (b) illustrates that BN is performing better than all the other techniques, in this scenario. There is strong evidence that BN median values are better than all other techniques. Moreover, it results in better average APFD values. In average, it produces 5% better APFD values than the second best technique(Chg_A_Cov), 11% better than the average of all techniques except optimal, and 17% better than the original order (Table 3).

Table 3. Average and Standard Error of Different Techniques

Technique	All Versions		More Than One Fault	
Name	Average	SD	Average	SD
Optimal	100.47917	1.03495	99.90429	0.89719
Original	52.62632	24.43825	66.03252	24.57651
Random	62.61275	9.54245	69.28956	6.47141
C_Cov	60.18787	30.75548	77.35928	8.79435
M_COV	63.94816	27.70506	73.09323	14.88074
C_A_Cov	79.80473	10.55892	72.11833	13.09055
M_A_COV	81.44635	10.32284	75.01233	7.09485
Chg_Cov	59.79584	29.16008	74.55728	11.42936
Chg_A_Cov	81.84868	11.73580	79.56256	11.04775
BN	67.66124	29.40874	83.19689	17.88581

To further inspect the effect of the number of faults, we depicted APFD of the techniques versus the number of faults. Fig. 5 shows when the fault count of the system grows, the APFD value of "additional" techniques decrease; whereas the BN see an increase in the value of APFD. This suggests that feedback employing techniques perform better when a very small number of faults are available, but as the potential number of faults grows BN is the most promising technique. This result sounds rational because BN is a model based on probabilities and the more number of trials, the more reliable the results of a probabilistic model.

Fig. 5 also shows another interesting phenomenon. While all "additional" techniques have a negative slop, the techniques with no feedback mechanism all see an increase in APFD with number of faults. This observation should be empirically evaluated because when generalized, it has a very important practical implication: when the software is believed to contain many faults, the use of feedback is not useful but in more reliable systems, when testers struggle to find the last faults, feedback can improve the rate of fault detection.

In conclusion, BN technique seems to perform better than any other technique inspected here, when there are more number of faults. In three out of four versions with more than one fault, the BN produced the best results. Therefore, authors believe that the BN technique will perform very well when applied in practice to software systems that typically contain much more faults.

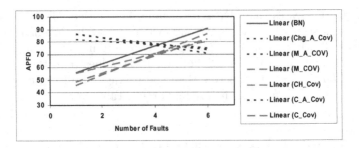

Fig. 5. APFD versus Fault Counts

6   Related Work

Many techniques for prioritization along with measures of assessing their performance have been introduced in literature. In [5], authors introduce APFD as a measure of fault detection rate and empirically evaluate their catalogue of techniques. In [9], more techniques with more than one criterion, are evaluated on larger case studies. In [8], the authors take a similar approach and evaluate similar techniques on Java programs and JUnit test cases.

Kim *et al.* [10] formulate test case prioritization based on the probability theory and focus on history-based prioritization to address the issue of continues software evolution and regression testing. They also introduce "total effort" and "fault-age" to measure cost-benefit trade-offs. Srivastava *et al.* have built Echelon [12] system to deal with prioritization in industrial environment. They propose extracting coverage information from byte-code for better performance and also provide some heuristics to address the high cost of gathering coverage information. Saff *et al.* [11] take a completely different approach by introducing continues testing. They developed a plug-in for Eclipse IDE and used developer behavior modelling to test software on the fly and during development. PORT [28] is another attempt in which potential defect severity and also issues related to testing of new code in regression testing are taken to account. More recently, Walcott *et al.* utilize Genetic Algorithms to solve the prioritization problem in a time-constrained situation [13].

On the other hand, employing Bayesian networks for testing has been addressed by some researchers. As early as 1997, in [29] authors described ways of modelling uncertainty in software into BN models that can be later used by testers and managers for either confirming, evaluating or predicting software uncertainties. In [30], authors use graphical models to provide a prediction model for the whole problem of software testing, and in [31] Bayesian networks is used to asses the overall software quality.

7   Conclusion and The Future Work

In this paper we first described test case prioritization problem from a probabilistic point of view, and then proposed a new approach to solve this problem using Bayesian networks. We introduced our framework to implement the approach and presented the results of a case study. The results suggest that the new approach can achieve high values of APFD, especially when the number of available faults are reasonable.

In the pursual of future research, first the results should be further inspected using empirical experiments and taking into account cost-benefit models. Also, the software faults in this case study are all hand-seeded and their representatives of real faults may be argued. Therefore, it is critical to evaluate this approach on programs that contain a reasonable number of real faults.

Moreover, the feedback mechanism as described in the problem statement section, can be added to this approach by simply making evidence nodes in BN after each test run. This may result in longer inference time, so cost-effectiveness should be carefully considered. The use of other metrics for fault-proneness and change analysis is another way of extending this work. Finally, other metrics of evaluation of prioritization techniques should be introduced and examined.

References

1. Leung, H.K.N., White, L.J.: Insights into regression testing. In: Proceedings on IEEE International Conference of Software Maintenance (ICSM). (1989) 60–69
2. Agrawal, H., Horgan, J.R., Krauser, E.W., London, S.: Incremental regression testing. In: Proceedings of the International Conference on Software Maintenance(ICSM). (1993) 348–357
3. Chen, Y.F., Rosenblum, D.S., Vo, K.P.: Testtube: A system for selective regression testing. In: Proceedings of the ACM International Conference on Software Engineering (ICSE). (1994) 211–220
4. Rothermel, G., Harrold, M.J.: A safe, efficient regression test selection technique. ACM Transactions on Software Engineering and Methodology 6 (1997) 173–210
5. Rothermel, G., Untch, R.H., Chu, C., Harrold, M.J.: Prioritizing test cases for regression testing. IEEE Transactions on Software Engineering 27 (2001) 929–948
6. Wong, W.E., Horgan, J.R., London, S., Bellcore, H.A.: A study of effective regression testing in practice. In: Proceedings of the IEEE International Symposium on Software Reliability Engineering(ISSRE). (1997) 264–274
7. Malishevsky, A.G., Rothermel, G., Elbaum, S.: Modeling the cost-benefits tradeoffs for regression testing techniques. In: Proceedings of the International Conference on Software Maintenance (ICSM). (2002) 204–213
8. Do, H., Rothermel, G., Kinneer, A.: Prioritizing JUnit test cases: An empirical assessment and cost-benefits analysis. Empirical Software Engineering: An International Journal 11 (2006) 33–70
9. Elbaum, S., Malishevsky, A.G., Rothermel, G.: Test case prioritization: A family of empirical studies. IEEE Transactions on Software Engineering 28 (2002) 159–182
10. Kim, J.M., Porter, A.: A history-based test prioritization technique for regression testing in resource constrained environments. In: Proceedings of the ACM International Conference on Software Engineering(ICSE). (2002) 119–129
11. Saff, D., Ernst, M.D.: Reducing wasted development time via continuous testing. In: Proceedings of the IEEE International Symposium on Software Reliability Engineering(ISSRE). (2003) 281–292

12. Srivastava, A., Thiagarajan, J.: Effectively prioritizing tests in development environment. In: Proceedings of the ACM SIGSOFT International Symposium on Software Testing and Analysis(ISSTA). (2002) 97–106
13. Walcott, K.R., Soffa, M.L., Kapfhammer, G.M., Roos, R.S.: Timeaware test suite prioritization. In: Proceedings of the IEEE International Symposium on Software Testing and Analysis(ISSTA). (2006) 1–12
14. Pearl, J.: Probabilistic Reasoning in Intelligent Systems: Networks of Plausible Inference. Morgan Kaufmann Publishers Inc., San Francisco, CA, USA (1988)
15. Okumoto, K., Goel, A.L.: Optimum release time for software systems based on reliability and cost criteria. Journal of Systems and Software 1 (1980) 315–318
16. Jensen, F.V.: Bayesian Networks and Decision Graphs. (2001)
17. Christian Collberg, Ginger Myles, M.S.: An empirical study of java bytecode programs. Technical Report TR04-11, Department of Computer Science, Univeristy of Arizona (2004)
18. Briand, L., Wüst, J.: Empirical studies of quality models in object-oriented systems. Advances in Computers 56 (2002) 98–167
19. Gyimothy, T., Ferenc, R., Siket, I.: Empirical validation of object-oriented metrics on open source software for fault prediction. IEEE Transactions on Software Engineering 31 (2005) 897–910
20. Elbaum, S., Gable, D., Rothermel, G.: Understanding and measuring the sources of variation in the prioritization of regression test suites. In: Proceedings of the IEEE International Symposium on Software Metrics(METRICS). (2001) 169–179
21. Chidamber, S.R., Kemerer, C.F.: Towards a metrics suite for object oriented design. In: Proceedings of the Annual ACM SIGPLAN Conference on Object-oriented Programming Systems, Languages, and Applications (OOPSLA). (1991) 197–211
22. Fenton, N.E., Pfleeger, S.L.: Software Metrics: A Rigorous and Practical Approach. PWS Publishing Co., Boston, MA, USA (1998)
23. : Apache Ant (2005) http://ant.apache.org.
24. : CKJM (2006) http://www.spinellis.gr/sw/ckjm/.
25. : Emma (2006) http://emma.sourceforge.net/.
26. : Genie/Smile (2005-2006) http://genie.sis.pitt.edu/.
27. Do, H., Elbaum, S., Rothermel, G.: Supporting controlled experimentation with testing techniques: An infrastructure and its potential impact. Empirical Software Engineering: An International Journal 10 (2005) 405–435
28. Hema Srikanth, Laurie Williams, J.O.: System test case prioritization of new and regression test cases. In: Proceedings of the International Symposium on Empirical Software Engineering. (2005) 64–73
29. Ziv, H., Richardson, D.J.: Constructing bayesian-network models of software testing and maintenance uncertainties. In: Proceedings of the International Conference on Software Maintenance(ICSM). (1997) 100–109
30. Wooff, D., Goldstein, M., Coolen, F.: Bayesian graphical models for software testing. IEEE Transactions on Software Engineering 28 (2002) 510–525
31. Fenton, N.E., Krause, P., Neil, M.: Probability modelling for software quality control. Journal of Applied Non-Classical Logics 12 (2002) 173–188

Redundancy Based Test-Suite Reduction

Gordon Fraser and Franz Wotawa*

Institute for Software Technology
Graz University of Technology
Inffeldgasse 16b/2
A-8010 Graz, Austria
{fraser,wotawa}@ist.tugraz.at

Abstract. The size of a test-suite has a direct impact on the costs
and the effort of software testing. Especially during regression testing,
when software is re-tested after some modifications, the size of the test-
suite is important. Common test-suite reduction techniques select subsets
of test-suites that achieve given test requirements. Unfortunately, not
only the test-suite size but also the fault detection ability is reduced
as a consequence. This paper proposes a novel approach where test-
cases created with model-checker based techniques are transformed such
that redundancy within the test-suite is avoided, and the overall size is
reduced. As test-cases are not simply discarded, the impact on the fault
sensitivity is minimal.

1 Introduction

Software testing is a process that consumes a large part of the effort and resources
involved in software development. Especially during regression testing, when
software is re-tested after some modifications, the size of the test-suite has a
large impact on the total costs. Therefore, the idea of test-suite reduction (also
referred to as test-suite minimization) is to find a minimal subset of the test-suite
that is sufficient to achieve the given test requirements.

Various heuristics have been proposed to approximate a minimal subset of the
test-suite. These techniques can reduce the number of test-cases in a test-suite
significantly. However, experiments have revealed that the quality of the test-
suite suffers from this minimization. Even though the test requirements with
regard to which the minimization was made are still fulfilled by the minimized
test-suite, it has been shown that the overall ability to detect faults is reduced.
In many scenarios, especially in the case of safety related software, such a degradation is unacceptable.

This paper introduces a novel approach to test-suite reduction. This approach
tries to identify those parts of the test-cases that are truly redundant. Redundancy in this context means that there are no faults that can be detected with

* This work has been supported by the FIT-IT research project "Systematic test case
generation for safety-critical distributed embedded real time systems with different safety integrity levels (TeDES)"; the project is carried out in cooperation with
Vienna University of Technology, Magna Steyr and TTTech.

M.B. Dwyer and A. Lopes (Eds.): FASE 2007, LNCS 4422, pp. 291–305, 2007.

the redundant part of a test-case, and not without. Instead of discarding test-cases out of a test-suite, the test-cases are transformed such that the redundancy is avoided. That way, the test-suite is minimized with regard to the number of test-cases and the total number of states, while neither test coverage nor fault detection ability suffer from the degradation experienced in previous approaches.

The approach uses the state information that is included in functional tests created with model-checker based test-case generation approaches. The model-checker is also used within an optimized version of the approach. An empirical evaluation shows that the approach is feasible.

This paper is organized as follows: Section 2 first introduces the problem of test-suite reduction and points out drawbacks of current solutions. Then, the necessary preliminaries for the remainder of the paper are discussed. Section 3 presents a new definition of redundancy in the context of test-cases, and shows how test-suites can be optimized in order to reduce redundancy. Section 4 describes experiments and results with regard to this optimization. Finally, Section 5 concludes the paper with a discussion of the results and an outlook.

2   Preliminaries

In this section, test-suite reduction and previous solutions are presented. Then, the necessary preliminaries for our approach are introduced.

2.1   Test-Suite Reduction

During regression testing the software is re-tested after some modifications. The costs of running a complete test-suite against the software repeatedly can be quite high. In general, not all test-cases of a test-suite are necessary to fulfill some given test requirements. Therefore, the aim of test-suite reduction is to find a subset of the test-cases that still fulfills the test requirements. The original test-suite reduction problem is defined by Harrold et al. [1] as follows:

Given: A test-suite TS, a set of requirements $r_1, r_2, , , r_n$ that must be satisfied to provide the desired test coverage of the program, and subsets of TS, $T_1, T_2, ..., T_n$, one associated with each of the r_is such that any one of the test-cases t_j belonging to T_i can be used to test r_i.

Problem: Find a representative set of test-cases from TS that satisfies all r_is.

The requirements r_i can represent any test-case requirements, e.g., test coverage. A representative set of test-cases must contain at least one test-case from each subset T_i. The problem of finding the optimal (minimal) subset is NP-hard. Therefore, several heuristics have been presented [1,2,3].

Test-suite reduction results in a new test-suite, where only the relevant subset remains and the other test-cases are discarded. Intuitively, removing any test-case might reduce the overall ability of the test-suite to detect faults. In fact, several experiments [4,5,6] have shown that this is indeed the case, although there are other claims [7]. Note that the reduction of fault sensitivity would also occur when using an optimal instead of a heuristic solution.

In this paper we introduce a new approach to test-suite minimization which does not have a negative influence on the fault detection ability. However, first we need to introduce some basic concepts and definitions.

2.2   Model-Checker Based Testing

In this paper we consider test-cases generated with model-checker based methods. A model-checker is a tool originally intended for formal verification. In general, a model-checker takes as input a finite-state model of a system and a temporal logic property and efficiently verifies the complete state space of the model in order to determine whether the property is fulfilled or not. If the property is not fulfilled then a counter-example is returned, which is a sequence of states beginning in the initial state and leading to the violating state. There are several different approaches that exploit this counter-example mechanism for automated test-case generation [8,9,10,11,12,13,14]. Model-checkers use Kripke structures as model formalism:

Definition 1. *Kripke Structure: A Kripke structure K is a tuple $K = (S, s_0, T, L)$, where S is the set of states, $s_0 \in S$ is the initial state, $T \subseteq S \times S$ is the transition relation, and $L : S \rightarrow 2^{AP}$ is the labeling function that maps each state to a set of atomic propositions that hold in this state. AP is the countable set of atomic propositions.*

A model-checker verifies whether a model M satisfies a property P. If M violates P, denoted as $M \nvDash P$, then the model-checker returns a trace that illustrates the property violation. The trace is a finite prefix of an execution sequence of the model (path):

Definition 2. *Path: A path $p := \{s_0, s_1, ...\}$ of Kripke structure K is a finite or infinite sequence such that $\forall i > 0 : (s_i, s_{i+1}) \in T$ for K.*

Informally, the states of a Kripke structure and its traces consist of value assignments to its input, output and internal variables. Input variables are those that are provided by the environment to the model, output variables are returned to the environment by the model, and internal variables are not visible outside of the model. A trace can be used as a test-case by providing the input variables to the system under test (SUT), and then comparing whether the outputs produced by the SUT match those of the trace. Therefore, a trace can be seen as a test-case:

Definition 3. *Test-Case: A test-case t is a finite prefix of a path p of Kripke structure K.*

The number of transitions a test-case consists of is referred to as its *length*. E.g., test-case $t := \{s_0, s_1, ..., s_i\}$ has a length of $length(t) = i$. We consider such test-cases where the expected correct output is included. This kind of test-cases is referred to as *passing* or *positive* test-cases. The result of the test-case generation is a *test-suite*. The aim of test-suite reduction is to optimize test-suites with respect to their size and total length:

Definition 4. *Test-Suite: A test-suite TS is a finite set of n test-cases. The size of TS is n. The overall length of a test-suite TS is the sum of the lengths of its test-cases t_i: $length(TS) = \sum_{i=1}^{n} length(t_i)$.*

Coverage criteria are used to measure test-suite quality. In the model-based scenario we assumed, we are mainly interested in model-based coverage criteria. A coverage criterion describes a set of structural items or aspects that a test-suite should cover. The test coverage is the percentage of items that are actually covered, i.e., reached during test-case execution. A model-based coverage criterion can be expressed as a set of properties (*trap properties* [8]) where a test-case covers an item if the according property is violated.

Definition 5. *Test Coverage: The coverage C of a test-suite TS with regard to a coverage criterion represented by a set of properties $\mathcal{P}$ is defined as the ratio of covered properties to the number of properties in total:*

$$C = \frac{1}{|\mathcal{P}|} \cdot |\{x | x \in \mathcal{P} \wedge covered(x, TS)\}|$$

The predicate $covered(a, TS)$ is true if there exists a test-case $t \in TS$ such that t covers a, i.e., $t \nvDash a$.

The fault detection ability describes the potential of a test-suite at detecting faults. The higher this ability, the more faults can be detected. In practice, the mutant score [15] is used as an estimate for the fault detection ability. A mutant results from a single syntactic modification of a model or program. The mutant score of a test-suite is the ratio of mutants that can be distinguished from the original to mutants in total. A mutant is detected if the execution leads to different results than expected.

Definition 6. *Test-case execution: A test-case $t = \{s_0, s_1, ...\}$ for model K is executed by taking the input variables of each state s_i, providing them to the SUT with a suitable test framework. These values and the produced output values represent an execution trace $tr = \{s'_0, s'_1, ...\}$. A fault is detected, iff $\exists (s'_i, s'_{i+1}) \in tr : (s'_i, s'_{i+1}) \notin T$ for K. (s_i, s_{i+1}) is referred to as a step.*

3   Test-Suite Redundancy

Previously, redundancy was used to describe test-cases that are not needed in order to achieve a certain coverage criterion. As the removal of such test-cases leads to a reduced fault detection ability, they are not really redundant in a generic way. In contrast, we say a test-case contains redundancy if part of the test-case does not contribute to the fault detection ability. This section aims to identify such redundancy, and describes possibilities to reduce it.

3.1   Identifying Redundancy

Intuitively, identical test-cases are redundant. For any two test-cases t_1, t_2 such that $t_1 = t_2$, any fault that can be detected by t_1 is also identified by t_2 and vice versa, assuming the test-case execution framework assures identical preconditions for both tests. Similarly, the achieved coverage for any coverage criterion is identical for both t_1 and t_2. Clearly, a test-suite does not need both t_1 and t_2.

The same consideration applies to two test-cases t_1 and t_2, where t_1 is a prefix of t_2. t_1 is subsumed by t_2, therefore any fault that can be detected by t_1 is also detected by t_2 (but not vice versa). In this case, t_1 is redundant and is not needed in any test-suite that contains t_2. In model-based testing it is common practice to discard subsumed and identical test-cases at test-case generation time [12].

This leads to the kind of redundancy which we are interested in: Model-checker based test-case generation techniques often lead to such test-suites where all test-cases begin with the same initial state. From this state on different paths are taken, but many of these paths are equal up to a certain state. Any fault that occurs within such a sub-path can be detected by any of the test-cases that begins with this sub-path. Within these test-cases, the sub-path is *redundant*.

This kind of redundancy can be illustrated by representing a set of test-cases as a tree. The initial state that all test-cases share is the root-node of this tree. A sub-path is redundant if it occurs in more than one test-case. In the tree representation, any node below the root node that has more than one child node contains redundancy. If there are different initial states, then there is one tree for each initial state.

Definition 7. *Test-Suite Execution Tree: Test test-cases $t_i = \{s_0, s_1, ...s_l\}$ of a test-suite TS can be represented as a tree, where the root node equals the initial state common to all test-cases: $root(TS) = s_0$. For each successive, distinct state s_j a child node is added to the previous node s_i:*

$$s_j : (s_i, s_j) \in t_i \rightarrow s_j \in children(s_i)$$

The depth of the tree equals the length of the longest test-case in TS. $children(x)$ denotes the set of child nodes of node x. Consider a test-suite consisting of three test-cases (letters represent distinct states): "A-B-C", "A-C-B", "A-C-D-E". The execution tree representation of these test-cases can be seen in Figure 1(a). The rightmost C-state has two children, therefore the sub-path A-C is contained in two test-cases; it is redundant. The execution tree can be used to measure redundancy:

Definition 8. *Test-Suite Redundancy: The redundancy R of a test-suite TS is defined with the help of the execution tree:*

$$R(TS) = \frac{1}{n-1} \cdot \sum_{x \in children(root(TS))} \mathcal{R}(x) \tag{1}$$

The redundancy of the tree is the ratio of the sum of the redundancy values $\mathcal{R}$ for the children of the root-node and the number of arcs in the tree ($n - 1$, with

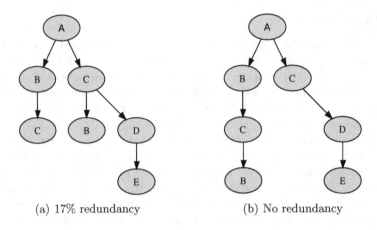

(a) 17% redundancy   (b) No redundancy

Fig. 1. Simple test-suite with redundancy represented as execution tree

n nodes). The redundancy value $\mathcal{R}$ is defined recursively as follows:

$$\mathcal{R}(x) = \begin{cases} (|children(x) - 1|) + \sum_{c \in children(x)} \mathcal{R}(c) & if \quad children(x) \neq \{\} \\ 0 & if \quad children(x) = \{\} \end{cases}$$

$$(2)$$

The example test-suite depicted as tree in Figure 1(a) has a total of 7 nodes, where one node besides the root node has more than one child. Therefore, the redundancy of this tree equals $R = \frac{1}{7-1} \cdot \sum_{x \in children(root(TS))} \mathcal{R}(x) = \frac{1}{6} \cdot (0 + (1+0)) = \frac{1}{6} = 17\%$.

A test-suite contains no redundancy if for each initial state there are no test-cases with common prefixes, e.g., if there is only one test-case per initial-state.

3.2   Removing Redundancy

Having identified redundancy, the question now is how to reduce it. This section introduces an approach to solve this problem. It has already been stated that the removal of test-cases from a test-suite has a negative impact on the fault detection ability, therefore this is not an option. Instead, the proposed solution is to transform the test-cases such that the redundant parts can be omitted.

For each test-case t_i of test suite TS a common prefix among the test-cases is determined. If such a prefix is found, then the test-case is redundant for the length of the prefix and only interesting after the prefix. If there is another test-case t_j that ends with the same state as the prefix does, then the remainder of the test-case t_i can be appended to t_j, and t_i can safely be discarded. This algorithm is shown in Listing 1. It is of interest to find the longest possible prefixes, therefore the search for prefixes starts with the length of the test-case under examination and then iteratively reduces the length down to 1. This also guarantees that duplicate or subsumed test-cases are eliminated.

The function *find_test* searches for a test-case that ends with the same state as the currently considered prefix, its worst time complexity therefore is $O(|TS|)$. The complexity of *has_prefix* is $O(n)$ as it depends on the prefix length. Appending and deleting test-cases take constant time. These operations are nested in a loop over $|TS|$, which in turn is called for all possible prefix lengths. Finally, this is done for each test-case in TS. Therefore, the worst-case complexity of this algorithm is $O(|TS|^2 \cdot n \cdot (|TS| + n))$; with realistic test-suite sizes it is still applicable. The algorithm terminates for every finite test-suite. In the listing, $t[n]$ denotes the nth state of test-case t, and $t[-1]$ the last state of t.

```
for each t in TS do
   for n := length(t) downto 1 do
      for each t2 in TS do
         if has_prefix(t2, t, n) and t2 != t then
            t3 := find_test(TS, t[n])
            if t3 != None then
               append_postfix(t3, t, n)
               delete(TS, t)
               break
            end if
         end if
      end for
   end for
end for
```

Listing 1. Test-suite transformation

The algorithm has to make non-deterministic choices when selecting a test-case as a source for the prefix, when selecting a test-case to look for the common prefix and when searching for a test-case to append to. These choices have an influence on how fast a test-suite is processed. In addition, the number of test-cases remaining in the final reduced test-suite also depends on these choices. The success of the reduction depends on whether there are suitable test-cases where parts of other test-cases can be appended. A test-case that is necessary for removal of a long common prefix might be used to append another test-case with a shorter common prefix earlier. In that case, the long prefix could not be removed unless there was another suitable test-case. Determination of the optimal order would have to take all permutations of the test-suite order into consideration and is therefore not feasible. In practice, the algorithm is implemented such that test-cases are selected sequentially in the order in which they are stored in the test-suite.

Figure 1(b) illustrates the result of this optimization applied to the Figure 1(a). The test-case A-C-B has the common prefix A-C, and there is a test-case ending in C, therefore the postfix B of A-C-B is appended to A-B-C, resulting in A-B-C-B.

This algorithm optimizes the total costs of a test-suite with respect to two factors: It reduces the total number of test-cases (test-suite size), and it reduces the overall number of states contained in the test-suite (test-suite length). In the resulting test-suite individual test-cases can be longer than in the original test-suite. We assume that the costs of executing two test-cases of length n are higher than that of executing one test-case of length $2 \cdot n$ because of setup and pull-down overhead. Therefore, it is preferable to have fewer but longer test-cases instead of many small ones. This assumption is for example also made in [16], where the test-case generation aims to create fewer but longer test-cases.

While the computational complexity of the algorithm is high, the success depends on the actual test-suite. A test-suite might contain significant redundancy but have few test-cases that are suitable for appending, in which case not much optimization can be achieved. In addition, the order in which test-cases are selected has an influence on the results.

As we assumed a model-checker based test-case generation approach, we can make use of the model-checker for optimization purposes. If appending is not possible, then the model-checker can be used to create a 'glue'-sequence to append the postfix to an arbitrary test-case. Of course the model-checker is not strictly necessary to perform this part; there are other possibilities to find a path in the model. However, the model-checker is a convenient tool for this task, especially if it is already used for test-case generation in the first place. Listing 2 lists the extended algorithm. The function *choose_nondeterministic(TS)* chooses one test-case out of the test-suite TS non-deterministically. This choice has an influence on the length of the resulting glue-sequence. An optimal algorithm would have to consider the lengths of all such possible glue-sequences, and therefore calculate all of them. A distance heuristic is conceivable, which estimates the distance between the final state of a test-case and the state the glue sequence should lead to. For reasons of simplicity, the prototype implementation used for experiments in this paper makes a random choice.

The function *create_sequence* calls the model-checker in order to create a suitable glue sequence. A sequence from state a to state b can be created by verifying a property that claims that such a path does not exist. If such a sequence exists, the counter-example consists of a sequence from the initial state to a, and then a path from a to b. For example, when using computation tree logic (CTL) [17], this query can be stated as: AG a -> !(EF b).

The presented algorithms reduce both the number of test-cases and the total test-suite length, while previous methods selected subsets of the test-suite. Therefore, the effects on the quality of the resulting test-suite are different.

Each step of a test-case adhering to Definition 3 fully describes the system state. A model-checker trace consists of the values of all input and output variables as well as internal variables. A fault is detected if the actual outputs of the implementation differ from those of the test-case. Therefore, any fault that

```
for each t in TS do
  for n := length(t) downto 1 do
    for each t2 in TS do
      if has_prefix(t2, t, n) and t2 != t then
        t3 := find_test(TS, t[n])
        if t3 != None then
          append_postfix(t3, t, p)
          delete(TS, t)
          break
        end if
      else
        t3 := choose_nondeterministic(TS)
        if t3 != t then
          s = create_sequence(t3[-1], t[n])
          append(t3, s)
          append_postfix(t3, t, n)
          delete(TS, t)
          break
        end if
      end if
    end for
  end for
end for
```

Listing 2. Test-suite transformation with glue sequences

occurs deterministically at a certain state can be detected with a step of a test-case, no matter when this step is executed. As the test-suite reduction guarantees that only redundant steps as parts of prefixes are removed, any fault that can be detected by a test-suite TS, can also be detected by the test-suite resulting from reduction of TS. It is conceivable that there are faults that do not deterministically occur at certain system states. For example, a fault might only occur after a certain sequence has been executed, or if a state is executed a certain number of times. However, we have not found such a fault in our experiments. Furthermore, it is equally possible that the transformation leads to such test-cases that can detect previously missed non-deterministic faults.

Definition 5 allows arbitrary properties for measuring test coverage. Whether the test-suite reduction has an impact on the test coverage depends on the actual properties. If the coverage depends on the order of not directly adjacent steps in the test-case, then splitting a prefix from a test-case and appending the remainder to another test-case can reduce the coverage. For example, transition pair coverage [18] requires all pairs of transitions to be covered. A transition pair can be split during the transformation. However, the appending can also lead to transition pairs previously uncovered. In practice, many coverage properties do not consider the execution order, e.g. transition or full-predicate coverage [18], or coverage criteria based on the model-checker source file [9].

4   Empirical Evaluation

This section presents the results of an empirical evaluation of the concepts described in the previous sections. The evaluation aims to determine how much reduction can be achieved with the presented algorithms, and how they perform in comparison to other approaches. Furthermore, the effects on coverage and mutant score are analyzed.

4.1   Experiment Setup

The experiment uses three examples, each consisting of a model and specification written in the language of the model-checker NuSMV [19]. For each model, 23 different test-suites are created with different methods (various coverage criteria for coverage based methods, different mutation operators for mutation based approaches, property based methods). The details of these methods are omitted for space reasons and because they are not necessary to interpret the results. In addition, a set of mutant models is created for each model. The use of a model-checker allows the detection of equivalent mutants, therefore only non-equivalent mutants are used for the evaluation of a mutant score. Car Control (CA) is a simplified model of a car control. The Safety Injection System (SIS) example was introduced in [20] and has since been used frequently for studying automated test-case generation. Cruise Control (CC) is based on [21]. A set of faulty implementations for this example was written by Jeff Offutt. The presented algorithms are implemented with Python, and the symbolic model-checker NuSMV is used.

4.2   Lossy Minimization with Model-Checkers

For comparison purposes, a traditional minimization approach is applied to the model-checker scenario, similarly to Heimdahl and Devaraj [6]. Model-based coverage criteria can be expressed as *trap properties* [8] (Section 2.2). The test-cases are converted to models and then the model-checker is challenged with the resulting models and the trap properties. For each trap property that results in a counter-example it is known that the test-case covers the according item.

A minimized subset of the test-suite achieving a criterion can be determined by calculating the covered properties for each test-case, and then iteratively selecting the test-case that covers the most yet uncovered properties. We choose *transition coverage* as first example coverage criterion. Black [13] proposed a test-case generation approach based on mutation of the reflected transition relation. The mutated, reflected properties can be used similarly to trap properties for test-case generation, to determine a kind of mutant score and also for minimization. In order to distinguish this from the mutant score determined by execution of the test-case against mutant models we dub the former *reflection coverage*.

4.3   Results

Tables 1, 2 and 3 list the average values of the minimization of the 23 test-suites for the three example models. "Redundancy" denotes the algorithm in

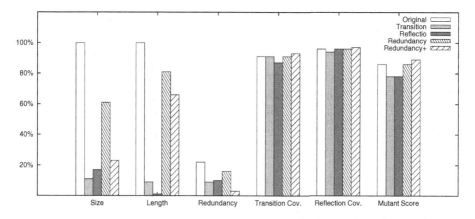

Fig. 2. Comparison of reduction methods, average percentage over all three example models and 23 test-suites each

Listing 1, and "Redundancy+" the extended version of Listing 2. In all cases the coverage-based reduction techniques result in smaller test-suites than the direct redundancy based approach. The extended redundancy based approach comes close to the coverage based approaches with respect to test-suite size. The test-suite length is reduced proportionally to the test-suite size for coverage based techniques, while as expected the redundancy based length savings are not as significant. Again, the extended algorithm achieves better results, showing that the potential saving in redundancy is bigger than what is added by the glue sequences. In general, even though the reduction in the total length is smaller with the redundancy approaches than with the coverage approaches, it is still significant and shows that the approach is feasible.

The test coverage of coverage minimized test-suites is not changed for the criterion that is used for minimization, while a degradation with the other criterion is observable. In contrast, the redundancy based approach has no impact on the coverage of either criterion. The extended redundancy approach even leads to a minor increase of the coverage, due to the glue sequences. As for the mutant score, the coverage based approaches lead to a degradation of up to 16%, while the redundancy approach has no impact on the mutant score, and the extended redundancy approach again results in a slight increase. Figure 2 sums up the results of the experiments for all models and test-suites. As these experiments use only models and mutants of the models, this raises the question whether the results are different with regard to actual implementations. Therefore, the Cruise Control test-suites are run against the set of faulty implementations. Table 4 lists the results. They are in accordance with those achieved with model mutants, which indicates the validity also for implementations.

Figure 3 illustrates the effects of the order in which test-cases are selected at several points in the algorithm as box-plots. The box-plots illustrate minimum, maximum, median and standard deviation for the achieved reduction with the 23 test-suites per example, each randomly sorted 5 times. Figure 3(a) shows the

Table 1. Results in average for Cruise Control example

Method	Size	Length	Redundancy	Transition Coverage	Mutant Score (Reflection)	Mutant Score
Original	36,55	213,77	44,55%	89,16%	95,93%	87,31%
Transition	6,23	35,6	32,00%	89,16%	94,46%	79,70%
Reflection	6,59	37,36	30,30%	78,67%	95,93%	73,42%
Redundancy	27,91	186,09	36,99%	89,16%	95,93%	87,31%
Redundancy+	8,95	152,73	4,82%	89,86%	96,44%	89,13%

Table 2. Results in average for SIS example

Method	Size	Length	Redundancy	Transition Coverage	Mutant Score (Reflection)	Mutant Score
Original	21,87	644,04	10,45%	89,28%	95,15%	78,29%
Transition	3,26	84,17	2,51%	89,28%	93,42%	68,72%
Reflection	4,91	126,3	4,53%	87,63%	95,15%	72,70%
Redundancy	14,48	440,39	6,15%	89,28%	95,15%	78,29%
Redundancy+	5,52	268,78	0,46%	91,23%	96,19%	81,42%

Table 3. Results in average for Car Control example

Method	Size	Length	Redundancy	Transition Coverage	Mutant Score (Reflection)	Mutant Score
Original	54,09	1351,91	10,44%	95,78%	96,07%	92,84%
Transition	3,36	71,32	3,05%	96,78%	93,76%	85,09%
Reflection	7,68	152,27	5,30%	95,54%	96,07%	87,62%
Redundancy	25,68	1182,82	4,69%	95,78%	96,07%	92,84%
Redundancy+	11,36	1058,05	1,17%	99,03%	97,53%	95,16%

effects on the test-suite sizes. As the use of glue sequences makes it possible to append to any test-case, the order has no effect on the resulting test-suite size in our experiments, therefore there is no deviation. There is insignificant variation when not using glue sequences, and also only minor variation in the test-suite length (Figure 3(b)). In contrast, the choice of a test-case to append to using a glue sequence has a visible influence on the resulting test-suite length. This suggests the use of a distance heuristic instead of the random choice.

Both presented algorithms have high worst-case complexity. However, many factors contribute to the performance: the test-suite size, the lengths of the

Table 4. Mutant scores for cruise-control implementation mutants

Original	Transition	Reflection	Redundancy	Redundancy+
75,8%	39,1%	37,2%	75,8%	76,5%

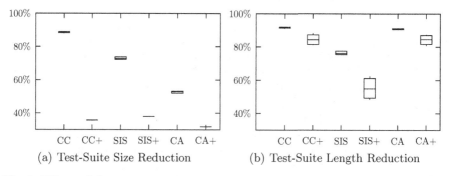

Fig. 3. Effects of the test-case order, as percentage value of original sizes and lengths. Minimization using glue sequences is denoted by a '+' after the example name.

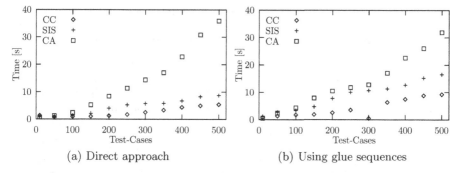

Fig. 4. Minimization time vs. test-suite size

test-cases, the contained redundancy, the suitability of test-cases for the transformation, the order in which test-cases are selected, the effort of calculating glue sequences, etc. Figure 4 depicts the performance of the minimization for the three example models for different test-suite sizes executed on a PC with Intel Core Duo T2400 processor and 1GB RAM. Notably, the computation time for the car controller example increases more than for the other examples. This example has a bigger state space, therefore appending is not easily possible. Figure 4(b) shows that there is less difference in the increase in computation time when using glue sequences. The additional computational effort introduced by the generation of the glue sequences is very small, compared to its effect. However, performance measurement is difficult, as the redundancy is not constant along the test-suites used for measurement. In order to examine the scalability of the approach, minimization was also tested on a complex example with a significantly bigger test-suite. The example is a windscreen wiper controller provided by Magna Steyr. For a set of 8000 test-cases, basic minimization takes 35m22s. This example also shows the effects of the model complexity, as the calculation of glue sequences is costly for this model: Minimization with glue sequences takes 2h1m56s. Obviously, the performance is specific to each application and test-suite, but it seems to be acceptable in general.

5   Conclusion

In this paper we have introduced an approach to minimize the size of a test-suite with regard to the number of test-cases and the total length of all test-cases. The approach detects redundancy within the test-suite and transforms test-cases in order to avoid the redundancy. In contrast to previous approaches the quality of the resulting test-suites does not suffer with regard to test coverage or fault detection ability from this minimization under certain conditions. In fact, experiments showed that the resulting test-suites can even be slightly improved. The experiments also showed that the reduction is significant, although not as large as with approaches that heuristically discard test-cases.

One drawback of this approach is the run-time complexity of the algorithm. However, even without further optimizations the approach is applicable to realistic test-suites without problems. The transformation relies on information that might not be available in all test-suites. Complete state information is necessary, as is provided by model-checker based test-case generation approaches. There are several possibilities to continue work on this approach:

- It would be desirable to optimize the basic algorithm with regard to its worst case execution time.
- The non-deterministic choice might not always lead to the best results. Heuristics for choosing test-cases could lead to better reduction.
- The algorithms presented in this paper sequentially analyze the test-cases in a test-suite. Therefore, a single run might not immediately eliminate all the redundancy. It is conceivable to iteratively call the algorithm until the redundancy is removed completely. This is likely to lead to test-suites of very small size, where each test-case is very long.
- In this paper, a scenario of model-checker based testing was assumed. It would be interesting to evaluate the applicability to other settings.
- The presented definition of redundancy only considers common prefixes. However, common path segments might also exist within test-cases. Consideration of this kind of redundancy might lead to further optimizations.

References

1. Harrold, M.J., Gupta, R., Soffa, M.L.: A methodology for controlling the size of a test suite. ACM Trans. Softw. Eng. Methodol. 2(3) (1993) 270–285
2. Gregg Rothermel, Mary Jean Harrold, J.v.R.C.H.: Empirical studies of test-suite reduction. Software Testing, Verification and Reliability 12(4) (2002) 219–249
3. Zhong, H., Zhang, L., Mei, H.: An experimental comparison of four test suite reduction techniques. In: ICSE '06: Proceeding of the 28th international conference on Software engineering, New York, NY, USA, ACM Press (2006) 636–640
4. Jones, J.A., Harrold, M.J.: Test-suite reduction and prioritization for modified condition/decision coverage. IEEE Trans. Softw. Eng. 29(3) (2003) 195–209
5. Rothermel, G., Harrold, M.J., Ostrin, J., Hong, C.: An empirical study of the effects of minimization on the fault detection capabilities of test suites. In: ICSM '98: Proceedings of the International Conference on Software Maintenance, Washington, DC, USA, IEEE Computer Society (1998) 34

6. Heimdahl, M.P.E., Devaraj, G.: Test-Suite Reduction for Model Based Tests: Effects on Test Quality and Implications for Testing. In: ASE, IEEE Computer Society (2004) 176–185

7. Wong, W.E., Horgan, J.R., London, S., Mathur, A.P.: Effect of test set minimization on fault detection effectiveness. In: ICSE '95: Proceedings of the 17th international conference on Software engineering, ACM Press (1995) 41–50

8. Gargantini, A., Heitmeyer, C.: Using Model Checking to Generate Tests From Requirements Specifications. In: ESEC/FSE'99: 7th European Software Engineering Conference, Held Jointly with the 7th ACM SIGSOFT Symposium on the Foundations of Software Engineering. Volume 1687., Springer (1999) 146–162

9. Rayadurgam, S., Heimdahl, M.P.E.: Coverage Based Test-Case Generation Using Model Checkers. In: Proceedings of the 8th Annual IEEE International Conference and Workshop on the Engineering of Computer Based Systems (ECBS 2001), IEEE Computer Society (2001) 83–91

10. Hamon, G., de Moura, L., Rushby, J.: Automated Test Generation with SAL. Technical report, Computer Science Laboratory, SRI International (2005)

11. Callahan, J.R., Easterbrook, S.M., Montgomery, T.L.: Generating Test Oracles Via Model Checking. Technical report, NASA/WVU Software Research Lab (1998)

12. Ammann, P., Black, P.E., Majurski, W.: Using Model Checking to Generate Tests from Specifications. In: ICFEM. (1998)

13. Black, P.E.: Modeling and Marshaling: Making Tests From Model Checker Counterexamples. In: Proc. of the 19th Digital Avionics Systems Conference. (2000)

14. Okun, V., Black, P.E., Yesha, Y.: Testing with Model Checker: Insuring Fault Visibility. In Mastorakis, N.E., Ekel, P., eds.: Proceedings of 2002 WSEAS International Conference on System Science, Applied Mathematics & Computer Science, and Power Engineering Systems. (2003) 1351–1356

15. Ammann, P., Black, P.E.: A Specification-Based Coverage Metric to Evaluate Test Sets. In: HASE, IEEE Computer Society (1999) 239–248

16. Hamon, G., de Moura, L., Rushby, J.: Generating Efficient Test Sets with a Model Checker. In: Proceedings of the Second International Conference on Software Engineering and Formal Methods (SEFM'04). (2004) 261–270

17. Clarke, E.M., Emerson, E.A.: Design and synthesis of synchronization skeletons using branching-time temporal logic. In: Logic of Programs, Workshop, London, UK, Springer-Verlag (1982) 52–71

18. Offutt, A.J., Xiong, Y., Liu, S.: Criteria for generating specification-based tests. In: ICECCS, IEEE Computer Society (1999)

19. Cimatti, A., Clarke, E.M., Giunchiglia, F., Roveri, M.: NUSMV: A New Symbolic Model Verifier. In: CAV '99: Proceedings of the 11th International Conference on Computer Aided Verification, London, UK, Springer-Verlag (1999) 495–499

20. Bharadwaj, R., Heitmeyer, C.L.: Model Checking Complete Requirements Specifications Using Abstraction. Automated Software Engineering 6(1) (1999) 37–68

21. Kirby, J.: Example NRL/SCR Software Requirements for an Automobile Cruise Control and Monitoring System. Technical Report TR-87-07, Wang Institute of Graduate Studies (1987)

Testing Scenario-Based Models*

Hillel Kugler[1], Michael J. Stern[2], and E. Jane Albert Hubbard[1]

[1] New York University, New York, NY, USA
kugler@cs.nyu.edu,
jane.hubbard@nyu.edu
[2] Yale University, New Haven, CT, USA
Michael.Stern@yale.edu

Abstract. The play-in/play-out approach suggests a new paradigm for system development using scenario-based requirements. It allows the user to develop a high level scenario-based model of the system and directly execute system behavior. The supporting tool, the Play-Engine has been used successfully in several projects and case-studies. As systems developed using this method grow in size and complexity, an important challenge is maintaining models that are well understood in terms of their behaviors and that satisfy the original intension of the system developers. Scenario-based methods are advantageous in early stages of system development since behaviors can be described in isolated fragments. A trade-off for this advantage, however, is that larger models comprising many separate scenarios can result in executable behavior that is difficult to understand and maintain. A methodology for facile testing of scenario-based requirements is needed. Here, we describe a methodology and supporting prototype implementation integrated into the Play-Engine for testing of scenario-based requirements. We have effectively applied the method for testing a complex model containing several hundred scenarios.

1 Introduction

Scenarios have been used in many approaches to describe system behavior [1,22,19], especially in the early stages of system design. This paper deals with a scenario-based approach that uses the language of live sequence charts (LSCs) [5] and the Play-Engine tool [11,12] and extends it to support the testing of scenario-based models.

One of the most widely used languages for specifying scenario-based requirements is that of message sequence charts (MSCs, adopted in 1996 by the ITU [24]), or its UML variant, sequence diagrams [23]. Sequence charts (whether MSCs or their UML variant) possess a rather weak partial-order semantics that does not make it possible to capture many kinds of behavioral requirements of a system. To address this, while remaining within the general spirit of scenario-based visual formalisms, a broad extension of MSCs has been proposed, called

---

* This research was supported in part by NIH grant R24 GM066969.

M.B. Dwyer and A. Lopes (Eds.): FASE 2007, LNCS 4422, pp. 306–320, 2007.
© Springer-Verlag Berlin Heidelberg 2007

live sequence charts (LSCs) [5]. Among other features, LSCs distinguish between behaviors that must happen in the system (universal) from those that may happen (existential). A universal chart contains a *prechart*, which specifies the scenario which, if successfully executed, forces the system to satisfy the scenario given in the actual chart body. Existential charts specify sample interactions between the system and its environment, that must be satisfied by at least one system run. Thus, existential charts do not force the application to behave in a certain way in all cases, but rather state that there is at least one set of circumstances in which a certain behavior occurs. The distinction between mandatory (hot) and provisional (cold) behavior applies also to other LSC constructs, e.g., conditions and locations, thus creating a rich and expressive language. In addition to required behavior, LSCs can also explicitly express forbidden behavior ("anti-scenarios").

A methodology for specifying and validating requirements, termed the "play-in/play-out approach", and a supporting tool called the Play-Engine is described in [11,12]. Play-in is an intuitive way to capture requirements by demonstrating the behavior on a graphical representation of the system, while play-out is a method for executing LSC requirements, giving the feeling of working with an actual system. The expressive power of universal charts, based on the pattern "prechart implies main chart", forms the basis of an executable semantics for an LSC requirement model. In play-out mode, the Play-Engine monitors progress within charts and performs system events in the main charts for universal charts that have been activated, trying to complete all universal charts successfully. As the events are being executed, their effects are visualized via a Graphical User Interface (GUI), thus providing an animation of system behavior. The combination of an expressive specification language, a convenient method for capturing the requirements by playing them in on a GUI, and an executable framework that uses the same GUI for visualization, makes the Play-Engine a promising approach for modeling and system development, as shown by several projects [16,15,4,9,21].

In general, systems developed in any language are difficult to validate as they become large and complex, and a variety of verification and testing techniques have been developed to aid this process. For a number of reasons, the fragmented nature of scenario-based behavioral specifications makes large-scale modeling efforts that use languages and tools like LSCs and the Play-Engine particularly difficult to validate. First, unanticipated violations of the requirements may occur during play-out due to the interaction between several different LSCs. Furthermore, while the LSC language contains techniques for representing systems that contain significant levels of behavioral non-determinism, non-deterministic language structures increase the complexity of avoiding such LSC violations. Second, debugging LSC models is aided by the ability to visualize active LSCs during execution, showing graphically the progress along each active chart. However, visualization in the current Play-Engine implementation does not scale well for systems with hundreds of simultaneously active charts.

This work has been motivated by a project on modeling biological systems using tools for software and system design. Biological systems are in general very complex. Even the relatively small and well-defined subsystem we have focused on - VPC fate specification in the nematode C. *elegans* – involved constructing and testing a model of several hundred LSCs [17,15]. The size and complexity of this model (which is significantly larger than that of other Play-Engine models and also of most models used in other scenario-based approaches reported in the literature) required us to address several issues that can typically be ignored when dealing with "text-book" examples or small case studies, and to find solutions that are efficient and scale well as the system grows. In this paper we propose a testing-based method to address these challenges. The main strengths of our approach is the ability to apply it to large LSC models, a smooth integration into the Play-Engine tool and development process, and a user-friendly presentation of the test results.

2   LSCs and Play-Out Definitions

This section reviews the main ideas and definitions underlying the language of live sequence charts and the play-out execution method. For a detailed and systematic treatment the reader is referred to [5, 11, 12]. The main strength of live sequence charts over classical message sequence charts is the distinction between existential and universal charts. Common to both universal and existential charts is the notion of a scenario, in which several objects described by vertical lines communicate by exchanging messages described using horizontal arrows. A scenario induces a partial order which is determined by the order along an instance line and by the fact that a message can be received only after it is sent.

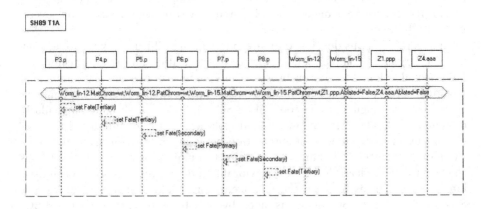

Fig. 1. Example of an existential chart

Existential charts have a semantic interpretation close to that of a basic MSC in classical MSCs. LSC semantics requires that for an existential LSC there must be at least one run of the system satisfying the scenario, it does not require that this scenario hold for all runs. The chart appearing in Fig. 1 is an existential chart as denoted by the dashed borderline. The scenario starts with a condition - an assertion that requires specific property values for some of the objects. The condition implies a synchronization over all participating objects. The scenario proceeds by objects sending (self) messages. For this chart to be satisfied all messages specified should occur but the ordering between them is not restricted since they appear on different object lines. This interpretation of existential charts is useful in early system design for demonstrating possible behavior, or in biological modeling for capturing experimental observations, but is too weak in terms of expressive power to define causality relations and provide executable semantics.

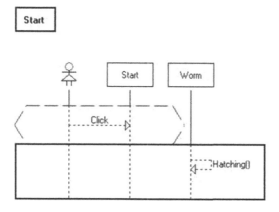

Fig. 2. Example of a simple universal chart

For this reason, LSCs introduce the concept of a universal chart, which describes requirements that must hold for all runs, and is therefore constrained to specific circumstances specified by a scenario appearing in the prechart. An example of a simple universal chart appears in Fig. 2. Universal charts are denoted by a solid borderline. According to the LSC in Fig. 2, if the Click method is sent from the user to the Start object, as specified in the prechart (dashed hexagon), the Hatching method appearing in the main chart must occur. The fact that this is a universal LSC means that this must hold for all system runs, i.e., for every run, each Click method must be eventually followed by a Hatching method.

The LSC language is rich and supports many constructs; a flavor of the language is demonstrated using a more complex universal chart appearing in Fig. 3. The prechart does not include a single message as in Fig. 2 but rather describes a more complex behavior. The condition labeled SYNC in the prechart restricts the ordering of events such that the prechart is satisfied and the main chart activated only if the `Hatching` method is followed by a `setFate(Primary)` message. The two `VPC` instances in Fig. 3 are symbolic instances, they represent the behavior of the VPC class, which can contain many concrete instances (in our biological model there are actually six VPCs). The behavior captured in Fig. 3 is that if the prechart holds, the relevant VPC will send the method `LS` to its right neighbor. An assignment appearing at the beginning of the main chart and binding conditions for the symbolic VPC instances (appearing in the ellipses) are used to capture this required behavior.

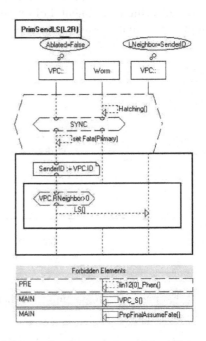

Fig. 3. Example of a more complex universal chart

We now present an outline of the formal definition of LSC semantics, capturing the requirements for a system to satisfy an LSC specification.

Formally, a **mode** of an LSC defines for each chart whether it is existential or universal.

$$mod : m \rightarrow \{existential, universal\}$$

An **LSC specification** is a pair

$$LS = \langle M, mod \rangle,$$

where M is a set of charts, and mod is the mode of each chart.

The **language** of the chart m, denoted by $\mathcal{L}_m$, is defined as follows:

For an existential chart, $mod(m) = existential$, the language includes all traces for which the chart is satisfied at least once.

For a universal chart, $mod(m) = universal$, the language includes all traces for which each time the prechart is satisfied the behavior specified in the main chart follows.

Next we define for a given system S, which is compatible with an LSC specification LS (i.e., the system includes all objects, properties and messages referred to in the LSC specification) when the system satisfies the LSC specification.

Definition 1. *A system S* **satisfies** *the LSC specification $LS = \langle M, mod \rangle$, written $S \models LS$, if:*

1. $\forall m \in M, \quad mod(m) = universal \Rightarrow \mathcal{L}_S \subseteq \mathcal{L}_m$
2. $\forall m \in M, \quad mod(m) = existential \Rightarrow \mathcal{L}_S \cap \mathcal{L}_m \neq \emptyset$

Here $\mathcal{L}_S$ is the language consisting of all traces of system S.

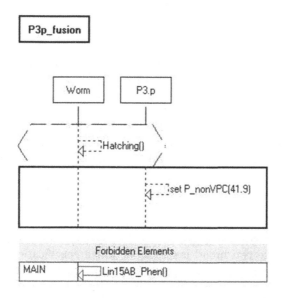

Fig. 4. Activated LSC

Play-out is a method that attempts to execute an LSC specification LS directly. This contrasts with a process in which a system S is constructed manually to satisfy the specification LS. The idea behind play-out is actually simple, yet leads to a surprisingly useful execution method. In response to an external event performed by the user, the Play-Engine monitors all participating universal LSCs to determine if a prechart has reached its maximal locations, thus activating the main chart. In our example, if the user has clicked on the Start button, the prechart of the LSC in Fig. 2 reaches its maximal locations and, as a result, activates the main chart. The Play-Engine, in response, will execute the method Hatching appearing in the main chart, thus fulfilling the requirement of this

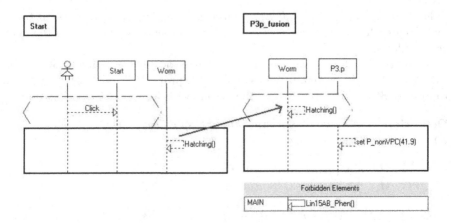

Fig. 5. Cascade of LSC activation

universal chart. Executing the method `Hatching` as specified in the main chart of Fig. 2, in turn will activate the LSC of Fig. 4, since the `Hatching` method is the only event appearing in the prechart of Fig. 4. The Play-Engine will then execute the message `setP_nonVPC(41.9)`. This is a typical situation in play-out, where executing a message in one LSC activates a new LSC, creating a cascade of events, as illustrated for our example in Fig. 5. A sequence of events carried out by the Play-Engine as a response to an external event input by the user is called a *superstep*. Play-out assumes that the Play-Engine can complete a superstep before the next external event is performed by the user.

While play-out is an effective method for executing LSCs, it does not guarantee satisfying the LSC specification. Thus, the system requirements for satisfying an LSC specification as presented in Definition 1 do not necessarily hold. Therefore, a mechanism is needed to test whether specifications have, in fact, been satisfied. There are two broad instances in which specifications can fail to be satisfied: (1) there may be existential charts that are never satisfied; and (2) some universal charts may be violated. The latter may be due to an unforeseen interaction between several different universal LSCs. A blatant example of universal LSC violation is when two charts are actually contradictory. One such simple example consists of two LSCs, both being activated by the same message **a** appearing in the prechart, and containing the two messages **b** and **c** in the main chart. One chart requires that the ordering between the events is **b,c** while the other chart requires that the ordering is **c,b**. A less blatant violation can occur if play-out is unable to execute the requirements correctly. The play-out mechanism of [11] is rather naive when faced with nondeterminism, and makes essentially an arbitrary choice among the possible responses. This choice may later cause a violation of the requirements, whereas a different choice could have satisfied the requirements. Technically, the nondeterminism has several causes: (1) the partial order semantics among events in each chart; (2) the ability to separate scenarios in different charts without having to state explicitly how they should be composed; and (3) an explicit nondeterministic choice construct, which can be used in conditions. This nondeterminism, although very useful in early requirement stages, can cause undesired under-specification when one attempts to consider LSCs as the system's executable behavior using play-out.

To address the challenge of arbitrary "dead ends" occurring in instances of non-determinism, [8] introduces a technique for executing LSCs, called *smart play-out*. It takes a significant step towards removing the sources of nondeterminism during execution, proceeding in a way that eliminates some of the dead-end executions that lead to violations. Smart play-out uses model-checking to execute and analyze LSCs. Smart play-out, like more ambitious synthesis methods, does not currently scale to handle large models, especially when using the full-range of LSC constructs, including symbolic instances [20] and time [11]. For this reason we have focused our work on using play-out and developing testing methods to detect those cases in which play-out does not execute the LSC requirements correctly. After the problems are detected and fixed, testing is used to increase the confidence in the correctness of play-out for the new model.

3   Execution Configurations

The testing of system behavior often requires the analysis of specific variations of distinct behavior fragments. These variations can be represented in related sets of "execution configurations". The execution configuration allows the user to specify the LSCs that should be considered by the Play-Engine while executing a model in play-out mode. An example of the execution configuration dialog is shown in Fig. 6. The dialog is composed of three sections: the first allows the user to select the participating universal LSCs, the second to select traced LSCs — either universal or existential charts, and the third designates the LSC search order. Charts selected as traced LSCs are monitored for their progress, but do not affect the execution itself. Thus, traced universal charts that are not in the set of participating LSCs will be monitored, and any activation or violation of them will be detected. However, a chart that is only traced will not cause any events in its main chart to occur. The LSC search order contained in the third section is used by the play-out execution algorithm while searching for the next event to be executed.

We have extended the Play-Engine to support handling and saving multiple execution configurations for the same model, allowing the user to select among them an active execution configuration. This allows the simultaneous maintenance of several variants of an LSC model, differing in the modeling of certain aspects of the system, values of various parameters, or corresponding to different levels of abstraction. The testing of these alternative models can be helpful in developing the system, in testing different possible implementation alternatives, and in fine tuning parameters.

Our extension allows the user to add, edit and delete execution configurations. There is always exactly one active execution configuration, specified by the user, which is used in play-out mode to determine the LSCs participating in the

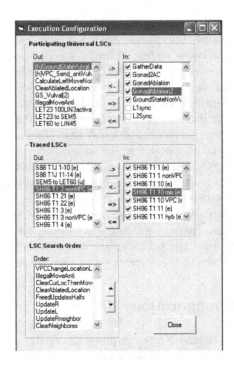

Fig. 6. The execution configuration dialog

execution, the traced LSCs and the search order. For certain applications, the ability to change the execution configuration while in the middle of play-out may be an interesting and useful feature. Currently, however, changing the active execution configuration is not allowed while in the middle of a play-out session. To set a new active execution configuration, play-out must first be stopped, the new active execution configuration set, and only then can play-out be reactivated.

4   The Testing Environment

We have created a testing tool that allows batch runs. Using the tool, the user designates a test plan that includes sets of initial configurations (also called jumpstarts) paired with iteration numbers, as shown in Fig. 7. The user specifies when to end an iteration by designating a specific universal LSC; upon the successful completion of that LSC, the iteration ends and a new one begins. This termination LSC, therefore, must be one that will be activated and successfully completed in every run, thus ensuring that the iteration will end and that the test plan execution can advance.

For each pair of initial configuration and iteration, the user can specify as part of the test plan which execution configuration to use. If no execution configuration is selected for a certain pair of initial configuration and iteration, the last active execution configuration is used. The ability to specify an execution

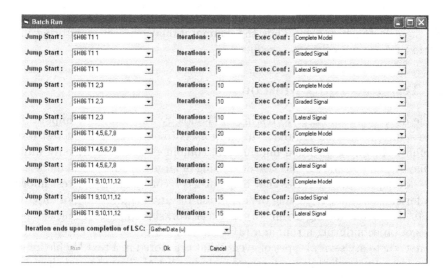

Fig. 7. Batch Mode Dialog

configuration permits testing several variants of a model as part of the same test plan, allowing convenient comparison of the test results.

We have added a number of additional features that are convenient for testing. One feature allows the user to develop a scenario-based model that does not depend on the search order or execution policy. This is effected by selecting a mode in which the LSC order is randomly permuted rather than fixed by the active execution configuration. This feature can help uncover problems that were not observable while running the model under a specific execution order.

Another set of features permits the user to allow running an unspecified number of iterations in order to satisfy a specific set of existential charts and an initial configuration. Under these conditions, the tool will run iterations until all of these existential charts are satisfied. Since it is often unknown a priori whether the model is indeed capable of satisfying all charts, an additional feature was implemented to avoid getting stuck in one initial configuration: the tool can be made to alternate between initial configurations that still have not satisfied all of their target charts, until all tests and charts are satisfied or until the tool is stopped by the user. The user can also set a maximum bound on the runtime or number of iterations after which the execution will be stopped, even if all of the existential charts have not been satisfied. These features are particularly necessary for the nondeterministic / probabilistic aspects of a model, where satisfying the relevant existential charts from a given initial configuration typically requires running multiple iterations.

Multiple execution configurations are also helpful for models that have large sets of existential charts that need to be satisfied, but only smaller subsets of these charts that need to be monitored per test. The user can create corresponding execution configurations that vary in the list of traced charts and use them in the test plan. Thus the computational price of monitoring many charts that are not relevant is reduced.

5   Test Recording Methods

While developing an effective testing methodology and tool, it is important to store sufficient information that will allow users to examine relevant test results carefully. Adequate recorded information, combined with user-friendly ways to display it, can provide for effective debugging of large scenario-based models. We have developed three features that help gather, record and display test information for effective understanding of simulation results: (1) a text log of important events that occur during a run; (2) an excel worksheet for recording key properties of objects during a run; and (3) a full run trace.

First, there are several types of events that are stored in a text log file for each of the runs. In the default mode, these include a list of all existential charts that have been traced to completion and universal charts that have been violated. In a more detailed mode, we additionally record when universal charts become activated (the prechart has completed successfully), and when universal charts are completed successfully. In addition, general information on the test plan, execution configurations used, and execution time is stored at the beginning and end of this log file.

Second, links to an excel worksheet have been enabled to store additional information from a simulation. The Play-Engine supports basic excel functions, which can be referred to in new or existing LSCs at specific time points to record relevant information, e.g., values of properties for participating objects. The user can determine exactly which information will be recorded, and at which relevant time points during a run. Typically, information for each iteration will be written at a distinct location in the excel sheet, for example in a new row. These results can then easily be examined in the excel file, and scripting options for excel and connection to existing tools may be used to allow manipulation and analysis of the collected data.

Finally, a full trace of the runs in batch mode can be recorded and saved. These traces can then be replayed after the test execution has ended to examine interesting results. A recorded run can be executed without the relevant LSCs participating, since the recorded run stores all event occurrences. All of the events are displayed on the graphical user interface (GUI) as in normal play-out mode, but the execution of recorded runs is much faster, allowing users to examine interesting traces more efficiently.

6   Applications and Testing Methodology

We have effectively applied our method to a complex biological model [16] containing several hundred scenarios, and are currently evaluating the method on a telecommunication application designed by France Telecom [4]. In this section we describe the basic steps performed in testing a model and outline some methodological guidelines derived from our initial experience. Some of the testing tool features have been designed with a goal of automating specific steps.

The batch run mode format for testing differs in certain fundamental ways from the standard manual play-out mode, thus necessitating some system reconfiguration prior to testing. Some of these adjustments are enabled by features of the Play-Engine tool itself, while others require altering some of the LSCs. The major difference between these two modes of play-out stems from the nature of the interactions between the system and its environment. The Play-Engine supports specification of reactive systems, providing an explicit distinction between the system and its environment. Environment objects are either an external user, a more abstract "environment", any object explicitly designated as external, or the global clock. In a manual play-out session, the user performs the events initiated by these environment objects, while the play-out execution engine performs all system events in response. By contrast, testing is performed in batch run mode with no user interaction, so it requires working with a closed system, where the environment is modeled and considered part of the system. To enable this closed-environment testing, the user creates interface system objects which appear in the LSCs instead of the environment objects, and all external objects are changed to system objects. In testing mode, time progresses automatically by the play-out mechanism according to the play-out execution semantics [10]. For testing behaviors that in manual play-out mode require user interaction due to external events, the interaction must be modeled explicitly using LSCs, by either modifying the existing LSCs or constructing new ones. Various initial system configurations can be pre-set in jumpstarts, obviating the need for the user to manually play these in. Jumpstarts can also serve as shortcuts in manual play-out mode as well.

Once the reconfigurations associated with system-environment interactions are in place, the user next prepares a test plan containing pairs of initial configurations and iteration numbers as described above. If there are several variants of models or large sets of traced LSCs, then appropriate execution configurations are created and used for the test plan. The user runs the test plan, a task that can typically run for several hours until all iterations are completed. Due to the size and complexity of current scenario-based models, the testing effort can also be distributed between several machines, each running a Play-Engine version and performing tests independently.

Next, the test results are examined by the user. Chart violations reported in the log file are worthwhile examining first, since these violations usually indicate problems in the model that must be fixed before investing much time in analyzing the other detailed results or viewing detailed simulations. Additional potential violations for universal charts can occur if the main chart was not completed successfully before the iteration ended. This may occur due to a real problem or just as a consequence of arbitrarily stopping the run when the designated LSC marking the end of the iteration is completed.

After several rounds of correcting the LSCs in the model and running the test suite, the user converges to a model with no test results showing violations of universal charts. The log file is next examined to determine if, for all tests, all relevant existential charts are satisfied. For existential charts that have not been satisfied, the user tries to determine whether they represent a possible outcome that was not observed (possibly due to probabilistic choices and a limited number of iterations) or an impossible outcome. The user can run this test again with a larger number of iterations if the former reason is suspected.

Runs that satisfy existential charts provide evidence of desirable behavior. To strengthen one's confidence that these are indeed the expected results, it is useful to examine the recordings for some of these runs and observe the simulation via the GUI. Runs that do not satisfy any existential charts represent potential new behaviors. In software or system development, the user should examine the run to decide if it is indeed a desirable behavior, and, if so, an appropriate matching existential chart can be added to the test suite. Otherwise the LSC model should be corrected to prevent this run. In the modeling of biological systems, if this run is clearly at odds with previous biological observations, the model must be corrected. Otherwise, this is a possible prediction of the model that can be tested experimentally. When the set of existential charts is rich enough, it is easier to find such interesting runs and then examine them more carefully.

7   Related Work

Scenarios have been recognized to be useful as part of the testing process. In [18] a methodology and tool called TestConductor is introduced that uses a subset of LSCs to monitor and test a UML model whose behavior is specified using statecharts. TestConductor is integrated into the Rhapsody tool [14]. A mapping and automatic translation for generating test descriptions in the standard test description language TTCN-3 directly from message sequence charts is described in [6]. Story boards are an alternative means for capturing scenarios; an approach utilizing these scenarios for testing, integrated into the Fujaba tool, is described in [7]. An approach for modeling use cases and scenarios in the abstract state machine language with applications for testing is described in [2]. Common to all of these approaches is that the scenarios serve as a requirement language, while the model or system that is to be tested is described in another language, e.g., statecharts or code. In this paper we use the same scenario-based language (LSCs) for describing the system model and the requirements. In fact, in our approach there is not such a clear separation between the system and the requirements, since the executable system model is directly based on running the requirements. Model-based testing [13, 3] is a general approach in which a model of the system under test is used for supporting and automating common testing tasks such as test generation, test execution and test evaluation. A major goal is to reduce the manual effort involved in the testing activity.

Acknowledgments

We would like to thank Dan Barak for his help in the implementation of the testing module and its integration into the Play-Engine, and Na'aman Kam for helpful discussions on the need for enhanced automation in the analysis of complex biological models. This research was supported in part by NIH grant R24 GM066969.

References

1. D. Amyot and A. Eberlein. An Evaluation of Scenario Notations and Construction Approaches for Telecommunication Systems Development. *Telecommunications Systems Journal*, 24(1):61–94, 2003.
2. M. Barnett, W. Grieskamp, Y. Gurevich, W. Schulte, N. Tillmann, and M. Veanes. Scenario-Oriented Modeling in AsmL and its Instrumentation for Testing. In *Proc. 2nd Int. Workshop on Scenarios and State Machines (SCESM'03)*, 2003.
3. M. Barnett, W. Grieskamp, L. Nachmanson, W. Schulte, N. Tillmann, and M. Veanes. Towards a Tool Environment for Model-Based Testing with AsmL. In *Proc. 3rd Int. Workshop on Formal Approaches to Software Testing (FATES '03)*, volume 2931 of *Lect. Notes in Comp. Sci.*, pages 252–266. Springer-Verlag, 2004.
4. P. Combes, D. Harel, and H. Kugler. Modeling and Verification of a Telecommunication Application using Live Sequence Charts and the Play-Engine Tool. In *Proc. 3rd Int. Symp. on Automated Technology for Verification and Analysis (ATVA '05)*, volume 3707 of *Lect. Notes in Comp. Sci.*, pages 414–428. Springer-Verlag, 2005.
5. W. Damm and D. Harel. LSCs: Breathing life into message sequence charts. *Formal Methods in System Design*, 19(1):45–80, 2001. Preliminary version appeared in Proc. 3rd IFIP Int. Conf. on Formal Methods for Open Object-Based Distributed Systems (FMOODS'99).
6. M. Ebner. TTCN-3 Test Case Generation from Message Sequence Charts,. In *Workshop on Integrated-reliability with Telecommunications and UML Languages (ISSRE04:WITUL)*, 2004.
7. L. Geiger and A. Zündorf. Story driven testing - SDT. In *Proceedings of the fourth international workshop on Scenarios and state machines: models, algorithms and tools (SCESM '05)*, pages 1–6. ACM Press, 2005.
8. D. Harel, H. Kugler, R. Marelly, and A. Pnueli. Smart play-out of behavioral requirements. In *Proc. 4th Intl. Conference on Formal Methods in Computer-Aided Design (FMCAD'02)*, Portland, Oregon, volume 2517 of *Lect. Notes in Comp. Sci.*, pages 378–398, 2002. Also available as Tech. Report MCS02-08, The Weizmann Institute of Science.
9. D. Harel, H. Kugler, and G. Weiss. Some Methodological Observations Resulting from Experience Using LSCs and the Play-In/Play-Out Approach. In *Proc. Scenarios: Models, Algorithms and Tools*, volume 3466 of *Lect. Notes in Comp. Sci.*, pages 26–42. Springer-Verlag, 2005.
10. D. Harel and R. Marelly. Playing with time: On the specification and execution of time-enriched LSCs. In *Proc. 10th IEEE/ACM International Symposium on Modeling, Analysis and Simulation of Computer and Telecommunication Systems (MASCOTS'02)*, Fort Worth, Texas, 2002.

11. D. Harel and R. Marelly. *Come, Let's Play: Scenario-Based Programming Using LSCs and the Play-Engine.* Springer-Verlag, 2003.
12. D. Harel and R. Marelly. Specifying and Executing Behavioral Requirements: The Play In/Play-Out Approach. *Software and System Modeling (SoSyM)*, 2(2):82–107, 2003.
13. A. Hartman and K. Nagin. The AGEDIS tools for model based testing. In R.L. Grossman, A. Nerode, A. Ravn, and H. Rischel, editors, *Proceedings of the 2004 ACM SIGSOFT international symposium on Software testing and analysis (ISSTA '04)*, pages 129–132. ACM Press, 2004.
14. Rhapsody. http://www.ilogix.com/, 2006.
15. N. Kam. *Formal Modeling of C. elegans Vulval Development: A Scenario-Based Approach.* PhD thesis, Weizmann Institute, 2006.
16. N. Kam, D. Harel, H. Kugler, R. Marelly, A. Pnueli, E.J.A. Hubbard, and M.J. Stern. Formal Modeling of C. elegans Development: A Scenario-Based Approach. In Corrado Priami, editor, *Proc. Int. Workshop on Computational Methods in Systems Biology (CMSB 2003)*, volume 2602 of *Lect. Notes in Comp. Sci.*, pages 4–20. Springer-Verlag, 2003. Extended version appeared in Modeling in Molecular Biology, G.Ciobanu (Ed.), Natural Computing Series, Springer, 2004 .
17. N. Kam, H. Kugler, L. Appleby, A. Pnueli, D. Harel, M.J. Stern, and E.J.A. Hubbard. Hypothesis Testing and Biological Insights from Scenario-Based Modeling of Development. Technical report, 2006.
18. M. Lettrari and J. Klose. Scenario-based monitoring and testing of real-time UML models. In *4th Int. Conf. on the Unified Modeling Language, Toronto*, October 2001.
19. S. Leue and T. Systä. Scenarios: Models, Transformations and Tools, International Workshop, Dagstuhl Castle, Germany, September 7-12, 2003, Revised Selected Papers. In *Scenarios: Models, Transformations and Tools*, volume 3466 of *Lect. Notes in Comp. Sci.* Springer-Verlag, 2005.
20. R. Marelly, D. Harel, and H. Kugler. Multiple instances and symbolic variables in executable sequence charts. In *Proc. 17th Ann. ACM Conf. on Object-Oriented Programming, Systems, Languages and Applications (OOPSLA'02)*, pages 83–100, Seattle, WA, 2002.
21. OMEGA - Correct Development of Real-Time Embedded Systems. http://www-omega.imag.fr/.
22. S. Uchitel, J. Kramer, and J. Magee. Incremental elaboration of scenario-based specifications and behavior models using implied scenarios. *ACM Trans. Software Engin. Methods*, 13(1):37–85, 2004.
23. UML. Documentation of the unified modeling language (UML), 2006. Available from the Object Management Group (OMG), http://www.omg.org.
24. Z.120 ITU-TS Recommendation Z.120: Message Sequence Chart (MSC). ITU-TS, Geneva, 1996.

Integration Testing in Software Product Line Engineering: A Model-Based Technique*

Sacha Reis[1], Andreas Metzger[1], and Klaus Pohl[1,2]

[1] Software Systems Engineering, University of Duisburg-Essen,
Schützenbahn 70, 45117 Essen, Germany
`{reis, metzger, pohl}@sse.uni-due.de`
[2] Lero (The Irish Software Engineering Research Centre),
University of Limerick, Ireland
`pohl@lero.ie`

Abstract. The development process in software product line engineering is divided into domain engineering and application engineering. As a consequence of this division, tests should be performed in both processes. However, existing testing techniques for single systems cannot be applied during domain engineering, because of the variability in the domain artifacts. Existing software product line test techniques only cover unit and system tests. Our contribution is a model-based, automated integration test technique that can be applied during domain engineering. For generating integration test case scenarios, the technique abstracts from variability and assumes that placeholders are created for variability. The generated scenarios cover all interactions between the integrated components, which are specified in a test model. Additionally, the technique reduces the effort for creating placeholders by minimizing the number of placeholders needed to execute the integration test case scenarios. We have experimentally measured the performance of the technique and the potential reduction of placeholders.

1 Motivation

Software product line engineering (SPLE) is a proven approach for deriving a set of similar applications at low costs and at short time to market [8][21]. SPLE is based on the planned, systematic, and pro-active reuse of development artifacts (including requirements, components, and test cases). There are two key differences between SPLE and the development of single systems [21]:

1. The development process of a software product line (SPL) is divided into two sub processes: domain engineering and application engineering. In domain engineering, the commonalities and the variability of the SPL are defined and reusable artifacts, which comprise the SPL platform, are created. In application engineering, customer-specific applications are realized by binding the variability and reusing the domain artifacts.

---

* This work has been partially funded by the DFG under grant PO 607/2-1 IST-SPL and by Science Foundation Ireland under the CSET grant 03/CE2/I303_1.

M.B. Dwyer and A. Lopes (Eds.): FASE 2007, LNCS 4422, pp. 321–335, 2007.

2. The variability of an SPL is modeled explicitly by variation points and variants. Variation points describe what varies between the applications of an SPL, e.g. the payment method in an online store. Variants describe concrete instances of this variation, e.g. payment by credit card, debit card, or invoice.

Because of the division of the development process into domain and application engineering, there are two major kinds of development artifacts that have to be tested. In domain engineering, the SPL platform has to be tested, in application engineering the derived applications have to be tested.

The SPL platform contains variability. This variability prevents the use of existing testing techniques for single systems, because the domain artifacts do not define a single application but a set of applications. With existing techniques from single system testing, each of these applications would have to be individually tested in domain engineering, resulting in an enormous test effort.

In the literature, several approaches for SPL testing have been proposed (e.g., [4][10][15][17][20][24]). However, these approaches cover unit and system testing only.

This paper presents a model-based, automated technique for integration testing in domain engineering. Our technique generates integration test case scenarios (ITCSs), which support the test of the interactions between the components of an integrated sub-system. An ITCS describes the order and the type of interactions that have to be performed during test execution. By augmenting an ITCS with test data, integration test cases can be derived.

The basic idea of our approach is to create placeholders for necessary variable parts and all components that are not part of the integrated sub-system. These placeholders are considered during the model-based generation of ITCSs. The benefits of our technique are as follows:

☐ Other failures than the ones uncovered in unit testing can be found, because the goal of integration testing is to uncover intercomponent failures (see e.g. [6]).
☐ Testing can be performed earlier compared to system testing. For integration testing the complete system is not needed. Missing components or variants can be simulated. Such an early test can significantly reduce costs (see e.g. [7]).
☐ Generally, not all possible interactions between components can be tested in integration testing. Our technique systematically selects a subset of all possible interactions by using a test model.
☐ The ITCSs are derived in such a way that the development effort for necessary placeholders is minimized. Thus, the testing effort is reduced.

2 Related Work

In the literature, several approaches for scenario-based integration test case derivation are presented (see [2][12][16][26][29]). All these approaches only support integration testing for the development of single systems, and therefore none of these approaches considers variability. As the consideration of variability is essential when testing in domain engineering, these approaches are not suitable for the use in the context of

SPLs without substantial extensions. Still, they substantiate that a scenario-based approach is one suitable approach towards integration testing.

Many approaches for test case derivation in SPLE can be found in the literature [25]. Representatives are approaches by Bertolino and Gnesi [4][15], Geppert et al. [10], McGregor et al. [17][18], and Nebut et al. [20]. These approaches focus on unit and system testing only. In our previous work, we have developed the ScenTED technique for system testing [24][15] and performance testing [23]. McGregor focused on unit [18] and system testing [17], but furthermore he pointed out that all common artifacts can already be tested in domain engineering by integration tests. However, he did not present a concrete technique for that.

In an approach by Muccini and van der Hoek [19] challenges in testing product line architectures are presented. For integration testing, they suggest to integrate all common components first and then to integrate the variant components. However, they do not present solutions for integration test case derivation. Cohen et al. [9] state that applying well-understood coverage criteria when testing the applications of an SPL could lead to a low coverage of the SPL platform. They have developed specific coverage criteria to improve on this situation. The approach by Cohen et al. [9] and our previous work [24][15] both support an early test in domain engineering by creating sample applications. However, creating a sample application assumes that all relevant components and variants have been developed. Consequently, this approach will be typically applied very late in the domain engineering process.

General approaches for deriving test case scenarios from control flow graphs also exist (e.g., [22][5][27]). In the approach of Wang et al. [27], all possible scenarios through a test model are derived by employing existing algorithms. Then, a mathematical optimization is performed to achieve the minimal set of these test case scenarios for branch coverage. Other criteria than branch coverage are also discussed. Because of the possible use of other coverage and also optimization criteria, this is a quite general approach. Still, variability and specifics of integration testing are not explicitly discussed.

Summarizing, none of the existing approaches for SPL testing support integration testing in domain engineering.

3   Overview of the Technique

In the following subsections, the test models that are used as input to our technique are described and an overview of the activities of the technique is given.

3.1   Test Models

Test models, which are used as input to our technique, are specified by UML 2.0 activity diagrams. We use UML 2.0 activity diagrams to define the control flow of the platform (i.e. the actions and the allowed transitions between these actions) and to define which components perform a given action. The components that perform an action are specified by activity partitions (as an example, see C1, C2, and C3 in Fig. 1). A set of these components has to be integrated before our technique is performed according to a defined integration strategy. For each new integrated subsystem, our technique can be applied again.

To model variability, we stereotype certain elements in the activity diagrams to denote variation points (see VP1 in Fig. 1) and merge points (see MP1 in Fig. 1). We define a merge point as a specific node in the diagram where all variant control flows of a variation point are merged together and continue in a single control flow.

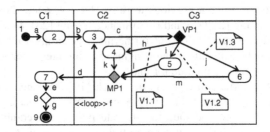

Fig. 1. Example of a Test Model

We assume that within the test model, variability always starts with a variation point. There are no variable parts that can be reached without passing through a variation point. Moreover, the control flows of all variants of a variation point are always merged together in exactly one associated merge point. The only exceptions are loops, which are explicitly marked by a stereotype (see <<loop>> in Fig. 1).

By using activity diagrams as test models, we follow other approaches where control flow graphs are used for this purpose (e.g. see [14]). In general, a test model can specify the behavior of the complete system or of the sub-system that should be integration tested. The abstraction level of the model strongly depends on the way the model has been developed. For example, the model can be developed on the basis of use cases from requirements engineering. If the scenarios of the use cases are documented in activity diagrams, these can be refined considering the architecture of the system. The abstraction level influences the quality of test results. The more abstract (i.e., less detailed) the model is, the less the coverage of the test object will be. Thus, the test model defines the quality of the test results.

3.2 Activities

Our technique for the generation of ITCSs for SPL consists of three main activities D1-D3. Fig. 2 shows these three activities together with their inputs and outputs.

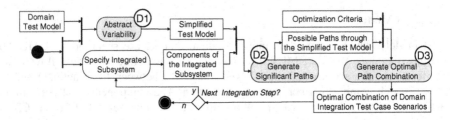

Fig. 2. Overview of our Technique

In the first activity D1, we abstract the variability of the given test model. The variability is the main problem that prevents the application of test techniques from single system development. Because of variability, no executable system exists in domain engineering. We abstract the variability and handle it as a black box for the ITCSs generation, because we want to test only the common parts of the platform (see Sec. 4.1). Thereby, the complexity of the test model is reduced. The relevant result of this activity is a simplified test model where the variability is abstracted.

In the second activity D2, all significant paths through the simplified test model are derived. For the derivation, we use Beizer's Node Reduction Algorithm [3]. Because the ITCSs that are generated with our technique only need to cover the interactions between the integrated components, we typically can reduce the number of paths (see Section 4.2). We refer to the reduced set of paths as significant paths.

In the third activity D3, we generate an optimal path combination, i.e. an optimal set of ITCSs, from the set of significant paths. We calculate the path combination with the minimal number of included abstracted variability. The variable parts within an ITCS have to be simulated by placeholders. In contrast to placeholders that are required for structural reasons, e.g. for enabling compilation, these placeholders are more complex because they have to simulate functionality. Therefore, the placeholders of the variable parts within the ITCSs represent a significant additional test effort in domain engineering that should be minimized to keep the overall testing effort reasonable.

4 Generation of Integration Test Case Scenarios

In this section, the activities of our technique are described in detail.

4.1 Abstraction of Variability (Activity D1)

In our technique, we consider variability in functionality (e.g. alternative control flows) as well as variability in the architecture (e.g. alternative components). If a component is a variant (i.e. it can be included in a customer-specific application or not), we will not integrate it in a sub-system for an integration test in domain engineering. The interactions between these components have to be tested in application engineering when the component is used as part of a specific application. Because variant components are not part of the integrated sub-system, they are simulated by placeholders in the same way that common components, which are not part of the integrated sub-system, are simulated.

In the test model, variability in functionality is represented by variation points, merge points and variants in the control flow. This variability is abstracted in the first activity D1. During this abstraction, the control flow between the variation point and the associated merge point as well as the variation point and the merge point itself are replaced by a new action. We define these new actions as abstracted variability.

Depending on the actual structure of the test model the abstraction is performed differently. We can differentiate between a normal arrangement of a variation point (see "A" in Fig. 3.) and a nested one (see "B" in Fig. 3.):

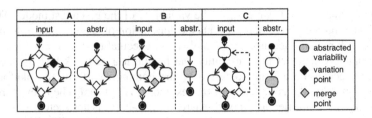

Fig. 3. Examples for Transformations for Abstracting Variability

Loops in a test model can be classified into three different types:

☐ A backflow within a variable part exists: This type poses no problem for abstraction and is already covered by the abstraction of a normal variation point ("A").

☐ A backflow out of a common part into a variable part exists: This type is not conforming to our assumptions from above. Because each variable part has to begin with a variation point, this composition is not allowed.

☐ A backflow out of a variable part into a common part exists: This type represents a valid violation of our above assumption that all variants have to be merged in one merge point. Because we stereotyped all backflows, they can be identified and thus abstracted accordingly (see "C" in Fig. 3.).

The implementation of our abstraction algorithm uses a relation matrix as a data structure to represent the test model. We have decided to use relation matrices, because in the subsequent activities of our technique for the generation of integration test cases, we will use existing algorithms that are based on matrices.

The dimension of the relation matrix corresponds to the number of nodes in the test model (i.e. actions, decision points, variation points etc.). The entries of the matrix represent the edges between the different nodes.

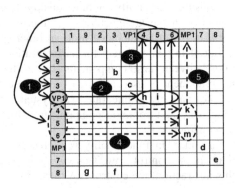

Fig. 4. Steps of the Abstraction Algorithm applied to the Example from Fig. 1

In Fig. 4. the steps of the abstraction algorithm are illustrated. The example test model consists of 11 nodes, including one variation point. The algorithm iterates through the rows of the matrix until a variation point is identified (see 1). With the entries of the identified row (see 2), the reachable nodes are identified (see 3). For these nodes, again the reachable nodes are identified in the same way (see 4, 5). This procedure is repeated until the merge point of the identified variation point is reached. If a loop is detected, the procedure is finished for the respective loop node before reaching the merge node. The rows and columns that are identified with the algorithm are eliminated from the matrix and are replaced by a new action that represents abstracted variability.

4.2   Generation of Significant Paths (Activity D2)

The second activity D2 of our technique is divided into five steps (D2a – D2e). These steps are illustrated by the example in Fig. 5., in which components C1 and C2 are integrated into the sub-system to be tested.

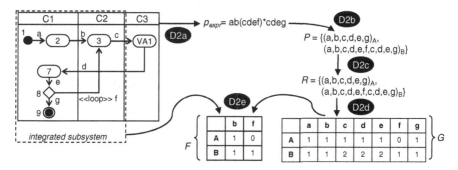

Fig. 5. Creation of an EP Matrix

Step D2a: Derivation of path expression. We start activity D2 with computing a path expression that represents all paths of the test model in a compact string. This path expression is generated by Beizer's node reduction algorithm of [3]. In the example, this leads to the expression "ab(cdef)*cdeg" (the asterisk '*' denotes an arbitrary repetition of the expression in parentheses).

Step D2b: Derivation of paths through the simplified test model. The path expression from step D2a can be used to derive all paths through the test model. However, if the test model contains loops, this can lead to an infinite number of paths. As we want to cover all interactions between the integrated components, we can limit the number of paths by restricting the loop iterations to at most one. This leads to a set $P := \{p_1, p_2, ..., p_n\}$ of paths p_i. In the example, P contains the two paths A = (a, b, c, d, e, g) and B = (a, b, c, d, e, f, c, d, e, g).

Step D2c: Selection of significant paths for the sub-system. For the integration test of a given sub-system, only paths that affect the integrated sub-system need to be considered. Therefore, all paths that do not contain any edges that are associated to a component of the integrated sub-system are deleted. Further, all infeasible paths should be eliminated. The identification of infeasible paths is nontrivial. Still, several approaches have been suggested to identify infeasible paths (e.g., [13]). We suggest using one of these existing approaches to eliminate the infeasible paths. Also, a domain expert could perform this step. The result of this step is a set $R \subseteq P$ that contains all significant paths. In the example, paths A and B are significant, thus $R = P$.

Step D2d: Creation of an EP Matrix. To prepare for the following activities of our technique, an edge-path frequency matrix (EP matrix) is created from the paths in the set R. The rows of an EP matrix G represent the paths. The columns of the matrix represent the edges, $e \in E$, of the test model. An element $G(p, e)$ of the matrix G represents how often an edge e is contained in a path p. In the example, the element $G(B, c)$ of the EP matrix contains a value of 2, because edge c appears twice in path B.

Step D2e: Reduction of the EP Matrix. As a final step, the EP matrix is reduced. In integration testing, the interactions between the components of the integrated sub-system are tested. Therefore, only edges of the test model that cross the component boundaries within the integrated sub-system have to be considered. As a consequence, all columns can be eliminated that represent other transitions, leading to a reduced matrix F. In the example, transition e is eliminated, because it is an internal transition of component C1. Transition c is eliminated, because it is not part of the component interactions within the integrated sub-system.

4.3   Generation of the Optimal Path Combination (Activity D3)

The third activity D3 generates a set of ITCSs based on the EP matrix F. The set of ITCSs has to cover all necessary edges of the test model, i.e. all interactions between the integrated components. Moreover, the set should lead to the minimal number of abstracted variability and thus required placeholders.

An ITCS is represented by a path through the simplified test model. The optimal set of ITCSs therefore is represented by a subset c of the paths R that are specified in the matrix F. We want to determine a path combination that guarantees a complete coverage of the interactions between the integrated components. The coverage for any given path combination c can be computed from the EP matrix F as follows.

Let $s(c, e)$ be

$$s(c, e) = \sum_{p \in c} F(p, e) \tag{1}$$

The coverage of the interactions between the integrated components is only achieved if $s(c, e)$ is larger than zero for all edges e. Otherwise, at least one edge has not been considered in the path combination.

The generation of an optimal path combination through the simplified test model obviously represents an optimization problem. We use the generalized optimal path selection model by Wang et al. [27] to generate the optimal path combination. This model can easily be used for different optimization criteria. Wang et al. define the objective function Z as follows:

$$Z = b^{\mathrm{T}} W^{\mathrm{T}} x \tag{2}$$

The vector of decision variables x contains one decision variable for each significant path through the simplified test model. The decision variable indicates, whether the path is selected for the path combination or not. Therefore, the decision variables are binary:

$$x = [(X_i \mid X_i = 0, 1)] \tag{3}$$

The vector b and the matrix W enable the weighting of the decision variables to upgrade or downgrade specific possible solutions.

The minimization of the abstracted variability that is contained in the significant paths is realized by the weighting matrix W. Thereto, we specify a matrix V. The rows of V represent the significant paths R. The columns of V represent the nodes v within the simplified test model that represent the abstracted variability. An element $V(p, v)$ of the matrix V is 1 iff the path p contains the node v, otherwise the element has the value 0. The matrix V is now used as weighting matrix W.

The vector b can be used to prioritize the complexity of the single abstracted variability. In contrast to this, the matrix V is used to optimize the number of abstracted variability in the path combination. Because the complexity of abstracted variability depends on many different factors (e.g., on the way of implementation), we currently do not use the vector b in our optimization. The resulting objective function thus becomes:

$$Z = 1^{\mathrm{T}} V^{\mathrm{T}} x \tag{4}$$

It should be noted that using the matrix V leads to an approximation with respect to minimizing the number of abstracted variability within the selected path combination. Because of an easier realization, the overall number of abstracted variability is minimized, not the number of different abstracted variability.

The desired coverage of the test model is achieved by defining auxiliary conditions:

$$A^{\mathrm{T}} x \geq r \tag{5}$$

The matrix A defines the elements that have to be covered (e.g., paths, branches, or nodes). The variable r specifies the desired degree of coverage. We specify the coverage of the interactions between the integrated components with the matrix F. Therefore, we can replace the matrix A with matrix F. To guarantee the coverage, it is sufficient to run through each needed edge once. Therefore, we can set the degree of coverage r to 1. The adapted auxiliary conditions are the following:

$$F^{\mathrm{T}} x \geq 1 \tag{6}$$

The optimization problem that is described in this manner can be solved with the branch-and-bound approach (see e.g. [1]). Branch-and-bound is a general algorithmic method for finding optimal solutions of integer optimization problems.

5 Evaluation of the Technique

In this section, we present the results of the experimental evaluation of our technique concerning the performance and the benefits of the technique.

5.1 Design of the Experiment

We have implemented a prototype for the complete technique in Java (JDK 1.4.2). The multi-constraint selection of an optimal set of paths through a graph is an NP complete problem. Therefore, the activity D3 of our technique is the most critical one and we focus on this activity in our evaluation. Our prototype uses for this activity D3 the Gnu Linear Programming Kit (GLPK, [11]) for solving the optimization problem with the branch-and-bound approach.

We have defined simplified test models by the random generation of EP matrices and W matrices. Then, we have generated the optimal set of ITCSs by applying our prototype. We have measured the computation time as well as the number of selected scenarios and the number of the contained abstracted variability. Altogether, we have generated and calculated over 2000 examples. All measurements have been performed on a standard PC with a 2.8 GHz Pentium IV processor and 1 GB RAM, running Windows XP (SP2).

The test models that have been used as input to activity D3 are represented by EP matrices and W matrices and can be characterized by six parameters:

1. the number of paths through the simplified test model (rows of the EP matrix)
2. the number of reduced interactions between the integrated components (columns of the EP matrix)
3. the number of entries of the EP matrix, i.e. how many cells of the EP matrix have a value greater than 0
4. the allocation of the EP matrix, i.e. the assignment of the values greater than 0 to the cells of the EP matrix
5. the number of abstracted variability in the simplified test model (columns of the W matrix)
6. the allocation of the W matrix, i.e. the assignment of the values greater than 0 to the cells of the W matrix

For the execution of the test runs, we have varied the number of paths and interactions of the EP matrix. We have started with 10 paths and 10 interactions and increased the values incrementally by 10. For each paths/interactions combination, we generated 5 examples with different kinds of allocations and different W matrices. Because of our experience with previous example test models, we have fixed the number of entries in the EP matrices to 50% and 25%. The allocation has been generated randomly. We prevent columns that contain a value greater than 0 in every row, because these columns would be covered by every path and therefore they would be needless and could be deleted. We also prevent columns that contain 0 in every row, because this would lead to a wrong test model. These columns could not be covered by any path through the simplified test model. The bounds of the number of abstracted variability, VA, in the simplified test models (i.e., the number of columns in the W matrices) are the following: $1 < VA < (10*(\text{columns of EP}))$. We assume that only 10% of the interactions of the original test model represent interactions between the integrated components. If more than 10% of the interactions represent interactions between the integrated components, the upper bound would be lower and less variability could be included in the model (e.g., 5*columns of EP for 20%). The number of entries and also the allocation of the matrix W have been generated randomly.

5.2 Validity Threats

We have analyzed different types of threats to the validity of the results of our evaluation (c.f. [28]). One threat leads to the necessity of using objective and repeatable measures. We have measured the computation time, the number of test case scenarios, and the number of reduced abstracted variability. These measures are objective, because it involves simple counting. Because the technique is automated, the measures are also repeatable.

The environment of our experimentation consists of a PC that has no network connection and there are no other applications running on the PC. We have performed all measurements on the same PC. Thus, the results are comparable. The implementation of the prototype has been intensively tested before we have performed the experiment.

Because of the high number of more than 2000 computations of different test models, in our opinion the results can be generalized and with a high probability they are also relevant for industrial practice.

5.3 Performance of the Technique

In our experiment, the performance is measured by computation time. We have applied our prototype to more than 2000 generated examples with different characteristics of EP matrices and W matrices.

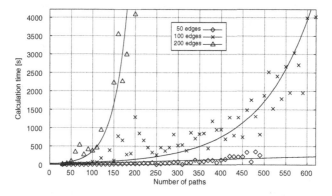

Fig. 6. Computation Times [s]

Fig. 6 shows the results concerning the computation time exemplary for EP matrices with 50, 100, and 200 edges and an allocation of 50%. The results in the diagram respectively represent average values of five computations. Moreover, the figure shows the regression curves for each data set. As expected, simplified test models with more included interactions need more computation time. The longest computation time of all executed computations was 9087 seconds for an example with 200 paths, 200 interactions (edges), and 1880 included abstracted variability. The variability in this example could only be reduced to 1842. Examples with 100 interactions have been smoothly calculated in an acceptable time, even if they have 600 paths. The computation time of examples with 50 interactions was minimal. Analyzing the results, we observed that the more variability could be reduced, the more computation time decreased. The most complex computations were those, where no variability could be reduced.

It should be noted that the measured computation times correspond to the dimensions of the simplified test model. Thus, directly determining computation time from the size of the (non-simplified) test model is not possible. However, the size of test models typically corresponds to a multiple of the size of the simplified test models. Because all computations of our experiment have been performed in an acceptable time (less than three hours), these results indicate that (non-simplified) test models of sufficient size can be calculated.

5.4 Benefit of the Technique

Our technique supports an early test in domain engineering because of the following aspects:

☐ The complete system is not needed for applying our technique, because missing parts (e.g., variability or not implemented components) can be simulated.
☐ The parts of the system that have to simulated are easily to identify. The variable parts can be identified by the nodes in the ITCSs that represent abstracted variability. The placeholders that are needed because of structural reasons can be identified by the architectural information within the ITCSs.
☐ The expected coverage is guaranteed. All common interactions between the components of the system are covered.

There are two additional benefits that could be measured in our experiment:

Low number of integration test case scenarios. Applying our technique leads to a small set of ITCSs that guarantees the coverage of all necessary interactions of the test model. A small test set can reduce the test effort during test execution.

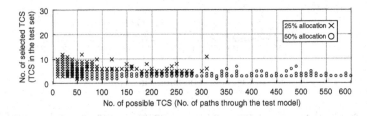

Fig. 7. Number of selected TCS

Fig. 7. shows the number of ITCSs within the generated test set in contrast to the number of possible ITCSs for 25% and 50% allocations of the EP matrix. The number of scenarios within the generated test set is very small, i.e. only a few ITCSs are sufficient to cover all necessary interactions of the test model. Although the number is not minimized during the computation and the generated test models are partially very complex, the average number of scenarios for 25% allocations of the EP matrix is 7.2 scenarios. On an average only 3.6 scenarios are sufficient for the coverage, if the EP allocation is 50%.

Minimal number of abstracted variability. Applying our technique leads to a test set that contains a minimal number of abstracted variability. The minimal number of abstracted variability reduces the test effort during the preparation of the test, because less placeholders have to be developed.

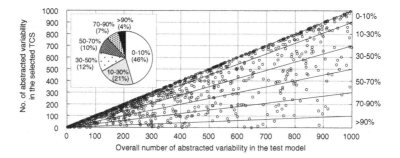

Fig. 8. Measured reduction of Variability

Fig. 8 shows the number of different abstracted variability in the selected ITCSs proportional to the overall number of different abstracted variability in the test model (50% allocation of EP). The difference between these numbers represents the reduction of variability and therefore a reduction of needed placeholders. In the diagram, the numbers of all performed computations are illustrated. The mean reduction is 25%. However, the standard deviation is very high and therefore the mean reduction is not really significant. Because of the high distribution of the values, we have divided the values in six categories. In 46% of the computations, only a reduction of less than 10% could be reached. But in more than 20% of the computations, a reduction of more than 50% could be reached. 4% of the computations lead to reduction of more than 90%. Summarizing, a high reduction is possible, but because of the high distribution of the results estimating the reduction for a given test model is not possible. The high distribution is due to the fact that the results are influenced by a set of parameters (e.g., allocation of the variability in the test model, size of the test model).

6 Conclusion and Outlook

In this paper, we have presented a model-based, automated technique for integration testing in domain engineering. The technique generates integration test case scenarios, based on which integration test cases can be developed. Our technique provides four significant benefits for software product line testing:

☐ The technique facilitates integration testing by considering a test model that describes the control flow as well as its assignment to the components of the software product line platform. Components and variable parts, which have to be simulated by placeholders, are explicitly modeled.

☐ The technique supports an early test in domain engineering. Variability is abstracted and placeholders can be used to simulate the abstracted variable parts of the software product line platform.

☐ The technique selects integration test case scenarios systematically. Based on the test model, the integration test case scenarios are derived by our technique such that the coverage of all interactions between the components of an integrated subsystem is guaranteed.

☐ The technique reduces the testing effort, because the variable parts within the selected integration test case scenarios, and thus the development effort for placeholders, is minimized. Our experimental evaluation has shown that on an average the number of variable parts in the scenarios can be reduced by about 25%.

Although the computations for minimizing the variable parts in the integration test case scenarios are quite complex, our experiments have shown that the technique can deal with large test models. However, the technique depends on the arrangement of variability in the test models. The abstraction of an unfavorable arrangement can – under rare circumstances – lead to an over-simplified test model, which prevents a reasonable application of the technique.

Currently, we are planning to apply our testing technique in an industrial setting. In addition, the reuse of the generated integration test case scenarios in application engineering is one topic of our future research. We are convinced that the testing effort can significantly be reduced, if the test case scenarios are systematically reused in application engineering.

References

1. Balas, E.; Toth, P.: Branch and Bound Methods. In: Lawler, E.L.; Lenstra, J.K.; Rinnooy Kan, A.H.G.; Shmoys, D.B. (eds.): The Traveling Salesman Problem, Wiley, New York (1985) 361-401

2. Basanieri, F.; Bertolino, A.: A Practical approach to UML-based derivation of integration tests, In: Proc. of the Quality Week Europe, paper 3T (2000)

3. Beizer, B.: Software Testing Techniques. Van Nostrand Reinhold, New York (1990)

4. Bertolino, A., and Gnesi, S. PLUTO: A Test Methodology for Product Families. In: Software Product-Family Engineering – 5th Intl. Workshop, LNCS 3014, Springer (2004)

5. Bertolino, A.; Marré, M.: Automatic Generation of Path Covers Based on the Control Flow Analysis of Computer Programs. IEEE Transactions on Software Engineering, Vol. 20, No. 12 (1994) 885-899

6. Binder, R.V.: Testing Object-Oriented Systems. Addison-Wesley (2000)

7. Boehm, B.; Basili, V.R.: Software Defect Reduction Top 10 List. IEEE Computer, 34(1) (2001) 135-137

8. Clements, P., and Northrop, L. Software Product Lines: Practices and Patterns. Addison-Wesley (2002)

9. Cohen, M.B.; Dwyer, M.B.; Shi, J.: Coverage and Adequacy in Software Product Line Testing. In: Proc. of the ISSTA 2006 Workshop on Role of Software Architecture for Testing and Analysis, ACM, New York (2006) 53-63

10. Geppert, B.; Li, J.; Rößler, F.; Weiss, D.M.: Towards Generating Acceptance Tests for Product Lines. In: Proc. of the 8th Intl. Conf. on Software Reuse, LNCS 3107, Springer, Heidelberg (2004) 35-48

11. GLPK (Gnu Linear Progrmming Kit), Gnu Project, http://www.gnu.org/software/glpk/.
12. Hartmann, J.; Imoberdorf, C.; Meisinger, M.: UML-Based Integration Testing, In: Harrold, M.J. (ed.): Proc. of the Intl. Symposium on Software Testing and Analysis, ACM, New York (2000) 60-70
13. Hedley, D.; Hennell, M.A.: The Causes and Effects of Infeasible Path in Computer Programs, In: Proc. of the 8th Intl. Conf. on Software Engineering, IEEE (1985) 259-267
14. Jorgensen, P.C.; Erickson, C.: Object-Oriented Integration Testing. Communications of the ACM, Vol. 37, No. 9 (1994) 30-38
15. Käkölä, T.; Duenas, J.C. (Eds.): Software Product Lines – Research Issues in Engineering and Management. Springer (2006)
16. Kim, Y.; Carlson, C.R.: Scenario Based Integration Testing for Object-Oriented Software Development, In: Proc. of the 8th Asian Test Symposium, IEEE (1999) 383-288
17. McGregor, J.D. Testing a Software Product Line. Technical Report CMU/SEI-2001-TR-022, Carnegie Mellon University, SEI (2001)
18. McGregor, J.D., Sodhani, P., and Madhavapeddi, S. Testing Variability in a Software Product Line. In Proc. of the Intl. Workshop on Software Product Line Testing, Avaya Labs, ALR-2004-031 (2004) 45-50
19. Muccini, H.; van der Hoek, A.: Towards Testing Product Line Architectures. In: Proc. of the Intl. Workshop on Test and Analysis of Component-Based Systems, Electronic Notes in Theoretical Computer Science, Vol. 82, No. 6 (2003)
20. Nebut, C.; Fleurey, F.; Le Traon, Y.; Jézéquel, J.-M.: A Requirement-based Approach to Test Product Families. In: Software Product-Family Engineering – 5th Intl. Workshop, LNCS 3014, Springer, Heidelberg (2004) 198-210
21. Pohl, K.; Böckle, G.; van der Linden, F.: Software Product Line Engineering – Foundations, Principles, and Techniques. Springer, Heidelberg (2005)
22. Prather, R.E.; Myers, J.P.: The Path Prefix Testing Strategy. IEEE Transactions on Software Engineering, Vol. 13, No. 7 (1987) 761-766
23. Reis, S.; Metzger, A.; Pohl, K.: A Reuse technique for Performance Testing of Software Product Lines. In: Proc. of the Intl. Workshop on Software Product Line Testing, Mannheim University of Applied Sciences, Report No. 003.06, (2006) 5-10
24. Reuys, A.; Kamsties, E.; Pohl, K, Reis, S.: Model-based System Testing of Software Product Families. In: Advanced Information Systems Engineering - CAiSE 2005, LNCS 3520, Springer, Heidelberg (2005) 519-534
25. Tevanlinna, A., Taina, J., and Kauppinen, R., Product Family Testing – a Survey. ACM SIGSOFT Software Engineering Notes, 29(2) (2004)
26. Tsai, W.T.; Bai, X.; Paul, R.; Shao, W.; Agarwal, V.: End-To-End Integration Testing Design. In: Proc. of the 25th Annual Intl. Computer Software and Applications Conf., IEEE, Los Alamitos (2001) 166-171
27. Wang, H.S.; Hsu, S.R.; Lin, J.C.: A Generalized Optimal Path-Selection Model for Structural Program Testing. The Journal of Systems and Software, Vol. 10 (1989) 55-63
28. Wohlin, C.; Runeson, P.; Höst, M.; Ohlsson, M.C.; Regnell, B.; Wesslen, A.: Experimentation in Software Engineering – An Introduction. Kluwer Academic Publishers (2000)
29. Wu, Y.; Chen, M.-H.; Offutt, J.: UML-Based Integration Testing for Component-Based Software. In: Proc. of the 2nd Intl. Conf. on COTS-Based Software Systems, LNCS 2580, Springer (2003) 251-260

Practical Reasoning About Invocations and Implementations of Pure Methods

Ádám Darvas[1] and K. Rustan M. Leino[2]

[1] ETH Zurich, Switzerland
`adam.darvas@inf.ethz.ch`
[2] Microsoft Research, Redmond, WA, USA
`leino@microsoft.com`

Abstract. User-defined functions used in the specification of object-oriented programs are called *pure methods*. Providing sound and practical support for pure methods in a verification system faces many challenges, especially when pure methods have executable implementations and can be invoked from code at run time. This paper describes a design for reasoning about pure methods in the context of sound, modular verification. The design addresses (1) how to axiomatize pure methods as mathematical functions enabling reasoning about their result values; (2) preconditions and frame conditions for pure methods enabling reasoning about the implementation of a pure method. Two important considerations of the design are that it work with object invariants and that its logical encoding be suitable for fully automatic theorem provers. The design has been implemented in the Spec# programming system.

1   Introduction

The notion of using user-defined functions in program specifications is both natural and useful. In object-oriented languages, such functions are known as *pure methods*—"pure" because their evaluation does not have an effect on the caller's program state [11]. The use of pure methods facilitates abstraction. To illustrate that, consider the postcondition

ensures this.IsPremium() ==> balance == **old**(balance) * 1.02;

of a method Bonus in an Account class. The condition expresses that if the Account object is a "premium" account, then its balance gets increased by 2%. The advantage of using pure method IsPremium in the condition is that its specification need not be repeated, which makes the condition more concise and comprehensible. Furthermore, even if the meaning (that is, specification and implementation) of the method changes over time, the postcondition of method Bonus need not be modified.

State-of-the-art languages such as Eiffel [15], Java with JML [11], and Spec# [3] support the use of pure methods. Common to these specification-enriched object-oriented languages is that their specifications are executable, and in particular their pure methods are executable. Like ordinary methods, pure methods

M.B. Dwyer and A. Lopes (Eds.): FASE 2007, LNCS 4422, pp. 336–351, 2007.
© Springer-Verlag Berlin Heidelberg 2007

have associated pre- and postconditions that we use in static verification to reason about invocations and implementations of the methods. But pure methods are different from ordinary methods in three ways.

First, pure methods can be used in specifications, which are expressions to assert properties of the code in a program. Since code also contains expressions, it is tempting to treat specifications like other expressions appearing in the code. But if the evaluation of specifications were treated as ordinary code, then it would be difficult to allow quantifications in specifications: quantifications in code are treated as loops, to reason about loops one needs loop invariants, and expressing these loop invariants, in general, requires quantifiers! So, we would like to treat specifications like mathematical expressions, not like code with control flow and side effects. And this means that we want to treat pure-method invocations in specifications like mathematical functions, not like procedure calls with side effects. Hence, when reasoning about the program, we introduce a mathematical function for every pure method, and this entails the task of turning the pure method's pre- and postconditions into well-founded mathematical definitions.

Second, to reason about invocations of pure methods (in our experience, more so than for ordinary methods), it is useful to specify the *read effects* of pure methods. Such specifications restrict what the result value of a pure method may depend on, which lets callers determine if various state changes have any effect on the pure method.

Third, there are situations in code where it is appropriate to allow a pure method to be invoked, but not an ordinary method. Such invocations thus require that pure methods be given weaker (*i.e.*, more applicable) preconditions than ordinary methods. We have found that with these weaker conditions, the abstraction techniques used to formulate frame conditions for ordinary methods lose too much precision when reasoning about implementations of pure methods.

In this paper, we describe the design of pure methods in the static program verifier Boogie [2] for Spec# [3]. The design addresses the issues mentioned above. It also addresses an important engineering issue arising from the fact that Boogie uses a fully automatic theorem prover, Simplify [7]. This automation comes at a price; relevant to our work here is the incompleteness of the handling of quantifiers, and specifically the prover's apparent inability to deal with reachability and to find witnesses for existential quantifiers.

We call our design *practical* because it is simple to realize and is capable of handling all cases we encountered in practice. However, it is not *universal* in the sense that there are programs that our design cannot handle. Nonetheless, we believe that the design is a practically useful solution. Parts of the design that are not specific to the Boogie methodology can be adapted to work with other program verifiers too, for example, Krakatoa [14]. The parts that are specific to the Boogie methodology may not be directly adaptable to some other verifiers, but the issues that those parts of the paper bring out are still relevant to any verification system aiming for modular reasoning.

We have implemented our design in Boogie, which has allowed us to start experimenting with its practicality. One of the benchmarks we have used is the source code of Boogie itself, which comprises some 45K lines of Spec#. Although much work remains to actually specify and verify the Boogie source code, all uses of pure methods in the source code pass our admissibility checks.

Section 2 briefly sketches the basic encoding and axiomatization of pure methods. Section 3 presents our design for the axiomatization which takes into account the constraints of Spec#. In Section 4, we give an overview of the Boogie methodology to prepare the reader for the remaining sections. Sections 5 and 6 study typical situations that occur during the verification of pure methods and propose axioms for their treatment. Finally, we list related work and conclude.

2   Encoding of Pure Methods and Their Return Values

In this section, we describe how methods in an object-oriented program are encoded as methods with first-order pre- and postconditions, uninterpreted functions, and a variety of axioms. These encodings can then be subjected to standard verification techniques based on, for example, Hoare logic [17] or verification-condition generation [14,2]. As is standard, our encoding represents the heap explicitly, so where the object-oriented notation would write $o.f$ to denote the f field of an object referenced by o, our encoding writes $h[o, f]$, which denotes the value at location (o, f) in the object store (that is, heap) h.

Pure methods and their uses in specifications are encoded by uninterpreted functions and function applications, respectively [5,6]. For each pure method M, the encoding introduces a function $\#M$, which we refer to as a *method function*. The method function takes one argument for each parameter of the method, including the receiver parameter, and an additional argument for the object store in which it is evaluated. For instance, a pure method declared as:

> [**Pure**] **int** Exmpl(**int** x)
>   **requires this**.f $<=$ x;
>   **ensures result** $<=$ x $-$ **this**.f;
> { **return** (x $-$ **this**.f) / 2; }

where **result** denotes the return value of the method, introduces a method function $\#Exmpl$ with the signature $ref \times int \times heap \rightarrow int$, where ref, int, and $heap$ are the sorts for references, machine integers, and object stores, respectively. We can use a function, because it is standard to require pure methods to be deterministic [11].

Pure methods and their implementations also give rise to method declarations in the encoding. These method declarations are used to reason about calls to pure methods from code and to reason about the implementations of pure methods. To make a connection between calls to a pure method M in code and calls to M in specifications, we follow [5] and our encoding adds a postcondition that ties the result of M to the value of $\#M$. This is needed when the method specification does not completely determine the result value. For method Exmpl, the additional postcondition in the encoding is **result** $= \#Exmpl(\textbf{this}, x, h)$;

where h denotes the object store. This postcondition allows us to verify code like: "v = o.Exmpl(23); **assert** v == o.Exmpl(23);" in the source program, since the expression in the assert statement is a specification expression.

Method function $\#M$ is axiomatized based on the specification of method M. In essence, the axiom states that if the precondition of the method holds, then the method returns a value that is consistent with the postcondition. Formally, for a pure method M with pre- and postconditions Pre and $Post$, we would like an axiom like:

$$(\forall\, t, p, h \bullet\ Pre[t/this]\ \Rightarrow\ Post[t/this, \#M(t, p, h)/result]\,) \tag{1}$$

where t and p range over the possible values of the receiver object and other parameters, respectively, and h ranges over well-formed heaps. The substitutions replace every occurrence of **this** by the bound variable for the receiver object and every occurrence of the special variable **result** by the function application of $\#M$. For method Exmpl, the axiom (after substitutions) is:

$$(\forall\, t, x, h \bullet\ h[t, f] \leqslant x\ \Rightarrow\ \#Exmpl(t, x, h) \leqslant x - h[t, f]\,)$$

Unfortunately, formula (1) does not necessarily give rise to a well-founded definition for $\#M$, because the postcondition $Post$ might be unattainable (for example, $Post$ might be $false$) [6]. This is not a problem for a verification system when verifying ordinary code, because it will not be possible to prove the correctness of any terminating path in the implementation. However, an unattainable postcondition would be a problem for a verification system if it caused the generation of an unsound axiom, because such an axiom would let every part of the program be verified, including the implementation of the pure method.

Formula (1) *is* sound if for all relevant values of the arguments, there is some value that $\#M$ can take on. More precisely, if M's specification does not call any pure methods, then the soundness of (1) follows from:

$$(\forall\, t, p, h \bullet\ Pre[t/this]\ \Rightarrow\ (\exists\, w \bullet\ Post[t/this, w/result]\,)) \tag{2}$$

Thus, in this case, a sound axiomatization of method function $\#M$ is the implication $(2) \Rightarrow (1)$. If M's specification calls pure methods, then soundness additionally requires that any recursion be well-founded, which can be expressed by a much more complicated form of (2) that takes into account the values of all applications of all method functions involved in the recursion.

3   Practical Issues of Method Functions

The idea of using $(2) \Rightarrow (1)$ as the axiom that defines the method function $\#M$ suffers from two practical problems, which we describe in this section. We also describe how we overcome these problems in our design, which is an adaptation of previous work by Darvas and Müller [6].

3.1   Well-Founded Definitions of Method Functions

One problem with using $(2) \Rightarrow (1)$ to axiomatize $\#M$ is the alternating quantifiers in (2), which do not work well with our automatic theorem prover. Some simple experiments we conducted showed that Simplify does not discover even very simple witnesses w for the existential quantifier. In this section, we show how some simple syntactic checks guarantee the existence of a witness, thus satisfying the antecedent (2) once and for all.

As a first step in our heuristic process, we identify a *candidate witness expression* for the pure method. Then, we check that the candidate witness expression lies below the method function in a well-founded order (that is, a partial order with no infinite descending chains). If this process yields a well-founded candidate witness expression, then (2) is satisfied, so our encoding will simply include (1) as the axiom that constrains $\#M$. Since the heuristics look for syntactic patterns, they might not always discover a witness even if a witness does exist.

Identifying a candidate witness expression. Our heuristics consider a method to have a candidate witness expression E if and only if the method has exactly one **ensures** clause and it has the form "**result** *op* E" or "E *op* **result**", where *op* is one of the reflexive operators ==, $\leqslant$, $\geqslant$, $\Rightarrow$, or $\Leftrightarrow$, and E is an expression that does not contain the literal **result**. The syntactic nature of the heuristics might require postconditions to be rewritten in order to have the witness discovered.

Expression ordering. An expression E lies below (an application of) a method function $\#M(t, p, h)$ if and only if every method function in E lies below $\#M(t, p, h)$. Method functions are ordered by a lexicographic ordering: method function $\#N(s, q, h)$ lies below $\#M(t, p, h)$ if and only if:

- s is the term $h[t, f]$ where f is a field declared with the **rep** modifier (we explain later what **rep** fields are; for now, it suffices to know that **rep** fields induce a well-founded order on the objects in any program state), or
- s and t are the same term, pure methods N and M are declared in the same class, and that class orders N before M.

A suitable well-founded ordering on pure methods within a class, if one exists, can be inferred by building a call graph based on how the postconditions of the pure methods of the class call each other [6]. Our design uses a cruder inference that associates a number with each method and orders the methods accordingly. We let programmers override this inference by marking a pure method with a new attribute called RecursionTermination that takes a natural number as parameter. The inference uses the programmer-specified number, if present; otherwise, if the method's postconditions does not call any other pure methods, the inferred number is 0; otherwise, the inferred number is infinity.

Our experience with the specification of Boogie suggests that the annotation overhead may not be too bad in practice. We had to annotate only one method in mscorlib, the Microsoft Common Object Runtime Library. This was partly due to the simple yet helpful inference mechanism. The advantage of the approach is its simplicity compared to building and analyzing the call graph of each class.

3.2   Tension Between Dynamic Execution and Static Verification

The other problem stems from a tension between our desire to encode a pure-method invocation in a specification as an application of the corresponding method function, which does not alter the heap, and our desire to allow the implementation of a pure method, which will be executed at run time, to make some changes to the heap. In this section, we describe that problem and the solution our design uses.

Pure methods are side-effect free. That is, they are not allowed to change the state of existing objects. However, in many practical cases it is convenient to permit them to allocate new objects and freely modify their state. For example, a pure method to find the median value in a collection may allocate a temporary *List* object and apply a number of mutating operations to it as part of computing the result of the pure method. This means that a call to a pure method may change the heap, but only in a way that does not change the state of objects that were allocated before the call.

We would like our encoding to evaluate each specification expression, including all the method calls it contains, in a single state. But this raises some concern, since at run time the pure methods may be invoked in different states. To illustrate that this is a real concern, consider the specification expression "o.M() == o.M()", where the implementation of pure method M allocates and returns a new object. At run time, the specification evaluates to *false*, but its encoding $\#M(o, h) = \#M(o, h)$ equals *true* [6].

One way to overcome this problem is to disallow pure methods to *return* newly allocated objects—while still permitting the allocation and modification of new objects [6]. This restriction makes the encoding indistinguishable from the run-time behavior, because the objects allocated in a call are not observable by specification expressions evaluated after the call. Although this solution leads to a simple encoding, we found it to be too restrictive in many practical cases.

We take a more liberal approach, allowing pure methods to return newly allocated objects provided that does not cause any discrepancy between the dynamic execution and static verification. In the remainder of this section, we outline the analysis.

New attributes. The analysis requires the introduction of two new attributes. A reference-type pure method marked with attribute ResultNotNewlyAllocated says that the returned object has been allocated before the method was called. We encode this property as an additional postcondition

$$\textbf{ensures result} == \textbf{null} \lor \textbf{old}(h)[\textbf{result}, \textit{allocated}];$$

where **old**(h) refers to the value of the heap on entry to the method, and *allocated* is a special field that encodes whether or not the object has been allocated.

A method marked with the attribute NoReferenceComparison says that the method implementation does not perform any reference comparison (*i.e.*, use any operator == or != with reference-type operands). Two simple compile-time checks enforce this property: (1) the method may use reference comparison only if one of the operands is the literal **null**; (2) for any call contained in the implementation, the callee must be marked with NoReferenceComparison.

By default, the attributes are not attached to methods, that is, methods may return newly allocated objects and may compare references.

Definition of allocating expressions. We introduce the notion of an *allocating expression* to describe an expression that may yield a newly allocated object. An expression e is considered to be allocating if and only if e is of reference type and is either (a) a constructor or method call where the callee is not marked with ResultNotNewlyAllocated; or (b) a composite expression with any allocating sub-expression.

The rationale behind (a) is self-evident; (b) is more subtle. Consider a field access "**this**.M().f" where method M is allocating, *i.e.* not marked with ResultNotNewlyAllocated. Then M might return a newly allocated object whose field f refers to a newly allocated object too. Our definition of allocating over-approximates the set of expressions that yield newly allocated objects; however, this keeps the analysis sound and simple.

Checks on specification expressions. Having defined allocating expressions, we can spell out the restrictions our analysis enforces on specifications: (1) reference comparisons may have at most one operand that is allocating; (2) if two or more parameters (possibly the receiver) of a method call are allocating, then the callee must be one that is marked with NoReferenceComparison.

Attribute inheritance. Finally, to ensure soundness in the presence of subtyping, we need a rule that forces an overriding method to be at least as restricted in what its implementation is allowed to do as the overridden counterpart. That is, if an overridden method is marked with one of the attributes then the overriding method must be marked with that attribute too.

Limitations. There are two main limitations of our design: methods need be annotated manually by users, and the syntactic nature of our analysis leads to over-approximation. We believe a more accurate analysis that goes beyond syntactic checks (*e.g.*, points-to analysis) could lessen these limitations: most annotations could be inferred and more methods could be annotated with NoReferenceComparison (since our requirements are not minimal).

On the other hand, as far as our experience went with the specification of Boogie, we only had to mark two methods with ResultNotNewlyAllocated (one in Boogie and one in mscorlib) and none with NoReferenceComparison. Furthermore, we did not encounter specifications that were rejected because of how over-approximative our analysis is.

Summary of contributions. In this section, we showed two new techniques that yield a simple and practical encoding and axiomatization of pure methods. A combination of simple syntactic measures can let the theorem prover off the hook for dealing with the quantifiers in formula (2): the identification of witness candidates, and the association of methods with numbers, most all of which can be inferred by a simple syntactic analysis. Our simple syntactic allocating-expression analysis provides a plentiful solution to the tension between dynamic execution and static verification. These techniques do not rely on the specifics of the Spec# system, thus they can be adapted by other languages and program verifiers, too.

4   The Boogie Methodology

The remainder of the paper describes encodings that build on a particular state-of-the-art discipline of object invariants known as the *Boogie methodology* [1]. In this section, we review the parts of the methodology that are necessary for the understanding of the encodings.

Invariants and reentrancy. Any verification system needs to provide a way to specify and verify invariants. The basic idea of a condition declared to be an invariant is that by checking the condition at certain program points, one can safely assume that it holds at certain other program points. In the object-oriented setting, it is not clear where to check and assume the invariants of objects. For example, consider the simple approach of checking object invariants at the end of constructors, assuming them on entry to methods, and checking them again at the end of methods. This simple approach is not sound if a call from inside a method (where the object invariant may be temporarily broken) instigates a chain of (perhaps dynamically dispatched) calls that reenter a method of the object (where the simple approach said to assume invariants).

An approach that solves this problem is to explicitly track whether or not an object is in a state where its object invariant is certain to hold [1]. Following that approach, we say in this paper that an object is either *consistent*, which implies its object invariant holds, or *exposed*, which allows the object's fields to be updated and allows the object invariant to be violated. In this approach, known as the Boogie methodology, an appropriate precondition for a typical method is that the receiver object is consistent. The implementation then typically changes the state of the object from consistent to exposed, makes desired updates on the object's fields, and finally changes the state of the object back to consistent, at which point the object invariant is checked. Spec# has a special block statement, the **expose** statement, that performs the state change from consistent to exposed at the beginning of the block and back at the end of the block.

Aggregate objects. One other important thing in object-oriented specification and verification is the handling of aggregate objects. An aggregate object is a collection of separately allocated objects that together form one logical object. For example, an *Engine* may be an aggregate object that contains several *Cylinder* objects and a *FuelPump* object. A typical situation is then that a method of the Engine object, whose precondition says that the engine is consistent, calls methods on the Cylinder and FuelPump objects, whose preconditions say that those respective objects are consistent. The correctness of the Engine method thus relies on that the engine's cylinders and fuel pump are consistent, but explicitly mentioning the consistency of those objects in the precondition of the Engine method would be a violation of information hiding.

An approach that solves this problem is structuring the heap according to a hierarchical *ownership* relation [4]. For example, one would specify that an engine is the owner of its cylinders and fuel pump. We say that the cylinders and fuel pump are representation objects, or just *rep* objects, of the engine object. Using the ownership relation, a verification approach can ensure that the consistency of an object implies the consistency of the objects it owns [1]. This addresses the typical situation outlined above, because it allows an Engine method to meet the preconditions of the calls it makes to various Cylinder and FuelPump methods.

For this approach to be sound, one needs to make sure that an object's state is changed from consistent to exposed only if the object's owner is already in the exposed state. Consequently, any method whose implementation exposes the receiver object needs to include in its precondition that the receiver object's owner is exposed. We say that an object is *committed* when its owner is consistent. In summary, an appropriate precondition for a typical method is that the receiver object is consistent and not committed.

In the sequel, we refer to the *ownership cone* of an object o to mean the set of objects that includes o (pictured on top of the cone), the rep objects of o (pictured one level below o), the rep objects of the rep objects (pictured yet another level below), and so on. That is, the ownership cone of o is a hierarchical collection of objects that includes o and all objects transitively owned by o.

Frame conditions. An important part of a method specification is its *frame condition*, which describes, as a postcondition, which locations in the heap the method may modify. Commonly, the frame condition is produced partly from a user-specified *modifies clause* and partly from rules prescribed by the methodology. For example, a standard rule is to allow fields of newly allocated objects to be modified.

A typical method implementation modifies the fields of the receiver object, the fields of its rep objects, the fields of their rep objects, and so on—that is, it modifies the heap locations in the ownership cone of the receiver object. We must therefore make it possible to include an object's entire ownership cone in a method's frame condition.

It is not possible to list all the locations of an ownership cone by name in the modifies clause, because doing so would violate information hiding. One approach is to instead use some encoding that yields the fields of all transitive rep objects, which can be done by quantifying over field names and using some transitive closure or reachability operator. However, experience shows that such a closure or reachability construct is hard to process well with an automatic theorem prover (*cf.* [9]).

The Boogie methodology takes a simple approach that over-approximates the heap locations that an implementation is able to modify: it says that, in addition to heap locations explicitly indicated in the modifies clause and heap locations that belong to newly allocated objects, a method's frame condition includes the fields of all committed objects. More precisely, a modifies clause W gives rise to the following frame condition:

$$(\forall o, f \bullet \; h[o,f] = \mathbf{old}(h)[o,f] \vee (o,f) \in \mathbf{old}(W) \vee \qquad\qquad (3)$$
$$\neg\mathbf{old}(h)[o, allocated] \vee (o \text{ is committed in } \mathbf{old}(h)) \;)$$

where o ranges over non-null object references, f over field names, and a heap location is a pair (o, f). This encoding has the advantage that it uses a simple quantification—it avoids transitive closure and reachability—and gives an implementation the license to modify fields of its transitive rep objects. One can also give an argument for why callers need not be adversely affected by the over-approximation [1].

5   Encoding Lightweight Read-Effects

In this section, we describe an encoding and reasoning technique that makes use of lightweight read-effect annotations of pure methods. By *lightweight* we mean that users need not prescribe precisely the effects but rather in an abstract, (over-)approximative way in terms of ownership cones.

In our attempts to run Boogie to verify Spec# code, we repeatedly find code patterns like the following, where M is a pure method:

if (o.M() != **null**) { r.P();   y = o.M().f; }

This code dereferences o.M() after checking that it is not null. One way to show that it does not throw a null-pointer exception is to prove that the two calls to o.M() return the same value. The basic verification support needed in such situations is knowing whether some heap changes (such as those performed by the call to r.P() in the example above) affect the value returned by a pure method.

Determining whether a heap change has any effect on the value returned by a pure method depends on what the pure method reads. We find it useful to consider three kinds of pure methods: (1) those that do not read any mutable part of the heap (called *state-independent* pure methods); (2) those that confine what they read to heap locations in the ownership cone of the receiver object (so-called *read-confined* pure methods, which are the most common kind of pure methods); and (3) those without any restrictions on what they might read (called *read-anything* methods). We require that every pure method be declared to be of one of these three read levels.

We do not go into details of how to enforce read restrictions. In our implementation of Spec#, we currently use a variation of the data-flow analysis prescribed by Sălcianu and Rinard [18].

Since a state-independent method M does not depend on the heap, we drop the heap argument from the signature of function $\#M$. This encoding makes it evident that the value returned by M in code patterns like the one above is not affected by heap changes.

Methods that can read anything are always potentially sensitive to changes in the heap, so we do not do anything extra for these methods.

For the most common kind of pure methods, the read-confined ones, we would like to provide an axiom that says, "if the values of the heap locations in the ownership cone of an object o are the same in two object stores h and k, then the return value of o.M() is the same in h and k". There are two problems with trying to supply such an axiom.

One problem is that describing, in the axiom, all heap locations in the receiver's ownership cone requires transitive closure or reachability, which makes it difficult to apply automatic theorem provers. The other problem is that even if the axiom mentions the entire ownership cone, frame condition (3) does not say anything about how the state of a committed object changes. Hence, a call like r.P() in the example above is viewed as possibly having an effect on the committed objects in the ownership cone of o. That is, with frame condition (3), an axiom that mentions the entire ownership cone is too weak to be useful.

To find a solution, we recall how the state of the ownership cone of an object can change in the Boogie methodology. The methodology enforces that a field s.x is updated only when s and all transitive owners of s are exposed. Consequently, an object's ownership cone remains unchanged through any time period during which the object remains consistent. We will seek to encode this fact by recording a *snapshot* of an object's ownership cone at the time the object transitions from exposed to consistent. The snapshot may become out-of-date when the object is in the exposed state, so we need to make sure to use snapshots only for consistent objects. Equipped with snapshots, which we represent by adding a field *snapshot* to every object (transparent to users), we obtain the following property:

$$(\forall o, p, h, k \bullet \ (o \text{ is consistent in } h) \wedge (o \text{ is consistent in } k) \wedge \\ h[o, snapshot] = k[o, snapshot] \ \Rightarrow \ \#M(o, p, h) = \#M(o, p, k)) \quad (4)$$

where o ranges over non-null object references, p ranges over the possible values of M's other parameters, and h and k range over heaps. Note the limited role of p in (4); this is due to the read-confinedness of the method, *i.e.* it may not read heap locations in the ownership cones of parameters. Axiom (4) lets us prove the example above—provided r.P() does not change o.snapshot, of course.

Encoding. To make the idea described here a reality in a checker, we need to design a suitable encoding for updating snapshot fields (to be used by the static verifier) and an appropriate formulation of axiom (4).

We update the snapshot field of an object o at the end of the constructor of o (when the object first becomes consistent) and at the end of **expose** blocks. We might consider the update of the field as an assignment statement like:

$$o.snapshot := (o.x, o.y, o.z, \ldots, o.r.snapshot, o.s.snapshot, \ldots) \quad (5)$$

where the right-hand side is a tuple of the (non-snapshot) fields x, y, z, ... of o and the snapshots of the rep fields r, s, ... of o. This works if the right-hand side represents the entire ownership cone of o. But in Spec#, we allow an unbounded number of rep objects (à la Leino and Müller [12]), so it is not sufficient to include the snapshots of rep fields. Instead, we abstract over the actual snapshot and assign to o.snapshot an arbitrary value satisfying property (4). Given that we postulate the property as an axiom, the assignment simply becomes "**havoc** o.snapshot" where **havoc** is a command that sets its l-value argument to an arbitrary value (satisfying postulated axioms).

Like for other fields, if a method has an effect on the snapshot field of a non-new, non-committed object, then it must account for the effect in the method's modifies clause. To make this easier on the programmer, our implementation implicitly adds **this**.snapshot to the modifies clause of every non-pure method. In addition, for any term explicitly mentioned in the modifies clause, say p.f.g where p is either **this** or another method parameter, our implementation implicitly adds p.snapshot and p.f.snapshot to the modifies clause.

As for axiom (4), we do not encode it the way we just showed it above, because quantifying over pairs of heaps does not give rise to good performance in the theorem prover. The axiom really states that, for any consistent object o and parameters p, $\#M(o, p, h)$ depends only on the reference o, the values p, and o.snapshot, that is, $\#M(o, p, h)$ is a function of o, p, and o.snapshot. So, we abstract again and introduce an uninterpreted function symbol $\#\#M$ and write the axiom simply as:

$$(\forall\, o, p, h \bullet \ (o \text{ is consistent in } h) \ \Rightarrow \\ \#M(o, p, h) = \#\#M(o, p, h[o, snapshot]) \ ) \tag{6}$$

This encoding solves the problem in the example above and it is the encoding we use in Boogie.

6   Preconditions and Frame Conditions for Pure Methods

This section discusses how to write preconditions for pure methods, motivating that a more relaxed condition is needed than the one used by the Boogie methodology. Then, we discuss what is an appropriate frame condition for pure methods and introduce axioms to regain some precision lost by the relaxed preconditions.

6.1   Consequences of the Standard Precondition

Let us take a closer look at a typical method, which will lead us to some considerations for the preconditions of pure methods. Consider the Engine class example mentioned in Section 4 and suppose it has the following method, which does the typical thing of calling a method on a rep object:

```
void RevUpEngine()
  requires this is consistent and not committed;
  { expose (this) { this.pump.IncreaseVolume(); } }
```

Let's review why this code needs the **expose** statement around the call. Typically, the form of the precondition of the called method, IncreaseVolume, is the same as that of the precondition of the caller, RevUpEngine: the receiver (here, pump) is consistent and not committed. To meet the precondition "not committed" of IncreaseVolume, it is necessary for method RevUpEngine to expose the engine object before invoking the method on the rep object.

Now, consider the situation where both the calling method and the called method are pure, for example where a pure GetRevStatus method calls a pure GetVolume method on the pump. In this situation, which occurs in practice, the pure caller method is not allowed to change the state of objects, thus it cannot expose the receiver object, and thus it cannot establish the called method's precondition that the rep object not be committed. To allow this situation, we need a more liberal precondition for pure methods. In particular, we would like to drop the part about the receiver not being committed. That part of the precondition was needed to support exposing and mutating an object, which pure methods are not allowed to do anyway.

In summary, an appropriate precondition for a pure method says that the receiver object is consistent, but says nothing about whether the object is committed or not, *i.e.*, whether the object's owner is consistent or exposed.

6.2   Frame Conditions of Pure Methods

It is clear that a pure method must have an empty modifies clause. However, it is not equally clear if the frame condition for a pure method is prescribed in the same way as it is for a mutating method.

Initially, we had thought of dropping the fourth disjunct of the frame condition (3) for pure methods. Such a design had seemed to make sense, because pure methods are not allowed to modify the committed objects in the cone of the receiver or other parameter. However, consider a pure method with the body "**return** (**new** T()).P();" where P is a method that mutates its receiver and the cone of the receiver. It seems reasonable to want to allow this code, because it operates only on newly allocated objects (the third disjunct). However, since both the T constructor and the P method include the fourth disjunct in *their* frame conditions (since they are mutating methods), it will be difficult to prove that M has no effect on the state of committed objects.

Instead, we propose keeping the fourth disjunct in the frame condition of pure methods. This gives pure method M the license to modify committed objects, thus it is allowed to call the T constructor and P method, whose frame conditions give them the license to modify committed objects. Despite having the license, we will see below that pure methods cannot actually modify committed objects.

The appropriate precondition for pure methods (which does not say whether or not the receiver is committed) and the frame condition of methods (which does not constrain the state of committed objects) interact. We discovered this bad interaction when we tried to verify code of the following form:

[**Pure**] **int** M()
{ **int** a = **this**.x;   **int** b = N();   **assert** a == **this**.x;   **return** b − a; }

where N is some pure method (whose frame condition, like the frame condition of all methods, includes the fourth disjunct). So, N is seen as having an arbitrary effect on the state of committed objects. This is a problem for the verification of the assert if the receiver is committed, which the appropriate precondition for pure methods (in particular, the precondition of M) allows it to be.

Intuitively, we can justify why the assert above will hold as follows. Any effect N has on **this**.x must happen when **this** is exposed. But **this** is consistent on entry to (M and) N, so N must at some point expose **this**. Exposing an object can only be done if its owner is already exposed. Thus, if **this** is committed on entry to N, then N must first expose the owner of **this**, and this same argument applies to the owner of **this**, and so on. Every committed object has some transitive owner that is consistent and not committed. In fact, that transitive owner is unique in any given state, let's call it the "first non-committed owner". So, if **this** is committed, then in order to expose **this**, one must start with exposing the first non-committed owner of **this**. This, according what we have described in Section 5, will have an irrevocable effect on the *snapshot* of that first non-committed owner. Since the first non-committed owner is both allocated and not committed, the only way its snapshot is allowed to be changed is if it is included in W, the set of modifiable locations of the method. Since pure methods have empty modifies clauses, we conclude that N does not have any effect on the snapshot of the first non-committed owner of **this**, and thus no effect on **this**.x.

We encode the idea of a first non-committed owner using a field *FirstNon-CommittedOwner* (*fnco*, for short), which has a meaningful value for any allocated, committed object. We do not want to give a precise axiomatization of fnco, because doing so would mean we need transitive closure or reachability. Instead, we just encode the properties we need, namely that fnco is allocated and not committed (which excludes it from the third and fourth disjuncts of the frame condition):

$$(\forall o, h \bullet \ h[o, allocated] \wedge (o \text{ is committed in } h) \ \Rightarrow$$
$$h[o, fnco] \neq \textbf{null} \wedge h[h[o, fnco], allocated] \wedge (h[o, fnco] \text{ not committed in } h) \ )$$

And we also need to say that a change to a field of a committed object requires a change in the snapshot of the object's first non-committed owner.

$$(\forall o, f, h \bullet \ h[o, allocated] \wedge (o \text{ is committed in } h) \ \Rightarrow$$
$$(h[o, f] \text{ is a function of } o, f, \text{ and } h[h[o, fnco], snapshot] \ ) \ )$$

Finally, o.fnco can change only if o.fnco.snapshot does, a property that we formalize into a postcondition assumption after each call.

With these axioms and assumptions, we are able to regain information about the values of fields and can prove the correctness of pure method M above.

Summary of contributions. We presented an axiom that exploits methods' read-confinedness, investigated what the proper precondition of pure methods is, and proposed axioms to regain information due to that precondition. Without these results, many code patterns often encountered in Spec# could not be handled.

7   Related Work and Conclusion

The work closest to ours on the sound axiomatization of pure methods is that of Darvas and Müller [6]. In fact, we follow all their proposals with adaptations required due to the different settings of our work. For example, our design is more liberal in allowing pure methods to return newly allocated objects.

Jacobs and Piessens [8] present a reasoning technique for confined methods that is very similar to our approach of using snapshots (Section 5). Their notion of confinedness is extended to method parameters too—which could be encoded in our settings as well with a slight adaption of axiom (6). They record their snapshots, which are represented as fields f_{state}, explicitly from the state fields of the rep objects. This works only if the rep objects can be enumerated syntactically (*cf.* (5)). However, it seems that they could use a havoc statement instead, like we do, to overcome that limitation.

Separation logic divides up the heap and keeps track of accessible regions of it. For example, the work of Parkinson and Bierman [16] can be used to encode the basic Boogie methodology. Read and write effects can be handled, but the approach has not been developed into a practical tool for a language like Spec#.

Kassios introduces a promising and powerful way to specify and reason about changes in the heap [10]. The technique is not tied to any particular methodology. We look forward to seeing it implemented in a tool.

In many ways, pure methods look like *model fields*, abstract variables whose values are defined in terms of more concrete fields. There are, however, some differences; for example, a model field has to be listed in the modifies clause of a method if the method changes its value. We would like to study the relation between pure methods and the model-field encoding by Leino and Müller [13].

Conclusion. We have presented encoding, axiomatization, and reasoning techniques for pure methods as implemented in the Spec# system. The techniques work with an automatic theorem prover and fit into a methodology for object invariants. Our work contributes a list of verification differences between ordinary and pure methods, an adaptation and extension the results on axiomatizing pure methods in [6], and an axiomatization of the special properties of read-confined pure methods that makes them insensitive to changes in other objects, an exploration of how to write preconditions and frame conditions for pure methods and how to provide a practical axiomatization to support these.

Acknowledgments. We thank Peter Müller for helpful discussions and Mike Barnett for discussions and his help with the implementation. The idea of taking a "snapshot" of an object's state is originally from Bart Jacobs. Diego Garbervetsky implemented the effects analysis in the Spec# system.

References

1. M. Barnett, R. DeLine, M. Fähndrich, K. R. M. Leino, and W. Schulte. Verification of object-oriented programs with invariants. *JOT*, 3(6):27–56, 2004.

2. M. Barnett, R. DeLine, B. Jacobs, B.-Y. E. Chang, and K. R. M. Leino. Boogie: A modular reusable verifier for object-oriented programs. In *FMCO*, volume 4111 of *LNCS*, pages 364–387. Springer, 2006.

3. M. Barnett, K. R. M. Leino, and W. Schulte. The Spec# programming system: An overview. In *CASSIS*, volume 3362 of *LNCS*, pages 49–69. Springer, 2005.

4. D. G. Clarke, J. M. Potter, and J. Noble. Ownership types for flexible alias protection. In *OOPSLA*, volume 33(10), pages 48–64. ACM, 1998.

5. D. R. Cok. Reasoning with specifications containing method calls and model fields. *JOT*, 4(8):77–103, October 2005.
6. Á. Darvas and P. Müller. Reasoning about method calls in interface specifications. *JOT*, 5(5):59–85, June 2006.
7. D. Detlefs, G. Nelson, and J. B. Saxe. Simplify: A theorem prover for program checking. Tech. Rep. HPL-2003-148, Systems Research Center, HP Labs, 2003.
8. B. Jacobs and F. Piessens. Verification of programs using inspector methods. In *Formal Techniques for Java-like Programs*, 2006.
9. R. Joshi. Extended static checking of programs with cyclic dependencies. Technical Note 1997-028, Digital Equipment Corporation Systems Research Center, 1997.
10. I. T. Kassios. Dynamic frames: Support for framing, dependencies and sharing without restrictions. In *FM*, volume 4085 of *LNCS*, pages 268–283. Springer, 2006.
11. G. T. Leavens, A. L. Baker, and C. Ruby. Preliminary design of JML: A behavioral interface specification language for Java. *ACM SIGSOFT Software Engineering Notes*, 31(3):1–38, 2006.
12. K. R. M. Leino and P. Müller. Object invariants in dynamic contexts. In *ECOOP*, volume 3086 of *LNCS*, pages 491–516. Springer, 2004.
13. K. R. M. Leino and P. Müller. A verification methodology for model fields. In *ESOP*, volume 3924 of *LNCS*, pages 115–130. Springer, 2006.
14. C. Marché, C. Paulin-Mohring, and X. Urbain. The KRAKATOA tool for certification of JAVA/JAVACARD programs annotated in JML. *Journal of Logic and Algebraic Programming*, 58(1–2):89–106, Jan.–Mar. 2004.
15. B. Meyer. *Eiffel: The Language*. Prentice Hall, 1992.
16. M. Parkinson and G. Bierman. Separation logic and abstraction. In *POPL*, pages 247–258. ACM, 2005.
17. A. Poetzsch-Heffter and P. Müller. A programming logic for sequential Java. In *ESOP*, volume 1576 of *LNCS*, pages 162–176. Springer, 1999.
18. A. Sălcianu and M. C. Rinard. Purity and side effect analysis for Java programs. In *VMCAI*, volume 3385 of *LNCS*, pages 199–215. Springer, 2005.

Finding Environment Guarantees

Marsha Chechik, Mihaela Gheorghiu, and Arie Gurfinkel

University of Toronto, Toronto, ON M5S 3G4, Canada
{chechik,mg,arie}@cs.toronto.edu

Abstract. When model checking a software component, a model of the environment in which that component is supposed to run is constructed. One of the major threats to the validity of this kind of analysis is the correctness of the environment model. In this paper, we identify and formalize a problem related to environment models — *environment guarantees*. It captures those cases where the correctness of the component under analysis is due solely to the model of its environment. Environment guarantees provides a model-based analog to a property-based notion of *vacuity* by identifying cases when the component is irrelevant to satisfaction of a property. The paper also presents a model checking technique for the detection of environment guarantees. We show the effectiveness of our technique by applying it to a previously published study of TCAS II, where it finds a number of environment guarantees.

1 Introduction

As software is controlling more and more critical aspects of our lives, its reliability is ever more important. Formal verification can help increase confidence in the software systems being built. Among the verification methods, model checking is gaining popularity due to its automated approach. In this approach, a model of the software component being analyzed is closed with a model of the environment in which the component is expected to run. Correctness properties of the component are then checked on the resulting model. One of the major threats to this kind of analysis is the correctness of the environment model. Creating a faithful model of the environment is error-prone, as often the environment consists of parts of the physical world whose behavior is only partially understood, or it is a complex system, *e.g.*, an operating system, whose behavior is also hard to capture in a unified model. Moreover, the model of the environment is often simplified to enable effective model-checking, potentially leading to errors.

To illustrate the kinds of modeling errors we address, consider, for example, model checking a traffic light controller. In this system, cars arrive at an intersection, trip sensors, and wait for the green light. The controller, which is the component being analyzed, uses the sensors, that represent the environment, to maximize the flow of cars through the intersection. An essential property of the system is that if a sensor is ever tripped, an appropriate light eventually turns green. This property is formalized in CTL (defined in Sec. 2) as $\varphi = AG\,(\mathsf{Sensor\_Tripped} \Rightarrow (AF\,\mathsf{Light} = \mathsf{green}))$. Suppose there is a bug in the environment model due to which Sensor_Tripped is always off. The property then holds regardless of the correctness of the controller. Thus, although the desired property is satisfied, the component should not be deemed correct. Instead, we want the model checker to detect that the environment model may be wrong.

M.B. Dwyer and A. Lopes (Eds.): FASE 2007, LNCS 4422, pp. 352–367, 2007.

Industrial researchers noted that in practice properties with implication (such as φ) may hold for the wrong reasons, referring to the problem as "antecedent failure". IBM researchers generalized this notion to properties that are not necessarily implications, naming it *vacuity* [2]. The definition of vacuity is *property-based*: a formula α is vacuous in a subformula β in a given model if β does not influence the value of α in the model. That is, in the traffic light example above with the faulty environment model, the property φ is vacuous in Light=green: it is satisfied independently of the color of the light because the antecedent of the implication is false. [2] also defined a vacuity detection method for a restricted class of CTL formulas and noted that when found, vacuity always pointed to a problem in either the component, its environment, or in the property, which was observed for 20% of the properties checked. Other researchers [16,1,13] extended vacuity detection to general properties expressed in CTL and other common languages. All these approaches, however, remain property-based, and are not adequate to detect errors in the *model*. Vacuity information is not sufficient to decide when the environment model is faulty. Consider the property φ again — it is also vacuous in Light=green in a model where the activation of the sensors depends on a flag being set by the controller independently of the environment, and the controller never sets that flag. In this case, the vacuity is due to the *component*, and not to its *environment*, and is often not effective for finding problems with the model.

In contrast to the property-centric approach of vacuity detection, Shlyakhter *et al.* [21] devised a technique to debug models more directly. They identified the problem of "overconstraining" declarative models, and pointed out that overconstraining occurs most often in the definition of the models being checked rather than in the specification of their correctness properties. They have developed a technique for extracting and displaying the part of the model used for establishing satisfaction of a property. When most of the model was unnecessary to prove a property, the authors were able to conclude that was due to overconstraint, caused by subtle modeling errors. This technique, however, is restricted to declarative models, and does not exploit the view of the model that separates the component from its environment.

In our work, we also aim to provide a technique for model debugging, but in the case of operational models, such as those specified by state-machines, and we target the analysis toward debugging environment models. We consider a model to be "overconstrained" if a property that should hold of the software component in the given environment is guaranteed solely by the environment. In other words, the component can be replaced by another, *arbitrary*, component in the same environment, without affecting the satisfaction of the property. We say that such properties are *environment guarantees*. Environment guarantees always indicate a problem: either the desired property is not a property of the component, and should rather be reconsidered as a property of its environment, or there is an error in the model of the environment or in expressing the property. The naive approach to detect environment guarantees is to generate all possible components, compose each with the given environment, and check whether the property holds on all the composed models. This is clearly infeasible. Instead, we show how to model the environment as an open system and check properties on it directly, using a symbolic model-checking algorithm.

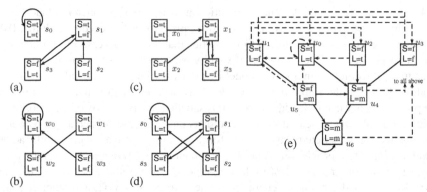

Fig. 1. An example Kripke structure (a). A four-valued Kripke structure of an open system (e), and its three completions (b), (c), and (d)

A similar approach, called *robust satisfaction* was proposed and studied in [15]. It is aiming to identify whether a property holds in *all* possible environments, and is the same as environment guarantees with the roles of the environment and the system reversed. While the method in [15] is complete (it always finds errors when they are present), it is rather expensive (see Sec. 7 for a detailed discussion).

Our paper makes the following contributions: (1) We argue that a way to discover faulty environment models is to detect cases where properties are guaranteed solely by the environment. Although this process does not find all possible environment modeling errors, the errors reported by this analysis *always* point to some error in understanding of the model-checking results. (2) We formalize the meaning of a property being guaranteed by the environment by modeling the environment as an open system (Sec. 3). (3) We show how to model open systems and define a model-checking algorithm which can lead to a scalable technique for discovering environment guarantees (Sec. 4). (4) We describe a simple implementation for checking environment guarantees for true universal properties (Sec. 5). (5) We show that our technique finds real errors and is scalable for handling non-trivial systems by applying it to the well-known example of the Traffic Collision and Avoidance System (TCAS II) [18,4] (Sec.6). In our case study, we found that several essential properties of TCAS II, including some analyzed by Chan *et al.*in [4], hold as the result of environment guarantees: the model of the environment used in verifying this system has been simplified too much.

2   Background

In this section, we review the model-checking process and fix the notation.

Definition 1. *A model* $\mathcal{M}$ *consists of a set* $V = \{v_1, \ldots, v_n\}$ *of variables and a set* Δ *of rules describing the temporal behavior of those variables. A state of the model* $\mathcal{M}$ *is a valuation of all variables in* V. *A rule is an expression over the model variables that relates their values in a state at time* t *(current) with those at time* $t + 1$ *(next).*

Without loss of generality, we assume that the variables are boolean. Therefore, the set S of states consists of all n-tuples of boolean values. For instance, consider our previous

$\mathcal{K}_\mathcal{M}, s \models p$ iff $I(p, s)$ $\mathcal{K}_\mathcal{M}, s \models \neg\varphi$ iff $\mathcal{K}_\mathcal{M}, s \not\models \varphi$

$\mathcal{K}_\mathcal{M}, s \models \varphi \wedge \psi$ iff $\mathcal{K}_\mathcal{M}, s \models \varphi \wedge \mathcal{K}_\mathcal{M}, s \models \psi$ $\mathcal{K}_\mathcal{M}, s \models EX\varphi$ iff $\exists t \in S, (s,t) \in R \wedge \mathcal{K}_\mathcal{M}, t \models \varphi$

$\mathcal{K}_\mathcal{M}, s \models EG\varphi$ iff $\exists$ path $s = s_0, s_1, \ldots$ s.t. $\forall j \cdot \mathcal{K}_\mathcal{M}, s_j \models \varphi$

$\mathcal{K}_\mathcal{M}, s \models E[\varphi\ U\ \psi]$ iff $\exists$ path $s = s_0, s_1, \ldots$ s.t. $\exists j \cdot \mathcal{K}_\mathcal{M}, s_j \models \psi \wedge \forall k \cdot k < j \Rightarrow \mathcal{K}_\mathcal{M}, s_k \models \varphi$

Fig. 2. Semantics of CTL

example of a traffic light system. It can be modeled by a variable Light, which is true iff the light is green (Light=green), and a variable Sensor, which is true iff the sensor is tripped. For a variable v, we use v (unprimed) and v' (primed) to denote its current and next state value, respectively, and define $V' = \{v'_1, \ldots, v'_n\}$.

We assume that rules are described in the style of the SMV language [6]. Each rule is an assignment of the form $v'_i \leftarrow \delta$, where $v'_i \in V'$ and δ is a boolean formula over the variables in $V \cup V' \setminus \{v'_i\}$. We assume no circularity in the rules, *i.e.*, no variable depends on itself if we follow any chain of the rules, and there is at least one assignment for each variable. In our example, the rules may be Sensor' $\leftarrow \neg$Sensor $\vee$ Light and Light' $\leftarrow$ Sensor, which indicate that the sensor is on in the next state if it is currently off or the light is on, and the light is on in the next state if the sensor is currently on. It is convenient to think of each assignment as an equivalent boolean formula, i.e., $v' \leftarrow \delta$ iff $(v' \wedge \delta) \vee (\neg v' \wedge \neg\delta)$. Multiple assignments per variable are used to indicate that the variable changes non-deterministically, *e.g.*, when the model $\mathcal{M}$ contains rules $v' \leftarrow$ true and $v' \leftarrow$ false, it means that v' can be either true or false in the next state of $\mathcal{M}$.

Given a model $\mathcal{M}$, we associate with it a state-transition graph $\mathcal{K}_\mathcal{M}$, known as a *Kripke structure*: The *Kripke structure* $\mathcal{K}_\mathcal{M}$ is a tuple $\langle S, R, I \rangle$, where S is the set of states, $R \subseteq S \times S$ is the transition relation, and $I : V \times S \rightarrow \{$true, false$\}$ is the interpretation of variables. For each variable v_i and state s, $I(v_i, s)$, or $s(i)$ for short, is the value of v_i in s. Let s and s' denote valuations of all unprimed and primed variables, respectively. The relation R is the set of all pairs of states (s, s') such that s and s' satisfy at least one of the rules of Δ for every variable in V.

The Kripke structure for our example is shown in Fig. 1(a). For brevity, we use S for Sensor and L for Light in the diagrams. For example, in state s_0, the right hand sides of the rules for both Sensor and Light are true. Thus, both Sensor and Light have to be true in the successor state, creating the self-loop at s_0.

Properties of a model $\mathcal{M}$ are formulated in the temporal logic CTL, whose semantics is given in Fig. 2, and evaluated in the states of the associated Kripke structure $\mathcal{K}_\mathcal{M}$. For example, $E[\varphi\ U\ \psi]$ is true in s if along some path from s, φ continuously holds until ψ becomes true. The following derived CTL formula is also commonly used: $EF\ \varphi \equiv E[$true $U\ \varphi]$. For instance, in the structure of Fig. 1(a), the formula EF Light (the light eventually becomes green) is true in all states, whereas the formula AG (Sensor$\vee$Light) (always the sensor is tripped or the light is green) is true in states s_0, s_1, s_3 and false in s_2. The subclass of CTL formulas containing only universal path quantifiers is called ACTL. Often, some state of a Kripke structure, say, s_0, is designated as *initial*. In this case, we say that a formula φ holds in a Kripke structure $\mathcal{K}_\mathcal{M}$ to mean that $\mathcal{K}_\mathcal{M}, s_0 \models \varphi$. A model $\mathcal{M}$ *satisfies* a CTL formula φ if $\mathcal{K}_\mathcal{M} \models \varphi$.

3   Environment Guarantees

In this section, we formalize the notion of environment guarantees. A model described in Sec. 2 is a composition of the software component being analyzed, called the *component* from now on, with its environment. The boundary between them is often blurred during verification: they are simply specified using a collection of rules. In what follows, we make this boundary more explicit.

We assume that the set V of model variables is partitioned into a set C of *component variables* and a set E of *environment variables*. We further assume that this partition can be determined *syntactically*, (*e.g.*, by the names or types of the variables, or their location, etc.), or by the model documentation. Environment variables represent the inputs to the software, coming from the environment. Component variables represent the outputs from the software to the environment. The variable partition induces a partition on the rules of a model into *component rules* and *environment rules*.

Definition 2. *A partitioned* model $\mathcal{M}$ *is a tuple* $\langle (C, E), (\Delta_C, \Delta_E) \rangle$, *where* $V = C \cup E$ *and* $\Delta_C \cup \Delta_V = \Delta$, *such that* Δ_C *consists of assignments to* v' *for each* $v \in C$, *and* Δ_E *consists of assignments to* v' *for each* $v \in E$.

Definition 3. *Given a partitioned model* $\mathcal{M} = \langle (C, E), (\Delta_C, \Delta_E) \rangle$, *the* environment *of* $\mathcal{M}$ *is a tuple* $\mathcal{E} = \langle V, \Delta_E \rangle$.

That is, the environment consists of its rules together with all variables in the model. In our traffic light example, Sensor is an environment variable, whereas Light is a component variable. Consequently, the rule Sensor' $\leftarrow$ ¬Sensor $\vee$ Light is the environment rule, and Light' $\leftarrow$ Sensor is the component rule. Models in which all variables have associated rules are called *closed*. For example, the combination of the sensor and the light controller for the model in Fig. 1(a) is a closed system. A model that does not contain rules for all of its variables is called *open*. The *environment* is the open model obtained by removing the component rules from a closed model. In our example, it consists of a single rule Sensor' $\leftarrow$ ¬Sensor $\vee$ Light, and variables Sensor and Light.

When does the environment guarantee a property? Intuitively, when satisfaction of some property of the model depends solely on the environment rules. For instance, if the environment rule in our example were Sensor' $\leftarrow$ true, then in any state where Sensor is true, the property AG (Sensor $\vee$ Light) would be guaranteed by the environment. In this case, it is obvious that the environment alone guarantees the property; in real-life models, however, such as the one considered in our case study (see Sec. 6), the intricate logic may hinder the easy detection of such environment guarantees.

To define when the environment satisfies a property, we construct all possible "closures" of the environment with component rules, and then use the standard semantics of temporal logic over the resulting closed models. In our example, one closure was shown earlier, where the component rule Light' $\leftarrow$ Sensor is added to the rules of the environment. We can construct another closure by adding component rule Light' $\leftarrow$ ¬Sensor to the rules of the environment.

Definition 4. *A* model $\mathcal{M} = (V, \Delta)$ *is a* closure *of an environment* $\mathcal{E} = (W, \Lambda)$ *if* $V = W$ *and* $\Lambda \subseteq \Delta$, *where* $\forall$ *component variables in* $\mathcal{M}$, $\exists$ *a rule in* $\Delta \setminus \Lambda$.

Rules are identified modulo logical equivalence, so $v' \leftarrow \delta$ and $v' \leftarrow \neg\neg\delta$ are the same.

Definition 5. *An environment* $\mathcal{E}$ guarantees a satisfaction *of temporal property* φ *in state* s, *written* $\mathcal{E}, s \models \varphi$, *if and only if* all of its closures *satisfy* φ *in* s. *An environment guarantees a failure of* φ *in state* s, *written* $\mathcal{E}, s \models \neg\varphi$, *if and only if* φ *fails in* s *in all closures of* $\mathcal{E}$. *Finally, an environment* $\mathcal{E}$ guarantees *a property* φ *in state* s *iff* $\mathcal{E}, s \models \varphi \vee \mathcal{E}, s \models \neg\varphi$.

4. Environment Guarantees: Modeling and Algorithms

Given the environment rules, the rules closing them represent the behavior of a possible component in that environment. Intuitively, our notion of environment guarantee, given in Sec. 3, means that regardless of the component the environment is combined with, the resulting model still satisfies the property. This suggests the following naive approach to detecting environment guarantees: generate and model check all closures of the environment. Since there are exponentially many such closures, this approach is clearly infeasible. To solve this problem, in this section we use another representation of the environment that implicitly encodes all of its closures, and define a model-checking algorithm over this representation that checks all closures at once.

4.1 Logics for Open Systems

We aim to model open systems as state-transition graphs that can be model-checked directly. However, it is possible that an open system does not guarantee either the property, or its negation. That happens when the truth of the property depends on *how* the system is closed: in some closures the property is false; in the others, it is true.

Consider the model of the environment described in Sec. 3, with variables Sensor and Light and a single rule Sensor′ ← ¬Sensor ∨ Light. Suppose we want to check a property that the sensor does not stay off for two consecutive states, *e.g.*, if the sensor is off in a given state, it will be on in all of its next states, formalized as $\psi_1 = AG\ (\neg\text{Sensor} \Rightarrow AX\ \text{Sensor})$. We check this property in a state where both the sensor and the light are on. Note that the rule of the environment guarantees that ψ_1 is true, independently of Light. Therefore, this is an environment guarantee and will evaluate to true on all of the closures. On the other hand, consider a slightly different property: in any state, if the sensor is off, it remains off for one more time step, or $\psi_2 = AG\ (\neg\text{Sensor} \Rightarrow AX\ \neg\text{Sensor})$. In this case, we can find two closures of the environment that disagree on the value of this property. In one of them, the environment is closed with rule (1) Light′ ← true, in the other – with (2) Light′ ← false. With (1), in any state, after at most two steps, the sensor becomes on and stays on forever. With (2), the sensor alternates between on and off. If checked in a state where both the sensor and the light are on, ψ_2 is true in the first closure, but false in the second. In this case, we want the property to evaluate to "unknown" on the model of the environment alone, meaning that the environment by itself does not have enough knowledge to satisfy or refute the property. By this discussion, classical Kripke structures are not appropriate for modeling open systems since they limit reasoning to only two values. Instead, multi-valued structures have been employed for this task [10]. In our approach, we use the 4-valued logic known as Belnap [3] (see Fig. 3). We use this logic instead of the 3-valued approach of [10] because it enables a more precise analysis by distinguishing between the

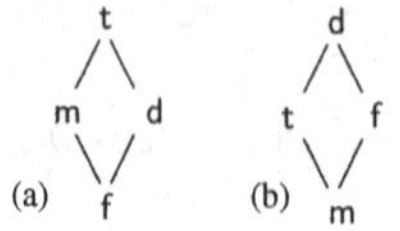

Fig. 3. Belnap logic **4**: (a) truth ordering, (b) information ordering, (c) truth table

partiality in the behavior of the component and that of the environment. We denote by **4** the set of values $\{t, f, m, d\}$: t and f stand for "known to be true" and "known to be false", respectively; m (maybe, or unknown) represents the lack of evidence to decide truth or falsity ("possibly true or false"); and d (definite) represents "necessarily true". Their information content defines an *information ordering* (see Fig. 3(b)) $\preceq$: $m \preceq t, f$ and $t, f \preceq d$.

The usual boolean operations are extended to **4**. For example, conjunction of m with t is m since m may be resolved to true, in which case the result is true, or to false, and then the result is false. Fig. 3(c) presents a table for computing conjunction and negation of values of this logic. These operations are computed on the *truth ordering* pictured in Fig. 3(a), by using greatest lower bound for conjunction and symmetry for negation. We denote by **3** the subset $\{t, f, m\}$ of **4**, and by **2** the subset $\{t, f\}$.

4.2 Representing an Open System as a State-Transition Graph

So far, we have established the requirements that a model of an open system should satisfy in order to help us in detecting environment guarantees: (1) it should support direct model-checking, (2) it should allow properties to evaluate to more values than just true or false, (3) it should represent all closures of the open system, and (4) its model-checking result should be equivalent to model-checking all those closures. In the rest of this section, we show that we can extend Kripke structures to the 4-valued logic so that these requirements are satisfied.

The 4-valued Kripke structure for our example open system is shown in Fig. 1(e). It captures the interaction of the environment with all possible machines. Values of variables for which the environment does not have rules are unknown to the environment, captured by the logic value m. The transitions between states are 4-valued. In the figure, solid and dashed lines are used to represent d and m transitions, respectively. Definite transitions, d, indicate local environment guarantees. For example, the d transitions from u_2 and u_3 to u_4 in Fig. 1(e) indicate that in a state where the sensor is off, the environment guarantees that it will next become on, which can be inferred from the corresponding rule. The value of Light is unknown in u_4 since the environment cannot guarantee anything about it, as it does not have rules allowing changes to this variable. The m transitions capture what the machine can do, subject to environment restrictions. For example, the two m transitions from u_5 indicate that the machine has full control of the light. The absence of m transitions from u_5 to u_2 and u_3 means that the machine cannot violate the environment guarantee for sensor to be on.

Definition 6. *A* 4-*valued Kripke structure* $\mathcal{M}$ *over a set of variables* $V = \{v_1, \ldots, v_n\}$ *is a tuple* $\langle S_\mathcal{M}, I_\mathcal{M}, R_\mathcal{M} \rangle$, *where* $S_\mathcal{M}$ *is the set of states, consisting of all possible n-tuples of values from* **3**; $I_\mathcal{M} : V \times S_\mathcal{M} \to \mathbf{3}$ *is the interpretation of the variables that associates to every variable, in every state, a value from* **3**, *i.e., for every* $s \in S_\mathcal{M}$ *and* $1 \leq i \leq n$, $I_\mathcal{M}(v_i, s) = s(i)$; *and* $R_\mathcal{M} : S_\mathcal{M} \times S_\mathcal{M} \to \mathbf{4}$ *is a* 4-*valued transition relation. For an n-tuple s, we denote by* $s(i)$ *its ith component.*

Given an open system described by a set of rules Δ, for every pair of 3-valued states (s, s'), (1) transition (s, s') is m if s' is boolean (*i.e.*, every variable in this state has a value in **2**); (2) transition (s, s') is d if for each variable v_i that is boolean in s', s and s' satisfy some rule $v_i' \leftarrow \delta \in \Delta$, and s and s' do not violate some rule $v_i' \leftarrow \delta \in \Delta$; (3) otherwise, the transition is false. The 4-valued structure in Fig. 1(e) has been constructed using this algorithm.

4.3 Checking for Environment Guarantees

Our method for detecting whether the environment guarantees a property is as follows. Given the environment rules, (1) construct the associated 4-valued Kripke structure (using Definition 6); (2) use the multi-valued model-checking algorithm to check the property on this structure; (3) if the algorithm answers t or f, the property is guaranteed by the environment. An interpretation of CTL formulas over multi-valued Kripke structures and a corresponding model-checking algorithm have been defined [5], and apply to our 4-valued Kripke structures without modification. We illustrate how the property "there is a next state where the light is on", written as EX Light, is model-checked in state u_5 of the structure in Fig. 1(e). In the classical case, the property is true if and only if there exists a next state where Light is true. Equivalently, the value of the property in a Kripke structure $\mathcal{K} = \langle S_\mathcal{K}, I_\mathcal{K}, R_\mathcal{K} \rangle$ is given by the boolean formula $\bigvee_{s' \in S_\mathcal{K}} R_\mathcal{K}(s, s') \wedge I_\mathcal{K}(s', \text{Light})$, where $R_\mathcal{K}(s, s')$ is true if and only if $(s, s') \in R_\mathcal{K}$. The same formula is used in the 4-valued case, where the operations involved are interpreted over **4**, and for our example, we get:

$(\text{m} \wedge \text{t})$	// transition (u_5, u_0)	$\vee (\text{d} \wedge \text{m})$	// transition (u_5, u_6)
$\vee (\text{m} \wedge \text{f})$	// transition (u_5, u_1)	$\vee \text{f}$	// all missing transitions

which evaluates to m. This is expected, because this property evaluates to true in the first closure of our example, and to false in the second. Model-checking of other CTL operators uses the evaluation of EX as a basic step. For example, for any formula p, "eventually p", or EF p, is expanded as $p \vee EX$ $(p \vee EX$ $(...))$, and this expansion is finite since the system is finite-state. A property "always p", or AG p, is equivalent to $\neg EF$ $\neg p$. If we check properties ψ_1 and ψ_2 on the structure of Fig. 1(e) using this algorithm, we obtain t and m, respectively. Our algorithm points to an environment guarantee if the property evaluates to either true or false, as it does for ψ_1.

Correctness. To show that the method presented in Sec. 4.3 is sound, we need to show that if the model-checking algorithm answers t, then all of the closures of the environment satisfy the property. In Sec. 3, we showed that each closed system is mapped to a classical Kripke structure. Thus, such a structure exists for every closure of the environment. For example, the structures for the two closures in our example are shown in

Fig. 1(b)-(c). We first define *state compatibility* by extending the information ordering to tuples of values component-wise.

Definition 7. *Let u be a 3-valued state and w be a boolean state over the same variables. w is more informative than u, e.g., $u \preceq w$ if, for all $1 \leq i \leq n$, $u(i) \preceq w(i)$.*

The compatibility relation between the boolean and 4-valued structure is defined as follows: a 3-valued state u is compatible to all boolean states w where $u \preceq w$; for any two compatible states, any d transition out of the 3-valued state is matched by a transition out of the boolean state; conversely, any transition out of the boolean state is matched by an m transition out of the 3-valued state. The matched transitions mean that the destinations of these transitions are compatible. We can verify compatibility of the structures in Fig. 1(b)-(c) with the 4-valued structure in Fig. 1(e). For example, state u_5 is compatible with w_3. The d transition (u_5, u_4) is matched by (w_3, w_0), since u_4 and w_0 are compatible. The d transition (u_5, u_6) can also be matched by (w_3, w_0) since u_6 is also compatible with w_0. Conversely, a transition (w_3, w_0) is matched by the m transition (u_5, u_0).

Any classical Kripke structure compatible with a 4-valued Kripke structure is called its *completion*.

Definition 8. *A classical Kripke structure $\mathcal{K} = (S_\mathcal{K}, I_\mathcal{K}, R_\mathcal{K})$ is a completion of a 4-valued Kripke structure $\mathcal{M} = (S_\mathcal{M}, I_\mathcal{M}, R_\mathcal{M})$ if for any $u \in S_\mathcal{M}$ and $w \in S_\mathcal{K}$, $u \preceq w$ implies: (1) for all $u' \in S_\mathcal{M}$ such that $R_\mathcal{M}(u, u') \succeq$ t, there exists $w' \in S_\mathcal{K}$ such that $u' \preceq w'$ and $(w, w') \in R_\mathcal{K}$, and (2) for all $w' \in S_\mathcal{K}$ such that $(w, w') \in R_\mathcal{K}$, there exists $u' \in S_\mathcal{M}$ such that $u' \preceq w'$ and $R_\mathcal{M}(u, u') \preceq$ t.*

The structures in Fig. 1(b)-(c) are thus completions of that in Fig. 1(e). In fact, all classical structures corresponding to the closures of an open system are completions of the 4-valued structure associated with this system.

Theorem 1. *Let $\mathcal{E}$ be an open system and $\mathcal{M}_\mathcal{E}$ be its associated 4-valued Kripke structure. Then, every closure of $\mathcal{E}$ corresponds to a classical Kripke structure that is a completion of $\mathcal{M}_\mathcal{E}$.*

Thus, we can conclude that if all completions of the 4-valued Kripke structure satisfy a property, then all closures of the open system do so as well. To complete our soundness argument, we note that the multi-valued model-checking algorithm has the following property: *If on a given structure and a given property φ, the answer of the model-checking algorithm is* t *(f), then all completions of that structure satisfy (violate) φ, and thus φ is guaranteed by the environment.*

Theorem 2. *Let $\mathcal{E}$ be an open system and $\mathcal{M}_\mathcal{E}$ be its associated 4-valued Kripke structure. For any CTL formula φ and any boolean state s, if the result of the multi-valued model-checking algorithm on $\mathcal{M}_\mathcal{E}$ is* t *or* f, *then $\mathcal{E}$ guarantees φ in state s.*

When model-checking yields t (f), we can further conclude that φ holds (fails to hold) in the composition of $\mathcal{E}$ with every component.

Our method is not complete, *i.e.*, if the answer of the model-checking algorithm is m, the environment may or may not guarantee the property.

5   Implementation

The multi-valued model-checking algorithm that reasons over 4-valued Kripke structures has been implemented in the tool XChek [5]. We can use XChek to check models of the environment directly or reduce the multi-valued model-checking problem to two classical ones, via a reduction described in [12], and then use a classical model-checker such as NuSMV [6]. In either case, this approach is more efficient than checking all possible closures of the environment. Unfortunately, while XChek can provide an effective reasoning over models once they have been constructed, building such models from text-based descriptions remains a challenge. Specifically, the case study in Sec. 6 involved a model specified in SMV [6], where the full generality of the SMV modeling language was used.

In what follows, we discuss a simple implementation that can decide environment guarantees of true ACTL formulas. An example ACTL property is AF (Sensor∨Light). Intuitively, since any ACTL property refers to "all paths", if it holds on the model with the most paths, it will hold on any model having a subset of those paths. It was shown in [12] that truth of ACTL properties can be decided by restricting the model-checking algorithm only to the m transitions. In the 4-valued structures we use to model open systems (see Sec. 4.2), a destination of an m transition is always a boolean state. Thus, the reachable state space of a structure restricted to those transitions is completely boolean. Furthermore, this boolean structure corresponds to a composition of the environment with the component that changes its variables nondeterministically.

Let us consider the *most nondeterministic component* to be the one where all variables change nondeterministically, *i.e.*, for every $c \in C$, the rules for c are $c \leftarrow$ true and $c \leftarrow$ false. The closure of the environment with this component results in the model with the most paths. If this closure satisfies an ACTL property, the closure with any other component will satisfy the property as well. Thus, to check if an ACTL property is an environment guarantee, it is sufficient to check if it is satisfied by the closure of the given environment with the most nondeterministic component. Consider the environment in our example, consisting of the rule Sensor′ $\leftarrow$ ¬Sensor ∨ Light. The most nondeterministic component in this case is described by rules Light′ $\leftarrow$ true, Light′ $\leftarrow$ false. The Kripke structure associated with their composition is shown in Fig. 1(d). With s_0 as the initial state, the property AF (Sensor ∨ Light) holds in this structure. Three other closures of the same environment, shown in Fig.s 1(a)-(c), satisfy the property as well. Correctness of using the most nondeterministic component for checking environment guarantees also follows from the fact that the closure of the environment with such component simulates all other closures of that environment. For instance, the Kripke structure in Fig. 1(d) is a simulation of models in Fig. 1(a)-(c). By [11], simulation preserves true ACTL properties, giving us a correct algorithm. Because of the duality of CTL operators, the same result holds for false existential properties.

Theorem 3. *Let $\mathcal{E}$ be an environment, φ be a true ACTL property, and $\mathcal{M}$ be the closure of $\mathcal{E}$ with the most nondeterministic component. $\mathcal{E}$ guarantees φ iff $\mathcal{M}$ satisfies φ.*

The most nondeterministic environment is routinely used for checking correctness of true universal properties of the component, e.g., [9]. However, we believe we are the first to propose the use of this technique for finding environment guarantees. It is trivial to construct the composition between the environment and the most nondeterministic component syntactically from a text-based description of a system. Specifically, we have implemented this method for the modeling language of NuSMV, to facilitate reasoning about the TCAS II system (see Sec. 6). The language of NuSMV is similar to ours, and its semantics is such that if for any variable a rule is not given, the variable is assumed to change nondeterministically. Thus, to implement the detection of environment guarantees for true ACTL properties, it suffices to remove the component rules from a model[1], and then check the properties on the remaining model using NuSMV [6]. The implementation is also highly efficient: increasing nondeterminism reduces the sizes of the decision diagrams used by NuSMV, and hence its running time.

6   Case Study: Checking the TCAS II System

We illustrate our approach with the Traffic Collision Avoidance System, TCAS II [22]. TCAS II implements a protocol for conflict detection and resolution between an aircraft and neighboring aircraft so as to avoid collisions during flight. This is a safety-critical system required on every U.S. commercial aircraft transporting more than thirty passengers, and has also been deployed in other countries. TCAS II has also been used as a classical case study for requirements modeling [18] and formal verification [14,19,4].

An SMV model of TCAS II has been translated from RSML [18] by Chan *et al.* [4] and is part of the NuSMV distribution. It views TCAS as consisting of two main modules: Own Aircraft, which is the aircraft having TCAS II installed, and Other Aircraft, which is a neighboring aircraft that may or may not have TCAS installed. An instance of Own Aircraft may communicate with several instances of Other Aircraft. Own Aircraft maintains information about the state of the host aircraft, including its altitude, direction, horizontal and vertical speeds, and it also receives similar information from Other Aircraft. Based on this information, Own Aircraft assesses possible threats and, in case it finds any, computes an escape maneuver (*e.g.*, climb, or descend) and the strength of this maneuver (*i.e.*, the altitude rate at which it is to be carried out) and outputs both as advisory to the pilot. TCAS II escape maneuvers are limited to the vertical plane. The SMV model we looked at contains one instance of the Own Aircraft state machine and one instance of an abstraction of Other Aircraft that behaves mostly nondeterministically. In this work, we view Own Aircraft as the component and Other Aircraft as its environment. Even with many features of TCAS II abstracted away, this SMV model is non-trivial for the NuSMV model-checker: computing the reachable states of this model takes 17 minutes on our machine (a Dell PC with an Intel Pentium 4 CPU at 2.8 GHz and 1 GB of RAM, running Red Hat Linux 7.3) yielding 1,349,878 BDD nodes. The model comes with several CTL formulas capturing essential properties of the system. All of these properties are in ACTL and happen to hold in the implementation provided. Therefore, our implementation described in Sec. 5 could be applied. We used it to check these properties, as well as a few additional ones. For the summary of results, please refer to Table 1.

---

[1] If the language did not have this default semantics, we would have to also insert rules $v' \leftarrow$ true and $v' \leftarrow$ false for every component variable v, which is simple to do syntactically as well.

Table 1. Results of checking properties of TCAS II

Properties	Results		Time (sec.)		BDD nodes	
	Full	Env.	Full	Env.	Full	Env.
0 reachability	—	—	1034.61	4.2	1349878	145246
1 $AG \neg$ND_Composite_RA	true	true	20.63	3.8	173041	37846
2 AG (New_Increase_Climb $\Rightarrow AX \neg$New_Increase_Descend)	true	true	20.81	3.84	175280	37991
3 AG (OA.in_Sense_Climb_Positive $\wedge$ Composite_RA = Descend $\wedge$ OA_Not_Evaluated_Meantime $\Rightarrow$ CRA_Not_Changed_Meantime)	true	true	27.83	3.87	341216	38352
4 AG (Composite_RA_Evaluated_Event $\Rightarrow \neg$DMG_Inconsistent)	true	maybe	40.67	6.1	224611	39709

Our analysis focuses on two SMV variables: Composite_RA which encodes the escape maneuver, or Resolution Advisory, and Displayed_Model_Goal, which encodes its strength. A desirable property of Composite_RA is that it should change deterministically [14]: this is essential for ensuring that Own Aircraft has predictable behavior and does not decide on different maneuvers under similar conditions. We checked that nondeterminism is not attained using a macro ND_Composite_RA defined in the model to encode possible nondeterminism (row 1 of Table 1). We performed the check on the original system and on the open model of the environment, and the property evaluated to true under both checks, which shows that it is in fact guaranteed by the environment. It seems that the modeler oversimplified the state machines, eliminating much of the logic that computes Composite_RA, which is essential in TCAS II. Table 1 summarizes the performance of the check in terms of time and BDD node allocation, on the full model (Full) and the environment alone (Env.).

Next, we verified a property which we expect to hold in any aircraft controller system: no aircraft can immediately switch from increasing the rate of climbing to increasing the rate of descending, *i.e.*, an aircraft must stop climbing before descending. The model defines macros New_Increase_Climb and New_Increase_Descend to encode the respective resolution advisories, which we used to formulate the question (row 2 in Table 1). It also passed in both the original model and the environment only, hence being guaranteed by the environment. This confirms the modeling error we have noticed before, *i.e.*, that Other Aircraft controls the resolution advisories of Own Aircraft. We also checked whether it is possible for the direction (up or down) of Other Aircraft to change without being noticed by Own Aircraft. More precisely, we checked whether it is possible for Composite_RA of Own Aircraft to remain constant if Other Aircraft changes from climb to descend (row 3 of Table 1). Using Dwyer *et al.*'s property patterns [8], we expanded OA_Not_Evaluated_Meantime as $A[(\neg$OA_Evaluated_Event $\vee$ $AG \neg$OA.in_Sense_Descend_Positive) U OA.in_Sense_Descend_Positive] and used a similar expansion for CRA_Not_Changed_Meantime. This property is also guaranteed by the environment. The antecedent of the implication fails both in the full model and in the environment. This reveals an environment assumption, rooted in the semantics of RSML: environment variables cannot change without being evaluated by the component. Discovering such assumptions is important [9] to make verification experts aware of conditions under which their analysis is valid.

Finally, we checked one of the original properties of the TCAS II system [4]. It states that when Composite_RA is evaluated, Displayed_Model_Goal is computed "consistently", *i.e.*, the cases by which its value is decided are mutually exclusive. A macro

DMG_Inconsistent, defined in the model, captures the inconsistency conditions, resulting in the formula shown in row 4 in Table 1. Since the property holds in the full model, but not on the environment, the environment alone does not guarantee it, and the property does depend on the component. A vacuity check [16], however, indicates that the antecedent of the implication is vacuous, potentially misleading the user into thinking that something is wrong. [4] notes that in this model, Composite_RA sometimes disagrees with Displayed_Model_Goal (*e.g.*, the advisory indicates climb, but the strength of the maneuver is negative), but does not provide an additional explanation. Our method helped us in identifying the reason for these anomalies: the logic for computing the escape maneuver *does not* depend on the component, whereas that for computing its strength *does*. As we argued in Sec. 5 and observed in our experiments in Table 1, for true universal properties, verifying the environment alone is much more efficient than checking the full model. This suggests that at least for this class of properties, checking whether the environment guarantees the property can precede the verification process: if the property evaluates to true on an environment alone, it will yield this answer also when the environment is composed with the system.

How representative is our experience of finding a model with only true ACTL properties to verify? [4] indicates that the value of Displayed_Model_Goal is computed by a case analysis consisting of seven cases. These cases are supposed to be mutually exclusive. The property $AG \neg$DMG_Inconsistent checks whether this is indeed the case. This property was initially found false[2]. Upon manual inspection of the counterexample produced by the model-checker, *the environment model was identified as the cause of the violation*, and it was fixed so that the property finally passed. Thus, we have evidence that false universal properties exist "in the wild", and detecting environment guarantees for those is a worthwhile task which would eliminate the manual analysis of the counterexample. A yet more important class of properties to handle is CTL properties with mixed path quantifiers. For example, it is conceivable to demand that a reactive system can always be reset. One way to implement it is to have an initial state *Init* and require a property $AG\ EF\ Init$, *i.e.*, from every state of the system, state *Init* is always reachable. Whether such a property holds or fails, a counterexample for it cannot be generated, and a special-purpose technique for detecting environment guarantees, such as the one proposed in Sec. 4 is required. We leave implementing a technique for checking environment guarantees of arbitrary CTL properties for future work.

7   Related Work and Discussion

The original definition of vacuity attempted to capture the conditions under which satisfaction of a property in the model does not indicate that the model behaves correctly. This definition was motivated by practical experience at the IBM Haifa Research Lab in applying model-checking to verifying hardware systems [2]. This definition was developed in a context of a rather restricted fragment of a temporal logic, in which a property is divided between a stimulus provided by the environment and an expected response of the component. In this context, this work provided an efficient algorithm for vacuity

---

[2] Unfortunately, we were unable to obtain this erroneous model.

detection that identifies errors in practice. However, it does not work for more general properties and when the placed assumptions are not satisfied.

Over the years, the algorithm for vacuity has been generalized, extended, and implemented for various temporal logics, *e.g.*, see [16,2,1,20]. However, this work has concentrated on the technical definition of vacuity, *i.e.*, whether every subformula of a property is important for its satisfaction. Without additional assumptions used by Beer *et al.*, these techniques can produce false positives, *i.e.*, cases of vacuity that are not indicative of errors in the system. Instead of detecting trivial satisfaction, they indicate when a property can be simplified. Although this may be useful for model-checking, by itself it does not help in identifying problems.

For example, consider the property $\varphi = AG$ (Sensor_Tripped $\Rightarrow (AF$ Light $=$ green)) from Sec. 1. It is vacuous in Sensor_Tripped in a model where the light changes color periodically, whether there is a car waiting at the intersection or not. Thus, a stronger property, AG AF(Light $=$ green), holds in the model, but does not necessarily signal any errors. Suppose that φ was given by the requirements stakeholder for creating a more optimal traffic controller system, and the model is just one implementation of the controller that does not require the assumption of the sensor being tripped. Another example is when Sensor_Tripped is under the control of the component (and not the environment), so vacuity in it may not lead to a problem either: the controller might have some values of the sensor hard-coded into it, just to make sure that the rest of the controller behaves correctly. We refer to such cases as *property overengineering* – requiring a property that is weaker than the one that actually holds in the model by making potentially unnecessary assumptions about the environment or the state of the system. Industrial experience [7] indicates that properties are hard to get right. This process is expensive, and the properties, once deemed correct and validated with all stakeholders, remain fixed throughout the duration of the project, and even between different releases of the system. So, engineers are often reluctant to modify overengineered properties, and vacuity reports that point to such cases only distract from finding real problems.

In our paper, we have shown that Kripke structures based on 4-valued Belnap logic can be used to approximate open systems. Godefroid [10] has also proposed to use multi-valued logic, in his case 3-valued Kleene logic, to model open systems. He shows that under the assumption that the component can block the environment, his 3-valued model-checking technique is equivalent to module-checking. However, we believe that this assumption is highly unrealistic – a component can interact with the environment, but cannot deter its progress.

The setting of work on *robust satisfaction* [15] and *module checking* [17] is similar to ours: given a system M, determining whether a property holds in all environments composed with M (for environment guarantees, the roles of the system and the environment are reversed). This algorithm is complete, and the authors note that for checking satisfaction of ACTL, robust satisfaction has the same complexity as model-checking and can be decided using the same implementation as ours. For other properties, robust satisfaction is exponentially more expensive than model-checking. In contrast, our algorithm is partial, *i.e.*, in some cases it may fail to detect that a property is guaranteed by the environment, but is of the same complexity as model-checking.

The work of [21] is the closest to ours in spirit: determining which part of the model is needed for checking the correctness property can alert the user to the presence of an overconstraint in their declarative models and help him/her locate its source. As in our case, the algorithm of [21] is efficient but not complete, and the authors report of several overconstraints that were not detectable by it.

8   Conclusion and Future Work

In this paper, we argued for the need to provide support for debugging environment models used in model-checking software systems. Specifically, we noted that when the environment single-handedly guarantees (truth or falsity of) property which is expected of the component, then either the property should be reconsidered as part of the environment, or there is an error in the model of the environment. We have called this problem *environment guarantees* and argued that it can be found if the environment is modelled as an open system. We also discussed how to construct open models of the environment from rule-based descriptions of state-machine models, such as those created by SMV specifications, and implemented this technique for checking whether true ACTL properties are guaranteed by the environment. We reported our experience with a model of the TCAS II system which showed that environment guarantees present a real threat, especially when the modeler attempts to create abstractions of their systems to overcome the state explosion problem of model-checking. We also argued that the problem is not limited to true ACTL properties, and while we have a theoretical decision procedure for arbitrary CTL properties, its implementation and evaluation is left for future work.

Our work opens a number of questions related to debugging models of the environment: (1) We assumed that every variable belongs to the environment or to the component (but not both), *i.e.*, the environment and the component do not have shared variables. Moreover, we considered only cases of synchronous parallelism between the two. To make our approach applicable to more general domains, we plan to address these limitations. (2) Clearly, there are environments that may not guarantee a property by themselves; however, there are additional constraints imposed on them by components, *i.e.*, via communication channels, that lead to environment guarantees. We intend to study this problem in future work. (3) We also assumed that there is a clear separation between the component and its environment, and thus the environment can be captured and its model constructed. This may not always be the case. For example, we may aim to verify a collection of components compositionally, so while checking one component, all remaining ones form its environment. This environment might be simply too big to analyze. There might also be cases when the component is composed with multiple environments, or when determining what constitutes an environment is difficult. One potential direction to remedy these problems is to follow the approach of Shlyakhter *et al.* [21], aimed at computing and highlighting the part of the overall system on which the property depends. The user can then see whether the highlighted part is the environment and decide whether this constitutes a problem. Of course, highlighting is useful even when the boundary between the component and the environment is well understood: it points the user to the part of the environment that is entirely responsible for satisfying the desired property, facilitating debugging.

Acknowledgments. We thank Shoham Ben-David for her comments on an earlier draft of this paper. Financial support has been provided by NSERC and IBM.

References

1. R. Armoni, L. Fix, A. Flaisher, O. Grumberg, N. Piterman, A. Tiemeyer, and M. Vardi. "Enhanced Vacuity Detection in Linear Temporal Logic ". In *Proceedings of CAV'03*, volume 2725 of *LNCS*, pages 368–380, July 2003.
2. I. Beer, S. Ben-David, C. Eisner, and Y. Rodeh. "Efficient Detection of Vacuity in Temporal Model Checking". *FMSD*, 18(2):141–163, March 2001.
3. N.D. Belnap. "A Useful Four-Valued Logic". In Dunn and Epstein, editors, *Modern Uses of Multiple-Valued Logic*, pages 30–56. 1977.
4. W. Chan, R.J. Anderson, P. Beame, S. Burns, F. Modugno, and D. Notkin. "Model Checking Large Software Specifications". *IEEE TSE*, 24(7):498–520, July 1998.
5. M. Chechik, B. Devereux, S. Easterbrook, and A. Gurfinkel. "Multi-Valued Symbolic Model-Checking". *ACM TOSEM*, 12(4):1–38, October 2003.
6. A. Cimatti, E.M. Clarke, E. Giunchilia, F. Giunchiglia, M. Pistore, M. Roveri, R. Sebastiani, and A. Tacchella. "NUSMV Version 2: An Open Source Tool for Symbolic Model Checking". In *Proceedings of CAV'02*, volume 2404 of *LNCS*, pages 359–364, 2002.
7. F. Copty, A. Irron, O. Weissberg, N. Kropp, and G. Kamhi. "Efficient Debugging in a Formal Verification Environment". *STTT*, 4(3):335–348, May 2003.
8. M. Dwyer, G. Avrunin, and J. Corbett. "Patterns in Property Specifications for Finite-State Verification". In *Proceedings of ICSE'99*, May 1999.
9. D. Giannakopoulou, C. S. Pasareanu, and H. Barringer. "Assumption Generation for Software Component Verification". In *Proceedings of ASE'02*, pages 3–12, 2002.
10. P. Godefroid. "Reasoning about Abstract Open Systems with Generalized Module Checking". In *Proceedings of EMSOFT'03*, volume 2855 of *LNCS*, pages 223–240, October 2003.
11. O. Grumberg and D.E. Long. "Model Checking and Modular Verification". In *Proceedings of CONCUR'91*, 1991.
12. A. Gurfinkel and M. Chechik. "Multi-Valued Model-Checking via Classical Model-Checking". In *Proceedings of CONCUR'03*, volume 2761 of *LNCS*, pages 263–277, 2003.
13. A. Gurfinkel and M. Chechik. "Extending Extended Vacuity". In *Proceedings of FMCAD'04*, volume 3312 of *LNCS*, pages 306–321, November 2004.
14. M. Heimdahl and N. Leveson. "Completeness and Consistency in Hierarchical State-Based Requirements". *IEEE TSE*, SE-22(6):363–377, June 1996.
15. O. Kupferman and M. Vardi. "Robust Satisfaction". In *Proceedings of CONCUR'99*, volume 1664 of *LNCS*, pages 383–398, 1999.
16. O. Kupferman and M. Vardi. "Vacuity Detection in Temporal Model Checking". *STTT*, 4(2):224–233, February 2003.
17. O. Kupferman, M.Y. Vardi, and P. Wolper. "Module Checking". *Information and Computation*, 164(2):322–344, January 2001.
18. N.G. Leveson, M.P.E. Heimdahl, H. Hildreth, and J.D. Reese. "Requirements Specification for Process-Control Systems". *IEEE TSE*, 20(9):684–707, September 1994.
19. J. Lygeros and N. Lynch. "On the Formal Verification of the TCAS Conflict Resolution Algorithms". In *Proceedings of Conf. on Decision and Control*, December 1997.
20. M. Purandare and F. Somenzi. "Vacuum Cleaning CTL Formulae". In *Proceedings of CAV'02*, volume 2404 of *LNCS*, pages 485–499, July 2002.
21. I. Shlyakhter, R. Seater, D. Jackson, M. Sridharan, and M. Taghdiri. "Debugging Overconstrained Declarative Models Using Unsatisfiable Cores". In *Proceedings of ASE'03*, 2003.
22. US Dept. of Transportation. "Introduction to TCAS II". FAA, March 1990.

Ensuring Consistency Within Distributed Graph Transformation Systems

Ulrike Ranger and Thorsten Hermes

RWTH Aachen University
Department of Computer Science 3 (Software Engineering)
Ahornstraße 55, 52074 Aachen, Germany
{ranger,thermes}@i3.informatik.rwth-aachen.de

Abstract. Graph transformation systems can be used for modeling the structure and the behavior of a software system in a visual way. In our project, we extend existing graph transformation systems to model and execute distributed systems. One challenge in this context is the simultaneous and correct modification of the local runtime graphs of the participating applications by visual distributed graph transformations.

As the execution of these transformations may cause inconsistencies in the local runtime graphs, we present an approach to avoid inconsistencies: A runtime mechanism translates invalid graph transformations into valid transformations. This translation is based on predefined rules describing the substitution of invalid transformation parts. Thus, new graph transformations are dynamically built at runtime. Furthermore, the runtime mechanism controls access within a distributed system.

1 Introduction

For the software development process, the use of visual modeling languages becomes more and more important. The most famous representative of such a language is the Unified Modeling Language (UML). By using different diagram types, like use-case, class and sequence diagrams, the UML supports the different phases of a software development process. These diagrams are advantageous as they serve as basic development artifacts and allow the visualization of different abstraction levels of the software system.

There are several tools enabling the drawing of UML diagrams, e.g. Rational Rose and Poseidon. They allow the generation of class templates according to UML class diagrams. Unfortunately, they do not support the generation of source code for UML behavior diagrams representing modifications on object structures.

Graph transformation systems (GTS) fill this gap, as they support the specification of static and dynamic software aspects and the generation of source code from the specification. Graphs are descriptive data structures and mathematically founded. A lot of efficient algorithms already exist for solving problems on graphs. Two representatives of GTS are PROGRES [1] and Fujaba [2], which have been used to model software system with complex data structures, e.g. process management systems, authoring tools, and systems for reverse

M.B. Dwyer and A. Lopes (Eds.): FASE 2007, LNCS 4422, pp. 368–382, 2007.

engineering. The structure of the software system is defined by a graph schema. The dynamic aspects are modeled as graph transformations, allowing the creation and modification of a runtime graph conforming to the graph schema. Both schema and transformations can be specified textually as well as visually.

Based on the specification, the GTS generates source code, from which a *visual prototype* may be created e.g. using the UPGRADE framework [3]. As UPGRADE is an extensive framework, the prototype can be configured and adapted to the user's need. With this abstraction from the runtime graph and the graph transformations, the prototype allows the developers to observe the modeled software system and its behavior from a desired view.

GTS are restricted to the modeling of local systems. Our project aims at the extension of GTS for the modeling and execution of *distributed systems*. In a distributed system, each participating application is based on a separate specification and stores its own runtime graph. Every application (acting as a *server*) defines its interface. It provides graph elements, which can be used in specifications of other applications (*clients*). A client can either call pre-defined transformations contained in interfaces or model new graph transformations visually, by using interface elements as remote objects. In this paper, we focus on the visual modeling of distributed transformations, as the textual modeling is studied in [4]. The execution of visually defined transformations modifies the client runtime graph as well as the server runtime graphs. Since an interface does not and even cannot cover *all* graph constraints of an application's specification, the execution may lead to inconsistencies in the different runtime graphs. A transformation causing inconsistencies is called an *invalid transformation*.

In [5] we described the modeling and execution of visual distributed graph transformations disregarding the mentioned inconsistencies. In this paper, we present our concepts to avoid the execution of invalid transformations by enabling the server to modify these transformations dynamically at runtime. With the use of queries on the runtime graph and predefined rules describing how invalid transformation parts are translated into valid parts, *valid graph transformations* are built from the invalid transformations. This mechanism can also be used for introducing access rights.

The paper is structured as follows: In Section 2 we introduce the general structure of a distributed system and show how such a system can be modeled with a GTS. We explain these concepts considering an example of a simplified process management system. Section 3 describes our approach for avoiding inconsistencies within the distributed system, which may be caused by the execution of invalid distributed graph transformations. We present similar approaches and compare them to our approach in Section 4. A summary and an outlook to future work is given in Section 5.

2   Specifying Distributed Systems with GTS

In this section, we introduce how distributed systems can be specified with GTS. We first describe the general architecture of a distributed system and then show

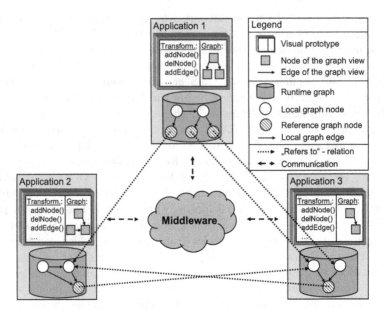

Fig. 1. Basic architecture of a distributed system

the modeling of its structure and behavior. The modeling is shown by means of an *abstract graph language* resembling the PROGRES language.

2.1   Architecture of a Distributed System

In our approach, a distributed system consists of several applications, which are all built according to the tool construction process described in section 1:
(1) specifying the desired software application with the graph language of the GTS, (2) generating appropriate source code from the specification, and (3) creating a visual prototype. Figure 1 shows the basic architecture of a distributed system consisting of three applications[1]. For every application, the visual prototype and the runtime graph is depicted. The *prototype* shows the application's state, which is stored in the runtime graph. The user can call graph transformations modeled within the specification and observe their impacts on the runtime graph. The graph transformations can vary from simple graph modifications, like addNode for adding a new node of a certain type, to complex graph modifications, like produceDoc which will be described in Section 2.3.

The coupled applications perform different tasks and are used separately by different users. For coupling the applications and exchanging data between them, they require access to runtime graphs of other applications. For restricting the access to all data, every application has to specify an interface defining the nodes

---

[1] For sake of simplicity, we assume that all coupled applications have well-defined tasks and thus are based on different specifications. I.e. every specification is not executed more than once within a distributed system.

and edges which may be used by other applications (clients) (see Section 2.2). Our approach is general enough that an application may act as client and server simultaneously, but in this paper we restrict the applications to act either as client or as server. Instead of replicating remote nodes with their data, we use *reference nodes* in the client runtime graphs allowing the direct access on remote server nodes[2]. Reference nodes do not store any data but the location of the remote object. They are helper structures supporting the realization of relations between nodes located in different applications.

The communication between the applications, like propagating modifications to remote nodes, is done by a *middleware*. The middleware uses existing technologies like RMI or CORBA. At the moment, we use a synchronous communication model, which supports distributed transactions guaranteeing a defined and consistent state of the entire system. In the following, we will not focus on its implementation but on modeling a distributed system in a visual way. The code generation of the GTS is responsible to generate code for the middleware.

2.2 Structure of a Distributed System

In this section, we show how the static structure of a distributed system is modeled with the abstract graph language. For this purpose, we introduce the *simplified process management system* SPMS as example, which is the first distributed and extensive system we have modeled with our new concepts. The SPMS manages the tasks, documents, and resources needed for complex processes, like the development of a software system. These aspects are modeled and executed as separate applications, which have to be coupled at runtime to form a comprehensive process management system. In Figure 2 the class diagrams of the applications, the SPMS consists of, are depicted. The class diagrams represent the graph schemas[3] of the applications, in which the classes correspond to node types and associations between classes correspond to edge types.

The *Resource Manager* handles all human and computer resources needed for executing and performing the tasks of complex processes. A resource is modeled by node type R, which has an attribute rName for its name and a boolean attribute occupied indicating the activity state. Additionally, a resource can be assessed by using node type A (abbreviation for assessment). In the *Document Manager* the documents (modeled by node type D) are managed, which serve as input for tasks and are produced by tasks. The Document Manager stores all documents alphabetically ordered in a linear list using edge type nextElem. This list is needed for giving the local users of the Document Manager a clear overview of all existing documents. Furthermore, edge type basedOn models dependencies between documents. In the *Task Manager* the actual process is designed by dividing and structuring it into several smaller tasks using node type T. These tasks have to be executed in a specific order determined by edges of type nextTask.

In the SPMS, the Task Manager is used for coupling the applications, although another application could have also been used. As the applications are developed

---

[2] In contrast to reference nodes, we do not store reference edges as they are of no use.

[3] We use directed node- and edge-labeled graphs, in which nodes may be attributed.

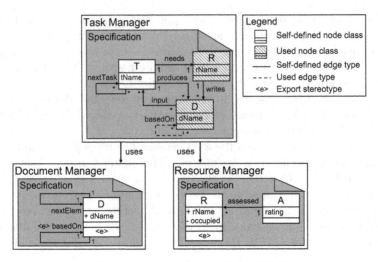

Fig. 2. Static structure of the SPMS

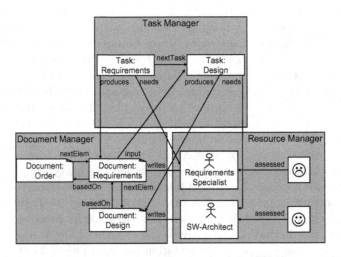

Fig. 3. Sample runtime-graph of the SPMS

separately, the Task Manager does not have any knowledge about the other applications. Therefore, the Resource Manager and the Document Manager define *interfaces* containing the types, which may be used by the Task Manager. The interfaces are not separated from the implementations, but implicitly defined by marking the respective visual elements with the <e>-stereotype (including the public attributes of node types). The interface of the Resource Manager consists of node type R and its attribute rName. Node type D, its attribute dName and the edge type basedOn compose the interface of the Document Manager.

Interface elements are *read only* and thus must not be changed by a client, e.g. by adding an attribute to a node type. This fact is emphasized in the specification by illustrating the used graph elements by striped rectangles and dashed arrows. To integrate interface elements, the used graph elements and the self-defined elements can be related by defining edge types between them. For example, if a resource performs a certain task, this is modeled by an edge type needs in the Task Manager relating the self-defined node type T and the used node type R (see Figure 2). In that way, the interrelations between the different applications can be modeled using local edges.

Figure 3 shows an example of a SPMS runtime graph, which is a possible instantiation of the model (graph schema) depicted in Figure 2. The Task Manager has several tasks for the development of a software system, which refer to documents and resources in the other applications.

2.3   Modeling the Behavior

Based on the static structure of the SPMS shown in Figure 2, the behavior of the distributed system can be specified by graph transformations. In this paper, we focus on the *visual specification of distributed graph transformations*.

Basically, a visual graph transformation[4] consists of a left-hand side (LHS) and a right-hand side (RHS). The LHS defines a *graph pattern*, which is searched for in the runtime graph. A sub-graph in the runtime graph conforming to the LHS is called *match*. If several matches are found, one of them is chosen non-deterministically. The RHS of the transformation defines the modifications of the match, e.g. creating nodes. For the definition of visual transformations, graph languages offer an expressive variety of language constructs. The graph languages provide also the definition of *graph queries*, which only search for a match.

One essential advantage of specifying graph transformations visually is the modeling of the behavior in a *declarative* way, i.e. the modeling of *what* the transformation does instead of *how* the specified modifications can be achieved. In distributed graph transformations, the specified behavior lead to the simultaneous modification of several runtime graphs belonging to different applications. Distributed graph transformations are executed as *transactions*, i.e. either all modifications or no modification at all are performed, fulfilling the ACID properties known from databases. As the syntax and semantics of distributed transformations are described in [5], we only present a simple example here.

Figure 4 shows the distributed graph transformation produceDoc for producing a new document by a task. This transformation is specified in the Task Manager, but its execution affects also the state of the Document Manager. A task t and a document d, representing a remote node in the Document Manager, are given as input parameters. The LHS consists of these nodes and an edge of type input incident to them. Furthermore, it contains a resource r referencing a node in the Resource Manager, which is needed by the task t. On the RHS, all nodes and edges of the LHS are preserved and additionally a new document nd is created. For integrating the new document nd in the existing graphs, a writes-edge is created connecting r and nd showing that nd is written by r. Furthermore, a

---

[4] In some GTS approaches, a visual graph transformation is called a *production* or *rule*.

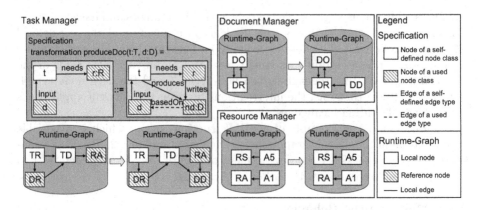

Fig. 4. Transformation for producing a new document

produces-edge incident to task t and the document nd is created. As nd is based on d, a edge of type basedOn is created connecting both documents.

When executing produceDoc, the runtime graphs of the Task Manager and the Document Manager are modified, as node and edge types of both are used in the transformation. These modifications are depicted in the runtime graphs in Figure 4 affecting local and reference nodes. For example, in the Document Manager a new local node with id DD for the new document nd in the transformation is created, while in the Task Manager only a reference node pointing to node DD is created. This behavior is founded in the fact that node type D is specified in the Document Manager and the Task Manager acts only as client for this type. Thus, every node of type D logically belongs to the Document Manager and coupled applications may only have references on these nodes. The resulting runtime graphs depicted in Figure 4 correspond to the SPMS state shown in Figure 3 (for lack of space only the initials of nodes are shown in Figure 4).

2.4   Execution of Distributed Transformations

The search of a graph pattern has an exponential worst-case complexity and becomes even more cost-intensive when concerning different applications. [6] presents an approach to divide the LHS specified in a client into several sub-patterns, each affecting exactly one application. The sub-patterns are sent to the server applications at runtime using GTXL [7], instead of querying the applications for every single pattern element. The server applications respond with appropriate matches, thus reducing the communication costs. After determining the match for the LHS in the client, the modifications are performed according to the RHS. We use a similar mechanism for them: We divide the distributed graph transformation of the client into several sub-transformations, each affecting one application. The sub-transformations are sent to the server applications using GTXL and are then executed. For example, the transformation on the left in Figure 5 is a sub-transformation of produceDoc sent to the Document Manager.

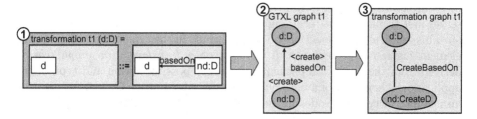

Fig. 5. Representations of a visual graph transformation

GTXL provides a XML-based format for exchanging graphs and transformations. The structure of a transformation in GTXL may be regarded as graph, in which the nodes and edges are marked with stereotypes describing their modification. Figure 5 shows an example of a graph transformation ① and its abstract graph representation in GTXL ② (③ will be explained in Section 3).

When executing a sub-transformation, inconsistencies in the runtime graph of the server application may occur. These can be caused by *create operations*, which insert new nodes and edges in the server's runtime graph, *delete operations*, destroying nodes and edges of a server, and *attribute operations*, which change the attribute values of server objects. All these operations transform the server runtime graph without considering its internal constraints. For example, when executing transformation produceDoc depicted in Figure 4, a new document is created in the Document Manager. As the Task Manager does not know that the Document Manger stores all documents in a linear list, he has not specified the insertion of the new document in the list. This causes local inconsistencies, because the linear list does not contain all documents of the Document Manager, but it relies on a consistent list structure. This problem is called *graph rewriting dilemma* [8]: The interfaces have to provide node and edge types, which are visually available in client specifications, but due to data abstraction the interfaces do not cover entire graph schemas with all specification constraints. Since this is an important aspect in software engineering, we present an approach for preserving information hiding and solving the graph rewriting dilemma.

3 Meta-transformations

In this section, we describe a mechanism to deal with invalid graph transformations specified in a client application: The server dynamically translates them into valid graph transformations, which also update the *internal data* hidden by the interface. The translation mechanism is invoked by the server application for every incoming query or transformation received from a client (via GTXL). This mechanism can also be used for access control (e.g. as described in [9]).

3.1 The Meta-transformation Approach

Since we use graph transformations to describe the applications's behavior, it is only natural to use the same approach for ensuring consistency. As illustrated

in Figure 5, an incoming graph transformation[5] can be viewed as a graph. The
server first translates the incoming GTXL graph ② into a transformation graph
③. This graph stores the actions to be performed in the type information of each
element instead of stereotypes. It is based on a *transformation graph schema*
derived from the application schema: For every possible action and type in the
application schema, a combined type is generated, e.g. type CreateD for creating
an instance of type D. Nodes in the transformation graph are called *operations*.

The transformation graph is then transformed using a pre-defined set of rules,
which we call *meta-transformations*. These are transformations that operate on
transformations represented by transformation graphs. They are written by the
specifier of the server application without knowledge of the transformations that
might be modeled by clients. Their application is performed at runtime, when
a transformation is received. Each meta-transformation deals with a single aspect of consistency or access control, and does not have to match the entire
incoming transformation. Since a big transformation may be matched by multiple meta-transformations, the specifier defines a total order over the meta-
transformations. Each meta-transformation works on the intermediate result of
previous ones. The final result is a transformation graph that represents a valid
transformation, which is then executed by the application.

We require that either at least the changes specified in the incoming transformation are performed (*minimal semantics*), or that no changes are performed at
all. In the later case an error is reported to the client and the distributed transformation is aborted. This ensures that distributed transformations are predictable
from the client's perspective. There are two types of meta-transformations:

Simple Meta-Transformations. The only difference to regular graph transformations is that simple meta-transformations are not defined over the application's graph schema, but the graph transformation schema described above. If a
match for a LHS is found in the incoming transformation, the meta-transformation is applied, either once or to every match, as defined by the specifier.

Complex Meta-Transformations. In order to deal with large incoming transformations and perform sophisticated checks, complex meta-transformations use
the control structures of the graph language to combine queries and simple
meta-transformations (equivalent to PROGRES transactions). For their notation, we will use the visual flow notation of Fujaba in Section 3.2. Complex
meta-transformations do not have a LHS or RHS, and are invoked for every incoming transformation. In addition to queries on the transformation graph, we
provide runtime graph queries (specified using the application's graph schema).
This allows reactions depending on the current runtime graph, e.g. rejection of
a transformation that attempts to create a document if a document with that
name already exists. The control flow together with the queries can be used to
simulate advanced features like *negative application conditions* [10].

---

[5] We only discuss graph transformations, but the same mechanism applies to queries.

3.2   Examples

Maintaining an Ordered List. The Document Manager maintains a linked list of all stored documents, ordered by their dName attribute. This implementation detail is hidden, so any document created by the Task Manager will have to be inserted into this list by the Document Manager itself.

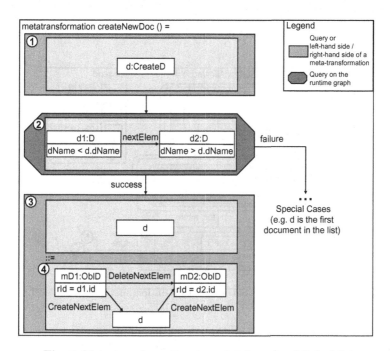

Fig. 6. Meta-transformation to maintain ordered linked list

The complex meta-transformation in Figure 6 begins with a query on the transformation graph ① that is matched when an incoming transformation attempts to create a document. The runtime graph query ② is then executed to find two documents between which the new document should be inserted. If a suitable position is found, the simple meta-transformation ③ is invoked. It modifies the incoming transformation so that it does not only create the document d, but also creates appropriate edges to d1 and d2 and deletes the existing edge between them. Figure 7 shows the effect of createNewDoc() on the transformation from Figure 5, translated into the standard transformation notation.

We use attributes to relate runtime graph elements with the operations on them, e.g. to ensure that we create edges to the same documents we found in the runtime query. The attribute id for documents in the runtime graph is used to access the internal identifier assigned by the GTS. On the transformation graph level, operations that affect a specific document store its identifier in the attribute rId. Using attribute assignments in ④, we add ObID operations for d1 and d2, meaning the corresponding documents will appear on both LHS and RHS

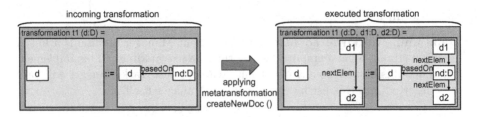

Fig. 7. Result of applying the meta-transformation createNewDoc()

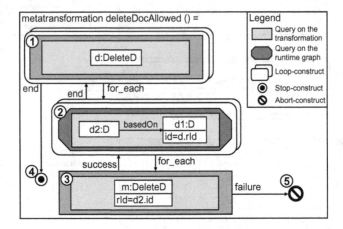

Fig. 8. Meta-transformation preventing deletion of documents that are still referenced

of the transformation. The failure branch for handling special cases is omitted due to space limitations. Usually, we would perform the initial query ① inside a loop (see next example) to deal with incoming transformations creating more than one document.

Access Control. Documents in the Document Manager must not be deleted while there are other documents based on them. In this case, we ensure consistency not through translation, but rejection of incoming transformations.

This access control is realized by the complex meta-transformation in Figure 8. The initial query ① matches the deletion of a document d in the incoming transformation. Its enclosing for_each loop iterates through all matches for a document deletion operation. For every such document d1, a runtime graph query ② searches for a document d2 based on it. d1 is identified using the rId from the corresponding deletion command d. Again, the for_each loop enclosing ② ensures that we process all possible matches for d2. We perform a query ③ on the transformation graph to check whether this document will also be deleted by the incoming transformation. If not, this would cause an inconsistency, and thus the failure branch leads to a special symbol ⑤, which results in the rejection of the incoming transformation. If no consistency violation is detected, the loop ends with ④, and processing of this meta-transformation is finished.

3.3   Evaluation

Existing GTS, like PROGRES, address some concerns of meta-transformations by other mechanisms. We will compare them to our approach and give some estimates regarding runtime and specification complexity.

Constraints and Repair Actions. Constraints specify invariants on the runtime graph that are verified after every transformation. If a violation is detected, processing is halted. This is not acceptable in a distributed system where the client specifier cannot keep the server graph consistent because of a limited interface. Repair actions [8] are an extension of constraints. Instead of terminating the application, a transformation may be triggered to return the graph to a consistent state. This is different from the meta-transformation approach, where inconsistencies are not allowed to occur in the first place. While this approach allows repair actions to perform iterative graph manipulation, they suffer from several disadvantages: First, they have less available information, e.g. when deleting a node, a meta-transformation can still evaluate its attributes and incident edges before the node is deleted. A repair action is invoked after the deletion, and thus all information about the node is lost. Second, repair actions are not independent: The specifier of a repair action must assume that every repair action is the first action performed on a runtime graph with multiple inconsistencies, making it hard to correctly perform the repairs. Third, constraints and repair actions require the whole graph to be searched for inconsistency patterns after every modification, meaning their execution time grows with the graph size.

Runtime Complexity of Meta-Transformations. Meta-transformations operate on the transformation graph, which typically contains only few elements. For runtime graph queries, knowledge of the incoming transformation can be used to avoid global searches on the runtime graph. Only when this is not possible, these queries exhibit the same complexity as constraints/repair actions. This means that, except for these worst cases, the runtime complexity of meta-transformation does not depend on the size of the runtime graph, making them much more scalable.

Number of Meta-Transformations. To cover all possible operations (creation, deletion, and, for nodes only, attribute modification), $3 * n + 2 * e$ meta-transformations have to be specified, where n is the number of node types and e the number of edge types in the interface. Operations that require neither consistency enforcement nor access control may be omitted. We are currently investigating possibilities to support the specifier in this task.

4   Related Work

The presented meta-transformations may not be confused with the *meta transformation rules* introduced in [11]. They translate generic graph transformations applying type variables into several concrete transformations without type variables at specification time. At runtime, the concrete transformations are executed instead of the generic transformations, improving the performance. These rules can also be used for increasing the maintainability of transformations. In contrast to meta-transformations, the meta rules of [11] operate on static transformations known at specification time, and are performed at specification time.

In [12], the GTS Fujaba is extended by defining the life-cycle of software components and their interactions. This is modeled by using existing diagrams and introducing new diagram types in Fujaba, which e.g. offer the specification of deploying components located on different machines. Furthermore, fault tolerance in case of hardware failures is considered. For the interaction of components, distributed graph transformations are needed. In contrast to our approach, no means for modeling the distributed transformations in a visual way is provided, thus [12] is more related to the textual specification presented in [4]. As only textual interfaces and calls of remote procedures are used, the graph rewriting dilemma as presented in Section 2.4 does not arise in [12].

In context of GTS, many projects deal with the integration of different models, e.g. by using triple graph grammars [13]. Most of these approaches use only one specification containing the different models and one runtime graph. They focus on synchronizing the different models instead of modeling distributed systems as presented in this paper. Furthermore, they do not concentrate on the abstraction of implementation details, as provided by specification interfaces.

For modeling distributed systems, [14] introduces *hierarchically distributed graph transformations* for GTS. Basically, a network graph defines the topology and the relations between applications of a distributed system. Each application is represented as a node in the network graph and in turn stores its runtime state within a local graph. Instead of using references as described in Section 2.1, objects are replicated in the applications. Distributed transformations are modeled on the level of the network graph and not on application level, making the applications *passive* components within the distributed system. Another difference between the two approaches is the level of data abstraction: We provide abstraction on the graph schema level, while [14] offers the more fine-granular abstraction on object level. Thus, for every object shared by two applications an explicit relation has to be defined, which leads to the extensive definition of object relations. However, the approach is only rudimentarily implemented and does not offer means for solving the graph rewriting dilemma.

5   Conclusion

Our project extends existing GTS by modeling structure and behavior of a distributed system in a visual way. To achieve information hiding, applications of a distributed system only exchange interfaces. As a drawback, distributed graph transformations specified in a client cannot consider all constraints internally imposed by the servers. Since this may lead to inconsistencies within the runtime graphs, we introduce meta-transformations for translating invalid transformations into valid transformations dynamically.

Meta-transformations are based on existing concepts for visual graph transformations, but operate on graph transformations themselves instead of modifying runtime graphs. As incoming transformations are not known at specification time, the server specifier defines a number of *translation rules*, which are applied by a runtime mechanism. This also allows queries on the runtime graph, so that the local state may be taken into account when performing the translation. Meta-transformations provide a general mechanism, which can also be used for realizing access control within a distributed system.

The graph rewriting dilemma [8] has been originally described for local systems, which are built from different *sub-systems* using one common graph. Meta-transformations can be used for ensuring the consistency of all sub-systems in this local case as well. As all graph transformations which will be performed on the sub-systems are known at specification time, meta-transformations can be applied in a pre-processing step just before generating code for the system. Thus, the runtime infrastructure is not needed for local systems.

We have tested our concepts on a large distributed process management system and they have shown to be suitable for solving the graph rewriting dilemma. As a next step, we will formalize the presented concepts and integrate them into the existing formalism of PROGRES. Additionally, we are analyzing concepts for improving the interface mechanism presented in Section 2.2 by introducing *virtual graph views*. They define an explicit view on an application instead of implicitly determine the interface by a proper part of the graph schema. For the realization, meta-transformations can be used for translating queries conforming to the virtual graph view into queries conforming to the internal structure.

References

1. Schürr, A.: Operationales Spezifizieren mit programmierten Graphersetzungssystemen. PhD-Thesis, RWTH Aachen University (1991)
2. Fischer, T., Niere, J., Torunski, L., Zündorf, A.: Story diagrams: A new graph rewrite language based on the Unified Modelling Language and Java. In Ehrig, H., Engels, G., Kreowski, H.J., Rozenberg, G., eds.: 6th International Workshop on Theory and Application of Graph Transformations, TAGT'98. Volume 1764 of LNCS., Springer-Verlag, Heidelberg, Germany (2000) 296–309
3. Böhlen, B., Jäger, D., Schleicher, A., Westfechtel, B.: UPGRADE: A framework for building graph-based interactive tools. In Mens, T., Schürr, A., Taentzer, G., eds.: 1st International Workshop on Graph-Based Tools, GraBaTs'02. Volume 72 of ENTCS., Elsevier Science Publishers (2002)
4. Böhlen, B., Ranger, U.: Concepts for specifying complex graph transformation systems. In Ehrig, H., Engels, G., Parisi-Presicce, F., eds.: 2nd International Conference on Graph Transformations, ICGT'04. Volume 3256 of LNCS., Springer-Verlag, Heidelberg, Germany (2004) 96–111
5. Ranger, U., Schultchen, E., Mosler, C.: Specifying distributed graph transformation systems. (2006) , presented at the 3rd International Workshop on Graph-Based Tools, GraBaTs'06.

6. Ranger, U., Lüstraeten, M.: Search trees for distributed graph transformation systems. In Karsai, G., Taentzer, G., eds.: 2nd International Workshop on Graph and Model Transformation, GraMoT'06. Volume 4 of Electronic Communications of the EASST., European Association of Software Science and Technology (2006) (to appear).

7. Taentzer, G.: Towards common exchange formats for graphs and graph transformation systems. In Ehrig, H., Ermel, C., Padberg, J., eds.: 1st International Workshop on Uniform Approaches to Graphical Process Specification Techniques, UNIGRA'01. Volume 44(4) of ENTCS., Elsevier Science Publishers (2001)

8. Winter, A.: Visuelles Programmieren mit Graphtransformationen. PhD-Thesis, RWTH Aachen University (2000)

9. Heckel, R., Ehrig, H., Engels, G., Taentzer, G.: A view-based approach to system modeling based on open graph transformation systems. In Ehrig, H., Engels, G., Kreowski, H.J., Rozenberg, G., eds.: Handbook on Graph Grammars and Computing by Graph Transformation: Applications, Languages, and Tools. Volume 2. World Scientific, Singapore (1999) 639–668

10. Habel, A., Heckel, R., Taentzer, G.: Graph grammars with negative application conditions. Fundamenta Informaticae **26** (1996) 287–313

11. Varró, D., Pataricza, A.: Generic and meta-transformations for model transformation engineering. In Baar, T., Strohmeier, A., Moreira, A., Mellor, S., eds.: 7th International Conference on the Unified Modeling Language, UML'04. Volume 3273 of LNCS., Springer-Verlag, Heidelberg, Germany (2004) 290–304

12. Tichy, M.: Durchgängige Unterstützung für Entwurf, Implementierung und Betrieb von Komponenten in offenen Softwarearchitekturen mittels UML. Diploma Thesis, University of Paderborn (2002)

13. Schürr, A.: Specification of graph translators with triple graph grammars. In Mayr, E.W., Schmidt, G., Tinhofer, G., eds.: 20th International Workshop on Graph-Theoretic Concepts in Computer Science, WG'94. Volume 903 of LNCS., Springer-Verlag, Heidelberg, Germany (1995) 151–163

14. Fischer, I., Koch, M., Taentzer, G.: Visual design of distributed object systems by graph transformation. Technical Report 98-15, Tech. University of Berlin (1998)

Maintaining Consistency in Layered Architectures of Mobile Ad-Hoc Networks

Julia Padberg, Kathrin Hoffmann*, Hartmut Ehrig,
Tony Modica, Enrico Biermann, and Claudia Ermel

Institute for Software Technology and Theoretical Computer Science
Technical University of Berlin, Germany

Abstract. In this paper we present a layered architecture for modeling workflows in Mobile **A**d-Hoc **NET**works (MANETs) using algebraic
higher order nets (AHO nets). MANETs are networks of mobile devices
that communicate with each other via wireless links without relying on
an underlying infrastructure, e.g. in emergency scenarios, where an effective coordination is crucial among team members, each of them equipped
with hand-held devices.

Workflows in MANETs can be adequately modeled using a layered architecture, where the overall workflow, the team members' activities and
the mobility issues are separated into three different layers, namely the
workflow layer, the mobility layer and the team layer. Dividing the AHO
net model into layers immediately rises the question of consistency. We
suggest a formal notion of layer consistency requiring that the team layer
is given by the mapping of the individual member's activities to the gluing of the workflow and the mobility layer. The main results concern the
maintenance of the layer consistency when changing the workflow layer,
the mobility layer and the team layer independently.

1 Introduction

Mobile Ad-Hoc Networks (MANETs) consist of mobile nodes, communicating independently of a stable infrastructure. The network topology is changed continuously depending on the actual position and availability of the nodes. A typical
example is a team of team members communicating using hand-held devices and
laptops as e.g. in the disaster recovery scenario in Section 2. Formal modeling
of workflows in MANETs using algebraic higher order nets (AHO nets) has been
first introduced in [5]. AHO nets are Petri nets with complex tokens, namely
place/transition (P/T) nets as well as rules and net transformations for changing these nets. On this basis we present a layered architecture of the model that
allows the separation of support activities concerning the network from activities
concerning the intended workflow. This yields better and conciser models, since
supporting the network connectivity has a much finer granularity than the more

---

* This work has been partly funded by the research project forMA₁NET (see
http://tfs.cs.tu-berlin.de/formalnet/) of the German research Council.

M.B. Dwyer and A. Lopes (Eds.): FASE 2007, LNCS 4422, pp. 383–397, 2007.

or less fixed workflow execution. The layered architecture of AHO net models of workflows in MANETs distinguishes three layers, the workflow layer, the mobility layer and the team layer. The workflow layer describes the overall workflow that is to be achieved by the whole team. The mobility layer describes the workflows in order to maintain the MANETs connectivity. The team layer describes the individual activities of the team members. Moreover, we provide a set of rules in each layer for the transformation of corresponding P/T-nets expressing different system states. As we distinguish different layers in which transformations are applied independently, the question comes up how these layers fit together. Layer consistency means that these layers together form a valid AHO net model of workflows in MANETs. In a mobile setting it is not realistic to expect consistency at all moments, so there are different degrees of inconsistency that are feasible during maintenance of consistency. Consider the subsequent possibilities for maintaining consistency in a layered AHO net model of workflows in MANETs: *Checking consistency* means that in all states of the AHO net modeling the workflows in MANETs consistency can be checked. *Guaranteed consistency* is given if each state of the AHO net is a consistent one, that is the rules are only applied when the conditions that guarantee consistency are satisfied. *Backtracking consistency* is the possibility to reach an inconsistent state, and to have then the possibility to backtrack the transformations until a consistent state is reached. *Restoring consistency* is the possibility of inconsistent states in the AHO net, but with a "recipe" to fix them. (So, backtracking could be considered as a special case.) This recipe provides conditions for the application of the next transformations. The notion of consistency we present in this paper can be used for all four possibilities. Consistency maintenance depends on the precise AHO net model. More precisely, the way consistency is maintained is given by the way rules are applied during the firing of the transitions of the AHO net model. Orthogonally, there are other notions of consistency that are relevant for an AHO net model of workflows in MANETs, e.g. the intended workflow of the whole team is covered by the individual activities of the team members. Another important consistency notion concerns the distributed behavior that means in which way the behavior of each member is interrelated with the behavior of the other team members. In the conclusion we hint at the possible formalization of such a team work consistency or behavior consistency in our approach.

The formal approach presented in this paper was developed in strong collaboration with some research projects[1] where an adaptive workflow management system for MANETs, specifically targeted to emergency scenarios, is partly realized resp. going to be implemented. Section 2 introduces an exemplary scenario of disaster management to illustrate our notions and results, while in Section 3 we discuss our approach to model workflows in MANETs using a layered architecture. The formalization to maintain consistency in layered architectures can be found in Section 4. Finally, we discuss future work.

---

[1] MOBIDIS - http://www.dis.uniroma1.it/pub/mecella/projects/MobiDIS, MAIS - http://www.mais-project.it, IST FP6 WORKPAD - http://www.workpad-project.eu/

2 Scenario: Emergency Management

As a running example we use a scenario in archaeological disaster/recovery: after an earthquake, a team (led by a team leader) is equipped with mobile devices (laptops and PDAs) and sent to the affected area to evaluate the state of archaeological sites and the state of precarious buildings. The goal is to draw a situation map in order to schedule restructuring jobs. The team is considered as an overall MANET in which the team leader's device coordinates the other team member devices by providing suitable information (e.g. maps, sensible objects, etc.) and assigning activities. A typical cooperative process to be enacted by the team is shown in Fig. 1(a), where the team leader has to select a building based on previously stored details of the area while team member 1 could take some pictures of the precarious buildings and team member 2 (after a visual analysis of a building) could fill in some specific questionnaires. Finally, these results have to be analyzed by the team leader in order to schedule next activities.

In the following we exemplarily present P/T-nets called token nets for our scenario. As described above, Fig. 1(a) presents the workflow W_0 that has to be cooperatively executed by the team. The dashed lines are an additional information illustrating the relation among tasks and team members and are not a part of the P/T-net itself. There is a corresponding workflow $\underline{W}_0$ where the place **p** is represented by two places **p1** and **p2** (and similar place **p'**) to integrate movement activities. In Fig. 1(b) the token net M_0 presents the mobility aspect of team member 1 stating that he/she has to go to the selected destination while team member 2 stays put. Finally, in Fig. 2 there are three separate nets for the team layer showing the local view of each team member onto the workflow and the mobility net.

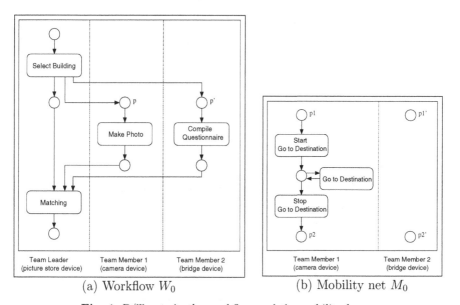

(a) Workflow W_0 (b) Mobility net M_0

Fig. 1. P/T-nets in the workflow and the mobility layer

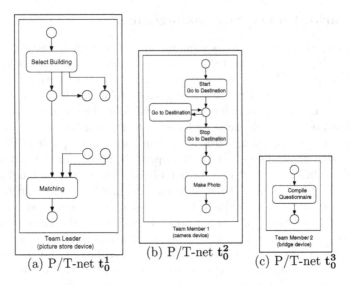

Fig. 2. Team member nets in the team layer

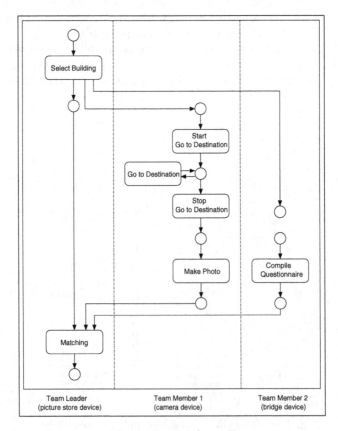

Fig. 3. Teamwork net T_0

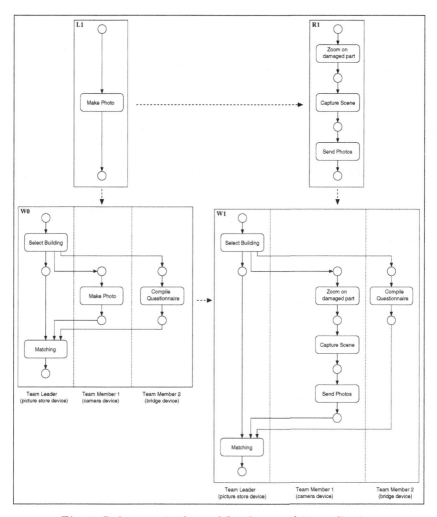

Fig. 4. Rule r_{photo} in the workflow layer and its application

To maintain consistency in a layered architecture first of all the teamwork net T_0 (see Fig. 3) has to be produced by gluing the workflow $\underline{W}_0$ and the mobility net M_0 (see Fig. 1). In more detail, the place **p** in the workflow W_0 is refined by the movement activities of team member 1. Moreover, the local view of each team member (see Fig. 2) is achieved by an inclusion into the teamwork net, called activity arrow that realizes the relation of team members to their activities. Thus, we start with a consistent layer environment (see Section 4).

In a particular scenario the movement of the device equipped with the camera could result in a disconnection from the others. To maintain the network connectivity and ensure a path among devices a layered architecture should be able to alert the mobility layer to select a possible "bridge" device (e.g. the one owned by team member 2) to follow the "going-out-of-range" camera device.

In general this may result in a change of the MANET topology. Specifically, the current mobility net and the P/T-net of team member 2 have to be transformed in order to adapt it to the evolving network topology.

Thus, according to the requirements of our scenario, the structure of the token nets in Figs. 1 and 2 has to be changed to react to incoming events, e.g. to avoid a "going-out-of-range"-situation. In general we consider the change of the net structure as rule-based transformation of P/T-nets. This theory is inspired by graph transformation systems [12] that were generalized to net transformation systems [7]. The existence of several consistency and compatibility results for net transformation systems is highly profitable for maintaining consistency of workflows in MANETs. The basic idea behind net transformation systems is the stepwise development of P/T-nets by appropriate rules. Think of these rules as replacement systems, where the left-hand side of a rule is replaced by the right-hand side. A transformation from a P/T-net N_0 to a P/T-net N_1 by a rule r is denoted by $N_0 \overset{r}{\Longrightarrow} N_1$.

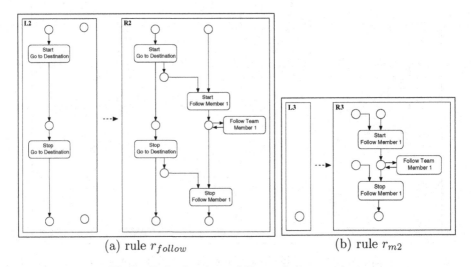

(a) rule r_{follow} (b) rule r_{m2}

Fig. 5. Rules for the mobility and the team layer

In our example team member 1 has to refine his/her activity of making photos. For this reason the structure of the workflow W_0 in Fig. 1(a) is changed using the rule r_{photo} depicted in the upper row in Fig. 4 resulting in the new workflow W_1 in Fig. 4. Assume a probable disconnection while team member 1 is going to the previously selected destination. Here the rule r_{follow} in Fig. 5(a) maintains the network connectivity by adding movement activities for team member 2 to follow team member 1, i.e. $M_0 \overset{r_{follow}}{\Longrightarrow} M_1$. Analogously, the net structure of the local view of team member 2 has to be adapted to include these movement activities. So, we provide the rule r_{m2} in Fig. 5(b) for the team layer to change the structure of the token net t_0^3 (see Fig. 2(c)), i.e. $t_0^3 \overset{r_{m2}}{\Longrightarrow} t_1^3$. Note that these rules are applied independently so that consistent transformations cannot be guaranteed in general. But we present in Section 4 layer consistency conditions to maintain consistency of a layered architecture in MANETs, i.e. after the application of specific rules we have again a consistent layer environment.

3 Layered Architectures of Mobile Ad-Hoc Networks

In [5] a model for MANETs is described by a global workflow and its transformation by a global set of rules. Following the observation that a workflow in MANETs consists of different aspects we provide a layered architecture as depicted in Fig. 6(a) to get a more adequate model. We separate movement activities from general activities and allow a local view of team members that is most important in such an unstable environment. From a practical point of view the MANET topology often has to be restructured to maintain the network connectivity resulting in a change of movement activities while general activities are more or less fixed during the workflow execution. Thus, the global workflow, based on a predictive layer, is separated into three different layers. Each of these layers is equipped with its own P/T-nets and transformation rules. The advantage is that we exploit some form of control on rule application by assigning a set of rules to a specific layer. Under these restrictions transformations can be realized in a specific layer of our model.

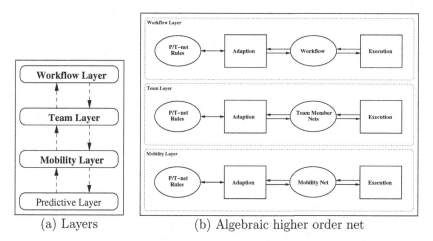

    (a) Layers   (b) Algebraic higher order net

Fig. 6. Layered architecture for supporting cooperative work on MANETs

The predictive layer signals probable disconnections to the upper mobility layer. The predictive layer implements a probabilistic technique [6] that is able to predict whether in the next instant all devices will still be connected. The mobility layer summarizes movement activities of the involved team members and is in charge of managing those situations when a peer is going to disconnect. The team layer realizes the local view of team members onto the workflow and the mobility net. Here, a P/T-net describes those activities being relevant for one team member. Finally, the workflow layer represents in terms of a P/T-net[2] the cooperative work of the team but excludes movement activities.

The layered architecture is formalized by a layered AHO net (see Fig. 6(b) for a schematic view), so that rules in a certain layer are provided for transformations of corresponding P/T-nets, e.g. to react to some incoming events. In general, AHO nets [8] combine an algebraic data type part and Petri nets by the inscription of net elements with terms over the given data structure. Technically, the data type part of the AHO net in Fig. 6(b) consists of P/T-nets, the well-known token game, rules and rule-based transformation in the sense of the double pushout (DPO) approach [7], where all of them specified by appropriate sorts and operations. In this way, P/T-nets and rules can be used as tokens in our model, and the token game and rule-based transformations can be implemented in the net inscriptions. Moreover, places in the layered AHO net are either system or rule places, i.e. the state of our model is given by an appropriate marking consisting of token nets and token rules. Token rules are static, i.e. rules represented as tokens do not move and remain unchanged on the corresponding rule places (indicated by the double arrow). In short, firing a transition **Adaption** changes the structure of a corresponding token net according to an appropriate token rule (for details we refer to [8]). Specifically, the mobility layer is in charge of catching disconnection events incoming from the predictive layer and modifying the mobility net (e.g. adding a "Follow Member X" activity) by applying transformation rules.

The P/T-nets presented in Section 2 are possible markings of our AHO net model in Fig. 6(b). Fig. 1(a) depicts the token net W_0 for the workflow layer, i.e. it represents the current marking of the place **Workflow** in Fig. 6(b). For the mobility layer in Fig. 1(b) the token net M_0 is depicted (token net on the place **Mobility Net** in Fig. 6(b)). Finally, the team member nets in Fig. 2 are a marking on the place **Team Member Nets** in our model. Note that in general we consider the marking of the token nets. This requires switching from P/T-nets to P/T-systems so that firing a transition **Execution** in our model (see Fig. 6(b)) computes the successor marking of a token net. But in this paper we prefer the notion of P/T-nets because our main results focus on the structure of token nets. Analogously, for each layer a specific transformation rule is depicted in Figs. 4 and 5.

4   Concepts and Results for Layer Consistency

In this section we discuss the basic concepts for maintaining consistency in our approach. Consistency is defined for the layered architecture of workflows in MANETs, that is, the *workflow layer*, the *mobility layer* and the *team layer*. We present a notion of consistency, that relates the layers to the team members' activities. Moreover, as discussed in Section 2 we have rules and transformations for changes at the level of the workflow layer, of the mobility layer and for

---

[2] Note that we have a P/T-net that describes the workflow, but this needs not be a workflow net in the sense of [14].

changing the individual activities of the team members. These rules and transformations allow the refinement of the token nets according to the imperatives of the network maintenance. To support the local views they have to be applied independently but must allow precise consistency maintenance. So, we give a precise definition of layer consistency and provide precise conditions that allow maintaining consistency. The main theorem states the conditions under consistency can be maintained stepwise. This result can be extended, so that certain degrees of inconsistency are allowed, while restoring consistency is still possible. In Subsection 4.3 we pick up the discussion on maintaining consistency in view of the notions we present subsequently. Here, we present these notions and results at a more informal level, but the notions are defined formally and the results have been proven mathematically in [4].

4.1   Consistent Layer Environment

Based on the layered architecture for MANETs we have for the *workflow layer* a P/T-net W, for the *mobility layer* a P/T-net M and for the *team work layer* for each team member $m = 1, ..., n$ a P/T-net $\mathbf{t^m}$ representing their individual activities. Moreover, we have the relation to the activities of the whole team and rules changing these activities. Here, we assume merely that $\mathbf{t^m}$ are P/T-nets. Alternatively we could require workflow or process nets. The activities of the team members consist of parts concerning their workflow as well as parts concerning their mobility. Team members can change their team member nets according to specific rules. The main goal of our approach is modeling the changes that occur for reasons of the tasks to be achieved as well as the changes that are required because of the mobility issues. To this end we need the workflow W and rules r^W for transforming W, the mobility net M and rules r^M for transforming M as well as each team member's net $\mathbf{t^m}$ and rules $\mathbf{r^m}$ to transform these. These rules are given as net rules and transformations in the DPO approach [7] (see for example the P/T-net rules in Figs. 4 and 5 in Section 2). The nets W, M and $\mathbf{t^m}$,

as well as the rules r^W, r^M and $\mathbf{r^m}$ are the tokens in the AHO net depicted in Fig. 6(b). Firing in this AHO net causes the transformation of the nets W, M and $\mathbf{t^m}$. Consistency of such a layered AHO net means in a broad sense that W, M and $\mathbf{t^m}$ have to be related as depicted in Fig. 7. The interface net I is assumed to be fixed throughout this paper, but it is straightforward to adapt our constructions to changing the interface as well.

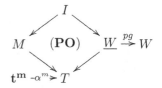

Fig. 7. Consistent layer environment

Definition 1. *A* consistent layer environment *according to the layers in Fig. 6(b) is given for the the workflow W, the mobility net M and team members' nets $\mathbf{t^1}, ..., \mathbf{t^n}$ if the following conditions are satisfied:*

1. *In order to have refinement of places in W with subnets of M we allow replacing W by $\underline{W} \xrightarrow{pg} W$, where pg is a place gluing morphism (bijective on transitions and surjective on places).*

2. *There is the fixed interface net I included in M and $\underline{W}$, so that a teamwork net T is obtained by the gluing of M and $\underline{W}$ along I, written $T = M +_I \underline{W}$.*
3. *There are activity arrows for each team member $\mathbf{t^1} \xrightarrow{\alpha^1} T, ..., \mathbf{t^n} \xrightarrow{\alpha^n} T$ that are net morphisms relating a team member's activities – given by the net $\mathbf{t^m}$ – to the teamwork net T.*

The nets $W, M, (\mathbf{t^1}, ..., \mathbf{t^n})$ and T correspond in our example to the nets given in Figs. 1, 2 and 3, respectively. $\underline{W}_0$ is obtained from W_0 by splitting $\mathbf{p}$ in Fig. 1(a) into two places $\mathbf{p1}$ and $\mathbf{p2}$ that are unconnected (and similar $\mathbf{p'}$ into $\mathbf{p1'}$ and $\mathbf{p2'}$). I consists of the places $\mathbf{p1}$, $\mathbf{p2}$, $\mathbf{p1'}$ and $\mathbf{p2'}$ included in $\underline{W}_0$ and also in M_0 in Fig. 1(b) where these places are the entry and exit places.

4.2   Transformations at Different Layers

As mentioned before we want to model changes using transformation rules at the different layers we have. The transformation of the mobility net M, the workflow W and the team members' activities $\mathbf{t^m}$ is achieved using net transformations (see [7]) as illustrated in Section 2.

Example 1. Starting at a consistent layer environment firing of the AHO net transitions **Adaption** in Fig. 6(b) yields various transformations in the different layers. So, at the level of the tokens (i.e. nets and rules) we then have e.g. the situation depicted in Fig 8: There are rules in the mobility layer, in the workflow layer and three rules in the team layer that have been applied, yielding the following transformations $M_0 \xrightarrow{r^M} M_1, W_0 \xrightarrow{r^W} W_1$ as well as rules for each team member $\mathbf{t_0^1} \xrightarrow{r^1} \mathbf{t_1^1}, \mathbf{t_0^2} \xrightarrow{r^2} \mathbf{t_1^2}$ and $\mathbf{t_0^3} \xrightarrow{r^3} \mathbf{t_1^3}$. This is the situation as discussed in Section 2 if we assume additional rules for the team leader and team member 1.

According to the discussion in Section 1, we now need conditions that allow to maintain consistency. We have to obtain the teamwork net that integrates the changes induced by the transformations above. The results for net transformations yield a variety of independence conditions for the sequential and parallel application of rules and for the compatibility with pushouts (see [7]). Subsequently we develop the conditions for maintaining layer consistency based on transformations at the mobility and the workflow layer. Later, in Corollary 1, we assume not only transformation steps, but transformation sequences.

Let there be the transformations $W_0 \xrightarrow{r^W} W_1$ and $M_0 \xrightarrow{r^M} M_1$. We first need to ensure *compatibility with place refinement*. This means that the rule r^W is also applicable to $\underline{W}_0$ and there exists a place-gluing morphism $pg_1 : \underline{W}_1 \rightarrow W_1$, such that the diagram (1) in Fig. 9 commutes.

Provided the *preservation of the interface I*, that is, the applications of the rules r^W and r^M are independent of I, there is the parallel rule $r = r^W + r^M$, so that the application of r to the teamwork net T_0 yields the transformation $T_0 \xrightarrow{r} T_1$, with $T_1 = M_1 +_I \underline{W}_1$. So, the first step to the next consistent layer environment is achieved. Now we restrict the transformation $T_0 \xrightarrow{r} T_1$ to the transformations $\mathbf{t_0^m} \xrightarrow{r^m} \mathbf{t_1^m}$ for each team member $m = 1, ..., n$. Since the team members' activities are represented by activity arrows, the rules have to be compatible with arrows. The *existence of activity rules* ensures that for each team member the rule $r = (L \leftarrow K \rightarrow R)$ is restricted to an activity rule $\mathbf{r^m} = (\mathbf{L^m} \leftarrow \mathbf{K^m} \rightarrow \mathbf{R^m})$, where $\mathbf{K^m}$ has to be the pullback (roughly an intersection) of $\mathbf{L^m}$ and K as well as the pullback of $\mathbf{R^m}$ and K.

Moreover, each activity rule $\mathbf{r^m}$ has to be the reduction of the corresponding rule r to that part being relevant for the team member m. The *conformance of activity rules and team member nets* means that $\mathbf{L^m}$ is additionally the pullback of $\mathbf{t_0^m}$ and L, and the application of an activity rule $\mathbf{r^m}$ to a team member net $\mathbf{t_0^m}$ yields the transformation $\mathbf{t_0^m} \overset{\mathbf{r^m}}{\Longrightarrow} \mathbf{t_1^m}$.

Then we can state our first main result, that provides the conditions for stepwise consistency maintenance.

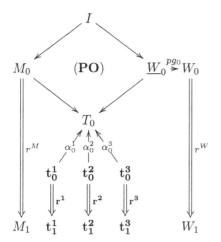

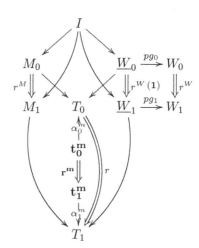

Fig. 8. State after some transformations

Fig. 9. A new consistent layer environment for $m = 1, 2, 3$

Theorem 1 (Stepwise Consistency Maintenance)

Given a consistent layer environment $T_0 = M_0 +_I \underline{W}_0$ with the place gluing $\underline{W}_0 \overset{pg_0}{\rightsquigarrow} W_0$ and the activity arrows $\mathbf{t_0^m} \overset{\alpha_0^m}{\rightarrow} T_0$ for each member $m = 1, ..., n$, then the transformations $W_0 \overset{r^W}{\Longrightarrow} W_1$, $M_0 \overset{r^M}{\Longrightarrow} M_1$ and the transformations $\mathbf{t_0^m} \overset{\mathbf{r^m}}{\Longrightarrow} \mathbf{t_1^m}$ yield again a consistent layer environment $T_1 = M_1 +_I \underline{W}_1$ with the place gluing $\underline{W}_1 \overset{pg_1}{\rightsquigarrow} W_1$ and the activity arrows $\mathbf{t_1^m} \overset{\alpha_1^m}{\rightarrow} T_1$ for each m, provided the layer consistency conditions *hold:*

1. *compatibility with place refinement, i.e. the rule r^W is compatible with the morphism pg_0,*
2. *preservation of the interface I, i.e. the application of the rules r^W and r^M is independent of I,*
3. *existence of activity rules, i.e. for each m there are activity rules $\mathbf{r^m}$ over the parallel rule $r = r^W + r^M$ and*

4. *conformance of activity rules and team member nets, i.e.* $t_0^m \overset{r^m}{\Longrightarrow} t_1^m$ *is compatible with* $T_0 \overset{r}{\Longrightarrow} T_1$.

Proof. It is shown in [4] that given the four layer consistency conditions above, the properties for a consistent layer environment are fulfilled: existence of place gluing morphism, compatibility of parallel rule application and gluing of W and M, and existence of activity arrows for each team member net.

Example 2. Considering the example in Section 2, outlined in Fig. 8 we have the following situation: The rule r_{photo} is compatible with place refinement because it preserves all involved places. For the same reason, the rules r_{photo} and r_{follow} are independent of the interface given by the overlapping of the workflow $\underline{W}_0$ and the mobility net M_0 and we obtain the parallel rule r consisting of both r_{photo} and r_{follow}.

In a next step we focus on the rule r_{m2} in Fig. 5(b) that is compatible on the one hand with the parallel rule r, i.e. the reduction to those activities of rule r being relevant for team member 2 is equivalent to rule r_{m2}; on the other hand the transformation $t_0^3 \overset{r_{m2}}{\Longrightarrow} t_1^3$ is compatible with the transformation $T_0 \overset{r}{\Longrightarrow} T_1$, because there is a corresponding inclusion of the resulting token net t_1^3 into the teamwork net T_1. Thus, we have the pushout $T_1 = M_1 +_I \underline{W}_1$ and the construction of the activity rule for each team member yields the activity arrows $t_1^m \overset{\alpha_1^m}{\to} T_1$. So, we obtain the consistent layer environment depicted in Fig 9, where $r^W = r_{photo}$ and $r^M = r_{follow}$.

If we allow transformation sequences instead of transformation steps in Theorem 1 we may obtain inconsistent states. For recovery of consistency we need additional conditions. At the different layers rule application need to be checked with respect to the last known consistent state, because there cannot be made assumptions on the actual state of the layers. Technically this can be achieved using parallel independent rules, where the independence is considered with respect to the last known consistent state. The subsequent corollary states that restoring consistency under these conditions is achieved using Theorem 1 twice.

Corollary 1 (Restoring Consistency). *Given a consistent layer environment, shortly* $(t_0^m \overset{\alpha_0^m}{\to} T_0 = M_0 +_I \underline{W}_0 \overset{pg_0}{\to} W_0)$, *and transformation sequences* $M_0 \overset{*}{\Longrightarrow} M_{n_M}$ *via* r_i^M *and* $W_0 \overset{*}{\Longrightarrow} W_{n_W}$ *via* r_j^W *and the transformation steps* $t_0^m \overset{r^m}{\Longrightarrow} t_1^m$ *leading to a possibly inconsistent state (see Fig. 10). It is possible to get an intermediate consistent layer environment* $(t_1^m \overset{\alpha_1^m}{\to} T_1 = M +_I \underline{W} \overset{pg}{\to} W)$ *and a next consistent layer environment* $t_2^m \overset{\alpha_2^m}{\to} T_2 = M_{n_M} +_I \underline{W}_{n_W} \overset{pg_{n_W}}{\to} W_{n_W}$ *(see Fig. 11) if the following conditions hold:*

1. *The transformation sequence* $M_0 \overset{*}{\Longrightarrow} M_{n_M}$ *can be decomposed, such that* $(M_0 \overset{*}{\Longrightarrow} M_{n_M}) = (M_0 \overset{r^M}{\Longrightarrow} M \overset{\bar{r}^M}{\Longrightarrow} M_{n_M})$ *for suitable rules* r^M *and* $\bar{r}^M$.
2. *The transformation sequence* $W_0 \overset{*}{\Longrightarrow} W_{n_W}$ *can be decomposed, such that* $(W_0 \overset{*}{\Longrightarrow} W_{n_W}) = (W_0 \overset{r^W}{\Longrightarrow} W \overset{\bar{r}^W}{\Longrightarrow} W_{n_W})$ *for suitable rules* r^W *and* $\bar{r}^W$.

3. *The layer consistency conditions in Theorem 1 hold for* (r^W, r^M) *with* $\mathbf{r^m}$.
4. *There exist transformation steps* $\mathbf{t_1^m} \overset{\bar{\mathbf{r}}^{\mathbf{m}}}{\Longrightarrow} \mathbf{t_2^m}$, *such that the layer consistency conditions in Theorem 1 hold for* $(\bar{r}^W, \bar{r}^M)$ *with* $\bar{\mathbf{r}}^{\mathbf{m}}$.

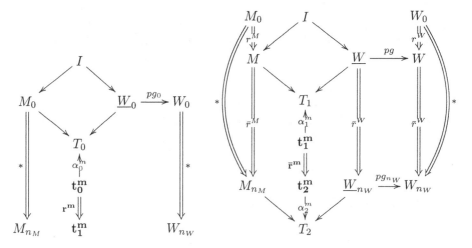

Fig. 10. Possibly inconsistent state

Fig. 11. Restoring the next consistent layer environment

4.3 Maintaining Consistency

The notions and results we have introduced above concern the fundamental understanding of consistency in MANETs. As mentioned in the introduction other notions of consistency are possible and desirable. The AHO net model given in Fig. 6(b) merely presents the rough structure but abstracts especially from the details of the firing conditions. The exact formulation of the firing conditions models the way the rules are applied in the different layers and constitutes the way consistency is dealt with. The discussion below abstracts from realization issues, as e.g. the complexity of the task to find morphisms between nets. Considering the possibilities discussed in the introduction we have:

- *Checking consistency:* The AHO net in Fig. 6(b) allows the application of arbitrary rules and it can be checked whether a certain state of an AHO net model for MANETs is a consistent layer environment. There need to be the fixed interface I, the token nets M and W on the places **Mobility Net** and **Workflow**, respectively, and the token nets $\mathbf{t^m}$ for each team member m on the place **Team Member Nets**, so that there are nets T and $\underline{W}$, so that there is a place gluing morphism $\underline{W} \rightarrow W$, T is the gluing of M and $\underline{W}$ along I, and there are m activity arrows $\mathbf{t^m} \overset{\alpha^m}{\rightarrow} T$.
- *Guaranteed consistency:* Theorem 1 ensures transformations so that each state is consistent. Then the AHO net in Fig. 6(b) may allow only the application of rules that satisfy these conditions. Moreover, the parallel firing of

the transitions in the different layers has to be ensured to have consistency in each state.

- *Backtracking:* Since all rules are symmetric (as one of the characteristics of the DPO approach) the inverse rules can be applied in inverse order. Then the AHO net in Fig. 6(b) may allow the application of arbitrary rules, but requires a storage of the transformations. Then an explicit backtracking can be achieved by firing the transitions in the AHO net but using only the inverse rules.
- *Restoring consistency:* Corollary 1 gives conditions for restoring consistency. Then the AHO net in Fig. 6(b) may allow only rule application which satisfy these conditions. An explicit restoration is possible using the transformations constructed in the corollary. Note that here we merely treat transformation sequences for the mobility and the workflow layer. Restoring consistency after transformation sequences at theteam layer is very closely related to the question of team work consistency and hence not treated here (see Section 5 for a short discussion).

5   Conclusion

The use of a layered architecture for modeling workflows in MANETs has the advantage of separating different views with different granularity, but immediately rises the question of consistency. In this paper, we have presented the notion of layer consistent environment stating that the views in the workflow layer, the mobility layer and the team layer fit together. Since the main modeling advantage of AHO nets is the possibility to model net transformations we have introduced maintenance means for the AHO net for workflows in MANETs that take changes modeled by net transformation into account.

Related work on distribution of workflows in a possibly mobile setting can be found e.g. in [15, 3, 10] where a unique workflow is divided on the one hand in different autonomous workflows and on the other hand the resulting workflows are adapted by using inheritance resp. graph rules. In contrast we present a layered architecture, where a global workflow and its transformation are separated into three different parts, each of them relevant for a specific aspect of workflows in MANETs.

In this paper we present the first results of a line of research[3] concerning formal modeling and analysis of MANETs. So, there is a large amount of most interesting and relevant open questions directly related to the work presented here. The behavior of token nets has been treated in previous papers [5] and has been excluded here deliberately. Nets in different layers have their own behavior that is executed by firing the corresponding transitions in the AHO net (see Fig. 6(b)). This directly leads to a challenging consistency issue, namely how the individual processes relate to each other. A solution would be to use the theory for open nets [2]. Other relevant notions of consistency concern e.g. the consistency between each team member's activities and the complete team work. It should be ensured

---

[3] The research project *Formal modeling and analysis of flexible processes in mobile ad-hoc networks* (forMA₁NET) of the German research Council.

that the team members' activities together cover the complete team work. Again, team consistency has to be maintained during transformations in the different layers. Especially in the area of workflow modeling, properties like safety and liveness are of importance. In [13, 11] inheritance preserving rules and property preserving rules, respectively, are formalized, so that restructuring of workflows preserves properties. Thus, another interesting aspect of future work is to study an integration of preserving rules into the AHO net in Fig. 6(b).

We plan to develop a tool for our approach. For the application of net transformation rules, this tool will provide an export to AGG [1], a graph transformation engine as well as a tool for the analysis of graph transformation properties like termination and rule independence. Furthermore, the token net properties could be analyzed using the Petri Net Kernel [9], a tool infrastructure for Petri nets different net classes.

References

1. AGG Homepage. http://tfs.cs.tu-berlin.de/agg.
2. P. Baldan, A. Corradini, H. Ehrig, and R. Heckel. Compositional Semantics of Open Petri Nets Based on Deterministic Processes. *MSCS*, 15(1):1–35, 2005.
3. L. Baresi, A. Maurino, and S. Modafferi. Workflow partitioning in mobile information systems. volume 158 of *IFIP International Federation for Information Processing*, pages 93–106, 2005.
4. E. Biermann, T. Modica, and K. Hoffmann. Categorical Foundation for Layer Consistency in AHO-Net Models Supporting Workflow Management in MANETs. Technical Report 2006/13, TU Berlin, Fak. IV, 2006.
5. P. Bottoni, F. De Rosa, K. Hoffmann, and M. Mecella. Applying Algebraic Approaches for Modeling Workflows and their Transformations in Mobile Networks. *MIS*, 2(1):51–76, 2006.
6. F. De Rosa, A. Malizia, and M. Mecella. Disconnection Prediction in Mobile Ad hoc Networks for Supporting Cooperative Work. *IEEE Pervasive Comp.*, 4(3):62–70, 2005.
7. H. Ehrig and J. Padberg. Graph Grammars and Petri Net Transformations. volume 3098 of *LNCS*, pages 496–536. Springer, 2004.
8. K. Hoffmann, T. Mossakowski, and H. Ehrig. High-Level Nets with Nets and Rules as Tokens. volume 3536 of *LNCS*, pages 268–288. Springer, 2005.
9. E. Kindler and M. Weber. The Petri Net Kernel - An Infrastructure for Building Petri Net Tools. *Software Tools for Technology Transfer*, 3(4):486–497, 2001.
10. A. Maurino and S. Modafferi. Partitioning Rules for Orchestrating Mobile Information Systems. *Personal and Ubiquitous Computing*, 9(5):291–300, 2005.
11. J. Padberg and M. Urbasek. Rule-Based Refinement of Petri Nets: A Survey. volume 2472 of *LNCS*, pages 161–196. Springer, 2003.
12. G. Rozenberg. *Handbook of Graph Grammars and Computing by Graph Transformations, Volume 1: Foundations.* World Scientific, 1997.
13. W. M. P. van der Aalst and T. Basten. Inheritance of Workflows: An Approach to Tackling Problems Related to Change. *TCS*, 270(1-2):125–203, 2002.
14. W. M. P. van der Aalst and K. van Hee. *Workflow Management: Models, Methods, and Systems.* MIT Press, 2002.
15. W. M. P. van der Aalst and M. Weske. The P2P Approach to Interorganizational Workflows. volume 2068 of *LNCS*, pages 140–156. Springer, 2001.

Towards Normal Design for Safety-Critical Systems

Derek Mannering[1], Jon G. Hall[2], and Lucia Rapanotti[2]

[1] General Dynamics UK Limited
[2] Centre for Research in Computing, The Open University

Abstract. Normal design is, essentially, when an engineer knows that the design they are working on will work. Routine 'traditional' engineering works through normal design. Software engineering has more often been assessed as being closer to radical design, i.e., repeated innovation. One of the aims of the Problem Oriented Software Engineering framework (POSE) is to provide a foundation for software engineering to be considered an application of normal design. To achieve this software engineering must mesh with traditional, normal forms of engineering, such as aeronautical engineering. The POSE approach for normalising software development, from early requirements through to code (and beyond), is to provide a structure within which the results of different development activities can be recorded, combined and reconciled. The approach elaborates, transforms and analyses the project requirements, reasons about the effect of (partially detailed) candidate architectures, and audits design rationale through iterative development, to produce a justified (where warranted) fit-for-purpose solution. In this paper we show how POSE supports the development task of a safety-critical system. A normal 'pattern of development' for software safety under POSE is proposed and validated through its application to an industrial case study.

1 Introduction

Vincenti ([1]) defines 'normal design' as what the engineer is engaged in when s/he knows from the outset

> "how the device in question works, what are its customary features, and that, if properly designed along such lines, it has a good likelihood of accomplishing the desired task."

Much of the routine design encountered in traditional engineering disciplines works 'normally'. Some have recently observed that software engineering does not: Maibaum [2] states that

> "SE ignores the principles of engineering design and almost always adopts radical design methods, to its detriment."

M.B. Dwyer and A. Lopes (Eds.): FASE 2007, LNCS 4422, pp. 398–411, 2007.

Jackson [3] states that

> "Though less conspicuous than radical design, normal design makes up by far the bulk of day-to-day engineering enterprise. Unfortunately, this is not true of software engineering."

Through regulation, standardisation and its co-location with traditional engineering disciplines, safety-critical software intensive systems engineering may be tending to normality. This view has something to recommend it: typically, industrial standards and practices require integration with other normal engineering processes.

Vincenti [1] characterises normal design processes as: (a) relying on engineering judgement in the searching of past experience; (b) allowing the conceptual incorporation of the novel features that come to mind in solving a problem; and (c) allowing the "mental winnowing of the conceived variations" to pick out those most likely to work.

In a previous case study [4], we made a record of a current industrial safety-critical software intensive design process, using the Problem Oriented Software Engineering (POSE) framework [5]. Working from this record, the goal of this paper is to show how it might reflect Vincenti's three characteristics, and so be called 'normal'. To do this, we apply the record in the design of a different, functionally unrelated avionics system component and find that the record is a good fit to the needs of safety-critical development and consider this to be evidence that—to some limited extent—POSE offers an approach to normal design for software engineering.

The paper is organised as follows: background and related work are presented in Section 2. The basics of the POSE framework are described in Section 3. Section 4 demonstrates the use of POSE on a case study involving the development of requirements and high level architecture for a component of an aircraft defensive aids system. Section 5 contains a discussion and conclusions.

2   Background and Related Work

POSE is an extension and generalisation of Jackson's Problem Frame approach [6]. Problem Frames attempt to keep the focus of the software engineer on developing their understanding of the problem to be solved, rather than on a (premature) move to solution of a poorly understood problem. Problem Frames make certain fundamental assumptions: primary is the separation of descriptions of what is given—the *indicative* parts of a problem—from what is required—the *optative* parts of a problem. Originally confined to Requirements Engineering, the influence of Problem Frames has spread to the fields of domain modelling, business process modelling, software architectures and early design—see [7,8,9] for collections of recent work.

The case study work presented in this paper is based on a multi-level safety analysis process typical of many industries. For example, commercial airborne systems are governed by ARP4761 [10]. ARP4761 defines a process incorporating Aircraft FHA (Functional Hazard Analysis), followed by System FHA, followed by PSSA (Preliminary System Safety Assessment, which analyses the proposed architecture). This paper is concerned with the latter, PSSA, but uses PSA (Preliminary Safety Analysis, a combination of hazard identification and preliminary hazard analysis as required by the safety standards) in place of PSSA. In this paper requirements follow the fundamental clarification work of Jackson [20] and Parnas [12] which distinguishes between the given domain properties of the environment and the desired behaviour covered by the requirements. This work also distinguishes between requirements that are presented in terms of the stake-holder(s) and the specification of the solution which is formulated in terms of objects manipulated by software [13]. Therefore there is a large semantic divide between the system level requirements and the specification of the machine solution. One of the reasons for applying POSE is that it bridges the divide by transforming system level requirements into requirements that apply directly to the solution.

The POSE notion of problem used in this work fits well with the Parnas 4-Variable model. This has been used by Parnas *et al.* as part of a table driven approach [12], which is particularly well suited to defining embedded critical applications as shown by its use in SCR [14] and the RSML methods. The RSML work led to the SpecTRM [15] methods, which form part of a human centred, safety-driven process which is supported by an artefact called an Intent specification [16]. The work in this paper is located in the area of the second-level System Design Principles of the Intent specification, and thus may be complementary to the third, Blackbox level provided by SpecTRM.

The work of Anderson, de Lemos, and Saeed [17] share many of the principles and concepts that have driven the development of this work. Particularly the notions that safety is a system attribute and the need to apply a detailed safety analysis to the requirements specifications. The main advantages of the POSE approach over that work are: (a) it provides a framework for transforming requirements; (b) it is rich in traceability; and (c) the models it uses are suitable for safety analysis. The latter means it is efficient as there is no need to develop 'new' models (with all their attendant validation problems) to be able to perform a PSA. Further, its support for traceability makes it particularly suited for use with standards such as DS 00-56 [18] and the DO-178B [19] software guidelines.

3   Problem Oriented Software Engineering

POSE (see [5] for the formal definition) recognises that software engineering processes by necessity include the identification and clarification of system requirements, the understanding and structuring of the problem world, the structuring and specification of a hardware/software machine that can ensure satisfaction of the requirements in the problem world, and the construction of arguments, convincing both to developers, customers, users and other stake-holders that the developed system will provide the functionality and qualities that are needed.

Briefly, POSE generalises and extends fundamental ideas expressing the completeness of requirements engineering [20,21] and those of problem orientation (see, for instance, [6]) to apply to software engineering.

In POSE, software development is viewed as solving a *problem*, the *solution* (S, a labelled double-barred box in the figures that follow) being a *machine*— that is, a program running in a computer—that will ensure satisfaction of the *requirement* (R, the dotted oval in the figures) in the given *problem world* (W) consisting of real-world domains (the labelled but otherwise undecorated boxes in the figures). Typically the requirement concerns properties and behaviours that are located in the problem world at some distance from its interface with the machine. Like Problem Frames, POSE views the problem world W as a collections of *domains* described in terms of their known, or indicative, properties, which interact through their sharing of *phenomena*, i.e, events, commands, states, *etc* (that decorate the arcs in the figures).

POSE is defined as a Gentzen-style sequent calculus that allows problems to be transformed into problems that are easier to solve, or that will lead to other problems that are easier to solve. A set of transformation rule schema defined in the calculus capture (atomic) discrete steps in development. Each requires a justification of application in order for the transformation to be solution preserving, although justifications need not be formal. The combination of the justifications is an argument that the solution is adequate as a solution to the original problem. The interested reader should consult [5] for a fuller presentation of POSE.

POSE problem transformations transform problems in ways that respects solution adequacy: simplifying only slightly, this means that a solution to a transformed problem is also a solution to the original problem.

In the following section we will give highlights of a POSE development of an avionics case study (more detail of the case study is given in [4]). For brevity, we present the development in graphical form, using a Problem Frame-like notation rather than the Gentzen-style presentation in [5]. Moreover, we present only the relevant details of Problem Frames in this paper as and when they are needed; a thorough presentation is beyond the scope of this paper, and can be found in [6].

3.1 A Problem-Oriented Approach to Safety Analysis

From previous work [4], we observe that POSE transformations can be combined to form re-usable process templates or "patterns" [22] for safety-critical development. One such process is shown in Fig. 1 as a UML activity diagram. The activities in the figure include the following POSE transformations[1]:

Domain and Requirement Interpretation used to capture increasing knowledge and detail in the context and requirement of the problem (used in activities 1 and 4);

Solution Expansion used to structure the solution according to a candidate architecture (used in activity 2);

Problem Progression by which the problem is simplified by removing domains (used in activity 3).

The choice point (labelled 5) in the figure is the PSA by which the candidate architecture is assessed for suitability. The outcome of the PSA determines whether

---

[1] Defined and described in [5,23,24].

the current architecture is viable as the basis of a solution or whether backtracking in needed so that another candidate architecture can be chosen.

The pattern is iterative, ending when an architecture suitable for solution development is found. This process is iterative in that design choices, through the choice of candidate architecture, influence requirements, and vice versa.

As we shall see, POSE allows the capture of many important other artefacts of the process, including a record of the choices that have been made, the rationale for the revision of requirements statements.

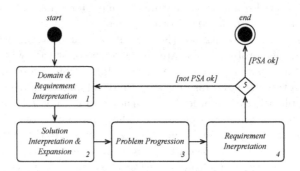

Fig. 1. POSE Safety Pattern

4   The Case Study

The POSE pattern emerged from the realisation that PSA feasibility checks can identify the inadequacy of the architecture early in a development, and avoid the cost associated with rework. The case study from which it was derived and that of this paper are real developments, underdone by the first author, based on systems flying in real aircraft. The case studies are cut-down only in the sense that some detail has been removed for brevity, and they retain all essential complexity. The POSE pattern was applied (retrospectively) in the context of the first case study to confirm that architecture inadequacy could be identified earlier in development (and, perhaps, therefore result in cost savings). In this paper, we use the POSE pattern to guide a safety critical development process capable of satisfying the provisions of DS 00-56 [18].

The case study concerns the development of the *Decoy Controller* (*DC*) component of a defensive aids system on an aircraft, as shown in Fig. 2. The *DC*'s role is to control the release of decoy flares providing defence against incoming missile attack. The *DC* interfaces with the *Defence System* (*DS*) computer, which is responsible for controlling and orchestrating all the defensive aids on the aircraft. The *DS* and other domains (see Fig. 2) already exist (and so appear as undecorated boxes in the figure).

As is common practice in the industry, we will assumes that an aircraft level safety analysis has been completed with safety requirements being allocated to the main aircraft systems, including the defensive aids system. This analysis

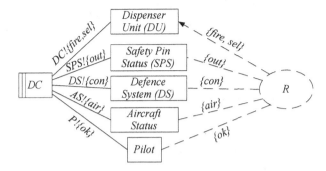

Fig. 2. The DC Problem ($P_{Initial}$)

has allocated requirements to the defensive aids sub-system, including the DC:
in fact, there are two safety hazards allocated to the DC, concerned with the
inadvertent firing of the decoy flares, as follows:

H1. Inadvertent firing of decoy flare on ground. Safety Target: safety critical,
10^{-7} fpfh[2]; and

H2. Inadvertent firing of decoy flare in air. Safety Target: safety critical, 10^{-7}
fpfh.

These hazards have both systematic (safety related) and probabilistic components. To counter these hazards, the architectural design of the overall defensive
aids system introduces a number of safety interlocks as input to the DC to provide safety protection. These are: an input from the pilot indicating whether the
release should be allowed; an input indicating whether the aircraft is in the air;
and an input indicating whether the safety pin, present when the aircraft is on
the ground, is in place. The expected behaviour is that flare dispensing should
be inhibited if any of the following conditions hold: a) the pilot disallows flares;
b) the aircraft is not in the air; or c) the safety pin has not been removed. It
transpires that these interlocks provide extra assurance for hazard **H1** but not
for **H2**. Therefore, the safety task is to demonstrate that **H2** can be satisfied,
with the knowledge that if **H2** can be satisfied, then so can **H1**.

4.1 The process

The first activity in the POSE pattern—"Domain and Requirement Interpretation and Expansion," (labelled 1 in Fig. 1)—details the problem context and
requirement. This works by identification of the major system components, and
the description of their phenomena and their behaviour. The initial problem representation is problem $P_{Initial}$ shown in Fig. 2, with interface phenomena given
in Table 1. Here we summarise the problems components.

The decoy flare DU (Dispenser Unit) has a number of different flare types
which can be selected by control messages from the DC—the chosen type being

---

[2] *fpfh* is 'failures per flight hour.'

communicated in the *sel* phenomena ($DC!\{fire, sel\}$[3], in the figure). The *DC* is told which flare type to select by phenomena controlled by the Defence System ($DS!\{con\}$)[4].

The selected flares are released by the *fire* command (in $DC!\{fire, sel\}$) from the *DC* to the *DU*. The *Pilot* domain inputs the allow release ($P!\{ok\}$) to the *DC*. The Aircraft Status domain inputs the in air status ($AS!\{air\}$) to the *DC*. The *SPS* provides the safety pin status (*out*) to the *DC*.

Table 1. Phenomena of *DC* Problem

Phenomenon	Designation
fire	Command to release the selected flare
sel	Indicates which flare type should be selected
out	Pin status; *out* = *yes* indicates pin has been removed
con	Contains command to fire and selected flare type
air	Aircraft status; *air* = *yes* indicates aircraft is in the air
ok	Pilot intention; *ok* = *yes* indicates allow release

The customer requirement for the *DC* can be expressed as follows:

Ra. The *DS* shall command which flare is selected using a field in its *con* message issued to the *DC*. The *DC* shall obtain the selected flare information from this field in the *con* message, and use it in its *sel* message to the *DU* to control the flare selection in the *DU*.

Rb. The *DS* shall command the *DC* to issue a *fire* command in its *con* message. This shall be the only way in which a flare can be released.

Rc. The *DC* shall cause a flare to be released by issuing a *fire* command to the *DU*, which will fire the selected flare.

Rd. The *DC* shall only issue a fire command if its interlocks are satisfied, i.e. aircraft is in air (*air* = *yes*), *SPS* safety pin has been removed (*out* = *yes*) and *Pilot* has issued an allow a release command (*ok* = *yes*).

As well as **Ra** to **Rd**, the *DC* must also satisfy its safety targets set by the aircraft system level safety analysis. Recognising this, we add safety requirement **RS** to **R**:

RS. The *DC* shall mitigate **H1** & **H2** (Target: safety critical 10^{-7} fpfh).

Therefore, the overall requirement is **R = Ra & Rb & Rc & Rd & RS**, and is indicated in the dotted ellipse in Fig. 2. A complete statement of **R** should also include requirements that cover space, weight, environmental performance, interfaces and so on, but these are beyond the scope of this initial work.

---

[3] That *fire* and *sel* are controlled by *DC* is indicated by the ! on the arc.

[4] Note, flare selection and timing are not safety related, it is only applying an inadvertent fire command to any flare that is regarded as a safety issue.

4.2   A DC Candidate Architecture

The next POSE pattern activity—"Solution Interpretation and Expansion", labelled 2 in Fig. 1—introduces the candidate architecture for *DC* shown in Fig. 3. The *DC* architecture consists of three components, Safety Controller (*SC*), Decoy Micro-controller (*DM*, shown in Fig. 3(b)) and Interlock Input (*II*), as shown in Fig. 3(a). This choice of architecture is typical of industrial safety design strategies that attempt to minimise the number and extent of the safety related functions, localising them to simple, distinct blocks. These strategies justify the candidature of the architecture, and are recorded, under POSE, as part of the justification for the transformations involved.

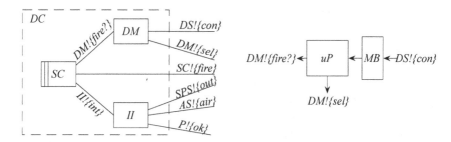

Fig. 3. (a) The *DC* Candidate Architecture and (b) *DM* Internal Architecture

Briefly, component *II* collects together the interlock inputs and passes their status to *SC* (*int*). Component *DM* is a microcontroller used to decode messages from the Defence System (*con*), and when appropriate to issue the fire command request to the *SC* (via *fire?*). The Message Buffer (*MB*, in Fig. 3(b)) holds the received control message *con* from the *DS*. The micro-controller *uP* decodes this message to extract: a) the fire command request status (*fire?*) sent to the *SC*, and b) the selected flare type (*sel*) sent to the *DU*. The *SC*, the component to be designed, is intended as a simple block that handles the safety critical elements of the interlocking. *SC* is, therefore, expected to relate an active *fire?* request to the *DU* (through phenomenon *fire*) if the interlocks are satisfied.

The introduction of the *DC* architecture affects the requirement **R** as terms in *DC* are replaced by terms in *DM*, *SC* and *II* as appropriate. The result is a new requirement statement

$$\textbf{R'} = \textbf{R'a} \,\&\, \textbf{R'b} \,\&\, \textbf{R'c} \,\&\, \textbf{R'd} \,\&\, \textbf{R'S}$$

in which **R'a** is **Ra** with *DC* replaced by *DM*; similarly for **R'c** and **R'd**, *mutandis mutatis*. The most significant change occurs for **R'b** (changes in bold):

R'b. The *DS* shall command the **DM** to issue a **fire?** command in its *con* message. **The DM will request the SC to send the fire command.** This shall be the only way in which a flare can be released.

The result of the transformation step is problem $P_{Interpreted}$ shown in Fig. 4.

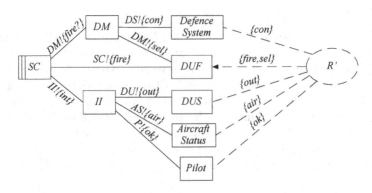

Fig. 4. Solution Interpretation of DC (problem $P_{Interpreted}$)

4.3   Problem Simplification

Of course, this candidate architecture is not guaranteed to lead to a solution; and we will use a PSA to determine whether the DC architecture can safely be the basis of the DC. Performing a PSA on the problem shown in Fig. 4 is an unnecessarily complex task that can be simplified by removing some of the contextual domains. Domain removal is achieved in POSE through "Problem Progression" (labelled 3 in Fig. 1), which simultaneously allows us to transform the requirement **R'** to apply directly to the safety controller, SC, used in the simplified PSA.

For brevity, we show only the removal of the *Pilot* and the associated requirements transformation. To remove the *Pilot* we must alter the requirement so that shared phenomena constrained by the *Pilot*'s actions are recorded: in this case, only that the release command ($ok = yes$) can occur[5]. In this case the requirement is rewritten to include the assumption $A1$ "the input $ok=yes$" as well as including "II observes the pilot input $ok = yes$". Given this rewriting of the requirement, the *Pilot* domain can be removed.

Transforming **R'** in this way yields a new requirement statement, that we will call **R1**, in which **R'a** becomes **R1a**, **R'b** becomes **R1b**, **R'c** becomes **R1c** and **R'S** becomes **R1S** without change. **R'd** becomes (changes shown in bold):

R1d. The SC shall only issue a *fire* command if its interlocks are satisfied, i.e. aircraft is in air ($air = yes$), the SPS safety pin has been removed ($out = yes$) and **II observes pilot input $ok = yes$.**

There are a number of domain removals (and assumptions to the requirement) that follow which, for brevity, we do not describe fully[6]; they result in the problem shown in Fig. 5 which is a better basis for the PSA.

---

[5] Because the *Pilot* is an autonomous agent. If we fail to make this assumption, the problem becomes trivial.

[6] See [25] for more details.

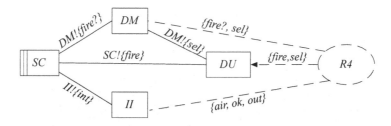

Fig. 5. The Reduced SC problem (problem $P_{Reduced}$)

4.4 Formalising the Requirements

The next activity—"Requirements Interpretation" in Fig. 1—is the formalisation of **R4** for input into the PSA. One must ensure that the justification of the transformation properly relates informal and form requirements, in this case a simple task. The non-safety aspects of the requirement can be formalised into a Parnas Table-like form, shown in Table 2, with the safety targets and assumption appended as shown.

Table 2. Formalised Requirement R4, prior to PSA

Monitor Condition	Output Constraint
$air = yes \land out = yes \land ok = yes \land fire? \land sel$	$fire \land sel$
$\neg(air = yes \land out = yes \land ok = yes) \land fire? \land sel$	$\neg fire \land sel$
$\neg(air = yes \land out = yes \land ok = yes) \land \neg fire? \land sel$	$\neg fire \land sel$
R4S: **H1** & **H2** safety targets satisfied and Assumptions A1 to A4 are valid	

4.5 Preliminary Safety Analysis (PSA)

Many techniques can be applied to perform a PSA. The work of this case study uses a combination of mathematical proof, Functional Failure Analysis (FFA) [10] and functional Fault Tree Analysis (FTA) [26].

The goal of a PSA is to: (a) confirm any relevant hazards allocated by the system level hazard analysis; (b) identify if further hazards need to be added to the list; and (c) analyse an architecture to validate that it can satisfy the safety targets associated with the identified relevant hazards. The solution preserving nature of problem transformation under POSE means that any solution of the progressed $P_{Reduced}$ problem will be a solution to the $P_{Initial}$ problem[7]. Simply, if the PSA fails, there is no feasible solution to $P_{Reduced}$.

The structuring provided by the POSE framework and the phased development means that it is relatively straightforward to develop a formal Parnas table-like requirement (as in Table 2) that applies directly to the solution machine.

---

[7] We do not, of course, yet know that either has a solution; it is also worth noting that $P_{Initial}$ may have a solution without $P_{Reduced}$ having one.

Table 3. FFA Summary for *SC*

Id.	Failure Mode	Effect	Hazard
F1	No *fire?* signal	Flare release inhibited	No
F2	*fire?* signal at wrong time	Inadvertent flare release	Yes
F3	*fire?* signal when not required	Inadvertent flare release	Yes
F4	Intermittent *fire?* signal	Could inhibit flare release	No
F5	Continuous *fire?* signal	Inadvertent flare release	Yes

Simple logic proofs demonstrate that **R4** (Table 2) has the required functional properties. The remaining feasibility check at this level is to demonstrate that the behaviour of the design blocks (*SC*, *DM*, and *II* in Fig. 5) can satisfy **R4S**.

The FFA can be used to identify any additional relevant hazards and, more likely, it will identify credible failure modes that result in an existing hazard. The FFA should be applied to each architectural component in turn. Functional FTA can then be used to analyse if the events identified by the FFA satisfy the targets contained in **R4S**. There is insufficient space to present the full PSA, and so we summarise only its main elements to demonstrate the process followed. The significant results from applying FFA to the *DM* are shown in Table 3.

The functional FTA requires a suitable model and the architecture of Fig. 3(b) has an appropriate form. A functional FTA can be applied to this block diagram, using the three FFA problem cases (i.e. those with 'Yes' in the Hazard column) F2, F3 and F5 as top events. The FTA indicates that a failure in *uP* (systematic or probabilistic) could result in the *fire?* failing on. The *Pilot* allow input provides some mitigation, but as soon as this is set (*ok = yes*) a flare will be released, which is undesirable behaviour. Making the *fire?* signal integrity safety related (not safety critical) would provide sufficient integrity, but this is contrary to the design aim of making the *DM* non-safety involved.

The conclusion of the PSA is, then, that the selected *DM* architecture is not a suitable basis for the design—no adequate solution can be derived from its parametrisation. Choices at this point include: a) designing the *DM* to be safety related, or b) re-structuring the *DM* architecture to partition the safety and non-safety elements. The first option is undesirable due to the expense and long term impact, i.e. timing and selection are not safety functions and are expected to be fine-tuned to support different flare types. Making this safety-related would have a detrimental impact on the affordability of the solution. The second option is more appealing, and a second candidate architecture is shown in Fig. 6 in which the simple safety functions (those associated with the *fire?* request) are routed separately through *MB* and *FPGA* (a Field-Programmable Gate Array, [27,28]), while the other complex functionality is routed through *MB* and *uP*. This means that the *MB* and *FPGA*, which have simple functionality, have to be designed to a safety related standard, but this is still economic compared with the alternative of making the *uP* safety related.

The failed PSA leads to iteration of the process. We note, only the information associated with the revised architecture is new, the remainder of the performed transformations can be carried across from the first iteration, simplifying the second (and any subsequent) iteration. The second iteration of the POSE pattern will be similar to the first. Indeed, the revised *DM* of Fig. 6 has the same interfaces as that of Fig. 3(b), hence the requirement resulting from the second set of reductions is the same as that obtained from the first, that shown in Table 2. Although we do not show it, the PSA applied to this revised architecture shows that the modified architecture satisfies **R4S**; the revised architecture model obtained from the second run through of the POSE pattern can form a suitable basis for the remainder of the development.

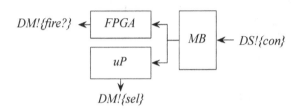

Fig. 6. Revised Candidate Architecture for *DM*

There is still work to do—we do not have *SC* as yet; a fresh application of the process would be possible at this point. This concludes our description of the controller synthesis.

5   Discussion and Conclusions

We have illustrated the synthesis of a controller for a safety-critical system under POSE. We have had, from necessity, to omit many details of the process, but we hope that some of the complexity of the development has remained, in particular, those showing how POSE structures and guides development of the product whilst recording the related justifications and, hence, the adequacy argument for it.

The process by which the synthesis was achieved was captured and re-used from a previous unrelated safety-critical development. The process appears to exhibit Vincenti's three characteristics, namely:

- The safety analysis of Section 4.5 demonstrated that failures in the DM domain could result in the safety targets not being satisfied. This is a form of "winnowing of the conceived variation" in that choices are restricted by the need to satisfy extra constraints, in this the safety analysis.
- A revised (but not new) architecture was developed, by which "engineering judgement was used to search past experience";
- And this was used to mitigate failure; novel features "that come to mind" were incorporated.

We might therefore conclude that the study provides early validation that the pattern may be suitable as the front-end of an integrated safety critical development approach for embedded applications, hence supporting the goal of extending the normal design concept to critical software. Of course, further and more conclusive validation is still required and we are working closely with industrial partners to exercise the framework on further real-world safety critical problems. A wider application of the pattern to other software engineering domains is also under investigation.

The case-study as presented was cut-down to its most important, and complex, aspects to fit within the page limit. Most of the routine detail was omitted, but in its original form it was based directly on an industrial avionics example, and from a conceptual viewpoint the POSE pattern worked well. However, as size and complexity grow the desirability for tool support to handle the detail, the more mundane tasks and keeping track of progress is greatly increased. Tool support for POSE is ready to start development, based on an existing, successful commercial tool for safety-critical analysis and assurance.

Acknowledgements

We are pleased to acknowledge the financial support of IBM, under the Eclipse Innovation Grants. Thanks also go to our colleagues in the Centre for Research in Computing and the Computing Department at The Open University, especially Michael Jackson. The comments of the three anonymous reviewers have helped in improving the paper greatly.

References

1. Vincenti, W.G.: What Engineers Know and How They Know It: Analytical Studies from Aeronautical History. The Johns Hopkins University Press (1990)
2. Maibaum, T.: Mathematical foundations of software engineering: a roadmap. In: ICSE 2000, King's College, London (2000)
3. Jackson, M.: Problem frames and software engineering. Information and Software Technology **47**(14) (2005) 903–912
4. Mannering, D., Hall, J.G., Rapanotti, L.: Relating safety requirements and system design through problem oriented software engineering. Technical Report 2006/11, Open University, Dept. of Computing (2006)
5. Hall, J.G., Rapanotti, L., Jackson, M.A.: Problem oriented software engineering. Technical Report 2006/10, Open University, Dept. of Computing (2006)
6. Jackson, M.A.: Problem Frames: Analyzing and Structuring Software Development Problem. 1st edn. Addison-Wesley Publishing Company (2001)
7. Cox, K., Hall, J.G., Rapanotti, L., eds.: Proceedings of ICSE 1st International Workshop on Applications and Advances of Problem Frames, IEEE CS Press (2004)
8. Cox, K., Hall, J.G., Rapanotti, L., eds.: Journal of Information and Software Technology: Special issue on Problem Frames. Volume 47. Elsevier (November 2005)

9. Hall, J.G., Rapanotti, L., Cox, K., Jin, Z.: Proceedings of the 2nd International Workshop on Advances and Applications of Problem Frames, ACM SIGSOFT (2006)

10. SAE: ARP4761: Guidelines and methods for conducting the safety assessment process on civil airborne systems and equipment. Technical report (December 1996)

11. Zave, P., Jackson, M.: Four dark corners of requirements engineering. ACM Transactions on Software Engineering and Methodology **VI**(1) (1997) 1–30

12. Courtois, P.J., Parnas, D.L.: Documentation for safety critical software. In: 15th International Conference on Software Engineering, Baltimore, USA (1997) 315–323

13. van Lamsweerde, A.: Requirements engineering in the year 00: A research perspective. In: ICSE'00, 22nd International Conference on Software Engineering, Limerick (2000)

14. Bharadwaj, R., Heitmeyer, C.: Developing high assurance avionics systems with the SCR requirements method. In: Proceedings. DASC. The 19th. Volume 1. (2000) pages 1D1/1 –1D1/8

15. Leveson, N.G.: Completeness in formal specification language design for process-control systems. Proceedings of the third workshop on Formal methods in software practice 2000, Portland, Oregon. ACM Press (2000) 2000

16. Leveson, N.G.: Intent specifications: An approach to building human-centered specifications. IEEE Transactions on Software Engineering **Vol. 26**(1) (2000) 15–35

17. de Lemos, R., Saeed, A., Anderson, T.:   On the integration of requirements analysis and safety analysis for safety-critical systems. Technical Report http://citeseer.ist.psu.edu/536230.html, University of Newcastle upon Tyne (1998)

18. UK-MoD: Safety management requirements for defence systems part 1 requirements. Interim Defence Standard 00-56 Issue 3, MoD (17 December 2004)

19. RTCA/DO-178B: Software considerations in airborne systems and equipment certification. Technical report (December 1 1992)

20. Zave, P., Jackson, M.A.: Four dark corners of requirements engineering. ACM Transactions on Software Engineering and Methodology **6**(1) (1997) 1–30

21. Gunter, C.A., Gunter, E.L., Jackson, M., Zave, P.: A reference model for requirements and specifications. IEEE Software **17**(3) (2000) 37–43

22. Coad, P.: Object oriented patterns. Communications of the ACM **35**(9) (1992) 152–160

23. Rapanotti, L., Hall, J.G., Jackson, M.: Problem-oriented software engineering: solving the package router control problem. Technical report 2006/07, Open University, Dept. of Computing (2006)

24. Rapanotti, L., Hall, J.G., Li, Z.: Deriving specifications from requirements through problem reduction. **153**(5) (October 2006) 183–210

25. Mannering, D., Hall, J.G., Rapanotti, L.: A problem-oriented approach to normal design for safety-critical systems. Technical Report 2006/14, Centre for Research in Computing (2006)

26. Vesely, W., Goldberg, F., Roberts, N., Haasl, D.: Fault Tree Handbook. Volume NUREG-0492. U.S. Nuclear Regulatory Commission (1981)

27. Hilton, A.J., Townson, G., Hall, J.G.: FPGAs in critical hardware/software systems. In: FPGA 2003, Proceedings of the ACM/SIGDA International Symposium on Field Programmable Gate Arrays. (2003) 244

28. Hilton, A., Hall, J.G.: Developing critical systems with PLD components. In Margaria, T., Massink, M., eds.: FMICS '05: Proceedings of the 10th international workshop on Formal methods for industrial critical systems, New York, NY, USA, ACM Press (2005) 72–79

A Clustering-Based Approach for Tracing Object-Oriented Design to Requirement

Xin Zhou[1] and Hui Yu[2]

[1] IBM China Research Lab, China
zhouxin@cn.ibm.com
[2] Peking University, China
yuhui04@sei.pku.edu.cn

Abstract. Capturing the traceability relationship between software requirement and design allows developers to check whether the design meets the requirement and to analyze the impact of requirement changes on the design. This paper presents an approach for identifying the classes in object-oriented software design that realizes a given use case, which leverages ideas and technologies from Information Retrieval (IR) and Text Clustering area. First, we represent the use case and all classes as vectors in a vector space constructed with the keywords coming from them. Then, the classes are clustered based on their semantic relevance and the cluster most related to the use case is identified. Finally, we supplement the raw cluster by analyzing structural relationships among classes. We conduct an experiment by using this clustering-based approach to a system – Resource Management Software. We calculate and compare the precision and recall of our approach and non-clustering approaches, and get promising results.

Keywords: Object-oriented software development, Requirement Traceability, Use Case, Class, Clustering.

1   Introduction

Keeping the traceability between software requirements and other artifacts generated by each software development phase is well recognized as significant in multiple areas, including software maintenance, software evolving and software reuse [1][2]. Such traceability can be obtained from two approaches: one is to record the tracing relationships during the development duration by developers. The other one is to identify the un-recorded tracing relationships by analyzing the requirements and the artifacts.

In current object-oriented software development, use case [3] is widely used to model the user requirement, and class model [4] is the dominant means used to describe the static aspect of software design that realizes requirement. If the corresponding relationships between elements in class model and use cases are well understood, the designers can more easily analyze how requirements have been satisfied by their design, can more precisely locate to and modify the design elements impacted by changing requirements, and so forth. Although designers can accurately record and maintain such relationships while designing, they are usually reluctant to do this due to the heavy overload brought to them.

M.B. Dwyer and A. Lopes (Eds.): FASE 2007, LNCS 4422, pp. 412–422, 2007.
© Springer-Verlag Berlin Heidelberg 2007

The paper addresses the problem of object-oriented design to requirement traceability by automatically identifying the potential tracing relationships. As the designers only need to verify the generated potential tracing relationships, they will not feel much troubled. Our approach leverages the ideas and technologies from Information Retrieval (IR)[5][6] and Text Clustering[7][8] area. A premise of our work is that system analyzers and designers use meaningful identifiers and descriptions in use cases and class model so as to describe their semantic exactly. According to the approach, the use case and the classes are represented as vectors in a vector space constructed with the identifiers coming from them. Then, the semantic relevance among class vectors is calculated, and those closely related classes identified are grouped into clusters. The centroid vector of each cluster is generated and its similarity with the use case vector is evaluated so that the cluster most closely related to the use case is identified. Considering some classes might be missed by the clustering process, we finally supplement some classes that have generalization or association relationships to the selected cluster.

The following part of this paper is organized as below: we illustrate our tracing approach in section 2. In section 3, we experiment the approach with a case. Related works is introduced in section 4. Section 5 concludes and forecasts future works.

2   Approach Description

Given one use case UC and a set of classes $\{C_1, C_2, ..., C_n\}$, the approach for identifying the classes that realize UC out of the whole class set includes four major steps. As shown in Figure 1, the first step is to extract keywords from the use case and classes, use these keywords to construct a vector space and represent the use case and each class as vectors in the vector space. This step is a prerequisite for further clustering and matching. The second step is to build class clusters according to their

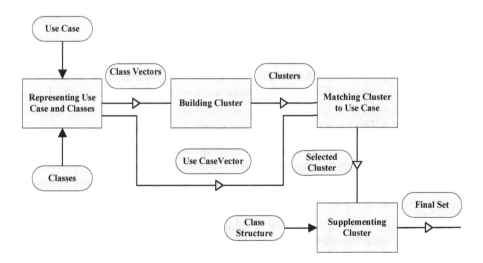

Fig. 1. Approach Overview

semantic relevance since we believe that classes collaboratively realizing the feature described by a use case should have closer semantic relevance. The third step is to generate the centroid vector that summarizes and characterizes a cluster and evaluate its similarity with the use case vector. The cluster with the highest similarity is the post possible one that realizes such use case. As we might have missed some actually relevant classes while constructing the cluster, in the final step we supplement the raw cluster by analyzing generalization and association relationships among all classes. We will introduce each step in detail in the following sub-sections.

2.1 Representing Use Case and Classes

Representing the use case and all classes in vector format is for the convenience of further clustering and matching, which consists of three activities including keyword extraction, vector space building and vector generation.

We take the names and description of the use case, classes, class attributes, and class methods as the source to extract the keywords that implicate the use case's and classes' semantics. The standard practice in information retrieval should be followed while extracting keywords. Namely, only nouns and verbs are extracted and they should be transformed to the original form (i.e. the single form of nouns and the infinitive form of verbs). After the extraction, we can get two keyword sets: one set includes all of the keywords from the use case, and the other set includes all of the keywords from all classes.

An intuitive way for building the vector space is to use the keywords from the union of use case keyword set and class keyword set to build the vector space. The number of dimensions of the resulting vector space will be scores or even hundreds, which causes large computational cost of clustering and matching. Considering that we only care the common part of the use case's semantic and the classes' semantic while conducting the clustering and matching, the keywords from the intersection of use case keyword set and class keyword set are used instead to build the vector space. This way reduces computational cost by decreasing the overall dimensions of the vector space without losing useful information.

With the built vector space, representing the use case and classes as vectors is simple. If the keyword on the x-th dimension of the vector space is one keyword of the use case, then the x-th dimension of the use case's vector is assigned as "1", otherwise is assigned as "0". Similarly, the vector of each class can be generated.

2.2 Building Cluster

We believe that a use case is realized by a group of classes collaboratively and the classes in a group have higher semantic relevance. So in this step, we group classes into clusters according to their semantic relevance, and the resulting clusters will be further processed in next step so that the one closest to the given use case can be identified.

One straightforward approach for building cluster can be: firstly calculating the semantic relevance between any two classes using the cosine of the angle between their vectors, then creating a graph that takes all classes as its nodes and adding one edge between two classes if the relevance value between them is larger than a given threshold value, finally identifying all the complete sub-graphs that cannot be contained by other complete sub-graphs. The classes in each identified complete sub-graph compose a cluster. However, the exponential time complexity of finding maximal complete sub-graph prevents the approach to be practical. With the increasing graph size, the calculating may exhaust all computation resource.

In this paper, we modify the approach above by changing the relevance calculating criterion and cluster creation method, which reduces the computation complexity of clustering. We firstly choose a constant I ($1 \leq$ I $\leq$ N), which is the number of dimensions that we will consider while calculating the class vector relevance. Given a determined constant I, there are totally (C_N^I) possible combinations of dimensions. For each dimension combination {D_{j1}, D_{j2}, ..., D_{jI}} ($1 \leq$ j $\leq C_N^I$), all those classes, whose vector has value '1' on all these I dimensions, are grouped to one cluster. So totally, we can get C_N^I clusters. By merging the same clusters, and removing nested clusters, the candidate class clusters are finally determined for further matching with the given use case.

2.3 Matching Cluster to Use Case

In this step, the cluster that has the closest semantic relevance to the given use case will be found out. We calculate the centroid of a cluster, which summarizes and characterizes all classes in the cluster. So, the semantic relevance between all classes in the cluster and the use case can be gotten by calculating the relevance between the cluster centroid and the use case.

In our approach, we map each class and each use case onto a vector, and each element of the vector corresponds to a key word extracted from the class and use case. We use the simplest method to represent the vector, either 1 if the i-th key word occurs in the class or use case, or 0 otherwise. This representation helps us simplify the process of building cluster. But when we match cluster to use case, we have to consider the frequency of a word in the use case. The frequency of the key word reflects the importance of the word in representing the semantics of the use case.

We use a well known IR metric called *tf-idf* [9]. According to this metric, we derive the vector element of cluster centroid from the term frequency tf_i, and the inverse use case frequency iuf_i (represented as *idf* in IR area). We use tf_i to reflect the importance of the i-th key word within a use case description; it is the ratio of the number of the occurrences of the i-th key word to the total occurrences that all keywords in the vector space appearing in use case description. And iuf_i is a global weight that reflects the overall value of the i-th keyword as an indexing term for the entire collection, and the inverse use case frequency iuf_i is defined as the ratio of total number of use cases to the number of use cases containing the i-th key word. For example, considering a very common word like "class", it is likely to be contained in most use case descriptions. It is not import in our retrieval process; sometimes it even makes our retrieval result inaccurate. So a small value of global weight *iuf* should be appropriate.

Given $\{C_1, C_2...... C_k\}$ are the classes in a cluster, and each C_i is represented by a vector $\{c_{i1}, c_{i2}...... c_{iN}\}$, the centroid $G=\{g_1, g_2......g_N\}$ of the cluster can be calculated following the formula given below:

$$g_i = tf_i * \log(iuf_i) * \frac{1}{n}\sum_{j=1}^{n} c_{ij} \qquad (1)$$

And we use a similar way to represent the query vector Q, the vector element qi in Q is:

$$q_i = tf_i * \log(iuf_i) \qquad (2)$$

The semantic relevance between each cluster and the given use case is computed as the cosine of the angle between the cluster centroid vector G and the query vector Q:

$$Revelance(G,Q) = \frac{\sum_{i=1}^{N} g_i q_i}{\sqrt{\sum_{i=1}^{N}(g_i^2) * \sum_{i=1}^{N}(q_i^2)}} \qquad (3)$$

The classes in the cluster with the highest relevance to the given use case are regarded as the most probable realization of the use case.

2.4 Supplementing Cluster

Although we have generated the closest cluster, some actual relevant classes still might be missed from the cluster. This is caused by several reasons. The first one is that semantic information may be lost while keywords are extracted from natural language sentences. The second reason is that description of some use cases or classes may be not complete or accurate enough as expected. The third reason is that our cluster building requires all classes in a cluster to be relevant to each other, which is a strong precondition. Actually, there are some "common" classes in design, such as the ones realizing database accessing, human-computer interaction, and so forth. Although they actually contribute to the realization of some use cases, they might be excluded from the cluster since its semantic relevance to the classes in the identified cluster is very low. In a word, we might lose some potential relevant classes if no extra supplement is conducted.

In order to make our approach generate more accurate result, we use relationships in class diagram to supplement the raw cluster built. These relationships can help us find classes missed due to the insufficiency of the semantic search algorithm, the strong precondition of clustering approach, or lack of information in the use case description. Three rules are followed while supplementing the raw cluster, as stated below:

● If class A is in the raw cluster and class B is the super class of A, then B should be added to the cluster.

- If class A is in the raw cluster and class B is a subordinate class of A, then B should be added to the cluster.
- If class A is in the raw cluster and A has a unidirectional association to class B, then B should be added to the cluster.

The major reason for supplementing cluster at the final step instead of performing it before matching cluster to use case is that supplemented classes, especially the common classes, might dilute the semantic correlation of the original cluster and then cause imprecise cluster matching.

3 A Case Study

We use the approach introduced above to trace the design to requirement of Resource Management Software developed by Electrical Engineering and Computer Science Department of Milwaukee School of Engineering. This software schedules and visualizes the availability of specific resources, like consultants, office spaces, and equipment. The detailed description for each use case and the design is provided by [10], which is the basis for our traceability analysis. Requirement of the software is represented by 26 use cases, and the design consists of 45 classes located in five major packages: View, Controller, Entity, Database and Util. In the case study, we only deal with 11 use cases and 22 classes that closely relate to the business logic.

We respectively follow our clustering-based approach and other existing approach to identify the relative classes for each use case. Then, we carefully understand the software's pertinent documents and manually identify the relative classes for each use case, which is used as the correct answer for comparing the results got by those approaches. Two metrics, Precision and Recall, are used to quantitatively denote an approach's completeness and correctness. For each use case, precision is the ratio of actual relevant classes retrieved a certain approach over all the relevant classes regarded by this approach, and recall is calculated as the ratio of actual relevant classes identified by a certain approach over the total actual relevant classes.

3.1 Experiment Clustering-Based Approach

We experiment our clustering-based approach by assigning the constant I mentioned in sub-section 2.2 as 1 and 2 respectively. Table 1 illustrates the experiment result. The first column lists all the use cases to be traced, the second and third columns list the result of the approach with the constant I assigned as 1, and the fourth and fifth columns list the result of the approach with the constant I assigned as 2. We can find that if the constant I is assigned a higher value, the precision will increase while the recall will decrease. That means we can balance the precision and recall by tuning the value of the constant I. Usually, we prefer a higher recall value to higher precision value, since we believe the time spent on discarding a non-relevant class will be lower than time required for recovering a missed class.

Table 1. Precision and recall of the clustering-based approach

Use Case	Clustering Method (I = 1)		Clustering Method (I = 2)	
	Precision	*Recall*	*Precision*	*Recall*
Add Client	66.67%	100.00%	80.00%	66.67%
Modify Client	60.00%	100.00%	80.00%	66.67%
Delete Client	85.71%	100.00%	80.00%	66.67%
Add Resource	75.00%	100.00%	100.00%	66.67%
Modify Resource	83.33%	100.00%	100.00%	10.00%
Delete Resource	83.33%	100.00%	100.00%	60.00%
Add Project	63.64%	100.00%	80.00%	57.14%
Modify Project	81.82%	100.00%	87.50%	77.78%
Delete Project	70.00%	100.00%	100.00%	87.50%
Add Resource Allocation	72.72%	72.72%	72.72%	72.72%
Delete Resource Allocation	72.72%	100.00%	72.72%	100.00%

3.2 Comparing Clustering-Based Approach with Non-clustering Approach

IR technologies, especially the probabilistic model [11] and the Vector Space Model (VSM) [12], are widely used in tracing code to requirement documents [13][14]. The basic idea for the VSM-based approaches is: code elements and requirement are represented by corresponding vectors, and the requirement vector is used as a query condition to search relevant code element vectors. The code elements, whose semantic similarity with the query larger than a given threshold, are regarded as the implementation of the requirement. We experiment to use such kind of non-clustering approach to identify relevant classes for use cases in Resource Management Software. The first time, we select a loose threshold so that higher recall can be obtained. The second time, we select a more strict threshold so that higher precision can be obtained. The result is illustrated in Table 2.

As illustrated in Figure 2, we compare the results of clustering-based approach and non-clustering approach. It shows that: if a strict threshold is used, the non-clustering approach's precision values are as good as those of the clustering-based approach, but its recall values are much worse, and if a loose threshold is used, the non-clustering approach's recall values are almost as good as those of the clustering-based approach, but its precision values are much worse. Thus, we can conclude that in this experiment our clustering-based approach wins over the non-clustering approach.

Table 2. Precision and recall of the non-clustering approach

Use Case	Non-Clustering Method (Loose Threshold)		Non-Clustering Method (Strict Threshold)	
	Precision	Recall	Precision	Recall
Add Client	46.15%	100.00%	75.00%	50.00%
Modify Client	46.15%	100.00%	42.86%	50.00%
Delete Client	40.00%	100.00%	50.00%	50.00%
Add Resource	52.94%	100.00%	61.54%	88.89%
Modify Resource	62.50%	50.00%	100.00%	40.00%
Delete Resource	50.00%	100.00%	50.00%	50.00%
Add Project	50.00%	100.00%	80.00%	57.14%
Modify Project	52.94%	100.00%	75.00%	66.67%
Delete Project	50.00%	100.00%	70.00%	100.00%
Add Resource Allocation	68.75%	100.00%	72.72%	72.72%
Delete Resource Allocation	50.00%	100.00%	80.00%	100.00%

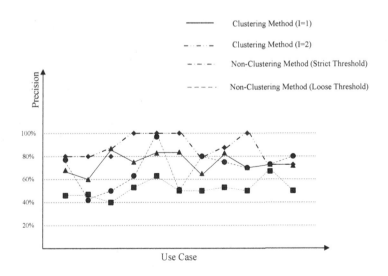

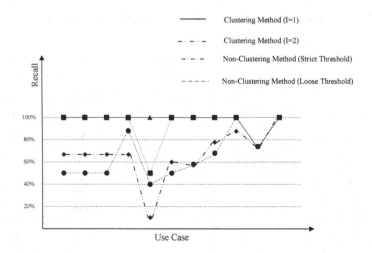

Fig. 2. Comparing clustering-based approach and non-clustering approach

4 Related Work

4.1 IR-Based Traceability Identification

Current literature provides partial solutions to the problem of traceability in various fields of computer science. The proposed solutions are related to areas of Information Retrieval[10][11], Database Management[15], Rule-based System[16][17], Concept-based approach[18], etc.

Some most popular solutions are related to the area of Information Retrieval. Papers [13][14] presented by Antoniol G. introduced a semi-automated process to recover traceability between code and documentation. Their process starts with processing the artifacts, then using a classifier to generate a ranked document list. Their solution uses two IR methods as classifiers. The probabilistic method and the vector space method are used to recover traceability links between code and documentation. Their solution also assumes that the artifacts follow the OO paradigm and the use of common vocabulary between code and documentation.

It's important to note that when we use the approach mentioned above to trace from requirement to classes, it doesn't have high precision and recall. In our approach, presented in section 2, we use a clustering-based approach to get the traceability from requirement to classes. Our work uses the potential semantic relationship between classes to get clusters, which allows our approach to lead to a more accurate result. Moreover, in order to avoid the incompleteness and imprecision of nature language which is used to describe use case, we use a supplementing process after cluster retrieving process based on the IR technology. Thus, our approach has higher precision and recall when tracing from use case to classes.

4.2 Clustering-Based IR Technology

One of the common Information Retrieval (*IR*) technologies is clustering-based approach. In practice of information retrieval, it is not possible to match each analyzed document with each analyzed search request because the time consumed by such operation would be excessive. Various solutions have been proposed to reduce the number of needed comparisons between information items and requests, among which, clustering technique is an effective way to do this, and therefore it is imported to the area of information retrieval.

There is a basic hypothesis in Clustering-based Information Retrieval: closely associated documents tend to be relevant to the same requests. This inspires us to introduce clustering technique into our research. We do clustering by analyzing the inherent semantic relevance between classes. The experiment reveals that such a mechanism brings a higher recall for the traceability process.

5 Conclusions and Future Works

In this paper, we have presented an approach for identifying the group of classes in object-oriented software design that realizes a given requirement represented in a use case. We use the Information Retrieval (*IR*) and text clustering technologies as the basis of our approach to retrieve relevant classes of a given use case. Our premise is that system analysts and designers use common meaningful keywords for use cases, classes, attributes, methods, parameters, etc. We represent the use case and the classes as vectors in a vector space constructed with the keywords coming from them. Then, we cluster the classes based on their semantic relevance and find out the cluster most related to the use case. Finally, we supplement the raw cluster by analyzing generalization, association relationships among all classes. An experimental study is also reported in this paper. This clustering-based approach is used to create traceability between the classes and use case from a system – Resource Management Software. We calculate and compare the precision and recall of our approach and other non-clustering approaches, which reveals that our approach works well on most occasions.

At present, we still cannot claim that we will get similar results on all other systems although it might be quite imaginable. In the future, we will focus on enhancing the supplement process in order to get a more precise result. For instance, we will consider the weight of each inter-class relationship while supplementing a class to a cluster. Also, we will experiments more on other real systems to evaluate and enhance the approach.

References

1. M. Jarke. "Requirements Tracing". Communications of the ACM, Vol. 41, No. 12, pp. 32-36, December 1998.
2. Pohl, K. PRO-ART: Enabling Requirements Pre- Traceability, In Proceedings of the Second International Conference on Requirements Engineering, IEEE Computer Society Press, 1996 pp. 76-84.

3. I. Jacobson. Object-Oriented Software Engineering. Addison-Wesley Publishing Company, 1992.
4. R. Brooks. Towards a theory of the comprehension of computer programs. International Journal of an-Machine Studies, 18:543–554, 1983.
5. C.J.van Rijsbergen. Information Retrieval. Butterworths, 1979.
6. Frakes, W. and Baeza-Yates, R. Information Retrieval: Data Structures & Algorithms. Prentice Hall, 1992.
7. Bhatia, S.K., and Deogun, J.S. 1998. "Conceptual clustering in information retrieval", IEEE Transactions on Systems, Man and Cybernetics, Part B, 427-436.
8. Kaski, S. 1998. "Dimensionality reduction by random mapping: fast similarity computation for clustering", Proceedings of the 1998 IEEE International Joint Conference on Neural Networks Proceedings, 413-418.
9. G.Salton, C.Buckley. Term-weighting approaches in automatic text retrieval. Information Processing and Management, 24(5):513–523, 1988.
10. http://people.msoe.edu/~barnicks/courses/cs400/199900/teamrpts.htm
11. KS Jones, S Walkerr, SE Robertson. A probabilistic model of information retrieval: development and status. Information Processing and Management, 2000
12. D.Harman. Ranking algorithms. In Information Retrieval: Data Structures and Algorithms, pages 363-392. Prentice-Hall, Englewood Cliffs, NJ, 1992.
13. G. Antoniol, B. Caprile, A. Potrich, and P. Tonella, "Design-Code Traceability for Object Oriented Systems," The Annals of Software Eng., vol. 9, pp. 35-58, 2000.
14. G. Antoniol, G. Canfora, G. Casazza, A. DeLucia, and E. Merlo, "Recovering Traceability Links between Code and Documentation," IEEE Transactions on Software Engineering, vol. 28, no. 10, pp. 970-983, Oct.2002.
15. P.K. Garg, W. Scacchi. SODOS: a software documentation support environment-its definition. IEEE Transactions on Software Engineering, August 1986
16. A. Zisman, G. Spanoudakis, E. Perez-Minana, P. Krause. Tracing software requirement artifacts. The 2003 International Conference on Software Engineering Research and Practice, Las Vegas, Nevada, USA. 2003.
17. C. Nentwich, W. Emmerich, A. Finkelstein, E. Ellmer, Flexible Consistency Checking. ACM Transactions in Software Engineering and Methodology, 12(1), 28-63, 2003.
18. M. Jarke, R. Gallersdoerfer, M. Jeusfeld, M. Staudt, and S. Eherer, TMConceptBase–A Deductive Object Base for Meta Data Management,° Int'l J. Intelligent Information Systems, vol. 5, no. 3, pp. 167-192, 1995.

Measuring and Characterizing Crosscutting in Aspect-Based Programs: Basic Metrics and Case Studies

Roberto E. Lopez-Herrejon[1] and Sven Apel[2]

[1] Computing Laboratory, University of Oxford, England
[2] School of Computer Science, University of Magdeburg, Germany
`rlopez@comlab.ox.ac.uk, apel@iti.cs.uni-magdeburg.de`

Abstract. Aspects are defined as well-modularized crosscutting concerns. Despite being a core tenet of Aspect Oriented Programming, little research has been done in characterizing and measuring crosscutting concerns. Some of the issues that have not been fully explored are: What kinds of crosscutting concerns exist? What language constructs do they use? And what is the impact of crosscutting in actual Aspect Oriented programs? In this paper we present basic code metrics that categorize crosscutting according to the number of classes crosscut and the language constructs used. We applied the metrics to four non-trivial open source programs implemented in AspectJ. We found that for these systems, the number of classes crosscut by advice per crosscutting is small in relation to the number of classes in the program. We argue why we believe this result is not atypical for Aspect Oriented programs and draw a relation to other non-AOP techniques that provide crosscutting.

1 Introduction

Aspects are defined as well-modularized crosscutting concerns, that is, concerns whose implementation would usually involve (crosscut) multiple traditional modular units such as classes. Despite the increasing interest and research in *Aspect Oriented Programming (AOP)*, very little attention has been paid to measuring and characterizing crosscutting in actual programs [8].

In this paper we present a set of basic code metrics that categorize crosscutting according to the number of classes crosscut and their language constructs. To facilitate the description, we present them semi-formally using a functional programming style. Our metrics rate a crosscutting within a spectrum that goes from *homogeneous* to *heterogeneous*, depending on the number of classes crosscut by pieces of advice in relation to the number of classes crosscut by all crosscutting mechanisms of AspectJ. This distinction helps drawing a relation with other technologies that also provide support for crosscutting [7].

By analysing actual programs and categorizing their crosscutting, our metrics shed light on the impact of aspects on the overall program structure. We applied our metrics to four non-trivial AspectJ programs. We found that for these programs, the number of classes crosscut by advice per crosscutting is small in relation to the

M.B. Dwyer and A. Lopes (Eds.): FASE 2007, LNCS 4422, pp. 423–437, 2007.

number of classes in the program. We argue why we believe this result is not atypical for Aspect Oriented programs and draw a relation to other non-AOP techniques that provide crosscutting.

2 Aspect Oriented Programming

Aspect Oriented Programming (AOP) is a novel software development paradigm that aims at modularizing *aspects*, which are defined as well-modularized crosscutting concerns [10][25]. This type of concerns cuts across traditional module boundaries such as classes and interfaces, and their implementation is scattered and tangled with the implementation of other concerns. *AspectJ* is the flagship language of AOP [10]. This is the implementation language of the case studies we evaluated, thus we use AspectJ to illustrate and define our metrics. This section explains the basic constructs of the language. In AspectJ, an application consists of two parts: *base code* which corresponds to standard Java classes and interfaces, and *aspect code* which contains the crosscutting code. Next we describe the two types of crosscuts that AspectJ provides.

2.1 Static Crosscuts

Static crosscuts affect the static structure of a program [26]. We consider *Inter-Type Declarations (ITDs)*, also known as *introductions*, that add fields, methods, and constructors to existing classes and interfaces[1]. Let us consider the example in Figure 1a. It contains an aspect A and three classes X, Y, and Z. The symbols s_i stand for any statement. Aspect A has four ITDs that introduce: 1) field q in class X, 2) method n in class Y, 3) constructor for class Z, and 4) method foo to class X.

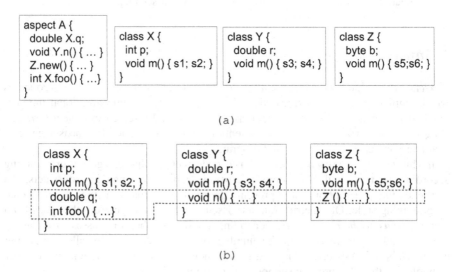

(a)

(b)

Fig. 1. Static Crosscut Example

---

[1] AspectJ provides further kinds of static crosscuts which we do not consider for our basic metrics.

The process of applying the crosscutting code to the base code is known as *weaving*. This is performed with an AspectJ compiler such as `ajc` with a command as follows:

```
ajc A.java X.java Y.java Z.java
```

The result of weaving is shown in Figure 1b. Class X is augmented with field q and method foo, class Y has a new method n and class Z has a new constructor. Thus, aspect A crosscuts all 3 classes in this example as depicted with a dashed line in Figure 1b[2].

2.2 Dynamic Crosscuts

Dynamic crosscuts run additional code when certain events occur during program execution. The semantics of dynamic crosscuts are commonly described and defined in terms of an event-based model [27][38]. As a program executes, different events fire. These events are called *join points*. Examples of join points are: variable reference, variable assignment, execution of a method body, method call, etc. A *pointcut* is a predicate that selects a set of join points. *Advice* is code executed `before`, `after`, or `around` each join point matched by a pointcut.

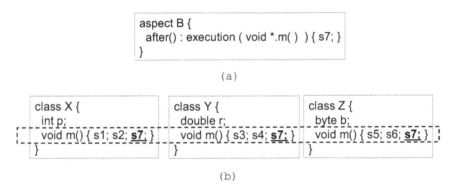

Fig. 2. Dynamic Crosscut Example

Let us consider the example in Figure 2a. Aspect B contains a single piece of advice. This advice captures the `execution` of methods m, with no arguments and that return `void`, of any type (denoted with *). It executes an additional statement, labelled s7, `after` the execution of the bodies of method m. The result of weaving aspect B with classes X, Y, and Z of Figure 1a is shown in Figure 2b, where the additional statement s7 is added at the end of the method m of the 3 classes. Thus in this example the advice in aspect B crosscut the 3 classes as depicted with a dashed line in Figure 2b (underlined and bold).

---

[2] AspectJ generally uses more sophisticated rewrites than those shown in this paper. The composed code snippets we present simplify illustration and are behaviourally equivalent to those produced by `ajc`.

3 Basic Crosscutting Metrics

In this section we provide a semi-formal description of our crosscutting metrics. A goal is to distinguish the contribution to crosscutting stemming from static and dynamic crosscuts. This on one hand sheds light on how the different language constructs are used and on the other it helps to relate aspects with other technologies that can modularize crosscutting concerns.

We describe our using a functional programming style (similar to Haskell [14]) over a simplified abstract program structure. This notation provides a more concise description than natural language and can serve as a guideline for the implementation of tools that automatically gather these and related metrics. We start by describing the abstract structure of our programs, followed by the description of auxiliary functions used to define our metrics.

3.1 Abstract Program Structure

Aspects do not work in isolation. Their functionality is typically implemented in conjunction with a set of classes and interfaces [18][29]. Thus we modularize programs and present our metrics in terms of *features* [39], sets of aspects, classes, and interfaces. Defining our metrics in terms of features permits their application to product line (families of related programs [17]) case studies, an area of increasing interest for the AOP research community [7].

We define a program P to be a set of features F_i, denoted with the following list:

P=[F_1, F_2, . . . , F_n]

Where P is of type `program` and F_i is of type `feature`. Figure 3 summarizes the abstract representation of our programs in the form of a grammar.

A feature F consists of a list of feature elements that can be classes, interfaces or aspects. A `class` is a list of `class_element` which can be of type `method`, `constructor`, `field`, etc. An `interface` is a list of `interface_element` which can be of type `field` or method declaration (`methoddecl`). An `aspect` is a list of method (`methodITD`), constructor (`constructorITD`), and field (`fieldITD`) inter-type declarations, and pieces of advice (`advice`). These ITDs are denoted as tuples of class and the corresponding element definition. For example, the tuple for `methodITD` is of type (`class, method`). For pieces of `advice` we focus only on the pointcut expression `pce` and a `body`. We consider both named and anonymous pointcuts but we focus only on the pointcut expression formed with poincut designators and their combinations denoted with operators `&&`, `||`, `()`, and `!`.

Finally we define an auxiliary type `shadow` with a tuple whose elements are a `program_element` (elements of classes, interfaces and aspects), a `class`, and a pointcut expression `pce`. A *shadow* is a place on the source code whose execution creates join points [32]. We represent a shadow with a tuple of three elements. The first element of `shadow` contains the program element that has the shadow (a `method` for example for a `execution` join point), the `class` that contains the program element, and pointcut expression pce that casts the shadow in that program element. This data structure is not created when programs are originally parsed, instead it is the result of a weaving mechanism.

In this paper we use only the subset of program structures of AspectJ shown in Figure 3. However this abstract program representation can be extended, the same is true for the set of auxiliary functions and metrics we describe in next subsections.

```
program :: [feature]

feature :: [feature_element]
feature_element :: class | interface | aspect

class :: [class_element]
class_element :: method | constructor | ...

interface :: [interface_element]
interface_element :: methoddecl | field

aspect :: [aspect_element]
aspect_element :: methodITD | constructorITD | fieldITD | advice

methodITD :: (class, method)
constructorITD :: (class, constructor)
fieldITD :: (class, field)

advice :: (pce,body)
pce :: pointcut_expression
shadow :: (program_element, class, pce)
program_element :: class_element | interface_element | aspect_element
```

Fig. 3. Abstract Program Representation

3.2 Auxiliary Functions

The following functions provide the basic building blocks of the definitions of our metrics. Note that the names of some of these functions are the plural of the type of element they return as result.

count. This function returns the number of elements in a list. It has signature (where a is any type and n is a number):

```
count :: [a] -> n
```

loc. This function returns the number of lines of code (LOC). It has signature (where a is any type and n is a number):

```
loc :: [a] -> n
```

union. N-ary and polymorphic disjoint set union. It receives any number of arguments, unions them and eliminates any repeated elements. We denote its signature with n entries of type b that when unioned return a list of b elements:

```
union :: [b₁] -> ...-> [bₙ] -> [b]
```

sum. Receives as input a list of numbers and performs the summation on them. It has the following signature where n is a number:

```
sum :: [n] -> n
```

foreach. Receives as input a list and a function. which applies to all the elements in the list. It has signature (where a and b are any type):

```
foreach :: [a] -> a -> b -> [b]
```

classes. Receives a feature and returns the list of classes in that feature. It has signature:

```
classes :: feature -> [class]
```

interfaces. Receives a feature and returns the list of interfaces in that feature. It has signature:

```
interfaces :: feature -> [interface]
```

aspects. Receives a feature and returns the list of aspects in that feature. It has signature:

```
aspects :: feature -> [aspect]
```

advices. Receives as input a list of aspects and returns the list of pieces of advice contained in the aspects.

```
advices :: [aspect] -> [advice]
```

methodITDs. Receives as input a list of aspects and returns the list of method ITDs or introductions contained in the aspects.

```
methodITDs :: [aspect] -> [methodITD]
```

constructorITDs. Receives as input a list of aspects and returns the list of constructor ITDs or introductions contained in the aspects.

```
constructorITDs::[aspect] -> [constructorITD]
```

ccclasses. This function computes the crosscutting classes from a list of method ITDs, constructor ITDs or field ITDs, and removes any repeated elements. It has signature (where symbol | stands for logical or):

```
ccclasses :: [ methodITD | constructorITD | fieldITD ] -> [class]
```

pointcuts. Receives as input a list of aspects and returns a list of pointcut designators (pce).

```
pointcuts :: [aspect] ->[pce]
```

shadows. This function receives as input a list of pointcuts, finds the join point shadows in a program and returns them in a list:

```
shadows :: [pce] -> [shadow]
```

sclasses. This function receives a list of shadows, extracts their classes (second elements in the shadow tuples), and removes any duplicates.

```
sclasses :: [shadow] -> [class]
```

3.3 Program Structure Metrics

The metrics in this section highlight the contribution of aspects to the overall structure of programs measured in lines of code.

Let P be a program. We define the following metrics:

NOF. *Number Of Features.* Counts the number of features in a program.

```
NOF (P) = count (P)
```

NOA. *Number Of Aspects.* Counts the number of aspects in a program.

```
NOA (P) = sum(foreach (P, λf.(count (aspects (f)))))
```

The way to understand this definition is as follows. For each feature f in program P extract its aspects and count them. Sum up all the counts of the aspects in all the features.

NCI. *Number of Classes and Interfaces.* Counts the number of classes and interfaces in a program.

```
NCI (P) = sum(foreach (P, λf.(count (union (classes (f)) (interfaces(f))))))
```

BCF. *Base Code Fraction.* Corresponds to the number of lines of code that come from standard Java classes and interfaces relative to the lines of code in a program.

```
BCF(P)= sum(foreach (P, λf.(sum (loc (classes (f)))
                                (loc (interfaces (f))))))
        / loc(P)
```

ACF. *Aspects Code Fraction.* Corresponds to the number of lines of code that come from aspects relative to the lines of code in a program.

```
BCF (P) = sum(foreach (P, λf.(loc (aspects (f))))) / loc(P)
```

IF. *Introductions Fraction.* Corresponds to the number of lines of code that come from introductions or inter-type declarations relative to the lines of code in a program.

```
IF (P) = sum (foreach (P, λf.(sum (loc (fieldITDs (aspects (f))))
                                  (loc (methodITDs(aspects (f))))
                                  (loc (constructorITDs (aspects (f)))))))
         / loc(P)
```

AF. *Advice Fraction.* Corresponds to the number of lines of code that come from pieces of advice relative to the lines of code in a program.

```
AF (P) = sum (foreach (P, λf.(loc (advices (aspects (f)))))) / loc(P)
```

3.4 Feature Crosscutting Metrics

In AOP literature, an *homogenous concern* is one that applies a same piece of advice to several places; whereas an *heterogeneous concern* applies different pieces of advice to different places [7][18]. The metrics in this section adapt these concepts to features and provide a quantitative criteria to classify features within a spectrum that goes from *homogeneous* to *heterogeneous* according to the number and type of crosscuts they implement.

Let f be a feature of a program P, we define the following metrics:

FCD. *Feature Crosscutting Degree.* Corresponds to the number of classes that are crosscut by all pieces of advice in a feature and those crosscut by the ITDs.

```
FCD(f,P)= count(union(ccclasses(methodITDs(aspects (f))),
                      ccclasses(constructorITDs(aspects (f))),
                      ccclasses(fieldITDs(aspects(f))),
                      sclasses(shadows(pointcuts(advices(aspects(f)))),P))))
```

ACD. *Advice Crosscutting Degree.* Corresponds to the number of classes that are crosscut exclusively by the pieces of advice in a feature.

```
ACD(f,P)= count(sclasses(shadows(pointcuts(advices(aspects(f))),P)))
```

HQ. We define *Homogeneity Quotient* as the division of the advice crosscutting degree (ACD) by the feature crosscutting degree (FCD):

```
HQ(f,P) = ACD(f,P)/FCD(f,P) if FCD(f,P)!=0
        = 0                 otherwise
```

PHQ. *Program Homogeneity Quotient.* It corresponds to the summation of the homogeneity quotients for all the features in a program, divided by the number of features NOF.

```
PHQ(P) = sum(foreach(P, λg.HQ(g,P)))/NOF(P)
```

3.5 Homogeneous vs. Heterogeneous Features

We can categorize features according to their Homogeneity Quotient (HQ) within a continuum that has at its ends:

- *Fully Homogenous Feature*: Its pieces of advice crosscut all the classes crosscut by the feature. That is ACD=FCD and thus HQ=1.
- *Fully Heterogeneous Feature*: It is either base code (no crosscutting) or all the crosscutting it does is via ITDs. That is HQ=0.

If the Program Homogeneity Quotient or PHQ tends to value 1 the program is exploiting the crosscutting capabilities of advice. Also, if PHQ tends to value 0, it can have two interpretations: 1) majority class crosscuts are due to inter-type declarations, 2) majority of features have no crosscuts at all. Next section we apply our metrics to four case studies.

4 Case Studies

We applied our set of metrics to four different AspectJ product line systems developed by us and other researchers. They are:

- **ATS.** *AHEAD Tool Suite* is a set of stand alone and language-extensible tools [3] which implement *Feature Oriented Programming (FOP)*, a technology that studies feature modularity in program synthesis for product lines [13]. We performed our study in the AspectJ implementation of five core tools of ATS [30]. Its code is available upon request.
- **FACET.** *Framework for Aspect Composition for an EvenT* channel is an AspectJ implementation of a CORBA event channel, developed at the Washington University [24][3]. The goal of the FACET project is to investigate the development of customizable middleware using AOP. Features in FACET are for example different event types, synchronization, the CORBA core, or tracing.

---

[3] Source code available at http://www.cs.wustl.edu/~doc/RandD/PCES/facet/

	AHEAD	FACET	Prevayler	AJHotDraw
Program Total Lines Of Code	56727	6364	3964	22104
NOF - Number Of Features	48	34	19	13
NOA - Number Of Aspects	503	113	55	10
NCI - Number of Classes & Interfaces	524	181	107	351
BCF - Base Code Fraction	0.68	0.81	0.69	0.99
ACF - Aspect Code Fraction	0.32	0.19	0.31	0.01
IF - Introductions Fraction	0.19	0.05	0.08	0.01
AF - Advice Fraction	0.01	0.06	0.13	0.00
Other Aspect Code	0.12	0.08	0.10	0.00

Fig. 4. Program Structure Metrics Summary

- **Prevayler.** Prevayler is a Java application that implements transparent persistence for Java objects. In other words, it is a fully-functional main memory database system in which a business object may be persisted. Prevayler was refactored at the Universtiy of Toronto using AspectJ and horizontal decomposition [21][4]. Features are for example persistence, transaction, query, and replication management.
- **AJHotDraw.** AJHotDraw is an aspect-oriented refactoring of the JHotDraw two-dimensional graphics framework. It is an open source software project that provides numerous features for drawing and manipulating graphical and planar objects [1].

4.1 Program Structure Metrics

We applied the first set of metrics to our four case studies. We obtained the following results, summarized in Figure 4:

- **ATS.** The core tools are formed with 48 features for a total 56727 LOC. To the best of our knowledge, we are not aware of any product line in AspectJ of scale comparable to this case study. Base code constitutes 68% of the program code implemented in 524 standard Java classes and interfaces. Aspect corresponds to 32% implemented in 503 aspects. Of this percentage, 19% comes from ITDs, while approximately 1% was contributed by from pieces of advice. The remaining 12% correspond to other constructs such as package imports.
- **FACET.** It consists of 34 features implemented in 6364 LOC. Base code is 81% of total LOC using 181 classes and interfaces. Aspect code is 19% of which 5% are ITDs, 6% are pieces advice, and the remaining 8% comes from other aspect constructs such as aspect methods.
- **Prevayler.** The code base of Prevayler is 3964 LOC modularized into 19 features. Base code is 69% of features LOC and its implemented in 107 classes

---

[4] Source code available at http://www.msrg.utoronto.ca/code/RefactoredPrevaylerSystem/

and interfaces. The other 31% of total LOC is aspect code, of which 8% comes from ITDs, 13% from pieces of advice, and the remaining 10% from other aspect constructs.

- **AJHotDraw.** It consists of 13 features for a total of 22104 LOC. It is implemented with 351 classes and interfaces and only 10 aspects. Not surprisingly 99% percent of the code is standard Java and only 1% of aspect code, of which almost all comes from ITDs.

4.2 Feature Crosscutting Metrics

ATS. Figure 5 shows the histogram of the homogeneity quotient of the 48 features of ATS. As expected, given the program structure metrics of ATS, most features have no crosscutting, homogeneity quotient of 0. The program homogeneity quotient (PHQ) is 0.03 which indicates a very small use of pieces of advice.

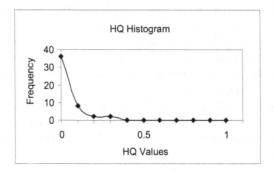

Fig. 5. ATS Homogeneity Quotient Histogram

FACET. Figure 6 shows the homogeneity quotient histogram of the 34 features of FACET. This histogram, as opposed to the one for ATS, has a more balanced distribution, with a program homogeneity quotient whose value is 0.5098.

However, this number has to be put in context. Out of the 34 features of FACET, 22 use pieces of advice. Almost all features that use advice crosscut between 1 and 4 classes, on average 1.3 classes. The exception is a tracing feature that crosscuts all the 181 classes of FACET. Thus, even though around a half of the features are homogeneous the actual impact of advice is limited in terms of the number of classes they crosscut, and the percentage of code they constitute.

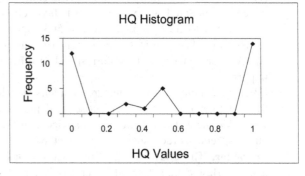

Fig. 6. FACET Homogeneity Quotient Histogram

Prevayler. Figure 7 shows the homogeneity quotient histogram of the 19 features of Prevayler. This histogram shows that most of Prevayler's features are homogeneous with a program homogeneity quotient of 0.7805. Again this result is put in context. On average, each feature crosscuts 3.5 classes, a small percentage of the 107 classes that form Prevayler.

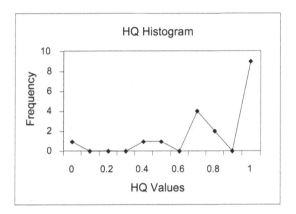

Fig. 7. Prevayler Homogeneity Quotient Histogram

AJHotDraw. Figure 8 shows the homogeneity quotient histogram of the 13 features of AJHotDraw. Given that most of its code is standard Java, its program homogeneity quotient is close to zero 0.0854. Only three of the thirteen features implement crosscuttings: one fully homogenous (uses advice and crosscuts 12 classes), one fully heterogeneous, and one where most crosscutting comes from ITDs (uses advice and crosscuts one class, HQ is 0.1111).

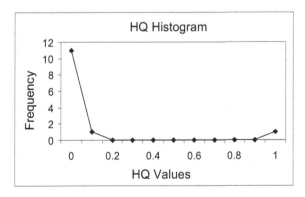

Fig. 8. AJHotDraw Homogeneity Quotient Histogram

5 Collaborations and Heterogeneous Features

Aspects are not the only technique that provides support for crosscutting. There are several techniques categorized as *collaboration-based designs* that also have crosscutting capabilities. This line of research is at least a decade old [23][34][36][37]. A *collaboration* is a set of objects (hence the crosscutting) and a protocol that determines how the objects interact. The part of an object that enforces the protocol in a collaboration is called a *role* [35][37]. One of their goals is to provide a more flexible modularity unit to improve reuse in multiple configurations or compositions for the development of different programs. Thus, collaborations are mechanisms to implement features for product lines [12].

Collaborations can be implemented using several Object Oriented techniques. The kinds of program increments these techniques support are ultimately bound by the Object Oriented ideas they rely upon (i.e. inheritance, polymorphism, encapsulation, etc.). A technique that implements collaborations is FOP and its implementation in AHEAD [13]. For example, using FOP the crosscutting implemented in aspect A of Figure 1a is implemented as follows:

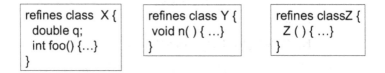

Fig. 9. Crosscutting Example in FOP

The kinds of crosscutting that AHEAD and other collaboration-based designs techniques support correspond to AspectJ's static crosscutting inter-type declarations that we considered. In other words, the distinctive characteristic of aspects is its support for dynamic crosscuts implemented with pieces of advice.

We have seen that in the four case studies we analysed, the pieces of advice crosscut a relatively small number of classes in comparison with the number of classes in the entire programs. Furthermore, the percentage of lines of code is also small, ranging from 1% to 13% in our examples, on average 6%. These numbers beg the questions: Are these results typical? What is the real impact of aspects in software development if their distinctive trait is advice?

We claim that these results are not atypical. Our experiences and other's working with product lines and aspect programs lead us to conjecture that most of the features or crosscuttings in programs are of heterogeneous nature, and that pieces of advice crosscut few classes relative to the number of classes that build a system [8][30][18]. Intuitively, the reason behind this conjecture is that large programs are not synthesized by adding the same piece of code in different places, but rather, adding different pieces of code in different places [6].

Our response to the second question is that aspects can be extremely useful for modularizing crosscutting that involves many classes such as logging, however these types of crosscutting are not pervasive in all software systems and constitute a small fraction of the overall code.

6 Related Work

Several metrics have been proposed for aspects. Zhao and Xu describe metrics for aspect cohesion based on aspect dependencies graphs [41]. Zhao also utilizes a similar framework to define measurements for aspect coupling [40]. Their metrics are formally described, however they lack concrete architectural interpretation and, to the best of our knowledge, have not been applied to actual case studies.

Coupling metrics have been proposed by Ceccato and Tonella [15]. They extend and adapt to AOP some of Chidamber and Kemerer's metrics for Object Oriented systems [16]. This set of metrics is defined informally and it is applied to a tiny case study (250+ LOC), Hannemann's implementation of the Observer Pattern [22]. However, its is unclear how these metrics would extrapolate to larger case studies and their architectural significance.

Bartsch and Harrison evaluate five metrics in Ceccato and Tonella's work [11]. They argue that only one of the evaluated metrics can be considered well-defined (lacks any interpretation ambiguities), and none of them are completely valid from a measurement theory point of view. Along the same lines, Mehner proposes a series of steps to validate AOP metrics and their application [33].

An extensive study on modularizing design patterns have been performed by Garcia et al. [20]. They use Hannemann's implementation of GoF patterns to apply seven metrics that extend and adapt to AOP Chidamber and Kemerer's metrics [16]. Their metrics are informally defined and their results are given an interpretation in terms of improvement of separation of concerns and reuse.

Coupling metrics for AOP certainly depend on the crosscutting capabilities of aspects. Our metrics focus only on crosscutting relations produced by pointcut shadows and ITD's, and do not consider cases such as method calls or field references which the above coupling metrics account for.

7 Conclusions and Future Work

In this paper we present a semi-formal description of a set of crosscutting metrics. Our metrics categorize crosscutting within an spectrum from heterogeneous to homogeneous depending on the number of classes crosscut by pieces of advice in relation to the number of classes crosscut by all crosscutting mechanisms of AspectJ. This distinction helps draw a relation with other technologies that also provide support for crosscutting.

We applied our set of metrics to four case studies. We found that for these programs, the number of classes crosscut by advice per crosscutting is small in relation to the number of classes in the program, and that crosscuttings are mostly heterogeneous. We argued that this finding is not atypical as programs are not synthesized by adding the same piece of code in different places, but rather, adding different pieces of code in different places. We are in the process of applying our metrics to other case studies to provide more empirical arguments to further support our conjecture.

Earlier work of the first author described a preliminary definition of our metrics that were applied to a single case study [31]. Work of the second author categorizes crosscuts in two dimensions [7][9]. We plan to integrate these two dimensions into the set of metrics presented here. We also intend to extend our metrics to address issues such as cohesion and coupling for features. These extended metrics could help identify opportunities for feature refactoring.

We collected the Program Structure Metrics with the *AJStats* tool. This tools is under development at the University of Magdeburg and it is publicly available [2]. Currently we are collecting the Feature Crosscutting Metrics manually. We are exploring different possibilities to extend AJStats to collect this set of metrics. Our goal is to develop tool infrastructure that would allow the implementation of these and other metrics in a simple and extensible way.

References

1. AJHotDraw project web site http://sourceforge.net/projects/ajhotdraw .
2. AJStats tool project website http://wwwiti.cs.uni-magdeburg.de/iti_db/forschung/ajstats/ .
3. AHEAD Tool Suite (ATS). http://www.cs.utexas.edu/users/schwartz
4. Alves, V., Matos, P., Cole, L., Borba, P., Ramalho, G.: Extracting and Evolving Game Product Lines. SPLC (2005)
5. Anastasopoulus, M., Muthig, D.: An Evaluation of Aspect-Oriented Programming as a Product Line Implementation Technology. ICSR (2004)
6. Apel, S.: The Role of Features and Aspects in Software Development. PhD Dissertation. School of Computer Science, University of Magdeburg, 2007.
7. Apel, S., Leich,T., Saake. G.: Aspectual Mixin Layers: Aspects and Features in Concert. ICSE (2006)
8. Apel, S., Batory, D.: When to Use Features and Aspects? A Case Study. GPCE (2006)
9. Apel, S., Batory, D.: On the Structure of Crosscutting Concerns: Using Aspects or Collaborations?. AOPLE (2006)
10. AspectJ, *http://eclipse.org/aspectj/*.
11. Bartsch, M., Harrison, R.: An Evaluation of Coupling Measures for AspectJ. LATE Workshop AOSD (2006)
12. Batory, D., Cardone, R., Smaragdakis, Y.: Object-Oriented Frameworks and Product-Lines. SPLC (2000)
13. Batory, D., Sarvela, J.N., Rauschmayer, A.: Scaling Step-Wise Refinement. IEEE TSE, June (2004)
14. R. Bird.: Introduction to Functional Programming using Haskell. Prentice Hall (1998)
15. Ceccato, M., Tonella, P.: Measuring the Effects of Software Aspectization. First Workshop on Aspect Reverse Engineering. Delft, The Netherlands (2004)
16. Chidamber, S., Kemerer, C.: A Metrics Suite for OOD Design. IEEE TSE 20(6) (1994)
17. Clements, P., Northrop, L.: Software product lines: practices and patterns. Addison-Wesley (2002)
18. Coyler, A., Clement, A.: Large-scale AOSD for Middleware. AOSD (2004)
19. Coyler, A., Rashid, A., Blair, G.: On the Separation of Concerns in Program Families. TRCOMP-001-2004, Computing Department, Lancaster University, UK (2004)
20. Garcia, A., Sant'Anna, C., Figueiredo, E., Kulesza, U., Lucena, C., von Staa, A.: Modularizing Design Patterns with Aspects: A Quantitative Study. Transactions on TAOSD I. LNCS 3880 (2006)
21. Godil, I., Jacobsen, H.-A.: Horizontal Decomposition of Prevayler. CASCON (2005)

22. Hannemann, J.: AspectJ implementation of GoF patterns. http://www.cs.ubc.ca/~jan/ AODPs
23. Holland, I.: Specifying Reusable Components using Contracts. ECOOP (1992)
24. Hunleth, F., Cytron, R.: Footprint and Feature Management Using Aspect-Oriented Programming Techniques. In Proceedings of the Joint Conference on Languages, Compilers, and Tools for Embedded Systems & Software and Compilers for Embedded Systems (LCTES/SCOPES), pages 38~V45 (2002)
25. Kiczales, G., Hilsdale, E., Hugunin, J., Kirsten, M., Palm, J., Griswold, W.G.: An overview of AspectJ. ECOOP (2001)
26. Laddad, R.:. AspectJ in Action. Practical Aspect-Oriented Programming. Manning (2003)
27. Lämmel, R.: Declarative Aspect-Oriented Programming. PEPM (1999)
28. Lopez-Herrejon, R.E., Batory, D., Cook, W.: Evaluating Support for Features in Advanced Modularization Techniques. ECOOP (2005)
29. Lopez-Herrejon, R.E., Batory, D., Lengauer, C.: A disciplined approach to aspect composition. PEPM (2006)
30. Lopez-Herrejon, R.E., Batory, D.: From Crosscutting Concerns to Product Lines: A Function Composition Approach. Tech. Report UT Austin CS TR-06-24. May (2006)
31. Lopez-Herrejon. R.E.: Towards Crosscutting Metrics for Aspect-Based Features. AOPLE Workshop at GPCE (2006)
32. Masuhara, H., Kiczales, G.: Modeling Crosscutting Aspect-Oriented Mechanisms. ECOOP (2003)
33. Mehner, K.: On Using Metrics in the Evaluation of Aspect-Oriented Programs and Designs. LATE Workshop AOSD (2006)
34. Reenskaug, T., Anderson, E., Berre, A., Hurlen, A., Landmanrk, A., Lehne, O., Nordhagen, E., Ness-Ulseth, E., Ofdetal, G., Skaar, A., Stenslet, P.: OORASS : Seamsless Support for the Creation and Maintenance of Object-Oriented Systems. Journal of Object Oriented Programming, 5(6): (1992)
35. Smaragdakis, Y., Batory, D.: Mixin Layers: An Object-Oriented Implementation Technique for Refinements and Collaboration-Based Designs. ACM TOSEM April (2002)
36. Van Hilst, M., Notkin, D.: Using C++ Templates to Implement Role-Based Designs. JSSST International Symposium on Object Technologies for Advanced Software. Springer-Verlag (1996)
37. Van Hilst, M., Notkin, D.: Using Role Components to Implement Collaboration-Based Designs. OOPSLA (1996)
38. Wand, M., Kiczales, G., Dutchyn, C.: A Semantics for Advice and Dynamic Join Points in Aspect Oriented Programming. TOPLAS (2004)
39. Zave, P.: FAQ Sheet on Feature Interaction. http:// www.research.att.com/~pamela/ faq.html
40. Zhao, J.: Measuring Coupling in Aspect-Oriented Systems. Technical Report SE-142-6. Information Processing Society of Japan (IPSJ), June (2003)
41. Zhao, J., Xu, B.: Measuring Aspect Cohesion. FASE (2004)

Author Index

Lecture Notes in Computer Science

For information about Vols. 1–4310

please contact your bookseller or Springer

Vol. 4335: S.A. Brueckner, S. Hassas, M. Jelasity, D. Yamins (Eds.), Engineering Self-Organising Systems. XII, 212 pages. 2007. (Sublibrary LNAI).

Vol. 4334: B. Beckert, R. Hähnle, P.H. Schmitt (Eds.), Verification of Object-Oriented Software. XXIX, 658 pages. 2007. (Sublibrary LNAI).

Vol. 4333: U. Reimer, D. Karagiannis (Eds.), Practical Aspects of Knowledge Management. XII, 338 pages. 2006. (Sublibrary LNAI).

Vol. 4332: A. Bagchi, V. Atluri (Eds.), Information Systems Security. XV, 382 pages. 2006.

Vol. 4331: G. Min, B. Di Martino, L.T. Yang, M. Guo, G. Ruenger (Eds.), Frontiers of High Performance Computing and Networking – ISPA 2006 Workshops. XXXVII, 1141 pages. 2006.

Vol. 4330: M. Guo, L.T. Yang, B. Di Martino, H.P. Zima, J. Dongarra, F. Tang (Eds.), Parallel and Distributed Processing and Applications. XVIII, 953 pages. 2006.

Vol. 4329: R. Barua, T. Lange (Eds.), Progress in Cryptology - INDOCRYPT 2006. X, 454 pages. 2006.

Vol. 4328: D. Penkler, M. Reitenspiess, F. Tam (Eds.), Service Availability. X, 289 pages. 2006.

Vol. 4327: M. Baldoni, U. Endriss (Eds.), Declarative Agent Languages and Technologies IV. VIII, 257 pages. 2006. (Sublibrary LNAI).

Vol. 4326: S. Göbel, R. Malkewitz, I. Iurgel (Eds.), Technologies for Interactive Digital Storytelling and Entertainment. X, 384 pages. 2006.

Vol. 4325: J. Cao, I. Stojmenovic, X. Jia, S.K. Das (Eds.), Mobile Ad-hoc and Sensor Networks. XIX, 887 pages. 2006.

Vol. 4323: G. Doherty, A. Blandford (Eds.), Interactive Systems. XI, 269 pages. 2007.

Vol. 4322: F. Kordon, J. Sztipanovits (Eds.), Reliable Systems on Unreliable Networked Platforms. XIV, 317 pages. 2007.

Vol. 4320: R. Gotzhein, R. Reed (Eds.), System Analysis and Modeling: Language Profiles. X, 229 pages. 2006.

Vol. 4319: L.-W. Chang, W.-N. Lie (Eds.), Advances in Image and Video Technology. XXVI, 1347 pages. 2006.

Vol. 4318: H. Lipmaa, M. Yung, D. Lin (Eds.), Information Security and Cryptology. XI, 305 pages. 2006.

Vol. 4317: S.K. Madria, K.T. Claypool, R. Kannan, P. Uppuluri, M.M. Gore (Eds.), Distributed Computing and Internet Technology. XIX, 466 pages. 2006.

Vol. 4316: M.M. Dalkilic, S. Kim, J. Yang (Eds.), Data Mining and Bioinformatics. VIII, 197 pages. 2006. (Sublibrary LNBI).

Vol. 4314: C. Freksa, M. Kohlhase, K. Schill (Eds.), KI 2006: Advances in Artificial Intelligence. XII, 458 pages. 2007. (Sublibrary LNAI).

Vol. 4313: T. Margaria, B. Steffen (Eds.), Leveraging Applications of Formal Methods. IX, 197 pages. 2006.

Vol. 4312: S. Sugimoto, J. Hunter, A. Rauber, A. Morishima (Eds.), Digital Libraries: Achievements, Challenges and Opportunities. XVIII, 571 pages. 2006.

Vol. 4311: K. Cho, P. Jacquet (Eds.), Technologies for Advanced Heterogeneous Networks II. XI, 253 pages. 2006.

M. Kano, X. Li, Q.
natorics and Graph

i, F. Fages, M.-S.
nici, P. Shvaiko, J.
n Data Semantics

(Eds.), Perspec-
pages. 2007.

logy – CT-RSA

elshohn (Eds.),
rocessing. VII,

Düntsch, J.
owski (Eds.),
I, 499 pages.

ireless Sen-

ds.), Graph

), Compu-
15 pages.

M. Soto,
elization

. Geske,
amming
. (Sub-

pproxi-
07.

m, D.
ibed-
007.

owé
lex-
rary

er-

er
M
I,

07:
293

eclar-

se The-

jan, T.-S.
edia Mod-

Rajan, T.-S.
media Mod-

, Verification,
ation. XI, 395

kardt, E. Ploed-
ference Manual.

nformation Infras-
06.

1. Leucker, J. van de
cations and Technol-

avarda, V. Koutkias, R.
Medical Data Analysis.
ary LNBI).

o (Eds.), Software Archi-

Orłowska, G. Schmidt, M.
Applications of Relational
istruments II. X, 373 pages.

Ed.), Progress in Cryptology -
85 pages. 2006.

F. Fahringer, Grid Computing.

, G. Baumgartner, J. Ramanujam,
Languages and Compilers for Par-
476 pages. 2006.

S. Peleg (Eds.), Computer Vision,
Processing. XV, 965 pages. 2006.

n-Kumar, N. Garg (Eds.), FSTTCS
s of Software Technology and Theo-
Science. XIII, 430 pages. 2006.

Basili, H.D. Rombach, K. Schneider, B.
. Pfahl, R.W. Selby, Empirical Software
sues. XVII, 194 pages. 2007.

Lecture Notes in Computer Science

For information about Vols. 1–4310

please contact your bookseller or Springer

Vol. 4360: W. Dubitzky, A. Schuster, P.M.A. Sloot, M. Schroeder, M. Romberg (Eds.), Distributed, High-Performance and Grid Computing in Computational Biology. X, 192 pages. 2007. (Sublibrary LNBI).

Vol. 4358: R. Vidal, A. Heyden, Y. Ma (Eds.), Dynamical Vision. IX, 329 pages. 2007.

Vol. 4357: L. Buttyán, V. Gligor, D. Westhoff (Eds.), Security and Privacy in Ad-Hoc and Sensor Networks. X, 193 pages. 2006.

Vol. 4355: J. Julliand, O. Kouchnarenko (Eds.), B 2007: Formal Specification and Development in B. XIII, 293 pages. 2006.

Vol. 4354: M. Hanus (Ed.), Practical Aspects of Declarative Languages. X, 335 pages. 2006.

Vol. 4353: T. Schwentick, D. Suciu (Eds.), Database Theory – ICDT 2007. XI, 419 pages. 2006.

Vol. 4352: T.-J. Cham, J. Cai, C. Dorai, D. Rajan, T.-S. Chua, L.-T. Chia (Eds.), Advances in Multimedia Modeling, Part II. XVIII, 743 pages. 2006.

Vol. 4351: T.-J. Cham, J. Cai, C. Dorai, D. Rajan, T.-S. Chua, L.-T. Chia (Eds.), Advances in Multimedia Modeling, Part I. XIX, 797 pages. 2006.

Vol. 4349: B. Cook, A. Podelski (Eds.), Verification, Model Checking, and Abstract Interpretation. XI, 395 pages. 2007.

Vol. 4348: S.T. Taft, R.A. Duff, R.L. Brukardt, E. Ploedereder, P. Leroy (Eds.), Ada 2005 Reference Manual. XXII, 765 pages. 2006.

Vol. 4347: J. Lopez (Ed.), Critical Information Infrastructures Security. X, 286 pages. 2006.

Vol. 4346: L. Brim, B. Haverkort, M. Leucker, J. van de Pol (Eds.), Formal Methods: Applications and Technology. X, 363 pages. 2007.

Vol. 4345: N. Maglaveras, I. Chouvarda, V. Koutkias, R. Brause (Eds.), Biological and Medical Data Analysis. XIII, 496 pages. 2006. (Sublibrary LNBI).

Vol. 4344: V. Gruhn, F. Oquendo (Eds.), Software Architecture. X, 245 pages. 2006.

Vol. 4342: H. de Swart, E. Orłowska, G. Schmidt, M. Roubens (Eds.), Theory and Applications of Relational Structures as Knowledge Instruments II. X, 373 pages. 2006. (Sublibrary LNAI).

Vol. 4341: P.Q. Nguyen (Ed.), Progress in Cryptology - VIETCRYPT 2006. XI, 385 pages. 2006.

Vol. 4340: R. Prodan, T. Fahringer, Grid Computing. XXIII, 317 pages. 2007.

Vol. 4339: E. Ayguadé, G. Baumgartner, J. Ramanujam, P. Sadayappan (Eds.), Languages and Compilers for Parallel Computing. XI, 476 pages. 2006.

Vol. 4338: P. Kalra, S. Peleg (Eds.), Computer Vision, Graphics and Image Processing. XV, 965 pages. 2006.

Vol. 4337: S. Arun-Kumar, N. Garg (Eds.), FSTTCS 2006: Foundations of Software Technology and Theoretical Computer Science. XIII, 430 pages. 2006.

Vol. 4336: V.R. Basili, H.D. Rombach, K. Schneider, B. Kitchenham, D. Pfahl, R.W. Selby, Empirical Software Engineering Issues. XVII, 194 pages. 2007.

Vol. 4335: S.A. Brueckner, S. Hassas, M. Jelasity, D. Yamins (Eds.), Engineering Self-Organising Systems. XII, 212 pages. 2007. (Sublibrary LNAI).

Vol. 4334: B. Beckert, R. Hähnle, P.H. Schmitt (Eds.), Verification of Object-Oriented Software. XXIX, 658 pages. 2007. (Sublibrary LNAI).

Vol. 4333: U. Reimer, D. Karagiannis (Eds.), Practical Aspects of Knowledge Management. XII, 338 pages. 2006. (Sublibrary LNAI).

Vol. 4332: A. Bagchi, V. Atluri (Eds.), Information Systems Security. XV, 382 pages. 2006.

Vol. 4331: G. Min, B. Di Martino, L.T. Yang, M. Guo, G. Ruenger (Eds.), Frontiers of High Performance Computing and Networking – ISPA 2006 Workshops. XXXVII, 1141 pages. 2006.

Vol. 4330: M. Guo, L.T. Yang, B. Di Martino, H.P. Zima, J. Dongarra, F. Tang (Eds.), Parallel and Distributed Processing and Applications. XVIII, 953 pages. 2006.

Vol. 4329: R. Barua, T. Lange (Eds.), Progress in Cryptology - INDOCRYPT 2006. X, 454 pages. 2006.

Vol. 4328: D. Penkler, M. Reitenspiess, F. Tam (Eds.), Service Availability. X, 289 pages. 2006.

Vol. 4327: M. Baldoni, U. Endriss (Eds.), Declarative Agent Languages and Technologies IV. VIII, 257 pages. 2006. (Sublibrary LNAI).

Vol. 4326: S. Göbel, R. Malkewitz, I. Iurgel (Eds.), Technologies for Interactive Digital Storytelling and Entertainment. X, 384 pages. 2006.

Vol. 4325: J. Cao, I. Stojmenovic, X. Jia, S.K. Das (Eds.), Mobile Ad-hoc and Sensor Networks. XIX, 887 pages. 2006.

Vol. 4323: G. Doherty, A. Blandford (Eds.), Interactive Systems. XI, 269 pages. 2007.

Vol. 4322: F. Kordon, J. Sztipanovits (Eds.), Reliable Systems on Unreliable Networked Platforms. XIV, 317 pages. 2007.

Vol. 4320: R. Gotzhein, R. Reed (Eds.), System Analysis and Modeling: Language Profiles. X, 229 pages. 2006.

Vol. 4319: L.-W. Chang, W.-N. Lie (Eds.), Advances in Image and Video Technology. XXVI, 1347 pages. 2006.

Vol. 4318: H. Lipmaa, M. Yung, D. Lin (Eds.), Information Security and Cryptology. XI, 305 pages. 2006.

Vol. 4317: S.K. Madria, K.T. Claypool, R. Kannan, P. Uppuluri, M.M. Gore (Eds.), Distributed Computing and Internet Technology. XIX, 466 pages. 2006.

Vol. 4316: M.M. Dalkilic, S. Kim, J. Yang (Eds.), Data Mining and Bioinformatics. VIII, 197 pages. 2006. (Sublibrary LNBI).

Vol. 4314: C. Freksa, M. Kohlhase, K. Schill (Eds.), KI 2006: Advances in Artificial Intelligence. XII, 458 pages. 2007. (Sublibrary LNAI).

Vol. 4313: T. Margaria, B. Steffen (Eds.), Leveraging Applications of Formal Methods. IX, 197 pages. 2006.

Vol. 4312: S. Sugimoto, J. Hunter, A. Rauber, A. Morishima (Eds.), Digital Libraries: Achievements, Challenges and Opportunities. XVIII, 571 pages. 2006.

Vol. 4311: K. Cho, P. Jacquet (Eds.), Technologies for Advanced Heterogeneous Networks II. XI, 253 pages. 2006.